THEORIES
OF THE POLITICAL SYSTEM

David Easton, *Consulting Editor*

If we divest ourselves of historicist preconceptions about the appropriate way to study the great theories, we shall be in a position to appreciate why political theory is central for the development of reliable political knowledge.

David Easton, *The Political System*

Third Edition

THEORIES
OF THE POLITICAL SYSTEM

*CLASSICS OF POLITICAL THOUGHT AND MODERN POLITICAL
ANALYSIS*

William T. Bluhm, 1923 –
The University of Rochester

PRENTICE-HALL, INC., ENGLEWOOD CLIFFS, NEW JERSEY 07632

Library of Congress Cataloging in Publication Data

Bluhm, William Theodore, 1923-
    Theories of the political system.

    Includes bibliographical references and index.
    1. Political science—History. I. Title.
JA81.B625 1978   320.5   77-15522
ISBN   0-13-913327-5

For Elly

Printed in the United States of America

10   9   8   7   6   5   4   3   2   1

Prentice-Hall International, Inc., *London*
Prentice-Hall of Australia Pty. Limited, *Sydney*
Prentice-Hall of Canada, Ltd., *Toronto*
Prentice-Hall of India Private Limited, *New Delhi*
Prentice-Hall of Japan, Inc., *Tokyo*
Prentice-Hall of Southeast Asia Pte. Ltd., *Singapore*
Whitehall Books Limited, *Wellington, New Zealand*

Contents

Preface
to the Third Edition

Since the publication of the first edition of this book in 1965, one important objective of its composition has been achieved—an increased recognition of the importance of the classics for the understanding of contemporary politics. This recognition has been the result of many and diverse causes, perhaps the least important of which have been the arguments of unreconstructible classicists like myself. More significant have been the cultural malaise and anomie of our youth in the wake of burnt-out New Left enthusiasms, the graceless close to the debacle of Vietnam, and the demoralizing experience of Watergate and associated revelations of iniquity and law-breaking in high places.

A need for fixed points of ethical certainty and moral inspiration have led many to seek the solaces afforded by irrationalist religious cults. Another reaction has been a return to the philosophical tradition in the search for ethical and political guidance within the categories of reasoned discourse. This is as true among those who stand to the left as among the more conservative elements of our college population. The moral concern with which students these days approach the Great Books, and their perfect openness to philosophical argument is a new and exhilarating experience for the teacher of political philosophy. It also underlines the need for increased conscientiousness and an increased sense of responsibility on the part of the teacher in his classroom exegesis of the classic writings. He is called upon now more than ever to discipline himself against the ready temptation of sliding into a simplistic ideological position in the development of his interpretations.

Somewhat different causes have led professional political scientists to join undergraduates and graduate students in a new openness to the classics. One has been the successful demonstration by political philosophers like

Charles Taylor and John Gunnell that every conceptual framework arises from a special way of viewing and evaluating the world. Values, defined as metaphysical, epistemological, and ethical assumptions, determine the selection and definition of terms of reference and the shape of the political landscape to be researched in all of our scientific paradigms. This has been cogently demonstrated within the philosophy of science by men like Kuhn, Toulmin, Feyerabend, and Shapere. Hence it is incumbent upon the researcher to be self-conscious about the philosophical position he embraces, for to be unconscious is to become an ideologist—a pitfall to be avoided by theory-builders, empirical researchers, and philosophers alike. It is precisely from the tradition of political philosophy that we can learn to be systematically self-conscious about these primary questions. For self-conscious reflection on principles of knowing (epistemology) and reality (metaphysics) is the very definition of philosophical endeavor.

I have argued in the earlier editions of this book that, for the most part without realizing it, the authors of major political research paradigms which are widely employed in American political science, incorporate in their theories many of the metaphysical and ethical positions of the tradition. This book, I hope, may be of use in making the appropriation of these assumptions a self-conscious and reflective affair, based on philosophical conviction rather than mere taste and habit. And I continue to hope that it will also promote a much-needed willingness to talk across the boundaries of discrete paradigms in the search for philosophical and scientific synthesis. What I call for with this book is not a return to Classical Truth and to tradition, but moving forward from what is true in the classics and usable in the tradition. Each persuasion claims to be the sole orthodoxy, yet each gives us insights into only some aspects of politics and neglects the whole. What is required is snythesis, the building of bridges from theory to theory. It is my hope that a comparative review of the classic theories in the context of this problem, and of the modern studies which build on them, may bring us some way on the road to such a goal.

In this third edition I wish to highlight the interplay of two themes that have been central to the tradition of political philosophy from the beginning, and whose interrelationship has become peculiarly problematic in our time—the theme of virtue, or moral goodness, and the theme of freedom. From Plato to Machiavelli, it was supposed that good men made good laws, and that good laws in turn produce good men, and therewith the public happiness. In this context, freedom was defined by an over-arching moral order, shared by gods and men—except in the case of Machiavelli. Machiavelli radically redefined the concept of virtue to eliminate absolute goodness, and paved the way for the ascendancy of a new concept of freedom, a concept that is first spelled out by Hobbes as a natural right to be unrestrained by man or god in the exercise of autonomous individual will.

Since Rousseau, the problem of combining so extreme an individualism with coherent social order has led to a variety of attempts to build freedom back into a public order of right and virtue. These attempts, for the most part, have avoided resorting to traditional concepts of transcendence, which are uncongenial to the empirical bent of the modern mind. A workable partnership of freedom and goodness in a public system of right has not yet emerged, and this is manifest in two dilemmas of our democracy. One is the problem of finding a non-arbitrary welfare function containing a transitive (rational) ordering of national priorities in a system of public choice based on the free play of group interests. The other is the problem of sorting out the rationally acceptable from the non-acceptable in the myriad demands of liberation groups.

In order to trace the story of virtue and freedom through the book in a connected fashion, parts of several chapters have been rewritten, and the selection of modern writers that I compare with the classic philosophers has been modified. I have also dropped some classics that appeared in the first two editions—e.g., Thucydides and Harrington—and added others who fit better the central theme and who are attracting large public interest today because of their concern with the relationship of freedom to virtue. Most notable among the additions are wholly new chapters on Kant and Hegel. I have also expanded my treatment of Marx to include the humanist as well as the dialectical materialist interpretation of his work, by adding material on the Economic and Philosophic Manuscripts of 1844.

I should like to say a word of thanks to my teachers, especially Daniel J. Boorstin, Guy H. Dodge, Carl J. Friedrich, Jerome Kerwin, Hans Morgenthau, and Leo Strauss, each of whom taught me to appreciate a different aspect of political theory. Janice Brown and Lee McQuinn, my efficient and uncomplaining secretaries, labored long hours in preparing the typed copy.

W.T.B.
Rochester, New York

Chapter 1

Perspectives on Political Theory: Noumenalism, Naturalism, Virtue, and Freedom

Political Theory and Political Ideology

We are all philosophers, or theorists of sorts. (I am using the words interchangeably.) Or rather we all use political theories, if we have any conscious political life at all, if we think at all about politics. For a political theory is an explanation of what politics is all about, a general understanding of the political world, a frame of reference. Without one we should be unable to recognize an event as political, decide anything about why it happened, judge whether it was good or bad, or decide what was likely to happen next. A theory helps us identify what is happening in a particular case of politics—it tells us whether to call the brawl outside a street fight or a civil war. It helps us to explain why an event occurred and to predict future events—e.g., why Jones beat Smith in the mayoralty race, and whether Jones is likely to be reelected for a second term. Theory also is a tool for evaluating what is happening and for guiding our political choices—e.g., it tells us whether a civil rights program is good or bad, whether federal medical insurance for the aged is good or bad, whether we should vote for candidates for public office who support or condemn these things. An alternative term is "ideology."

The Structure of an Ideology

Here is a more extended example. When an historian recently characterized the practice of the Presidency during the Johnson, and especially the Nixon years, as an "Imperial Presidency," he created an expression that has come to signify more than the expansion of Presidential authority.[1] The expression serves as a shorthand for an entire theory of politics, based on an elitist and hedonistic theory of human nature. The believer in an "Imperial Presidency" is an egoist, and he casts all others in his own image as narrowly self-concerned individualists. He also thinks that the ability of individuals to get what they want is differentially distributed throughout society. For such a person, politics is the province of the capable few, men with organizational know-how, who are adept at strategic calculation and maneuver, and who, as a consequence are able to manipulate the many and win power. Concepts such as truth, moral goodness, friendship, love, community, and equality do not stand for real things, though they may be useful in political rhetoric.

The election of 1976 has brought to the Presidency a man who appears to espouse a radically different view of human nature and a correspondingly different conception of the Presidency. In the "Inauguration Walk" down Constitution Avenue to the White House, in his rejection of "Ruffles and Flourishes," in the elimination of staff limousines and exclusive dining rooms, by enrolling daughter Amy in a local public school, and in other symbolic ways, Jimmy Carter has been telling the public that he rejects the distinction of the "few" and the "many." He thinks people are basically alike, in political office and out. In his sweater-clad first fireside talk, in the "call-in" program, in discussions with the grass roots of the Federal bureaucracy, and in plans for common-man visits to the White House, Carter is trying to say that community is important and that its fulfillment requires intensive democratic communication between leaders and the people they are leading. From the beginning of his campaign and through Inauguration Day, the new President has stressed the importance of trust and openness in our society, which implies a capacity for sharing and loving that the "Imperial" theory rejects as a dangerous illusion. And he sees politics as a cooperative, not a zero-sum game.[2] He has also spoken openly of his personal religious experience and of its significance in relation to his public acts, which implies the existence, for him, of a world of genuine moral principles, Divinely ordained and sanctioned.

Each of us, in reacting positively or negatively to each of these two ideologies of the Presidency—the "Imperial" theory and the "Populist" theory—is implicitly giving his or her consent to a theory of human nature *and* to a general theory of politics that are logically correlative. Of course, this will be the case only for the perfectly self-consistent person. Ideologies are in fact usually fragmentary, unsophisticated, and sometimes composed of parts that do not fit together. But no matter how internally consistent or inconsistent, they serve as frames of reference which guide citizens and

[1] See Arthur M. Schlesinger, Jr., *The Imperial Presidency* (Boston: Houghton Mifflin, 1973), esp. Chs. 8, 10, 11.

[2] See Chapter 7 below.

rulers in the making of public policy. A moment's reflection will show that you, too, (like Molière's prose-speaker) have been thinking and speaking political theory all your life.

The political theories which we shall examine in this book differ from the commonplaces of ideology in their greater elaborateness and sophistication, sometimes in their greater consistency. At least some of them contain a more accurate picture of the political world than the beliefs which the average man carries around in his head. And this is why they are worth studying. All the great political theorists have at least *thought* that by their work they might supplant opinion with knowledge, folklore with science. Every author of a political theory has aspired to be the guide both of statesmen and of citizens.[3]

Political theory is important not only for the conduct of politics but also for the practice of political inquiry. None of the great political theories gives us a truly comprehensive political science. Each has great insights, but each contains flaws and gaps, and the process of political investigation proceeds, more elaborately today than ever before, to add to the landmarks on the map of the wilderness of politics which preceding generations have drawn. For the professional student of politics, political theory, in one of its definitions, stands for an abstract "model" of the political order which he is examining, a guide to the systematic collection and analysis of political data. Ideology is also, of course, a guide to collection and analysis but on a different level; an example of it might be the research work of liberal or conservative pressure groups. What distinguishes the theorist is the tentativeness of his axioms, his willingness to discard hypotheses that prove fruitless or false after conscientious examination and his effort to maintain a dispassionate stance toward the subject of his inquiry, by contrast with the frank admission of the ideologist that he believes his basic assumptions to be proven gospel. Whether the kind of objectivity to which the scientific model-builder aspires is really possible is itself, however, a basic question of political theory.

We have indicated that the structure of formal political theories is the same as that of the ideologies by which we live our daily political lives, and that they differ from ideologies in such things as elaborateness, sophistica-

---

[3]Cf. the rather different use of the concept "ideology" in Andrew Hacker, *Political Theory: Philosophy, Ideology, Science* (New York: The Macmillan Company, 1961), Chapter 1. Professor Hacker distinguishes theory as ideology from theory as science and philosophy by criteria of "interestedness" and honesty in formulation. Science and philosophy he describes as the product of "disinterested search for the principles of the good state and the good society . . . [and] for knowledge of political and social reality." Ideology he describes as "a rationalization for current or future political and social arrangements . . . [and] a distorted description or explanation of political and social reality." (Page 5.) He finds elements both of ideology and of science and philosophy in the formal theory of the study. He does not use the concept of ideology to distinguish popular opinions from formal theory.

tion, clarity, internal consistency, erudition, and possibly degree of truth. Let us see now what the structure of a political theory is like, what kinds of questions compose a comprehensive theory.

The Structure of a Political Theory

A definition of "politics" is a good starting point for this discussion, but it is not an unambiguous place to begin. For one of the chief means of distinguishing political theories is by referring to the conception of the "political" which they embody. Are there any historical constants which cut across all the various conceptions of politics?

Most ideas of politics include the notion of government (defined as rule-making or decision-making) as the social function of political activity, and the notions of power and influence, both as individual and group goals and as the means whereby decisions are produced and enforced. But definitions diverge sharply when one asks what the purposes of the rules are, and what kinds of power and influence are characteristically "political." Some writers call the object of rule-making the definition and creation of "the good life" for a society. But they are divided as to its nature, some of them seeing it as a life of moral perfection, others as the realization of human freedom. Others attempt to combine concepts of "freedom" with "goodness" in their vision of the purpose of political life. Still others settle simply for order or control as the end of political activity.

If one asks about the characteristics of political influence, again there are many different views. By "political" rule the ancient Greeks meant government by pure persuasion, and they spoke of force in governing as a "prepolitical" phenomenon.[4] Nineteenth-century nationalists like Treitschke, by contrast, spoke of war and violence as "politics in the highest degree." Some writers' definitions include both ideas, for example, that of Heinz Eulau, who says that "what makes a man's behavior political is that he rules and obeys, persuades and compromises, promises and bargains, coerces and represents, fights and fears."[5] Some writers stress the cooperative and harmonious aspects of political activity, others emphasize rivalry and conflict.

Most political theories have associated the "political" with "public government." And it is certainly true that all the great political theories were developed to explain activity connected with public authority, the activity of kings, armies, parliaments, courts, city councils, and of parties, pressure groups, paramilitary formations, and conspiracies. Nevertheless, it is possible to speak of "private politics" as well, politics in the university, the

[4]Hannah Arendt, *The Human Condition* (Garden City: Doubleday & Company, Inc., 1959), pp. 29-30.

[5]Heinz Eulau, *The Behavioral Persuasion in Politics* (New York: Random House, Inc., 1963), pp. 4-5.

business corporation, the labor union, the church, even in the streetcorner gang. And in recent years, political scientists have been studying "small groups" experimentally, on the assumption that the behavior of these "laboratory phenomena" corresponds to the behavior of public political bodies.

Reduced to its universal elements, then, politics is a social process characterized by activity involving rivalry and cooperation in the exercise of power, and culminating in the making of decisions for a group.

Now what do political theorists want to know about this activity? Their object is to understand politics in the most comprehensive fashion possible, but with the greatest possible parsimony of explanatory terms. They want to discover the general order and pattern in political facts, to explain these facts adequately and to construct rules of political action based on this analysis.

Order and Good Order

The inquiry into order proceeds at two levels. The theorist attempts to describe and explain the nature and the manner of generation of the various patterns which are found in the empirical world, the world of phenomena, and also to explicate the nature of the good, best, right, or rational order. In some theories the rational order is identified with a transcendent pattern of "essential" reality and radically distinguished from empirical patterns, which are considered mere appearance. In others it has the character of a logical construct, developed from empirical data but not identical with any observable political system. Others find the good order embodied in or emerging from a phenomenal system. Still others equate the rational with every historical reality.

Inquiring into the patterns of the empirical world, the theorist asks what the typical motives, goals, values are of people who are politically engaged. Are these values universal, or do they vary from culture to culture? If they vary, what are the influences, both physical and social, which condition them? He seeks to descibe and classify the political systems through which men pursue their goals—the main forms of government, and their typical functions, structures, and processes. He asks how the behavior of individuals and groups differs in the various systems. He seeks to learn about the conditions which give rise to particular forms of government and to individual institutions. And he tries to discover the causes of both evolutionary and revolutionary change. He asks about the role of class structure, personality structure, economic organization, geography, climate, historical experience in the determination and alteration of the political system.

Investigating the "rational" or "best" order, the theorist first of all seeks to determine the "rational" or "best" or "right" order of human ends or values. He may ask whether there is available a model of man in his perfection from which these values can be deduced, what its metaphysical status is, and how it can be known. Or he may attempt to understand the "best" in terms of the realization of freedom rather than virtue, or by combining the two concepts. He may decide that ultimate values should be identified by observing what are actually pursued as values, or by what men say are the best values. Having established a system of ultimate goals, the theorist of the rational order must then consider what instrumental values, i.e., what structures and processes, are logically required and empirically feasible for their realization.

Questions concerning order are sometimes contemplative in character. The theorist answers them in the attitude of an observer who stands outside the system, in detachment from his citizen duties—as in the work of Plato, Aristotle, Machiavelli and Hobbes. But sometimes the description of order is accomplished in an activist frame of reference, in which the work of description carries a normative project of change and reform forward. In such a framework, thought and action are closely woven together, and the truth is not understood as a reality to be dispassionately contemplated from the outside, but as something created in political action. The dialectical systems of Hegel and Marx are leading cases in point. But the contemplative theorist also has a regard for problems of reform and change, and makes it his business to prescribe rules of action, both for himself and for others, a "practical" theory in the strict sense of the word. In this enterprise he adopts a new attitude toward the world. Now he sees it as malleable, as indeterminate but subject to determination through human agency.

Criteria of Political Choice

In the realm of prescriptions for action the theorist may see his task as having either an ethical or a purely technical character. If he chooses to construct a political ethics, he must decide whether or not there are any rules, either specifying ends or specifying means, which carry an unqualified moral obligation to their performance, and the grounds of that obligation. If he finds ultimate values "open," he must work out a rubric for filling them in, for building or creating them, since he does not consider them as given and discoverable. He must decide whether variations in empirical circumstance affect obligations or the manner of applying obligatory rules. He must order political values in a hierarchy. He must work out principles for situations which involve value conflicts, in which to pursue one good involves the destruction of another. If his work is to be useful, he must at all times work within the limits set by psychological and physical "givens" of the empirical world.

The theorist who denies the absolute obligation of any ends or means, or who refuses to work out a rule for the creation of values or ordering of values, and who equates the valuable and obligatory with whatever ends men happen to desire has a somewhat different task from that of the ethical theorist. His work in the realm of action is to demonstrate the compatibility or incompatibility of posited ends and to prescribe rules of technical efficiency for the realization of particular values.

In both cases, however, the work of the theorist of political choice can be understood as casting into prescriptive form the causal statements already generated in the examination of order, both empirical and rational. The form of argument of the ethical theorist would be, "By A I mean x, y, and z. A is good. Here is the demonstration of its goodness and obligatory character." The technical theorist would say, "By A I mean x, y, and z. I posit A as a value to be realized." (Each of these statements is descriptive, a statement about order.) Each would then continue, "If you wish A, you ought to do b under condition c, and d under condition e." This is a prescriptive statement, but it is essentially the same as the descriptive statement, "A is a function of $b(c)$ or of $d(e)$."

Causal Theory and Value Theory

It has been the fashion to speak of propositions about the empirical order of politics as "causal theory" and of propositions about the good order as "value theory." But these terms are not adequate for our purposes, because they are to a certain extent misnomers and imply a false distinction. The theorist of the good or rational order customarily specifies the conditions requisite to the establishment of his good polity, and specifications of this sort involve statements about causation. Plato, for instance, said that his utopia could not be established unless philosophers became kings and unless they "wiped the slate clean." And he described an elaborate system for breeding and educating his Guardian class. Now all of these things involve causal relationships, and Plato's statements about them can be cast into an "If—then" form. His theories may be in error, and the causal relationships which he posited may not in fact obtain. Whether they do or not is irrelevant to our concern for the form of statement, which does have a causal character. Yet Plato's work as a whole (and especially the part just referred to) is usually consigned to the category of "value theory," because it is concerned with the character of the good order rather than with the empirical order.

The expression "causal theory" is also usually taken to mean only theory which can be tested in some empirical fashion. Yet many of the great theories contain causal notions, both about the empirical order and about the rational order, which cannot be so tested, or which at least at present *seem* not to be testable by scientific means; for example, the Thomistic theory concerning the way in which the Natural Law is made known to men. But this is no reason to deny the causal character of the idea in classifying it for analysis.

Similarly, many social scientists today speak of questions of fact and questions of value, as though a radical separation of these two were possible. But the "fact-value" idea, developed by the sociologist Max Weber, represents a special philosophical position, a variety of positivism, and implies a whole range of judgments about the character of political facts and values which are not universally accepted. In this view the only "facts" are empirical; there can be no metaphysical or ethical facts, only empty definitions. And all matters of ultimate value are judged by this philosophy to be "nonrational preferences," though means-values are considered rational if they are technically efficient in the pursuit of passionately established goals. The "order-good order" dichotomy which I have chosen permits the examination of political reality without prejudgment of metaphysical as well as empirical approaches, and provides a category for the examination of moral judgments which does not prejudge their rationality nor limit the notion of rationality to technical efficiency.

Philosophy and Method.   It is clear from the foregoing that every political theory is formed within the framework of a broader system of philosophy, from which it derives basic axioms and assumptions. We must give special attention to the metaphysical, ethical, and epistemological bases of a political theory in order to understand it adequately. The answers a writer gives to the questions "What is ultimately real?", "What is ultimately good?", and "What can I know about the good and the real, and how can I know it?" are crucial for the kind of political theory he writes. Plato's belief, for example, that reality is found in a world of abstract and ideal essences, which is also the standard of good, led him to construct a best political order which had an intellectual existence only and no counterpart in empirical reality. Plato's metaphysics also accounts for his use of a dialectical and deductive rather than an inductive method of analysis.

The ideal polity of Hobbes is likewise derived deductively from a set of universal principles of order. But, by contrast with those of Plato, these are principles of psychological motivation, conceived as analogous to the laws of physical motion, and abstracted from the empirical motions of the material world, which Hobbes thought to be the only reality. Plato's *Republic* was an effort to capture in words an image of a Divine Idea; Hobbes' *Leviathan* was a blueprint for a political "machine," grounded in the laws of physics.

Plato's and Hobbes' metaphysics, as different as they are from one another, both produce ahistorical, "eternal" models of good political order. In striking contrast, Hegel believed that ultimate reality (as an ideal order) is immanent in the historical process, enshrined in the freedom of an "Absolute Spirit" which is coming into being, but is not yet complete. This led him to adopt an historical–dialectical method of explanation which is entirely different from the ahistorical dialectics of Plato.

A theorist's philosophical assumptions constitute the basic axioms of his organon, or method, for understanding the political world. It is in the light of these axioms that the theorist constructs his conceptual framework, which designates the significant variables of the political system, and selects his techniques for collecting and analyzing data and presenting findings. The conceptual framework in particular reveals a writer's philosophical persuasion. Marxian method, for example, makes use of such notions as social class, class consciousness, false consciousness, ruling class, exploitation, ideology, labor value, surplus value, dialectical development, mode of production, forces of production. These concepts designate the main elements in the political order and its environment, and form part of an entire Marxian world-view. The Marxian will be primarily interested in dynamic rather than static analysis. And he will give primary attention to data about the economy in seeking for causal factors in a given political pattern.

Techniques for collecting and analyzing data also vary from theorist to theorist, and to a somewhat lesser extent reveal philosophical commitments. Self-consciousness and sophistication in the matter of empirical research techniques (e.g., opinion surveys, psychological analysis, "small group" experiments), as we shall see, have been little evident in the work of political theorists during the whole period from the death of Aristotle to recent times, though they are now receiving an extraordinary amount of attention among behaviorally oriented political scientists. For the most part, the classical theorist worked with the data of his own common-sense experience of politics as man and citizen, plus a smattering of historical knowledge, and supposed that this was a representative and accurate cross-section of political experience. And today, also, some scholars consider this public world of common sense adequate for meaningful reasoning about political things. However, "method," conceived as the canons of valid reasoning and as epistemology, was of great concern to the classic writers, especially to such theorists as Locke, Hume, and Mill.

These, then, are the components of "method" in political analysis: (1) a set of philosophical judgments about the nature of reality, of goodness, and of human cognitive faculties; (2) a conceptual framework, which is either consciously or unconsciously derived from a set of assumptions about the good and the real, and ways of knowing them; (3) a set of methods for collecting, analyzing, and presenting data.

Kinds of Political Theories

Our conception of method indicates a useful way of classifying the theorists with whom we shall deal in this book. We have said that a writer's conceptual framework and the techniques he employs for collecting and studying data depend upon and are in a sense derived from a set of judgments he makes about the real, the good, and the knowable. This suggests that the most significant classification of theories will be made in terms of these judgments. If we proceed to classify in this way, we find that the theories with which we shall be concerned fall into one of two categories which represent two broad schools of thought about the real, the good, and about ways of knowing them. (In several cases we shall find a writer who has made a valiant effort to bridge the gulf between the two metaphysics, while retaining his base of operations on one side of it.) The labels which I shall use for these schools are "noumenalism" and "naturalism." I subdivide the "noumenalist" world into "transcendentalist" and "immanentist" parts. I should put the reader on notice that the meanings I shall assign to these words may not conform fully to accepted usage, but I shall try to be quite explicit about the connotations I give to them.[6]

Noumenalist Theory

Noumenalist theory equates the "best" or "rational" political order with a divinely ordained set of values (i.e., ends, goals) and rules of behavior which are understood as having the fullest or most perfect reality. Noumenalists divide into two groups when it comes to stating the relationship which exists between this good order and the empirical order. Those whom I shall call "transcendentalists" (Plato and Kant are examples) set the two radically apart. They view the good order as wholly transcending the world of sense, the empirical world, incapable of any complete or permanent embodiment in a historical polity. The second group, whom I call "immanentists" (Aristotle and Hegel are examples) on the contrary find the rational order immanent in the world of sense as potentiality and as causal principle, giving form and meaning, and furnishing a principle of growth and development to empirical things. It is possible, as they see it, for a historical polity to grow into perfection.

Both groups of noumenalists hold that the good order is known by an intuitive faculty which we shall speak of throughout the book as the "teleological reason," a useful term coined by Professor Carl J. Friedrich.[7] Some noumenalists (e.g., St. Augustine, St. Thomas Aquinas) add faith, inspired by divine grace, as a second and superior faculty by which we grasp the perfect order.

---

[6]I derive the word "noumenalism" from Immanuel Kant's "noumenon," which stands for ultimate reality as it is in itself, as contrasted with "phenomenon," appearance. The theories which I describe as "noumenalist" all affirm the existence of such a reality, though they differ with Kant and with one another on the manner and extent to which it can be known by us. Most of the writers I call "noumenalists" are more commonly called "essentialists" or "realists," but not all of them (e.g., Augustine).

[7]See Carl J. Friedrich, *Inevitable Peace* (Cambridge, Mass.: Harvard University Press, 1948), p. 129.

Noumenalists conceive the divine political order as part of a total social pattern which embodies a best way of life. The citizens of the best political order are all morally perfect men. Noumenalists do not agree, however, on the extent to which empirical men are perfectible, capable of living the best life in the here-and-now. They also differ on the question of how we determine what our obligations are under less than ideal circumstances.

Naturalist Theory

The common denominator of the "naturalists" is an assumption that reality, at least as far as we can know it, consists only of phenomena (the theory of Hobbes is a classic example of naturalism). Reality is coextensive with the empirical world in this view. No intelligible essences or other forms of nonempirical reality lie beyond or behind this world to lend it being and significance. We order this phenomenal world with names which we ourselves create and which stand only for the appearances manifest to us through sense experience and introspection. The most striking thing about the world of appearances is its dynamic character. The images are in constant motion, ever changing from one into another. To understand it as an order, we impute causality to the relationships of the images one to another. This is our own construction, however, as are the names we use for the appearances. The naturalist considers this theoretical construction more important as an instrument of prediction and control than as a means of understanding, since he regards the world as essentially unintelligible.

The purposes for which we wish to predict and control the order of images are also essentially unintelligible in the naturalist view. They are not fashioned by us, however, but are laid upon us. We experience them as nonrational urges, as desires or aversions for whose objects we use names like "good" and "evil," "beautiful" and "ugly," "just" and "unjust." Ultimate values are not the objects of a teleological reason towards which we are also emotionally inclined, but simply the objects of the strongest human passions. Reason enters naturalist theory as instrumentality. It supplies efficient means for the fulfillment of the demands of passion, and it orders and balances the passions in such a way as to prevent their mutual frustration. The rational polity of the naturalist is made up of men who efficiently maximize their values. Usually it is contrasted with the empirical order, where frustration is rife, though in some cases examples of a close approach to ideal efficiency are found by naturalists in the empirical order (as in Machiavelli's appraisal of Rome). When rules of action are prescribed by naturalists, they are not thought of as containing either an absolute or contingent moral obligation, but as "precepts of reason," as Hobbes put it, rules of efficient behavior.

In a strict logical sense, the two metaphysics which we have outlined are mutually exclusive. We must opt for one or the other school. It is not possible to embrace all the elements of both in a consistent scheme. Nevertheless, we find writers in each camp who can be called metaphysical bridge builders, attempting to incorporate in their work some elements of theory which are typical of the thinkers of the opposite school. Aristotle is such a bridge builder. His treatise on metaphysics and the first three and last two books of the *Politics* seem to place him squarely in the noumenalist camp. But his psychology book, the *De Anima,* and the central three books of the *Politics* are strongly naturalistic in flavor. (Some interpreters of Aristotle have, in fact, considered him a naturalist.)

There are also traces of naturalistic analysis to be found in Augustine's *The City of God.* The divine history and the profane history which Augustine traces in that work are spelled out in parallel but are never fused with one another. The psychological theory which is the chief explanatory instrument of the profane history is the same as that used by naturalists such as the Sophists. Augustine draws much of his analysis of the rise and fall of the Roman Empire, for example, from the work of Sallust, a naturalistic historian.

Bridge builders are also found among the naturalists we shall study, especially beginning with Rousseau, and including Marx, and, most notably, J. S. Mill. The pure naturalists are largely hedonists and individualists in their psychology, i.e., in their reading of the pattern of passionate desires. They see men as egoists who want things like glory, power, security, and material well-being. They view man in his natural (i.e., original) condition as radically antisocial, as a creature who conforms to social rules only against the grain. The inhabitants of the empirical world and of the rational world of the pure naturalist all have the same pattern of narrowly selfish motives. The only difference between them is one of efficient behavior. Empirical men are often frustrated. Rational men are satisfied.

The modified naturalists, or teleo-naturalists as we may call them, by contrast, find sympathetic, benevolent, altruistic motives operating as a part of the fundamental, given order of human values. Some of them even insist on the reality of ideals of perfection, though they assign these ideals only a status as psychic facts, rather than the status of noumenal realities. They people their best polities not with efficient hedonists but with men who look much like those who populate the good order of the noumenalists. These rational men are also thought of as in some sense morally better than the average empirical man.

Some of the teleo-naturalists (e.g., Mill) even distinguish between higher and lower values, and think it important to train men to give more regard than they now do to the higher goods. These writers seem to be operating with some faculty such as the teleological reason of the noumenalists (hence the label I have given them). Yet they expressly deny that they have insight into any divine or objectively right order and claim that they are merely describing the actual, given content of the human psyche. The problem of this kind of theory lies in the fact that not all empirical psyches evidently *do* contain the "higher values." There seems to me to be some hope for the eventual construction of a viable bridge from this kind of theory, which begins with its feet firmly planted on empirical ground, to the transcendent reality of the noumenalists if its proponents become aware of the logical incompatibility of their conceptions of value with their naturalistic assumptions about the limits of intelligible reality.

The distinctions which we have made between noumenalists and naturalists concerning their various views of the good, the real, and the knowable show up in their political theories primarily in their conceptions of the good or rational order. Our categories are not as helpful in distinguishing the various ways in which theorists describe the empirical order. One might suppose that naturalists would give a larger place in their work to descriptions of empirical systems than would the noumenalists as a group. Some do. But this is not consistently the case. The political theory of Hobbes, a leading naturalist, is wholly devoted to eliciting the principles of the rational order. He gives us no purely empirical descriptions. Aristotle, whom many consider a noumenalist, by contrast, in the central books of the *Politics* presents us with an exhaustive catalog of the structures and processes of empirical polities.

The distinction between theorists who employ an inductive and those who use a deductive method of analysis also fails to square with the classification we are using. Plato, a noumenalist, and Hobbes, a naturalist, both use a deductive method in constructing and presenting their theories. By contrast, Aristotle, a noumenalist, and Machiavelli, a naturalist, employ inductive procedures. Rousseau, a teleo-naturalist, uses a largely deductive method and Mill, another teleo-naturalist, recommends a combined deductive-inductive approach to analysis.

Theories of "Virtue" and Theories of "Freedom"

It is useful to classify theories in terms of the historical pattern mentioned in our Preface—the counterpoint of "Virtue" and "Freedom." For these terms do much more than designate two conceptions of political purpose. They signify totally different ways of conceiving the entire political process. Pre–modern theories of "Virtue" enshrined the view that the stability of political systems, as well as their perfect fulfillment of purpose, depended on the moral character of both rulers and citizens, whether noumenalistically or naturalistically defined. Even for Machiavelli, the viability of a political system required moral integrity. If the "matter" (the citizen body) is corrupt, republican institutions must be reduced to a royal form. And if no prince of *virtū* can be found, anarchy is the alternative. Noumenalist and naturalist theories differ on the question of how virtue is produced—the first stressing the role of education, the second the importance of social and economic circumstance (equality–inequality), and of manipulating motives such as fear and love. But they agree that the purpose of law, whether directed to the first or second of these sets of factors, is to produce goodness. Theories based on the concept of "Virtue" also assume that different forms of regime signify different ways of life, different agreements about what is good and valuable, and that if the agreement alters, the form of government necessarily varies *pari passu.*

If "Freedom" is the focal concept of a theory, stability is assessed in terms of the degree to which citizens are secure in their freedom, whether this is the freedom of Hobbesian or Lockean property owners, or freedom conceived as moral independence, embodied in a Rousseauistic "General Will." Naturalistic theories conceive of freedom wholly in terms of external liberty to act without restraint, while teleo-naturalist and noumenalist theories stress internal, or moral freedom. And this, of course, means that the word "Freedom" becomes in such theories a conception of "Virtue," or goodness. But it is a conception which, in contrast to the pre–modern tradition of goodness, is substantively empty. It does not imply conformity to a detailed model of perfection, but rather the absence of dominantly egoistic impulses, openness of the self to the other, and openness to the concept of universal procedural rules of right: the idea of law as such, abstractly conceived. This is especially true of Rousseau's *moi commun* who shares in a "General Will," of Kant's man of good will who obeys the Categorical Imperative by treating all men as ends rather than merely as means, of Hegel's carrier of the "Absolute Idea," seeking self-realization in freedom, and of Marx's post–revolutionary communist who experiences his freedom as a "species being," or universal self.

Theories of "Virtue" and theories of "Freedom" also differ (in most cases) on the question of the historicity of politics. Pre–modern theories envisage political life as a series of endless cycles of goodness and corruption which, taken together, have no over–arching historical significance. (In Christian thought, history, of course, leads to the Kingdom of Heaven, but this is transcendent history, which lies mysteriously behind the veils of the empirical, and does not explain what goes on in the temporal pattern of daily political life. That is, one cannot discern movement toward the City of God by examining the politics of the City of this World.) Modern theories of freedom, by contrast, make the historical process a teleological one: the story of the vindication and realization of human freedom. Hobbes is an exception; his thought is universalist and ahistorical. And in Locke and Rousseau there is only a fragmentary historical analysis. But the works of Kant,

Hegel, Mill, Marx, and Nietzsche are all radically historical in their conception of freedom's fulfillment.

The Political Classics
and Modern Political Analysis

Much of this book will be taken up with the description and analysis of the great political theories of Western political culture, arranged in order of historical sequence, from Plato to Nietzsche. It therefore shares considerable common ground with the traditional theory text. The reader will find, however, that my approach to the interpretation of the classics differs considerably from that of the traditional treatment. I am not interested in these works primarily as reflections of or influences on the political ideologies of the societies in which they were created, but rather in the universal ideas contained in the classic theories. What do they have to say about rational political order and about the empirical order, which is as relevant to our concerns in twentieth-century America as to the problems of ancient Athenians and Romans, of the citizens of the medieval *Respublica Christiana,* of Renaissance absolutists and republicans, of eighteenth- and nineteenth-century revolutionaries, liberals, and conservatives? In what way can their study transform *our* ideologies into knowledge, or at least stimulate such a transformation? In what way can they contribute to this transformation by rendering more sophisticated the model building of professional students of politics?

I attempt to show how the classic theories can perform this work by showing that they are already performing it. Their central concepts find restatement in the theories of modern students of politics. Modern scholarship in fact contains few fundamental assumptions about the nature of political reality and about what the vital political questions are which are not expressed in one or other of the great books. The new behavioral approaches, despite their great originality, build on the past, some on the naturalism of Machiavelli or Hobbes, others on the Aristotle of *Politics* IV–VI, still others on the teleo-naturalism of J. S. Mill. And beside them we find noumenalist theories in profusion which also draw freely from the classical fountainhead—neo-Platonist, neo-Augustinian, and neo-Thomist theories.

It is my hope that this text will help to integrate courses in the classics with the general political science curriculum by pointing out this relationship between the materials taught in the traditional theory course and the various kinds of modern scholarship which form the materials of other courses in the discipline, and by underscoring the relevance of the classics for the current methodological debate and the larger debate about values which is going on throughout our society. I present an analysis of the classics of our political tradition as methodologies and as general theories of the political system, and I examine some representative examples of the main tendencies in modern political studies as extensions and modifications of one or other of the great general systems of political theory. Thus, with the analysis of Plato I couple a discussion of the work of Leo Strauss and his students. With Aristotle I discuss the writings of political sociologists such as Seymour Lipset and philosophers of the school of Ludwig Wittgenstein. The chapter on Machiavelli relates the thought of that writer to the "Chicago School" of political science, and to modern theories of "group process." And so with the other classic and modern theorists.

Caveat about What this Book is and What It is Not

I should like to make it clear that this is not intended as a study in the history of ideas, within the accepted meaning of that expression. The comparisons which I make of the old and the new are not meant to imply a direct causal relationship between the classical writing and the modern work, nor am I interested, for its own sake, in the matter of who influenced whom. Some of the likenesses I observe may be accidental, though I suspect that in most cases some sort of indirect influence could be established. But this is quite irrelevant to my purpose. I am not interested in tracing influences but in noting significant similarities and differences. What I wish to show is that current political research both of the behavioral and nonbehavioral (including the antibehavioral) variety can be most fully appreciated if it is understood within some general theoretical order, and I have tried to relate the modern writings which I examine to the classical systems with which they have a clear affinity. On the one hand, this should demonstrate that the great theories are not of antiquarian interest only, but have a perennial value and a vital significance for the understanding of the politics of our time. On the other hand, it should help the student build a broad theoretical system in which to anchor the particular bits of modern political analysis which make up his daily assignments in political science courses, and open to him new dimensions of meaning in these assignments. Hopefully, it will also help the student transform his ideologies into carefully reasoned theory.

Let it also be understood that I do not claim a one-to-one identity between the philosophical framework of the great theory and that of the modern writing. To make such a claim would be absurd on its face. No restatement of a great idea by a sophisticated scholar is a pure return to an earlier statement. Consciously or unconsciously, the writer refines and modifies the idea in the light of the continuing historical dialogue which results from the fact that every closed system is only a partial apprehension of reality. Even Jacques Maritain, who more self-consciously than the others I have written about attempts to build upon a single one of the great theories, incorporates in his politics many ideas which are clearly closer to the systems of Bergson and Kant than to that of St. Thomas. The resemblances which I have pointed out, therefore, are between some of the most accented concepts of the modern writing and the dominant ideas of a particular classic. The comparisons are a heuristic device and should be understood as such.

Since the publication in 1953 of David Easton's book *The Political System* there has been a growing recognition of a need for a general theory of politics which can give coherence and significance to the many diverse narrow-gauge studies that are written every year. Some of the modern writings which I consider in this book have been offered as attempts at general-theory building. By relating each of them to a comprehensive philosophical system I hope to throw some light on the validity of these claims. By focusing on their underlying assumptions I perhaps help to show how these schools of thought complement one another in such a way as to furnish elements of a comprehensive theory, if no one is adequate taken alone. I hold no brief for noumenalist philosophy as opposed to naturalistic science, or for a science opposed to philosophical inquiry into the transcendent political good. Rather, in my final chapter I have tried to show how we may proceed to construct a bridge between the various tendencies within political studies today, though its actual construction lies beyond the limits of this book.

Organization of the Chapters

I open each chapter with a brief intellectual biography of a classic theorist and a sketch of the political and intellectual climate of his time. Next I present the theorist's "method," in the broad sense of his world-view, conceptual framework, and techniques for collecting and analyzing political data. (In the Mill chapter, for special reasons, part of the discussion of method is the third rather than the second element.) This I follow with an explication and critique of the political theory proper. Then I present in comparison a summary and analysis of a modern political theory which develops some of the central ideas of the classic theory and applies them to the contemporary scene. Throughout I attempt to estimate the strengths and weaknesses, major insights and major blind spots of the type of political theory under scrutiny.

I have chosen for analysis those theories which I believe speak most clearly to us in America today and those which have received significant development in modern political studies. The interested reader will, I am sure, seek out for himself the other great theories not treated in this work.

Bibliographical Note

The historicist conception of political theory, which forms the framework of most of the textbooks in political ideas, is developed in capsule form by its chief practitioner, George Sabine, in "What Is a Political Theory?" *The Journal of Politics,* Vol. I, 1939, pp. 1–16, and also in the preface to his textbook, *A History of Political Theory,* 3rd ed., New York: Holt, Rinehart & Winston, Inc., 1961. The conception has been severely criticized both by the "naturalist" political scientists and by "noumenalist" political philosophers. For a naturalist critique, see David Easton, *The Political System,* New York: Alfred A. Knopf, Inc., 1953, Chapter 10. A noumenalist critique is contained in Leo Strauss, *Natural Right and History,* Chicago: University of Chicago Press, 1953, Chapter 1. Barrington Moore, *Political Power and Social Theory,* Cambridge, Mass.: Harvard University Press, 1958, describes the quarrel between the "moral absolutists" and the "empirical relativists," who correspond roughly to my "noumenalists" and "naturalists."

For a survey of the various uses of the concept "political theory," see Vernon Van Dyke, *Political Theory: A Philosophical Analysis,* Stanford, Calif.: Stanford University Press, 1960, Chapter 9. A variety of conceptions of political theory and of the relationship of theory to political studies in general are found in Roland Young, ed., *Approaches to the Study of Politics,* Evanston, Ill.: Northwestern University Press, 1958. See in particular the articles by Carl J. Friedrich, Louis Hartz, and Frederick M. Watkins. The papers in the volume were presented at a conference on political theory and the study of politics held at Northwestern University in 1955. For a conference report see Harry Eckstein (rapporteur), "Political Theory and the Study of Politics: A Report of a Conference," *American Political Science Review*, Vol. L. June 1956, pp. 475–87. In the Young volume, Mulford Q. Sibley has an article on "The Place of Classical Political Theory in the Study of Politics."

A spate of book-length studies of the nature of political theory appeared in the late 1960s. Dante Germino, *Beyond Ideology: The Revival of Political Theory,* New York: Harper & Row, Publishers, 1967, evaluates behavioral theory as ideology and calls for a revival of classical modes of political philosophizing. Eugene Meehan, *Contemporary Political Thought, A Critical Study,* Homewood, Ill: Dorsey Press, 1967, standing within the positivist and behavioral tradition, stresses the need to bring value theory together with causal theory. Fred Frohock, *The Nature of Political Inquiry,* Homewood, Ill.: Dorsey Press, 1967 and Thomas A. Spragens, Jr., *The Dilemma of Contemporary Political Theory: Toward a Post-Behavioral Science of Politics,* New York: Dunellen Publishing Co., 1973, are two important efforts to show how ethical analysis may be fused with behavioral inquiry.

PART ONE

Theories
of
Political Virtue

The philosophic tradition of "Virtue" arises from the decay of the aristocratic mythology of Homeric political culture in Greece whose heyday was the tenth century B.C. As late as the sixth century B.C., indeed, it was a common assumption that nobility or virtue (areté, human excellence) went with noble blood and was inherited from divine ancestors. And an analysis of the literature of the tribal period, the age of the Illiad and the Odyssey, reveals what things were traditionally admired. Physical courage was central, but this was combined with kindness and displayed in accord with a code of gentlemanly conduct. Most important was the quality of aidos, respect for self and for others, which restrained the powerful from acts of brutality and shrewd persons from greediness. Aidos was based on a regard for public opinion and on a sense of social obligation. This is what was meant by "honor"—performing one's obligations, doing what was expected of one. Generosity, bravery, courtesy, hospitality, and loyalty to the group are all included in the notion of aidos.[1]

To underline the significance of divine ancestors is to show that the context of the concept of "virtue" described above was a closed tribal society based on ties of kinship. In such a setting, the individual was swallowed up in his social roles and acted the part allotted to him by the gods and the fates. Tribal religion legislated the values of the society, which were expressed in the way of life of the divinely-descended aristoi (the aristocrats), and established these values as authoritative for all members of the closed group. The obligation to be virtuous was the primary moral reality. Individual freedom did not exist.

The individual as a free agent, free of obligatory religious mores imposed by the tribe, began to emerge about two centuries after tribal life had evolved (in the

---

[1]W.R. Agard, *What Democracy Meant to the Greeks* (Chapel Hill, N.C.: University of North Carolina Press, 1942), pp. 26-27. See also Werner Jaeger, *Paideia* (New York: Oxford University Press, 1939), I, pp. 1-8.

eighth century B.C.) into the territorially defined citizenship of the Polis, the Greek city-state. First noticeable in the colonial cities of Ionia, where life had been urban from the beginning, and where "the old sanctities of tribal life had never found a home," humanist liberalism became a prominent feature of life on the Greek peninsula, especially in Athens, during the democratizing experience of radical social, economic and political change of the sixth and fifth centuries.[2] The intellectual context was one of skepticism and naturalism, both associated with the beginnings of an atomistic and mechanistic view of things in which there is a tendency to bring non-organic, animal, and human nature together as a single physical reality.

Greek liberalism received its chief expression in the writings of the Thracian atomist philosopher Democritus, and in those of the Sophists, the itinerant teachers of fifth-century Athens, all of whom were foreigners in Athens, and therefore uninfluenced by its pre-democratic traditions.[3] None of these writers produced a major systematic philosophic statement, however. And the liberal movement quickly declined from an effort by Democritus and Protagoras to solve pragmatically the problem of democratic consensus on the basis of enlightened individualism, to the cynical and bitter doctrines of individual withdrawal from politics and society penned by Antiphon, terminating in the imperalist individualism of Callicles. The latter was ready to reduce the conception of objective public interest and purpose to the self-interested will of the clever and the strong. All this was against the background of the withering of Athenian democracy during the Peloponnesian War (431-404 B.C.), after a brief heyday of a free and consensual democratic order during the generalship of Pericles. The political themes abortively set forth by the Greek liberals were not to find adequate phiiosophical development until the modern era, in the writings of Hobbes, Locke, Rousseau and Bentham.[4]

Despite the fact that their intention was to understand and institutionalize freedom, the Greek liberals continued to employ the traditional language of virtue (areté). They redefined it, of course, and they developed an interest in whether virtue could be taught, since in the traditional view the transmission of virtue was by inheritance. Democritus and Protagoras focused on civic virtue, the bond of social and political order. Antiphon developed the theme of personal integrity and the virtue of the individual in isolation from society. For the run-of-the-mill Sophist rhetors, who were numerous in fifth-century Athens, virtue signified the ability to "win friends and influence people" with the spoken word in democratic debate, and the business of the Sophists was to instill this ability by the teaching of rhetoric, for a fee. For Callicles virtue was the prowess of the strong man displayed in his ability to secure and hold power—a herald of the Machiavellian concept.

[2] See Ernest Barker, *Greek Political Theory: Plato and his Predecessors*, 3rd ed. (London: Methuen, 1947), p. 45.

[3] See Eric Havelock, *The Liberal Temper in Greek Politics* (New Haven & London: Yale University Press, 1957), and the critique by Leo Strauss, in *Liberalism: Ancient and Modern* (New York: Basic Books, 1968), Ch. 3.

[4] Havelock makes express comparisons between the Greek liberals and these modern theorists. *The Liberal Temper*, pp. 132, 155-56, 258, 262.

With Socrates and Plato, freedom receded into the background, and virtue or goodness became a word once more endowed, as in the tradition, with transcendent meaning and absolute moral value. In their thought it was a subtler, gentler, and more spiritualized concept than in traditional teachings, however. And its conception and achievement were to be the result of intellectual-erotic endeavor by the individual rather than through kinship. Its categories were those of rational philosophy, not of fideist religion. We shall examine in detail in the next chapter the political implications of this view of human excellence, focusing on the work of Plato and that of the modern Neo-Platonist school of Leo Strauss.

In the philosophy of Aristotle, the noumenal conception of virtue was translated from Plato's "Heaven above the heavens" to historical life as an immanent impulse to moral perfection.[5] Aristotle also made an effort to incorporate the naturalistic insights and the democratic values of the liberals in his analytical politics. We classify him as a noumenal bridge-builder. The politics that flow from this position are analyzed in Chapter 3. We shall see that while Aristotle tried to tie the noumenal and naturalistic world views together, some of the modern political scientists who find Aristotelian categories congenial, separate the two by attempting to divorce theoretical description from normative comparison and ethical prescription.

With the death of Aristotle, which occurred at the same time as the moral and political death of the polis, the conception of "virtue" moved out onto the world stage of the oecumene (the entire civilized world). In the thought of the early Stoa (336-204 B.C.), "virtue" lost all connection with politics and became a purely private and inward affair—as it was for Antiphon. However, in a mystical way the lone philosopher, pursuing virtue, was conceived as a member of a world community that lived passively behind the veils of the fragmented world political society, a quiet communion of hearts and minds, at peace in the midst of clashing empires. In the second and third periods of the Stoa, however (204-43 B.C., 43 B.C.-ca. 565 A.D.), in the context of Roman life, virtue became once again connected with politics - as the moral achievement of the philosopher who engages in politics for the sake of the common good, solely out of a sense of duty, but without experiencing personal fulfillment through the commitment. In the polis, individual virtue and the moral and institutional health of society were mutually dependent. For the Stoic, however, virtue was something cultivated in private which profited the respublica, the commonwealth, in its application to political tasks. Its measure and standard was absolute right, now conceived as a Law of Nature. During the last years of the republic this concept functioned as a principle of constitutional government, while during the centuries of empire it progressively mitigated the worst features of the institution of slavery and facilitated the development of a vast and complex code of universally applicable principles of legal right (the Jus Gentium).

In the thought of the Christian Fathers such as Augustine, whose political theories we consider in Chapter 4, the Greek and Roman traditions of virtue became

[5]See chapter 1 for definition of "noumenal."

mingled with Judaic concepts of human goodness. Virtue was now the quality of the saint, whose evil will had been regenerated by Divine Grace, through the death and resurrection of Jesus Christ. And it was made manifest in works of love and justice, the former defined in the terms of the Sermon on the Mount, the latter by the norms of the Mosaic Code. Its culmination now lay beyond the temporal in membership in the City of God in Heaven (the Church Triumphant). Virtue was neither generated by political life, nor expected to generate political virtue. Politics was reduced to the maintenance of peace and order—a politics of preservation rather than perfection. And its cycles were explained in terms of the presence or absence not of Christian virtue, but of the ancient pagan virtue of moderation.

The imminent demise of the ancient world was clearly evident in the pessimistic pages of Augustine's City of God (426 A.D.). When its death came at last in the sixth century, political philosophy, as systematic reasoning about society, disappeared. Europe lay down for six centuries of philosophical sleep. Political doctrine we find aplenty, in the encyclicals of popes, in glosses of monks on Holy Writ, in canon law, in the edicts of kings, and in the polemical literature that developed out of conflict between the papacy and a variety of secular rulers. But it was not until the thirteenth century that anything approaching the speculative literature of ancient philosophy was written. When it finally appeared, the central theme was, as before, "virtue."

Thomas Aquinas was more optimistic than Augustine, and more complex in his thinking on virtue. He defined two kinds of virtue: that of the natural man of reason, and that of the regenerated Christian, the man of faith. The first was the province of the civil order, the latter, that of the Church. Comparing it with earlier models, Aquinas's treatment of temporal virtue was more Stoic than Hellenic. For despite the influence of Aristotle on his work, Aquinas did not assert that participation in political life made men good, or that the goodness or badness in the citizenry produced good or bad rulers. Nor was the ruler improved as a man by ruling; his motives in ruling well were duty and the hope of salvation, not temporal fulfillment. In carrying out his duty, his role was to restrain men from behavior adverse to the interests of society, not to inculcate in them the highest virtue. That was for the Church to do, with transcendent salvation as its goal rather than the temporal perfection of natural man. We review Thomas's thought, and that of a modern Thomist in Chapter 5.

The dominant scholasticism of Medieval thought, like its Aristotelian model, was essentialist (noumenalist) in its assumption that reality was teleological, and was knowable by reason. A counter-current in Medieval intellectual life was the nominalist (not to be confused with noumenalist) school represented by Marsiglio of Padua and William of Occam, whose lives bridged the thirteenth and fourteenth centuries. This was a school of thought which derived its basic assumptions from Augustinian pessimism about the corruption of reason as the result of the Fall of Adam. For them our universal concepts were just names we give to the phenomena we observe, not representations of the real structures of the world, of "essences," which are foreclosed to us.

As they unfolded, the categories of nominalist thought became strongly reminiscent of the antique naturalism of Democritus and the Sophists. Not surprisingly, the theme of freedom, in a secularist mode, was sounded by these thinkers, as the Respublica Christiana passed its zenith. Marsiglio was certainly no individualist. However, his theoretical concern was not with moral virtue, but with problems of community control through representative institutions, always a central concern of theories of freedom. And his conception of social policy was utilitarian. Occam, in his denial of the reality (knowability) of essences, or universals, certainly laid a groundwork for individualism in his insistence that only particulars are real.

From Marsiglio and Occam there was but a short historical step to Niccolo Machiavelli, for whom the individual alone was real, and who in his Discourses was explicitly concerned with the construction of a commonwealth in which individuals felt secure and were free to pursue the objects of their desire. Ironically, virtue was his chief theme—the virtue of the absolute prince and of the free citizenry of a republic. But its definition had altered radically from that of the moral tradition. Machiavelli, in fact, inverted the traditional terms of reference, by asserting that a virtuous prince must know "how not to be good and to use his knowledge or refrain from using it as he may need." Machiavellian virtue could not be taught. It was not inherited from divine ancestors, but was inborn nevertheless, as animal strength and cunning.

With Machiavelli we are on the threshold of a new way of ideas and a new world of naturalistic freedom. We have also arrived at the foundations of the modern natural science of politics. We meet both Machiavelli and representatives of that science in Chapter 6.

Chapter 2

Platonic Goodness and the School of Leo Strauss

Plato was born into one of Athens's noble families, and according to tradition his lineage could be traced back to the god Poseidon. While Plato's rationalism of course led him to repudiate such myths of divine descent, his philosophy incorporated and transformed the moral values that had been an integral part of the myth–based tradition. His purpose in philosophizing was to understand these values more clearly than they had been understood in his time, and to demonstrate their ground in moral reason. In Plato's philosophy, virtue ceased to be a legacy and became instead a teachable "knowledge of the Good."

The Intellectual and Political Context

Naturalistic Political Science

Plato's search for the transcendent good, the foundation of his political philosophy, can only be understood in the light of the earlier Greek science of politics, and the connection that Plato drew between this science and the tragic story of the Peloponnesian War, the great struggle between Athens and Sparta for the hegemony of the Greek world (434–404 B.C.). The beginnings of that science are found in the work of the Ionian philosophers of the sixth and fifth centuries B.C., who were the first to propose a general naturalistic theory of causation as a substitute for the traditional reliance on religious myth. In the poems of Homer, all events, both natural and human, were caused by the gods, who acted at the prompting of whim and caprice in a universe unregulated and unpredictable. But by the sixth century, Greek thinkers began to perceive regularity in the world, and in place of the gods they saw natural forces at work in the causal order. In Miletus, one of the Ionian cities of Greek Asia Minor, Anaximander and Anaximines developed a crude theory of mechanical causation and explained all movement as the result of the interaction of opposing bodies or tendencies.[1] They did not arrive at their theory a priori, but only after a great deal of careful empirical observation, especially of the motions of the heavenly bodies. And they successfully employed the empirical data they had collected, in terms of their theories of natural regularity, to forecast future events, such as the solar eclipse of 585 B.C., predicted by Thales.[2]

Democritus. Ionian physics formed the background of the mechanistic atomism employed by Democritus of Abdera, an intellectual of the Age of Pericles, as the framework for understanding the workings of Athenian democracy. As Eric Havelock writes, "Democritus' political and social theory sufficiently establishes his conviction that even as all physical processes exhibit a configuration which is amenable to rational description, so also does the historical process which has generated human institutions."[3] Human atoms, clashing with one another and inflicting injury in the natural state, form themselves into patterns of political order to achieve security, according to Democritus. Unlike Hobbes, who much later carried forward this line of naturalistic analysis, Democritus did not argue that this is an adequate basis for consensus. Foreshadowing the approach of Rousseau, he built social agreement on a human capacity for altruism and compassion. This mitigates competition in society.

> Now it does not go "beyond reason" . . . . : men continue to seek power for themselves but within a formula set, not by custom law so much as the "utility of the commonwealth." This is a rational criterion of civic good.[4]

Democritus, as paraphrased by Havelock, is here celebrating the consensus of the Periclean moment of Athenian democracy and giving an account of it in terms of rational self-interest and empathy.

Protagoras. In the work of Protagoras, one of the elder generation of Sophists, and another of the Periclean intelligentsia, utilitarian rationalism has another important representative. Like Democritus, Protagoras was particularly concerned with the question of consensus-building in a secular democracy. And the curriculum that he taught was based on a theory of education designed to produce the responsible citizen. Central to this was

[1]Robert Scoon, *Greek Philosophy Before Plato* (Princeton, N.J.: Princeton University Press, 1928), p. 18.

[2]*Ibid.,* p. 20.

[3]Eric Havelock, *The Liberal Temper in Greek Politics* (New Haven: Yale University Press), 1957, p. 155.

[4]*Ibid.,* p. 146.

the inculcation of shared opinions about the "true" and the "just," even though within a naturalistic world view there was no way of establishing the validity of such views. In contrast to Democritus, Protagoras stressed custom and ideology, and the processes of political socialization, rather than rational interest and compassion, as the foundations of political consensus. In *Theaetetus*, Plato, probably exaggeratedly, makes him out to be a cynical cultural relativist:

> My position, then, is that whatever seems right and admirable to a particular city-state is truly right and admirable—during the period of time in which that opinion continues to be held; and that it is the wise man's task, when the people are afflicted with unsound beliefs, to substitute others so that they seem true and therefore *are* true. Thus the sophist, who trains his pupils on the same principle, thereby shows his wisdom and justifies his claim to a large fee when the course of training is over.[5]

Periclean Democracy and the Sophists

What was the political world like in which the naturalistic political science of Democritus and Protagoras held sway? It was a day of movement, a day of the opening of culture to culture, of the mingling of cultures, and consequently a skeptical and secular time, one very much like our own twentieth century. B. A. G. Fuller has admirably described the atmosphere of the times:

> Trade and travel and war had been raising the curtains of the surrounding world and revealing more intimately to the Greek the great foreign civilizations at his doors. The same influences had brought the Greeks themselves into close and irritating contact and confronted them with one another's peculiarities. And the development of her empire had opened the eyes of Athens to some of the political and social, if not to the philosophic and religious consequences of a world in which institutions and ideals, convictions and standards, were not of all one "stock" pattern. . . . Everywhere . . . the horizons of the mind were widening upon the vast confusion of human life. In the picture that was disclosed, crowded with the countless and multiform "cities of men" and the bewildering diversities of their "manners, climates, councils, governments," it might well seem that no final or single perspective could be found. The eye sought in vain some vanishing point of agreement, be it about the nature of the world or of the Gods or of the good, towards which all this diversity of thought and action converged. It met only an irreconcilable divergence and self-contradiction in ideals, beliefs, laws, institutions, rules of conduct, and even primitive instincts. The cherished truth of one school of philosophy was the detested falsehood of its neighbor . . . What was right here was wrong there.[6]

[5]*Theaetetus* 166. All references to the Dialogues are to the Jowett translation published in two volumes by Random House, New York, 1937.

[6]B.A.G. Fuller, *History of Greek Philosophy* (New York: Holt, Rinehart, & Winston, 1931), Vol. II, pp. 4-5.

Athens in the fifth century was an open society, in which talent and shrewd dealing could bring a man to the top. As a direct democracy, policy was made in the *Ecclesia,* a sovereign assembly of all male Athenians, whose power was legally unlimited. Furthermore, argument before the law courts, whose judgments were given by large popular juries chosen by lot, was carried on by the litigants themselves. The institution of professional counsel was unknown. And the bustling, competitive commercial life of the time kept the dockets of the courts filled with suits. Under these conditions it was an exceedingly valuable accomplishment to be able to speak persuasively. Leadership in the state no longer depended on inherited virtue. Nor did it depend on wealth. Under the democratic dispensation, leadership rested on wits and the ability to sway others with words. Rich young men in particular were eager for sophistic learning, realizing that their wealth was secure only so long as they could lead the common man.

The development of sophistic education was a response to the needs of the time. "In the new circumstances of democratic push and competition . . . the object of life lay in self-preservation. . . . Education must be . . . practical in its aim. Its prime, indeed its only function was to help every young man to get on with all speed and elbow his way vigorously to the front through the crowd."[7] At its best, this type of education produced the well-rounded, versatile individual who excelled in many things—the type of man celebrated by the Athenian leader Pericles in the Funeral Oration which Thucydides records in his *Peloponnesian War.* At the worst, it produced the immoral schemer who was ready to build a cogent argument for any point of view, and to make the worse cause appear the better and the better cause the worse. As a result of the influence of Plato, who was severely critical of the Sophists, it is this second type whose image is conveyed to us by the word "sophist" today.

The Sophist was a type of itinerant school teacher who taught in Athens from about the middle of the fifth century B.C. The schools of the Sophists represented the beginning of formal education in the Greek world, and were closely associated with the democratization of Greek life. The curriculum varied. In scope it ranged from training in a single type of rhetoric, such as the forensic rhetoric taught by Gorgias, to the encyclopedic curriculum of Hippias, which included courses in grammar, mythology, family history, archaeology, arithmetic, astronomy, geometry, and music. But no matter what the particular offering, the spirit of sophistic education was pretty much the same everywhere. Its object was to convey not truth but a technique, the art of successful living. In the early days of sophistry, in the work of Protagoras, as we have seen, this meant teaching civic virtue, good citizenship. But very soon thereafter sophistic education came to mean in-

[7]*Ibid.,* p. 10.

struction in the art of "getting ahead," social and political success. The Athenian young man of the fifth century turned to sophistic learning with much the same attitude as some young Americans today approach the winning of the bachelor's degree. A sophistic education was a ticket to worldly success.

The Peloponnesian War

In 431 B.C. Athens was at the height of her power. A bustling commercial state, her trade extended far and wide through the Mediterranean world. Colonies and other *poleis* throughout the Aegean and on the shores of Asia Minor paid her tribute as leader of the Delian League, a confederation Athens had led to victory over the Persians in 467 B.C., and converted thereafter into an empire. Fearful that the balance of power with her rival was about to be disastrously upset, Sparta and her allies of the Peloponnesian League brought on a showdown conflict with the Athenians. The showdown would take place at several levels: between land-based agrarian power and sea-based commercial economy; between traditional religious society and innovative-secular order; and between closed, aristocratic polity and open, democratic political order. In the final result, the decision would be given for Sparta.

Bred in the Sophistic culture we have described, and schooled also in the causal analysis that Hippocratic medicine had developed out of the physical speculation of the Ionians, the historian Thucydides presented a scientific account of the conflict between Athens and Sparta in naturalistic terms reminiscent of the work of Democritus and Protagoras. But unlike his two predecessors, Thucydides failed to draw utilitarian prescriptions for democratic stability and consensus from his descriptive explanations. His science described instead a pathology for which there was no cure.

Like Democritus and Protagoras, Thucydides found secular democracy quite compatible with social and political consensus during the Periclean heyday. He went further than they, to show that it was the energy, intelligence, and creativity released by the processes of democratization that were the chief causes of Athens' commercial prosperity and political power. But paradoxically, he found that these very democratic institutions were also the cause of the instability of that power. The conditions conducive to rational policy, of individuals and even more of groups, are difficult to maintain, he argued. And delicate reason is surrounded by pitfalls on every side. As Thucydides put it, "Human nature [is] always rebelling against the law [of reason]. . . . Indeed men too often take upon themselves in the prosecution of their revenge to set the example of doing away with those general laws [of reason] to which all alike can look for salvation in adversity, instead of allowing them to subsist against the day of danger when their aid may be required."[8] Times of distress, and of violent conflict in particular—times of war and revolution or plague—destroy reason.[9] Also, excessive deprivation of a basic value will lead to a reckless pursuit of that value. And at the other extreme, satiety, or complete fulfillment of one of the basic drives, will lead to the irrational pursuit of the value next highest in the hierarchy. Thus "plenty fills [men] with ambition which belongs to insolence and pride," and the impulse arises "to drive men into danger."[10] The iron necessity of the passions in these circumstances replaces the freedom of reason. And the result is the final frustration of the passionate person or state. Democracy, Thucydides believed, was peculiarly prone to the movements of the passions. Her institutions lent no support to reason in time of adversity. Democracy might facilitate the creation of great power, but it was helpless to maintain it. Athenian rationality rested on enlightened self-interest, which the institutions of democracy could produce but not sustain. Such a conscious, calculated awareness of the relationship between the individual good and the common good, and of the need for social unity and for cool, moderate policies was too fragile a thing to stand up in the face of the pressures of fear and honor deriving from empire, war, and the plague.

In Quest of Moral Order

Plato was born in 427 B.C., the fourth year of the Peloponnesian War, and his youth was spent amidst scenes of civil and international conflict that culminated in the destruction of Athens's empire and the collapse of her democratic institutions. In 404 B.C., the year the war ended, the ebullient and optimistic days of Periclean democracy seemed far away. The political scene was now one of defeat, conspiracy, and class domination. Civil strife continued far beyond the end of the war, and in 399 B.C. Plato saw his beloved teacher Socrates executed by the restored democracy as a scapegoat in a factional struggle.

Rationalist naturalism, originally a system of thought for legitimating and celebrating secular democracy, and an instrument of scientific prescription, had been transmuted in the work of Thucydides into the tragically detached description of ineluctable political pathology. It had run out of resources for dealing in an effectively human manner with the desperate situation faced by Athens and by the whole Greek world. Plato was to attempt an entirely new way of thinking about politics and ethics. He might well have commented in a vein adopted by a modern admirer of his, Profes-

---

[8]Thucydides, *The Peloponnesian War* (New York: Random House [Modern Library], 1951), 3.84.

[9]*Ibid.,* 3.82.

[10]See *Ibid.,* 3.45 and 3.46.

sor Eric Voegelin of Stanford University, that "the science of Thucydides explored the *idea* only of *kinesis,* of the disturbance of order," and that the thing which was vitally necessary in his time was rather a science of order.

> Thucydides' feat of transforming the knowledge of the craftsmen into a science . . . inevitably raised grave problems for the future of political science. The *kinesis* was a "Disease" of political order; the craftsmen who shaped and defined its *eidos* were the grave-diggers of Hellas . . . and the political science of Thucydides was a model study of the suicide of a nation but hardly a study of successful political order. If Cimon, Miltiades, and Pericles, according to a diagnosis of Plato, were poor statesmen who shaped a *kinesis* and thereby destroyed the order of the Athenian polis and its empire, where was the craftsman to be found, and what would he look like, who could shape a just order? . . . The science of Thucydides explored the *idea* only of *kinesis,* of the disturbance of order; Plato explored the idea of order itself. This relation between Thucydides and Plato needs emphasis, because on occasion one can still hear voiced the nostalgic sentiment: How marvellously could political science have advanced if others had followed in the footsteps of Thucydides, and if this promising beginning of a science of politics had not been cut off by the influence of Plato's philosophy. This preconception of the empiricists overlooks the fact that the two thinkers complement each other: Thucydides studied a political society in crisis, and created the empirical science of the lethal disease of order; Plato created the other half of politics, the empirical science of order.[11]

What precisely is meant when one says that Plato's intention was to create a "science of order"? Did not the story of imperial emergence and decline told by Thucydides reveal a pattern or an order? Perhaps, but Plato knew that this was not a good order; nor was it an inevitable order, as Thucydides had described it. A better way existed and could be chosen. Human life is not meant to be full of violence and conflict. Good order must be harmonious order. Nor are men condemned to be forever hedonists. A nobler life is possible. And men must be capable of developing social institutions which produce well-ordered lives and thereby civil peace.

But what is this good order, and how can it be known? Once known, how can it be instituted? Thucydides had restricted his science to empirical description, and in general he reserved judgment on the goodness of the things he observed. The heart of Plato's inquiry was the standard of goodness itself. And the pursuit of an answer to this question was to lead off into the most diverse and difficult fields of intellectual activity, including metaphysics—the study of ultimate reality—which had brought the Ionian and Eleatic philosophers to confusion. Plato embraced as an organic whole several lines of inquiry which today, in an age of great specialization and compartmentalization of knowledge, are most often pursued separately; though there are men of catholic mind now whose scholarship sweeps across

---

[11]Eric Voegelin, *Order and History*, Vol. II: *The World of the Polis* (Baton Rouge: Louisiana State University Press, 1957), p. 357.

an area almost as broad as that chosen by Plato. Like Reinhold Niebuhr and Jacques Maritain today, Plato was at once a theologian, metaphysician, epistemologist, moral philosopher, psychologist, and student of politics. And in social action he was, like them, a teacher of and preacher to the intellectuals. He was in addition something of an etymologist and semanticist, and paradoxically, at once a poet and a master logician.

Earlier in this chapter we spoke of the impact of sophistic culture on fifth and fourth-century Greece, and of the influence of the sophistic "professors" on Thucydides. Sophistry also pervades the writings of Plato, but in this case the influence is wholly negative. To Plato the Sophist is the great deceiver and therefore an arch foe, and the Dialogues constitute one long polemic against him. In all of the Dialogues it is a Sophist—Thrasymachus, Callicles, Gorgias, Protagoras—who articulates the doctrine of the false good on which Plato blamed the destruction of Athenian moral fiber and the terrible conflicts and the bestial behavior of his times.[12] Sophistic hedonism was the enemy, a doctrine which declared sensual pleasure to be the highest good in life and which made of the political system simply a device for maximizing the pleasure of the power elite. Through what kind of philosophy of the good life did Plato attempt to give it the lie, and how did he develop it?

Plato's Method

The Influence of Socrates

Plato's framework and method of investigation were, of course, not a wholly original system. Behind him stand all the early cosmologists and, most important of all, his teacher Socrates, a man who never wrote a book but who has had a most profound influence on more than 2,000 years of Western culture through his great pupil. The best scholarship today holds that it was chiefly from Socrates that Plato received the central concepts of his philosophy and the main elements of his scholarly method—his conception of the soul, his theory of Forms, the equation of knowledge of the Good with virtue, and dialectical inquiry.[13] At least in nucleus, these are all to be discovered in the interstices of Plato's earliest works, the so-called "Socratic Dialogues," a series of brief essays in which Plato's object was to present to the reader a faithful image of his master, and especially of the way in which his master went about the discovery of truth.[14]

[12]See *Republic* 1.338,344; *Gorgias* 452, 491–92.

[13]On this much disputed question I am following the English scholar, A. E. Taylor.

[14]This Group includes *Laches, Charmides, Euthyphro, Apology, Crito.* See Werner Jaeger, *Paideia,* trans., G. Highet (New York: Oxford University Press, 1945), Vol. II, p. 87 *ff.* and citations.

Socrates appears in all these little dialogues as a divinely sent gadfly, to use his own self-description. He is sent to arouse the citizens of Athens to a concern for the most important thing in life, what he called "the greatest improvement of the soul."[15] And he is constantly in the *agora* talking to his compatriots and annoying them into soul-improving activity. He tries to get them to think about and inquire into the meaning of the virtues and principles of right of the traditional ethical code, things which for most Athenians had become mere words, vague symbols to which they were accustomed to give lip-service, though sometimes hardly even that. He seems to assume that these traditional concepts embody a way of life which in an absolute sense constitutes the good of the human soul, the best way to live, but that they are badly understood, and are neglected by men who in general are more assiduous in acquiring the goods of the body than those of the soul. But they can be clarified. And virtue is knowledge of the Good—human goodness or excellence results from knowing what the good things are and how they are related to one another in the principle of Good itself. When Athenians have come to this knowledge, Athens will be reborn. It will become a good and well-ordered *polis*. Socrates is the midwife of this knowledge; he brings it to birth.[16]

An important point to emphasize here is that Socrates and Plato, in contrast to the Sophists, did not reject tradition. Their work was rather to reexamine it. And as we shall see, the result of their efforts was to reestablish traditional values on a new foundation. In place of the unthinkingness of the tradition, which relied on fable and myth as an anchor for value concepts, Socrates created a reasoned philosophy, or rather a sophisticated *method* of philosophizing by which the careful processes of clear thought would show the inherent reasonableness of the traditional virtues. As a young man Plato became a disciple of Socrates. He submitted to the discipline of dialectial examination of his own preconceptions about moral truth—to the give and take of earnest debate about the nature of the highest things. Even after Socrates' death the argument went on. Now Plato had a circle of his own, and the Academy was born—a formal school, or fourth-century B.C. Institute for Advanced Ethical Studies in which a little knot of scholars continued the pursuit of knowledge of the Good. And a doctrine began to emerge—about the Good, and about the political good, the best regime: *Republic, Statesman, Laws*.

Psyche

Now, let us look at the individual parts of the Platonic method. We have seen that one of its central notions, perhaps the starting point, is a certain conception of what the Greeks called *psyche,* which we usually translate

---

[15]*Apology*. 30.
[16]See *Apology* 21, 29, 30, 36, 38; *Laches* 187-90, 200-201; *Theaetetus* 148-51.

as "soul."[17] The expression *psyche* had been variously used by Greeks as far back as Homer.[18] But Socrates was the first Greek thinker to use this term to designate, as a unified whole, all of the invisible, nonphysiological parts of a man—what we call the "psychological" and the "spiritual" man put together—and Plato accepted and elaborated the Socratic conception.

The fundamental element of soul is life, defined as an immaterial and hence invisible substance, which is self-activating, self-moving, as contrasted with visible material substances which are moved by another.[19] This is a common-sense notion. The limbs of the body are moved by muscles and nerves, and these for their activity require the motion of blood through the body, which in turn requires the operation of certain nutritive processes, and so on. Every bodily movement or function can be referred back to another as its cause, or to some empirical agent outside the body in its physical environment. And as long as we stay in the realm of the empirical, we can expect to be able to reduce every observable cause of activity to the effect of some other observable cause of activity. At least this has always been the case. Biologists in probing for the principle or cause of life processes are looking for something empirical. And if they succeed in discovering this, they will still be faced with the problem of explaining the causal agent in empirical terms, and so on and on.[20] Plato supposed that to account for life or activity in empirical things one had to posit a nonempirical power which was self-sustaining—soul. We see life all around us, but we cannot reduce it to any empirical quantity. Therefore its nature must be nonempirical.

Knower and Known

The soul or life force in man, Plato observed, is intelligent. And intelligence he understood to be the ability we have to discern abstract and sensually invisible objects—those which we call concepts or universals. The organs of sight, hearing, taste, smell, and touch give the mind information about the empirical world—colors, sounds, flavors, odors, textures, and the like. But when the mind begins to reflect on these data and to seek for form and order in them by comparing sense objects with one another, it operates by a power of its own and uses abstract Ideas which no sense can perceive.[21]

[17]In the index of Jowett's four-volume translation of Plato's Dialogues (Oxford: Clarendon Press, 1953) the number of references to "soul" is rivaled only by the references to "art" and "God and gods."

[18]See John Burnet, "The Socratic Doctrine of the Soul," *Proceedings of the British Academy,* VII (1915-16), p. 245 *f.*

[19]*Laws* 10.892, 894–95; *Phaedrus* 245; *Timaeus* 36–37; *Phaedo* 80–81.

[20]See Robert K. Plumb, "Scientists Report Laboratory Clues to Origin of Life," *The New York Times,* Dec. 27, 1956, p. 1:3.

[21]*Theaetetus* 184–85; *Phaedo* 78–79.

These Ideas are of several different orders. Some are mathematical notions.[22] Others are ideas of physical qualities, such as greatness, health, strength.[23] Still other Ideas are moral qualities such as noble and base, good and evil, justice, holiness.[24] There are also aesthetic conceptions such as beauty.[25] And finally there are Ideas which are the "essential forms" or "absolute essences" of empirical creatures—Ideas which contain all those qualities which the particular members of classes of creatures have in common. There is for example an Idea of man, an Idea of table, an Idea of bed, all of which are different from the perceptual data of this man, this table, this bed.[26] In short, all of those invisible things of which we become aware upon reflection are Ideas. Knowledge is an awareness or comprehension of these Ideas and of their relations one to another. It begins with our reasoning or reflecting upon the impressions of sense.[27] And it ends with an understanding of things which in their inmost being are utterly independent of sense.

Plato's Metaphysics: The Form as the Real

Plato's own reflections on the world of Ideas and on the world of sense brought him to the conclusion that Ideas or Forms are the only truly real things that there are, and the only things that can be known. For they are permanent and unchanging, while the world of sense is one of incessant flux. In other words, he adopted what we have called the noumenalist view of reality. Things of sense cannot be known, "for at the moment that the observer approaches, they become other and of another nature, so that you cannot get any further in knowing their nature or state, for you cannot know that which has no state."[28]

Such meaning and purposive structure as empirical things have for us is only by virtue of their participation in the life of the Forms. The chaotic flux of matter receives transient impressions of Form. But the reality of such empirical things is that of a reflection in water, which is visible for a moment but then is rippled away by a movement of the wind. And the processes of change in the world of sensible objects are governed by "necessity," which produces a blind, purposeless chain of causes and effects that, like the sensible things themselves, is unintelligible, only the subject of opinion and statements of probability.[29]

[22]*Theaetetus* 185; *Republic* 10.602–603, 7.523, 524; *Phaedo* 74–75.

[23]*Theaetetus* 186.

[24]*Theaetetus* 186; *Phaedo* 75.

[25]*Phaedo* 75; *Republic* 5.476.

[26]*Phaedo* 76; *Republic* 10.596; *Parmenides* 130.

[27]*Theaetetus* 186.

[28]*Cratylus* 439; *Timaeus* 28.

[29]See *Timaeus* 48-52. On "mind" or "reason" and "necessity" in Plato's Dialogues, see Francis M. Cornford, *Plato's Cosmology* (New York: Harcourt, Brace & World, Inc., 1937), p. 159 *ff.* and citations.

In addition to the problems of knowledge posed by the dynamic character of empirical things, there are those posed by the fallibility of the organs of sense. They are "inaccurate witnesses."[30] True existence is revealed only in thought.

> And thought is best when mind is gathered into herself and none of these things trouble her—neither sounds, nor sights nor pain nor any pleasure, — when she takes leave of the body and has as little as possible to do with it, when she has no bodily sense or desire, but is aspiring after true being.[31]

Plato does not mean, however, that the mind knows in the Ideas things which it creates itself or which dwell only in the mind. He is not a subjectivist in any way. The Ideas which the mind knows he affirmed to have an existence outside the mind, in the "heaven above the heavens," as he poetically put it.[32] For thoughts cannot be thoughts merely, they must be thoughts of something which is. And Plato believed that "something" to be objective, consisting of "patterns fixed in nature,"[33] a region of "purity, and eternity, and immortality, and unchangeableness."[34]

Having discovered reality in Ideas, as he believed, Plato set about trying to discern the relationship of these only real things one to another. Where did the Ideas come from and how are they ordered? By what power are they known? What principle lies behind them at the very heart of the universe? This quest led him to the notion that all the Ideas can be referred back to one Idea as the principle of their unity—the Idea of Good. This Idea is at once the cause of the being and truth of the other Forms, and of the knowledge of them—"the cause of science." It is also the most beautiful of the Ideas, and is indeed equated with the Beautiful.[35]

But here a veil falls over his doctrine. Nowhere in the Dialogues does Plato give us a clear and adequate picture of the Good or of the manner of its being. Indeed, he tells us in the Seventh Letter that he has never written about the highest things, because they cannot be so communicated. And he implies that such knowledge is available only to a few persons who can climb with him a very steep and difficult road, involving not only the need for acute intellectual powers, but also moral discipline of a high order, love and devotion to the task of discovering the Good, and a rigorous preliminary training.[36] To understand what he meant by the Good, without

---

[30] *Phaedo* 65.

[31] *Idem.*

[32] *Phaedrus* 247.

[33] *Parmenides* 132.

[34] *Phaedo* 79.

[35] Sometimes also called "God." See *Republic* 5.452, 6.508–509, 10.597; *Lysis* 216.

[36] *Republic* 6.484–85, 490. See Glenn R. Morrow, *Studies in the Platonic Epistles*, Illinois Studies in Language and Literature, Vol. XVIII, Nos. 3–4 (Urbana: University of Illinois, 1935), p. 66.

any preparation for the task, Plato implies, is on the intellectual side like trying to understand the nature of the atom with no training in physics, and on the moral side like trying to attain to the Beatific Vision with mortal sin on one's soul.

Plato does tell us some things about the meaning of Good. For one thing "good" always implies defining characteristic, or essence, and it always implies function or purpose. Any "*X*" may be described as "good" if it has a recognizable, characteristic structure (if Form or Essence is present in it) and if it performs the function or purpose implied by its Form.[37] And Plato also makes an effort to describe the intellectual and moral processes whereby one can ascend to a full knowledge of what Good means, and to an experience of it. In the *Republic* he does this discursively, and he also does it poetically, in the famous Allegory of the Cave.[38] This knowledge achieved, all of the Forms or Ideas and their interconnections are open to one. The goodness and essential structure of the entire universe are laid bare.

Thus Plato reveals the real world as the world of value. And our experience as men, who possess value-knowing minds as the characteristic feature of our souls, must be interpreted primarily in terms of value, in terms of good and bad, which means in terms of purpose, if it is to be specifically human. To understand the eye we must not only describe its operations as a natural process, as the product of "necessity," without intelligible meaning, but in terms of its Form and its goodness—common sense says its purpose is to see, and it is good if it performs this function well. The purpose of the ear is to hear, of a horse to furnish transportation, of a pruning hook to cut off branches. And these things participate in their Forms, and consequently in Goodness, if they do their work properly.[39] The characteristic function, end, or purpose of the soul is to know the Ideas, and above all the True, the Good, and the Beautiful, and to love these ardently. (The acts of love and knowledge are inseparable.)[40] The soul is excellent (or virtuous, or good) which does this work well. And so the highest duty of man is to tend the soul.

Now the soul resembles the objects of its knowledge. For like the Ideas and the Divine Good, it is invisible, unchanging, and immortal (as the principle of life must of necessity be), by contrast with the body, which changes every moment, first in growth and then in decay and dissolution. Being thus akin to the Divine, the soul is plainly the superior of the mortal body, it has more real existence than the body, and therefore ought to con-

[37] See *Republic* 1.341-43, 353–54.

[38] See Books VI and VII.

[39] See *Republic* 1.352–53.

[40] See Voegelin, *op. cit.,* Vol. III, pp. 31—32; Richard L. Nettleship, *Lectures on the Republic of Plato* (London: Macmillan & Co., Ltd., 1929), pp. 157–58.

trol and rule it, give Form and Goodness to it.[41] This is its secondary function, derived from its ability to know the Ideas.

Governing the body is no easy task. Associated with it are other parts of the soul, which Plato calls mortal, and which war against the government of the rational or intelligent principle. These are the irrational appetites and passions—what we today call "drives"—invisible like the rational soul, but so closely assimilated to bodily functions as to be dissoluble, as the body is. One might say that the passions are soul only by analogy. Indeed, in *Timaeus,* Plato speaks of them as "another soul" which in its chief ingredients is the product of blind necessity rather than reason.

> Now of the divine, [God] was himself the creator, but the creation of the mortal he committed to his offspring. And they, imitating him, received from him the immortal principle of the soul; and around this they proceeded to fashion a mortal body, and made it to be the vehicle of the soul, and constructed within the body a soul of another nature which was mortal, subject to terrible and irresistible affections—first of all, pleasure, the greatest incitement to evil; then, pain, which deters from good; also rashness and fear . . . these things they mingled with irrational sense and with all-daring love according to necessary laws, and so framed man.[42]

The higher part of the mortal soul is the need or drive to compete or contend, to strive—"that part . . . which is endowed with courage and passion and loves contention."[43] The lower part is made up of the "drives" for food and drink, and other demands arising out of purely physical requirements, and these he likened to a "wild animal which was chained up with man."[44] All the parts of the soul—or rather both the immortal and the mortal souls—have their proper place in human life, and must be nurtured with their proper food.[45] But the irrational soul cannot of itself make decisions about its nurture. It will feed to the point of self-destruction, like a greedy dog, if it is not controlled. And the rational soul, itself feeding on the Good, must control it and establish the limits—reason must persuade necessity.[46]

Dialectic

By choosing the dialogue form in which to present his philosophy, Plato also intended to show us the method by which one could arrive at philosophic truth. The starting point is some everyday, commonsense no-

---

[41]*Republic* 1.353, 9.585; *Phaedo* 79–80; *Laws* 5.727.

[42]*Timaeus* 69.

[43]*Ibid.* 70.

[44]*Idem.,* cf. the description of the parts of the soul in *Republic* 4.431–41.

[45]*Timaeus* 70.

[46]See *Timaeus* 48.

tion. In *Euthyphro,* one of the early "Socratic" dialogues, for example, the problem which the interlocutors have set themselves is an examination of the concept "piety." The context of the inquiry is a discussion between Socrates and Euthyphro, a rich young man who is engaged in prosecuting his own father for murder. In anger, the father had a servant found guilty of wrongdoing bound and cast into a ditch, where he had died. Euthyphro, a self-righteous traditionalist, has taken it upon himself to set matters right with the law.

Socrates begins the dialogue by asking Euthyphro whether it is pious (that is, a fitting, proper, and righteous thing) for him to take his own father to law. Euthyphro replies that piety means prosecuting the wrongdoer. Socrates objects that this is only one example of a pious act, and that Euthyphro needs to understand the inner meaning of the term. This, he suggests, is to be found in its definition. Euthyphro then comes back with the idea that piety is what is pleasing to the gods—a typical traditionalist solution to the problem, which converts a cognitive problem into one of faith and established religious belief. Socrates then proceeds to point out that in the myths which are told about the gods they are represented as having many different opinions about what is pleasing. He has thus found a contradiction in Euthyphro's formula of definition; piety is both what pleases and what does not please the gods. This characteristic way of disproving a dialectical argument is decisive, and Euthyphro is compelled to try another approach.

Socrates tries to get his interlocutor to go beyond the categories established by formal religion. Do the gods love piety because it is pious, or is it pious because they love it, he asks. Euthyphro accepts the lead and replies that they love it because it is pious. Socrates then points out that this raises the question of essence, the essential "whatness" (or form) of piety. He suggests that a way of arriving at an answer might be to derive piety from a still more comprehensive form, justice. And he proceeds to inquire what part of justice piety might be. But here the traditionalist proves unable to break away from his fixed and unthinking opinions. He simply answers that it is that part of justice which concerns what is due to the gods. When Socrates asks him what attention is it that is due to the gods, he replies it is doing that which they love. And so the dialogue is back to its beginning, and the quest for the Form of piety remains unfulfilled.

The Political Problem.   One might ask what this has to do with political theory. We began this section with a question about Plato's method in the study of politics, but to this point we have been discussing his theory of knowledge, his metaphysics, his theology, his psychology, and his ethics. Actually, these are all a part of his method for studying politics, as will soon become apparent.

The good life has been revealed as the rational life, the life directed by knowledge of the Ideas, especially the Idea of Good. Now since man is a creature who lives in groups—the most comprehensive of which we call states or political communities—we may suppose that there are Forms or Ideas connected with the phenomena of this group life, if for all empirical things there are such Ideas. We may suppose that there is an Idea of the *polis* which is absolute, perfect, unchanging, which will be well or ill reflected in empirical *poleis*. We may suppose that there is an Idea of justice and of other qualities which are spoken of in the common language as characteristics of states and individuals. And we may conclude that men who are attempting to live the life of reason must have an understanding of the Ideal polity if they are to order their public affairs well. In human things the extent to which the Good and the other Forms are present in the empirical flux will depend on men's apprehension of these Forms and their conscious application to life. Good men and good states come into being only by an act of reason and of love of the Good made by men themselves. Society can be rescued from its formlessness, its chaos, its nonbeing, its necessity only by men who have seen and understood the Form of the *polis*.

The Political Theory of *The Republic*

Definitions of Justice

Plato's masterpiece is cast in dialogue form. It is a report of a philosophical discussion between Socrates and some of his companions held during a holiday banquet at the Piraeus home of Cephalus, a rich and respectable elder citizen of Athens.[47] The talk is about the nature of justice—a description of the best regime must take the form of a definition of an Idea. First the group canvasses various commonly held opinions on the question at hand.[48] Cephalus, and Polemarchus his son, give traditional definitions of justice considered as interindividual or private justice. But discussion reveals both definitions to be unsatisfactory—incomplete, ambiguous, and productive of inconsistent and absurd deductions. Then a sophistic conception is put forward. Thrasymachus argues that justice is simply whatever the interest of the stronger demands. He is talking about public rather than private morality, since by the stronger he means those who are able to control the governmental processes of society. Plato trips up his definition by giving a teleological definition of government. Government is an art, whose purpose must be the good of the ruled rather than of the ruler, because all arts are so understood; navigation as such regards the in-

---

[47]See Voegelin, *op.cit.,* Vol. III, pp. 52–53, 60, on Plato's symbolism in *The Republic.*

[48]*Republic* 1.331 *ff.*

terest of the passengers, medicine the good of the patient, and sheep-herding the good of the sheep, though the shepherd in *another* capacity may eat the sheep. The art *as such* must regard the interest of its subject. The whole structure of the argument plainly stands or falls with the validity of teleological explanations—the idea that something can be defined by reference to its purpose or function in the economy of the universe.

Returning to the traditional—though still obscure—semantics of justice, the conversation pursues the question of the comparative advantages and disadvantages of the just and unjust life. And Plato's young companion Glaucon and his brother Adeimantus demand to know how justice and injustice "inwardly work in the soul," leaving aside the question of their *external* "rewards and results."[49] But the question of the essential nature of justice remains to be settled before its internal effects can be assessed.

The Large Letters of the Polis. Plato suggests that the inquiry into the nature of justice will be facilitated if we pursue it by starting with the most revealing kind of data. Since justice is spoken of in the common language as a virtue or excellence of the *polis* as well as of the individual, i.e., as an ability which allows the soul and the *polis* to perform their respective work or tasks properly, Plato suggests that the "larger letters" of the *polis* will be more easily understood than those of the individual soul.

The Polis of Wards

We begin the investigation by examining a *polis* in the process of creation. This of course does not mean, in the Platonic framework, we must do historical research into the genesis of some particular *polis* or of all *poleis*. For justice, since it is a Form, will be found only in the good *polis*, not simply in any *polis*. And it may be that the good *polis* has never been generated; or if it has, that there is no record of it. How then shall we proceed? Beginning with the data derived from our everyday experience of any generated *polis*, our minds seek to envisage the institutions of the good *polis*. We seek to pass immediately beyond what is given by sense to thought. Our thoughts and their verbal expression, however, will not be identical with the Form, but only a human representation of it, i.e., something created or generated. The Ideas themselves are uncreated and eternal. As the geometer who discourses on the triangle and circle must draw visible, empirical triangles and circles to communicate about these Ideas, so must the political philosopher who would explain the Form of the *polis* come at it indirectly, and draw and discourse on a visible, empirical *polis*. He must construct in words an image of what the most perfect generated *polis* would be like if it were ever to be

---

[49]*Republic* 2.358.

brought into empirical existence. Only in this indirect fashion can the Form be communicated.[50]

The depiction of the Form of the *polis* begins with a teleological definition—the function of the *polis* is to supply all of the needs which individuals alone cannot supply.

> A [*polis*], I said, arises, as I conceive, out of the needs of mankind; no one is self-sufficing, but all of us have many wants. Can any other origin of a [*polis*] be imagined?[51]

The first needs which demand satisfaction are those of the body and of the mortal soul—the needs for food, shelter, and clothing. These needs are the work of "necessity."[52] Plato pictures men coming together to satisfy them by forming a simple economic society constructed on the principle of the division of labor and the principle of exchange. Everybody does one thing, that for which he is best equipped, and the products are exchanged. And so we have a society of farmers, craftsmen, and merchants. But strangely we find no one reflecting on the need for specialization and self-consciously bringing it about, either by private actions or through a public government. The society organizes spontaneously and thus receives Form not by human mind and reason but by that of God or some other nonhuman cause. The simple society is devoid both of human reason and of power. When the satisfaction of only the most basic material wants is demanded by "necessity," there is so perfect a complementarity of interests, and cooperation is so spontaneous, as entirely to eliminate the requirement of an over-all direction and a coercive function.

Plato describes this as the "true and healthy constitution of the [*polis*]."[53] But Glaucon rebukes him with having created a city of pigs. Such simplicity does not square with Glaucon's conception of the good life, nor with that of most people—"many will not be satisfied with the simpler way of life." And we suspect that it is really not Plato's view of the best society either. For in it there are no men who are exercising their specifically human capacity to know Good, or even attempting to exercise it. Presumably the Form of man and the Form of *polis* complement and imply one another, and exist together logically within the unity of the Good. But behind this generated simple society no Form of the *polis* is discernible which implies the Form of man. And where is justice? "Probably in the dealings of the

---

[50]*Republic* 2.369; *Timaeus;* and *Seventh Letter* 342–44.

[51]*Republic* 2.369. I have substituted "*polis*" for "state" in Jowett's translation, because the term "state" implies only a system of public law and government, not the undifferentiated total social organism which Plato was talking about here.

[52]See *Timaeus* 69-70.

[53]*Republic* 2.372.

citizens with one another," says Adeimantus.[54] But we are not told what it is. And so this primitive society must be an imperfect and incomplete one.

Plato and Adeimantus then go on to construct a more complicated and luxurious society. Necessity is still at work here. The desire for luxury leads to wars of conquest, as the original resources of the land will not supply the new needs. Thus a new function, the military, comes into being and the society takes on a more complicated structure. And, with this, power is born in society—an instrument of coercive control.

Who will be the soldiers? They must be men with an aptitude different from that of all our farmers, craftsmen, and merchants, an aptitude to prosecute war. And Plato tells us that they must be persons in whom spirit or anger—the higher element of the irrational soul—is a dominant characteristic. But how are these men bred and recruited for this new function? Do they come forward spontaneously, like the farmers and craftsmen? Or must they be consciously selected by some organ of society? And will they need some special training, or will they simply pick up the canons of their craft on their own, as apparently the farmers and tradesmen must? And how can we be sure that, invested with military power, and, characterized as they are by spirited natures, they will not abuse that power and devour their fellow citizens rather than the enemy? None of *these* problems are solved in Plato's good *polis* spontaneously or by a reason external to man. As soon as he has mentioned them, Plato turns to the problem of developing and institutionalizing human reason as the director of power and spirit. And the governmental or central policy-making function appears in society as the embodiment of directing reason.

And so a paradox unfolds. War has been declared by our good society. And it is "derived from causes which are also the causes of almost all the evils in States, private as well as public"[55]—the excessive love of material goods. But along with this, and indeed as a consequence of it, society has begun to seek the guidance of the Good through human reason, and to develop the philosophic man, who best reflects the Idea of man by embodying this reason. Thus from the Idea of man as a rational-spirited-appetitive animal, and from the Idea of the *polis* as an association through which all the needs of men are supplied (man as a social animal), Plato derives the Idea of a tri-functional system. To use the labels created by Francis Cornford, in the good society there must be separate social institutions which perform the "deliberative and governing, executive, and productive" functions.[56]

This system for its proper operation requires the development of some

---

[54]*Republic* 2.372–73.
[55]*Republic* 2.373.
[56]*The Republic of Plato* (New York: Oxford University Press, 1945), p. 129.

men who approximate the Ideal pattern of human nature—men who know Good and the other Forms, especially the Form of the *polis*. They will be the governing class, and will impress this Form upon the generated *polis*. The rulers should make policy, both domestic and foreign, in whatever they believe "is for the good of their country."[57] Their knowledge is that "which advises not about any particular thing in the [*polis*], but about the whole, and considers how a [*polis*] can best deal with itself and with other [*poleis*]."[58] They are expected to give special attention to certain problems of policy—national defense, keeping territorial expansion consistent with political unity, the prevention of excessive riches and poverty in the community (a chief cause of social conflict), and above all, the breeding, recruitment, and training of the next generation of rulers and executives. They will also enact regulations for the maintenance of order, a body of private law, and rules for the conduct of economic transactions, but if the primary problems have been adequately dealt with, Plato says that legislation in these areas can be minimal.[59]

The executive function is the province of the class of Auxiliaries who administer the policies of the rulers and make war—a combined civil service and officer corps. And the productive function is that with which we began—the production and exchange of economic goods required for bodily needs.

Now, paradoxically, while the fullest development of the *polis* into a tri-functional system is necessary in order for it to produce men modeled on the Idea of man, as we have conceived that Idea to now, the pre-eminently rational man, the same system seems to imply that there is not one but rather three Ideas of man—rational, spirited, and appetitive.

Is there an inconsistency here in Plato's thought? Probably not, for Plato appears to have developed these different images of the Form of human nature at different levels. Only the Form of man as pre-eminently a rational animal corresponds to man as a perfect and independent whole. The other natures are Ideas of man-as-functional-part of society. The three Ideas of man-as-part are logically necessary to the Idea of man-as-whole. This is at least a possible interpretation.[60] The important thing for our understanding of Plato's philosophy, however, is to recognize that nearly the whole structure of his good *polis* is derived by logical implication from an Idea, and is not the product of empirical observation, except as a stimulus to thought. Data of everyday experience stimulate in the observer's mind the Idea of man as a rational and social animal, but all the rest is a product of

[57]*Republic* 3.412.
[58]*Republic* 4.428.
[59]See *Republic* 4.422–27.
[60]Cf. Raphael Demos, "Paradoxes in Plato's Doctrine of the Ideal State," *Classical Quarterly,* New Series, VII (1957), p. 167.

logical inference. Some of it may be checked crudely against the data of sense—perhaps observation suggests three basic psychological types.[61] But since sense is a bad witness, it is not necessary to support in this way a judgment arrived at by the surer method of deductive logic.

The Education of the Guardians

The good *polis* is not yet complete. It requires institutions to sustain and renew the regime. The Idea of the tri-functional system implies the Idea of a system of recruitment and of training for the personnel of the parts. And much of the *Republic* is taken up with a discussion of these things.[62] But it is only the selection and education of the ruling classes—the Auxiliaries and the Guardians—that receives extended treatment. The holders of official power are the causes of good and evil in society, and therefore their recruitment and nurture is of the greatest importance.

In order to ensure the best raw material possible from which to renew his Guardian class each generation, Plato requires that the Rulers devise a mating system for the Guardians which will make certain that unions are effected among persons of the best moral, intellectual, and physical qualities, and discouraged among the inferiors. He makes the assumption that the eugenic methods employed in animal breeding are valid also for men.[63] But this does not result in an absolutely closed caste system. When men of "gold" or "silver" are discovered among the "iron and brass" of the productive class, they are to be promoted to Guardian rank. And similarly, if "baser metals" are found among the young of the Guardians, they are to be "thrust . . . out among the craftsmen and the farmers."[64]

The first step in the formal schooling of these choice natures is designed not to develop the reasoning faculty but to inculcate as habitual virtue such things as honesty, temperance, courage, endurance, humility, and the other moral qualities. This is the object both of the "musical" and "gymnastic" training of the young. Under the heading of "music" come all literary influences on the child—especially the stories of Homer and Hesiod about the gods and legendary heroes of Greece. The counterpart of this influence today is a complex collection of things made up of Bible stories read in Sunday school, Mother Goose, stories of our national heroes recounted in history books, and the entire comic-book literature which is so popular

[61] Professor William Sheldon, the American psychologist, has described three types—the ectomorph, mesomorph, and endomorph, which closely resemble the Platonic trilogy. See William H. Sheldon, *The Varieties of Temperament* (New York: Harper & Row, Publishers), 1942.

[62] See Books II, III, V, VI, VII.

[63] *Republic* 5.459-61

[64] *Republic* 3.415.

with the young today. What Plato means by "music" comprises all the materials in which persons both of human and of superhuman character are represented to the child as models to imitate. Plato would establish a rigid censorship over this material, forbidding the gods to be pictured as liars, thieves, murderers, drunkards, because persons with such characters should not be displayed to the impressionable child.

The Platonc institution of censorship is a favorite whipping boy of political theory textbooks and of professors of political theory in the United States, because it appears to be in conflict with the liberal democratic dogma of freedom of the intellect.[65] It should therefore be emphasized that the censorship is for the youth of Plato's society—the immature, malleable minds—not for adults. As such it is quite compatible with such liberal doctrines as those of John Stuart Mill, who in the famous *Essay on Liberty* says clearly that the liberties for which he argues are not meant for children but only for persons "in the maturity of their faculties."[66] Something like Plato's concern with screening the literary influences on his young Guardians is found in our present preoccupation with the problem of a possible connection between comics and television violence on the one hand and juvenile delinquency on the other.

Plato's program for gymnastic training involves the careful regulation of all the physical habits of the Guardian recruits—diet and sleep as well as exercise and sports—an entire physical regimen such as baseball and football players pursue. Virtue, particularly courage, depends on physical as well as on mental habits.

The formal training of the child is not the only thing which must be regulated if virtue is to be inculcated. The entire environment must be controlled. Now, if the specific function of the Guardian is to care for the common good, then his peculiar virtue will be a peculiar unselfishness, a perfect love of the *polis* and an utter unconcern for his private good. And it seemed to Plato that only conditions of communal living could sow such an unselfishness. This means that wives, children, and property must all be held in common, and the Guardian must be educated to regard the entire *polis* as his family. To be brought up with the ideas of *meum* and *tuum* is to nurture the seeds of selfishness which will lead one to see the common good in terms of the private good, rather than the reverse.

Plato recognizes the radical and unpopular character of his own proposal. He speaks of it as a "wave" of the argument, which may swallow up the philosophic swimmer if he does not bend all his energies to breast it. But if this *polis* is indeed to be built in the image of the Form, then the logic

---

[65]See Karl R. Popper, *The Open Society and Its Enemies,* rev. ed. (Princeton, N.J.: Princeton University Press, 1950), Vol. I.

[66]John Stuart Mill, *On Liberty,* (New York: Appleton-Century-Crofts, Inc., 1947), p. 10.

of the proposal is inexorable, once we grant that the kind of unselfishness he sought cannot be developed within the traditional framework of private property and private family.

It is significant that Plato's communal institution does not encompass the whole society. There is to be private property and family life aplenty for the productive class—the largest segment of his *polis*. It is only the holders of power, whose social function requires them to think every moment only of the common good, who must be prevented from developing private interests. So far as the productive class is concerned, it is sufficient to prevent radical inequality which might disrupt the community. It is also significant that Plato's communism is one of ascetic poverty and not of plenty. His Guardians are forbidden to handle gold and silver, and they are commanded to treasure only the gold and silver of their souls. Because of these things we have a theory here quite unlike the communism of Marx and Lenin and an institution which resembles a monastery rather than a proletarian paradise.

This is the schooling and way of life of all the Guardians—those who become rulers and those who serve in the lower capacities of soldier and civil servant. For the rulers, however, a special higher education is required. If they are to legislate well and establish sounds norms, they must have direct personal experience of the true fount of all norms and values, the Idea of Good. And so Plato provides them with a ten-year course of pure mathematics to develop their faculty of abstract reasoning, to prepare them for this experience. The objects of mathematics are independent of the material world, pure thought, and so are a fitting preparation for one who seeks to apprehend the Forms. This is followed by five years of training in dialectic, which leads the soul into the world of Forms and toward the Idea of Good itself. Then come fifteen years of practical experience in lesser positions in the service of the *polis*. Following this, the few who have excelled both in thought and in action will find themselves ready to enter the presence of Good itself. And after this ultimate moral and intellectual experience they take seats in the legislative council and lay down norms for the society. For having raised the "eyes of the soul to the universal light which lightens all things, and [having beheld] the absolute good," they have discovered "a pattern according to which they are to order the [*polis*] and the lives of individuals, and the remainder of their own lives also."[67]

The Ideal *polis* is now complete. The Form has been represented as a *polis* of the imagination. We have been given as close an approximation of the Form as possible in a generated thing, a *polis* of words analogous to the most perfect empirical *polis* which might be generated in time. And we are now ready in these large letters to discover the image of still another Form—justice. The virtue of wisdom has been located in our rulers—our *polis* has

[67] *Republic* 7.540.

the excellence which allows it to know Good. In the Auxiliaries the *polis* finds its courage—a true opinion about the things which are to be feared and the things which are not to be feared. And in the consensus of the classes on the system—both as to its processes and as to the distribution of power and authority—we find the virtue of temperance, "the agreement of the naturally superior and inferior, as to the right to rule of either."[68]

A word on the matter of temperance as consensus. Plato knew that this virtue would not arise automatically in his *polis,* as it apparently does in a beehive or in a hill of ants. All men, even though they be predominantly appetitive or spirited, are also rational animals. They think about their experience and seek to explain and justify it to themselves. They require an ideology. So Plato was faced with the need of providing the citizens of his *polis* with an explanation or justification of the distribution of power and functions in his society. But how could the complicated eithical truth underlying the system be conveyed to the duller minds? Only the Guardians would be capable of understanding in a perfect way the goodness of the institutional arrangements. The answer was the famous "Noble Lie" or "Royal Lie," as it is usually called, of Book III of the *Republic*—the story which Plato made up about the origin of the golden, silver, and iron men.

The word "lie" is really a misnomer in this context. "Myth" or "legend" are probably better translations of the Greek *pseudos.* Contrary to what many commentators have written,[69] it was not Plato's intention to have the Guardians deceive the ruled classes with falsehoods in order to produce agreement on the institutions of government. A myth is not a lie but a poetic or allegorical mode of conveying a difficult truth. Plato really believed that there are three kinds of men, i.e., three kinds of moral character. And the myth of the metal races was simply a convenient vehicle for carrying this truth to the average man. Its function is analogous to the Cave allegory of Book VII and the Myth of Er in Book X. Real deceit—the "Big Lie" of fascist and communist propaganda—is absolutely incompatible with the entire structure of Plato's moral philosophy.[70] Plato would no more call his legitimating ideology a lie in this sense than a theologian would use that word to describe the apple and serpent of the Garden of Eden, although he might not believe that an apple and a serpent were literally responsible for the first sin.

What justice is is now apparent to all—the proper performance of its function by each of the organs of the *polis* in perfect cooperation with the

---

[68]*Republic* 4.432.

[69]See, for example, Andrew Hacker, *Political Theory* (New York: The Macmillan Company, 1961), pp. 46-7. For an interpretation like mine see Francis N. Cornford's footnotes to his translation of *Republic* 414, in the Oxford University Press ed., 1945, p. 106, and his headnote on p. 68 of that volume.

[70]See *Republic* 6.490.

others—a virtue found at once in the whole and in all the parts. Each of our three kinds of men—rational, spirited, and appetitive—is doing his own proper work and not meddling with the business of the other: reason ruling, spirit administering and defending, appetite producing material requirements. Those whom necessity has made recalcitrant to the reception of the Form-of-man-as-whole can nevertheless receive the impression of the Form-of-man-as-spirited-part or the Form-of-man-as-appetitive-part.

Justice in the individual has also now been revealed. It is the Form of the control relationship of the parts of the soul to one another in the Form of man. The just man is he in whom reason commands spirit and appetite, with all three principles functioning cooperatively. We see now why Plato believed that individual and social justice were analogous concepts. The *polis,* as the individual, has a psychological structure, a moral character, a way of life. And Platonic justice is a principle of moral and psychological organization. It denotes an arrangement of psychological faculties (a moral structure) and a distribution of functions which produce harmony and health in a rational organism. As the man whose reason controls spirit and appetite is happy and at peace with himself—leads the best life—so is the *polis* whose spirited and appetitive classes are subject to the rule of the wise.[71]

A problem remains. Since reason is a dominant element in only a few men, shall we find in the just *polis* only a few just men and many unjust men? If this is the case, we have an element of terrible irony in Plato's theory. But it may be argued that the appetitive man and the spirited man who have functions in the just *polis* are controlled by reason, though not their own. They are "justified by faith," so to speak. In submitting themselves to the rule of the rational man they become just men, and the motions of their appetitive and spirited selves are held in due restraint. The Guardians are their reason.[72]

Can the Divine Polis be Instituted?

How will the Form be impressed on a historical *polis?* What is the least change required to bring it into being? The good *polis* must be consciously founded; it will not evolve of itself by a historical necessity, as some modern liberal and Marxist doctrines maintain. There must then be philosophic men who apprehend the Form, and they must be given power to enact reforms in existing societies. If these two conditions are met, the good *polis* may be generated in fact, though perhaps not in every detail, according to the word-picture which Plato has drawn of it.[73]

[71]See Voegelin, *op. cit.,* Vol. III, pp. 70, 86.

[72]Cf. the resolution of this problem by Raphael Demos, *op. cit.* On the nature of Platonic justice, see also Nettleship, *op cit.,* pp. 151-52, 160-61, 163-64.

[73]See *Republic* 5.472-73.

But the corrupt condition of society militates against the appearance of such a philosopher. While many fine natures are born, they are ruined by bad education—i.e., they are brought up to love television and sports cars and cocktail parties rather than the Good. And as a result, instead of becoming philosophers they become great rascals—Alcibiades instead of Socrates. Plato thought the democratic societies of his time were particularly blameworthy in this regard. Radically egalitarian in their principles, they vested all power in the majority and made majority opinion the only standard of right. Believing as he did that only the few can have insight into the Good, and that the many without the guidance of the few are morally blind, worse than wild beasts, Plato thought majoritarian democracy like that he had experienced in Athens one of the worst forms of government.

> And [does the public] not educate to perfection young and old, men and women alike, and fashion them after their own hearts?
> When is this accomplished? he said.
> When they meet together, and the world sits down at an assembly, or in a court of law, or a theatre, or a camp, or in any other popular resort, and there is a great uproar, and they praise some things which are being said or done, and blame other things, equally exaggerating both, shouting and clapping their hands, and the echo of the rocks and the place in which they are assembled redoubles the sound of the praise or blame—at such a time will not a young man's heart, as they say, leap within him? Will any private training enable him to stand firm against the overwhelming flood of popular opinion? or will he be carried away by the stream? Will he not have the notions of good and evil which the public in general have—he will do as they do, and as they are, such will he be?
> Yes, Socrates; necessity will compel him.[74]

Modern democratic culture has come in for similar strictures by writers from John Stuart Mill and Alexis de Tocqueville to Walter Lippmann and Alan Valentine, who fear the tyranny of majority opinion and the destruction of all high cultural values by egalitarianism.[75] Plato believed, nevertheless, that a few might weather the storm and become good. Perhaps his Academy could salvage these few from the moral shipwreck of society. And they might be compelled by a people weary of its own corruption to take power and enact a reform of institutions. Plato does not suggest that they seize power—he is not a revolutionary. Reform is possible only for the society "which will submit to their authority."[76] However, if the philosopher

---

[74]*Republic* 6.492.

[75]See Walter Lippmann, *The Public Philosophy* (New York: Mentor Books, 1955); Alan Valentine, *The Age of Conformity* (Chicago: Henry Regnery Co., 1954).

[76]This is the reading given by Cornford of *Republic* 6.49 and differs considerably from that of Jowett. See also the *Seventh Letter,* 331, in which Plato explicitly abjured force and violence: "[A wise man] should never use violence upon his mother city to bring about a change of government. If he cannot establish the perfect state without the exile and slaughter of men, he will keep his peace and pray for the welfare of himself and his city." In Morrow, *op.cit.,* p. 198.

is already a king, Plato gives him the right to enact the reform without asking popular consent.[77]

Philosophic reform virtually requires a surgical operation on the body politic. Plato speaks of the need to send out into rural isolation all the inhabitants of the city over ten years of age, and for the philosopher-king himself to take over the task of educating the uncorrupted young in the spirit of the new constitution. Only so extreme a measure would promise success. We are reminded of the forced movements of populations by modern totalitarian governments and of the terrible suffering involved. Though in Plato's plan such a measure would be adopted only if the population were willing, one might still wonder if it were really worthwhile to attempt the Platonic utopia, granting its goodness, if it could only be achieved by means involving the utter disruption of existing society. Also what people would willingly submit to so vast a reorganization of their lives?

But Plato nowhere says that he really expects his *polis* to be instituted. He only argues that *if* human perfection and happiness are to be achieved, this is the road which must be taken to the goal. Apparently for Plato, as later for Christians, perfection and happiness are possible only through conversion—a turning about, an upsetting of the established way—and by bearing a cross. But if no society will walk willingly the hard road, perhaps it can at least improve in a measure if it has before it a clear picture of what the Heavenly City is like—a national purpose of perfection which is always present as a goal to social reform.

The doctrine of the *Republic* is as much directed to the private person as to organized society. For in one place Plato indicates that even if the historical *polis* is fated to remain forever radically corrupt and never to see justice as a social fact, the private individual who has the image of the good *polis* before him can live as though he were a citizen of that *polis,* and have nothing to do with the way of life around him. It is possible for the individual who has disciplined his soul to become independent of his social environment and to lead the good life.

> In heaven . . . there is laid up a pattern of it, methinks, which he who desires may behold, and beholding, may set his own house in order. But whether such an one exists, or ever will exist in fact is no matter; for he will live after the manner of that city, having nothing to do with any other.[78]

After Plato has sketched out his picture of the Form of the *polis* and after he has canvassed the problems relating to its institution, he shows us how the system would break down were it ever to be instituted. For all generated things are unstable, subject to alteration. And in something which is perfect, alteration necessarily means decay.[79]

[77]*Republic* 6.49.
[78]*Republic* 9.592.
[79]See Voegelin, *op. cit.,* Vol. III, 122–23.

The decline begins with a technical error of the rulers. A mistake is made in calculating the most auspicious time for the mating of members of the Guardian class. As a consequence the children born of these unions are of poor moral quality—their natures are dominated by mesomorphic rather than ectomorphic traits, to use Professor Sheldon's terminology. And even the excellent education these people receive cannot make true Guardians of them, since it cannot prevail against nature but can only act within the limits laid down by nature. So they grow up as lovers of honor and glory rather than lovers of the Good. And coming to power with the rest of their generation, they naturally seek to enthrone their values as the dominant values of the society. Dissension breaks out in the ruling class, and the rebels win. Prestige is established as the chief good, and the ambitious man becomes the authoritative personality, the type held up for all to admire and emulate. The new system is called timocracy, the *polis* of ambition. And it is identified with two historical states—Crete and Sparta. But it, too, is unstable and gives way in turn to the *polis* of wealth (oligarchy) which yields to the *polis* of licentious freedom (democracy), which in turn gives way to the *polis* of the single frantic master-passion (tyranny). There is an inexorable logic in the progression— in an almost Hegelian fashion, each system is the father of its own antithesis. When the Spartan part of the soul has fallen, the lower appetites succeed one another in relentless fashion until the perfectly unjust city is established. And then, perhaps, the cycle may begin all over again. This is the fate of generated things—never to remain in the same condition but to pass continuously from state to state without rest, always becoming and never being.

Empirical Truth

Plato's representation of the revolutionary decline of the ideal state through four successive forms of polity was not meant to depict a historical cycle. It does not appear to correspond to any historical pattern of revolutionary change. Nevertheless, this part of the *Republic* is much closer to the empirical world than the depiction of the perfect polity. For one thing, it deals with the morally imperfect, which Plato held to be characteristic of all existing forms of government, a world of flux, change, and conflict. Particular propositions about the character of revolutions, some explicit, some implicit, are observably true of empirical revolutions. Plato undoubtedly based much of what he said in this section on observation of real revolutions.

That political change follows upon ideological change seems manifestly true of all major social revolutions. In eighteenth-century France we can trace the emergence of Enlightenment philosophy and the processes whereby in simplified form it filtered down through the various levels of French society, helping thereby to prepare the mind of the average Frenchman for radical institutional change.[80] Similarly, in nineteenth-century Russia we can see decaying the ideology which legitimated the old regime and witness the appearance of a host of contending new philosophies and value systems from liberalism to anarchism and Marxism. It is also interesting to note that the breakup of the nineteenth-century British Empire followed upon the education of the local African elites in liberal democratic institutions in Britain, like the London School of Economics, where they sat at the feet of apostles of change like Harold Laski; and then went home to make revolution against colonial administrators in the name of these very ideals.

That revolution is first heralded not by the activism of an insurgent class but by philosophical division in the ruling class is another proposition which Plato states quite explicitly and which appears to be a universally valid empirical theory. For it was in the ranks of the French and Russian ruling classes that some of the first ideologues of change (e.g., Prince Kropotkin) and also leading statesmen (for example, the Comte de Mirabeau) came. Also, the implicit proposition that when consensus is broken and revolution ensues, the end of the revolution does not restore consensus but brings rather an unstable compromise of opposite philosophical principles seems generally to hold of regimes which have emerged from revolutionary turmoil. In France, for example, for one hundred years (some would argue longer) after the revolution of 1789 the monarchist and republican principles continued to coexist in French society, side by side without coalescing or without one being eliminated, and with the regime of the day oscillating from the one to the other principle in a series of minor revolutions.

Finally, we might observe that Plato's critique of democracy—that the principles of freedom and equality when fully extended lead to the loss of all authoritative norms and to loss of respect for all authority, parental, social and governmental—seems to be borne out by the recent experience of unrest among the youth, and especially by the phenomenon of the "New Left." That it is the *principle* of democracy that is the root cause of unrest, rather than the failure of its perfect realization, however, is not fully clear.

Principles of Order in the Historical Polis

Plato's political inquiries did not terminate with the *Republic,* a product of his early maturity. In the very process of delineating the perfect *polis,* as we have already seen, he recognized the enormous difficulties involved in using it as a blueprint for reform. And his experience with the hurly-burly of practical politics from that time on confirmed these doubts.

[80]See, e.g., Daniel Mornet, *Les Origines Intellectuelles de la Révolution Fran-caise* (Paris: A. Colin, 1933).

Human life as it was lived in the empirical world was so formless, so corrupt, and so far removed from the life of the Good City, that it was vain to hope to make it conform directly to the Ideal.

How could philosophers be installed in power? What society could be sure it was not placing itself in the hands of a clever tyrant rather than in those of a philosopher? Might not even a true philosopher fall prey to the temptations which go with absolute power? And what hope was there for the tyrant already installed in power to become a philosopher? Was not the debacle of philosophic reform in Syracuse proof that young tyrants like Dionysius II are so corrupted by the circumstances in which they are raised as to be incapable of philosophy, even when they aspire to it? In the *Statesman,* Plato speaks quite frankly to these questions:

> Men are offended at the one monarch and can never be made to believe that anyone can be worthy of such authority, or is able and willing in the spirit of virtue and knowledge to act justly and holily to all.[81]

And in the *Laws:*

> No human nature invested with supreme power is able to order human affairs and not overflow with insolence and wrong.[82]

A Probable Politics

How, then, are *poleis* to be guided if the philosophic ruler is an impossibility? What is to be done if the political science of the Ideal is useless for reform? Since most men live not by science but by opinion and probable truth, perhaps opinion and probable truth can be used to help them. Perhaps an inquiry into how men have acted politically in the past—an examination of the changing world of generated things—may yield a clue to how men's behavior can be improved in the future. It should at least demonstrate better than Ideal science the limits within which improvement is possible. And so reluctantly and fearfully, Plato turned away from the serene permanence of the Forms to gaze at the dizzying kaleidoscope of history.

> Do not imagine, any more than I can bring myself to imagine, that I should be right in undertaking so great and difficult a task. Remembering what I said at first about probability, I will do my best to give as probable an explanation as any other,—or rather, more probable; and I will first go back to the beginning and try to speak of each thing and of all. Once more, then, at the commence-

---

[81]*Statesman* 301.
[82]*Laws* 4.713.

ment of my discourse, I call upon God, and beg him to be our saviour out of a strange and unwonted inquiry, and to bring us to the haven of probability.[83]

Under what circumstances might history yield information about prescriptive values? Somehow, somewhere, the principles of rational order must have been planted in the world of flux. We cannot know this, but it is probably true. Organized society could not exist at all if it were entirely devoid of Form. And if the good *polis* had never been historically generated, how would the irrational men of today have any order-preserving institutions at all, any Form? They must have inherited these vestiges of order from their ancestors.

In *Timaeus,* Plato's cosmology, or story of the generation of the universe, he tells us that the most ancient city, born fresh from necessity and the pure Idea, was probably like the *polis* of discourse.

> The city and its citizens, which you yesterday described to us in fiction, we will now transfer to the world of reality. It shall be the ancient city of Athens, and we will suppose that the citizens whom you imagined were our veritable ancestors, of whom the priest [in a tale told by Solon about the ancient world] spoke; they will perfectly harmonize, and there will be no inconsistency in saying that the citizens of your republic are these ancient Athenians.[84]

In *Statesman* and *Laws,* Plato refers to this time as the Age of Cronos, an age whose only record is an ancient oral tradition, a myth. It was an idyllic and blessed time for mankind, a kind of Garden of Eden. The rulers of the age governed as shepherds tend their flocks, and they were actually gods rather than men. As a consequence there was neither conflict nor violence, nor pain, nor suffering.[85] But a fatal cycle which governs the life of the generated cosmos decreed the end of this happy dispensation.

> There is a time when God himself guides and helps to roll the world in its course; and there is a time, on the completion of a certain cycle, when he lets go, and the world being a living creature, and having originally received intelligence from its author and creator, turns about and by inherent necessity revolves in the opposite direction.[86]

When God lets go the helm and all the gods withdraw from the direction of things, life becomes hard and full of pain. Men must now govern themselves, and as they ill remember the divine things, there is discord and tumult. The beasts, formerly gentle, now prey upon men, and men upon one another. Great natural cataclysms, such as earthquakes, caused by the

[83]*Timaeus* 48.
[84]*Timaeus* 26.
[85]Cf. *Timaeus* 25-27; *Critias* 109; *Statesman* 269-72; *Laws* 4.713.
[86]*Statesman* 269.

reversal of the motion of the planets, announce the end of each period of the cycle, and there is great destruction of human and animal life on the earth.

In this manner the Age of Cronos came to a violent end. A great deluge (Noah's Flood?) overwhelmed the earth, and only on the highest mountains was life preserved. Thus was ushered in the present age, the Age of Zeus. No longer are there gods or god-like men to act as shepherds and guardians. No philosopher-kings will be found in the Age of Zeus.[87]

But the "blessed rule and life" of the departed age was not entirely lost. The men who survived the great deluge remembered the happy way of life of the former ages and preserved it in their customs and habits. They believed the traditions about the gods and accepted the code of right handed down from the former age.[88] The rude and equal conditions of life were conducive to an orderly and peaceful existence and so reenforced habitual virtue.[89]

The first form of government to develop in this primitive age was patriarchal—the eldest in each family ruled the rest according to the precepts of ancient custom. Gradually, the isolated families came together, cities were built, and a more complex society developed. With this came conscious legislation and the establishment of modern institutions of government. But the principles of legislation were not new—they were distilled by the chiefs of the community out of the old family customs; the first lawgivers of the present age built on the past, and thus on a divine foundation.[90] In this way, laws, or social institutions, became the lieutenants of the divine rulers of Cronos.

An inquiry into these old institutions, closest in time to the one generated out of the Form, and an inquiry into the experience of mankind in preserving and in altering the old ways should teach us something about the political good. The best-ordered of modern states will be a copy of the ancient good *polis*. It will most successfully have preserved and adapted the traditional good law.[91]

> May we not conceive each of us living beings to be a puppet of the Gods. . . . [Our] affections are like cords and strings, which pull us different and opposite ways, and to opposite actions. . . . There is one among these cords which every man ought to grasp and never let go, but to pull with it against all the rest; and this is the sacred and golden cord of reason, called by us the common law of the [*polis*].[92]

[87]See *Statesman* 275.

[88]*Idem.*

[89]*Laws* 3.678–80.

[90]*Laws* 3.681.

[91]*Laws* 4.713. See Leo Strauss, *What is Political Philosophy?* (New York: The Free Press of Glencoe, Inc., 1959), pp. 29–34, for an entirely different interpretation of the *Laws.*

[92]*Laws* 1.644–45.

Historical inquiry then should reveal what institutions produce virtue and order, and how they are established. And from this study of political traditions a workable program of reform may be built up. It will be based on the assumption that in the Age of Zeus the reason of the *polis* will have to dwell not in the souls of a ruling class of philosophers but in the tradition-based laws and institutions of the society as a whole.[93] If the inferior classes of the *Republic* are justified by faith in the Guardians, who have a direct insight into the Good, the men of the *Laws* will be justified by their adherence to the law.

This is the approach to the study of politics which underlies the argument of Plato's later dialogues. Willy-nilly, Plato has left the certain world of philosophy and has entered, not without foreboding, the uncertain world of history. The end product of these efforts of his later years is found in the voluminous *Laws*, which Philip of Opus, a student of Plato's, published the year after his teacher's death.

Historical Method: The Laws

The participants in the dialogue, which is laid on the Island of Crete, are a Cretan, a Spartan, and an Athenian Stranger (Plato). They are represented as conversing as they walk from the city of Cnossus to "the cave and temple of Zeus." The theme of the dialogue is established in the opening statement.

> *Athenian Stranger:* Tell me, Stranger, is a God or some man supposed to be the author of your laws?
> *Cleinias:* A God, Stranger, in very truth a God: among us Cretans he is said to have been Zeus, but in Lacedaemon . . . they would say Apollo is their lawgiver.

In the Age of Zeus it is through the divinely given law that man comes to the Good.

The conversation turns to the objectives which the social institutions of Crete and Sparta seem to aim at, and the "Stranger" persuades his companions that the lawgiver must have had the entire good of man as the object of his legislation—the virtues of wisdom, temperance, justice, and courage, to which may be added material well-being, and through all these things, happiness.[94] We are reminded of the *Republic*, for all four of the cardinal virtues are present in the Ideal *polis*. But in the good historical *polis*, wisdom is somewhat differently defined and the virtues are differently distributed among individuals. The psychological order of the Age of Zeus is quite different from that of the Age of Cronos. There are two basic types of

[93]See *Statesman* 301.
[94]*Laws* 1.631.

empirical man. One inclines to "order and gentleness" (temperance) and the other to "quickness and energy and acuteness" (courage)—follower and leader types, respectively. If left in their naural condition, each nature corrupts, the orderly becoming over-fond of peace and cowardly, the energetic becoming madly violent. But in the good *polis,* wisdom, implanted in each class of souls, maintains a due proportion or balance in each, and establishes a cooperative relationship between the two classes. Wisdom is no longer defined as knowledge of the Good. It is now "true opinion about the honourable and the just and the good and their opposites."[95]—faith. And it takes the moral principles of the traditional law as its standard. As long as there is consensus on this law, "if only both classes [hold] the same opinions about the honourable and good," the *polis* will be wise, courageous, temperate, and thus good and just.[96]

The law should seek not only to create a cooperative relationship between the classes in this way, but to encourage the intermarriage or "weaving together" of the two natures, so that the end product will be a society in which all the virtues are present in all individuals, who will differ from one another only in degree and not in kind. In the historical context, Plato has moved far away from the radical elitism of the Idea toward the democratic principle. But he has also retreated from philosophy back toward tradition, his starting point.

In Book III of the *Laws* the characters undertake a historical survey of governments from the beginnings of social organization after the flood down to the Persian War, to investigate the success and failure of particular institutions in realizing this virtuous *polis.* Attention is focused on the three Dorian kingdoms of Sparta, Argos, and Messene, and on Persia and Athens. The survey yields an important lesson—that virtue and the other good things are impossible in a state where all governmental authority is concentrated, either in a single individual or in a single social group. Argos and Messene perished because their rulers lacked wisdom and temperance, and their rulers were absolute kings. In Persia and in Athens the intemperance of the absolute king in the one case and of the absolute *demos* in the other likewise destroyed these states by destroying all friendship and spirit of community. But Sparta endured because her rulers remained men of temperance, which Plato attributed to the institutions that divided authority among two kings, a council of elders, and the Ephorate. By this "arrangement the kingly office, being compounded of the right elements and duly moderated, was preserved and was the means of preserving all the rest."[97] None of the states which failed in virtue did so because they did not understand the difference between right and wrong. In each case traditional

[95]*Statesman* 309.
[96]*Statesman* 310.
[97]*Laws* 3.692.

laws prescribed sound codes of right conduct. But in the absolute states the rulers simply chose to violate these laws. The problem was one of the distribution and organization of official power.

The importance of the education of rulers is also revealed by the survey. Darius, who was not a king's son and therefore not educated in the luxurious atmosphere of the court, used his vast powers well. But his son Xerxes, who was raised in the royal fashion, became degenerate. And in Athens, it was the poets, the educators of the whole society, who corrupted the democracy and led them to set at nought the moral principles enshrined in the old law.[98]

In this way, general principles of good government for the Age of Zeus are brought to light. The happy and good *polis,* which is unified and strong, will rest on three foundations: (1) consensus on a fundamental law which inculcates right principles of action such as a philosopher-king would lay down and such as are found in the oldest laws; (2) an educational system which produces in the rulers the virtues of temperance and respect for the laws; (3) freedom, conceived as a distribution of power among governmental institutions and social groups so that no one person or partial interest may control the entire governmental apparatus. Plato describes this as a society governed according to the mean which lies between the extremes of royal despotism and democratic license. And its principles have come out of an examination of historical governments rather than from an inquiry into the Form of the *polis.* The classification of states which Plato uses in the *Statesman* is also apparently based on such a historical study as this.[99]

The Best Regime for the Age of Zeus. As Book III concludes, Cleinias, the Cretan, mentions that he has been appointed to serve on a constitutional commission which is to draw up a fundamental law for a new colony soon to be founded by the islanders. He expresses satisfaction at the good fortune which has put him in the company of two men learned in comparative politics and suggests that the three of them together lay out a blueprint of social institutions for the new community. Cleinias advises that they "make a selection from what has been said." Their recommendations will be based on the kind of analysis demonstrated in Book III. Book III itself must be understood as a mere exercise, a sample of the sort of research which underlies the prescriptions of the *Laws.*[100]

[98]*Laws* 3.694–702.

[99]This classification employs the dichotomy of law-abiding and lawless states. Plato places the rule of one (monarchy) first among the law-abiding states, the rule of a few under law (aristocracy) second, and the rule of the many under law (democracy) third. The order of lawless states is inverted, democracy coming first, oligarchy second, and tyranny last. See *Statesman* 300–303.

[100]*Laws* 3.701. See Glenn R. Morrow, *Plato's Cretan City* (Princeton, N.J.: Princeton University Press, 1960), pp. 5–6.

Plato's good state for the Age of Zeus is a new one, a virgin enterprise—a colony. The reform of existing societies requires above all the alteration of morals and manners. And this can be accomplished only by the rulers, and effectively and quickly only in societies in which power is highly concentrated —in a tyranny best of all.[101] But our historical research has shown that concentration of power breeds vice in the rulers, that a virtuous tyrant is an impossibility.[102] Men of virtue *will* be found in authority in mixed states, or polities, where power is broadly distributed. But their authority being limited, they are unable to effect a general reform of manners. However, they may, like Cleinias, get to serve on a legislative commission for a colony. And working in such a context, they are not faced with the need to change the bad habits of their colonists. They are able to select their raw material and choose only those persons who will fit into the society they contemplate. Colony-building gives the greatest freedom of choice to the legislator in laying down the social foundations of the moral and governmental order.

The legislator's best strategy is to choose men from many different cities rather than from one. If they are all drawn from one community they will inevitably bring their institutions with them out of force of habit, including those which caused faction and other trouble at home. And they will resist the legislator's plans. But if the colony is a melting pot, it will submit to the new order, though it may be difficult to make the colonists "combine and pull together.[103] The establishment of a spirit of community may take years.

What would Plato say of the American "experiment"? Much of its story accords with the prescriptions of the *Laws*. Immigrant groups coming here during the nineteenth and twentieth centuries from a variety of cultures have left their old political institutions behind them and have fervently attached themselves to the New World ideal of liberal democratic government—to the "*novus ordo seclorum.*" They have found community in a common attachment to the "American Dream" and to the constitutional system with which it is associated. And over the years an ever more complete community, a specifically American culture, has begun to emerge.[104] While the first settlers, who established the foundations of the system, came mostly from a single culture, there were Dutch, French, and Germans in addition to the English majority. And the dominant English group did not bring all of its institutions along to the New World, but made a kind of selection from the past, à la Plato. The aristocratic ways were left at home

[101]*Laws* 4.710.
[102]*Laws* 4.712.
[103]*Laws* 4.708.

[104]See Max Lerner, *America as a Civilization* (New York: Simon & Schuster, Inc., 1957).

and only the democratic ones were transplanted; though the legislator of this equality was circumstance—the wilderness rather than a man.[105]

Plato's human legislator also requires that equality be a chief principle of social organization for his colony. In the Age of Zeus, equality is the best substitute for the communality of the Ideal as a builder of community of interest and of virtue. And it must be established throughout society, for in the Age of Zeus all have a right to membership in the ruling class. No social group can claim a monopoly of power by virtue of its knowledge of the Good. Knowledge has departed and there is now only true belief, and all are potentially capable of true belief.

Equality is established at four levels—economic, political, temperamental, educational. But it cannot be an absolute but only a rough equality, because while there are no ineradicable differences in kind among men, there are different degrees of native talent and moral capability. All colonists must possess a minimum of property, and wealth four times the value of the basic unit is permitted. The extremes of wealth and poverty are thus lopped off, and a range of middling conditions established, conducive to social solidarity and the development of temperate living. To prevent conflict which might arise out of differences in kinds of property, i.e., the opposition of a distinctly urban to a distinctly rural interest, the constitution should lay down that half of every citizen's property must be located in or near the city and the other half in the hinterland. And the citizens will not specialize in an economic function. Such commerce as there is will be left to foreigners, while slaves will till the fields. The conflict-breeding plurality of interests that goes with large size is avoided by limiting the number of citizens to 5,040.

Attention to proportionate equality is found in the governmental system. Only electoral functions are to be performed by all the citizens without consideration of differences in property or other distinctions. The popular assembly chooses executive officers, some of the judiciary, an executive council (charged with the conduct of foreign affairs and rather vaguely defined domestic duties related to maintenance of the peace), a body of Guardians of the Law (a combined legislative, executive, and judicial authority which is to fill in details of the law omitted in the original legislation), a board of examiners (to review executive acts and punish malfeasances), and some of the members of a Nocturnal Council (whose chief function is to review and amend the whole system of legislation). Attendance in the electoral assembly is compulsory for the richest classes, but not for the others. And the composition of the executive council gives special weight to wealth—each of the four classes is equally represented

[105]See Alexis de Tocqueville, *Democracy in America* (New York: Alfred A. Knopf, Inc., 1951), Vol. I, p. 29.

without regard to its numbers. Such disunity as the recognition of these different economic interests might create is to be offset by provisions empowering each class to participate in the selection of representatives for the other classes. Thus the most disinterested —or general-interested— individuals will be chosen.

The principle of equality enters in some degree into qualifications for the various offices. Membership in the powerful body of Guardians of the Law and in the Nocturnal Council carries no property requirement, nor do many of the executive offices, though candidates for some offices, such as Warders of the City, must come from the wealthiest two classes. As in the *Republic,* the education of the young is subject to the strictest control. But all participate equally in its benefits, since all citizens are in the ruling class. And its object is to instill the same "true opinions" about right and wrong in all the citizens. Laws regulating marriage are designed to promote equality and solidarity by persuading the rich to marry the poor and the bolder to marry those of more cautious temperament. Thus, through the elimination of diversity and by instituting equality at a variety of levels, Plato sought the key to social unity and civic virtue.

A few more words about the common education of the citizenry. The Minister of Education is charged with the task of moral instruction and his "text" is the civil law of the *polis,* which prescribes a civic religion and an entire way of life. Half of the bulk of the *Laws* consists of an adumbration of just such a detailed rule of life—a veritable Greek counterpart of Leviticus and Deuteronomy, of the Sayings of Confucius, of the Code of Hammurabi, or the Rule of St. Ignatius. Each regulation carries at its head a long preamble, which is an explanation of the regulation, so that the citizens' "true opinion" may be as close to knowledge as possible.

Return to Elitist Principles   More must be said about the Nocturnal Council, the body which is to have charge of the amendment of the constitution. In the provisions which Plato lays down for this institution in the last portion of Book XI, he departs in considerable measure from the principles of equality and divided authority which provide the framework for the rest of the system. Reason in Plato's model society is concentrated in the laws. But the laws are static and inflexible things. They cannot amend themselves as circumstances may demand. Therefore a man or men must after all be given charge over them.

The members of the Nocturnal Council must be men of extraordinary virtue—the pre-eminently courageous, temperate, wise, and just. And they must also have a "more precise knowledge of virtue . . . than the many have."[106] They must understand the aims of the state as a single aim, the

---

[106]*Laws* 7.965.

creation of virtue, and they must understand in what way all the virtues are one, and order all things accordingly. They must understand the definition of virtue as well as the name.[107] And they must know in what way "the good and the honourable" are one.[108] All this is reminiscent of the search for the Good in the *Republic.* We seem to be back again on the dialectical ladder. And we are not surprised when Plato proceeds to recommend a special training for the members of the Nocturnal Council. But this time it is not mathematics or dialectic, but rather astronomy and theology—knowledge of the gods rather than of the Good—which are the special curriculum of the intellectual and moral elite.[109] Plato also specifies that the members of the Council must be always on the lookout both at home and abroad for new "kinds of knowledge which may appear to be of use and will throw light upon the examination."[110] They are perpetual inquirers, and their wisdom appears to approach but stop short of the "Knowledge" of the rulers of the *Republic,* yet exactly how is not clear.

Plato calls the Nocturnal Council the "anchor of the state" and says it is instituted "for the salvation of the state." At the end of the *Laws,* Plato advises that the city be "handed over" to it. If this is done, "the state will perfected and become a working reality." The limits of the Council's authority are left undefined.[111] The democratic principle is conserved in the requirement that some of its members—the priests and the ten eldest of the Guardians of the Laws—be elected by the citizenry. But the elder statesmen are given the right to co-opt younger men as colleagues. And what is to prevent the Council from using its power of constitutional revision to dispense altogether with devices of popular control?

The problem of constitutional revision is thus a great stumbling block to the egalitarian in Plato. If the divinely given constitution could remain forever fixed, then all the men of the Age of Zeus could be treated as essentially equal—as equally unable to know the Good, and equally capable of having good habits implanted by the laws, and therefore with an equal right to some control over public policy. But if the basic law needs to be changed and adapted, only those of extraordinary virtue, those whose virtue is not wholly the work of the law, can claim a right to act. The search for God-like men must begin again. And such legislators must have absolute freedom from control by the ignorant many if their work is to be rational. After his flirtation with equality, Plato returns at the close of the *Laws* to the elitist ideal of the *Republic.*

[107]*Laws* 12.962–65.
[108]*Laws* 12.966.
[109]*Laws* 12.966–67
[110]*Laws* 12.952.
[111]*Laws* 12.961, 968, 969.

Platonism Versus the Natural Science of Politics:
Leo Strauss and His "Academy"

Plato's theory of Forms, which posits a transcendental Idea of human perfection as the standard of justice, is one of the great answers to the problem of the political good. It has had proponents in every age since Plato's time, including our own. The modern British Platonist, Harold Cherniss, for example, argues that no normative ethics is rationally possible without metaphysical assumptions like those found in the theory of Forms:

> The "dialogues of search," by demonstrating the hopelessness of all other ex-pedients, show that the definitions requisite to normative ethics are possible only on the assumption that there exists, apart from phenomena, substantive objects of these definitions which alone are the source of the values attaching to phenomenal existence.[112]

Unless something like the Forms exists, "good" can only be a matter of sub-jective preference. Cherniss also argues that the theory of Forms demands the assent of our reason because it makes possible a "rationally unified cosmos." It enables us to solve with a single hypothesis the problems of on-tology, of ethics, and of epistemology—the problems of what is real, what is good, and what is knowable. And it establishes a connection among these separate spheres of experience—the experience of being, of valuing, and of knowing. Like the great hypotheses of modern natural science, Plato's theory has the virtues of simplicity and generality.

The enduring character of Plato's work is also indicated by the fact that though he has been dead these twenty-three centuries and more, he has become a controversial figure in the literature of political philosophy in the United States in recent years. Since 1945 a spate of polemical works has ap-peared, for and against his political theories. The flurry began with *The Open Society and Its Enemies,* in which Professor Karl Popper branded Plato the intellectual father of modern totalitarianism. Two extensive replies followed shortly, *Plato's Modern Enemies and the Theory of Natural Law,* written by John Wild, a Platonist philosopher at Harvard University, and Ronald R. Levinson's *In Defense of Plato.* Other scholars, like John Hal-lowell of Duke, also took up the cudgels in Plato's behalf.[113]

Chief warriors in the battling ranks of modern Platonists are a group known as the Straussians. They are teachers of political philosophy at col-leges and universities all over the United States, who take their common ap-

---

[112]Harold Cherniss, "The Philosophical Economy of the Theory of Ideas," *American Journal of Philology,* LVII (1936), p. 447.

[113]For a selection from these polemics see Thomas L. Thorson, ed., *Plato: Totalitarian or Democrat?* (Englewood Cliffs, N.J.: Prentice-Hall, Inc., 1963).

pelation from the name of their teacher, Leo Strauss, who achieved eminence as a professor at the University of Chicago during the two decades following the Second World War. After Strauss's retirement in 1967, his place in the Chicago Political Science Department was taken by Joseph Cropsey, a distinguished scholar who studied with Strauss at the New School for Social Research, before Strauss's removal to Chicago in 1948. Cropsey has carried forward and perfected the mode of textual exegesis developed by Strauss for the analysis of the classic writings, and he has also continued the critique of scientific naturalism begun by his teacher. Other well-known and eminent scholars in the Straussian tradition include Allan Bloom, Richard Cox, Werner Dannhauser, Martin Diamond, Harry Jaffa, Ralph Lerner, David Lowenthal, and Harvey Mansfield, Jr. Professor Bloom is the author of an extremely careful and subtle translation of Plato's *Republic,* which is widely used by political theory students around the country, and of an excellent commentary which is appended to the translation.[114]

In the late 1940s, the novelty of Leo Strauss's approach to the study of the classics was twofold. On the one hand, he was one of the first teachers of political theory to break with the historical approach that had been the generally accepted mode of studying the classics since late in the nineteenth century. On the other, he attacked the practitioners of the new natural science of politics that had its origins at the University of Chicago during the 1920s and 1930s, in the work of Charles Merriam and Harold Lasswell. Historicism was an enemy because it reduced the classic writings about politics to reflexes of the historical process. They were understood as thoughts engendered by special social and political circumstance, relevant only for that particular time and place. The proponents of the natural science of politics, or "behavioralism" as it also came to be called, though striving in their own theories for universal statement, had embraced a psychology that reduced human reasoning to a reflex of social and psychic structure. Both historicism and behavioralism had denied the human capacity to achieve objective knowledge about the political world as a world of moral purpose and moral responsibility. To the Straussians, this is the only political world that it is meaningful to study. And they further believe that there is available, to the inquiring mind, an objective order of Right.

Professor Strauss indicts the behavioralists for trying to construct a "value-free" political science, one which avoids questions of moral judgment and simply describes political events as though they were a part of the

---

[114]New York: Basic Books, Inc., 1968. See the grand barrage against behavioral political science written by a group of his students, to which Professor Strauss contributed the epilogue: Herbert Storing, ed., *Essays on the Scientific Study of Politics* (New York: Holt, Rinehart & Winston, Inc.), 1962.

mechanical course of nature. The human world cannot be understood with "value-free" categories, he argues.

> Political things are by their nature subject to approval or disapproval, to choice and rejection, to praise and blame. It is of their essence not to be neutral but to raise a claim to men's obedience, allegiance, decision, or judgment. One does not understand them as what they are, as political things, if one does not take seriously their explicit or implicit claims to be judged in terms of goodness or badness, or of justice, i.e., if one does not measure them by some standard of goodness or justice. To judge soundly one must know the true standards. If political philosophy wishes to do justice to its subject matter, it must strive for genuine knowledge of these standards.[115]

Professor Strauss arrives at this conclusion by reflecting on what people say and appear to think when they engage in political activity. In our everyday political experience we judge things to be "good" and "bad." And we have at least a vague opinion about a standard of goodness which guides our actions. In the normal course of things our opinion remains unquestioned, a "given." But if we stop to reflect on our opinion, "it proves to be questionable." We recognize its vagueness, its imprecision, its poverty. We feel uneasy. We are ready to question it—possibly after a Socratic "gadfly" has done his work. "The very fact that we can question it directs us towards such a thought of the good as is no longer questionable—towards a thought which is no longer opinion but knowledge. All political action has in itself a directedness towards knowledge of the good: of the good life, or of the good society. For the good society is the complete political good. If this directedness becomes explicit, . . . political philosophy emerges."[116]

The true political science, then, is political philosophy, conceived as a quest for moral truth, a quest by which we "attempt to replace opinion about the nature of political things by knowledge of the nature of political things."[117] But where is "power" in this definition of political studies? And where are all the nonrational (Strauss would say irrational) motives and processes which interest the behavioral scientist? Are they somehow subsumed in the idea of political science as a science of the good political order? Are they related questions which the student of politics should also try to answer, though with a method different from that with which he deals with questions of the political good? Are they irrelevant to a proper explanation of the political?

We will recall Plato's strictures on the behavioral science of his time in the *Phaedo*. He recounts there Anaxagoras' explanation of the causes of human action, which took the form of a description of physiological mo-

---

[115]Strauss, *What is Political Philosophy?*, p. 12.
[116]*Ibid.*, p. 10.
[117]*Ibid.*, pp. 11-12.

tions, and comments that he finds a "strange confusion of causes and conditions" in it. "It may be said," he remarks, "that without bones and muscles and the other parts of the body I cannot execute my purposes. But to say that I do as I do because of them, and that is the way in which mind acts, and not from the choice of the best, is a very careless and idle mode of speaking."[118] Plato seems to be saying here that the essential character of the political cannot be grasped by naturalistic or behavioral explanation, that a "causal theory" of politics must be framed in terms of human purposes. At best, behavioral analysis can describe certain conditions of political action. It is therefore never more than a subordinate and auxiliary discipline.

We are also reminded of Plato's attack on the Sophists. Their naturalistic political science made desire and passion the authors of human values, and reason an instrument for bringing irrational motives into balance with one another. For Thucydides, reason had lost even this instrumental power under the pressures of war and plague. Neither Protagoras nor Thucydides was able to conceive of reason as the human capacity to know "the Good." But without such a conception, for Plato, there could never be surcease from political conflict and trouble. For virtue is knowledge of the Good, and without virtue there can be no truly human politics.

The parallel between the naturalism of our modern political science and that of Democritus and the Sophists is more than accidental. For scientific naturalism is a recurrent philosophical phenomenon that achieves prominence among intellectuals in times when traditional pieties have become outworn and have come to obscure hypocrisies and inequities in political institutions. Naturalism criticizes accepted practices and engenders reform, usually of an equalizing kind, by claiming to see into the hard realities of political power and interest behind the veils of religious myth and moral tradition. As Sophistic naturalism accompanied the democratizing reform of the Athenian constitution in the fifth century B.C., so did the naturalism of Machiavelli accompany the formation of the secular state in the sixteenth century and that of Hobbes, Locke, and Rousseau, the liberal reform of the British and French constitutions in the seventeenth and eighteenth centuries A.D. The naturalism of the "Chicago School," drawing some of its categories and its philosophical inspiration from these great apostles of change, was also, in its beginnings, associated with a period of reform, the Progressive and "Muckraker" Movement, which culminated in the New Deal of the 1930's.[119]

Having accomplished equalizing change, naturalism does not always seem capable of filling the moral void produced by its acid dissolution of the

[118]*Phaedo* 99.

[119]Bernard Crick, *The American Science of Politics* (Berkeley: University of California Press, 1959), especially Chapters 6, 7, and 8.

outworn value conceptions it has undermined. Plato concluded that the decline of Athenian consensus during a time when scientific naturalism was an authoritative mode of thought showed that naturalistic analysis, unalloyed with inquiry into an objective order of right, was morally corrosive. Strauss and his students have reached the same conclusion about the natural science of politics in the United States today, and have made it their business to fill the void with a revival of Platonist rationalism.

Strauss seems to go further than Plato along these lines, calling the "political science" which "designates such investigations of political things as are guided by the model of natural science . . . *incompatible* with political philosophy."[120] But apparently this judgment flows from the behavioralists' intolerance of philosophy rather than Strauss's belief that the enterprise of the behavioral scientists is illegitimate in itself and unconnected with politics. For he says that naturalistic political science today "conceives of itself as *the* way towards genuine knowledge of political things."[121] It disdains philosophy as an intellectual sleight of hand. Science is the one true church. It is this claim rather than the nonrational investigations of behavioralists which leads Strauss to speak of this science's incompatibility with political philosophy. He goes on to add a word of praise for the "judicious collections and analyses" of the behavioralists. "The useful work done by the men called political scientists is independent of any aspiration towards 'scientific' political science," he writes, i.e., independent of any aspiration towards an exclusive right to explain politics. Unfortunately, however, Professor Strauss does not go on to show *how* the political philosopher, the seeker after the good order, can use the "judicious collections" of the naturalistic student of the empirical order. He himself makes no use of them whatever.[122]

What are the ill effects of considering the study of process and power the sole way of studying political things? Strauss thinks such a study leads to indifference to the idea of goodness, indeed to a nihilistic outlook on life. The scientist is dehumanized by his science, because he reduces the human to nonhuman terms. It is hard to see how the empirical evidence might sustain Strauss in this belief. While I have heard one behavioralist identify himself as a nihilist when asked about his value position at a meeting of the American Political Science Association, scores of others are found busily

[120]Leo Strauss, What is Political Philosophy? (New York: The Free Press of Glencoe, Inc., 1959), p. 14. Emphasis supplied.

[121]*Ibid.,* p. 13.

[122]For all the vehemence of their denunciations, this seems to be essentially the position taken by Professor Strauss's students vis-á-vis behavioralism in *Essays on the Scientific Study of Politics*—that the scientists' claim to sole orthodoxy makes them offensive to the philosopher, and that their concerns are not truly with the political, but with certain conditions of the political, with what Berns, e.g., calls the "subpolitical."

engaged in the creation of a "policy science" of democracy, designed to further the "dignity of man." The policy scientists may believe that their love of human dignity is a thing of the blood only, but they are nevertheless genuinely attached to the idea.

Strauss argues that the social scientist is obliged to say "that it is as legitimate to make the pursuit of safety, income, deference one's sole aim in life as it is to make the quest for truth one's chief aim. He then lays himself open to the suspicion that his activity as a social scientist serves no other purpose than to increase his safety, his income, and his prestige, or that his competence as a social scientist is a skill which he is prepared to sell to the highest bidder."[123] But Harold Lasswell, from whom Strauss borrows the restatement of Thucydides' "three greatest things," (fear, honor, and interest) has in fact for years been in the front ranks of the policy scientists of democracy and human dignity, and is not for sale to the highest bidder. Perhaps Mr. Strauss is only saying that people like Lasswell are not consistent. If they were, they *would* be for sale to the highest bidder. For a little later on he recognizes the regard which such social scientists actually have for democracy and for the truth. But the regard is a conformist and "philistine" regard, Strauss claims, for it rests on the notion that one does not have to think about these values. The modern behavioralist is not capable of defending his values, philosophically or scientifically.[124]

Professor Strauss continues his polemic against the behavioralists with the observation that they hide judgments of value beneath the surface of apparently scientific categories. He cites in particular the notions of an "authoritarian" and of a "democratic" personality used in studies like those of T. W. Adorno and his colleagues.[125] The first he thinks carries plainly pejorative connotations. It is a "caricature of everything which they as good democrats of a certain kind disapprove." Similarly, Max Weber's notion of "routinization of Charisma" he thinks "betrays a Protestant or liberal preference which no conservative Jew and no Catholic would accept."[126] That these things do occur, no behavioralist today would deny. He does deplore them, however, and seeks to erase value-laden concepts from his analysis whenever possible. Professor Strauss should recognize this. Some have tried to solve the problem by listing their political values at the head of research reports, so that any "corruption" of their scientific description can easily be detected.[127]

[123]Strauss, *op. cit.*, p. 20.

[124]See ch. 6 below for a discussion of the work of Lasswell and the Chicago School in comparison with the naturalism of Machiavelli.

[125]See T. W. Adorno et al., *The Authoritarian Personality* (New York: Harper & Row, Publishers, 1950).

[126]Strauss, *op. cit.*, p. 21.

[127]See, e.g., Arthur Maass, *Muddy Waters: The Army Engineers and the Nation's Rivers* (Cambridge, Mass.: Harvard University Press, 1951).

Another of Strauss's objections to the assumptions of behavioralism is that it is logically impossible to make *any* political inquiry without dealing with purposes as well as processes, or without at least *implying* the need for teleological analysis. The argument runs that the first step in political inquiry is to say what "political" means, what are and what are not political things. Professor Strauss thinks that we must conceive the political as "that which is related in a relevant way to the *polis,* the 'country' or the 'state'." One must therefore speak of a political *society,* but the political *society* cannot be defined without reference to its purposes. This admits a standard in the light of which one must judge political actions. Some behavioralists would argue in reply that it is possible to talk about political activities simply as a power process or as a decision-making process, which, indeed, is used by a society's members for a variety of purposes. The emphasis of the political scientist is not on the rightness or wrongness of the purposes involved, but on the characteristic pattern of the activity or process. If the decision-making notion is itself a teleological notion, it is indeed a minimal one. They would deny that any logical trap exists.

Professor Strauss continues the charges against behavioralism with the assertion that the claim of science to be the sole instrument for understanding the political world, i.e., the claim that conflicts between values are "essentially insoluble for human reason . . . has never been proven." He then moves from negative criticism to the positive work of showing how reason can in fact discover the political good. His method is simply to describe "the Classical Solution" of the problem, to recommend it to us, and to compare it unfavorably with the "Modern Solution," which begins with the heresy of Machiavelli and ends with that of Nietzsche.

It is regrettable that Professor Strauss remained content to explicate the ideas of others on the political good and never constructed a *Republic* of his own. Perhaps he saw himself only as the Socratic "gadfly" who helps others to their own discovery of the Good but who cannot supply them with the knowledge ready-made. The following passage from one of his discussions of Plato implies that this was his intention:

> No interpretation of Plato's teaching can be proved fully by historical evidence. For the crucial part of his interpretation the interpreter has to fall back on his own resources: Plato does not relieve him of the responsibility for discovering the decisive part of the argument by himself. The undying controversy about the meaning of the idea of the good is a sufficiently clear sign of this. Who can say that he understands what Plato means by the idea of the good if he has not discovered by himself, though guided by Plato's hints, the exact or scientific argument which establishes the necessity and the precise character of that "idea," that is, the argument which alone would have satisfied Plato and which he refused to present to us in the *Republic* or anywhere else.[128]

[128]Leo Strauss, "On a New Interpretation of Plato's Political Philosophy," *Social Research,* Vol. XIII (1946), p. 351.

For Plato and Strauss political understanding must be a matter of individual experience and of individual discipleship. The unrighteous and those who attempt no moral inquiry must either take on faith what Plato and Strauss allege or else assume an agnostic attitude. But they have no warrant, Strauss argues, to relegate ultimate values to the realm of mere preferences.

Bibliographical Note

An excellent new translation of *Republic* is by Allan Bloom, New York: Basic Books, Inc., 1968. The volume also contains a fine interpretive essay. Two standard, time-honored commentaries on Plato's political philosophy are Sir Ernest Barker, *Greek Political Theory: Plato and His Predecessors,* London: Methuen & Co., Ltd., 1947, and Richard Lewis Nettleship, *Lectures on the Republic of Plato,* London: Macmillan & Co., Ltd., 1929. Both are primarily descriptive and interpretive works. They are, in general, sympathetic accounts, particularly Nettleship's. Another useful interpretive study is Roger J. F. Chance, *Until Philosophers Are Kings,* London: University of London Press, 1928, a comparison of the political thought of Plato and Aristotle. Its analysis of the development in Plato's thought from the *Republic* through *The Statesman* to *The Laws* is particularly good. Glenn R. Morrow, *Plato's Cretan City*, Princeton, N.J.: Princeton University Press, 1960, is a definitive study of *The Laws.* A new and significant reinterpretation of Plato's theory of Forms is Gilbert Ryle, *Plato's Progress,* Cambridge: Cambridge University Press, 1966. A useful book, which attempts to make Plato contemporary, is Robert S. Brumbaugh, *Plato for the Modern Age,* New York: Crowell-Collier and Macmillan, Inc., 1962. R. H. S. Crossman, in *Plato Today,* New York: Oxford University Press, Inc., 1939, brings Plato to life in the modern world and asks him to examine critically the British cabinet system of government, presidential government and New Deal policies in the United States, and Russian communism.

A vigorous neo-sophistic attack on the whole structure of Plato's political philosophy is Karl R. Popper, *The Open Society and Its Enemies.* Vol. I, *The Spell of Plato,* rev. ed., Princeton, N.J.: Princeton University Press, 1950. Popper makes Plato the father of modern fascism and totalitarian nationalism. Two replies by neo-Platonist writers are Ronald R. Levinson, *In Defense of Plato,* Cambridge, Mass.: Harvard University Press, 1953, and John Wild, *Plato's Modern Enemies and the Theory of Natural Law,* Chicago: University of Chicago Press, 1953. Excerpts from these and other works in the modern polemic about Plato have been collected by Thomas L. Thorson, *Plato: Totalitarian or Democrat?* Englewood Cliffs, N.J.: Prentice-Hall, Inc., 1963. See also the vigorous assault on "sophistic" behavioral science by a group of Professor Strauss's students, Herbert J. Storing, ed., *Essays on the Scientific Study of Politics,* New York: Holt, Rinehart & Winston, Inc., 1962.

Chapter 3

Moral Virtue
and Sociological Process:
Aristotle, Lipset
and Situation Ethics*

Plato's pupil Aristotle lived to see the final phase of that moral and political disintegration of the world of the *polis* whose onset Thucydides had recorded and whose spread Plato had hoped to stem. He was forty-six years old when Philip of Macedon ended the system of independent *poleis* with his victory in 338 B.C. at Chaeronea and proceeded to lay the foundations of his son Alexander's empire. And he died in 322, one year after the death of the Conqueror.

Like Plato, Aristotle was no cloistered academician but an active participant in the political struggles of his time, though also as an adviser to politicians rather than as an office holder. (As a foreigner from Stagira, a town on the border of Macedonia, he was, of course, not eligible for office at Athens during his long stay there.) We might compare him with the scholarly counselors and politicians of our own time—the Tugwells, the Kissingers, the Moynihans. For several years he was able to study at first hand the inner working of a *polis* as a friend of Hermias, tyrant of the city of Atarneus in Asia Minor. And as tutor to the young Alexander at the court of Pella, Aristotle must have observed something of the development of imperial politics. Barker tells us that he had influence with Philip and laid down the principles which Philip used as a guide in the settlement of disputes among his Greek satellite states. He advised Alexander how to treat the conquered peoples of Asia and how to establish colonies. While he was head of the Lyceum from 335 until a year before his death in 322, he had close relations with Antipater, Alexander's vice-regent in the Greek area. Perhaps, indeed,

Some of the material in this chapter appeared originally in an article entitled "The Place of the 'Polity' in Aristotle's Theory of the Ideal State," The Journal of Politics, XXIV, (November, 1962), pp. 743-53. I am grateful to the editor for permission to reprint it here in modified form.

the *Politics* was meant as a handbook for Antipater in solving the constitutional difficulties of the Greek *poleis,* which in their subject condition continued to be riven by faction and were continuously in upheaval.[1]

The extant political writings of Aristotle deal entirely with the problem of order in the individual *polis,* and nothing remains on the politics of empire, if there ever were such writings. Like Plato, Aristotle was interested in delineating the ideal *polis* as a standard to guide reform of the troubled actual *poleis* of his time. But, unlike Plato, at no point in his career did Aristotle suggest that a blueprint of perfection in the hands of a philosophic tyrant was the best recipe for political improvement. Nor did he conclude, as did Plato, that no substantial amelioration of things was possible without either wiping the old slate clean, by violent means, or beginning anew with the fresh slate of a new colony. His conception of the good order and of the actual order, and of their relationship to one another, we shall see, differed considerably from Plato's, and he thought it useful to prescribe for various degrees of goodness, as well as for the perfect society. The problem of the best regime and the problem of stability, for example, became for Aristotle separate and independent questions, as they had never been for Plato. Aristotle also found it much more important than did Plato to understand and describe in detail the actual condition of the Greek *poleis* as a part of the work of defining the ideal and establishing the conditions of its realization. And he also seems to have found this an enterprise interesting and valuable for its own sake.

What elements in Aristotle's general intellectual makeup and in his way of thinking about politics account for these different emphases and interests? What were the tools with which Aristotle approached the inquiries which he set for himself? Let us look at Aristotle's method of studying politics.

A Method of Inquiry into the Political Good

Empiricism and Metaphysics

It is clear that despite his many years of study with Plato in the Academy, Aristotle never fully adopted his teacher's world-view or scholarly method. Plato's model of knowledge was the abstract world of mathematics, and he had a tendency to reduce the ultimate questions to a mystical calculus, as we have seen. By contrast, Aristotle's model was biology, a science which then as now rested on careful observation of the empirical world that Plato so disdained. The first line of the *Politics,* for ex-

[1]See Ernest Barker, *The Political Thought of Plato and Aristotle* (New York: Dover Publications, Inc., 1959), pp.213-17.

ample, begins with the words, "Observation shows. . . ."[2] And filtered through Plato's extreme rationalism and idealism, this empiricism produced a wholly new political science, in a way a hybrid of the approaches of Thucydides and Plato to the study of politics. Perhaps we should do better to describe Aristotle as a bridge-builder from the noumenalist to the naturalist world. He retains the Platonic conception of intelligible essences (though he revises that conception), and it is central to his idea of the rational, or best, polity. He was as much concerned as Plato to delineate a viable conception of political virtue. But his entire theory of the actual order could have been constructed without such a concept, as we shall see.

Empiricism may be seen in Aristotle's theory of the highest political good as well as in his description of actual politics. He found it impossible to accept Plato's theory of Forms, which was the metaphysical foundation of Plato's ideal state, because of its absolute divorce from the reality of common-sense experience. It was a dream world of impractical aspiration which most men would reject as fantasy. In the *Metaphysics,* for example, he goes so far as to say, "Now evidently the Forms do not exist." And later he adds:

> Above all one might discuss the question what in the world the Forms con-
> tribute to sensible things, either to those that are eternal or to those that come
> into being and cease to be; for they cause neither movement nor any change in
> them. But again they help in no wise either towards the knowledge of other
> things (for they are not even the substance of these, else they would have been
> in them), or towards their being, if they are not in the individuals which share
> in them. . . .
> But, further, all other things cannot come from the Forms in any of the usual
> senses of "from." And to say that they are patterns and the other things share
> in them is to use empty words and poetical metaphors. . . .[3]

Most of Aristotle's criticisms of Plato's *Republic* plainly stem from his recognition that the logical relationships which Plato found in his *polis* of Ideas could not be translated into empirical relationships, that only as ideal empirical relationships could they have significance as a standard for men. Thus, for example, Aristotle rejected communism as an institution for insur-ing the devotion of rulers to the common good. Plato's reasoning had run roughly as follows:

1. Every historical *polis* is in the long run unstable. It becomes dis-united and riven by faction. (Empirical hypothesis.)

---

[2] Perhaps it was his early experience as the son of a physician which developed Aristotle's high regard for sense evidence. According to Galen, Asclepiad families were of the custom of training their sons in dissection. See W. D. Ross, *Aristotle* (London: Methuen & Co., Ltd., 1923), p. 1.

[3] *Metaphysics* 1059b 1-2, 1079b 12-27. References to all of Aristotle's works except *Politics* are to the Jowett translation, in Richard McKeon, ed., *The Basic Works of Aristotle* (New York: Random House, 1946).

2. The historical *polis* is therefore evil, because it does not conform to the Form of the *polis,* which is presented to the teleological reason as a united and cooperative commonwealth in which all have a concern for the common good. (Moral judgment based on metaphysical insight and formal definition.)

3. Conflict in the historical *polis* arises from "a disagreement about the use of the terms 'mine' and 'not mine,' 'his' and 'not his' "; (*Republic* 5.462) i.e., each one is concerned only with his own interests, which he thinks of as distinct from and even opposed to those of his neighbors. The sense of distinct and conflicting interests arises from the distinction of possessions, from the institution of private property. (Empirical hypothesis.)

4. Conversely, harmony and unity in the ideal *polis* derive from the identification by each citizen of his own interest with the interest of all. This identification flows from the institution of common property. "Is not that the best-ordered State in which the greatest number of persons apply the terms 'mine' and 'not mine' in the same way to the same thing?" (*Ibid.*) (Logical deduction from metaphysical intuition of the Form?)

5. Therefore, the institution of common property will produce peace and concord in the historical *polis.* (Empirical prediction based on deduction from proposition stated under No. 4.)

Stated in summary, the argument appears to be:

If A (private property)$\rightarrow B$ (conflict),
then Non-A (community of goods)$\rightarrow$Non-B (nonconflict, harmony)

Aristotle discovered a double flaw in it. Plato apparently meant to argue that the community of goods would produce such an identity of individual interest with the interest of all that every citizen would think of the good of each other citizen as his own good. But as a matter of fact, Aristotle maintained, when people speak of the good of all as their own good, they do not mean "of each" by the expression "of all."

> They will all call them "Mine"; but they will do so collectively, and not individually. The same is true of property also: all will call it "Mine"; but they will do so in the sense of "all collectively," and not in the sense of "each separately." It is therefore clear that there is a certain fallacy in the use of the term "all." It is a term which . . . is liable by its ambiguity . . . to breed captious arguments in reasoning. We may therefore conclude that the formula of "all men saying 'Mine' of the same object" is in one sense . . . something fine but impracticable, and in another sense . . . in no wise conducive to harmony. Not only does it not conduce to harmony: the formula also involves an actual loss. What is common to the greatest number gets the least amount of care. Men pay most attention to what is their own: they care less for what is com-

mon; or, at any rate, they care for it only to the extent to which each is individually concerned.[4]

Not only was Plato using equivocal language in his argument, but his theory was also shown by experience to be wrong. Plato had not empirically checked his prediction. And observation demonstrated its fallacy:

> Fellow-travellers who are merely partners in a journey furnish an illustration: they generally quarrel about ordinary matters and take offence on petty occasions.[5]

Deductions must be checked with an empirical test. And they must be surrendered if they prove out of keeping with the facts.

> We are bound to pay some regard to the long past and the passage of the years, in which these things [advocated by Plato as new discoveries] would not have gone unnoticed if they had been really good.[6]

Experience is the acid test of a theory, even of a purely ideal system of the kind Plato delineated. The logical relationships of Plato's *polis* could be meaningful only if they could be translated into ideal empirical relationships. This could be done only if there was a correspondence between the causal principles, the "mechanisms," of the two worlds. Otherwise there would be no connection at all between the two realms, and the ideal *polis* would have no significance whatever for the real. But Plato *meant* it to have significance, and he insisted on the "participation" of the real in the ideal world. But he never specified the exact nature of this participation, and tended in fact radically to separate them, as his disregard for the empirical test shows.[7]

Aristotle's Immanentism: The Political Good as Entelechy and the Doctrine of the Four "Causes." But Criticism is one thing and constructive

---

[4]*Politics* 1261b 25-35. Barker's translation in Ernest Barker, ed., *The Politics of Aristotle* (New York: Oxford University Press, Inc., 1958). All subsequent references to the *Politics* will be to the Barker translation.

[5]*Ibid.*, 1263a 17-20.

[6]*Ibid.*, 1264a 1-3.

[7]Despite all this, empirical observation shows (e.g., in the studies of Dr. Bruno Bettelheim), that the generation raised as children of the community in the Israeli *kibbutzim* display just such a devotion to the common good as Plato had hoped for. Constituting only 4 percent of the population of Israel, they have produced a disproportionately large number of heroes and leaders. The children live together from an early age under teachers and apart from their parents. The entire arrangement is, of course, based on general consent, as Plato insisted it had to be. Whether communal living in the *kibbutzim* or the siege condition of Israel is the primary cause of the extraordinary civic devotion of these youngsters may, however, be debated.

thinking another. How did Aristotle go about finding in sense experience the "Good" which Plato knew only in abstract thought? That there are absolute values and ideal conditions, and that they are discoverable by reason, Aristotle affirmed. "Good" is not simply a name which I give to my preferences. And in working out his philosophy, Aristotle did not entirely abandon the notion of "Form" as a metaphysical principle. But he reshaped it. Plainly the world of sense has structure and order in it. Units of sense experience are not entirely unique, nor do they pass before our gaze in a chaotic tumble. Our experience is "intelligible." It makes sense to us. Now in what *ways* is it intelligible? *How* is it ordered?

Aristotle realized that by common judgment, "Forms" as universal concepts help us order experience. We can identify the "house" in houses, the "tree" in trees, the *"polis"* in *poleis*. But in doing this, he maintained, we are merely abstracting the elements that the particulars of our experience have as common characteristics. The universal is an organizing principle which designates the essential and characteristic structure of a substance. Plato went wrong when he made of these universals "things." Existentially, there is no universal or "Form" apart from the particular "primary substances." There is no *polis* of thought existing in a heaven above the heavens apart from historical *poleis*. The only things which exist are those things which cannot be predicated of other things, e.g., *this* house, *this polis,* Socrates. But the universal concept *"polis"* helps us to describe and understand *this polis*—Athens, Sparta, Corinth—because it designates in this *polis* its essential "whatness," the structure of its being. One scholar particularly well described this empirical anchoring of the Aristotelian notion of "Form" when he wrote that "The form is, in its own character, a *quale, . . .* but it is a form not *qua quale,* but *qua* that by virtue of which the primary substance in which it is present is a separate being of a certain kind."[8] It is in Aristotle's terminology a "secondary substance." And it is this universal, not the particular of sense, of which we have "knowledge." But we can have knowledge of it only by examining its manifestation in particulars.

Now what is it that we know when we know the Form or Universal? Aristotle's answer is fourfold.[9] First and foremost, the "essence" or "whatness" of a thing is a function or an end (*telos, entelecheia*). We explain something by referring to what it does or produces. The well-known Aristotle scholar J. H. Randall speaks of a "perfected activity, functioning without interference from outside."[10] Thus the function of a peach tree is to bear peaches, and of a chair to support a human body. It is primarily by referring

[8]Wilfrid Sellars, "Substance and Form in Aristotle," *Journal of Philosophy,* LIV (1957), 692.

[9]See *Physics* II, 3; *Metaphysics* I, 3, 5, 6, 7; II; V, 2, 4, 16; VIII; IX.

[10]John Herman Randall, *Aristotle* (New York: Columbia University Press, 1960), p.52.

to its *telos* that we can evaluate any particular thing and judge it good or bad. A peach tree which is barren is a bad tree. And a chair which breaks as one sits in it is a poor chair. It may be valuable as an antique decoration, but as a chair it is worthless. So to understand a *polis* we must discover the function of that class of things designated by the term *polis*.

So far we do not seem far removed from Plato. But to talk thus about the function of a thing does not of itself commit one to a doctrine of a world of transcendent and divine purposes or beings. Randall is most emphatic on this point and insists that the conception of function in Aristotle's work is quite independent of any theology.

> For although for Aristotle nature, apart from human arts, exhibits no discoverable purposes, it does exhibit natural ends or *tele*. . . . Events do not merely "happen," they have consequences, they achieve results, they exhibit a pattern of reaching outcomes that is repeated over and over again. . . . Nature is . . . full of ends, *tele,* that are achieved, of conclusions that are reached over and over. Only in human life are these ends and conclusions consciously intended, only in men are purposes found. For Aristotle, even God has no purpose, only man![11]

Function can be determined through empirical observation. But observations at a single point in time are inadequate. One must witness the entire life, the whole period of growth and decay, of many instances of a class of things in order to know the function or fulfillment proper to the class. After many such observations one comes to understand *telos* or entelechy as a capacity as well as an actuality, and as a principle of growth immanent in a substance, and guiding it toward its culmination, as a drive toward a specific end. The *telos* is in no sense a Platonic abstraction, living apart from, and only dimly mirrored in the empirical world of flux. It is the vital principle of the phenomenal world whose role is to form and shape the world. It has no existence apart from those phenomena. This is Aristotle's doctrine of the "final cause." One way to understand the nature of something is to seek to know what it tends to become as its fulfillment.

A second way of understanding something, according to Aristotle's analytical scheme, is through an examination of the "formal cause." Everything has an observable structure which is characteristic of the class to which it belongs, and to describe this structure adequately is to understand the entity. When a botanist classifies plants by leaf types, petal types, and the like, he is doing "formal cause analysis." And when a political scientist classifies political systems by types of electoral, legislative, and administrative procedures, party and pressure group organizations, and other criteria, he is also doing "formal cause" analysis. As the *telos* or end of an entity moves from potency to actuality, its form develops correspondingly to a perfect and complete condition—a characteristic structure is generated.

[11]*Ibid.,* p. 125.

Now "formal" and "final cause" analysis, while explaining the "what" and the "why" of a thing, are of no help in answering the question "how." For we naturally desire to know the processes through which ends and structures are evolved. Indeed these processes are today the primary object of scientific inquiry. Aristotle referred to them as the "efficient cause." The unfolding of *tele* is no mysterious or magical occurrence but a continuum of causally connected empirical events. It is, indeed, a mechanism whose logic can be laid bare by careful scrutiny of the phenomena. And in a sense, the "efficient cause" is prior to both the formal and final causes, because empirical motions and processes are the only things which we can directly observe to be active. "Ends, final causes—never 'do' anything. . . . Only motion can 'do' anything."[12]

The importance to Aristotle of understanding the efficient cause for the analysis of final causes is strikingly illustrated by comparing the discussion of the nature of soul in the *De Anima* with Plato's notion of soul. Aristotle agrees with Plato that the characteristic element of "soul" is "life." The two terms may in fact be used interchangeably. But he does not accept Plato's definition of life, or soul, as "the motion which can move itself."[13] Such an abstract and general definition is useless, because soul in general cannot be observed.

> It is . . . evident that a single definition can be given of soul only in the same sense as one can be given of figure. . . . It is true that a highly general definition can be given for figure which will fit all figures without expressing the peculiar nature of any figure. So here in the case of soul and its specific forms. Hence it is absurd in this and similar cases to demand an absolutely general definition, which will fail to express the peculiar nature of anything that is, or again, omitting this, to look for separate definition according to each *infima species.*[14]

Aristotle then proceeds to define "life" and "soul" according to the various empirical forms which it takes. Beings which we call "alive" have a capacity for self-nutrition. This is the basic meaning of "life." Some of these beings also have the power of sensation, another form of self-movement, and some, in addition, the power of local movement. Human life, or the human soul, contains all these capacities, and in addition, as its characteristic activity, mind, or the ability to think. Aristotle defines thinking as imagining (calling up mental images of sensible things) and judgment (registering the form of an object in the external world), two empirical processes. Each man can directly observe himself engaging in imagining and judging. And we can infer the existence of this activity in others from their words and deeds. Aristotle absolutely confines the definition of "thinking" and "mind" to this

[12]*Ibid.,* p. 128.
[13]*Laws* 10.896.
[14]*De Anima* 414b 20-28.

observable activity: "That in the soul which is called mind . . . is, before it thinks, not actually any real thing."[15]

Life, or soul, as the activity of thinking, is to Aristotle the essential characteristic of man—it is his "form" or "essence." A man is a substance composed of body, i.e., matter which potentially is a "this" or a "that," and soul, which gives form or actuality to the body as a substance with life of a certain kind—thinking—in it. Thinking life, in its perfection, is also the final cause of man, as life in its other forms is the final cause of other natural bodies.

> It is manifest that its soul is also the final cause of its body. For Nature, like mind, always does whatever it does for the sake of something, which something is its end. . . . All material bodies are organs of the soul.[16]

Thus we see that Aristotle's conception of final and formal causation is closely tied in with that of efficient causation. We can meaningfully talk of soul as final and formal cause only after reducing it to something observable, to an empirical motion or activity, and viewing it as efficient cause, i.e., as the source or origin of movements, such as bodily growth, local movement, or bodily sensation. Similarly, when Aristotle in the *Politics* tells us how the various kinds of regime operate and what the causes of their revolution and stabilization are, he is giving us information which we must have in order to deal intelligently with questions concerning the proper structure and purposes of the political system—the formal and final causes of politics. Necessity, or mechanical process, is not in competition with reason, as in Plato's work, but is its vehicle.

There is yet one more level of understanding, which involves answering the question "out of what," the "material cause." While there may be an ultimate uniform substratum, a primary matter out of which all things are generated, the immediate materials out of which the different classes of beings emerge are different. And these differences in raw material are crucial. For every structure and *telos,* and indeed every process of development, depends for the character it takes on the material with which it is associated. Oak trees will not grow out of hazel nuts but only from acorns. And if they are sown in sandy soil on the ocean front, and if the trees are constantly drenched by salt spray, they will always remain scrub growth. Similarly, in politics, one cannot expect a healthy *polis* to develop in a society dominated by impoverished urban workers or by a small class of overly rich oligarchs. Constitutions, both as *tele,* or ways of life (i.e., value systems), and as structures of government, are shaped out of and radically dependent upon the class structures of societies, one of their "material causes." And Aristotle devotes much attention in his *Politics* to the social bases of the good regime.

[15]*Ibid.,* 429a 23-4.
[16]*Ibid.,* 415b 15-18.

According to Aristotle, when we have answered the four questions "what," "why," "how," and "out of what," we have comprehended as fully as possible the subject of our inquiry. The empirical world has intelligible structure, and language can reveal it by answering these questions. The answers to the four questions give us a principle for classifying in universal categories the "primary substances" of our experience and a standard for evaluating their goodness. And they tell us whence these substances originate, and what the mechanics of their origin and development, the laws of their motion, are.

Immanent Good: Aristotle's Quest for the Best Regime

The focus of Aristotle's political thought, just as Plato's, is on the *polis*. Indeed, the title of his great treatise, *Politike,* ought to be translated "the theory of the common life of the *polis*," rather than by our word "politics."[17] And the first object of his analysis is to pin down the function or purpose of the *polis*. (In comparison with other forms of human association, what is it that the *polis* does, or produces, which is uniquely characteristic of it?) Aristotle does not separate out for inquiry the purpose of the political system of the *polis,* as modern students of politics do. His work is at one and the same time a sociology and a political science.

How did Aristotle proceed? He was aware that the *polis* had not always existed, but that it had a historical beginning and was preceded by more rudimentary village and family associations which continued to exist to his own day as "sub-organs" of the polis. This was common knowledge among learned Greeks of his time, as we have seen from our study of Plato. Placing these three entities side by side, and in order of historical development as three forms of the broader category "human association," Aristotle proceeded to ask whether a teleological development could be discerned in the phenomena. Could movement toward an end, or fulfillment, be discerned? He concluded that it could, that society seemed ordained to make possible for men the good and complete life, a life in which their highest capacities, and hence happiness, could be realized. This also was a common notion of the time, and Aristotle's own review of the facts confirmed it for him. Each level of society had something to contribute to human happiness, and the comprehensive society of the *polis,* which contained all the partial associations, was the form of social order in which complete fulfillment could be achieved. (This is the meaning of the famous Aristotelian dictum that "Man is a political animal.") The family and village existed for the sake of life, the *polis* for the good life. The *polis* is thus the culmination, the *telos*, of human society.

[17]Barker, Introduction to *The Politics of Aristotle,* p. lxvi.

> When we come to the final and perfect association, formed from a number of villages, we have already reached the *polis*—an association which may be said to have reached the height of full self-sufficiency; or rather . . . we may say that while it *grows* for the sake of mere life . . . it *exists* . . . for the sake of a good life. . . .
>
> Because it is the completion of associations existing by nature, every *polis* exists by nature, having itself the same quality as the earlier associations from which it grew. It is the end or consummation to which those associations move, and the "nature" of things consists in their end or consummation. . . . Again . . . the end, or final cause, is the best. Now self-sufficiency . . . is the end, and so the best.[18]

Now, at this point a modern student might throw up his hands and exclaim that Aristotle's analysis was hopelessly subjective and "culture-bound," and of no use for us today. Modern city-states like Andorra, Luxembourg, Liechtenstein are merely rather comical vestigial remains of an earlier historical order, and to think of them as the culmination of social development is ridiculous. But this would be dealing over-hastily and superficially with Aristotle's thought. For the notion of *"polis"* was to him not primarily a conception of territorial size, though size was an important factor, but rather a set of social and political principles which are capable of embodiment in geographical units of various size. The extent of the territorial unit in which they can be embodied is largely a function of technology. And given the technology of Aristotle's day, the *polis* seemed a better realization of these principles than any other political unit.

Yves Simon, a modern student of politics who stands in the Aristotelian tradition, writes that in our own time "dependence upon things, persons, and social structures lying outside one's own state or federal nation have become such a common and important occurrence that it may be wondered whether any society smaller than the world has the character of a civil society [i.e., a society of temporal fulfillment], except in a strongly qualified sense. Such a situation raises the problem of the world-state but does not demonstrate its possibility."[19]

The first of the principles of the perfect society is self-sufficiency, or autarky. Aristotle seeks to understand the form of social organization which contains within itself all things requisite for the complete happiness of its members. But what is the nature of that happiness, and how does Aristotle determine it?

Aristotle on Virtue

Aristotle expounded his idea of the good life in detail in two treatises on ethics. The last paragraph of the second of these works, the *Nicomachean Ethics,* points to a sequel on social organization, the *Politics.* What goes into

---

[18] *Politics* 1252b 27-1253a 1.

[19] Yves Simon, *Philosphy of Democratic Government* (Chicago: University of Chicago Press, 1951), pp. 67-68.

the making of a good and sufficient life, a happy life? It is more than security from injury, and material well-being. The end of the *polis* does not consist merely in providing an "alliance for mutual defence against all injury, or to ease exchange and promote economic intercourse." If this were the case, a *polis* could not be distinguished from other forms of alliance or from trade associations. "The Etruscans and the Carthaginians would be in the position of belonging to a single *polis;* and the same would be true of all peoples who have commercial treaties with one another."[20] The proper end of the *polis* is rather to make men good. And human goodness, just as the goodness of any creature, must be sought for in function. To know what the good human life is like, we must ask what the characteristically human activity is. What is it that a man does which distinguishes him from the rest of creation? The answer is the exercise of reason. Along with the lower animals, man has the faculties of nutrition, sensation, local movement, and perception. But in addition he has reason. "The function of man is an activity of soul which follows or implies a rational principle."[21] And so the good of man lies in the excellent (virtuous) performance of this activity.

But now we come to a new departure. For Aristotle has something new to say about what "reason" means. He distinguishes two kinds of reason, while Plato had spoken only of one. On the one hand, there is the reason which "contemplates the kinds of things whose originative causes are invariable." And on the other, there is the reason which regards "variable things." The objects of the contemplative reason comprise what we would today call the objects of scientific, mathematical, and metaphysical inquiry. The object of the practical reason is the good for man. The end of the contemplative reason is understanding only, theory. But that of the practical reason is moral action. The practical reason works out broad criteria of moral choice and also guides the particular choices of the moral agent. Practical wisdom is "a true and reasoned state of capacity to act with regard to the things that are good or bad for man."[22] Thus the rational activity of man will have two kinds of excellence, intellectual excellence and moral excellence.

Of the two activities, contemplation is the higher, because it is the activity of pure reason. It is a self-sufficient activity, because reason is a divine thing, because its objects are the best knowable objects, and because its pleasures are the purest and most enduring. And its purpose can be achieved in perfect isolation, apart from all human society. By contrast, moral virtue, which is a "state of character concerned with choice, lying in a mean . . . determined by a rational principle," involves our whole composite nature, the passions as well as reason. It is the excellence of that which is specifically human in us. And it requires society for its development. "The just man

[20]*Politics* 1280a 35-40.
[21]*Nicomachean Ethics* 1098a 7-8.
[22]*Ibid.,* 1140b 5-6.

needs people towards whom and with whom he shall act justly, and the temperate man, the brave man, and each of the others is in the same case."[23] It also requires abundant material goods. Liberality, for example, needs wealth for its exercise.

To a degree, Aristotle identifies the life of thought and the life of action as the lives of two different kinds of men, the philosopher and the man of affairs (*politikos*). But the separation is not complete, for the philosopher is not given leave to retire into the isolation of the wilderness. If he is to develop his humanity, even the philosopher must depend on society. "In so far as he is a man and lives with a number of people, he chooses to do virtuous acts; he will therefore need such aids to living a human life."[24] Society, then, and specifically the *polis,* exists to make possible one aspect of the life of reason—the life of practical reason and moral virtue—which is a life according to the principle of the mean.

Some actions are to be deemed bad in themselves and to be avoided altogether, such as envy, adultery, theft, murder. ("For all of these and suchlike things," Aristotle writes, "imply by their names that they are themselves bad and not the excesses or deficiencies of them."[25] He attempts no demonstration, but simply stays with tradition, invoking the connotation of "their names.") In most things one should guide the appetites, or passions, which activate us, by the principle of the mean, which is as good a rule as there is available in the world of "variable things" and contingencies, which is the world of moral choice. For example, with reference to feelings of fear and confidence, the excellent man is neither cowardly nor rash, but courageous. In matters of honor he will take proper pride in his accomplishments, and be neither unduly humble nor vainglorious. In the use of wealth he will be liberal, not miserly or prodigal. In bodily pleasures he will be neither ascetic nor self-indulgent, but temperate. With regard to pleasantness in social intercourse, the virtuous man is neither obsequious nor surly, but friendly. (Again in recommending the "mean" Aristotle presents no philosophical demonstration. Observation of the rule "is praised and is a form of success; and being praised and being successful are both characteristics of virtue."[26] Again, Aristotle derives his idea of *good* behavior from *actual* behavior—or rather from what is *in fact* approved and praised as good behavior. He refuses to divorce his normative order at any point from the existing Greek value system, which was under severe pressure from Sophistic and other quarters.)

How are the moral virtues, which make this good life possible, acquired? Not by teaching, Aristotle tells us. Intellectual virtue may be so ac-

[23]*Ibid.,* 1106b 35-1107a 1, 1177a 29-34.
[24]*Ibid.,* 1178b 5-7.
[25]*Ibid.,* 1107a 9-13.
[26]*Ibid.,* 1106b 26-7.

quired, but moral virtue is a result of habit. And good habits are acquired through the practice of good actions. As in the arts, we learn by doing. "We become just by doing just acts, temperate by doing temperate acts, brave by doing brave acts."[27]

But how are men brought to the performance of the noble actions from which good habits, a permanent disposition to act well, will arise? This is the question which leads us from the *Ethics* to the *Politics*. For it is the job of the laws and of the statesman to implant these habits in men. The statesman should receive his own education in these things from a study of the politico-ethical experience embodied in the laws and customs of mankind.

We have clarified the first principle of Aristotle's perfect social order, autarky. The perfect society contains within itself all the means for producing men who lead lives of noble action guided by the principle of the mean. If the *polis* is sufficient for the good life, it will make its members good. What does the experience of mankind tell us about how the perfect society is to be ordered? What are its structural principles?

A beginning of a revelation of the principles peculiar to "political" government is made in Book I of the *Politics* by a genetic analysis, which Aristotle calls his "normal method."[28] To understand the *polis,* we must understand the social forms out of which it emerged, the family and village. As these are only rudimentary and partial associations, they will be functionally and structurally different from the *polis.* And by seeing what these characteristics are, we shall, in a negative way, begin to understand what the *polis* is as we watch it grow out of them.[29]

> It is a mistake to believe that the statesman . . . is the same as the monarch of a kingdom, or the manager of a household, or the master of a number of slaves. Those who hold this view consider that each of these persons differs from the others not with a difference of kind, but . . . according to the number, or the paucity, of the persons with whom he deals. . . . This view abolishes any real difference between a large household and a small *polis;* and it also reduces the difference between the "statesman" and the monarch to the one fact that the latter has an uncontrolled and sole authority, while the former exercises his authority in conformity with the rules imposed by the art of statesmanship and as one who rules and is ruled in turn. But this is a view which cannot be accepted as correct.[30]

Aristotle describes the family or household group as an association whose primary object is to support life. Thus property as well as procreation comes

[27]*Ibid.,* 1103b 1-2.

[28]*Politics* 1252a 20.

[29]Book I appears to be incomplete, as it closes after a discussion of the elements of houshold management. There is no consideration at all of the village, here or elsewhere in the *Politics.*

[30]*Ibid.,* 1252a 17-18.

within the sphere of the household, since property (i.e., things, instruments) is necessary for life.

In this section Aristotle includes a long discussion of the slave as an "animate article of property," which has been much deplored in the commentaries and treated as a skeleton in the closet of an otherwise virtuous house. For Aristotle presents a justification of the institution of slavery as natural, in the teleological sense of the word "natural." All men who "differ from others as much as the body differs from the soul, or an animal from a man . . . are by nature slaves."[31] And it is best for them to be ruled by another, for being without reason, they are incapable of governing themselves. This is not the same as a justification of the *legal* institution of slavery, however, or an argument that everyone who is by law a slave is properly one by nature also. In fact Aristotle specifically says that nature's intention often miscarries, so that natural slaves have the status of free men, while men who should be free are bound in slavery.[32] In a sense even the very egalitarian philosophy of modern liberalism admits the conception of "slaves by nature" when it sanctions prisons for criminals and institutions for the confinement of the insane.

At any rate, Aristotle's main point in bringing up the whole question of slavery, an important established institution of his time, was not to praise or justify it, but by identifying the authority of the master as an aspect of household management, to distinguish it from the kind of authority properly exercised by a statesman over the citizens of a *polis*.

> The argument makes it clear that the authority of the master and that of the statesman are different from one another, and that it is not the case that all kinds of authority are, as some thinkers hold, identical. The authority of the statesman is exercised over men who are naturally free; that of the master over men who are slaves.[33]

It is all essentially a rebuttal of Plato's argument for a three-class *polis*. The *polis* as the association of human fulfillment must be an association of "freemen and equals," whose equality resides primarily in their common reason.

In discussing the other two interpersonal relations which are found in the household group, that between husband and wife, and that between father and child, Aristotle stresses the same point. The natural equipment of the persons in each of these relationships is different. Reason is developed only in the mature male. In the woman it takes a form "which remains inconclusive." (Aristotle merely asserts but does not defend this proposition.)

---

[31]*Ibid.*, 1254b 15-18.
[32]*Ibid.*, 1255a 3-1255b 15.
[33]*Ibid.*, 1255b 16-20.

And in the child it is immature. Hence hierarchy rather than equality is the applicable principle here. The husband and father is the naturally superior and should therefore rule, over his wife as "a statesman over fellow citizens," but with permanent tenure, over his children as "a monarch over subjects."[34] Moral goodness will be found in slave, wife, and child, to the extent that the person in question fulfills the duties of his status, which are primarily to obey the commands of the master or father. In none of these cases, however, do we find the perfection of human goodness. That is found only in the good master and father, whose reason is fully developed, and these are the citizens of the *polis.* Since the *polis* exists to make the good life possible, it must ideally offer a life of mature reason enjoyed equally by all its members. "The members of a political association aim by their very nature at being equal and differing in nothing."[35]

We have left Plato's elitist utopia far behind. The good life is not a life lived by most men in subjection to the dictates of a few philosophic Guardians who have achieved intellectual and spiritual communion with the "Good." It is a life lived by most men in subjection to the dictates of their own practical reason, which sees what is good for man in a rather imprecise way, guided only by the principle of the mean. But, with the help of a well-informed disposition to act aright, good habit, it is a life which moves prudently from problem to problem through the maze of moral choice. It is a life, for most men, of self-government rather than other-government.

Having completed this brief genetic analysis of the *polis,* Aristotle proceeds to elaborate his study with other methods. His object now is to discover that system, or constitution (*politeia*), which is ideal. And by ideal he means that one which best realizes the *telos* of the *polis,* the good life shared in common. The emphasis is now entirely on form and matter, the formal cause and the material cause. (The final cause has been sufficiently established.) Already we have some indications as to what it will be like. For in the genetic analysis, equality and rationality were posited as fundamental structural principles.

Book II pursues a formal cause analysis by reviewing what other writers have said about the best constitution, and by describing the characteristic institutions of actual states commonly reputed to be well organized. (Such a survey of the existing body of knowledge and opinion was a usual procedure of Aristotle in every field of inquiry.) His purpose is to point up the utter inadequacy in every respect of existing theory of the good regime. First he mercilessly criticizes Plato's *Republic,* as we have already seen, then the *Laws* as well; next he points out the defects of the utopias of half a dozen other writers, and finally he criticizes the constitutions of Sparta, Crete, and Carthage. The discussion is loose and rambling.

[34]*Ibid.,* 1259b 9-12.
[35]*Ibid.,* 1259b 6-7.

A large part of Book III is also devoted to an evaluation of current opinion. But the discussion this time is focused on the material cause, and the opinions surveyed are not those of academic theorists, or even of statesmen, but rather of social interests. Since the ideal must be found growing in the empirical world, rather than in the heaven above the heavens, it must be constituted out of matter which really exists, not out of imaginary stuff. Therefore one must see what materials are available, and what claims are made on behalf of each type.

Aristotle asks what claims to political power are commonly made, and which of them are valid. What is the best "matter" for the ruling class of the good *polis*? He introduces the theme by remarking that the citizens of a *polis*, whom he defines as those who "share in the offices and honors of the state" (from juryman to general), are the parts of a *polis*. And as the raw material out of which the parts are made varies, so will the whole. The character of the citizens determines the character of the constitution of the city in the broadest sense. "The civic body [the *politeuma*, or body of persons established in power by the polity] is everwhere the sovereign of the state; in fact the civic body is the polity (or constitution) itself."[36] The way of life of the citizens—their values, habits, virtues, vices—will be the way of life of the city. If it is a good and proper way of life, the *telos* of the city will be realized. If not, the city will be a poor thing. One must pay special attention to the composition of the "sovereign" authority.[37]

Claims are made on behalf of the "one," the "few," and the "many." The claim of the "one" (which establishes monarchy) is usually a claim of pre-eminent goodness, or virtue, though it may be the claim of the tyrant, which rests on force. The claim of the "few" may be that of the wealthy commercial minority, urging that wealth should rule (oligarchy). Or it may be that of the hereditary landed aristocracy, the patrician families, claiming greater goodness and capacity than others as the basis of their claim. The claim of the "many" is the claim of numbers, that the freeborn majority should rule (democracy or polity).

Something can be said for and against each of these actual claims to power. For the wealthy, it can be said that since the *polis* has need of financial resources for its very existence, their large share of these resources seems to constitute a valid claim to power. There is merit also in the claim of the "better sort," the aristocracy. Their social position always gives them prestige, and it is observable that noble families do in fact produce offspring of great merit and noble character, which is always the best claim to power. And since virtue is a sovereign claim, if one man in a *polis* is found to be pre-eminent over all others in goodness and statesmanship, who can deny him

[36]*Ibid.*, 1278b 11–12.

[37]The term used by Aristotle is *to kyrion*, which generally meant the deliberative assembly. See Barker *The Politics of Aristotle*, p. lxviii.

the right to rule over all, and be above all law, which is made for equals? The tyrant, presumably, can urge with some cogency that might is right and by superior force get his claim called legitimate. Aristotle actually does not detail his claim, though he lists the tyrant among the claimants. So far as "the people" or the "many" are concerned, it can be urged that though no one of them taken alone might be worth much, collectively they possess wisdom and an excellence of judgment which is of a superior sort.

But there are also important objections to each of these claims. The "many" are usually the poor, who have often in practice abused sovereign power by employing it to despoil the rich minority of their wealth, an act of manifest injustice and the ruination of a state. But a wealthy minority in the seat of power may as well use its authority to plunder the "many." Also, it is plain that the democratic conception of justice, that equality in the one point of free birth means equality in all things, and that of the oligarchs, that inequality in point of wealth means absolute inequality, are both mistaken notions. Neither conception takes cognizance of the true end of the *polis,* which is goodness, not mutual defense or the protection of property. So far as the rule of "the better sort" is concerned, though in a sense it is beneficial, by definition it bars all the rest of the community from public office and honors. And, by implication, this is an evil. Aristotle does not spell out the nature of the evil here. But we have already seen in Book I that the political relation, by its nature, and by contrast with those of the household, implies an equality among the members of the *polis.* To arrogate all authority to those few who are best is a slight to all the rest who by virtue of their rationality as mature freemen have a claim to power.

To accept the sovereignty of the one best man has the same disadvantage, since it disbars even more people from a share in the making of community decisions. Though Aristotle at the end of this section continues to argue that when such a god among men appears, all others are truly obligated to accept his rule, he plainly does not apprehend this as an ideal circumstance. In fact he is hardly ready to call such an association a *polis.* The man of singular goodness, he says, cannot "be treated as part of a [*polis*]." And in one place he gives qualified approval to the policy of ostracism, which was designed to prevent such a person from developing in a *polis;*[38] though usually, he notes, this policy has been applied in a spirit of faction, rather than in the disinterested spirit of Aristotle's analysis.

Where does this leave matters? What then *are* valid claims to power? Aristotle seems reluctant to answer the question flatly. All the *usual* claims have both merits and defects. All are valid, all are invalid. Much depends on the circumstances. Certainly in the case of any particular *polis* the decision would have to depend on its circumstances. But is there an *ideal* claim, corresponding to an *ideal* set of circumstances?

[38] *Politics* 1284b 15-34.

Aristotle seems particularly well disposed toward the "many," though not on the basis of the *usual* claim made on their behalf—numbers and free birth—but on the ground of a claim which *he* puts forward for them. Four times he speaks of the special claim which can be made for the "many's" right to sovereignty.[39] All of these defenses of the "many" embody the notion that, at least under *some* circumstances, the many can urge *all* the claims on their behalf, which the "one" and the "few" can never do. "The many may urge their claims against the few: taken together and compared with the few they are stronger, richer, and better."[40] Aristotle notes that these virtues will not be found in "all popular bodies and all large masses of men." But when they are found, then the many should rule. For example, "in a group whose members are equals and peers it is neither expedient nor just that one man should be sovereign over all others."[41]

Thus, when taken together, *all* the kinds of claims in the empirical order, not the claim of virtue alone, are valid for the ideal order. And an existing social group has been found which, under certain circumstances, can be considered the ideal ruling class, or *politeuma*.

A Method for Studying Actual Regimes

Book III has revealed that Aristotle is not content to think only in terms of ideal circumstances and ideal regimes. Observation made it evident that ideal circumstances were seldom, if ever, realized in human affairs, by contrast with physical nature, and that few, if any actual states could be found which measured up to an ideal standard.[42] Aristotle and his students had the evidence of studies of more than 150 different *poleis* that this was so. Yet there were many governments which, despite a certain amount of internal strife, were plainly going concerns, had some measure of worth, and were as good as circumstances permitted.

Aristotle's empiricism brought with it a strong appreciation of necessity in social relations. The social world, in all its variety, seemed much more fixed, much less plastic, than it had to Plato. The area in which human

[39]The first time is in Chapter XI, which follows upon the discussion in Chapter X of the particular defects of all the usual claims. The second is toward the beginning of Chapter XIII, following a listing of the virtues of the various claims. The third is later in Chapter XIII, following a further evaluation of the conflicting claims which concludes that no one principle urged by itself—wealth, birth, goodness, numbers—is adequate. And the fourth is in Chapter XV, which evaluates in detail the claim on behalf of absolute monarchy.

[40]*Ibid.,* 1283a 40–1283b 1.

[41]*Ibid.,* 1288b 1-3.

[42]See George Boas, "Some Assumptions of Aristotle," *Transactions of the American Philosophical Society,* New Series, Vol. XLIX, Part 6 (1959), pp. 44, 48, 49, 54, 56.

freedom might consciously mold conditions to its desire was very small. And "good" therefore had to contain a large element of the relative. "Good" must be measured in terms of that which rigid and various circumstance decrees as possible. Plainly, a comprehensive political science would have to take account of the normal persistence of actual regimes markedly different from the ideal regime, and some kind of relative standard of judgment would have to be found in addition to the standard of the *telos*. In one place, for example, he remarks that some men "come together and form and maintain political associations, merely for the sake of life; for perhaps there is some element of good even in the simple act of living, so long as the evils of existence do not preponderate too heavily."[43]

One standard which produces a very general but still useful principle of classification is that of the general interest. Governments which aim at the common interest are to be deemed right and just forms (even though the conception of interest they possess is not the same as the absolute good?), while those which seek only the private good of the rulers are wrong and perverted forms. This yields the six-fold classification of monarchy, aristocracy, polity (governments of the one, the few, and the many in the general interest), and tyranny, oligarchy, democracy (governments of the one, the few, and the many in the interest of the rulers). This is not original with Aristotle but is much like the commonly employed system of classification of the time.

It is also inadequate. Another standard of comparison is required. At the beginning of Book III, Aristotle tells us that we must distinguish the "good man" from the "good citizen." Only in the case of the ideal state will they be the same. In all other cases, the "good citizen" will be one who plays his proper role in the *polis* of which he is a member, thus contributing to its maintenance. And so stability, the continued endurance of a regime, is introduced by Aristotle as a third standard of evaluation.

A Bridge toward Naturalism

The need for this more elaborate analysis, going beyond a consideration of the ideal, is spelled out by Aristotle at the beginning of Book IV.

> First, [politics] has to consider which is the best constitution, and what qualities a constitution must have to come closest to the ideal when there are no external factors . . . to hinder its doing so. Secondly, politics has to consider which sort of constitution suits which sort of civic body. The attainment of the best constitution is likely to be impossible for the general run of states; and the good law-giver and the true statesman must therefore have their eyes open not only to what is the absolute best, but also to what is best in relation to actual conditions. Thirdly, politics has to consider the sort of constitution which de-

[43]*Politics*, 1278b 25–27.

pends upon an assumption. In other words, the student of politics must also be able to study a given constitution, just as it stands and simply with a view to explaining how it may have arisen and how it may be made to enjoy the longest possible life. . . . Fourthly, . . . politics has also to provide a knowledge of the type of constitution which is best suited to states in general.[44]

In Book IV, Aristotle continues to employ formal and material cause analysis but in a more complex way than in the earlier books. He is still seeking to delineate the structure of the ideal state which has been only partly completed. But he has indicated that the ideal structure is possible only in rare cases, under special circumstances, and that other structures may be considered good relative to the various nonideal circumstances which abound in the empirical world.

At this point, what began as a theory of the best regime has joined to it a theory of the empirical order. Aristotle catalogs all of the kinds of political systems which were in operation in his day. And as he shows what constitutions are suited to the various kinds of social circumstances, what "forms" go with what kinds of "matter," the language of freedom (the language of "good" and "ought") passes into the language of necessity. This is well illustrated in 1296b, for example, which begins the discussion of this question. Aristotle asks: "What and what sort of constitution is suited to (*symphero*) what sort of person?"[45] The Greek word *symphero* implies the notion of utility and advantage, which is the language of "good." But a few lines later, as the answers begin to emerge from the inquiry, we have such statements as:

> Where the number of poor is more than enough to counterbalance the higher quality of the other side, *there will naturally be* (*pephuken*) a democracy. . . . If they are mechanics and day-labourers, *we shall have* the extreme form. . . . Where the number of the members of the middle class outweighs that of both the other classes . . . a polity *can be* permanently established.[46]

These are purely descriptive, not evaluative, terms. Aristotle's theory of actual states, instead of being a theory of relative goods, turns out to be a theory of empirical correlations—what would be called "scientific description."

The four-cause scheme of analysis remains a useful instrument for the new enterprise. In place of perfection, the *telos* or final cause of the actual type becomes survival. ("There is some element of good even in the simple act of living.") And formal cause analysis, in place of a unique structure, must describe all the different types of system which are observed to survive

[44]*Ibid.*, 1288b 21-35.
[45]*Ibid.*, 1296b 13-14.
[46]*Ibid.*, 1296b 25-40. (Emphasis supplied.)

in the empirical world. We are in a Darwinian order now. The material cause reveals what social groupings produce what kinds of structures and the efficient cause tells us what behavior is characteristic of the various regimes, and the processes by which they change from one into another.

Aristotle's theory of the actual order seems very close both in its method and in its conclusions to that of the typical naturalist. The focal norm in each case is the survival of any given kind of system. It is a norm which is merely posited. And it corresponds to no noumenal purpose or entelechy. As far as it rests on a conception of the good, the particular good involved plays as large a role in the naturalistic as in the noumenalist theory of value. Aristotle assumes that most people desire preservation rather than destruction, a principle on which the arch-materialist Hobbes later erected his entire political theory. And it is this value, preservation, as related to *mere* order rather than the order of moral perfection, around which Aristotle constructs his theory of Books IV to VI of the *Politics*. It is a theory of the various ways in which a preservation-order is produced in the empirical world. Later, in Book VI, Aristotle combines with this theory of actual polities a theory of rational (or efficient) order which could also have been erected on purely naturalistic foundations. He considers the problem of constructing each of the actual systems in such a way as to make them more stable than they usually are found to be in their historical embodiments. We might state the theme in these terms: "Given the limitations which circumstance places on the kind of regime which can be stabilized, how, in any given situation, can the appropriate constitution be constructed so as to guarantee the maximum of stability?" A naturalist would frame the problem no differently.

A Dual Analysis. While Aristotle first announces the necessity for a dual analysis (of the empirical as well as of the ideal order) only at the beginning of Book IV, he actually begins to perform it in the last chapters (XIV—XVIII) of Book III. There he describes in considerable detail five different kinds of monarchy found to exist and indicates the conditions under which each should be considered "appropriate." He examines and finds wanting the claim of those who say that monarchy is the absolutely best form of government. But he tells us that there are special circumstances under which it can be considered good, or appropriate:

> The society appropriate to kingship is one of the sort which naturally tends to produce some particular stock, or family, preeminent in its capacity for political leadership. . . . Where it happens that a whole family, or even a single person, is of merit so outstanding as to surpass that of all the rest, it is only just that this family should be vested with kingship and absolute sovereignty, or that this single person should become king.[47]

[47]*Ibid.*, 1288a 8-19.

Then he describes five other existing varieties of monarchy and indicates the conditions under which each actually arises—to indicate the conditions under which each is "suitable." The difference between the good order and the empirical order simply evaporates in the course of description.

Book IV deals in this fashion with all the other forms of constitution. Most space is given to oligarchy and democracy, the forms most common in the Greek world of the time. The name "oligarchy" applies to any system in which the "rich and better born" (does he mean to include the hereditary aristocracy?), who are also a minority, control the government. And "democracy" is a constitution in which the free-born and poor, being also a majority, rule. In this section we again have evidence of Aristotle's empirical bent and of his feeling for the multiformity of political phenomena; for we discover that we have not two, but actually nine different kinds of constitution—five varieties of democracy and four of oligarchy. As to form, they are distinguished in each case by the kinds of qualification for office they employ and by the relative status of basic laws and decrees of the deliberative assembly. As to matter, they are distinguished by the social composition of the *poleis* in which they arise. For example, if the population is predominantly made up of small farmers, there will usually be a low property qualification. Meetings of the assembly will be kept to a minimum, since the people have little leisure to devote to politics because of the pressure of earning a living. But they are able to live by their moderate means. And as a consequence of these things, the fundamental law is supreme over and limits the scope of popular decrees. This is the first or "peasant form" of democracy. If the bulk of the population are mechanics and day laborers, there will be no property qualification. And a system of state payment for attendance at the assembly will provide leisure for the common man to engage in political activity. In this society the well-to-do will absent themselves from political meetings because of business affairs. As a consequence, decrees of the assembly will be paramount to law. This is the last form of democracy, which Aristotle calls the "extreme form."

The discussion of democracies and oligarchies is followed by a description of the system called "polity," which Aristotle defines as a "mean" between democracy and oligarchy, and as a mixture of the two.[48] Polities combine the institutions proper both to democracies and oligarchies. For example, a polity will adopt a rule fining the rich if they do not take part in the work of the law courts (an oligarchical rule), and combine it with a provision to pay the poor so that they may also sit in the courts

[48]This is different from the definition in the classification of constitutions of Book III, where "polity" is the general-interest form of rule by the "many." The democracies of Book IV, in which law is described as paramount over popular decree, seem to represent the polity of Book III, while the term now identifies another kind of regime.

(a democratic rule). Or it may combine the device of the lot (considered democratic) with that of election (an oligarchic institution) in the choice of executive officers.

In terms of its social base, the polity is also, in a sense, a mixture of democracy and oligarchy. For polity appears in societies which have a middle class that is larger and stronger than either the class of the very wealthy or of the very poor. Thus it combines the principles of numbers and free birth, which are characteristic of democratic government, with that of wealth, which is proper to oligarchy. That is, the dominant class is strong both in numbers and in material substance.

Polity: The Best Order as an Actual Order

Aristotle returns to the question of the ideal order in this portion of Book IV and showers great praise on the middle-class polity as the "constitution—short of the ideal—[which] is the most generally acceptable and the most to be preferred."[49] And from the description of the polity we come to see more clearly than we have to this point what the ideal order itself is like. Unlike Plato's state of the *Laws,* it is not an artificial construct, self-consciously created out of elements salvaged from the historical wreckage of an originally ideal order. It is rather the unself-conscious product of natural development toward the *telos* of the *polis.* The polity actually contains all the structural principles of the ideal order, though in an imperfectly developed form. To use a physical metaphor, it is like a late stage of development in an evolutionary series, like Cro Magnon man in comparison with modern man. The metaphor is not perfect, since an evolutionary series presumably has no fixed *terminus ad quem.* And our figure makes modern man just such a terminus, or rather *telos.* Yet, with this modification, the metaphor is a good way to illustrate Aristotle's thought. The polity is a close approximation to the formal cause of the ideal *polis,* and probably the closest that a historical state will come to its realization.

What are its great virtues? First, the members of its ruling class lead the best kind of social life. The introduction to this section is misleading. For Aristotle says that he intends to employ a standard of excellence not "above the reach of ordinary men, or a standard of education requiring exceptional endowments or equipment, or the standard of a constitution which attains an ideal height." He will be concerned with "the sort of life which most men are able to share and the sort of constitution which it is possible for most states to enjoy."[50] This seems to reject the *telos* or the ideal as a measure. But then he goes on to employ the standard of the mean, as he had worked it out in the *Ethics.*

[49]*Ibid.,* 1289b 1518.
[50]*Ibid.,* 1295a 25-31.

If we adopt as true the statements made in the *Ethics*—(1) that a truly happy life is a life of goodness lived in freedom from impediments, and (2) that goodness consists in a mean—it follows that the best way of life is one which consists in a mean, and a mean of the kind attainable by every individual. Further, the same criteria which determine whether the citizen body have a good or bad way of life must also apply to the constitution; for a constitution is the way of life of a citizen body.[51]

And so he does after all advance an ideal standard of measurement. The way of life of the philosopher may be the highest way. But it is really a divine rather than a human life, as we have seen. And the philosophic activity itself is a lonely activity. We are here concerned with the ideal *society,* and so the way of life of the polity, if it is a life according to the mean, must be the way of life of the ideal *polis* as well as of the ruling class of the best actual *polis.*

Legislators, whose function is to inculcate virtue in others, must be pre-eminently virtuous men if they are to legislate well. And Aristotle tells us that the best legislators have come from the middle class. The material circumstances of the middle class are conducive to the virtuous life. They are subject to none of the psychological pressures which make for vice in the very rich and the very poor. "Those who belong to either extreme . . . find it hard to follow the lead of reason." Virtue is a middle-class affair.[52]

The men of the middle class understand both how to rule and how to obey—a virtue, as we saw in Book III, both of the good man and of the citizen of the ideal state. And this too is a result of their middling condition. For "those who enjoy too many advantages . . . are both unwilling to obey and ignorant how to obey." They are fit only to be slave masters. At the other end of the social scale are the "mean and poor-spirited," who only know how to obey, and that as slaves.[53] This knowledge of the combined art of ruling and of obeying, and willingness both to rule and be ruled make for friendship and community in the middle classes, while the envious poor and the contemptuous rich have capacity for friendship neither with one another nor with the other classes.

Polity is also the most stable of constitutions and the freest of all from factions. This is particularly true of large polities where the middle class is more numerous than in small ones. Its chief strength lies not in the fact that it has the support of a majority, however, but that "no single section in all the state . . . would favour a change to a different constitution."[54] Its institutions and ideals have a general-interest appeal. It is therefore best in the order of preservation-values as well as an embodiment of the order of

[51]*Ibid.,* 1295a 36-40.
[52]*Ibid.,* 1295b 6-9.
[53]*Ibid.,* 1295b 14-19.
[54]*Ibid.,* 1294b 38-39.

perfection. The polity is the keystone of the arch of Aristotle's bridge from the noumenal to the naturalist world.

Lastly, the men of the dominant middle class are peers and equals, as are the citizens of the ideal state. For a "state aims at being as far as it can be, a society composed of equals and peers."[55]

It seems, then, that the only difference between the polity and the ideal state is a purely quantitative one. The ruling class of the polity, its way of life, its political institutions, are like those of the ideal state. The many, when thus organized, combine all three of the valid claims to power—numbers, wealth, and virtue. They are a true aristocracy. But while this class is only a majority in the polity, in the ideal state it would be coextensive with the entire society. Aristotle does not expressly say this, but it is quite compatible with what he does say about the principles of the ideal state in Books VII and VIII.

Thus by the end of Book IV we have seen fully revealed the structural principles of the ideal order, of the best order which has actually been constructed, and of *all* the main kinds of systems which have been historically constructed.[56] We have analyzed the final, the formal, and the material causes of the *polis* in both its ideal and empirical forms. (The analysis of empirical forms is organized, we have seen, around the same norm used by the naturalists, "survival.") Efficient causes remain to be discussed. To this subject Aristotle turns in Book V.

The Efficient Cause: Political Change

To study the "efficient cause" is to study the "how" of a thing, i.e., the mechanical order of all the little interrelated steps or events which end in a given result. It is therefore to study activity and change—"process" in today's terminology. This was the sole concern of Thucydides' political science, a science of the dynamics of empire. In Aristotle's work it is only part of an elaborate theoretical structure, and it is only incompletely treated. Aristotle was particularly interested in that aspect of the political process which involves the creation, destruction, and stabilization of organizations, i.e., the phenomenon of constitutional change. But he says virtually nothing about the processes of the stable system.

[55]*Ibid.,* 1295b 25-26.

[56]I think it better to speak of the polity as the "best system which has actually been constructed" rather than, as Barker does, of the "most practicable state," or as Aristotle himself does, of the "best constitution for the majority of states and men." For while in a sense this is a goal at which a majority of states may aim, its achievement will be rare. Aristotle specifically says that the polity is a rare occurrence: "A middle or mixed type of constitution has never been established—or, at the most, has only been established on a few occasions and in a few states." *Ibid.,* 1296a 36-37.

Book V opens with a discussion of the most general causes of change, both evolutionary and revolutionary, with emphasis on the latter. Aristotle tells us that the primary causes, or motor forces, are psychological, and are twofold—certain ideologies or "attitudes of mind," and certain drives or desires. As to the first, he suggests that revolutions are never made merely for material interest but always in the name of some ideal of justice. And a regime whose legitimating ideology carries conviction only with a particular social class is radically unstable and open to attack from many quarters. What we may term "radical oligarchy" and "radical democracy," the two most prevalent systems of Aristotle's time, were therefore peculiarly susceptible to sedition (*stasis*) because of the class ideologies of their ruling groups.

> Democracy arose in the strength of an opinion that those who were equal in any one respect were absolutely equal, and in all respects. (Men are prone to think that the fact of their all being equally free-born means that they are absolutely equal.) Oligarchy similarly arose from an opinion that those who were unequal in some one respect were altogether unequal. (Those who are superior in point of wealth readily regard themselves as absolutely superior.) Acting on such opinions, the democrats proceed to claim an equal share in everything, on the ground of their equality; the oligarchs proceed to press for more, on the ground that they are unequal—that is to say, more than equal. . . .
> But a constitutional system based absolutely, and at all points, on either the oligarchical or the democratic conception of equality is a poor sort of thing. The facts are evidence enough: constitutions of this sort never endure.[57]

Democracy is the more stable of the two, being plagued only by differences between the rich and the poor, while oligarchy suffers from factions within the wealthy classes as well. But more stable still is the regime whose legitimating principles have a universal appeal by recognizing numerical equality in some cases but "equality proportionate to desert" in others. The polity has just such a universal ideology and is the most stable of governments, as we have already noted.

Ideology does not operate alone to cause revolution. Associated with every such "attitude of mind" which disposes people to seek change are certain universal drives—the drive for material gain, the drive for prestige or status, the fear of loss and disgrace. Both ideological protest and the quest for material advantage through revolution are activated by still another type of cause—certain kinds of catalytic events which Aristotle calls "occasions and origins of disturbances." One is the distribution of income and prestige in a way which strikes an important social group as unjust. Another is "a disproportionate increase in some part of the state"—the sudden growth of a social class in numbers, wealth, or other power, or an unusual increment

[57]*Ibid.*, 1301a 28-35, 1302a 3-5.

of power in a certain political office. Election intrigues may set in motion the psychological causes of revolution, as may what Aristotle calls "dissimilarity of elements" in the makeup of a *polis*—ethnic or national heterogeneity in a population.

Revolutions sometimes are occasioned by the negligence of the ruling class. Men disloyal to the constitution may find their way into high positions which they then employ to subvert the entire order.

The Objects of Revolution. The object of sedition (*stasis*) according to Aristotle is not always a wholesale revolution of the regime. It may be to get control of the government into the hands of the party of change, while leaving the machinery of government intact. Or it may be to change only some parts of the constitution, so as to heighten or diminish the general character of the system, e.g., to make a democracy more or less democratic.

Particular Causes of Revolution. Aristotle follows his description of the general causes of revolution with a consideration of particular causes. These are catalytic events or circumstances peculiarly associated with each kind of regime. In democracies it is frequently the confiscatory policies of demagogues which precipitate sedition by the rich. When demagogues were also military men, the regime was often converted into a tyranny, though in Aristotle's time the coincidence of a popular following and military command was less frequent. He attributed this to the use of rhetoric as an art (the art of propaganda in the fourth century B.C.) which placed power over the mob in the hands of people with a glib and persuasive tongue. But such people, lacking military force, were unable to establish tyrannical power. Oligarchies are susceptible to a variety of threats arising both outside of and within the ruling class. Monarchies are overturned when the king loses moral authority—the respect of his subjects—or when the royal family is divided, or when the king attempts to enlarge his prerogative and move entirely beyond the restrictions of law. The discussion of the downfall of monarchies brings to mind aspects of three great modern upheavals, the English, French, and Russian revolutions.

Aristotle's discussion of revolution includes a critique of the Platonic theory of constitutional change set forth in Books VIII and IX of the *Republic*. His chief argument is that the cycle of change described by Plato, aristocracy—timocracy—oligarchy—democracy—tyranny, is empirically incorrect. Observation showed that democracy is more often and more readily converted into oligarchy than into tyranny. And tyrannies, instead of changing into philosophic monarchies, as Plato's theory implies, and thus inaugurating a new cycle, change rather into other forms of tyranny or into democracy or some other form. This criticism is in a way quite beside the point, because Plato did not intend to depict a process of empirical change but rather an ideal cycle—the logical process of corruption of the best system generated in imagination, the logic of moral decay. That Aristotle did not appear to understand this is further evidence of the empirical bent of his mind, and of his persuasion that discussion of politics in terms of purely abstract models, quite devoid of empirical reference, are not very rewarding affairs.

Conditions of Stability

Parallel to the problem of the cause of change is of course the question of the cause of stability. And this is Aristotle's next theme. Once more he reviews the various kinds of regime one by one and describes the policies which maintain them. The discussion is cast in the form of a structure-process analysis (formal and efficient causation), which carries us through the last half of Book V and all of Book VI. Book IV describes regimes as they are actually found to exist. In Books V and VI we are given a picture of the "rational" form (i.e., the most stable structure) of each kind of government, and of the measures necessary to create and maintain it.

What Herbert Spiro, a modern student of comparative government, calls "constitutional engineering" will go a certain way toward stabilizing a regime. In every state, for example, where the ruling class is relatively large, certain democratic institutions are desirable, even though the constitution is not democratic. There should be provisions for restricting the tenure of office to short periods, so that as many of the "peers" as possible have the right to enjoy office—status and glory must thus be well distributed in the ruling orders. And it is less easy for factions to get control of the governmental apparatus. This blocks one method whereby tyrannies are created in oligarchies and democratic states. In oligarchies and polities which use a property qualification, the property assessments underlying the qualification should be changed as the poorer class increases in wealth or as inflation occurs, else the regime will be automatically converted into a democracy. Increases in the property of one particular segment of the population pose problems which can be partially offset by constitutional engineering. Groups outside the prosperous circle may be compensated for their misfortune with the perquisites of public office. Measures to prevent the embezzlement of public funds are of the greatest importance.

All of the stabilizing devices recommended by Aristotle are designed to build social support for the political system, not to substitute for it. And Aristotle also recognizes their limited value in this area. Pure class rule, he points out, can never be stabilized by constitutional engineering. At least *some* access to control over policy must be provided for all major groups. Measures should be taken to build up the middle class as a buffer in the antagonisms of rich and poor. Leaders must learn to speak for the interests of classes other than their own. The most important stabilizer of regimes is adequate education of the citizens in the spirit of the constitution. There must be institutions for the political socialization of the population.

Aristotle's desire to be exhaustive in his analysis of political systems led him to examine the conditions of stability of even the tyrannical regime. Are there some circumstances under which tyranny can be considered a good order? It was certainly a *common* phenomenon in Aristotle's time, and certain kinds of circumstance seemed to generate it as a natural product. (We have already noticed how the notions of mechanical necessity and relative good tended to coalesce in Aristotle's mind.) Though its appearance under certain conditions might not be avoided, perhaps the worst aspects of tyrannical government could be mitigated. It is significant that the recipes which Aristotle puts forward for increasing the stability of tyrannies are all based on the principle that the successful tyrant should in his actions *appear* like the just king.

The analysis of tyranny begins with a description of the usual practices of tyrants in the maintenance of their power, "the method of government still followed by the majority of tyrants." The traditional policy aims at the prevention of opposition through social disorganization. Outstanding personalities in the country who might assume rival leadership positions are "lopped off." Social communication which might bind individuals together and produce community spirit is disrupted by the prohibition of all private societies for cultural purposes—the citizens are made strangers to one another and measures are taken to sow enmity and distrust between individuals and social groups. Efforts are even made to divide families, and set wife against husband. Public gatherings under government auspices are held frequently to facilitate surveillance of the population and to foster psychological dependence of the people on the ruler. A secret-police network is maintained to detect covert attempts at political communication and organization. Financial resources which might go into the development of an opposition organization are drained into the public treasury by heavy taxes and expended by the tyrant on showy public buildings. And the tyrant diverts the public mind from domestic ills and increases the general sense of dependence on his leadership by constant war-mongering.

After recounting the measures usually taken by tyrants to stabilize their regimes, Aristotle offers his own prescription, which, he argues, promises greater stability than the traditional methods. The tyrant should counterfeit the just king, "subject to the one safeguard that the reformed tyrant still retains power, and is still in a position to govern his subjects with or without their consent." He should deal responsibly with the public funds. He should seem grave without being harsh, and should seek to inspire awe rather than fear. He should display military prowess to engender respect. He should restrain his desires, and avoid giving offence to his subjects by molesting their women and children. In all his pleasures he should be moderate—or at least appear to his subjects to be so. He should appear godly. He should honor good men among his subjects, though avoiding the concentration of authority in any single pair of hands. The tyrant should attempt to satisfy both the rich and the poor, but if he is forced to choose one, he should be sure to base his power on the strongest social groups. In all things, so far as possible, he should appear a "trustee for the public interest, not a man intent on his own." Such a regime will be as good as the circumstances permit. It will be both morally better and more stable than the common tyranny.

The Ideal Polis

The last two books of the *Politics* take up once more and carry through to completion the theme of the ideal state. In Book I we were told that the *polis* in its ideal form is based on the principle of equality. It is a government by the many rather than by the few. In Book III we learned that the many may rightly lay claim to power when they are collectively richer and better, as well as more numerous, than the few; that the coincidence of these qualities in the many produces the ideal ruling class. And we were told that in the ideal *polis* the good man and the good citizen are identical. In Book IV we were shown this ideal order partly developed in the polity, a system governed by the many in the form of a large middle class which possesses the qualities of the ideal ruling class. These good citizens of the polity are also good men. They lead the sort of moral life described in the *Ethics* as the best life for man in society.

Throughout the *Politics,* intertwined with his analysis of actual states (both in their empirical and "rational" forms), Aristotle has been developing for us a picture of the ideal order. And he has identified elements of that order in the historical polity. We have been told a good deal about the final, material, and formal causes of the good *polis,* though nothing has been said of the efficient causes which establish the good order. Thus in the last two books the subject of the good *polis* needs only to be rounded out. The discussion proceeds on all four levels, but with emphasis on efficient causes.

Aristotle reaffirms the final cause of the best *polis* to be the realization of the good human life. "We may . . . expect that—unless something unexpected happens—the best way of life will go together with the best constitution possible in the circumstances of the case." Some scholars have been puzzled by the last words in this sentence. Ernest Barker, for example, writes:

> It is not quite clear . . . why Aristotle adds the words of qualification. The ideal constitution . . . presupposes ideal conditions or circumstances. . . . And it is not adjusted to given conditions or circumstances, such as an imperfect heterogeneous society.[58]

[58]Barker, *The Politics of Aristotle,* p. 279, footnote 2.

But if we keep Aristotle's metaphysic clearly in mind, this difficulty, I think, disappears. The metaphysic holds that the ideal order *is* adjusted to "given conditions." The Form must dwell in an empirical context if it is to be at all. It is a meaningless dream apart from the limiting conditions of that context. One may imagine in constructing an image of the best *polis* the best circumstances, but they must be real human circumstances, not those of a Platonic utopia. The "circumstances of the case" are the circumstances of the human case as we observe them to exist. It must be clear that the laws of efficient causation in the empirical world are capable of producing our imaginary system.

The good social life is the life of noble action guided by rational principle, which was described in detail in the *Ethics,*[59] and which we have already seen operating in the life of the ruling class of the polity. But now the notion "noble action" is given a new connotation. In the *Ethics,* the god-like life of thought was contrasted with the best human life, that of the virtuous man of action, in order to demonstrate that only the second way of life depended on society for its realization. But this seemed to imply that the philosopher, by virtue of his contemplative activity, had to be alien to the city, had to be an isolated, lonely, and passive being. Aristotle was not willing to conclude this. The contemplative reason, the divine faculty, might not need society for its development. But perhaps society could be served by philosophy. And surely the philosopher, to be fulfilled as a *man,* needed society. To resolve his dilemma, Aristotle in Book VII of the *Politics* tells us that philosophy is best understood as itself a kind of action, and thus may be assimilated to the life of action which is the life of the city.

> But the life of action need not be, as is sometimes thought, a life which involves relations to others. Nor should our thoughts be held to be active only when they are directed to objects which have to be achieved by action. Thoughts with no object beyond themselves, and speculations and trains of reflection followed purely for their own sake, are far more deserving of the name of action. "Well-doing" is the end we seek: action of some sort or other is therefore our end and aim; but, even in the sphere of outward acts, action can also be predicated . . . of those who, by their thoughts, are the prime authors of such acts.[60]

This does not mean, of course, that Aristotle has changed his conception of the final cause of the *polis* in the last pages of the *Politics.* He has not concluded that society exists for the sake of philosophy, nor that in the best *polis* every man will be a philosopher. He has simply tried to establish a place for the philosopher—*a* place among many, and not the *foremost* place—in the social life of man.

[59]See *Politics* 1332a 8-10, in which Aristotle makes specific reference to the standard set down in the *Ethics.*

[60]*Ibid.,* 1325b 17-23

Out of what kind of material will the best *polis* be constructed? Under this heading Aristotle deals with the size and character of the population and of the territory of the good society. The population should consist of the "greatest surveyable number required for achieving a life of self-sufficiency," a population large enough to support itself in all things but small enough so that its members can be well acquainted with one another and know each other's character. The people should have a natural endowment of spirit and intelligence, the foundation of courage and wisdom. And the territory should be large enough to make possible a life of leisure for the citizenry—the physical foundation of wisdom—and a life combining liberality with temperance, two of the other virtues of the good man.

Very little is said about formal causes—the social and political organization of the best *polis*. Perhaps Aristotle assumed that the description of the polity had supplied enough on this head. The economy is to be a "mixed one"; some property is to be state-owned, some privately. The citizens are all to be property owners, for the virtue of the man of action requires external goods for its development—"We have to remember that a certain amount of equipment is necessary for the good life, and while this amount need not be so great for those whose endowment is good, more is required for those whose endowment is poor."[61] Apparently they will all lead the leisure life of the gentleman farmer. For farm labor and all commercial and manufacturing functions are performed by slaves or serfs. "The truly good and happy man . . . has advantages at hand."[62] The state property is to be used to support the worship of the gods and such community-building institutions as common meals. This will allow the poor man, who can afford to make no financial contribution to their support, to take part in the activities of the city's common life.

The form of government is a democracy—all citizens share equally in the government. And all have the leisure necessary for participation in civic affairs, the noble actions through which human excellence is developed and made manifest. Aristotle divides these political functions into three parts and assigns each to a different age group. To the young citizen is given the responsibility of defending the state, the military function and the politics of force. To the older, and wiser, belongs the politics of words—the deliberative function. The oldest men staff the priesthood which fosters the cult of the gods of the community.

The resemblance of these citizens of the ideal state to the middle-class rulers of the polity (the entelechy in the process of development) is marked. Both groups are martial people and men of substance. Both groups are "peers and equals." Both groups know how to obey as well as rule. And they rule and are ruled in turn. The life enjoyed by the dominant class of the

[61]*Ibid.,*1329a 19-20; 1331b 40; 1332a 2.
[62]*Ibid.,* 1332a 20-25.

developing ideal is shared by all the citizenry of the *polis* in its fullest development.

Aristotle deals with all these questions concerning final, formal, and material causes in the first half of Book VII. The rest of the *Politics* is devoted to the problem of efficient causes. How is the endowment of our *polis* with excellent matter, both natural and human, and with excellent form, to be turned to account? How is this static potential to be converted into an actuality of virtuous activity, into "a perfected acti'ity functioning without interference from outside?"[63] What is the efficient cause of the good *polis?* The answer is, of course, a process—education. Only the right kind of education can guarantee that the good matter and good form will not be wasted but rightly used.

Aristotle's scheme of ideal education begins with the act of procreation. The first concern is to ensure a good physique for each generation, which requires regulation of marriage relations. The regulations are few, however, and relate chiefly to the ages and physical fitness of the marriage partners. There is no attempt à la Plato to distinguish types of moral character and to breed "gold" only with "gold," though it is assumed that all the parents are persons of spirit and intelligence. Monogamous family organization is the rule, and adultery is to be severely punished.

The next section deals with the nature of the young until the age of seven, and reads like a combination of the handbooks for modern parents by Doctors Spock and Gesell. In Aristotle's *polis,* of course, this would be a handbook for the public authorities charged with the oversight of all matters of child-rearing, as well as for parents, since the early training is carried on in the home. Only good models of behavior should be placed in the child's way. And all contact with things indecent, vulgar, or low must be avoided. In this way, right habits are implanted in the young. Play is supervised in institutions vaguely resembling the modern nursery school and kindergarten.

Formal education begins at seven, and lasts to age twenty-one. The basic subjects are reading, writing, physical training, and "music" (poetry, song, and instrumental music as a single discipline). The first two are useful for most of the ordinary concerns of life, but have little value for character building, the most important matter. And Aristotle excludes from his curriculum for "gentlemen citizens" all purely useful mechanical arts—what we today call "vocational training." "Music" is the important thing, for it is "music" which liberates the mind and soul and builds the good way of life. It serves to amuse us, to inculcate virtuous habit, and also contributes to the "cultivation of our minds and to the growth of moral wisdom"—the development of the practical reason.[64]

[63]Randall, *op. cit.,* p. 52.
[64]*Politics* 1339a 11, 1340b 20.

The discussion of education ends at this point. Nothing is said about the higher education, and most students of Aristotle believe that the section is incomplete. But we must remember that the *telos* of the *polis* is realized in producing men of practical reason. And "musical" education, to Aristotle, was the basic ingredient of moral training. The higher studies of the speculative intellect do not have the influence on character and on the quality of a citizen's life which Plato attributed to them. The *polis* does not exist to produce philosophers, nor is it ruled by them, as we have seen.

The *Politics* closes with this sketch of education as the chief efficient cause of the good *polis*. Of all the processes which affect the character of political systems, the learning process, to Aristotle, was the most significant single cause, for a political system is more than "an arrangement of offices." It embodies a set of values, indeed, an entire way of life. And as its education varies, so will the manners and morals of the *polis*. The emphasis was typically Greek, and one which, despite other marked differences in their work, Aristotle shared with his teacher Plato.[65]

Aristotle, Ordinary Language Philosophy, and Situation Ethics

We have seen that Aristotle's political science embraces a science of the best regime, conceived in terms of moral perfection, and a science of actual regimes which reminds us of the naturalistic descriptions of Thucydides. Aristotle gives us the latter under the rubric of "that which is good under various less than ideal circumstances." The "good" involved is not perfection but mere survival, the maintenance of some semblance of order, as opposed to absolute chaos (conflict). And the language of "good" (as a language of freedom) frequently turns into the language of necessity— into a description of what kinds of regime necessarily go with certain kinds of circumstance, with all considerations of "goodness" and "badness" suspended.

In his discussion of relative good and of necessity, however, Aristotle has not switched over to a purely naturalistic framework but remains within a noumenal frame of reference. What appears to be a naturalistic analysis rests upon the assumption that the degree of freedom necessary to construct the morally best regime does not exist under all circumstances, and that morality demands that we prescribe for all sorts of situations, not only for the ideal. The implication is that it would in fact be immoral to try to construct a regime in a given situation which is morally better than the situation will permit. The result would be conflict, chaos, and absolute disorder, which Aristotle judges to be even morally worse than a stable tyranny.

[65]See Werner Jaeger, *Paideia: The Ideals of Greek Culture,* 3 vols., trans. Gilbert Highet (Oxford: Basil Blackwell, 1939).

Hence he is willing to tell us how to construct any given kind of order, even a tyranny, which *seems* to be the very essence of sophistic naturalism. "Suppose one wishes to construct a democracy, an oligarchy, a tyranny; how should he go about it?" Aristotle does not give up the moral question, as did Thucydides. Nor does he try to answer it by looking only at the Form of perfect order, as did Plato. He tries rather to answer it in terms of "what the traffic will bear." The *telos* is there, but it grows up in the midst of empirical flux, and its realization is limited by the necessities of that flux.

No student of politics nor school of politics today, to my knowledge, has constructed so broad-ranging a political science as this, which combines an immanentist theory of the best regime with a technical and naturalistic approach to the relatively good. Most of the political philosophers and political scientists whom we can identify in one way or another with Aristotle have chosen to develop one or other of these emphases, but not both.

Probably closer than any other modern students of politics to Aristotle's approach to perfect order are the Neo-Thomists, who learn their Aristotelian categories from Thomas Aquinas' version of them. We shall examine their work in a later chapter. In two other schools of modern thought we find a conception of ethical action (unrelated to specific political regimes) which is markedly Aristotelian in flavor.[66] One has been partially developed by G.E.M. Anscombe, a British exponent of the "ordinary language" philosophy of Ludwig Wittgenstein, after self-conscious reflection on the Aristotelian model of ethics. The other is the work of a theologian, Joseph Fletcher, who tells us that his Christian conception of situation ethics is structurally similar to that of Aristotle, though it differs in its grounding principle.

Both Anscombe and Fletcher reject contemporary systematic "rule ethics" or "law ethics," approaches which have their historical origin in the Mosaic Code and in the Christian legal-moral tradition, but which today are largely utilitarian in character. Anscombe and Fletcher stress, like Aristotle, the character of lifestyle of the moral actor, which they see as the chief determinant of the morality of an action, rather than conformity to a rule of right.

Anscombe and the School of Ludwig Wittgenstein

Anscombe attacks the variety of rule ethics that she terms "consequentialism," which she claims "marks ... every English academic moral philosopher [since the time of Henry Sidgwick (1838-1900).]" According to this approach, a moral agent acts responsibly when he measures his intention against the foreseeable consequences of his intended act. The justice or

[66]See discussion of "criteria of political choice," p. 6-7 above, for the notion of ethical action employed here.

injustice of an act, and an understanding of what one ought to do, what it is one's duty to do, are determined by an estimate of consequences. This is the fundamental norm or rule of consequentialist ethics. Here we have a standard which appears to allow us to avoid the hard question of whether a given act is *intrinsically* right or wrong (in conformity with or in violation of a moral absolute), and it also disregards the quality of the actor's intention. One looks only to outcomes, and thus the problem of moral action is reduced to the measurement of facts.[67]

Anscombe points out that the consequentialist has not really escaped but merely ignored the hard questions, for he has in fact adopted the standards of his society as his basic criterion of judgment. He must decide what are good and bad consequences, and to do this he applies implicit social standards. This is especially evident in decisions about "permissibility" in borderline cases. For

> in order to be imagining borderline cases at all, [he] has . . . to assume some sort of law or standard according to which this is a borderline case. Where then does he get the standard from? In practice the answer invariably is: from the standards current in his society or his circle.[68]

Thus, Anscombe shows, that while the exponents of "law ethics" retain such legalist concepts as "moral obligation" and "moral ought," they have done away with the divine legislator which such concepts originally posited, and substituted the legislation of society, mere convention.

Anscombe closes her argument against consequentialism with a *reductio ad absurdum,* by showing that a proponent would have to entertain the idea that it would be morally permissible to punish the innocent (a conception of an *inherently* unjust act in the common language) if the consequence of doing so could be shown to be in some sense good or desirable.[69]

Anscombe proposes that "it is not profitable for us at present to do moral philosophy," and that an adequate approach to ethics must wait upon "an adequate philosophy of psychology."[70] By this she means that we should change the problem of ethical research from the question, "What is an adequate rule of right?" to the question, "What is a good moral character?" or "What is a just man?" This was the approach Aristotle employed, and it seems to Anscombe a potentially fruitful one, though we

[67]See G.E.M. Anscombe, "Modern Moral Philosophy," *Philosophy,* 33 (1958), 1-19. See also G.E.M. Anscombe and P.T. Geach, *Three Philosophers: Aristotle, Aquinas, Frege* (Oxford: Basil Blackwell, 1963), which contains an effort to vindicate Aristotle's metaphysics against the naturalistic critique of associationists such as Locke, and his successors in English philosophy.

[68]"Modern Moral Philosophy," *op. cit.,* p. 13.

[69]*Ibid.,* pp. 16, 17.

[70]*Ibid.,* p. 1.

cannot simply embrace Aristotle's model of man as our own. What we need to do is confront the fact that we do not know what a "good man" is, but that if we come to grips with this question in a meaningful way, we shall be able to come back to questions of right and wrong action without deluding ourselves as the seekers after a good "rule" do today.

> There is a huge gap, . . . which needs to be filled by an account of human nature, human action, . . . and above all of human 'flourishing'.[71]

In short, we need to address ourselves to the old question, "What is virtue?" We need to begin by giving "an account of what *type of characteristic* a virtue is."[72] And this leads us from ethics to conceptual analysis.

> There are several concepts that need investigating simply as part of the philosophy of psychology and . . . to begin with: "action," "intention," "pleasure," "wanting." More will probably turn up if we start with these. Eventually it might be possible to advance to considering the concept "virtue"; with which, I suppose, we should be beginning some sort of a study of ethics.[73]

Anscombe's notion of doing conceptual analysis derives from the later writings of Ludwig Wittgenstein, the well-known Viennese language philosopher, who did some of his most important philosophizing as a professor at Cambridge, where he had an enormous influence on the present generation of British moral philosophers. In his mature work, Wittgenstein turned from an earlier naturalistic effort to develop a "scientific" language of perfect logical proportions, to the investigation of the meanings and structures of ordinary language as a way of doing philosophy. This puts him and Anscombe procedurally in touch with Aristotle's basic method, for Aristotle always took his departure in ethical and political analysis from the language of daily experience. Wittgenstein himself avoided canvassing the traditional questions of ontology and ethics, but his students, such as Anscombe and Stephen Toulmin are evidently now moving in this direction.[74]

To come back to Anscombe's investigation of "Virtue": when we have made headway in the conceptual analysis of this central term, and have

---

[71]*Ibid.*, p. 18.

[72]*Ibid.*, p. 5.

[73]*Ibid.*, p. 15.

[74]See Ludwig Wittenstein, *On Certainty,* tr. D. Paul & G.E.M. Anscombe (New York: Harper & Row, 1969); *Philosophical Investigations,* tr. G.E.M. Anscombe, 3rd ed. (New York: Macmillan, 1968); "Wittgenstein's Lecture on Ethics," *Philosophical Review* 74 (1965), 3-26. American political philosophers are beginning to look to Wittgenstein for inspiration in doing political philosophy. See Hannah Pitkin, *Wittgenstein on Justice* (Berkeley: University of California Press, 1972.)

begun to fill in the gaps in our philosophy of psychology, we should have a clear idea, as did Aristotle, as to what acts are in themselves praiseworthy or blameworthy. For the rest, we would realize that decisions about moral behavior must rely upon an assessment of circumstance. "The circumstances can clearly make a great deal of difference in estimating the justice or injustice of such procedures as [not paying debts, not keeping contracts.]" And while "these circumstances may *sometimes* include expected consequences," this will not always be the case.[75] The just or virtuous person, like Aristotle's man of practical reason, will know what the circumstances require, because he *is* a just person—not because he has a good "rule."

Joseph Fletcher's "Situation Ethics"

Like Anscombe, Joseph Fletcher (who is Professor of Social Ethics at the Episcopal Theological School, in Cambridge, Massachusetts) opens his analysis of modern ethics with an attack on "law ethics," which he calls "legalism."

> Just as legalism triumphed among the Jews after the exile, so, in spite of Jesus' and Paul's revolt against it, it has managed to dominate Christianity constantly from very early days . . . . In many real-life situations legalism demonstrates what Henry Miller . . . calls 'the immorality of morality.'[76]

Religious legalism reduces ethical action to "directives to be followed. Solutions are preset, and you can look them up in a book."[77] In Judaism and Catholicism, legalism spins elaborate systems of ethical rules, which operate as a total guide to all life situations. Protestantism does not construct intricate systems, but insists instead on the rigid application of a few abstract moral rules. And the result is the attitude that "justice must be done, even though the world perishes." For Fletcher, the legalist "is the man Mark Twain called 'a good man in the worst sense of the word.' "[78]

Also anathema to Fletcher is the "antinomian" approach to ethical situations.

> This is the approach with which one enters into the decision-making situation armed with no principles or maxims whatever . . . . In every 'existential moment' or 'unique' situation, it declares, one must rely upon the situation itself, *there and then,* to provide its ethical solution.[79]

[75]"Modern Moral Philosophy," *op. cit.,* p. 15.

[76]Joseph Fletcher, *Situation Ethics* (Philadelphia: Westminster Press, 1966), p. 17.

[77]*Ibid.,* p. 18.

[78]*Ibid.,* p. 20.

[79]*Ibid.,* p. 22.

The antinomian either becomes a libertine, or a "Gnostic"—one who claims a special insight into situations, a "superconscience."[80] The Gnostic expects a special revelation from the Spirit to guide his every act. Instead of being characterized by undue rigidity and uniformity, the moral decisions of the antinomian are "random, unpredictable, erratic, quite anomalous."[81]

A third mode of ethical decision, "situationism," holds for Fletcher a kind of "Golden Mean" between the extremes of legalism and antinomianism. The situationist brings to the decision moment the ethical maxims of his religious heritage, and he uses them to illuminate the problems before him. But he is prepared "in any situation to compromise them or set them aside *in the situation* if love seems better served by doing so."[82] Fletcher's situationism rests on the assumption that Anscombe's problem of defining an adequate model of the "just" or "virtuous" person is not a matter for research, but has already been solved. The virtuous person is the person who is filled with Christian love, which completes and corrects what his reason, seeking to apply moral maxims, tells him is appropriate in a given situation.

In effect, Fletcher's "situationism" is a Christianized Aristotelianism. Like Aristotle, the rational situationist embraces "principled relativism."[83] He recognizes the importance of "principles or maxims or general rules" for illuminating decision-making problems. But he also recognizes that no *general* rule is adequate for decision-making, given the multiformity of empirical circumstance. One must employ reason to fit the rule to the situation, in a prudential way, like Aristotle's man of "practical reason." But above all, one must be guided by love. Thus, the principle of rational justice, that we should give each man his due, as Aristotle held, is redefined "Christianly."

> For what *is* it that is due to our neighbors? It is love that is due—*only* love. ("Owe no man anything except to love.") Love is justice, justice is love.[84]

Prudential reason is not *replaced* by love, but it is fully assimilated to it. Witness the following examples of how Fletcher puts the two together.

> This is a side of love that businessmen can appreciate, as when a production engineer tries to balance product quality against price in a low-income market; or a personnel manager has to choose between letting an illness-weakened supply clerk keep his job, on the one hand, and on the other, playing fair with line workers whose output and piece-rate pay are being cut down by the clerk's

[80]*Ibid.*, p. 23.
[81]*Ibid.*
[82]*Ibid.*, p. 26.
[83]*Ibid.*, p. 31.
[84]*Ibid.*, p. 89.

> delays. Love as prudence helps a field commander who has to decide whether a platoon or company, or even a regiment, is expendable. And if so, which one. Prudence, careful calculation, gives love the carefulness it needs; with proper care, love does more than take justice into account, it *becomes* justice.[85]

It is clear from this passage that when love and prudence are intertwined as Fletcher would have them, the act of loving is no mere gush of emotion or sentiment. It is rather an attribute of the actor's moral character, infusing prudence with generosity and concern for the subjects in the actor's care, but not preempting the role of judgment, which belongs always to reason. Love adds a new quality to the character of Aristotle's man of "practical reason." It does not abolish and supplant that character.

While situation ethics does not help us to evaluate political regimes, it is an important method for judging the morality of particular political decisions and for guiding the statesman who wishes to act conscientiously, no matter what the regime within which he must act. It is a procedural ethic like that presented by Aristotle in *Nicomachean Ethics,* VI. In illustrating the uses of his method, Fletcher presents several political examples. He argues, for instance, that situation ethics rules out an ideological approach to politics, for "doctrinaire by-the-book theory is too confining, too narrow." It also calls in question the "ethical code" solution to problems of corruption in society and government. Fletcher recalls serving on an ethics committee set up by President Kennedy to deal with matters of business ethics. The committee wrote a code "to cover all business, and found itself possessed of nothing but platitudes."[86]

By its nature, situation ethics cannot furnish a slide rule solution to specific political problems. It is fitting that Fletcher ends his book with an outline of the facts and moral dimensions of "Special Bombing Mission No. 13": the mission that destroyed Hiroshima.[87] Fletcher describes the ethical situation in detail, as a case study of great moral significance. But he renders no judgment as to the "right" or "wrong" of the final decision. This he leaves up to the man of good character, the man possessed of Aristotle's "practical reason," and of love.

Aristotle and Political Sociology

We turn to a modern expression of some of the themes of the "scientific" Aristotle, in the work of the eminent political sociologist, Seymour Martin Lipset. The distinguishing mark of the political sociologist is his assumption that the political system is quite unintelligible as only a set of legal

[85]*Ibid.,* p. 88.
[86]*Ibid.,* p. 138.
[87]*Ibid.,* pp. 167-68.

rules and institutions, and that it must be thought of, rather, as the entire social order functioning in one of its many dimensions. The legal order (the formal structure of public authority) and the political groups cannot be understood alone, but only in relation to the value system and way of life of a society, and only in relation to all of the institutions and all of the groups which compose the society. In the words of Lipset, "Many political scientists . . . have argued . . . that it is impossible to study political processes except as special cases of more general sociological and psychological relationships."[88] We will recall that Aristotle also takes this as a fundamental premise, that a government can be understood only in relation to the social whole of which it forms an aspect. Professor Lipset indeed prefaces his *Political Man: The Social Bases of Politics*, with two pages of quotations from Aristotle which sum up the community of thought which exists between him and Aristotle.

The Social Foundations of Democracy

Political Man is concerned with a somewhat narrower range of questions than the full title indicates. It is not a study of all politics, but specifically of democratic politics. Professor Lipset wishes to describe the social conditions under which a democratic order can be constructed and maintained. The form of analysis is like that which Aristotle uses in parts of Books IV to VI of the *Politics*. Among other questions, the reader will recall, Aristotle deals here with such problems as "the sort of constitution which depends upon an assumption . . . The student of politics must . . . be able to study a *given* constitution, just as it stands and simply with a view to explaining how it may have arisen and how it may be made to enjoy the longest life possible."[89]

Professor Lipset defines democracy as "a political system which supplies regular constitutional opportunities for changing the officials, and a social mechanism which permits the largest possible part of the population to influence major decisions by choosing among contenders for political office."[90] This is not equivalent to Aristotle's notion of democracy. In fact, Aristotle explicitly rejects a similar definition ("a form of constitution in which the greater number are sovereign"), because the word "democracy" in his time conveyed a notion of class rule. "Democracy" was commonly taken to mean rule by the many who are also freeborn and *poor*. The representative idea (the idea that democratic power is essentially electoral power) would have been strange to him.

[88]Seymour Lipset, *Political Man: The Social Bases of Politics* (Garden City, N.Y.: Doubleday & Company, Inc., 1960), p. 9.

[89]*Politics* 1288b 28-30

[90]Lipset, *op. cit.,* p. 45.

When we get into Professor Lipset's analysis of the social conditions under which a political order of this kind can be stabilized, however, we immediately find a counterpart in Aristotle's classification of governments. For Lipset shows that it is only a society constituted like Aristotle's "polity" which gives promise of a peaceful, orderly, stable, long-lived, government by the many. "From Aristotle down to the present," he writes, "men have argued that only in a wealthy society in which relatively few citizens lived at the level of real poverty could there be a situation in which the mass of the population intelligently participate in politics and develop the self-restraint necessary to avoid succumbing to the appeals of irresponsible demagogues."[91] Where the many are poor (democracy in Aristotle's sense), the regime quickly turns into the modern form of tyranny, the plebiscitary dictatorship of a Stalin, a Peron, a Hitler, a Nkrumah.

We noted in the introductory chapter that one of the things which distinguishes modern political science from all past inquiry into politics is its concern with getting good data and with demonstrating the reliability of its generalizations. Aristotle's comparative government researches were no doubt a model of scientific thoroughness for his day, yet in presenting empirical generalizations such as the proposition about the connection of a large middle class with political stability he took no pains to show the reader how he arrived at his judgment or to furnish more than illustrative evidence of its validity. Professor Lipset has supplied us with a scientific demonstration of it. Lipset's first step was to operationalize the hypothesis in terms of measurable entities which go with or are implied by the idea of a large middle class. He decided on four criteria—wealth, industrialization, urbanization, and education—and computed averages of these things for various European, Latin-American, and English-speaking countries. He discovered that in every case the average wealth, degree of industrialization and urbanization, and educational level were higher for the countries commonly classified as the most democratic states. His findings are substantiated by a similar survey of Middle Eastern states conducted by Daniel Lerner and the Bureau of Applied Social Research.[92] (See Table I.)

Lipset recognizes that while middle-class predominance may be a necessary basis for the stable functioning of government by the many, it is not a sufficient one. Important also are the effectiveness and legitimacy of the regime, prerequisites for the stability of any political order. The government must produce satisfactions for the groups in a society which have the power to destroy it. And there must be a widespread belief that the system is a just and appropriate one; the values implicit in the structure of the regime must be held by the powerful groups in the society. We are reminded of

[91]*Ibid.*, p. 50.

[92]Cf. *Political Man,* Chapter 2, and Daniel Lerner, *The Passing of Traditional Society* (New York: Free Press of Glencoe, Inc.), 1958.

Table I. *A Comparison of European, English-Speaking and Latin-American Countries, Divided Into Two Groups, "More Democratic" and "Less Democratic," By Indices of Wealth, Industrialization, Education, and Urbanization**

A. Indices of Wealth

Means	Per Capita Income	Thousands of Persons Per Doctor	Persons Per Motor Vehicle
European and English-speaking Stable Democracies	U.S. $695	0.86	17
European and English-speaking Unstable Democracies and Dictatorships	308	1.4	143
Latin-American Democracies and Unstable Dictatorships	171	2.1	99
Latin-American Stable Dictatorships	119	4.4	274
Ranges			
European Stable Democracies	420-1,453	0.7-1.2	3-62
European Dictatorships	128-482	0.6-4	10-538
Latin-American Democracies	112-346	0.8-3.3	31-174
Latin-American Stable Dictatorships	40-331	1.0-10.8	38-428

Means	Telephones Per 1,000 Persons	Radios Per 1,000 Persons	Newspaper Copies Per 1,000 Persons
European and English-speaking Stable Democracies	205	350	341
European and English-speaking Unstable Democracies and Dictatorships	58	160	167
Latin-American Democracies and Unstable Dictatorships	25	85	102
Latin-American Stable Dictatorships	10	43	43
Ranges			
European Stable Democracies	43-400	160-995	242-570
European Dictatorships	7-196	42-307	46-390
Latin-American Democracies	12-58	38-148	51-233
Latin-American Stable Dictatorships	1-24	4-154	4-111

**Source:* From *Political Man: The Social Bases of Politics* by Seymour Martin Lipset, pp. 51-54. Copyright © 1959, 1960 by Seymour Martin Lipset. Reprinted by permission of Doubleday & Company, Inc.

B. Indices of Industrialization

Means	Percentage of Males in Agriculture	Per Capita Energy Consumed
European Stable Democracies	21	3.6
European Dictatorships	41	1.4
Latin-American Democracies	52	0.6
Latin-American Stable Dictatorships	67	0.25
Ranges		
European Stable Democracies	6-46	1.4-7.8
European Dictatorships	16-60	0.27-3.2
Latin-American Democracies	30-63	0.30-0.9
Latin-American Stable Dictatorships	46-87	0.02-1.27

C. Indices of Education

Means	Percentage Literate	Primary Education Enrollment Per 1,000 Persons	Post-Primary Enrollment Per 1,000 Persons	Higher Education Enrollment Per 1,000 Persons
European Stable Democracies	96	134	44	4.2
European Dictatorships	85	121	22	3.5
Latin-American Democracies	74	101	13	2.0
Latin-American Dictatorships	46	72	8	1.3
Ranges				
European Stable Democracies	95-100	96-179	19-83	1.7-17.83
European Dictatorships	55-98	61-165	8-37	1.6-6.1
Latin-American Democracies	48-87	75-137	7-27	0.7-4.6
Latin-American Dictatorships	11-76	11-149	3-24	0.2-3.1

D. Indices of Urbanization

Means	Per Cent in Cities Over 20,000	Per Cent in Cities Over 100,000	Per Cent in Metropolitan Areas
European Stable Democracies	43	28	38
European Dictatorships	24	16	23
Latin-American Democracies	28	22	26
Latin-American Stable Dictatorships	17	12	15

Ranges	Per Cent in Cities Over 20,000	Per Cent in Cities Over 100,000	Per Cent in Metropolitan Areas
European Stable Democracies	28-54	17-51	22-56
European Dictatorships	12-44	6-33	7-49
Latin-American Democracies	11-48	13-37	17-44
Latin-American Stable Dictatorships	5-36	4-22	7-26

Aristotle's discussion of revolution in *Politics* V, in which he ties together as the primary causes of instability "(1) the state of mind which leads to sedition; (2) the objects which are at stake." By "state of mind" he means here ideological persuasion or value system. Revolutions are caused by a widespread sense of injustice, by a feeling that the existing order violates absolute principles of right and is therefore illegitimate. Aristotle describes two such fighting ideologies—democratic egalitarianism and aristocratic elitism. The objects at stake in revolutions are, according to Aristotle, "profit and honour . . . loss and disgrace," i.e., material satisfactions and pains.[93] Revolutions are caused by the ineffectiveness of a regime as well as by a widespread sense of its illegitimacy.

Both Aristotle and Lipset see crises of legitimacy as a function of social change. Aristotle, for example, speaks of "a disproportionate increase in some part of the state"—the sudden and disproportionate growth of a social class in numbers, wealth, or prestige—as one of the occasions of a crisis of legitimacy. But his analysis is very sketchy. He does not tell us, for example, under what conditions this will be true. Social change does not always bring political instability. Lipset tries to supply us with a theory of the conditions.

"Crises of legitimacy," Lipset writes, "occur during a transition to a new social structure, if (1) the *status* of major conservative institutions is threatened during the period of structural change; (2) all the major groups in the society do not have access to the political system in the transitional period, or at least as soon as they develop political demands. After a new social structure is established, if the new system is unable to sustain the expectations of major groups (on the grounds of 'effectiveness') for a long enough period to develop legitimacy upon a new basis, a new crisis may develop."[94] He gives as examples of societies in transition to democracy in which these conditions have obtained (and which have therefore had difficulty in sustaining democratic institutions despite the presence of a large middle class), France, Germany, and Italy. In each instance, political access

[93]*Politics* 1302a 21-35.
[94]Lipset, *op. cit.,* p. 78.

through the traditional institutions was denied to the new strata demanding a place in the sun, first to the rising bourgeoisie, then to the working class. "Where force was used to restrict access, the lower strata were alienated from the system and adopted extremist ideologies." The legitimacy of the traditional institutions and values was called in question by the new power groups. This in turn made the established groups more adamant in their conservatism.

By contrast, Lipset notes, the countries in which old elites provided access for the new groups preserved at least a shell of their old institutions intact, and with them the values of the old order. The new strata were able gradually and peacefully to fuse their new values and new institutions with the old. These came to be accepted by the conservative groups who did not feel their position radically threatened by the changes. The result is the phenomenon of the stable "crowned republic." "We have the observed fact that ten out of twelve stable European and English-speaking democracies are monarchies. ... The preservation of the monarchy has apparently retained for these nations the loyalty of the aristocratic, traditionalist, and clerical sectors of the population which resented increased democratization and equalitarianism."[95]

In relating legitimacy to effectiveness, Lipset argues that even though a regime be reasonably effective in producing material satisfactions, if the conservative groups are threatened during a period of transition, or if new groups are denied access to the political system, a crisis of legitimacy will occur which will unstabilize the system. But failures of effectiveness are also deadly for a regime, he believes, if they are repeated and if they continue for long periods. Even if a regime's legitimacy is not questioned for the reasons described above, long ineffectiveness will of itself produce a crisis.

Lipset sums up his theory with a diagram. (See Fig. 1.) "Societies which fall in box *A*," he writes, "which are, that is, high on the scales of legitimacy and effectiveness, have stable political systems, like the United States, Sweden, and Britain. Ineffective and illegitimate regimes, which fall in box *D*, are by definition unstable and break down, unless they are dictatorships maintaining themselves by force, like the governments of Hungary and Eastern Germany today."[96]

Lipset sees an important connection between effectiveness and industrialization, which, as we have seen above, he relates to middle-class predominance in the societies as a prerequisite of stable democracy. The new democracies of Africa and of Asia, he believes, cannot survive unless they can meet the test of effectiveness, which means that they must in-

[95]*Ibid.*, pp. 78-79.
[96]*Ibid.*, p. 81.

FIG. 1. *Legitimacy and Effectiveness of Regimes.**

EFFECTIVENESS

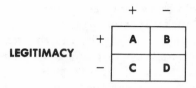

Source: Political Man by Seymour Martin Lipset, p. 81. Copyright © 1959, 1960 by Seymour Martin Lipset and reprinted by permission of Doubleday & Company, Inc.

dustrialize, and rapidly at that. But here a problem arises. For Lipset notes that in Europe "wherever industrialization occurred *rapidly* introducing sharp *discontinuities* between the pre-industrial and industrial situation, more rather than less extremist working-class movements emerged."[97] And conditions like these produce crises of legitimacy. The demands of effectiveness and of legitimacy may therefore be in irreconcilable competition with one another. In one place Lipset unhappily concludes, therefore, that "the prognosis for political democracy in Asia and Africa is bleak."[98] Perhaps we must look forward to long periods of *stasis,* alternated with absolute rule, before a working democratic order can be built in these areas. We think of Aristotle's conclusion that even tyranny (if it is enlightened) must be good under conditions much less than the ideal—or that it is at least inevitable under certain conditions.

At the end of his book Professor Lipset wishes to break out of the sad realism of the Aristotelian framework, however. "We must not be unduly pessimistic," he writes. "Democracy has existed in a variety of circumstances, even if it is most commonly sustained by a limited set of conditions. It cannot be achieved by acts of will alone, of course, but men's wills expressed in action can shape institutions and events in directions that reduce or increase the chances for democracy's development and survival. ... To clarify the operation of Western democracy in the mid-twentieth century may contribute to the political battle in Asia and Africa." [99] Would Aristotle agree, or would he, if he could speak in our idiom, call this "whistling in the dark"?

[97] *Ibid.,* p. 68.
[98] *Ibid.,* p. 94.
[99] *Ibid.,* p. 407.

Modern Approaches to Synthesis[100]

There is no reason why a modern theory of the best regime cannot be built upon theories of political stability developed by political sociologists like Lipset. Stability, it should be remembered, is a central value in all the great political philosophies which we commonly term "normative" and "absolutist," and which I have called "noumenalist." Plato for example tells us in a well known passage of *Republic* that unless "political power and philosophy meet together ... there can be no rest from troubles ... for states." The good state is the most unified, the consensual, the stable state. And characteristic of all the evil forms described in Book VIII is their radical instability, their short life and the ease with which they are overturned. By an inner logic of decay they produce their opposites. Miserly oligarchs breed spendthrift sons, who create by revolution a democracy. And democracy, again by the inner logic of its development, breeds tyrants from liberals (the licentious.) In *Politics* IV we have Aristotle saying "it is clear that the middle type of constitution is best. It is the one type free from faction; where the middle class is large, there is least likelihood of faction and dissension among the citizens." Both Plato and Aristotle maintain, of course, that it is the inherent goodness or rightness of their ideal orders which is the guarantee of their stability, not the other way around. The point is that the two are always associated in their thought. Stability is impossible without goodness. Therefore stability must be evidence of goodness.

There is also no reason why a new theory of the best order, as that enshrining the best values, cannot be built upon research into what values men actually pursue. We will recall that Aristotle, in the *Nicomachean Ethics,* proceeded in precisely this way in lining out the ethical rule to be followed in living the best life. Some beginning of such a theory has in fact been made by a political scientist who, like Aristotle, is also known for his descriptive work.

Philip Selznick, in an address before the Natural Law Forum in 1961, argued that "the study of normative systems is one way of bridging the gap between fact and value. At the same time, the objectivity and detachment of the investigator can remain unsullied. The great gain is that we can more readily perceive latent values in the world of fact. This we do when we recognize, for example, that fatherhood, sexuality, leadership, and many other phenomena have a natural potential for 'envaluation.' "[101]

[100]The following material was originally part of a paper entitled "Political Science and Political Ethics" delivered at the 1968 meeting of the New York State Political Science Association Convention, Saratoga Springs, March 29, 1968.

[101]Philip Selznick, "Sociology and Natural Law," *Natural Law Forum,* Vol. 16 (1961), p. 90. Cf. his descriptive essay about the politics of the Tennessee Valley Authority, *T.V.A. and the Grass Roots* (Berkeley: University of California Press, 1949).

A comprehensive understanding of ideals of leadership, for example, is clearly important for political theory, both descriptive and evaluative. That an investigation like this might well produce a universal concept of leadership, useful both as a normative and as a descriptive standard is evidenced by the manner in which the peoples of the world received the news of the deaths of John F. Kennedy and Pope John XXIII. The universal outcries of grief from primitives of Tanzania as well as from sophisticates of Manhattan are indications that there may be a universal concept of nobility of spirit which men look for in their leaders everywhere.

Selznick suggests further that the adequate study of social systems requires the investigation of their master ideals. To orient inquiry around the concept of survival or stability of the system he finds unsatisfactory, for while "*some* systems are indispensable if life is to exist at all . . . other systems are required if a certain *kind* of life is to survive."[102]

We are enjoined, then, by Selznick to engage in anthropological researches with a view to defining, " 'ends proper to man's Nature' and to discover objective standards of moral judgment."[103] To view the inquiry this way, it seems to me, also demands that we see our work as a metaphysical enterprise, as a search for the absolute—always admitting, of course, the possibility of factual or empirical error in our findings. I do not see how Selznick can logically say that in all of this he retains a first and basic "commitment to naturalism," even of the John Dewey variety,[104] since I do not believe that the naturalist vocabulary contains expressions like "ends proper to man's nature." Naturalism ultimately swallows norms up in practice—it can only tell us what ends are in fact pursued, not what should properly be pursued. The idea of a natural end is a teleological notion, and naturalism rejects teleology.

Some small beginnings have already been made in the anthropological study of shared principles of right. As far back as 1931 John M. Cooper reported a finding that "the peoples of the world, however much they differ as to details of morality, hold universally, or with practical universality" to a number of basic precepts which agrees closely with the Judaeo-Christian Decalogue:

Respect the Supreme Being or the benevolent being or beings who take his place. Do not "blaspheme." Care for your children. Malicious murder or maiming, stealing, deliberate slander or "black" lying, when committed against friend or unoffending fellow clansman or tribesman, are reprehensible. Adultery proper is wrong, even though there be exceptional circumstances

[102]*Ibid.*, p. 91.
[103]*Ibid.*, p. 94.
[104]*Ibid.*, p. 85.

that permit or enjoin it and even though sexual relations among the unmarried may be viewed leniently. Incest is a heinous offense.[105]

Cooper sums up the value consensus as one which enjoins divine worship and which "protects the fundamental rights of life, limb, family, property, and good name."

These are substantive values. Arnold Brecht has hypothesized also the existence of a procedural consensus, whose existence might be checked with the methods of social science research. As a "Tentative list of Universal Postulates of Justice" he suggests the following:

> First, *truth.* In the objective sense (as when we speak of an objectively just action) justice demands an accordance with objective truth; that is, all relevant statements on facts and relations must be objectively true. In the subjective sense (as when we speak of a just person) it demands an accordance with what is thought to be true. . . .
>
> Second, *generality* of the system of values which is applied. It is unjust to select arbitrarily different systems of values in considering one case and another.
>
> Third, *treating as equal what is equal under the accepted system.* It is unjust to discriminate arbitrarily among equal cases.
>
> Fourth, *no restriction of freedom beyond the requirements of the accepted system.* It is unjust to restrict freedom arbitrarily. . . .
>
> Fifth, *respect for the necessities of nature* in the strictest sense. It is unjust to inflict punishment or moral reproach for nonfulfillment of a law or command which is impossible of fulfillment.[106]

It is evident at a quick glance that these two lists taken together constitute some of the leading values of the modern secular Liberal tradition (in its broadest and most authoritative sense, *not* in the sense of the Classical Liberalism of Adam Smith) as well as of the preexisting Judaeo-Christian tradition of the West out of which it grew. This suggests that, although it may be dangerous to seek knowledge of human nature by living through the consequences of our ideologies, we may learn a great deal of use and gather a great deal of raw material by carefully scrutinizing the value content of the leading ideologies of our time. Surely, if we are to be realistic in hoping to propose a value theory which is intelligible and acceptable to the average man, we must begin with the thoughts which are already in his head. The ideological mores are important constraints which the philosopher ignores at his peril, as Charles Frankel recently pointed out in a paper on the "Philosophy of Practice."[107]

[105]John M. Cooper, "The Relations Between Religion and Morality in Primitive Culture," *Primitive Man,* IV (1931), 36 quoted in Heinrich Rommen, *The Natural Law* (St. Louis, Mo.: Herder, 1947), p. 227.

[106]Arnold Brecht, *Political Theory* (Princeton, N.J.: Princeton University Press, 1959), p. 396.

[107]International Philosophy Year Conference, State University of New York at Brockport, November 3, 1967.

With an inquiry into the operational norms of Liberal culture might be combined a dispassionate investigation of the norms of the Communist world, and both of these studied in relation to the traditional norms both East and West, which refuse to die as the world moves further along into the realm of scientific rationalism. What I am suggesting is an enterprise not far removed in intention, if in method, from that outlined twenty-five years ago by F.S.C. Northrop in *The Meeting of East and West*. "The task of the contemporary world," he wrote, "falls into four major parts: (1) the relating of the East and the West; (2) the similar merging of the Latin and the Anglo-Saxon cultures; (3) the mutual reinforcement of democratic and communistic values; and (4) the reconciliation of the true and valuable portions of the Western medieval and modern worlds."[108] The inquiry must include a study not only of the values held, but also of the grounds or reasons behind them—the underlying metaphysic of human nature. Such an enterprise would be in the spirit of Aristotelian synthesis of the noumenal and the natural. It would also constitute a new reform of the tradition.

Bibliographical Note

Standard full-length studies of Aristotle's thought are Donald James Allan, *The Philosophy of Aristotle*, London: Oxford University Press, 1952; George Grote, *Aristotle*, London: John Murray, Publishers, Ltd., 1872; Werner Jaeger, *Aristotle*, 2nd ed., Oxford: Clarendon Press, 1948; W.D. Ross, *Aristotle*, London: Methuen & Co., Ltd., 3rd rev. ed., 1937. A recent work which contains a good description of Aristotle's scholarly method and of his metaphysics, but which is rather skimpy in its treatment of the *Politics*, is John Herman Randall, *Aristotle*, New York: Columbia University Press, 1960. The leading analysis of the specifically political works of Aristotle is Sir Ernest Barker, *The Political Thought of Plato and Aristotle*, New York: Dover Publications, Inc., 1959. See also Barker's introduction to his translation of *The Politics of Aristotle*, New York: Oxford University Press, Inc., 1958.

For the application of Aristotelian ideas to special problems of modern political analysis see Charles L. Sherman, "A Latter Day Tyranny in the Light of Aristotelian Prognosis," *American Political Science Review*, Vol. XXVIII, No. 3, June 1934, pp. 424-35. Professor Sherman recognized in the new Nazi regime a reincarnation of the classic tyranny in 1934, when statesmen in the leading democratic states were still hailing Adolf Hitler as a savior of Germany. Using Aristotle's theory as his instrument, Professor Sherman also predicted the war policies of the *Fuehrer*, as the natural concomitant of the other features of tyranny. He also predicted the manner in

---

[108]F.S.C. Northrop, *The Meeting of East and West* (New York: Crowell Collier and Macmillan, Inc., 1953), p. 426.

which the regime would finally be destroyed. World War II was precipitated by the Nazi government five years after Sherman's prognosis, and the prediction that the regime would succumb from "external" causes was fulfilled nearly six years later. See also Fred Kort, "The Quantification of Aristotle's Theory of Revolution," *American Political Science Review,* Vol. XLVI, No. 2, June 1952, pp. 486-93, an endeavor to combine modern techniques of quantitative measurement with Aristotle's insights to produce an empirical weather vane of incipient revolution. See also Norton Long, "Aristotle and the Study of Local Government," *Social Research,* Vol. XXIV, Fall 1957, pp. 287-310.

Chapter 4

Transcendent Goodness and Power Politics: St. Augustine, Niebuhr, and Morgenthau

Augustine's political theorizing was stimulated by the crisis of the Roman Empire, as that of Plato and Aristotle had been prompted by the crisis of the *polis*. In A.D. 410 the city of Rome was taken and sacked by the Gothic hordes of Alaric, a rude shock to the civilized world of the time which for over four hundred years had looked to Rome as the sovereign political authority and protector of the high culture of the Mediterranean lands. The old order was rapidly passing, and new bearings had to be found. The new orientation would have to include, of course, an explanation of what had happened to the Imperial City whose rule all had supposed to be eternal.

One explanation of the catastrophe, which immediately gained popularity, represented an attempt to recover traditional bearings. We would probably call it a conservative or reactionary ideology today. It claimed that Rome had fallen because the Romans had deserted their old gods for a new religion. Christianity had received legal recognition and imperial protection in the previous century, just as the pressures of barbarian power began to develop on the borders of the empire. From that time on, there had been recurrent invasions, and the empire had gradually crumbled. Meanwhile, the new religion continued to spread, and from the concomitancy of these events people began to conclude a causal connection. The capture of the Imperial City was the signal for absolute doom. But if Romans returned to the old ways, and to their old gods, whose anger had produced the catastrophe, perhaps the decay could be halted and the empire restored to its old self. Such was the reasoning of the pagans of the empire who saw their world crumbling around them.

It was concern about the growing currency of this explanation of the empire's decline that set Augustine to thinking about politics, and to the composition of his *City of God (De Civitate Dei)* in which he defended

Christianity against the pagan attack and elaborated a theory of his own to explain the demise of the empire, and, indeed, the rise and decline of all political societies built by men.

Augustine's Method

Data and Basic Assumptions

As a Bishop of the Christian Church, Augustine naturally grounded his explanation in a Christian world-view, one which took the form of a divinely revealed theology. The starting point of the pagan writers, whose work we have been considering, had been reason—the natural power of the mind to understand the nature of things—and the sense data produced by the everyday experience of the alert and inquiring mind (as in the case of Plato) or by systematic compilation (as in the case of Aristotle).

The Christian thinker did not deny the importance of what could be discovered by experience and natural reason. St. Augustine was the son of a provincial Roman administrator and had received more than the ordinary education of a cultured gentleman of his time. He was indeed a scholar, well versed in Greek and Roman philosophy. The *City of God* is crowded with references to the work of Plato, of Neoplatonists such as Apuleius, Porphyry, and Plotinus, and of the Stoic philosophers Cicero and Seneca. His book also makes use of considerable historical data from the works of the Greek and Roman historians. There are innumerable citations of Sallust, Suetonius, Livy, Pliny, Varro, and Plutarch.

But to the Christian, reason and natural experience alone could provide no complete and fully satisfying answers to the great questions, for he believed that God had intervened in the life of the empirical world to communicate directly, in a special way, with his creature man. And it was to this Revelation that the Christian political theorist naturally turned for a frame of reference and starting point; or as we would put it today, for orienting concepts. To think significantly about politics, or about any large question, he would have to see what God himself had revealed which might open up a path to the questions puzzling him. The record of this Revelation was to be found in the extensive body of writings which we call the Judaeo-Christian Bible. Its composition extended over thousands of years, as its authors, Augustine believed, wrote under divine inspiration.

> The Scripture which is called canonical . . . has paramount authority, and to [it] we yield assent in all matters of which we ought not to be ignorant, and yet cannot know of ourselves . . . Accordingly, as in the case of visible objects which we have not seen, we trust those who have . . . so in the case of things which are perceived by the mind and spirit, i.e., which are remote from our

own interior sense, it behooves us to trust those who have seen them set in that incorporeal light, or abidingly contemplate them.

Of all visible things, the world is the greatest; of all invisible, the greatest is God. But, that the world is, we see; that God is, we believe. That God made the world, we can believe from no one more safely than from God Himself. But where have we heard Him? Nowhere more distinctly than in the Holy Scriptures, where His prophet said, "In the beginning God created the heavens and the earth." Was the prophet present when God made the heavens and the earth? No; but the wisdom of God, by whom all things are made, was there, and wisdom insinuates itself into holy souls, and makes them the friends of God and his prophets, and noiselessly informs them of his works.[1]

Form of Analysis

St. Augustine's political theory is cast in the form of a philosophy of history, a type of literature which was a new thing in the world of his time but which has since become a familiar vehicle for social interpretation. Hegel, Marx, Spengler, and Toynbee are among its most important exponents in modern times. A philosophy of history is a teleological interpretation of the whole of world history. It assumes that there was a beginning and that there will be an end to the sequence of temporal events, and that the totality of these events has meaning. There are ends immanent in history, purposes which are fulfilled through the historical process.

The pagan writers whose work we have examined had no such concept. They assumed that the world was eternal; that its life consisted of recurrent cycles of birth, growth, death, and renewal; and that there was no meaning to be discovered in these endless cycles. Aristotle's theory of the Forms as ends immanent in empirical beings striving for realization assigns meaning to particular historical sequences but not to the historical process as a whole. There is no assumption that the entelechy which informs a historical sequence will necessarily be realized. Aristotle has no doctrine, for example, that the good city of the last two books of the *Politics* will necessarily someday be generated in time, even though it represents the fulfillment toward which actual states tend. And if the political *telos were* someday fully realized, Aristotle would not dub this the culmination of history, nor would he regard it as a permanent achievement, a static condition of blessedness. The *polis* which reached the full flowering of its *telos* he would expect to decay as do all natural beings. He simply did not think of history as a purposive whole with a beginning and a fulfillment. But Judaeo-Christian theology (or, more properly, eschatology) treats history as a process for realizing a divine purpose and therefore quite naturally led

---

[1]St. Augustine, *The City of God,* trans., Marcus Dods (New York: Random House, Modern Library, 1950), p. 347. All references to *The City of God* will be to this edition.

Augustine to set forth his interpretation of politics within a philosophy of history.

What are the central ideas of the theory of history which forms the framework of Augustine's political thought? Contrary to the pagan writers who held that the world exists eternally, Augustine argued that it was created by God's fiat. The order of its movements and the world's beauty were evidence that it had been created and that God was its Creator. But the best testimony was that of God Himself, who announced His work through the inspired author of *Genesis*. This was also the beginning of time, for time cannot be measured unless there is motion and change, which are essential components of the life of this world. But God's nature which pre-exists the world and transcends it, is changeless and eternal.

God's purpose in creating the world was simply to express His own goodness. This is signified by the statements in *Genesis,* following the descriptions of each act of Creation, that "God saw that it was good." Some of the pagans had understood this, either because they had seen the Sacred Scripture, or by "quick-sighted genius." For "this also Plato has assigned as the most sufficient reason for the creation of the world, that good works might be made by a good God."[2] The natures of all things are therefore good. "No nature at all is evil, and this is a name for nothing but the want of good." But there is a hierarchy of goods—"From things earthly to things heavenly, from the visible to the invisible, there are some things better than others; and for this purpose are they unequal, in order that they might all exist."[3]

Emphasis on Will

Man, too, was made good by the good God: "God, as it is written, made man upright." Augustine adds, "and consequently with a good will. For if he had not had a good will, he could not have been upright. The good will, then, is the work of God; for God created him with it."[4] This passage is crucial for Augustine's political theory. Classical thought had described human excellence as consisting in the exercise of reason, both speculative and practical. And we have seen how pivotal this notion was for classical political theory. Augustine's shift of emphasis from reason to will in defining human goodness leads, as we shall see, to a wholly different kind of political theory. He does not, of course, deny man's rationality. Indeed, this is what is meant by being created in God's image. "God, then, made man in His own image. For He created for him a soul endowed with reason and in-

[2]*Ibid.,* pp. 364-65.

[3]*Ibid.,* p. 365.

[4]*Ibid.,* p. 457.

telligence, so that he might excel all the creatures of earth, air, and sea, which were not so gifted."[5] But Augustine does not single out rationality as the characteristic mark of human goodness, but rather, right intention, good will.

Though man, as created by God, was good, he was not perfect. The goodness of his original will directed him toward his proper end, his perfection. But Augustine did not identify the exercise of good will with perfection. While the happiness and perfection of the classical man was a temporal one, to be found here and now in the exercise of his reason, the happiness for which God ordained Adam was to pass out of the world of changing created things and to be assimilated to the changeless, uncreated Godhead. Adam was intended to enjoy "the vision of God" and to participate in "His unchangeable immortality."[6] Perfection was not to be found in Eden. The Paradise was to be only a preparation for perfection,[7] a test of man's will, for God created it free as well as good. Adam was not directed by necessary laws to his end, as are other creatures, but had freely to choose it.

> If he remained in subjection to His Creator as his rightful Lord, and piously kept His Commandments, he should . . . obtain, without the intervention of death, a blessed and endless immortality; but if he offended the Lord his God by a proud and disobedient use of his free will, he should become subject to death, and live as the beasts do—the slave of appetite, and doomed to eternal punishment after death.[8]

Human goodness for the Christian writer is thus signified by freely willed obedience to God's commands. Disobedience makes man bad by turning this will away from God, its proper end. And it also entails badness in the classical sense as well, making man a "slave of appetite," i.e., by impeding the activity of directing reason.

The second landmark in the Christian theology of history is the story of the Fall of Adam. Man chose to use his free will not to follow the commands of God but rather his own fancies. Saint Augustine says that the inclination to do this came from pride, which he defines as "the craving for undue exaltation." Adam chose to replace God as his true end with himself; his soul became a "kind of end to itself." The place rightfully occupied by the Creator was filled by the creature, and man fell into self-seeking. "The Holy Scriptures designated the proud . . . 'self-pleasers.' "[9]

How did the will become proud and vicious? Because it was made out

[5]*Ibid.*, p. 407.

[6]*Ibid.*, p. 402.

[7]*Ibid.*, p. 406.

[8]*Idem.*

[9]*Ibid.*, p. 460.

of nothing. "That it is a nature, this is because it is made by God; but that it falls away from Him, this is because it is made out of nothing."[10] Good is being, evil is nonbeing, nothing. And insofar as man's nature is created of nothing, it tends to evil, i.e., it is tempted to prideful acts of rebellion against God. "By craving to be more, man became less; and by aspiring to be self-sufficient, he fell away from Him who truly suffices him."[11]

The first overt act of disobedience, partaking of the fruit of the tree of the knowledge of good and of evil, was a result of pride, and the consequence for the whole human race was condemnation in the hereafter to eternal punishment and in temporal existence to labor and suffering. Having through sin lost even the guidance of his natural reason, man became a creature of his appetites, and therewith cruel and rapacious. But God chose not to abandon man to this lot and promised to send a Savior who would atone for Adam's wickedness, cure the evil will, and restore divine direction to human life, thus opening up again the possibility of eternal life hereafter with God. Temporal suffering and a continued inclination of the will, because of its nothingness, to pride and self-seeking (the struggle of the "old Adam" against the "new Christ") would, however, continue to the end of time. Salvation was made available to all who had faith in God's promise, even to those who lived before the coming of Christ but who led godly lives after God had sent His grace to them.

The Two Cities

These two signal events, the Fall and the Redemption of man, have given rise to two groupings of mankind, the Elect and the Damned. And Augustine says he will "mystically call [them] the two cities," the City of God (*Civitas Dei*) and the Earthly City (*Civitas Terrena*). Each is a community by virtue of the values which its members share, the things that its members love in common.

> Two cities have been formed by two loves; the earthly by the love of self, even to the contempt of God; the heavenly by the love of God, even to the contempt of self. The former, in a word, glories in itself, the latter in the Lord.[12]

The Earthly City lives "after the flesh" and "according to man"; its members are proud self-seekers. The Heavenly City lives "after the spirit" and "according to God." Its members are humble lovers of God. And the history of the human race is the history of these two mystical cities. "This whole time or world-age, in which the dying give place and those who are

[10]*Ibid.*, pp. 460, 461.
[11]*Ibid.*, p. 461.
[12]*Ibid.*, p. 477.

born succeed, is the career of these two cities which we treat." Throughout history they will remain "commingled and implicated with one another," "mingled together from the beginning down to the end."[13] But one day, God will come to destroy the world and separate them. The City of God will pass into eternal blessedness, while the Earthly City will be committed to eternal punishment, and time will be no more.

These are the basic outlines of the philosophy of history within which Saint Augustine constructed his political theory.

The Virtuous Regime as the Kingdom of Heaven

Augustine's theology produces a theory of the best regime quite different from that of Plato and Aristotle. The City of God, as a virtuous society which contains all things necessary for human happiness, cannot become a temporal city. Plato's *Republic* was, as we have seen, a description of the Form of the *Polis,* which as the permanent perfection of the political order, exists only in the "heaven above the heavens." Nevertheless, Plato supposed at least the possibility of its generation and brief existence in time. And the *polis* of the *Laws,* constructed out of institutions derived from the wreckage of the prehistorically incarnate Form, could be a stable approximation of the divine order. Aristotle's best regime was conceived as the natural *telos* of empirical processes, wholly realizable, though probably a rare occurrence. But Augustine's City of God cannot be generated in time as a political society.

Why is this so? St. Augustine's conception of human nature was such that no purely temporal organization could encompass and fulfill it. The neo-Augustinian theologian and political theorist, Reinhold Niebuhr, writes that the "classical wise man obscured [this nature] by fitting its mind into a system of universal mind and the body into the system of nature." The political problem was to organize man's environment so as to put mind into control of physical nature, and with this accomplished man would be perfected. For "the mind being the seat of virtue [had] the capacity to bring all impulses into order; and the body, from which came the 'lusts and ambitions,' [was] the cause of evil." But according to Augustine, Niebuhr writes, the self

> . . . is something more than mind and is able to use mind for its purposes. The self has, in fact, a mysterious identity and integrity transcending its functions of mind, memory, and will. . . . It must be observed that the transcendent freedom of this self, including its capacity to defy any rational and natural system into which someone may seek to coordinate it (its capacity for evil)

[13]*Ibid.*, pp. 344, 441, 478, 668.

makes it difficult for any philosophy, whether ancient or modern, to comprehend its true dimension . . .

[Augustine's] conception of the radical freedom of man, derived from the
Biblical view, made it impossible to accept the idea of fixed forms of human
behavior and of social organization, analogous to those of nature, even as he
opposed the classical theory of historical cycles.[14]

The Augustinian man is not malleable like the classical man. He cannot be
molded by the Reasonable Legislator to the same degree as the classical
man. He breaks out of every humanly devised rational order into chaos and
disorder.

The perfection of man, the realization of perfect virtue, is not then the
province of politics in Augustine's theology. Perfection is achieved through
grace and salvation, and the keys of the kingdom of the perfect are in the
hands of a church, which is not, as in the pagan theories, at one and the
same time a state. The temporal institutions of the church, ideally, are independent of the traditional political order—i.e., the city, the kingdom, the
republic, the empire. And the church is wider than its temporal institutions.
Its essential nature cannot be realized in empirical organization, for it is understood by St. Augustine to be the mystical community of the Elect, that is,
of all those who are saved by God's grace and who are united by a common
love of God—the City of God. Its membership transcends the composition
of any possible temporal organization. Some of them are now in Heaven;
others are alive but are not formally members of the Christian church, men
of good will who have been baptized only by desire. And not all those who
are formally members of the church are saved. Some will die in sin and be
cast into hell.

The member of the Holy City who is still in this life, though destined
for salvation, is not perfectly happy here and now. He remains subject to
physical sickness and deformity which may "destroy all beauty and grace in
the body." Madness may darken his mind. And his virtuous soul is not at
rest but must "wage perpetual war with vices—not those that are outside of
us, but within; not other men's, but our own. . . . For we must not fancy
that there is no vice in us."

Far be it from us, then, to fancy that while we are still engaged in this intestine
war, we have already found the happiness which we seek to reach by victory . . . .

Our very righteousness, too, though true in so far as it has respect to the true
good, is yet in this life of such a kind that it consists rather in the remission of
sins than in the perfecting of virtues.[15]

---

[14]Reinhold Niebuhr, *Christian Realism and Political Problems* (New York:
Charles Scribner's Sons, 1953), pp. 121, 133-34.

[15]*The City of God,* pp. 676, 677, 708.

Only at the end of history, when the empirical world has been destroyed, will the good regime, the kingdom of righteousness and happiness, be completed as the Kingdom of God in Heaven.

We should avoid supposing that because of its trans-historical character the Augustinian Heavenly City is simply a Christian version of the ungenerated Platonic Form of the *polis*. The two are radically different. Plato's good regime is pure idea, an abstraction. Augustine's is a community of flesh-and-blood men, men who come from the temporal city and who enter the Kingdom of Heaven in their bodies, although these bodies are transformed. Time is ordered to eternity in Augustine's theory, as it is not in Plato's. The entire succession of temporal cities has played a role in preparing the population of the City of God, though as a city of perfect men, it can exist only in eternity.

The Empirical City

What is the nature of temporal preparation for the Heavenly City? If politics is not a process for the perfection of man, what is it? And is there a best empirical regime and a hierarchy of temporal orders? Do some perform the work of preparation for eternity better than others? And what is the role of the empirical city for the *Civitas Terrena*, the community of the damned?

The Temporal City as the City of the Wicked

Many passages of Augustine's book actually identify the temporal political society with the mystical city of the damned. In one place, for example, Augustine says: "I promised to write of the rise, progress, and appointed end of the two cities, one of which is God's, the other this world's, in which . . . the former is now a stranger."[16] And in another he notes that "it is recorded of Cain that he built a city, but Abel, being a sojourner, built none. For the city of the saints is above, although here below it begets citizens, in whom it sojourns till the time of its reign arrives."[17] The empirical city was built by the murderer, not by the just man. And just men who now live *in* it are not *of* it—they are only pilgrims in the temporal city.

But there are other passages which appear to stand in sharp contrast to these. For example, at the end of Book XIV, Augustine makes a comparison of the two mystical cities in these terms:

> In the one, the princes and the nations it subdues are ruled by the love of the ruling; in the other, the princes and subjects serve one another in love, the lat-

[16]*Ibid.*, p. 609.
[17]*Ibid.*, p. 479.

ter obeying, while the former takes thought for all. The one delights in its own strength, represented in the persons of its rulers; the other says to its God, "I will love Thee, O Lord, my strength."[18]

This seems to imply that at least some empirical cities may be dominated by members of the Holy City, and that these cities would live a happier and morally better life than those dominated by the earthly man. And this is borne out in Augustine's definition of a political society. "A people," he writes, "is an assemblage of reasonable beings bound together by a common agreement as to the objects of their love . . . and it will be a superior people in proportion as it is bound together by higher interest, inferior in proportion as it is bound together by lower."[19] It appears from this that one can classify a state on a moral scale by assessing the character of its common values. Now if "justice" is characteristic of a society at the top of this scale, no pagan people would have the right to be called a just society. Because "justice is that virtue which gives every one his due." And "where . . . is the justice of man, when he deserts the true God and yields himself to impure demons?" In general, therefore, "the city of the ungodly . . . is void of true justice."[20]

Now, according to this definition of justice, presumably the empirical city in which the true God is worshipped would be a just society, and therefore deserving a high rank on the moral scale, a rank which would set it apart in *kind* from the ungodly pagan city. This would seem to be indicated by the fact that in his description of the history of the two cities Augustine identifies the City of God with the historical Jewish nation from Abraham to Christ, and the pagan nations of the same period with the Earthly City. And he says that the Christian church has succeeded to the place of the Jewish Kingdom as the City of God.

But apparently these identifications are only figurative, for the Holy City, as historical Jewish Kingdom and historical church, will contain wicked men, while failing to embrace all the just. Augustine writes, for example, of the Jews:

> In very deed there was no other people who were specially called the people of God; but they cannot deny that there have been certain men even of other nations who belong, not by earthly but heavenly fellowship, to the true Israelites, the citizens of the country that is above. . . . The holy and wonderful man Job, . . . was neither a native nor a proselyte, . . . but, being bred of the Idumean race, arose there and died there too.[21]

[18]*Ibid.*, p. 477.

[19]*Ibid.*, p. 706.

[20]*Ibid.*, pp. 699, 706.

[21]*Ibid.*, p. 658.

And in another place he refers to the historical Israel as

> ... Jerusalem the bond woman, in which some also reigned who were the children of the free woman, holding that kingdom in temporary stewardship, but holding the kingdom of the heavenly Jerusalem, whose children they were, in true faith, and hoping in the true Christ.[22]

Here the historical Jerusalem is in fact clearly identified with the Earthly City, though it was ruled from time to time by just men and worshipped the true God. And he writes of other kings of Israel and of Judah "who grievously offended God by their injustice, and, along with their people, who were like them, were smitten with moderate scourges." And of the church he writes, "There are many reprobate mingled with the good, and both are gathered together by the gospel as in a drag net."[23]

In still another place Augustine expresses "unlimited approval" of the idea of the pagan philosophers "that the life of the wise man must be social. For how could the City of God . . . either take a beginning or be developed, or attain its proper destiny, if the life of the saints were not a social life?"[24] But instead of going on to describe the high character of this society of saints, contrasting it with that of the city of the ungodly, he asks:

> But who can enumerate all the great grievances with which human society abounds in the misery of this mortal state?. . . Is not human life full of such things? Do they not often occur even in honourable friendships? . . . Who ought to be, or who are more friendly than those who live in the same family? And yet who can rely even upon their friendship, seeing that secret treachery has often broken it up, and produced enmity as bitter as the amity was sweet, or seemed sweet by the most perfect dissimulation? . . . If then, home, the natural refuge from the ills of life is itself not safe, what shall we say of the city, which, as it is larger, is so much the more filled with lawsuits civil and criminal, and is never free from the fear, if sometimes from the actual outbreak, of disturbing and bloody insurrections and civil wars?[25]

This seems to say that the saints on this earth can never live in a strictly closed society of their own. The holy pilgrims cannot build a temporal city exclusively their own, dominated by their love of God. They cannot escape association with the ungodly, who will always be present to pull down the moral tone of a temporal society. The good and bad are mixed together until the Judgment Day, and the consequence of this is to reduce all political societies to a common level. The temporal city is, after all, in all its forms,

[22]*Ibid.*, p. 591.
[23]*Ibid.*, pp. 607, 660.
[24]*Ibid.*, p. 680.
[25]*Ibid.*, p. 681.

including the Christian state, closer to the Earthly than the Heavenly City. There may be occasional just rulers in the empirical city. But in every society it is the wicked who predominate and set the moral tone of the society. The saints are few. They must live in Babylon until the end of time, though they do not suffer stain from the association. "For from Babylon the people of God is so freed that it meanwhile sojourns in its company."[26]

The Temporal Good

The life of the saints in Babylon brings some positive goods with it, though they are of a limited and utilitarian character. The empirical city provides the things necessary for the maintenance of life, material sufficiency—food, clothing, shelter, security of life and limb. And to ensure their acquisition, the citizens of the empirical city enter into an agreement to seek them as common ends, through peaceful cooperation.

> The earthly city, which does not live by faith, seeks an earthly peace, and the end it proposes, in the well-ordered concord of civic obedience and rule, is the combination of men's wills to attain the things which are helpful to this life.[27]

The social and governmental order are both based on material needs. The agreement is proposed by the Earthly City, but the citizens of the Heavenly City also enter into and accept it. They make "no scruple to obey the laws of the earthly city, whereby the things necessary for the maintenance of this mortal life are administered." And they form in fact a community with the disciples of the devil in the pursuit of these ends—"as this life is common to both cities, so there is a harmony between them in regard to what belongs to it."[28]

[26]*Ibid.*, p. 707. A common but, I believe erroneous interpretation of the relation of the Heavenly City to the temporal order appears in Francis W. Coker, *Readings in Political Philosophy* (New York: The Macmillan Company, 1938), p. 156: "The Assyrian and Roman empires, representative of the earthly city fell, as all pagan empires must fall. Only the Heavenly City endures; and the Christian Church, aided by a Christianized empire, will eventually bring about the union of all believers under the leadership of the Church. The Heavenly City will then be realized on earth," This is a medieval notion which Coker, unwarrantedly, reads back into St. Augustine. For a similar view see Charles H. McIlwain, *The Growth of Political Thought in the West* (New York: The MacMillan Company, 1932), pp. 155-60. My own view of the matter agrees with the older interpretations by J.N. Figgis and R.W. and A.J. Carlyle, with the recent exegesis by R. Niebuhr, and with the new monograph by Herbert Deane, *The Political and Social Ideas of St. Augustine* (New York: Columbia University Press, 1963).

[27]*The City of God*, p. 695.

[28]*Ibid.*, p. 696.

Once again we find a bridge raised by a noumenalist writer toward the naturalist bank of the metaphysical stream. Politics in Augustinian theory ceases to have a function for the realization of transcendent values and becomes a process for achieving purely material ends. The attitude of the saint toward these goods differs radically from that of the "self-pleaser" of the Earthly City, however. The latter makes material well-being an end in itself, and this is what causes his destruction; he is a complete hedonist. The just man, on the other hand, makes earthly goods and the earthly peace "bear upon the peace of heaven." He considers these things to be no more than necessary evils. He "makes use of this peace only because [he] must, until this mortal condition which necessitates it shall pass away." "The peace which [he] enjoys in this life . . . is rather the solace of . . . misery than the positive enjoyment of felicity."[29]

In this fashion, Augustine reduces the ideal temporal regime to a limited utilitarian order. It is not for the sake of the good life, but of life only. Unlike the classical good regime, it does not involve the whole man in all of his concerns but only the material aspects of life. The spirit is free of the city. There is a special reservation in the political agreement in favor of religious liberty. For the Christian "desires and maintains [this] common agreement" only "so far as [he] can without injuring faith and goodness," "so long as no hindrance to the worship of the one supreme and true God is . . . introduced."[30] And the community of interest which underlies the political order, being only a partial affair, is entirely lacking in the "communion" of the classical *polis*. For how can there be communion between saints and devils? The relationship of the city's members is more like that of the partners to a business contract than the spiritualized friendship (*koinonia*) of the classical ideal. And beyond the limited objects of the contract, there is an unbridgeable gulf between the heavenly and earthly members of the society.

Political Quietism

No particular form of government or society is preferable to any other, the Heavenly City "not scrupling about diversities in the manners, laws, and institutions whereby earthly peace is secured and maintained, but recognizing that, however various these are, they all tend to one and the same end of earthly peace."[31] But what if a government does not effectively guarantee the goods for which the saints enter into the social and political contract? Are they permitted, or enjoined, to rebel in the interest of a fair

[29]*Ibid.*, pp. 695, 696, 707.

[30]*Ibid.*, p. 696.

[31]*Idem.*

and equal distribution of temporal goods? And what about the reservation of religious liberty? Is there a right or obligation of resistance if it is violated?

Augustine's doctrine on all these points is quietistic. While it is profitable for all that "good men should long reign both far and wide,"[32] evil men will often be found in office. And Augustine finds no particular obligation for the Christian to drive them out. In fact he believed that God himself set wicked kings on their thrones as a punishment for sin. There is no demand for good-government crusades, no call for heroic acts of resistance to oppressive rule, no doctrine of political reform whatsoever, for:

> ... the dominion of bad men is hurtful chiefly to themselves who rule ... while those who are put under them in service are not hurt except by their own iniquity. For to the just all the evils imposed on them by unjust rulers are not the punishment of crime, but the test of virtue.[33]

The Christian is thus politically passive. He is enjoined to "pray for kings and those in authority."[34] Even in the matter of religion, he will not resist tyranny actively but suffer patiently the punishment attached to disobedience of the civil law.

This does not mean that the saint has no social responsibilities, but they are fulfilled through private rather than through political action. He will "injure no one, and . . . do good to everyone he can reach." He should especially "endeavour to get his neighbour to love God, since he is ordered to love his neighbour as himself." But there is no suggestion that he try to do this with the public sword. (Augustine is ambivalent on this point. There are passages in his letters which approve the suppression of heresy by public authority.) His responsibility in this regard, and in all social matters, is chiefly to his own circle. "Primarily . . . his own household are his care, for the law of nature and of society gives him readier access to them and greater opportunity of serving them."[35]

The Inevitability of Injustice. Augustine seemed to assume, indeed, that most governments would be radically unjust, that power would be used exploitatively. After all, the power relation itself was the result of sin— Cain built the first city. There was no control of man over man in Paradise. And since the temporal city belongs chiefly to the damned, with the saints only pilgrims in it, their values will permeate it for the most part. Since the lust of the "self-pleaser" for material goods is boundless, his pursuit of wealth,

[32]*Ibid.*, p. 112.
[33]*Idem.*
[34]*Ibid.*, p. 707.
[35]*Ibid.*, pp. 692, 693.

power, and glory leads inevitably to conflct and exploitation. He runs constantly after things which cannot give true order, peace, and justice. And the result is a temporal peace which is always unjust and always unstable.

The result of this radical pessimism about the human condition is to destroy, in Augustine's theory of the empirical city, virtually all notion of a good order to serve as a standard for statesmen. He accepts it as inevitable that injustice will be the norm of government, and "norm" in this context is simply a principle of actual behavior, not a rational standard. As Niebuhr puts it:

> Augustine's realism was excessive. On the basis of his principles he could not distinguish between government and slavery . . . , nor could he distinguish between a commonwealth and a robber band, for both were bound together by collective interest.[36]

One can meaningfully only describe the behavior of the empirical city; it is useless to prescribe for it. As in Book IV of Aristotle's *Politics,* the rational order is dissolved into the actual order and in a more thoroughgoing fashion. Augustine does not even prescribe for stability.

Order and Good Order

Augustine's rejection of political ideals appears to involve him in a dilemma. How can he identify the temporal city with the Earthly City and at the same time give the saints a share in its life, i.e., in the life of a radically unjust and exploitative order? Even though they are only called "pilgrims," their acceptance of the civil law for their temporal good appears to make them partners with the damned in injustice. How can a peace purchased at such a price be considered in any way a "good"?

Augustine recognized the problem and dealt with it in this way. Though the unjust earthly peace cannot be compared with the just peace of the Heavenly City, it is nonetheless peace, and this is a natural good, not an evil in itself.

> Even what is perverted must of necessity be in harmony with and in dependence on, and in some part of the order of things, for otherwise it would have no existence at all. Suppose a man hangs with his head downward, this is certainly a perverted attitude of body and arrangement of its members; for that which nature requires to be above is beneath, and *vice versa.* This perversity disturbs the peace of the body, and is therefore painful. Nevertheless the spirit is at peace with its body and labors for its preservation, and hence the suffering.[37]

[36]Niebuhr, *op. cit.,* p. 127.

[37]*The City of God,* p. 689.

While the hallmark of the Earthly City is strife and disorder, it does not seek strife for its own sake. Rather it seeks peace in order to enjoy the things of this world, while "it makes war in order to attain to this peace." And this "cannot justly be said to be evil."[38] "It abhors . . . the just peace of God, and loves its own unjust peace; but it cannot help loving peace of one kind or other. For there is no vice so clean contrary to nature that it obliterates even the faintest traces of nature."[39]

This is not the same as the doctrine that "whatever is, is right," but it resembles it. We might state Augustine's position rather as: "Whatever is, must have some minimal right in it, otherwise we could not even say that it 'is.' " Or more precisely, "Order is good, disorder is evil. Therefore any kind of order is better than chaos." If the alternative is anarchy and endless conflict, then even an unjust peace has some value. This judgment turns, of course, on the identification of "good" with "being," and of "evil" with "non-being" or "nothing," a heritage from the classical tradition which Augustine so radically reshaped in other respects.

Political Change: The Dynamics of Empire

The third element in Augustine's political theory is an explanation of political change. It is in this part of his theory that we find Augustine's answer to the pagan claim that Christianity, by seducing Romans from allegiance to their traditional gods, had destroyed the empire.

Augustine devotes the first three books of *The City of God* to a demonstration that the worship of the ancient gods of Rome had at no point in her history affected the fortunes of the Imperial City, either favorably or unfavorably. He recounts calamities which befell Rome long before there was a Christian religion, and asks how these could be accounted for if the worship of the municipal gods was supposed to yield power, social harmony, and well-being. If it is the chief work of divinity to bestow material rewards on the faithful, then "why did these gods permit disasters . . . to fall on their worshippers before the preaching of Christ's name offended them?[40] Where were the gods, for example, when, early in the days of the republic, the Gauls captured Rome and burnt the city?

> For at that time the whole city fell into the hands of the enemy, with the single exception of the Capitoline hill; and this too would have been taken, had not—the watchful geese aroused the sleeping gods![41]

[38]*Ibid.*, p. 481.
[39]*Ibid.*, p. 689.
[40]*Ibid.*, p. 42.
[41]*Ibid.*, p. 64.

How did it happen that Troy was destroyed by the Greeks, long before the advent of Christ, though it worshipped the same gods as the Romans, whose forefathers were refugees from the conquered city? And "where . . . was the wisdom of entrusting Rome to the Trojan gods, who had demonstrated their weakness in the loss of Troy?"[42] Augustine cites Sallust's record of innumerable troubles in pre-Christian Rome—class struggles between the First and Second Punic Wars; the terrific losses of men and materiel during the Second Punic War; disastrous floods and fires in Italy in the same period; a welter of cruel civil wars following the destruction of Carthage. The cruelty of Marius and Sulla during the civil wars was no less than that of the Goths in the sack of Rome in 410. And why did the gods not prevent it, since they were then still worshipped in Rome? Why did they not protect Saguntum, a faithful ally of Rome in the Punic Wars, from violent destruction by the enemy?

> Where, then, were the gods who are supposed to be justly worshipped for the slender and delusive prosperity of this world, when the Romans were harrassed by such calamities.?[43]

Finally, if the gods gave empire to the Romans, then who sustained the Assyrians, the Medes, the Persians, and the other empires which waxed and waned before Rome was heard of?

> If the Assyrians had gods of their own, who, so to speak, were more skillful workers [than those of the nations they subdued] in the construction and preservation of the empires, whether are they dead, since they themselves have also lost the empire; or, having been defrauded of their pay, or promised a greater, have they chosen to go over to the Medes, and from them again to the Persians, because Cyrus invited them, and promised them something still more advantageous?[44]

The Causes of Empire

If the *gods* do not give power, unity, and prosperity to states, nor withhold them, then what are the causes of these things? Augustine's answer is, of course, the will of the one true *God*. But, adds Augustine, He does not behave in this matter as the pagan pantheon was supposed to. He does not reward with temporal blessings only those who worship Him and make sacrifices to Him. Rather, He "gives kingly power on earth both to the pious and the impious, as it may please Him, whose good pleasure is always just."[45] "Throughout all the [first] three books already completed . . . we

[42]*Ibid.*, p. 79.

[43]*Ibid.*, p. 92.

[44]*Ibid.*, p. 115.

[45]*Ibid.*, p. 174.

have set forth how much succour God . . . has bestowed on the good and bad, according as it is written, 'Who maketh His sun to rise on the good and the evil, and giveth rain to the just and the unjust.' "[46] God does not, any more than the gods, play favorites in temporal affairs, as Scripture and events both show. St. Augustine has written the definitive answer to all those who in every political crisis from his time to our own have foolishly invoked the special favor of the Deity for their cause and have feverishly searched the auspices for signs of a divine blessing which does not exist.

According to what principles, then, does God give power? For though He acts as He pleases, His "good pleasure is always just." His will is a lawful will which moves according to a fixed pattern, and not at random.

> God, Himself gives earthly kingdoms both to good and bad. Neither does He do this rashly, and, as it were, fortuitously—because He is God, not fortune— but according to the order of things and times.[47]

What are these rules which distribute power independently of human holiness and recognition of the Godhead? We can know "something about the principles which guide His administration, in so far as it has seemed good to Him to explain it." Yet "the order of things and times" is in large part hidden from us. "It is too much for us, and far surpasses our strength."[48] Now, one might expect this sentence would be followed by a statement to the effect that the human mind is incapable of reading the intricacies of the divine heart. But instead Augustine writes that it surpasses our strength "to discuss the hidden things of *men's* hearts."—The Divine law does not operate mysteriously as a *deus ex machina,* but through natural causes. God's will is expressed through the wills of men.

> It does not follow that, though there is for God a certain order of all causes there must therefore be nothing depending on the free exercise of our own wills, for our wills themselves are included in that order of causes which is cer- tain to God, and is embraced by His foreknowledge, for human wills are also causes of human actions; and He who foreknew all the causes of things would certainly among those causes not have been ignorant of our wills. . . . Also by the wills of men I mean the wills either of the good or of the wicked.[49]

This removes the discussion from the transcendental to the empirical level, or, more precisely, adds an empirical dimension to the transcendental reaches of Augustine's thought; for if the heart of God is inscrutable, or is revealed directly only by special revelation, the hearts of men, though in

---

[46]*Ibid.,* p. 111. See also pp. 10, 41, 140.

[47]*Ibid.,* p. 140. See also p. 158.

[48]*Ibid.,* p. 174.

[49]*Ibid.,* pp. 154-55.

their fullness hidden from us, are far more accessible. If human will is a cause, the character of its motives can be inferred from human behavior, which can be empirically observed, and the causes of that behavior thereby made known.

More Planks in the Metaphysical Bridge

And this is precisely how Augustine proceeds to his analysis of the causes of empire. In effect, he asks what human behavior, and what motives underlying that behavior, can we observe which explain the rise and fall of states, for in the observable behavior of men we can trace the line of God's will and law. That is, law for man is not only to be found in what men *ought* to will, but in *what they in fact do will*. But this law does not, as in modern science, move in a meaningless void. The processes of nature remain subservient to the purposes of a just and rational God.

What are the motives that beget power? The chief is the desire for fame and glory. This was the foundation of the Roman Empire.

> Glory they most ardently loved: for it they wished to live, for it they did not hesitate to die. Every other desire was repressed by the strength of their passion for that one thing. At length their country itself, because it seemed inglorious to serve, but glorious to rule and command, they first earnestly desired to be free, and then to be mistress. . . . Eagerness for praise and desire for glory, then, was that which accomplished those many wonderful things, laudable, doubtless and glorious according to human judgment.[50]

It was the desire for glory that caused the overthrow of the Tarquins and the establishment of the republic, for the Romans were too proud to be ruled by kings. And self-government increased the general desire for glory. (Augustine throughout this section of Book V follows the analysis of Sallust and accepts it as a true picture of the causal relations involved. We are reminded of Thucydides.) The ambitions of the elite, the "men of eminent virtue," now led to the building of the empire. Caesar, in particular, "wished for a great empire, an army, and a new war, that he might have a sphere where his genius and virtue might shine forth." And so came wars and out of them the empire.

> Wherefore by the love of liberty in the first place, afterwards also by that of domination and through the desire of praise and glory, they achieved many great things.[51]

The love of glory leads first to the quest for freedom and then for empire.

[50]*Ibid.*, p. 159.
[51]*Ibid.*, pp. 159-60.

But the *desire* of glory alone does not produce the result; a certain discipline of soul must go with it. The ambitious man will even appear unselfish, for he can obtain glory only by serving the common good, conceived as common power. Caesar's desire for honor was realized only by building a powerful state which all could enjoy. The ambitious man may have to act against natural affection. Brutus and Torquatus, for example put their sons to death for the security and power of the state.[52] And by Romulus' crime (the murder of his brother in order to have the sole glory of founding the republic), "the empire was made larger indeed, but inferior."[53] The glory-seeker may also have to jeopardize his own safety, for he wishes "even after death to live in the mouths of [his] admirers." An example of this is found in the Roman general Regulus

> ... who in order not to break his oath, even with his most cruel enemies, returned to them from Rome itself, because ... he could not have the dignity of an honourable citizen at Rome after having been a slave to the Africans, and the Carthaginians put him to death with the utmost tortures, because he had spoken against them in the senate.[54]

The lover of glory will also suppress the desire for wealth and luxurious living, for these things are inimical to power and glory. The Romans exercised their arts "of ruling and commanding, and of subjugating and vanquishing nations ... with the more skill the less they gave themselves up to pleasures, and to enervation of body and mind in coveting and amassing riches."[55] Also, the love of glory will lead to moderate government, for the pursuit of glory is not the same as the pursuit of power for its own sake.

> Whosoever, without possessing that desire of glory which makes one fear to displease those who judge his conduct, desires domination and power, very often seeks to obtain what he loves by most open crimes.[56]

Only the few possess the disciplined character which leads to glory. The many are readily overcome by the other desires, especially the desire for wealth and the pleasures of the belly, and these things breed strife in the state, and weakness. The many (who are found in all social classes) can make no rational assessment of their own interest in glory, and only fear can restrain them from yielding to every whim of passion. Augustine quotes Cato to the effect that "even from the beginning of the state wrongs were

[52]*Ibid.*, pp. 167, 168.

[53]*Ibid.*, p. 462.

[54]*Ibid.*, p. 170.

[55]*Ibid.*, p. 160.

[56]*Ibid.*, p. 172.

committed by the more powerful, which led to the separation of the people from the fathers, besides which there were other internal dissensions.[57] Sound morals were, however, temporarily restored to the state by the Second Punic War, when "great fear began to press upon their disquieted minds, holding them back from those distractions by another and greater anxiety, and bringing them back to civil concord."[58]

The empire, then, was the work of the peculiar excellence of a few men, whose "wisdom and forethought . . . first enabled the republic to endure these evils and mitigated them." It was because of the few that it "waxed greater and greater."—Power in its construction depends upon the character of the elite. But once established, the Roman Empire became, as it were, self-sustaining. Once generated, power obtains a momentum of its own; so that even after the state "had been corrupted by luxury and indolence, again the republic, by its own greatness, was able to bear the vices of its magistrates and generals."[59] It could tolerate bad leadership for a long while. Witness the many emperors, who like Nero Caesar, were "despisers of glory . . . greedy of domination [exceeding] the beasts in the vices of cruelty and luxuriousness."[60]

But the free development of all the passions could not proceed forever without harm to the state, and ultimately produced such profligacy and discord in the state as to make it an easy prey to the barbarians. It was the "pride and effeminacy of the Romans," of long standing, which at last exposed them to the "affliction . . . [of] these latter days."[61]

> However admirable our adversaries say the republic was or is, it is certain that by the testimony of their own most learned writers it had become, long before the coming of Christ, utterly wicked and dissolute, and indeed had no existence, but had been destroyed by profligacy.[62]

And so it goes with all empires. They are founded on and are destroyed by the passions of men. And their peace and order are throughout painful and precarious, marked by intermittent wars, civil strife, violence, cruelty, and suffering. It is only by such "unnatural torments" that they can "attain the huge dimensions of a giant."[63] When men desire power and glory

[57]*Ibid.*, p. 162.

[58]*Idem.*

[59]*Ibid.*, p. 163.

[60]*Ibid.*, p. 172.

[61]*Ibid.*, p. 58.

[62]*Ibid.*, p. 63. See the entire section of Book II which runs from p. 54 to 73.

[63]*Ibid.*, p. 80.

so inordinately and as the highest things, "then it is necessary that misery follow and ever increase."[64]

Augustine, like Aristotle, has built a bridge from the noumenal to the naturalistic world in his description of the processes of proximate causation as they operate in the empirical world. This explains things without any reference to divine causation, and it is the same explanation which the naturalist makes of the same phenomena. Augustine does, of course, add a transcendent dimension to the explanation, completing it by accounting for the motives which the naturalist takes as simply given. But it is separable, nevertheless, from the naturalist parts of the theory.

Noumenalist Capstone. Augustine's transcendental explanation is formulated in the categories of revealed religion which we outlined at the beginning of the chapter. The passions which are the causes of political behavior are those of fallen men, who have turned from the true way. If all men were still either innocent or regenerated by grace, there would be neither power of man over man nor any strife.

> Pride in its perversity apes God. It abhors equality with other men under Him; but instead of His rule, it seeks to impose a rule of its own upon its equals.[65] The quarrel, then, between Romulus and Remus shows how the earthly city is divided against itself . . . . The wicked war with the wicked; the good also war with the wicked. But with the good, good men, or at least perfectly good men, cannot war.[66]

But men are not now good, nor will they be until the end of time—"the carnal lusts of two men, good but not yet perfect, contend together, just as the wicked contend with the wicked, until the health of those who are under the treatment of grace attains final victory."[67] And the whole story of human empires and wars, and the wild passions that underlie them, can be referred for its ultimate efficient cause to the Original Sin of Adam.

> This sickliness . . . is the punishment of the first disobedience. It is therefore not nature but vice.[68]
> Even when we wage a just war, our adversaries must be sinning; and every victory, even though gained by wicked men, is a result of the first judgment of God, who humbles the vanquished either for the sake of removing or of punishing their sins.[69]

[64]*Ibid.*, p. 482.

[65]*Ibid.*, p. 689.

[66]*Ibid.*, p. 483.

[67]*Idem.*

[68]*Idem.*

[69]*Ibid.*, p. 694.

Augustine makes a distinction between the motives of the lovers of glory, who serve their country well, and those dominated by the other appetites. He even speaks of the glory-seekers as "virtuous," and of their deeds as "admirable" and deserving of the reward of earthly glory which God grants them.

> Now . . . with regard to those to whom God did not purpose to give eternal life . . . in His own celestial city, . . . if He had also withheld from them the terrestrial glory of that most excellent empire, a reward would not have been rendered to their good arts—that is, their virtues—by which they sought to attain so great glory.[70]

And he tells us that their admirable self-restraint, in the service of earthly goods, should be a lesson to the servants of the true God.[71] But the love of human praise as the highest good remains a vice, and those who "restrain baser lusts" for such a good "are not indeed holy, but only less base."[72] And they are all members of the Earthly City and condemned to eternal torment.

Vice and the Divine Law.   But even vice has a functional role to play in the divine scheme of things. If the processes of conflict have no such positive role, the inferior orders of tyranny and empire which they produce, despite their wickedness, do have such a positive role to play in God's design, and their lives, which at one level are the result of human causation, at another level are subject to the direction of God. "He regulates [the extent of empire] according to the requirements of His providential government at various times." And "power and domination are not given even to such men [as Nero] save by the providence of the most high God, when He judges that the state of human affairs is worthy of such lords."[73] Even depraved nature is bound throughout by law, though God's law is not bound by this depravity. Indeed, God occasionally elevates to the seat of power a just man, like Constantine, so that those who worship Him for the sake of eternal life will not think that this world is in the control of a demoniacal power. However, to prevent religion from becoming a football of politics, He destroys the governments of the saints as well as those of the glory-lovers.

> Lest any emperor should become a Christian in order to merit the happiness of Constantine, when every one should be a Christian for the sake of eternal life, God took away Jovian far sooner than Julian, and permitted that Gratian should be slain by the sword of a tyrant.[74]

[70]*Ibid.*, p. 165.

[71]*Ibid.*, p. 163.

[72]*Idem.*

[73]*Ibid.*, pp. 172, 181.

[74]*Ibid.*, p. 179.

In the face of the great depravity of fallen nature, to give temporal power to the City of God is to corrupt that city and reduce it to its earthly counterpart. There is no just City of God except in heaven.

Tradition Transformed

In the work of Augustine, political philosophy has been transmuted into Christian theology. The result is radically to transform the traditional idea of the good life in the good society by removing the notion of perfection from earth to heaven. The change produces a fundamental alteration in man's attitude toward temporal politics. No longer the be-all and end-all of life, politics has become less important. The city no longer demands intense participation as a condition of virtue and happiness, because it can no longer bestow virtue and happiness.

Nonetheless, the transformation does retain much of the tradition. All the accepted ethical rules of social and political life are reaffirmed and sanctified. While Augustine shares the skepticism of the Sophist that they will not be closely observed, especially when they clash with interest, they remain the substance of moral obligation, not a calculated utility. The purposes of social life and political life are still divine purposes, though for the first time they become distinct from and humbler than the purposes of life itself, and it is expected that they will be much abused and perverted to unsocial ends. The same behavior is expected of the good man as in the traditional *Polis*. That it be forthcoming, however, is no longer a crucial matter.

Summary

Augustine's *City of God* contains the elements of a complete politics. It deals with all the major questions—the nature of the best regime, the problem of the best possible regime, and the mechanics of actual regimes. The theories in all three areas are carefully related to one another in a systematic whole, which in turn is articulated in a precise and careful way with a general philosophy of life. Based on a noumenalist view of reality, Augustine's theory also incorporates much that is typical of naturalist explanations. It is a broad-ranging synthesis.

Not all parts of the theory are fully developed however, except for the subject of the best regime, which is exhaustively treated. There is no institutional detail at all, though we have a few interesting hypotheses concerning the role of glory as a political motive, the generation of political momentum, the function and character of the elite, and the difficulties of establishing peaceful processes. Augustine's sketchiness in these areas is understandable in light of his orientation to the political problem as a whole.

His book is designed to demonstrate at once the inexorable character of existing political processes and their unimportance and vanity, and to direct the thoughts of his readers beyond these things, which they cannot change, to the private and interior life where they are free to act.

One particularly important gap in Augustine's theory is the absence of a detailed prescription for the behavior of the just man, or the man who would be just, who happens to get involved in the politics of the Earthly City. The just man is part of the political community; he has a contractual relationship with the Earthly City. Yet he appears to be an almost perfectly passive partner in the society; he accepts whatever regime is established. Augustine does at times speak of just men occupying the seats of authority, and he says that all persons benefit by their rule, but he gives them no guidelines for action. What kinds of institutions should they seek to establish? How should they deal with other citizens envying their power? Don't Christian rulers need more detailed information about the political behavior of the Earthly City to be able to control it? How should they act toward hostile powers abroad? If they govern a city which has become great through injustice, should they strive to maintain its power, and by what means? Or should they reduce the boundaries of empire? A Christian may be politically quiet in his home, but as legislator or administrator he must act. Augustine provides little direction, though he may have thought the good man would know how to act in any situation through God's grace.

But despite these weaknesses, Augustine's book has great value, and especially for our times. It is a wonderful tonic, as Augustine's modern disciples whom we deal with in the next section have shown, for those who think of the political problem as a technical rather than a moral issue, and who suppose it is practically possible to establish a rational political order in which the problem of equality and the problem of violence have been solved by scientific manipulation.

Augustinianism Today: The "Realist" School of Politics

The Augustinian approach to the study of politics experienced during the 1950s a significant revival in the work of a group of American scholars who came to be known as the "realist" school. The patriarch and first citizen of the group was Reinhold Niebuhr, the well-known theologian and student of politics. Other leading members include Hans Morgenthau and Kenneth Thompson, noted political scientists, and George Kennan and Charles Burton Marshall, two diplomats who are also scholars. The foreign policy of Henry Kissinger and the stance taken by Daniel Patrick Moynihan as Ambassador to the United Nations also revealed "realist" premises.

These men have arrived at an Augustinian position partly by independent roads and partly through Niebuhr's inspiration. And at least one of them, Professor Morgenthau, owes as much of this intellectual orientation to Edmund Burke as to St. Augustine. But Burkean and Augustinian theories share several fundamental assumptions and fit well together though there are some important nuances of difference.[75]

Realism versus Rationalism

Reinhold Niebuhr's book *Moral Man and Immoral Society* (1932) is the seminal work of the realist literature, most of which has appeared during and since World War II. All these writings represent a reaction to and a polemic against the rationalist assumptions of American thinking about politics, and especially about international politics, which had dominated the American scene from before the turn of the nineteenth century.

It seemed to the realist writers that one could give no adequate explanation of twentieth-century politics, and especially of the two great cataclysms, within the rationalist frame of reference which was a legacy of the neoclassical Enlightenment of the eighteenth century. They also believed that an American foreign policy which continued to be based on rationalist assumptions might prove disastrous to America and to her allies. The rationalist assumptions that the spread of democratic institutions around the world, the development of international law, and the creation of international institutions such as the World Court and League of Nations would "make the world safe" had proven false. The reality was one of increasing violence and brutality in international politics and the proliferation of iron-handed authoritarian governments.

[75]Morgenthau's image of the thought of the prerationalist age, with which he associates his own position, is distinctly more Augustinian than Burkean in flavor, as witness the following passage:

"The prerationalist age is aware of the existence of two forces—God and the devil, life and death, light and darkness, good and evil, reason and passion—which struggle for dominance in the world. There is no progress toward the good noticeable from year to year, but undecided conflict which sees today good, tomorrow evil, prevail; and only at the end of time, immeasurably removed from the here and now of our earthly life, the ultimate triumph of the forces of goodness and light will be assured.

Out of this everlasting and ever undecided struggle there arises one of the roots of what might be called the tragic sense of life, the awareness of unresolvable discord, contradictions, and conflicts which are inherent in the nature of things and which human reason is powerless to solve." Hans Morgenthau, *Scientific Man and Power Politics* (Chicago: University of Chicago Press, 1946), pp. 205-6.

This reads like a paraphrase of the argument of the *City of God;* it is decidedly more pessimistic about the realization of a good order in the here and now than is Thomism, which forms a main current of thought in what Morgenthau calls the "prerationalist age." And it is more pessimistic also than Burke (the prerationalist of the Age of Reason), whose antecedents are Thomistic rather than Augustinian. Burke thought of the Christian-aristocratic culture of pre-1789 Europe, which had been slowly developed over the ages, as a close approximation to an ideal order.

Hans Morgenthau stated the problem and the challenge especially well in his *Scientific Man and Power Politics* of 1946. "The very crisis of civilization," he wrote, "reveals itself in the tenacity with which it clings to its assumptions in the face of ever more potent signs that its rationalist philosophy cannot give meaning to the experience of the mid-twentieth century."[76] What was wrong with the rationalist approach? It embraced a fundamentally erroneous conception of man, of society, and of politics.

> [This school] believes that a rational and moral political order, derived from universally valid abstract principles, can be achieved here and now. It assumes the essential goodness and infinite malleability of human nature and attributes the failure of the social order to measure up to the rational standards to lack of knowledge and understanding, obsolescent social institutions, or the depravity of certain isolated individuals or groups. It trusts in education, reform, and the sporadic use of force to remedy these deficiencies.[77]

The reader will recognize in this characterization of the assumptions of neoclassical rationalism some elements of the original classical rationalism against which Augustine reacted in the *City of God* (noting, in addition, that the neoclassic rationalism displays a far greater optimism about the establishment of a perfect order in the here and now).

The proponents of the rationalist philosophy were found in all stations of American life—among the academic intelligentsia, in government, in the clergy, in the street. Niebuhr, in *Moral Man and Immoral Society,* singled out for special attack the rationalist intellectuals: the philosopher and educator John Dewey; sociologist and social psychologists Kimball Young, Floyd Allport, Clarence March Case, George M. Stratton, and Howard Odum; the economist Sir Arthur Salter, and certain rationalist clergy such as Justin Wroe Nixon and William Adams Brown.

Morgenthau has specialized his writing in the field of foreign policy and international politics, and has devoted much of his effort to a critique of the political theories and policies of rationalist statesmen such as Woodrow Wilson and Cordell Hull. In this area his work has been paralleled and supported by Kennan, Thompson, and Marshall.

The basic axioms of the realist position on the nature of man, society, and politics have been summarized by Morgenthau in these terms:

> [Realism] believes that the world, imperfect as it is from the rational point of view, is the result of forces which are inherent in human nature. To improve the world one must work with those forces, not against them. This being inherrently a world of opposing interests and of conflict among them, moral principles can never be fully realized, but at best approximated through the ever

---

[76]Morgenthau, *op. cit.*, p. 2.

[77]Hans J. Morgenthau, "Another Great Debate: The National Interest of the United States," *American Political Science Review,* XLVI (1952), pp. 961-62.

temporary balancing of interests and the ever precarious settlement of conflicts. This school, then, sees in a system of checks and balances a universal
principle for all pluralist societies. It appeals to historic precedent rather than
abstract principles, and aims at achievement of the lesser evil rather than of
the absolute good.[78]

The Augustinian elements in this capsule of realist theory are immediately
evident. With Augustine the realists reject the formulation of the political
problem as a problem of human perfection and aim rather at the limited
goods of peace and security. Even here they suppose that the most that can
be hoped for is a precarious peace and an unstable balance of interests.
Politics is and must remain a struggle for domination among competing
egos.

There is also a difference from the original Augustinian theory to be
seen in this passage, for the realists are not resigned to the fact of unjust
power but rather address themselves to the hard problem of developing
strategies for foiling the imperialistic intentions of the citizens of the Earthly
City—filling the gap in Augustine's work which we noted above (p. 149).
Unlike the rationalists, they do not assume that the behavior of the Earthly
City can be reformed by sweet reason, legal norms, or psychotherapy. The
struggle for power will go on for all time:

> The struggle for power is universal in time and space and is an undeniable fact
> of experience. . . . The decisive argument against the opinion that the struggle
> for power on the international scene is a mere historic accident can . . . be
> derived from the nature of domestic politics. . . . Both domestic and inter-
> national politics are a struggle for power, modified only by the different condi-
> tions under which this struggle takes place in the domestic and in the inter-
> national spheres.[79]

Nevertheless, aggression, the realists believe, can at least to some extent be
limited by the strategic employment of countervailing power and by the
development of a more cohesive international community.

The Principles of International Politics.   The writings of Morgenthau,
Kennan, and Thompson constitute a descriptive theory of international
politics, as well as an elaboration of the principles of statecraft for securing
the liberty of states against imperialist pressures and for mitigating and institutionalizing the use of force in international politics. The most
systematic statement of these theories is contained in Hans Morgenthau's
Politics Among Nations, which was first published in 1948. The traditional
writings in this field had either treated the subject nontheoretically, as recent

[78]*Ibid.,* p. 962.

[79]Hans Morgenthau, *Politics Among Nations,* 2d. rev. ed. (New York: Alfred
A. Knopf, Inc., 1954), pp. 30–31.

history, or they had focused on a description of existing international legal institutions, without inquiring into the reasons for their inadequacy or into the political and social forces which underpin them. Or they had speculated about the ideal order and blueprinted utopian schemes of international and supranational organization.[80] Morgenthau's new approach, which attempted a theoretical understanding of the social, psychological, and moral forces determining the relations of states, immediately received a wide response and soon became one of the most widely adopted college texts in international politics courses.

The Balance of Power. A chief element in Morgenthau's theory of international politics is the balance of power concept. In any political system, if the parts are to be secure and autonomous, and if the system is to be stable, an equilibrium of forces must arise.

> The equilibrium must aim at preventing any element from gaining ascendance over the others. The means employed to maintain the equilibrium consist in allowing the different elements to pursue their opposing tendencies up to the point where the tendency of one is not so strong as to overcome the tendency of the others, but strong enough to prevent the others from overcoming its own.[81]

The principle is not limited to application in the international field. Many instances of its use are found in domestic politics, Morgenthau notes. Multiparty systems in parliamentary bodies frequently produce two leading minority groups in opposition to one another. A third group will act as the holder of the balance, joining the weaker of the two to impose a check upon the stronger. The phenomenon is also found in two-party systems such as that of the United States.

> Congress displayed the typical configuration of this checking and balancing process when, especially in the last years of the administration of Franklin D. Roosevelt and during most of Truman's, the Southern Democrats constituted themselves a third party, voting on many issues with the Republican minority. They thus checked not only the Democratic majority in Congress, but also the executive branch, which, too, was controlled by the Democratic party.[82]

The equilibrium concept also appears as an organizing principle of the constitutional order, as in the checks and balances system which the Framers quite self-consciously wrote into the Constitution of the United States.

In international politics, from the time of the establishment of the

[80]*Ibid.*, p. 3. Citation of comment on the state of the discipline by Grayson Kirk.

[81]*Ibid.*, p. 157.

[82]*Ibid.*, p. 158.

state system on a stable footing in 1648, following the close of the wars of
the Reformation, balance of power politics had been consistently pursued
down to the First World War by all states desirous of preserving the state
system. But following the First World War, many Western statesmen,
shocked at the magnitude and terrible cost of the war, became disillusioned
in it as a principle of foreign policy and tended to blame the war on the principle. A substitute had to be found for a system which could maintain itself
only through the constant hazard of conflict and, frequently, the actuality of
extensive wars. It was supposed that formal organizations such as the
League of Nations, based on the principle of collective security, could
provide this substitute.

It is Morgenthau's argument that in an international society such as
ours, in which there is little felt community of interest and in which
ideological consensus is nonexistent, this is necessarily a vain hope. One
cannot legislate a free, peaceful, and cooperative society through formal
legal norms. And Morgenthau thinks that the experience of the 1930s proves
his case. The German aggressor was able to take advantage of the Allies'
lack of concern for the balance of power to build a Central European empire
without opposition between 1934 and 1939. And when the West finally
realized what was happening, a more terrible war resulted than the limited
conflict which might have been the upshot of an earlier attempt to restore
the power equilibrium.

The apparently continued hope of Western statesmen after World
War II that collective security might still work as a substitute for the balance
of power sparked Morgenthau's crusade for a return to the equilibrium
principle:

> In recent times, the conviction that the struggle for power can be eliminated
> from the international scene has been connected with the great attempts at
> organizing the world, such as the League of Nations and the United Nations.
> Thus Cordell Hull, then Secretary of State, declared in 1943 on his return from
> the Moscow Conference, which laid the groundwork for the United Nations,
> that the new international organization would mean the end of power politics
> and usher in a new era of international collaboration. Mr. Philip Noel-Baker,
> then British minister of State, declared in 1946 in the House of Commons that
> the British government was "determined to use the institutions of the United
> Nations to kill power politics in order that, by the methods of democracy, the
> will of the people shall prevail."[83]

Morgenthau's message is spelled out in *Politics Among Nations* and
also in a volume of 1951 entitled *In Defense of the National Interest*. The
argument against legalism and for the balancing principle as a foundation of
rational foreign policy has also been made with extreme cogency by George

[83]*Ibid.*, pp. 29, 30.

F. Kennan in his *American Diplomacy, 1900–1950*, which appeared in the same year. Since that time the realist position seems to have won quite wide acceptance in a kind of Hegelian fusion with our traditional legalist and moralist proclivities, both in government circles and in public opinion at large, as William Carleton indicates:

> Americans were in world politics . . . to stay; and they were learning. They were learning that foreign policy is never-ending and that it cannot be turned on and off; that tensions and crisis situations are more or less normal; that there are many aspects and many values involved in any given international situation; that problems are rarely solved; . . . that the "solutions" to given problems are likely in turn to lead to new problems and challenges.
>
> Americans were learning, too, that there is no single approach to international relations. At first the American approach had been legalistic and moralistic. Then after 1945 Americans discovered the importance of power, of power-politics, . . . and they tended to put too much reliance on armaments and military alliances. Now they were learning that power, vastly important as it is, is not the only or even always decisive factor in international relations. Americans were learning that foreign policy, if it is to touch reality at all points, must avoid the single-track approach and be positively and avowedly pluralistic, as diverse and varied as history, as inclusive as life itself.[84]

Building World Community. Realist political theory does not argue that the stable system can rest on a power equilibrium alone. Morgenthau's work, in fact, stresses the weakness of the balancing principle taken alone. He writes, for example:

> The new balance of power is a mechanism which contains in itself the potentialities for unheard-of-good as well as for unprecedented evil. Which of these potentialities will be realized depends not upon the mechanics of the balance of power, but upon moral and material forces which use that mechanism for the realization of their ends.[85]

To the balancing principle must be added the principle of hard-headed and perennial negotiation of differences between the opposing camps, and pragmatic compromises of nonvital interest. A skilled diplomacy of negotiation is a second vital institution for the maintenance of peace and security. And beyond this, the realists recognize, work must go constantly forward on the construction of the material and psychological foundations of a world community. As St. Augustine pointed out, the chief foundation of every peaceful order is a community of interest and desire. And in temporal societies that order can proceed from *any* kind of common interest; it need

[84]William G. Carleton, *The Revolution in American Foreign Policy* (New York: Random House, 1957), p. 152. Copyright 1954, 1957 by Random House, Inc.

[85]*Politics Among Nations*, 1948, p. 285.

not be community based on the highest values possible. Robber bands and kingdoms, are, with reference to their principle of unity, not fundamentally different.

At what level, then, can there be a realistic approach to the construction of a world community of interest? On this question Morgenthau quotes with approval a statement by David Mitrany of the philosophy underlying the social and economic activities of the specialized agencies of the United Nations. The object is:

> to overlay political divisions with a spreading web of international activities and agencies, in which and through which the interests and life of all the nations would be gradually integrated. . . . Any effective international system . . . must care as much as possible for common needs that are evident, while presuming as little as possible upon a social unity which is only latent and unrecognized. . . . The community itself will acquire a living body not through a written act of faith but through active organic development. . . . That trend is to organize government along the lines of specific ends and needs, and according to the conditions of their time and place, in lieu of the traditional organization on the basis of a set constitutional division of jurisdiction of rights and powers. . . . The functional approach . . . would help the growth of such positive and constructive common work, of common habits and interests, making frontier lines meaningless by overlaying them with a natural growth of common activities and common administrative agencies.[86]

It may be possible to build, if only gradually, a world community of interest through the work of international agencies which administer to very basic material human needs, needs which are shared by thieves and honest men, by the citizens of the Earthly and the Heavenly Cities.

Power Politics and Right. The ethical problem of the just man involved in the toils of power politics, a great gap in Augustinian theory, has been extensively treated by the realists. The leading book in this area is Morgenthau's *In Defense of the National Interest.* The central thesis of the volume is that one cannot choose between moral principles and power politics but that the two must be married to one another in any valid ethical system.

> The fundamental error that has thwarted American foreign policy in thought and action is the antithesis of national interest and moral principles. The equation of political moralizing with morality and of political realism with immorality is itself untenable. The choice is not between moral principles and the national interest, devoid of moral dignity, but between one set of moral princi-

[86]David Mitrany, *A Working Peace System* (London: National Peace Council, 4th ed. with new Introduction, 1946), quoted in Morgenthau, *Politics Among Nations*, 2d. rev. ed., p. 493.

ples divorced from political reality, and another set of moral principles derived from political reality.[87]

The pursuit of abstract moral principles without attention to the realities of the distribution of power, Morgenthau argues, can in fact lead to an immoral result. It may lead a state to commit national suicide, and thereby destroy the common good of an entire society of men. The national interest itself has a moral dignity. And there is no principle of morality that a state, like an individual, should lay down its life for others. To do so would in fact simply invite further injustice, for the power with which the suicide might have defended the right would be gone. Further, real meaning can be given to moral principles only within an integrated society. (Communities are held together by the things their members love in common.) In disorganized societies, like the community of nations as a whole, principles such as justice and equality have no concrete and universally accepted meaning. Morgenthau also discusses the other side of the coin. Moralizing has often been simply a facade for political aggrandizement, either conscious or unconscious, and cruel wars have been fought in the name of God and for the establishment of justice. Like Augustine, Morgenthau argues that the more modest values of temporal security and peace be given primary status as social ends.[88] By defining a rule of ethical behavior, Morgenthau has closed a gap in the Augustinian synthesis of "fact" with "value."

Realist Method

Though Morgenthau occasionally speaks of his work as a science of politics, he differs from the so-called behavioral writers in the field, who stand more in the rationalist tradition, in his Augustinian skepticism about the extent to which the order of international politics can be discovered and about the degree of prediction and control possible.[89] In the introduction to the first edition of *Politics Among Nations*, for example, he writes:

> The first lesson which the student of international politics must learn and never forget is that the complexities of international affairs make simple solutions and trustworthy prophecies impossible. It is here that the scholar and the charlatan part company. Knowledge of the forces which determine politics

[87]Hans Morgenthau, *In Defense of the National Interest* (New York: Alfred A. Knopf, Inc., 1951), p. 33.

[88]See also Kenneth W. Thompson, *Christian Ethics and the Dilemmas of Foreign Policy* (Durham, N.C.: Duke University Press), 1959.

[89]In Chapter 5 of his *Scientific Man and Power Politics*, Morgenthau has elaborated a detailed critique of the natural science approach to the study of politics.

among nations, and knowledge of the ways by which their political relations proceed, reveals the ambiguity of the facts of international politics. In every political situation contradictory tendencies are at play. One of these tendencies is more likely to prevail under certain conditions than others. But which tendency actually will prevail is anybody's guess. The best the scholar can do, then, is to trace the different tendencies which, as potentialities, are inherent in a certain international situation. He can point out the different conditions which make it more likely for one tendency to prevail than for another, and, finally, assess the probabilities for the different conditions and tendencies to prevail in actuality.[90]

This recognition by the realists of the enormous complexity of social phenomena and their belief that these phenomena cannot be reduced to a precise scientific order probably underlie their lack of interest in the various techniques for the quantitative measurement of political patterns developed by the behavioralists. Morgenthau and Thompson in particular seem to assume that they can sufficiently understand the basic patterns and causes of political behavior from a sophisticated reading of history and from common-sense analysis of public and private records. So only general rules of thumb can be developed by the scholar for the guidance of the statesman, not precise calculative and predictive instruments. And for the elaboration of such principles of prudence no elaborate scientific apparatus is necessary. Insight plus the traditional methods of historical and political scholarship are adequate.

Sources of the Realist Postulates.   The assumptions of the realists about the nature of man and of politics rest in large part on theological foundations similar to those of the parallel assumptions of St. Augustine. Niebuhr, for example, in the foreword to *The Children of Light and the Children of Darkness* says that the political philosophy contained in the book was "informed by [a] belief in a Christian view of human nature." And in the first chapter he presents a new variation of the Augustinian theme of the origins of bad will and self-interest in pride.

Possessing a darkly unconscious sense of his insignificance in the total scheme of things he seeks to compensate for his insignificance by pretensions of pride. The conflicts between men are thus never simple conflicts between competing survival impulses. They are conflicts in which each man or group seeks to guard its power and prestige against the peril of competing expressions of power and pride.[91]

In another place he says the "Christian doctrine of original sin . . . makes an important contribution to any adequate social and political theory the lack

[90]*Politics Among Nations*, 1948, pp. 6–7.

[91]Reinhold Niebuhr, *The Children of Light and the Children of Darkness* (New York: Charles Scribner's Sons, 1944), pp. xiii, 20.

of which has robbed bourgeois theory of real wisdom; for it emphasizes a fact which every page of human history attests."[92]

Hans Morgenthau, too, grounds his view of man and of politics in large part on theological foundations. In speaking of man's drive for power, for example, he usually uses the expression "lust for power," which implies an ethical frame of reference, rather than the ethically neutral expression "power drive" preferred by the psychologist. In explaining the roots of man's selfishness he cites Luther (who was an Augustinian monk) to the effect that "concupiscence is insuperable." He speaks of the ubiquity of the craving for power, and says that "here is the element of corruption and sin which injects even into the best intentions at least a drop of evil and thus spoils it." And he attributes man's boundless desire for power to his desire to dethrone God:

> While man's vital needs are capable of satisfaction, his lust for power would be satisfied only if the last man became an object of his domination, there being nobody above or beside him, if he became like God.[93]

Nevertheless, it does not seem necessary that one be committed to Judaeo-Christian theology to accept the principles of realist political theory. Many of the basic assumptions of the realists, as we shall see, are shared by skeptics and materialists, such as Niccolo Machiavelli, Thomas Hobbes, and Friedrich Nietzsche. Also Niebuhr has pointed out the similarity of the Augustinian view of human nature to that developed by Freudian psychology. Niebuhr, in fact, is more like the modern psychologist than like St. Augustine in his belief that at least to some degree progress can be made gradually to a more just and rational world society than we now have, that the influence of the irrational "Id" can be gradually reduced. And he sees an important role for the secular social scientist in this development.

> The development of reason and the growth of mind makes for increasingly just relations not only by bringing all impulses in society into reference with, and under the control of, an inclusive social ideal, but also by increasing the penetration with which all factors in the social situation are analyzed. The psychological sciences discover and analyse the intricate web of motivation, which lies at the base of all human actions. The social sciences trace the consequences of human behavior into the farthest reaches of social life. They are specialised and yet typical efforts of a growing human intelligence, to come into possession of all facts relevant to human conduct. If the psychological scientist aids men in analyzing their true motives, and in separating their inevitable pretensions from their actual desires, which they are intended to hide, he may increase the purity of social morality. If the social scientist is able to point out that traditional and customary social policies do not have the

[92]*Ibid.*, p. 16.

[93]See *Scientific Man and Power Politics*, pp. 187-96.

results, intended or pretended by those who champion them, honest social intentions will find more adequate instruments for the attainment of their ends and dishonest pretensions will be unmasked.[94]

Yet Niebuhr and the others retain at bottom a skepticism about a very great extension of rationality and order in social life, which probably can have no other foundation than a theological principle like the doctrine of Original Sin. A few pages following the optimistic passage just quoted, Niebuhr writes:

> but the limits of reason make it inevitable that pure moral action, particularly in the intricate, complex and collective relationships, should be an impossible goal. Men will never be wholly reasonable, and the proportion of reason to impulse becomes increasingly negative when we proceed from the life of individuals to that of social groups, among whom a common mind and purpose is always more or less inchoate and transitory, and who depend therefore upon a common impulse to bind them together.[95]

Bibliographical Note

For a biography of Augustine, see Peter R.L. Brown, *Augustine of Hippo*, Berkeley: University of California Press, 1967. The leading analysis of Augustine's political theory is Herbert Deane, *The Political and Social Ideas of St. Augustine,* New York: Columbia University Press, 1963. This supplants John Neville Figgis, *The Political Aspects of Saint Augustine's "City of God"*, London: Longmans, Green & Company, Ltd., 1921, for years the leading commentary. Two briefer studies are Norman H. Baynes, *The Political Ideas of Saint Augustine's "De Civitate Dei,"* Historical Association Pamphlet No. 104, London: G. Bell & Sons, Ltd., 1936, and Hans Daniel Friberg, *Love and Justice in Political Theory, A Study of Augustine's Definition of the Commonwealth,* University of Chicago Ph.D. Thesis, 1944. A new study focusing on Augustine's philosophy of history is Gordon L. Keyes, *Christian Faith and the Interpretation of History*, Lincoln: University of Nebraska Press, 1966.

The realist literature is extensive. In addition to the works cited in the footnotes, see Reinhold Niebuhr, *Christianity and Power Politics*, NewYork: Charles Scribner's Sons, 1940, and *The Structure of Nations and Empires*, New York: Charles Scribner's Sons, 1959. A selection of Niebuhr's political writings is found in Harry R. Davis and Robert C. Good, eds., *Reinhold Niebuhr on Politics,* New York: Charles Scribner's Sons, 1960. An interesting discussion of the intermingling of Kantian and other liberal con-

---

[94]Niebuhr, *Moral Man and Immoral Society* (New York: Charles Scribner's Sons. 1932), p. 32.

[95]*Ibid.*, pp. 34–35.

cepts with Augustinianism in Niebuhr's political theory is Wilson Carey McWilliams, "Reinhold Niebuhr: New Orthodoxy for Old Liberalism," *American Political Science Review,* Vol. LVI, No. 4, Dec. 1962, pp. 874-85. Additional books by Hans Morgenthau are *Dilemmas of Politics,* Chicago: University of Chicago Press, 1958, and *The Purpose of American Politics,* New York: Alfred A. Knopf, Inc., 1960. See also Kenneth W. Thompson, *Political Realism and the Crisis of World Politics,* Princeton, N.J.: Princeton University Press, 1960.

The realist thesis has stirred up one of the stormiest polemics ever carried on in the literature of American political science. Opponents of the Augustinian axiology have rallied around an "idealist" banner and have produced a large number of scholarly broadsides against what they mistakenly have called the Machiavellianism of the realist school. See especially Frank Tannenbaum, "The Balance of Power versus the Coordinate State," *Political Science Quarterly*, Vol. LXVII, June 1952, p. 173 ff, and Robert W. Tucker, "Professor Morgenthau's Theory of Political Realism," in *American Political Science Review,* Vol. XLVI, Mar. 1952, p. 214 ff. Also see Morgenthau's answer, "Another 'Great Debate': The National Interest of the United States," *American Political Science Review,* Vol. XLVI, Dec. 1952, p. 961 ff. A full-length reply to the realists is Thomas I. Cook and Malcolm Moos, *Power Through Purpose: The Realism of Idealism as a Basis for Foreign Policy,* Baltimore: Johns Hopkins University Press, 1954.

Chapter 5

Temporal Virtue
in the Christian Commonwealth:
St. Thomas and Maritain

Thomism has received among its proponents the name *philosophia perennis* because of its long existence as a school of thought and its recurrent revitalization after periods of decay. Originally a designation of the work of the thirteenth-century Dominican scholar Thomas Aquinas, Thomism now refers to a large body of philosophical and theological writings produced in continuous stream from medieval times down to the present, in which we find the principles of St. Thomas adapted and reformulated to meet the intellectual challenges of new historical situations. Particularly in its political aspects, the original Thomist doctrine has undergone significant variations in every age, yet retained its kernel of fundamental assumptions. St. Thomas himself wrote during the heyday of the medieval *Respublica Christiana,* and his political thought reflects the institutions of feudal Europe, united by the government of the Catholic Church. In the sixteenth and seventeenth centuries, following the collapse of this order and the emergence of the modern system of sovereign and secular states, Francis of Vittoria and the Jesuit scholars Molina, Suarez, and Bellarmine added to Thomist political and legal theory a whole new branch of international legal principles and a new theory of church and state. The present crisis of the liberal order, both in its domestic and international aspects, has given rise to yet another spate of Thomist political writings.

This latest revival, signaled by the social encyclicals of Pope Leo XIII in the last quarter of the nineteenth century, has produced Thomist treatises by clerics and laymen, and by Catholics and non-Catholics alike. Here in the United States the new Thomism is perhaps best known in the work of a French Catholic layman, Jacques Maritain, who has traveled widely in this country lecturing at our principal universities. Maritain's presence at the University of Chicago, in fact, stimulated the development of a Thomist circle there which included such prominent non-Catholic scholars as Robert Maynard Hutchins, President (later Chancellor) of the University from 1929 to 1951, and Mortimer Adler, professor of the philosophy of law at Chicago from 1930 to 1952, and now director of the Institute for Philosophical Research in San Francisco. After the departure of these three men, Thomism continued to be represented in the Chicago curriculum in the teaching of Yves Simon, a former pupil of Maritain, who was on the faculty of the Committee for Social Thought until his death in 1961.

A Thirteenth Century Optimist

The thirteenth century was a time of revived hope for a rational world, a natural emotion in the building of a new culture after a period of flux. While the doctrines of St. Augustine were conceived in a context of political and social decomposition, the death throes of antique civilization, Thomism represented the soaring hopes of a new Europe. By the thirteenth century the barbaric peoples who overran the Roman Empire had settled down in fixed territorial jurisdictions and were in process of civilizing themselves. This meant the exchange of the unthinking ways of ancestral custom for a self-conscious and rational approach to life. And just as the adolescent, full of ideals, challenges the unjust world he has inherited, so the young Europe set out with idealism to achieve Augustine's "City of God." This was no longer the weary pilgrim's home in a far-off heaven, but an earthly *Respublica Christiana* to be built in the here and now. It would not mean the end of violence. But the Papal-Imperial conflicts, the Crusades, the Albigensian suppression were growing pains rather than a death agony.

Monsignor D'Arcy epitomizes the age well when he writes:

> The thirteenth century, in particular, was an age in which men tried to move mountains. The Papacy and the Empire alike dreamed of universal jurisdiction; the universities, lately established, were packed with youth, anxious and determined to explore and master all the far continents of thought. In the perspective of history we can now see that the characteristic of the century was architectural or formative. In England and France common law and jurisprudence took shape, Magna Carta was signed, St. Louis dispensed justice under an oak tree at Vincennes, and universities like Paris received their permanent charters and statutes. Not that this quest for "the tranquillity of order" brought with it peace. . . . As is usual in a period of vaulting ambition . . . order is sought at the point of a sword. . . .
>
> We see, then, that the times in which St. Thomas lived needed a philosophic and Christian genius to shape architecturally the many tendencies now freely manifesting themselves. Europe had passed out of the dark ages, and with that liberation had come a race of great personalities and a spirit of daring enterprise.[1]

[1]M. C. D'Arcy, *Thomas Aquinas* (Boston: Little, Brown & Co., 1930), pp. 3-4, 8.

Thomist political theory is therefore optimistic about the politics of this world where Augustinianism is pessimistic. Augustinians like Reinhold Niebuhr have gone so far in remarking the contrast as to compare Thomistic rationalism with that of the French Enlightenment. This optimism is epitomized in St. Thomas' maxim, *"Gratia non tollit naturam, sed perficit"* ("Grace does not do away with the natural order, but rather perfects it"). And it stands in radical contrast to the Augustinian insistence on the depravity of human nature since the Fall. To the Augustinian, natural inclinations have become wholly corrupt and evil. By nature, every man is a citizen of the *Civitas Terrena*. Grace must conquer nature and chain it up in order to release citizens for the Heavenly City. But Thomas saw grace and nature in an entirely different relationship, not locked in struggle but rather cooperating for the perfection of man, a state reflecting the temporal dimension of classical theory as well as the new note of salvation.

Crosscurrents

Our own time, by contrast with both the fifth and thirteenth centuries, is full of ambiguities. On the one hand, the brutalities of totalitarian concentration camps and organized terror, the decline of traditional morality and the surge of criminal violence in the world's growing urban centers, the growing stockpiles of atomic weapons, deep and widespread alienation from the life-style of the modern state, and massive pollution of the environment—all seem to herald a new collapse of civilization. On the other hand, there are absolutely opposite indicators in the political and social emancipation of the black and other colored peoples of the world in the last few years, and in the promise now held out by modern sicence for the eventual freedom of all humanity from disease, drudgery, and poverty.

These ambiguities perhaps explain why Augustinian pessimists and Thomist optimists can both flourish in today's world. They may also explain the presence of antithetical elements in the writings of each school. We have already noted the modified doctrine of rational progress strangely present in Niebuhr's Augustinianism. Conversely, in Maritain's Thomism there is a troubled note, a doubt about the resources of reason, and an apocalyptic rather than a rationalist conception of the good temporal order.

St. Thomas as a Political Actor

Thomas Aquinas was born in 1225 at the castle of Roccasecca in central Italy, into a highly political noble family. As a child and young man he played the part of a pawn in the political chess game of his day. At the age of five he was sent by his father, Landolf, Count of Aquino, as an oblate to the nearby Benedictine monastery of Montecassino. But there is a high degree of probability that family ambitions, not piety, underlay this offering to the Lord. Count Landolf's estate adjoined the property of the monastery. Some years earlier Landolf had seized the abbey (on behalf of the Emperor Frederick II) and held it for ransom—a move which was a part of Frederick's larger conflict with the Pope, to whom the abbey was loyal. Sending Thomas as an oblate to Montecassino was in the nature of a "fifth-column" penetration of the place. Some day he might become abbot, and in that capacity hold the lands of the monastery for his family and for the Emperor.[2]

Later, when Thomas as a young man of twenty decided to enter the Dominican rather than the Benedictine order, the threat to family ambitions posed by the decision led his brothers to waylay him on the road and to hold him captive for a year in the hope of changing his mind. Still later, when he had become a learned scholar, St. Thomas continued to have contact with the world of politics, though in a less melodramatic fashion. He was frequently a guest at the table of the saintly Louis IX, King of France, and two of his treatises are extant which were written as policy recommendations to rulers of the time. One is a letter to the Duchess of Brabant *On the Governance of the Jews (De Regimine Judaeorum)* and another is a treatise *On Kingship (De Regno)*[3] addressed to Hugo II, King of Cyprus.

The Revival of Aristotle

Political involvements, however, were the exception rather than the rule of St. Thomas's life. He was pre-eminently a man of thought, not of action. His greatness is associated with the broad intellectual innovation of his time, the thirteenth-century revival of the full corpus of Aristotelian learning and its synthesis with the tenets of the Christian faith, a movement which represented a revolution against the established edifice of Augustinian thought. Why should not the knowledge of the pagans contribute to the building of the Christian Commonwealth? Aristotle was the greatest and wisest of them all. Surely the regenerate Christian intellect was capable of separating the gold from the dross of antique science. St. Thomas put himself at the forefront of the Aristotelian revival and devoted most of his mature life to the incorporation of Aristotle's thought into the Christian scheme of things.

[2]See Étienne Gilson, *The Philosophy of St. Thomas Aquinas,* 2d. rev. ed. (Cambridge, England: W. Heffer and Sons, Ltd., 1929), p.2.

[3]The latter is perhaps better known by the title incorrectly given it by editors of the early manuscript, *De Regimine Principum.* See I. Th. Eschmann's introduction to St. Thomas Aquinas, *On Kingship,* trans., Gerald B. Phelan (Toronto: Pontifical Institute, 1949), for a discussion of the history of the text. All references to the essay *On Kingship* will be to this edition.

Conceptual Framework
and Methodological Assumptions

Universal Law

St. Thomas' political thought is cast within the framework of a natural law theory which represents an intricate fusion of concepts derived from classical philosophy, Christian theology, and Roman law. The teleological metaphysics and ethics of Plato and Aristotle, translated from the tiny *polis* to the cosmos as a system of universal laws by Stoic jurisprudents like Cicero, became the "word vessels into which the Church Fathers were able to pour the first conception of the Christian natural law."[4] It was this theory of the early Fathers which was St. Thomas' starting point, the matrix which he filled with Aristotelian concepts.

St. Thomas defines a law as the "dictate of reason emanating from the ruler who governs a perfect community." He envisages God ruling a perfect universe through the decrees of His divine reason.

> The very Idea of the government of things in God the Ruler of the Universe has the nature of a law. And since the divine reason's conception of things is not subject to time but is eternal, . . . therefore it is that this kind of law must be called eternal.[5]

How does the eternal law operate to produce its effects? It is "imprinted" on things, and from that impression, creatures derive their inclinations to behave in a certain way; in each case, a way proper to the achievement of their end or essence. In the case of irrational beings, their subjection to the eternal law is a mechanical process. Men, however, are guided by a rational apprehension of the eternal law. It is imprinted on them not as instinct but as precept, and St. Thomas calls the imprinted precepts the natural law.[6] The natural law is nonetheless supported by instinct in men. The principles of action are *known* to men by reason, but they are also *inclined* to follow them by appetite. The inclination, in fact, precedes the knowledge. God has given men an initial "push" toward their proper end.

> All those things to which man has a natural inclination are naturally apprehended by reason as being good . . .

[4]Heinrich Rommen, *The Natural Law* (St. Louis, Mo.: Herder, 1947), p. 12. For the classical Greek, stoic, and patristic background of scholastic natural law see Chapter 1. See also John Wild, *Plato's Modern Enemies and the Theory of Natural Law* (Chicago: University of Chicago Press, 1953), Chapters 3-6.

[5]*Summa,* I-II, Q. 91, A. 1, in Dino Bigongiari, ed., *The Political Ideas of St. Thomas Aquinas* (New York: Hafner Publishing Co., Inc., 1953), p. 12.

[6]*Ibid.,* I-II, Q. 91, A. 2, in *Ibid.,* pp. 13-14.

All the inclinations of any parts whatsoever of human nature . . . in so far as they are ruled by reason, belong to the natural law. . . .

Every act of reasoning is based on principles that are known naturally, and every act of appetite in respect of the means is derived from the natural appetite in respect of the last end.[7]

Unlike irrational creatures, however, man is autonomous. He must order his impulses, and he must choose to observe the law of nature by an act of free will. Since some men choose not to do so but will to violate the eternal law, does this mean that human freedom allows man to escape the action of the law? Thomas answers "no," for the imperfect subjection of the wicked to the law, in their actions "is supplied on the part of passion in so far as they suffer what the eternal law decrees concerning them, according as they fail to act in harmony with that law." And thus, since it is by "the eternal law that some are maintained in a happy state, others in an unhappy state, . . . both the blessed and the damned are under the eternal law."[8]

Natural and Supernatural Perfection

Despite the fall of Adam, according to St. Thomas, natural reason remains essentially incorrupt. Reason can still discern man's natural end, and it continues to receive the support of appetite in its realization. There is a natural as well as a supernatural fulfillment for man. Moreover, politics plays a part in producing it, because human laws are understood by Thomas as dictates of the practical reason of men which derive from the "general and indemonstrable principles" of the natural law as "particular determinations of certain matters."[9] They are either deductions from the natural law or the application of general principles to particular situations. Human reason is fallible, however, and may err at any point in the process of apprehending and applying the natural law. Furthermore, passion may distort its work. A rational empirical order is only a possibility, not a certainty.

Still another form of law is needed for a perfect world, divine law, which speaks to man through a special revelation—e.g., the Decalogue, the law of Moses, the precepts of the Sermon on the Mount. This is needed because natural law cannot direct man to his *transcendent* end, because of the uncertainty of human law applying law in particular cases, and because human law is neither competent to direct interior acts of the soul nor to "punish and forbid all evil deeds.[10] Divine law supplements natural law and corrects its human interpretations.

[7]*Ibid.,* I-II, Q. 94, A. 2, c and ad 2; Q. 91, A. 2, in *Ibid.,* pp. 45, 46, 14.

[8]*Ibid.,* I-II, Q. 93, A. 6, in *Ibid.,* pp. 40, 41.

[9]*Ibid.,* I-II, Q. 91, A. 3, in *Ibid.,* p. 15.

[10]*Ibid.,* I-II, Q. 91, A. 4, in *Ibid.,* pp. 17-18.

This grand theory of a universal order of law forms the unifying frame of reference for the Christian and Aristotelian and other classical elements in Thomistic political theory. Let us now turn to the conception of political science which it implies.

Politics as a Scientific and a Prudential Discipline

It should be clear at this point that for St. Thomas the science of government lies partly in the domain of reason and partly in the domain of faith and revelation. It is founded on natural and divine law, and is therefore philosophical, scientific, and theological in its principles. It is indeed a broad discipline. Witness the following from Thomas' *Commentary* on Aristotle's *Politics,* in which he sets forth the method and system of political science.

> It proceeds in similar manner . . . to the speculative sciences, which study some unity, completing their knowledge by observation of its parts and principles and by throwing into relief the actions and changes of the whole. So our present science by studying the principles and various parts of the city teaches us more about it by throwing light upon its elements, its movements and its changes; and being also a practical science, it shows us also how these various elements may be perfected; for this is necessary in every practical science.[11]

St. Thomas thus envisages a comprehensive political science, embracing a theory of the rational order, a theory of the actual order, and a body of practical precepts.

But this is Thomas' conception of the elements of a complete politics, not a description of what he himself actually accomplished. Thomas never wrote a comprehensive treatise on politics. His writings describe some aspects of the rational order and set down a method for developing practical precepts. We find nothing in them like the detailed empirical comparisons of the central books of Aristotle's *Politics.*

However, St. Thomas did not intend precepts for political action to hang in a utopian void, entirely out of contact with the hard "givens" of the empirical world. As Heinrich Rommen points out, natural law theory "is not in the least some sort of rationalistically deduced, norm-abounding code of immediately self-evident or logically derived rules that fit every concrete historical situation."[12] John Courtney Murray notes that the doctrines of the *philosophia perennis* are "orientated toward constant contact with reality and the data of experience."[13] The given, determined elements of our condition are accorded due weight by Thomas.

[11]*Commentary on the Politics,* I, Lect. I, in Aquinas, *Selected Political Writings,* ed. A. P. D'Entrèves, (Oxford: Basil Blackwell, 1948), p. 199.

[12]Rommen, *op. cit.,* p. 216.

[13]John Courtney Murray, *We Hold These Truths* (New York: Sheed & Ward, 1961), p. 331.

Laws should not seek to suppress natural instincts or to straitlace their functions. Even arbitrary conventions . . . are primarily means of the enlarging,
not the cramping, of human activity. . . .

Human motions which issue from sub-rational depths were not obscene in
themselves, but healthy; even jungle law was adapted to the balance of nature
and to the preservation of species and individuals.[14]

In the Aristotelian-Thomistic metaphysics, "*ratio* or meaning was an actor,
not a spectator, a shaping purpose, not just a logical essence," working in
and through empirical reality.[15]

Thus St. Thomas included the study of the *conditions* of political
prudence, as well as the rules of prudence themselves, in the scope of
political science, though he did not go on to elaborate a descriptive or
"behavioral" theory. He obviously knew the empirical descriptions of
Aristotle and would no doubt have appreciated the efforts of our modern
students of political behavior, for rational political action presupposes
"behavioral" knowledge as much as training in ethics. It is wanting if the actor is deficient in either area.

The Good Political Order

Immanentist Premises

The immanentist Aristotelian metaphysics which forms the foundation of St. Thomas' natural law doctrine has important results for his conception of the good political order. It requires that we look at civil society
and government not as conventions erected to dam up the irrational forces
of a corrupt nature, hobbles on a wild horse (*à la* Augustine), but as instruments for the release of nature, for the development of naturally good
tendencies.

Life in a community . . . enables man . . . to achieve a plentitude of life; not
merely to exist, but to live fully, with all that is necessary to well-being. In this
sense the political community, of which man forms a part, assists him not
merely to obtain material comforts, such as are produced by the many diverse
industries of a state, but also spiritual well-being.[16]

The Thomist conception of the political and social good is thus elevated to a
higher ethical level than the Augustinian, and broadened considerably in
scope as well. The classical notion of civil society as the agent of virtue is
restored.

[14]Thomas Gilby, *The Political Thought of Thomas Aquinas* (Chicago: University of Chicago Press, 1958), pp. 120, 140, citing *Summa,* I-II, Q. 91, A. 6, *c* and ad 3.

[15]*Ibid.,* p. 113.

[16]*Commentary on the Nicomachean Ethics,* I, Lect. 1 in Aquinas, *Selected
Political Writings,* p. 191.

Government and the Common Good

Thomas says that government, like society, is natural. It arises out of the need for a central agent of a commonwealth which itself arises out of the needs of nature.

> If then it is natural for man to live in the society of many, it is necessary that there exist among men some means by which the group may be governed . . There must exist something which impels towards the common good of the many, over and above that which impels towards the particular good of each individual.[17]

Government is the directive agency of a society.

The ancients felt no need to elaborate such a justification of government because they could not imagine a society without one. St. Thomas' object was to challenge the patristic view of government which, in stressing government's coercive functions—as the fruits of sin rather than the instruments of nature—quite neglected its directive work. The Church Fathers, whose political theory dominated the early Middle Ages, supposed that in a state of innocence or of perfection, government would be superfluous, because they could see in it only the violence of sanctions against recalcitrant wills, the public sword. St. Thomas admits that in such a condition, indeed, "there would have been no need for protection, there being no hostility either internal or foreign, and no need for correcting transgressions, all men desiring the real good."[18] But a ruler would nonetheless have been needed. His function would have been "to guide in active life and in the field of studies according as one was wiser and intellectually more enlightened than another."[19] St. Thomas thinks it useful to demonstrate that the directive aspects of government are its irreducible feature, implicit in the idea of social living.

> Slavery—the *subiectio servilis* . . . can only be explained as a consequence of sin. But the political relationship—the *subiectio civilis* of man to man which is necessary for the attainment of the common good—is not a consequence of sin, for it is founded upon the very nature of man. Authority and obedience would still have been required even if the state of innocence had been preserved.[20]

Thomas thus rules out all forms of anarchy as impossible political ideals under any social conditions whatsoever. Society is necessary for the

[17]*On Kingship*, I, 1 (8, 9), pp. 5, 6.
[18]II *Sentences* 44.1.3, quoted in Bigongiari, *op. cit.*, pp. xii-xiii.
[19]*Idem.*
[20]Aquinas, *Selected Political Writings*, p. xvii.

170

fulfillment of human nature, and the common good which it makes possible, and which flows back on all its members and perfects them, can be produced only through a specific organ. Even a society of saints would need to be governed to safeguard the common good. By nature, a man alone can pursue only his particular good, rationally look out only for his own interest. Even if he is disposed to seek it, he is unable to frame a true conception of the public interest. And the free pursuit of private interests, according to Aquinas, does not automatically generate the public welfare.

> The common welfare of the city and the individual welfare of one person are distinguished not only by a quantitative but also by a formal difference: for the common welfare is different in nature from that of the individual, just as the nature of the part is different from that of the whole.[21]

Men in society must define and implement their common good through a common decision-making organ, government. An example frequently employed by modern Thomists to demonstrate the point is the picture of a busy intersection without traffic light or policeman. Society and government are both natural to man and are inseparable.

A Dual Good. The political good of the ancients was the highest good for man. To them, it was through the life of the city, and especially by participation in its government, that a person most became a man. Human perfection was possible only within the city, and a man living outside the *polis* had to be either a beast or a god. Christianity had ended this monopoly of the city over the good life, for in the idea of salvation it carried the idea of human perfection beyond natural fulfillment to a supernatural level.

> Man is not formed for political fellowship in his entirety, and in all that he has . . . but all that a man is, and can do, and has, must be directed to God.[22]

Indeed, even supernatural man remained a social animal, requiring the help of others for his perfection. But this need could be filled only by the supernatural society of the church, through its sacraments and its fellowship, not by the civil order. Human perfection was the work of two societies, the one the vessel of an immanent, the other of a transcendent, good.

What implications does this conception of the duality of life have for the Thomist idea of the civil order as an agent of virtue and the good life? What precisely are the things which civil society should accomplish through its temporal government? In discussing the duties of a king in his study *On Kingship,* St. Thomas maps out three areas of action.

---

[21]*Summa,* I-II, Q. 58, A. 7, ad 2, in *Ibid.,* p. 165.
[22]*Summa,* I-II, Q. 21, A. 4, ad 3, quoted in A.P. D'Entrèves, *The Medieval Contribution to Political Thought* (London: Oxford University Press, 1939), p. 29.

To establish virtuous living in a multitude three things are necessary. First of all, that the multitude be established in the unity of peace. Second, that the multitude . . . be directed to acting well . . . In the third place, it is necessary that there be at hand a sufficient supply of the things required for proper living, produced by the ruler's efforts.[23]

This seems to be a rather comprehensive mandate. The second task, of directing the multitude to "acting well," seems to swallow up the moral direction which one would expect to see reserved to the church and to restore the secular classical concept. This impression is reinforced by other passages which tell us that "it pertains to the kingly office to promote the good life of the multitude in such a way as to make it suitable for the attainment of heavenly happiness."[24] Other parts of the essay *On Kingship,* however, and many passages in St. Thomas' other works, in saying what is involved in directing the multitude to virtuous living, qualify and limit the concept considerably. Unlike the classical philosopher-king, St. Thomas' civil ruler does not invade the personality of a man. The king is concerned only with external acts, with deeds, not thoughts, and leaves the fashioning of the interior person to the conscience of the individual, to the family, and to the ministrations of the Church.

St. Thomas required the State's action to be confined to what is external, public, and measurable by standard patterns. . . . Its business was not to train its subjects, heart and soul, to what on the official view was the highest virtue. . . . It could command certain virtuous deeds, but not that they should be performed virtuously. For men could make laws only on matters they were able to judge, and they were able to judge only external appearances.[25]

In some passages St. Thomas even seems to return to the patristic view that *coercion* is the essential element of human law.

Since some are found to be depraved and prone to vice, and not easily amenable to reason, it was necessary for such to be restrained from evil by force and fear, in order that, at least, they might desist from evil doing and leave others in peace, and that they themselves, by being habituated in the way, might be brought to do willingly what hitherto they did from fear, and thus become virtuous. Now this kind of training which compels through fear of punishment is the discipline of laws.[26]

In another place he says that the compulsion of a law derives chiefly from "fear of penalty," and therefore only those things are "strictly under the

[23]*On Kingship,* II, 4 (118), p. 65.
[24]*Ibid.,* II, 4 (115), p. 64.
[25]Gilby, *op. cit.,* p. 303. See also Aquinas, *Selected Political Writings,* p. xx.
[26]*Summa,* I-II, Q. 95, A. 1, in Bigongiari, *op. cit.,* p. 56.

precept of law for which a legal penalty is inflicted."[27] And in still another instance he tells us that "the notion of law contains two things: first, that it is a rule of human acts; secondly, that it has coercive power."[28]

But though Thomas confines civil government to external regulation and denies to the statesman the function of value builder for society, he still sees government as an agent of moral virtue in the Aristotelian sense. Its actions are not merely to create restraints, but to create rules which free the inner inclinations of men to their natural perfection and which also contribute to the work of salvation.

If we define political good to mean objects pursued by public authority, the Thomist political good is indeed not narrower but broader than the classical ideal. While Augustine's transformation of the tradition restricts, Thomas' expands the role of politics in perfection, but without confusing the terrestrial with the celestial. The bifurcation of value into temporal and eternal, lacking in the classical tradition, is specifically Christian. Whatever autonomy Thomas salvages for the individual vis-à-vis the civil ruler he hands over to the church, and his system culminates in theocracy. In medieval thought and practice, the category of public government is not exhausted by civil rule. The members of civil society in Christian Europe are also members of a church, whose government has public status. They are thus subject to the commands of *two* public powers, one temporal and one spiritual, which direct man respectively to his natural and his supernatural ends.

How are these jurisdictions related to one another? In the debate which raged throughout the Middle Ages on this question, St. Thomas took what has been called a moderate papal position. He declared that while the temporal order, the province of reason and of temporal perfection, is organizationally autonomous, it cannot be sovereign. It is necessarily subordinate to the order of faith, as natural ends are subordinate to supernatural ends: "In the law of Christ, kings must be subject to priests."[29] The ecclesiastical authority may intervene in temporal policy to protect faith and morals, and the temporal government enforces external religious uniformity as a prerequisite of civil peace.

Thus we see that while St. Thomas limits civil government by denying it the right to designate the highest goods and to mold man's inner life, he gives charge of these things to another public jurisdiction, not to a private society, nor wholly to individual conscience. The civil government, as partner with ecclesiastical authority in a unified Christian Commonwealth, is given a supporting, if not a primary, role in the work of salvation, besides

[27]*Ibid.,* I-II, Q. 111, A. 9, in Aquinas, *Selected Political Writings.* p. 147.
[28]*Ibid.,* I-II, Q. 96, A. 5, in Bigongiari, *op. cit.,* p. 73.
[29]*On Kingship,* II, 4 (111), p. 63.

its function in the natural perfection of man and in the provision of his material necessities.

These assumptions of a sacral age are, of course, repugnant to those of liberal societies in a secular time like our own. Finally, in the Thomist thought of today the idea of the church as a public authority has given way to a theory of individual and corporate liberty.

Rules for the Decision-Maker

Discovering Natural Law Norms

If, according to Thomas, the function of the positive law created by the human decision-maker is primarily to embody and give coercive force to the principles of the natural law in the form of authoritative directives, how does the decision-maker apprehend the natural law norm to start with?

As the fundamental concept with which the contemplative reason works is "being," that which "is," so the basic category of the practical reason, according to St. Thomas, is "good." The primary and only self-evident injunctions of the natural law are "Do good" and its corollary, "Avoid evil." All other principles are derived by reflection on the question, "What is good?" This is answered in the first instance empirically—by observing to what "goods" men are inclined (a notion comparable to the "drives" of modern psychology). Men are, however, inclined to many things—they seek a great variety of "goods." St. Thomas indicates that they should be ordered in the same way as the natural inclinations are ordered.

Reflection tells us that man's first inclination, which he has in common with other animals, is self-preservation. This is the basic good for man as a member of the animal kingdom (though not specific to him as man). Other inclinations which man shares with the animals involve sexual intercourse and the nurture of the young produced thereby. Specific to man are the inclinations to know the truth and to live in society. And reflection on all these impulses produces a set of norms to govern the relations which they create.[30]

Now, from the precept to preserve life and avoid its wanton destruction we may derive the principle that one should not wrongfully harm another, and from this in turn the conclusion that murder is wrong, and the norm "Thou shalt not kill." (The second table of the Decalogue is simply a reaffirmation by Divine Revelation of principles known to the natural reason.) From this and from the principle that the social order must be preserved as necessary to man's development, we may derive the authority of the ruler to enact the norm "Thou shalt not kill" into a coercive law.

[30]See *Summa*, I-II, Q. 94, AA. 1, 2, in Bigongiari, *op. cit.*, pp. 43-46.

Positive laws of this kind are valid always and everywhere, as embodiments of clear natural law principles.

The Role of Circumstance

The natural law gives specific direction to the statesman in only a few instances, however. For the most part, laws are not direct embodiments of the natural law but additions to it, applying general principles to particular situations. For example, the natural law proclaims that evildoers should be punished, but human law must specify particular kinds of punishment. These can be various and must depend on the circumstances of the situation, *not* on the principle. In a survey of the world's penal laws one would be struck by their variety and relativity to the particular culture, not by evidences of agreement. But relativity of this sort, Thomists argue, does not demonstrate the fallacy of the natural law idea, as some sociologists have claimed. The principle of just punishment can be variously embodied. It is not a moral straitjacket.

Circumstance is so various that in some cases even necessary conclusions from universal natural law principles must be suspended. For example, the principle that deposits ought to be returned to the rightful owner on demand cannot properly be applied when it is known that they would be used for a wrongful purpose. Gilby gives us another striking example of the relativity of applied natural law norms to cultural factors.

> Differences of physical condition [affect] judgments, especially with regard to social morality. The sugar-intake of the medievals through their ordinary diet was less than ours; their drinking and therefore their drunkenness had a different quality about it.[31]

All of this points to the large pragmatic element in Thomist natural law theory, both individual and political. Its universal principles are very few and very abstract, and the form of their application is determined by social and psychological conditions rather than by the abstract norms themselves. Here we have another effort, resembling Aristotle's, to fuse "fact" with "value."

One important result of this for St. Thomas' counsel to decision-makers is that they should set their sights according to what the "traffic will bear." No matter how noble an enactment might appear to be, if it is unenforceable it should not be passed.[32] It would only place an unbearable burden on the executive power and weaken its authority. The folly of an Eighteenth Amendment will lead inevitably to the passage of a Twenty-first.

[31]Gilby, *op. cit.*, p. 137.
[32]*Ibid.*, p. 184.

Natural law theory also holds that it serves the common good better to tolerate a positive moral evil than to attempt to enforce virtuous behavior which is beyond the capacity of the population to observe. A utopian law does more harm than good. This is how St. Thomas puts it.

> Now human law is framed for a number of human beings, the majority of whom are not perfect in virtue. Wherefore human laws do not forbid all vices from which the virtuous abstain, but only the more grievous vices from which it is possible for the majority to abstain and chiefly those that are to the hurt of others, without the prohibition of which human society could not be maintained: thus human law prohibits murder, theft, and suchlike. . . .
> The purpose of human law is to lead men to virtue not suddenly, but gradually. Wherefore it does not lay upon the multitude of imperfect men the burden of those who are already virtuous, *viz.,* that they should abstain from all evil. Otherwise these imperfect ones, being unable to bear such precepts, would break out into greater evils.[33]

The prudent ruler divests himself of unrealistic reform aims. He moves within the realm of the possible rather than of the desirable.

Another consequence of Thomistic empiricism is its experimental and tentative attitude toward positive law enactments. The purely human authority of laws which have the form of additions to the natural law (as in the example of the penal code above) means that they are always subject to reconsideration and repeal. A government must not absolutize its enactments as the will of God or the embodiment of the natural order, which it might be mistakenly interpreting. The force of laws does not depend on their inherent morality but rather on their enactment by lawful authority.[34]

Gilby's interpretation of St. Thomas actually puts public policy of this order outside the realm of right and wrong into the category of the socially convenient and advantageous. The principle which he finds in Thomistic writings is pragmatic and utilitarian.

> Purely political decisions . . . and positive laws . . . were expected not to contravene the principles and conclusions of morality but they were not implied in them. Right or wrong was not the only question, or indeed the decisive one. What was feasible and advantageous, that was the point, and moral theory could not settle it.[35]

[33]*Summa,* I-II, Q. 96, A. 2, c and ad 2, in Bigongiari, *op. cit.,* p. 68.
[34]See Gilby, *op. cit.,* pp. 145-46.
[35]*Ibid.,* p. 169. Gilby probably stretches Thomas' meaning too much here. Cf. A. P. D'Entrèves' Introduction to Aquinas' *Selected Political Writings,* and Jacques Maritain, *Man and the State* (Chicago: University of Chicago Press, 1951), p. 62.

The upshot of this is that the political good *concretely* understood must remain subject to ever new determinations as situations alter. The statesman must be a pragmatist and enact "what works" from case to case. This does not mean a constant reshuffling of laws, however, since the extreme of change is a danger to social stability.[36] But it does mean flexibility and experimentalism in the law.

Political Institutions

Natural Law Pragmatism

Unlike his classical predecessor, St. Thomas gives us no theory of a hypothetically best regime for ideal circumstances. His discussion of political institutions employs a frame of reference which is more like that of Books III and IV of Aristotle's *Politics,* which deal with actual regimes, than of Books VII and VIII on the ideal state. Governments of the one, of the few, and of the many are all legitimate forms, according to St. Thomas, if they serve the common good rather than the private interest of the rulers. In any given instance the circumstances must determine what kind of regime will best serve the common good. Thus he quotes Augustine approvingly as follows:

> If the people have a sense of moderation and responsibility and are most careful guardians of the common weal, it is right to enact a law allowing such a people to choose their own magistrates. . . . But if, as time goes on, the same people become so corrupt as to sell their votes and entrust the government to scoundrels and criminals, then the right of appointing their public officials is rightly forfeit to such a people, and the choice devolves to a few good men.[37]

While tyranny (the government of one in the private interest) is illegitimate, and the worst form of government, even it should sometimes be tolerated. For "if there be not an excess of tyranny, it is more expedient to tolerate the milder tyranny for a while than, by acting against the tyrant, to become involved in many perils more grievous than the tyranny itself."[38]

There is, nevertheless, in St. Thomas' writings a conception of a best regime to serve as a beacon for the statesman cast adrift in the sea of contingency. But it is found in all its fullness among actual historical regimes; it is not deduced from the intuition of an entelechy, half-fulfilled in practice,

---

[36]See Gilby, *op. cit.,* p. 305, citing *Summa,* I-II, Q. 97, A. 1, c and ad 1, 2.

[37]*De libero arbitrio,* i.6, quoted in *Summa,* I-II, Q. 97, A. 1 in Bigongiari, *op. cit.,* p. 79.

[38]*On Kingship* I, 6 (44), p. 24.

à la Aristotle. St. Thomas identifies it with the ancient polity of the Jews, whose principles were established by the divine law.[39] God himself has revealed and also instituted the best political order. It is a mixed government, which combines the elements of all the simple forms.

> The best form of government is to be found in a city or in a kingdom in which one man is placed at the head to rule over all because of the preeminence of his virtue, and under him a certain number of men have governing power also on the strength of their virtue; and yet a government of this kind is shared by all, both because all are eligible to govern and because the rulers are chosen by all. For this is the best form of polity, being partly kingdom, since there is one at the head of all; partly aristocracy, in so far as a number of persons are set in authority; partly democracy, i.e., government by the people, in so far as the rulers can be chosen from the people and the people have the right to choose their rulers.[40]

While this form of government was established by divine law, its principles can also be discerned by reason in the natural law. So far as its democratic aspects are concerned, St. Thomas writes that the very notion of government by law requires some participation by its subjects in the enunciation of law.

> Only a community of responsible citizens could receive law strictly so called, for law was not merely a command to be carried out but also a reason to be consented to and possessed. It was not given to slaves or even to sons, but to freemen; it supposed "civil conversation."[41]

The Aristotelian roots of the idea are evident. Expediency as well as principle dictate "that all should take some share in the government, for this form of constitution ensures peace among the people, commends itself to all, and is most enduring, as stated in *Politics* ii, 6."[42]

Unlike Aristotle, however, Thomas does not make widespread active participation in government, beyond some sort of electoral function, a necessary condition of the highest virtue. As a pragmatist, he does not see it as an ideal for actual conditions. "Most men had their work to do and enjoyed little time for narrowly political occupations. More important than a rota of public jobs was a temper of freedom, confirmed by the law and defended by the leisure class of contemplatives."[43] Perhaps we see here the germ of a characteristic assumption of modern liberalism, that the good life

---

[39]*Summa,* I-II, Q. 105, A. 1, in Bigongiari, *op. cit.,* p. 88.

[40]*Idem.*

[41]Gilby, *op. cit.,* p. 296, citing *Summa,* I-II, Q. 98, A. 2; VI *Ethics* Lect. 7; II *Ethics* Lect. 11; III *Politics* Lect. 3, 4, 7.

[42]*Summa,* I-II, Q. 105, A. 1, in Bigongiari, *op. cit.,* p. 87.

[43]Gilby, *op. cit.,* p. 297.

is found in participation in the life of society at large, not peculiarly in the affairs of public authority, which regulates only an aspect, not the whole, of life. Possibly some such notion as this lies behind the Thomistic modification of the Aristotelian formula that man is a "political animal" to read "political and social animal."

The aristocratic principle, as an ingredient of the best regime, requires that there be procedures for enlisting the virtue of the most enlightened and talented citizens in the making of public policy. In the Jewish polity, "seventy-two men were chosen, who were elders in virtue; for it is written: 'I took out of your tribes men wise and honourable, and appointed them rulers.' "[44]

The ultimate direction of affairs must be in the hands of one man, however. The best form of administration is therefore royal. "Moses and his successors governed the people in such a way that each of them was ruler over all, so that there was a kind of kingdom."[45] For group government, be it democratic or aristocratic, breeds faction and civil conflict, as Thomas sees it, which destroy the primary political good, peace and order, the prerequisite of all other goods.[46] In the essay *On Kingship* he attempts to establish the point by an elaborate argument, based on reason ("What is itself one can more efficaciously bring about unity than several") on analogy ("Every natural governance is governance by one. . . . Among bees there is one king bee and in the whole universe there is one God"), and on experience ("For provinces or cities which are not ruled by one person are torn with dissensions and tossed about without peace").[47]

The Thomistic best form of government can be described as a constitutional monarchy in which the concentration of administrative power is combined with legal controls to prevent its arbitrary use. Those responsible for designating the king should scrutinize the character of the candidate with care. And, secondly, "the government of the kingdom must be so arranged that opportunity to tyrannize is removed. At the same time his power should be so tempered that it cannot easily fall into tyranny."[48] St. Thomas does not go on to explain what he means by *temperetur,* but he appears to have had some kind of baronial council in mind, like the medieval parliament, which could serve as a bridle on the king. If Thomas were living today, he would probably point to the impeachment process and congressional power of the purse in a presidential system, and the convention of ministerial responsibility in a cabinet system as examples of tempered government. Each of these orders seeks to combine unity of executive

---

[44]*Summa,* I-II, Q. 105, A. 1 in Bigongiari, *op. cit.,* p. 88.

[45]*Idem.*

[46]*On Kingship,* I, 2 (17), p. 11.

[47]*Ibid.,* I, 2 (17, 19, 20), pp. 12, 13.

[48]*Ibid.,* I, 6, (42), p. 24.

leadership with responsibility to a popular body. In the event of the extensive abuse of power by the king, St. Thomas favored the right of deposition vested in some constitutional authority—in the "multitude" if it enjoyed the right of election, or in a "higher authority" if the right of choice rested there (e.g., Caesar's exile of Archelaus from Judaea).[49]

Cabinet Government or Presidential System?

If St. Thomas were living today, it is likely that he would find the cabinet system, despite the plural character of its executive, a better embodiment of his ideal than the presidential scheme, for when he spoke of the need for unity in administration he meant the whole field of policymaking. "Administration" in his day embraced what we call legislation as well as administration, the parliament being called into action only in the extraordinary case to supply funds when the king's own revenues failed, or to demand some redress of grievances from the king which was not forthcoming in the normal course of things. The concentration of control over public policy in the British Prime Minister is, of course, much greater than that in the office of the American President, the Parliament today serving not truly as a legislative body but as a constitutional check on executive abuses. St. Thomas might even describe the parceling out of policy-making powers to the President and Congress, and within the Congress to a host of semi-autonomous committees, as an example of the polyarchy which he thought a weak and dangerous form of government.

The Right of Resistance

If constitutional devices fail, recourse may be had in extreme cases to tyrannicide and revolution, for no one is bound by unlawful commands, such as orders contrary to God's law, or measures taken *ultra vires*. A tyrant may also be a ruler who seizes power violently and against the popular will. If there is no appeal open to a higher authority, he may be killed, apparently even by a private person.[50] Tyrannicide and revolution in such cases may not strictly be called sedition, which is a crime. But Thomas urges that such extralegal resort to force be reserved for extreme abuses of power. Rebellions may result in greater disorder and suffering for the community than the continuance of the tyranny. No one can predict the result once authority is shaken.[51] If the rebellion fails, it may create factions and dissension, or it

---

[49]*Ibid.,* I, 6 (49-52), pp. 27-29.

[50]*Sentences,* Book II, Dict. 44, Q. 2 (2), in Aquinas, *Selected Political Writings,* p. 185.

[51]*Summa,* I-II, Q. 42, A. 2, in *Ibid.,* p. 161.

may bring a harsher tyranny than the first in its train.[52] The legitimacy of tyrannicide by a private person Thomas is very reluctant to admit, since it seems to make the legitimacy of government a matter of every man's private judgement. Thomas would have praised the Founding Fathers for pointing out in the Declaration of Independence that the act of the Continental Congress declaring the separation of the colonies from Great Britain came only in the wake of "a long train of abuses and usurpations," and that "Governments long established should not be changed for light and transient causes."

The legitimacy of revolution and tyrannicide in extreme cases was an idea which had never been expressed in the classical political theories that we have been studying. Socrates chose to suffer execution by an unjust government, following an unjust judgment, rather than flee, let alone lift up his hand in rebellion. The seed of the idea of rightful resistance to injustice was sown in Western political culture by the Stoics, who were the first to speak of a universal law of nature not made by man to which all human laws should conform. Before this one might call an act of government immoral and wicked, but still feel obligated to obey it as the constituted law, with all the majesty that term implies. But when the idea of a higher law developed, human acts not in conformity with it were considered simply not law. Cicero wrote that neither the Senate nor the Roman people may repeal the law of nature. And it is easy to move from this notion to the idea that such unlawful acts have no obliging force. Fused with the Judaeo-Christian idea of a law of God overshadowing human acts and with primitive Germanic notions of the paramountcy of the people's custom over the will of the king, the Stoic ideal of universal law eventually produced the medieval doctrine of rightful resistance to tyrannical government. In the work of St. Thomas we find a typical and eloquent expression of the idea.

St. Thomas' Legalism

What of the way of life, the system of education, and the social and economic structure which go with St. Thomas' best regime? It is noteworthy that in his longest expressly political essay, St. Thomas says virtually nothing of these things. This is a testimony to the influence on his thought of the legalistic spirit of Rome which permeated the life of the Middle Ages. The legalist deals with questions of law and governmental structure independently of their social, psychological, and economic foundations. We see this tendency most markedly in Cicero, who treated the whole matter of republican government in Rome in terms of the balancing of legal principles, rather than of the character and relations of social classes, as Aristotle would have done.

[52]*On Kingship,* I, 6 (44, 45), pp. 24-25.

There are a few paragraphs at the end of *On Kingship,* however, which discuss the physical setting of a good state, in which Thomas compares the virtues of hot, cold, and temperate climates, and of highland with lowland locations. There are also a few passages on the need to limit commercial pursuits because of their corrupting influence on morals. But as a pragmatist, Thomas does not exclude trade altogether, "since one cannot easily find any place so overflowing with the necessaries of life as not to need some commodities from other parts. Also, when there is an overabundance of some commodities in one place, these goods would serve no purpose if they could not be carried elsewhere by professional traders. Consequently, the perfect city will make a moderate use of merchants."[53]

The last chapter argues that the city ought not to "superabound in delightful things," which make men "dissolute through pleasures . . . neglecting necessary matters and all the pursuits that duty lays upon them."[54] This is not a call for asceticism, however, but, in Aristotelian fashion, for bourgeois moderation, life according to the mean.

> It is best to have a moderate share of pleasure as a spice of life, so to speak, wherein man's mind may find some recreation.[55]

These, then, are the principles which St. Thomas lays down as guidelines to the architects of a political regime. Knowledge of them, however, is no guarantee of good government. Imperfection may always creep in due to adverse circumstance, to the fallibility of reason, or to the vice which is a consequence of sin.

The Neo-Thomism of Jacques Maritain

The Situation of the Neo-Thomist

The ideal of thirteenth-century Europe, as we saw earlier, was to create a City of God, a *Respublica Christiana,* which would reveal in its way of life the perfection both of the natural and the supernatural man. It would be the vessel of natural justice as well as of Christian sanctity. The political science of St. Thomas was intended to contribute to the enterprise of eliciting from the resources of experience and faith, and especially from reason, the principles and rules of the naturally just order.

In our time, Jacques Maritain, as a Neo-Thomist, has been the apostle of a new *Respublica Christiana,* a new Christendom. And like Thomas, he writes as a challenger of established patterns of thought and a herald of the

[53]*Ibid.,* II, 7 (142), p. 78.
[54]*Ibid.,* II, 8 (148, 147), pp. 80, 79.
[55]*Ibid.,* II, 8 (148), p. 80.

new. But the situations of the two thinkers are not alike. First, Thomas wrote for a Christian culture while ours is dominantly secular, or rather, pluralistic. Secondly, Maritain wrote in the ruins of the first Christendom, and in the aftermath of hundreds of years of destructive criticism both of Thomistic faith and of Thomistic reason. And lastly, the experience of two world wars, the accelerating pollution of the environment, and the constant threat of a nuclear cataclysm make it hard for modern man to be very optimistic about human reason. These differences in historical situation make for a considerable difference in the tone and the content of thirteenth and twentieth-century Thomism, as we shall see, though the fundamental frame of reference remains the same.

The Nature of Political Science

In typical Thomist fashion, Maritain describes political science as a practical science. It is "policy-oriented," and aims at controlling and transforming, rather than at merely understanding, the world. Nevertheless, it *"remains speculative or explanatory in mode* in regard to the general or fundamental cognitional equipment," and it employs the concepts of the contemplative disciplines which aim at pure understanding. Since political action involves moral choice as well as technique, political science must draw on the concepts and findings of both branches of contemplative knowledge, the ontological (philosophical, metaphysical) as well as the "empiriological" (scientific), each of which has its own proper objects and procedures. "It cuts right through the whole field of knowledge, from the metaphysical heavens from which it is suspended, to the world of experience, on which it must needs rest."[56]

With ontological tools the political scientist *"sees into* the nature of things," says Maritain, and grasps their essential character, in a kind of Aristotelian intuition; with the instruments of "empiriological" analysis he observes and measures phenomenal motions, the outside of things. In this realm the intellect remains *"external* to [the] work," acting as a "witness and regulator of the senses."[57] How the findings of ontology and of science are to be combined to produce a political ethics or policy science he nowhere makes clear, however. The intention to create a synthesis of noumenal insight with naturalistic science is stated but not carried through.

> The degrees or instances of moral science where its normative character, its *thou shalt* is the surest, themselves require as wide as possible a basis of experimental knowledge. . . .

[56]Jacques Maritain, *The Degrees of Knowledge,* trans. Bernard Wall and Margot Adamson (London: G. Bles, The Centenary Press, 1937), p. 312.

[57]Jacques Maritain, *Scholasticism and Politics,* ed. Mortimer Adler (New York: The Macmillan Company, 1940), pp. 30-31, 50, 54.

Today we have developed a large number of scientific disciplines—e.g. in sociology and economics and in what is called *Kulturwissenschaften*—which are a sort of methodical and scientific investigation of the field of experience which is preparatory to moral science and vested in it. They concern moral questions. And they appear in the form of "positive" sciences concered with what is and not with what ought to be.[58]

Let us now review the main theses of Maritain's political theory.

"Personalism" and the Political Good

The first and central question which the student of politics must answer is the question of the political good, or the proper objects of political life. Maritain seeks an answer to this problem through metaphysical inquiry, by discovering the character of man's essential nature, or "being." From this he deduces an understanding of the human good in general, of which the political good is an aspect. The fruit of this metaphysical analysis is Maritain's doctrine of "personalism," which rests on two concepts that reveal the interior character of human nature, "individuality" and "personality."

On the one hand, the intellect perceives that we are individuals, beings in which prime matter is precariously united to form, tending to fragmentation and decomposition like all material things, yet struggling and narrowly managing to retain form and unity. As individuals we are but parts of the whole, moving within the physical order.

But we are also persons, autonomous wholes, not rooted in matter but in spirit, "in so far as the latter stands by itself in existence and superabounds in it." Unlike the "individual," therefore, the "person" is serene and secure in its being. And it is free of the laws of the material universe. The person proceeds from God, and like Him it has the ability to know and to love. By these faculties we turn outward toward other persons, both human and divine. The person is generous, outgoing, expansive. It seeks to communicate, to give itself and to receive other persons in knowledge and in love. By these faculties we are capable "of being elevated by grace to participate in the very life of God, so as to finally love Him and know Him even as He knows and loves Himself."[59]

How do we know that all this is so? From our experience in daily living, Maritain tells us. We all know well enough the effects of individuality in hurts given and received in the hurly-burly of the market place. But we also have known, in the experience of love, the person, for "love does not aim at qualities, or at natures, or at essences, but at persons. . . . What I love is the

[58]Jacques Maritain, *Science and Wisdom,* trans. Bernard Wall (New York: Charles Scribner's Sons, 1940), p. 169.
[59]Maritain, *Scholasticism and Politics,* p. 64.

deepest reality, the most substantial, hidden, *existing* reality in the beloved—a metaphysical centre, deeper than all qualities and essences which I can discover and enumerate in the beloved."[60]

Now all this does not mean that there are two beings in a man. Rather, individuality and personality are aspects of the one self who acts. This self chooses freely what it will do, and may "follow either the slope of personality or the slope of individuality,"[61] the life of "passion and the senses" or that of "spirit and of freedom."[62] Since personality is the best which is in us, the image of the divine, it is our calling as moral agents to realize its mastery of the self. Personality is the true self, something to be achieved. Individuality is to be mastered, limited by the person.

What has all this to do with politics? The concept of the "individual" helps us to understand the propriety of political subordination. As individual, a man is but a part of the social whole and can be required to give up his life and property for the whole. In this sense a man is obliged to accept restrictions on his conduct laid down by the whole for the common good. The concept of the "person," on the other hand, tells us that every man also transcends the polity, which exists only to serve the person and whose activities are limited by the superior rights of the person. As person, a man is an independent whole, not a part, and exists only for his own sake.

The concepts of the "individual" and the "person," and especially the latter, help us to specify the objects of the civil community and of the authority set over it. As persons we crave society; we must communicate and share ourselves with one another. Society makes possible a "communion in the good life" of human persons. What are the ingredients and conditions of this shared good?

> It involves, as its *chief* value, the highest possible attainment (that is, the highest compatible with the good of the whole) of persons to their lives as persons, and to their freedom of expansion or autonomy—and to the gifts of goodness which in their turn flow from it.[63]

The common good is thus summed up in the idea of a "freedom of expansion and autonomy which consists above all in the flowering of moral and rational life, and of those . . . interior activities which are the intellectual and moral virtues."[64] The condition of the full realization of this freedom of persons is the liberation of man from all of the things which hamper

[60]*Ibid.,* pp. 63, 62.

[61]*Ibid.,* p. 65.

[62]*Ibid.,* p. 66.

[63]Jacques Maritain, *The Rights of Man and Natural Law,* trans. Doris C. Anson (New York: Charles Scribner's Sons, 1943), p. 9.

[64]*Ibid.,* p. 44.

spiritual and intellectual growth—the bondage of physical nature, political bondage, and economic and social bondage.[65] The realization of this condition in turn implies an entire constellation of rights of the person, which ought to be enforced by authority against individuals, and against authority itself.

The Rights of Man

Maritain lists three categories of rights—human rights, civic rights, and rights of the working person. Human rights include the rights to life, to personal freedom, including freedom of expression and association, and the right to the pursuit of happiness. The latter is conceived as the pursuit of "moral righteousness, of the strength and perfection of the soul, with the material and social conditions thereby implied," i.e., freedom of conscience. Human rights include also the right to private property, as a safeguard of individual liberty, and the right to marry and raise a family, with the due liberties involved. "All these rights are rooted in the vocation of the person (a spiritual and free agent) to the order of absolute values and to a destiny superior to time."[66]

Civic rights relate chiefly to the conduct of public affairs. Free men ought to choose those who are designated to lead them toward the common good. "Universal suffrage has a wholly fundamental political and human value, and is one of those rights which a community of free men can never give up."[67] The right to form political parties is correlative to this right, as is the right of the people as a whole to establish by constitutional enactment the forms of government which will guarantee all other rights. Political equality, equality before the law, and equal admission of all citizens to public employment and to the professions without respect to race or color also belong in the category of civic rights.

The last group of rights, of the social person as worker, include the right to choose one's work, the right to a just wage, the right to organize vocational groups, the right to work, the right to joint ownership of an economic enterprise, the right to relief and insurance against unemployment and sickness.[68]

No right may be taken out of the context of its exercise and declared absolute and unlimited in its application. All rights must be used in conformity with the common good and are therefore subject to limitation by authority. Some will nevertheless be unrestricted, for it would impair the

[65]*Ibid.*, pp. 44-45.
[66]*Ibid.*, p. 80.
[67]*Ibid.*, p. 85.
[68]*Ibid.*, pp. 111-114.

common good if the right to exist and the right to pursue happiness were not absolute (though murderers may lose their right to exercise the right to live). Others, such as the right of association or of free speech, must be subject to regulation. They are "inalienable only substantially."[69] Maritain would no doubt think that something like Justice Holmes's "clear and present danger" test is a useful rule of thumb for determining at what point free expression impairs the common good and may therefore be restricted.

The Historical Evolution of the Natural Law

Maritain finds the most fundamental of his catalog of rights, the rights of the human person, to be grounded in the natural law, while the others depend indirectly on the natural law.

> The dignity of the human person? The expression means nothing if it does not signify that by virtue of natural law, the human person has the right to be respected, is the subject of rights, possesses rights.[70]

The reader may well ask at this point why, if the rights of the person flow from the natural law, they were not discovered by St. Thomas, whose political theories are also founded on the natural law idea, as we have seen. St. Thomas himself might reply that natural law is differently applied according to differences of social circumstance, and that the secondary precepts of the natural law are not equally well-known in all places and at all times. They may be blotted out by sin and corrupt habits. For example, theft is not deemed sinful in all places.[71] But these statements do not constitute an adequate answer to the question. Maritain attempts to supply one with a philosophy of history and culture.

Knowledge of the natural law, Maritain tells us, develops with the moral evolution of the human race. Parallel to the line of technical progress we may discern in the data of history the progressive development of conscience, attested to by the findings of social anthropology. Like St. Thomas, Maritain emphasizes the role of inclination, by contrast with conscious conceptualization, in our knowledge of the natural law. These inclinations "rooted in man's being as vitally permeated with the preconscious life of the mind" have gradually been "developed or were released as the movement of mankind went on." They were at first "expressed in social patterns rather than in personal judgments," and continue to unfold in the context of our social experience.[72] We are given a picture of the moral conscience as an

[69]Jacques Maritain, *Man and the State,* p. 101.
[70]*Ibid.,* p. 65.
[71]*Summa,* I-II, Q. 94, A. 6, in Bigongiari, *op. cit.,* pp. 53-54.
[72]Maritain, *Man and the State,* pp. 90, 94.

Aristotelian entelechy (though Maritain does not call it that), developing from potency to act over the whole span of human history. This idea does not come from Aristotle, who had no philosophy of history, but probably owes as much to Kant as to St. Thomas for its formulation.[73]

Out of the classical and medieval experience developed the notion of man's obligations, says Maritain, and out of that of the eighteenth century "the root *inclinations* of human nature as regards the right of the human person were set free."[74] From this came our knowledge of man's natural rights. The development has continued down through the nineteenth and twentieth centuries with the manual worker's achievement of a consciousness of himself as a person, after centuries of animal-like existence. A result has been a new elaboration of natural law principles in the form of a recognition of the rights of the social and working person. The entire movement is toward ever greater freedom for the expansion of personality, toward the creation of a "city of persons," a genuine democracy.

The line of progress is uneven, however. And there is no guarantee that the "city of persons" will be realized. Sound development has brought distortions in its wake, Maritain tells us. Modern individualist ideologies, in stressing rights, have neglected obligations, and have rigidly absolutized these rights, abstracting them from their proper relationship to the common good. In reaction have come distortions in the opposite direction in the form of totalitarianisms which completely destroy the autonomy of man and reduce him to a mere function of the social whole.[75]

Progress to the "city of persons" is, therefore, neither automatic nor necessary. As moral and technical advances create freedom, they thereby make successive stages in the developmental order ever more dependent on free and conscious choice.

> Progress, if it is to continue, will not take place by itself. Evolution, by means of the very mechanism of its syntheses, takes unto itself ever increasing liberty.[76]

Contemplating the moral and physical wreckage of two world wars, Maritain is not sure that the resources of natural reason are at all sufficient to make sound choice, in keeping with the dictates of natural law, a real

[73]John Courtney Murray, another prominent Neo-Thomist, also writes of the natural law in terms of historical development. In *We Hold These Truths,* for example, he says that "in view of its immanent aspect . . . the natural law constantly admits the possibility of 'new orders,' as human institutions dissolve to be replaced by others." (p. 332).

[74]Maritain, *Man and the State,* p. 94.

[75]See Jacques Maritain, *The Range of Reason* (New York: Charles Scribner's Sons, 1952), p. 193.

[76]Maritain quoting Pierre Teilhard de Chardin, in *The Rights of Man and Natural Law,* p. 31.

probability. Throughout his political essays Maritain speaks of the need for an "evangelization" of the natural order if the democracy of persons is to be realized.

> Democracy can only live on Gospel inspiration. It is by virtue of the Gospel inspiration that democracy can progressively carry out its momentous task of the moral rationalization of political life.[77]

This appears to be a considerable departure from the original Thomist conception of the relationship of faith to reason. According to St. Thomas, while divine law reveals both the proper objects and right structure of government, these can be, and historically have been, also known by natural reason. The divine law confirms but does not supplant natural law. Nowhere does Thomas suggest that a sound natural polity is impossible unless it is also penetrated by Christian ideals. In the essay *On Kingship* he does indeed say that an important safeguard against tyranny in a particular polity is a ruler who seeks salvation as his chief reward, rather than wealth, power, or earthly glory. But he also says that love of human esteem alone may ensure good government. Thomas stresses the importance of the cooperation of the spiritual (i.e., the supernatural) and the temporal (i.e., natural) order, each established on its own principles, but not the need for a spiritual penetration of the natural system.

A Theology of History

Maritain discusses the relationship of faith to reason within the framework of a theory of history. The "evangelization" of the natural order is a "relation of fact" rather than of "right." While the canons of the natural law are in principle knowable by reason alone, in the historical order it has been through the influence of Christian Revelation on men's souls that they have in fact become known.

> The consciousness of the dignity of the person and the rights of the person remained implicit in pagan antiquity, over which the law of slavery cast its shadow. It was the message of the Gospel which suddenly awakened this consciousness, in a divine and transcendent form, revealing to men that they are called upon to be the sons and heirs of God in the Kingdom of God. Under the evangelical impulse, this same awakening was little by little spread forth, with regard to the requirements of natural law, over the realm of man's life here on earth, and of the terrestrial city.[78]

Christianity has acted as a moral leaven in history, producing growth "in the depths of the profane and temporal consciousness itself," and work-

---

[77]Maritain, *Man and the State*, p. 61.

[78]Maritain, *The Rights of Man and Natural Law*, p. 68.

ing even in distorted natural law theories such as that of the eighteenth century.

> Even under mixed and aberrant forms . . . is it not the Christian leaven that is still seen fermenting in the bosom of human history, while the unhappy adventure of individualist democracy is unfolding itself?[79]

But the Christian leaven does not work without the active cooperation of men of good will, so there is an ever present need to preach the gospel, not only for salvation hereafter but for the well-being of the temporal order as well. Secular ideologies are destroying the vital principle in modern democracies. If democracies are to escape destruction they must experience "a complete turn about toward spirit," and this can only come from the spread of a vital Christianity and the arousal of Christians to a sense of social mission.[80] Furthermore, moral rebirth must be accompanied by social reorganization "according to justice and human dignity and with the free cooperation of the labouring classes, in order to go beyond the capitalist system and the social cult of material goods and material power."[81]

Sometimes Maritain writes apocalyptically about the coming of the "city of persons," and we are led to believe that there *is* a guarantee of its realization after all. In one place, for example, in speaking of the growing release of man "from the external and internal constraints of Nature," flowing from technical progress and from the growth of political and social democracy, he writes:

> In this way, certain conditions and certain means are prepared, and certain beginnings of spiritual freedom, of the freedom *purely and simply terminal,* whose conquest and achievement transcend the proper order of nature and the civil community.[82]

The flowering of democracy in the temporal order constitutes an immediate preparation for the coming of the Heavenly Kingdom itself, "when every form of servitude shall have disappeared—under the 'new Heavens' of the resurrection." And in another of Maritain's works, the fulfillment of the temporal good is actually fused with the coming of the millennial society.

> Our age appears as an apocalyptic age, a liquidation of several centuries of history. We are picking the grapes of wrath. We have not finished suffering. But at the end of the crisis a new world will emerge. . . .
> The renewal of civilization that we hope for, the age of integral humanism, the time when science and wisdom are to be reconciled, the advent of a fraternal

[79]Maritain, *Scholasticism and Politics,* p. 86.
[80]*Ibid.,* p. 87.
[81]*Ibid.,* p. 246.
[82]*Ibid.,* p. 137.

commonwealth and of true human emancipation—all this we do not await on the morrow. But we await them the day after the morrow, on that day which St. Paul announced will be, after the worst darkness, like a springtime of splendor and renovation for the world.[83]

St. Thomas prescribes a perfect political regime for fallen, though not depraved, man in the here and now. Maritain is a prophet of the "New Jerusalem."

Church and State

The intricate web which Maritain thus weaves of temporal and transcendental threads paradoxically enough does not involve the fusion of church and state; precisely the opposite. A new Christendom would not aim at the restoration of ecclesiastical power but would depend rather on "the vivifying inspiration of the Church."

> The very modality of her action upon the body politic has been spiritualized, the emphasis having shifted from power and legal constraints to moral influence and authority. . . . The superior dignity of the Church is to find its ways of realization in the full exercise of her superior strength of all-pervading inspiration.[84]

Maritain does not condemn the sacral order of medieval Christendom, in which the church dominated the civil order. In terms of the historical evolution of the good society, this was a proper relationship for that time. It allowed the church "to assert the freedom of the spirit in the face of the ruthlessness of the temporal power, and to impose on it such restraints as the truce of God." It also enabled the church to civilize a barbarous Europe and to fill the gaps of a still inchoate civil order. But today, freedom of conscience has become a "crucial asset to civilization," and its importance must be stressed if we are to avoid state totalitarianism.[85] Maritain insists, as a corollary, on the freedom of the church to teach and to preach.

Ethical Behavior under a Bad Regime

True to his Aristotelian heritage, Maritain does not confine his political theory to the best regime. In *Man and the State* and in the chapter entitled "The End of Machiavellism" in *The Range of Reason,* he considers the moral problem of the good man in a bad state, say under a totalitarian

---

[83]Maritain, *The Range of Reason,* pp. 203, 204.
[84]Maritain, *Man and the State,* p. 162.
[85]*Ibid.,* pp. 158, 161.

tyranny. Must he abstain from political activity, because no moral means are available to him to combat it? Or is he obliged to violate his conscience and the moral law in order successfully to combat the tyranny, hoping that somehow the end will justify the means?

Maritain answers that the question is not a valid one, for it supposes a moral law with rigid rules of universal applicability. Thomist natural law theory emphasizes the importance of the situation in determining how a moral principle is to be applied.

> The application of moral rules immutable in themselves takes lower and lower forms as the social environment declines. . . . In utterly barbarized societies like a concentration camp, or even in quite particular conditions like those of clandestine resistance in an occupied country, many things which were, as to their moral nature, objectively fraud or murder or perfidy in ordinary civilized life cease, now, to come under the same definition and become . . . objectively permissible or ethical things.[86]

Thus the manufacture of false papers in convents during the Second World War, objectively fraud, was a morally right and commendable activity *under the circumstances.* This does not mean that anything whatsoever is permissible in time of war or in combatting tyranny. But the line of demarcation between good and evil acts is shifted downward by the barbarization and disorganization of society. *Precisely* where it runs in a particular case is the hard problem of the individual conscience, acting with prudence, to determine. There is no slide-rule method for determining what is right or wrong in a given instance. One must rely on goodness of will and the virtuous habits built up over a lifetime as the chief guides. Maritain would probably argue that even the best will and highest virtue are no absolute guarantees against bad, or objectively wrong, decisions. Errors of judgment are always possible, and the rightness or wrongness of a decision may be determinable only by hindsight, after the act, if, indeed, at all. This may not be an entirely satisfying theory of moral choice, but it is at least not a utopian one.

Conclusion

Maritain's political theory, like that of St. Thomas, is confined to partially explicating the good order and to stating a method for choosing rules of behavior. Maritain has written no empirical political theory, attempted no "empiriological" description of actual regimes. Has he even used the findings of "empiriological" political and social science in developing his theories of rational order and his ethical precepts, a principle of procedure which he himself recognizes to be of the first importance? Aside from a few references to the literature of anthropology, the answer is unfortunately

[86]*Ibid.,* p. 73.

"no." This is a large fault in a day like our own in which the natural sciences of social and individual behavior have had a rich development, and doubly a fault for a person who has himself recognized the prime importance of these disciplines for ethical theory. The thirteenth century produced no empirical political and social science, but such empirical knowledge as St. Thomas had—the *Politics* of Aristotle—he took into account in constructing a political philosophy.

An extended discussion of Freudian psychology does indeed appear in *Scholasticism and Politics.* But it is not intended to establish Maritain's philosophy on an empirical foundation and is rather a criticism of the philosophical postulates of Freud's thought. Its chief object is to expose and destroy what Maritain considers a naive and false philosophy implicit in Freud's assumptions. A discussion of the significance for political philosophy of the clinical findings of Freudian and other psychologists would have been a great contribution to the study of politics.

As a consequence of this neglect, Maritain's "personalism" exists in a utopian void, quite out of contact with the real world, despite the fact that Maritain likes to call it a "concrete historical ideal." The influence on the theory of St. Thomas' doctrine of material individuation and of his theory of personality in the Trinity are clear. Not evident in its formulation, however, is the influence of hard empirical facts uncovered by the disciplines of geography, economics, sociology, psychology, and political science. In fact, Maritain entirely escapes from the world of our experience by identifying his personalist utopia, as we have seen, with the transcendent New Jerusalem, in which "all things are made new." The promise of synthesis is not fulfilled.

Maritain's philosophy of history, which explains the generation of the personalist good society, also contains problems. Even if we grant the main assumptions of Maritain's moral philosophy, it is by no means a self-evident fact that a consciousness of natural rights developed as a result of the influence of the Gospel. The concept of "leaven" may be lovely poetry, but it is imprecise and makes for poor historical and philosophical analysis. Maritain is not troubled by the fact that the eighteenth-century theorists of the Rights of Man were not only non-Christian but violently anti-Christian, and that the elaboration of the rights of labor in the nineteenth and twentieth centuries has been largely the work of atheist and agnostic socialists. Surely these facts pose difficulties for his thesis, but Maritain makes no effort to deal with them.

Maritain does recognize the difficulties faced by any philosopher of history. In *Three Reformers* he goes so far as to say that he doubts that anything precise or certain can be done in this field:

> The Angels, who see all the happenings of this universe in the creative ideas, know the *philosophy of history;* philosophers cannot know it. For history itself

is not a science, since it has to do only with individual and contingent facts; it is a memory and an experience for the use of the Prudent. And as to detecting the causes and the supreme laws working through the stream of incident, to do that we should need to share the counsel of the supreme Fashioner, or be directly enlightened by Him. That is why it is properly a prophetic work to deliver to men the philosophy of their history.[87]

Nevertheless, Maritain casts himself in the role of philosopher, not prophet, and a philosophy of history forms the heart of his political philosophy.

Maritain is impelled to this, I believe, because of the importance of the concept of evolution in modern thought, and because of the substantial knowledge about our world which that concept has begotten during the nineteenth and twentieth centuries. He speaks of the "idea of dynamism and evolution" as "the real conquest of modern thought," and he holds that "it is perfectly right to emphasize the need for Thomistic philosophy, in the various phases of its conceptualization, to give greater scope" to this idea.[88] Yet his own contribution to the philosophy of history is poetic prophecy, not philosophy.

Charles Fecher, Maritain's intellectual biographer, remarks the poetic flavor of Maritain's work as a whole and describes his style as "rich in imagery and metaphor, in poetic allusion." "It may seem a bit strange," he writes "that the disciple of Aristotle and St. Thomas Aquinas should prefer to their dry, emotionless method the less exact one used by their celebrated antagonist," Plato.[89] Maritain has answered the challenge posed by this choice of style with the claim that in philosphy it is more provocative of thought than a mathematically precise mode of expression. "A certain margin of imperfection in language obliges the mind constantly to revitalize and to go beyond signs. . . . In philosophy as in poetry verbal equivocations occasionally guarantee the most fertile and the truest intuitions."[90] But this raises the much debated question as to whether one can properly be said to be thinking when one tries to go beyond words and concepts.

Another problem of Maritain's work stems from the relationship which he sets up between philosophy and theology, a relationship which is not entirely clear. On the one hand he speaks of philosophy as autonomous, working from premises that are "self-supported," and guided by the "light of *reason,* which is its own guarantee." On the other hand, he subjects philosophy to the "negative government" of theology, and rejects as "false

[87]Jacques Maritain, *Three Reformers* (New York: Charles Scribner's Sons, 1934), p. 93.

[88]Maritain, *The Range of Reason,* pp. 35-36.

[89]Charles Fecher, *The Philosophy of Jacques Maritain* (Westminster, Md.: The Newman Press, 1953), p. 332.

[90]*Ibid.,* p. 333.

any philosophic affirmation which contradicts a theological truth."[91] It is hard to see how he can have it both ways. Philosophy cannot have its own guarantee in reason and at the same time maintain, in theology, an external censor which may reject what reason alone confirms.

An example of this confusion is found in Maritain's treatment of the concept of the "person" in *The Rights of Man and Natural Law*. On one page he says that the description he expounds "does not belong exclusively to Christian philosophy," but is "common to all philosophies which in one fashion or another recognize the existence of an Absolute superior to the entire order of the universe, and the supra-temporal value of the human soul." Then on another page he says that "it was first in the religious order, and through the sudden pouring forth of the evangelical message, that this transcendent dignity of the human person was made manifest."[92] Here it is a peculiarly Christian concept.

The over-all impression which one receives from Maritain's work is that he has made philosophy the handmaiden of theology in a more radical mode than Aquinas ever imagined. He likes to speak, for example, of "Christian philosophy" and of himself as a "Christian philosopher." And in one place he has written:

> I have no intention of suggesting that theology ought to be confined to its center, to the mysteries of faith, and should abandon all the mysteries of the human world to another wisdom. Theology has jurisdiction over the whole human world and it may even seem especially important today that it should extend its views to matters of ethnology, politics, and sociology, as well as the interpretation of profane history.[93]

His politics is, in fact, a theological politics throughout. Its basic premises derive from Christian Revelation, and it will have its greatest appeal to persons of the Christian faith who accept these premises.

This does not mean, of course, that all Christians, nor even all Catholics, will accept Maritain's political theories. Nor does it mean that all Christians, or all Catholics, will feel compelled to accept *any* theological politics. It remains an open question among Christians whether political theory need be tied in any direct way to theology.

I have dealt up to this point with the weaknesses in Maritain's political philosophy. Yet Maritain has made a real contribution to contemporary political theory in his defense of metaphysical analysis against the claim that "empiriological" science and the world of knowledge are coextensive. In

---

[91]*Ibid.*, p. 76.

[92]Maritain, *The Rights of Man and Natural Law*, pp. 5, 73.

[93]Jacques Maritain, *Science and Wisdom* (New York: Charles Scribner's Sons, 1940), p. 120, quoted in Fecher, *op. cit.*, p. 308.

Scholasticism and Politics, for example, he criticizes the assumptions of the Vienna circle of logical positivism, arguing that our common-sense experience testifies to the meaningfulness of ontological statements.

> Let them be silent! For we cannot say "I," we cannot utter a noun of the language, without testifying that there are objects in things, that is, centres of visibility, which our senses do not reach but which our intellect does.[94]

He further argues that the models, or "ideal constructions," which sciences such as physics and experimental psychology build as explicative devices also attest to the reality of the ontological order.

> The *essence,* the *substance,* the *explicative reasons,* the *real* causes, are thus reached in a certain fashion, in an oblique and blind manner, through substitutes which are well-grounded myths or symbols, ideal constructions, which the mind elaborates from the data of observation and measurement, and with which it goes out to meet things.[95]

If the explanations of the physical sciences thus point blindly toward metaphysical reality, and are incomplete sciences apart from an understanding of that reality, the claim of the sciences of human behavior to autonomy is even less well grounded, Maritain argues in *Science and Wisdom:*

> This field of knowledge . . . suffers throughout its length the attraction of a final term and a typical function (which is intellection at work) and the regulation of human action, which has relation to the ends of human life, and to the last end as well as to intermediate ends. . . . The positivist conception of the disciplines of observation and verification . . . appear[s] as a great illusion . . . These disciplines are in no sense autonomous sciences comparable with physics or chemistry. . . . They are empirical preparations for science, they form experimental material for what is properly called moral science.[96]

This does not mean that he would make a moral philosopher out of the behavioral scientist. On the contrary, the scientists' work "should be abstracted as far as possible" from judgments of value. If the behavioral sciences were "used for this purpose of making explicit value-judgments they would run the risk of changing the material and of forestalling conclu sions that it is not their job to reach." The task of making explicit moral judgments is not theirs but belongs to "the science to which they are subordinated in the same category of practical knowledge."[97] Unfortunately,

[94]Maritain, *Scholasticism and Politics,* p. 50.
[95]*Ibid.,* p. 35.
[96]Maritain, *Science and Wisdom,* p. 170.
[97]*Ibid.,* p. 172.

as we have seen, Maritain, as a representative of the superordinate ethical science in the field of politics, has chosen to ignore the work of his self-designated empiricist subordinates.

Bibliographical Note

Leading full-length studies of Aquinas' thought are Étienne Gilson, *The Christian Philosophy of St. Thomas Aquinas,* L.K. Shook, trans., Random House, 1956, and Martin Grabmann, *Thomas Aquinas: His Personality and Thought,* Virgil Michel, trans., New York: Longmans, Green & Co., Inc., 1928. The standard commentary on Thomistic political theory is A. P. D'Entrèves, *The Medieval Contribution to Political Thought,* London: Oxford University Press, 1939, Chapter 2. See also his introduction to Aquinas, *Selected Political Writings,* New York: The Macmillan Company, 1949. A new, more detailed analysis of Thomas' political theory is Thomas B. Gilby, *The Political Thought of Thomas Aquinas,* Chicago: University of Chicago Press, 1958. This study has many virtues which are missing in D'Entrèves' treatment, though the author may stress too much the pragmatic element in Thomas' theory. Since most commentators miss this, perhaps Gilby's exaggeration is excusable and may serve a useful purpose. A study of the natural law theme in Aquinas' work is Daniel J. O'Connor, *Aquinas and Natural Law,* New York: St. Martin's Press, Inc., 1968.

An extensive Maritain bibliography is found in the footnotes to this chapter. For a commentary see Hwa Yol Jung, *The Foundations of Maritain's Political Philosophy,* Gainesville: University of Florida Press, 1960. The most recent commentary on Maritain, which attempts to place his last work, *The Peasant of the Garonne,* into the perspective of his life's work, is written by Brooke W. Smith, and is entitled, *Jacques Maritain, Antimodern or Ultramodern? An Historical Analysis of his Critics, his Thought, and his Life,* New York: Elsevier, 1976. Smith concludes that this is not a conservative retreat from an earlier liberal stance, but continuous with the main stream of Maritain's thought, which he regards as independent of the liberal-conservative dichotomy. Another leading Neo-Thomist political theorist, who is not as well known as Maritain but whose thought is clearer and better disciplined, and who is perhaps also a more orthodox Thomist than Maritain, is Yves Simon. See his *Philosophy of Democratic Government,* Chicago: University of Chicago Press, 1951, and *A General Theory of Authority,* Notre Dame, Ind.: Notre Dame University Press, 1962. See also the work of another modern Thomist who is a natural law scholar, Heinrich Rommen, *The Natural Law,* trans., T. R. Hanley, St. Louis, Mo.: B. Herder Book Co., 1947. Leading non-Catholic Thomists are Mortimer Adler and Robert Maynard Hutchins. See Mortimer Adler, "A Question about Law," in Robert E. Brennan, *Essays in Thomism,* New York: Sheed & Ward, 1942, and Robert M. Hutchins, *St. Thomas and the World State,* Milwaukee: Marquette University Press, 1949. An interpretation of the history of Western political theory from a Thomist standpoint is Charles N. R. McCoy, *The Structure of Political Thought,* New York: McGraw-Hill, Inc., 1963.

Chapter 6

Machiavellian Virtú and the Emergence of Freedom Values: Machiavelli, the "Chicago School," and Theories of Group Process

In the preface to his *Discourses* on Livy's history of Rome, Niccolo Machiavelli describes his object as the discovery of "new ways and methods"; and he likens his work to a search for "new seas and unknown lands."[1] Scholars today are engaged in hot debate over the value of the continent he discovered. To some it is the promised land of an exact science; to others a submoral continent not fit for human habitation.[2] But whatever its value, there is no disagreement that Machiavelli discovered something strikingly new. The movement is sharply away from tradition.

In its naturalistic frame of reference, Machiavelli's political science resembles that of Democritus, Protagoras, and Thucydides. Political science becomes a technique for the successful manipulation of power, in the service of posited ends whose value is not examined. The test of means is based on efficiency rather than legitimacy.

Variations on the principles laid down by Machiavelli have been developed down through the years by a grand array of minds. In the seventeenth century, Thomas Hobbes and James Harrington built on Machiavellian foundations. The eighteenth-century theories of Alexander Hamilton and James Madison, which underpin the structure of the American Constitution, represent still another version of Machiavellism.

---

[1] *The Discourses of Niccolo Machiavelli*, trans., Leslie J. Walker (New Haven, Conn.: Yale University Press, 1950), I. Preface, 1. All references to the *Discourses* will be to this edition. References to *The Prince* will be to the Bergin translation (New York: Appleton-Century-Crofts, Inc., 1947).

[2] Compare Max Lerner, Introduction to *The Prince and the Discourses* (New York: Random House [Modern Library], 1940), and Leonardo Olschki, *Machiavelli the Scientist* (Berkeley, Calif.: Gillick Press, 1945), with Leo Strauss, *Thoughts on Machiavelli* (New York: Free Press of Glencoe, Inc., 1958), and *What is Political Philosophy?* (New York: Free Press of Glencoe, Inc., 1959), p. 40.

And in our own century we find a spate of Machiavellian works of the first order. Notable in the early part of the century are the writings of an Italian group, Vilfredo Pareto, Gaetano Mosca, and Robert Michels (a German socialist invited to Italy by Mussolini). And in the American political science of our time we find a number of representatives. Later in this chapter we shall examine the work of Charles Merriam and Harold Lasswell, prominent members of the "Chicago School" of political science, who introduced empiricist methods of observation and measurement into American political studies that are strongly reminiscent of Machiavelli's radically empirical approach, and who espoused a naturalistic theory of human nature like Machiavelli's. We shall also look at the work of the theorists of group process who build on the Harringtonian version of Machiavellian naturalism.

Machiavelli was born in 1469, into a minor aristocratic family of Florence. Italy was at the time entering a period of extraordinary political turbulence which marked the emergence of the modern state, and the radical decline, both politically and morally, of the Catholic Church as an all-European government. France and Spain were developing into powerful centralized monarchies, whose ambitions naturally led them into adventures in Italy, where no government capable of unifying the plethora of quarreling small city-states had arisen to fill the power vacuum. The Church, weakened in its authority by the low level to which the morals of its higher clergy had fallen, suffered further loss of prestige by entering the game of Italian politics as a temporal state, unable to expand its sway beyond the central portions of the peninsula. In the *Discourses,* Machiavelli predicts the proximate scourging or ruin of the Church, which was in fact being prepared even as he wrote his book.

Machiavelli's own fortunes were no happier than those of his country. From 1498 to 1512 he served in an administrative position connected with the conduct of the foreign affairs of Florence but was forced into retirement by the fall of the republic in the latter year, when Lorenzo de Medici, supported by Spanish arms, established a tyranny there. From then until his death most of his time was spent on his small farm near the village of San Casciano. Appeals to Lorenzo to make use of his talents, and the dedication to this ruler of *The Prince* were of no avail in restoring Machiavelli to office. When at last the republic was revived for a brief period in 1527, the new rulers refused to give Machiavelli a place because of suspicions engendered by his efforts to ingratiate himself with the Medici. Machiavelli died the same year.

Frustrated personal ambition, humiliation at the sight of his country's domination by foreign armies, resulting from the weakness and instability of her governments, and cynical disillusionment in the moral authorities of his time—such was Machiavelli's experience. What kind of political theory would it beget? It must necessarily register a radical disenchantment with tradition. It would prompt a "voyage of discovery" to a new moral world, culminating in the planting of a radically new standard of "virtue."

Machiavelli's Object and Method:
To Glory and Freedom Through the Understanding of Practice

The starting point of Machiavelli's political theorizing is an Augustinian view of human nature. Despite their pious mouthings, the only things that men really want and which determine their behavior, he believes, are the goods of the "Earthly City"—power, glory, and material well-being. Their hunger for these things is insatiable, and desire constantly outruns the power of attainment; hence, perpetual dissatisfaction with their lot, resulting in animosities and conflict.[3] Men are "ungrateful, fickle, and deceitful, eager to avoid dangers and avid for gain."[4] "It must needs be taken for granted that all men are wicked and that they will always give vent to the malignity that is in their minds when opportunity offers."[5]

This is the permanent moral condition of mankind. Machiavelli in effect agrees with Augustine that the way of life of the "Earthly City" will always be that of the empirical city. It seems clear to him that a result of this way of life is massive frustration and suffering, such as he found in Italy and such as he himself experienced. But, unlike Augustine, he is unwilling to resign himself to this condition as inevitable and to play the role of a humble pilgrim in a woebegone world, hoping for temporary release from misery under the government of the occasional just ruler enthroned by God. Machiavelli cannot be a pilgrim because he does not have the mentality of a pilgrim. He wants more than just a modicum of temporal security and well-being to help him on his road to heaven. He is not interested in heaven but is frankly a citizen of the "Earthly City," who wants to enjoy the goods of that city, especially glory, in abundance. And he hopes that he can obtain earthly glory by showing his fellow citizens of the Earthly City how to escape their dilemma—a way of avoiding frustrations and of heaping up the things they desire without changing their selfish natures.[6] For some this means glory and power, for others the security of property, and for all, freedom:— freedom from domination and exploitation by other selfish men.

Since the distribution and use of power in society affect the distribution of all the other good things, Machiavelli's problem was to discover a system of government which could produce this abundance of hedonistic values, yet remain stable. It would have to be a system which presumed no alteration in the basic patterns of human behavior, and would therefore be

[3]*Discourses*, I.37.1.
[4]*The Prince*, Chapter 17, p. 48.
[5]*Discourses*, I.3.1.
[6]See Strauss, *Thoughts on Machiavelli*, pp. 282-87.

fundamentally different from the utopias of Plato, Aristotle, and St. Thomas that rested on assumptions of educability and perfectibility.

> Since it has been my intention to write something which may be of use to the understanding reader, it has seemed wiser to me to follow the real truth of the matter rather than what we imagine it to be. For imagination has created many principalities and republics that have never been seen or known to have any real existence, for how we live is so different from how we ought to live that he who studies what ought to be done rather than what is done will learn the way to his downfall rather than to his preservation.[7]

The Precepts of Practice

Where could Machiavelli discover the rules of such a system? From time to time there had been powerful and united states in the past, whose citizens had enjoyed greater worldly satisfactions than weak and turbulent Renaissance Italy. Ancient Rome in particular had been a happy and prosperous polity. Would not a careful scrutiny of the careers of the great state-builders of history, both individuals and peoples, reveal the principles underlying their successes and the causes of their failures? This knowledge could lead the way to variations of their procedures, producing even more powerful, more prosperous, and more stable states in the future.

> If one examines diligently the past, it is easy to foresee the future of any commonwealth and to apply those remedies which were used of old; or, if one does not find that remedies were used, to devise new ones.[8]

A Purely Natural Order. Machiavelli expressly, though subtly, rules divine or supernatural causes out of the picture. Only natural forces work on the political destinies of man. Thus, when listing the greatest captains of antiquity in *The Prince,* Machiavelli places Moses first, and says:

> I shall cite as the most excellent Moses, Cyrus, Romulus, Theseus, and the like. And though we should not speak of Moses, as he was merely an agent of things ordained by God, he yet deserves our admiration, if only through the special grace which allowed him to speak with God. But observing Cyrus and the others who acquired or founded kingdoms, we shall see that they are all admirable, and if we study their particular measures and actions they will be found not unlike those of Moses though he had so great a Preceptor.[9]

A quick reading, such as a censor might give this passage, leaves the pious thought that God intervenes in human affairs to guide His chosen agents.

[7]Niccolo Machiavelli, *The Prince,* trans., Thomas G. Bergin (New York: Appleton-Century-Crofts, Inc.), p. 44. Copyright 1947, F.S. Crofts & Co., Inc.

[8]*Discourses,* I.39.1.

[9]*The Prince,* Chapter 6, p. 14.

But a slow reading, plus a second thought, tells the reader that there are no divine interventions, since those leaders who act without such help pursue precisely the same courses as those who claim divine guidance.

The pages of Machiavelli's books are crowded with examples of all the typical kinds of political behavior that he was able to discover from a reading of the historians and biographers of the ancient world—Livy, Polybius, Plutarch, Sallust, Tacitus, Thucydides—and from his own extensive administrative and diplomatic experience in the modern world. The reader is presented with a parade of witnesses whose actions illustrate the principles and maxims that Machiavelli lays down—the "captains" of antiquity, Moses, Theseus, Cyrus, Alexander; the heroes of the Roman republic and the emperors of Rome; and the "captains" of his own time, Francesco Sforza, Piero Soderini, Cesare Borgia, Popes Alexander VI, Julius II, Leo X, Savonarola, the Medici, the Orsini, and so on *ad infinitum.* From the actions of these witnesses, Machiavelli generates his rules. Both *The Prince* and the *Discourses* are case books, collections of particular instances which illustrate general principles. For example, we have the "case of Oliverotto da Fermo," who became ruler of Fermo by killing off all the leading citizens of the city at a banquet that he had cleverly arranged for the purpose. The story illustrates two generalizations: (1) that a new and illegitimate government can be made secure if all power groups likely to be dissatisfied with it are annihilated at the outset, and (2) that cruel measures taken to establish a new and illegitimate government are not a threat to its stability if employed summarily, but only if extended over a period of time. And the chapter in which the "case" is reported closes with a maxim, or prescription, derived from the generalizations:

> A prince occupying a new state should see to it that he commit all his acts of cruelty at once so as not to be obliged to return to them every day. And then, by abstaining from repeating them, he will be able to make men feel secure and can win them over by benefits.[10]

Let us now examine the systematic theory of politics which arises out of the wealth of case materials that Machiavelli compiled.

Prescriptions for State Building

The Few and the Many

First we must consider Machiavelli's theory of the "matter" out of which, and for whose happiness, the state is to be constructed. Every society, in Machiavelli's schema, contains two kinds of people, to whom he

[10]*The Prince,* Chapter 8, p. 26.

refers as the "few" and the "many." These words signify social classes—the nobility and commons of Machiavelli's day, the patricians and the plebs of ancient Rome—and also two different psychological types which divide on class lines. The few are those who have an unquenchable thirst for domination, whose primary drive is for power over others. They are also the more intelligent members of society. The basic demand of the many, by contrast, is for security of person and property, and for freedom from domination by others. Or, as Machiavelli puts it, "the nobility desire to dominate, the common people not to be dominated."[11]

This does not mean that the many do not love power. All men do. But in the many, the power drive is often dormant, perhaps because they recognize that they are neither as clever nor as wealthy as the few. Machiavelli says that their *"hope* of usurping dominion over others will be less than in the case of the upper class."[12] Their desire for power can, however, be awakened when they suffer hurt at the hands of the few. The Roman plebs, for example, demanded a share in authority, the tribunate, in order to defend themselves from patrician exploitation. This taste of power whetted their appetite for more and more power.[13] But popular ambition to dominate, and even to be free and self-governing, can be put to sleep again. Under certain conditions, the many will exchange their freedom for such values as economic security.

Such is the "matter" of every political order–the few and the many. Now every "matter" will be found to be in one of two conditions: it will be either "virtuous" or "corrupt." (I put these words in quotation marks, since they have a special meaning in Machiavelli's vocabulary.) And it will be the "virtue" or "corruption" of the "matter" which determines what kind of regime must be instituted to produce the maximum of satisfactions demanded by the citizens of the "Earthly City." To employ the Aristotelian categories that Machiavelli uses, as the "matter" varies in quality, so must the "form" of the polity vary, if the object of political organization (material gratification) is to be achieved.[14] When the "matter" is in a "virtuous" state, a republic can be instituted. And it is through republican forms that the greatest quantity of satisfactions for all and sundry is obtained. If the "matter" is "corrupt," however, absolute government must be introduced. General satisfaction is impossible under these conditions, but at least the many and some of the few can get what they want under such a regime. The alternative is general frustration following upon the anarchy which results from efforts to fit the wrong form to the wrong matter.

[11]*Discourses*, I.5.3.
[12]*Idem.* (Emphasis supplied.)
[13]*Ibid.*, I.3.
[14]See *Discourses*, III.8.5.

Now what precisely does Machiavelli mean by "virtue" and "corruption," and what are the characteristics of the republican and royal orders which fit these two conditions of the "matter"? Machiavelli's doctrine on these things is contained in two works which are companion pieces, *The Prince* and the *Discourses.* The first is chiefly concerned with principalities, the second with republics. Each is a "how to" book, a set of rules for the construction of a strong and stable political order. Let us begin with the anatomy of republics as Machiavelli presents it to us in the *Discourses.*

The Organization of the Discourses

The larger of Machiavelli's two political studies has the form of a commentary on the first ten books of Livy's history of Rome, in which the historian described the development of the empire. As a commentary, the organization of the work is determined chiefly by Livy's chronology, and the theory is therefore presented in a rather rambling and apparently unsystematic fashion. The 142 brief chapters, some of them only one paragraph in length, are grouped together in three books, but the rationale of their organization is in dispute among scholars. Leslie Walker, a recent translator and editor of the *Discourses,* thinks the book is arranged in terms of the things which made Rome great—"(i) her constitution, (ii) her military organization, prowess, and skill, and (iii) the virtues of a long succession of outstanding men."[15] Another scholar proposes that Book I is a consideration of "the internal affairs of Rome that were transacted on the basis of public counsel," Book II a study of the foreign affairs of Rome that were transacted on the same basis, and Book III an analysis of "both private and public affairs of Romans that were transacted on the basis of private counsel."[16] Machiavelli is an extremely subtle and complex writer, and both of these interpretations present problems. The student will, of course, wish to work out his own answer to the puzzle. Whatever the ambiguities concerning the threefold arrangement of the book, however, its main themes are clear. It deals with the social and political conditions under which republican virtue is generated and destroyed, the procedures which statesmen may take for creating, maintaining, and renovating republics, and the procedures for destroying republics.

To get into our analysis, let us first ask what Machiavelli understands by a republican system of government. He uses the term broadly, to include all governments which are not monarchies. The dual classification is exhaustive. "All states . . . that have held authority over men, are or have been either republics or monarchies."[17] Republican rule has two subcategories,

[15]*Ibid.,* Walker Introduction, Vol. I, p. 60.
[16]See Strauss, *Thoughts on Machiavelli,* p. 97.
[17]*The Prince,* Chapter 1, p. 1.

the aristocratic and the popular republic, the first limiting participation in public affairs to the upper classes, the second giving a share of authority to the poor as well. Venice is the model of the aristocratic polity, republican Rome of the popular type. The aristocratic republic is distinguished from a feudal monarchy by the fact that its rulers, unlike the feudal baronage, are not hereditary princes with subjects of their own, but simple citizens. The essential mark of the republic is citizen participation, both directly and through elected and responsible officials, in the making of public policy.

Founding a Republic

The creation of the republican order presents a paradox, for it can be instituted only by an absolute ruler.

> One should take it as a general rule that rarely, if ever, does it happen that a state, whether it be a republic or a kingdom, is either well-ordered at the outset or radically transformed vis-à-vis its old institutions unless this be done by one person. It is likewise essential that there should be but one person upon whose mind and method depends any similar process of organization.[18]

When the legal rules for the exercise of power are suspended, as they are at the institution or renovation of a regime, no holds are barred in the pursuit of power. Society in such a condition is a wild thing, and its members cannot cooperate for the common good, since cooperative behavior is generated only by fear activated by the threat of punishment at the hands of public authority. In such a state of things "diversity of opinion will prevent them from discovering how best" to create a frame of government.[19] Therefore, one man must establish his authority, if need be by violence, and frighten all into submission. Romulus found it necessary to kill his own brother in order to create a stable regime.

The absolute power should not last beyond the founder's lifetime, however, for the founder's successor may wish to make it a permanent tyranny. In any case, if the "matter" is virtuous, "what he has organized will not last long if it continues to rest on the shoulders of one man."[20] One aspect of republican virtue is a love of liberty, a desire to be self-governing, spread throughout the society; and liberty-loving people will not tolerate one-man government for long, though they will abide by the institutions which the legislator has created for them. Therefore the founder should begin to devolve authority on others as soon as his single right to legislate has been established. In this fashion Machiavelli has begun to redefine "virtue" in terms of "freedom," an effort which is carried forward throughout

[18]*Discourses,* I.9.2.
[19]*Ibid.,* I.9.3.
[20]*Idem.*

the modern philosophies we discuss in Part Two of this book. An important aspect of Machiavelli's "new way" is to blaze a path from "virtue" to "freedom," the axial concept of modern political thought.

The legislator's problem is twofold. He must restrain the ambitions of the elite and of the lower classes, while at the same time guaranteeing satisfactions to each. And he must channel the intellectual power of the few and the physical power of the many into the service of the power and glory of the state, from which both groups derive enjoyment. What principles should guide him in the distribution of authority? What institutions should he create?

After a careful canvassing of the arguments for aristocratic vis-à-vis popular republics, Machiavelli comes down firmly on the side of the popular order. Large and spirited armies are required for the creation of empire, from which all receive satisfactions, and even a conservative state may find itself forced to expand as a defensive measure. But an aristocratic order cannot safely arm its plebs, for they will either use their arms against the regime or lack spirit, and there are not sufficient numbers in the upper classes to fill the ranks of a powerful army. Thus the generality of the population must be given a share in authority so that they may be available for military purposes.[21]

Machiavelli assumes that dissension between the social classes in a popular republic cannot be avoided. This will be true despite, or rather perhaps because of, the "virtue" of the "matter," which a republican system presupposes. The ambition of the upper classes to dominate will run up against the lower classes' love of liberty and desire to escape oppression, so there will be endless squabbles. But class antagonism, if properly channeled, can actually be beneficial to the republic and produce individual behavior directed to the public good. The opposition of interests serves both to limit the power exercised by each side and to keep the parties honest and public-spirited, another component of republican "virtue." Thus a sound popular republic will not grant sovereign authority to a democratic assembly. But it will establish an institution through which the lower classes can exercise control over and share in the patrician initiative in policy-making. The Roman tribunate is an example.

The inevitable ambitions and animosities of particular individuals, which may combine with group antagonisms to breach the regular procedures of peaceful and legal conflict, must also be channeled by legal processes. Again, the Romans should be imitated in this matter. Their system of requiring that all charges of knavery against individuals take the form of public indictments before a competent public authority, rather than private calumnies, permitted the airing and peaceful settlement of ill feelings which might otherwise have led to factionalism and class war. The indigna-

[21]*Ibid.*, I.5, 6, 60.

tion of the plebs at an antiplebeian measure proposed to the senate by Coriolanus, for example, was handled in this way. Coriolanus was cited by the tribune to appear in a public defense of his measure and was impeached. This settled the affair in an orderly manner, while a riot, ending in his murder, would have caused class warfare. On the other hand *false* charges of patrician wickedness brought by Manlius Capitolinus, who sought to curry popular favor out of purely personal ambition, were exposed and quashed by the same system.[22]

The Problem of the Few. The procedure of elections guarantees a republic a ready supply and a constant succession of capable leaders, according to Machiavelli. Elections produce good leaders because a virtuous public, which identifies the private with the public interest, will choose the ablest men to lead. Two factors operate to restrain the ambitions of this elite. The mere number of them will produce a balance of forces within the group. (In Rome "there were so many that one looked after the other.")[23] And the system of public indictments described above will make them hesitate to break the rules of the republican game for short-run private advantage.

> So carefully did [the Roman leaders] maintain their integrity and so studious were they to avoid the least semblance of ambition lest it should cause the populace to attack them as ambitious persons, that, when there came to be a dictator, he acquired the more fame the sooner he resigned.[24]

The carrot works as well as the stick in keeping the elite honest. A virtuous public will shower them with rewards for the services which they render the state; each will get the glory and adulation that he craves. Private ambition is thus channeled into courses which produce public benefits.

> A well-ordered republic, therefore, should . . . make it open to anyone to gain favours by his service to the public, but should prevent him from gaining it by his service to private individuals. And this is what we find Rome did; for she rewarded those who labored well in the public cause, by giving them triumphs and all the other honours she was wont to bestow on her citizens, while she condemned those who under various pretexts sought by private measures to acquire greatness and ordered them to be prosecuted.[25]

The development of a custom requiring that persons who have held high post should not consider it dishonorable to accept a lower one—serving as a congressman, for example, after one has been President—also

[22]*Ibid.*, I.7,8.
[23]*Ibid.*, I.30.3.
[24]*Idem.*
[25]*Ibid.*, III.28.3.

contributes to the ability and honesty of the leadership. The Romans found that the presence of elder statesmen in the lower leadership echelon provided inexperienced top leaders with needed information and also acted as a brake on their ambition.

The Problem of the Many. Institutions are also required to restrain the ambitions which the lower classes of a virtuous society will display and to channel their physical force into socially useful courses. According to Machiavelli, religion is of prime importance in this connection. By religion Machiavelli means any superstition concerning occult and supernatural forces which can produce awe and fear in the common mind. (Here too his break with tradition is complete.) The elite are too clever to be deluded by it, and employ it to manipulate the masses. Numa, for example, who introduced the Roman religion, is to be accorded higher praise than Romulus, who founded the state. Numa "pretended to have private conferences with a nymph who advised him about the advice he should give to the people."[26] The Roman people, overawed, accepted the institutions which he introduced. The nobility were able to trick the plebs into appointing nobles to the tribunate by manipulating their religious fear, and thus succeeded in limiting the effect of that institution on their own power.

Time and again, Roman generals employed the civic religion to put courage into people and force them to defend the state. Scipio after the defeat at Cannae, when many were talking of removing to Sicily, made the citizens swear an oath not to abandon their country. And they kept it, out of superstitious fear. Oracular predictions of victory over Veii so heightened the spirits of a Roman army that they took the town by storm after a futile siege of ten years. Roman generals frequently found it useful to manipulate the auspices so that the army would be encouraged to fight vigorously and win the day. Religion thus serves to "reduce [the populace] to civic obedience conjoined with the arts of peace," and also makes it "easy to teach men to use arms."[27]

A wise elite will also practice other deceptions on the many which will redound to the general benefit. To induce the plebs to choose consuls and tribunes from the nobility rather than from their own ranks, the patricians customarily nominated their own most able and public-spirited members, while scattering known rascals among the plebeian candidates. Ashamed to choose inferior persons from their own ranks, the virtuous plebs voted for the patricians. Machiavelli treats this as a wholesome trick, for while it operated to limit the ambitions of the plebs, it also produced government in the general interest.[28]

[26]*Ibid.*, I.11.3.
[27]*Ibid.*, I.11.1 and 3.
[28]*Ibid.*, I.47,48.

As long as the many remain virtuous, and as long as a capable and public-spirited few are on hand to propose measures to the many and lead them, Machiavelli believes that the people's policy choices will be as sound as their electoral judgment. Public opinion needs to be guided and enlightened; but when enlightened, it will be sound.

> Not without good reason is the voice of the populace believed to be that of God; . . . when two speakers of equal skill are heard advocating different alternatives, very rarely does one find the populace failing to adopt the better view or incapable of appreciating the truth of what it hears.[29]

In the event that excessive fear or passion should momentarily sway the popular judgment, a remedy against foolish and dangerous policies is found in the ability of the great to overawe the populace with the dignity and gravity of their bearing and the authority of their pronouncements. The experience of Rome provides many examples of senatorial grandeur performing this function.

Emergency Government.   Despite his belief in the goodness of plural authorities for ordinary times, Machiavelli considers it vital for a republic to provide for the temporary centralization of authority to meet emergencies. Normal republican institutions move too slowly to deal efficiently with crises, for too many people must be consulted and diverse opinions reconciled. Consequently, an institution like the Roman dictatorship, which vested absolute authority in one man for a limited period of time, is of the greatest utility. It was not this office but the growing corruption of the Roman people in Caesar's time—their loss of interest in liberty—which led to the destruction of the republic, for the appointments both of Sulla and of Caesar by improper procedures, and the extension of the term of office of the dictator, would have been unthinkable in the virtuous days of the early republic.

When the "Matter" Is Corrupt.   The institutions which we have described are only capable of reinforcing the virtue of a society, not of producing or sustaining it. An examination of the fundamental causes of virtue leads us outside the order of political institutions into economic and social conditions. The most important foundation of virtue lies in the equal distribution of property. If the many have a moderate income, they will cherish their freedom and have the will to operate the intricate system which we have just described. The few will seek the rewards of honor for public service. But if property is unequally distributed, with the many in a condition of abject poverty, and the few living in luxury, both classes will violate the rules of republican order. The many will consent to the transgression of

---

[29]*Ibid.,* I.58.6. See also III.34.

the principles and procedures of republican government if they think it will help fill their stomachs. They will elect to office demagogues who bribe them with material benefits, rather than choose public-spirited leaders. The sting of poverty will make them irreligious and lawbreakers, and they will kick over the traces by which the few had managed their physical power for the common good.

On the other hand, luxurious living destroys the republican discipline of the few. They lose their taste for the honors which are gained only by difficult and faithful public service, and they seek to create private followings. Their arrogance is no longer restrained by fear of condemnation by the law on the indictment of a liberty-loving plebs. On the contrary, the new condition of the many is an invitation to the few to break the law and to seek power by playing the demagogue. The few lose all solidarity with one another and are reduced to a plethora of rival factions, competing for popular support, or entrenched for armed conflict again with the many. No longer will they join hands with one another and with the many to suppress would-be tyrants like Manlius Capitolinus. Each seeks to be a tyrant, and all sense of a public good is lost.

Long periods of peace and the absence of foreign threats also tend to corrupt a society. When Rome became secure and had no longer need to fear enemies, leaders were chosen for their popularity rather than for their virtue and fighting ability. And later those who could muster the strongest force came to the fore.

Renovation.   Public-spirited statesmen may observe corruption growing in society and, seeing the handwriting of impending destruction on the wall, they may take measures to stem it, for the corruption of a people cannot be completed in a lifetime. Republics must be renovated from time to time by what Machiavelli calls bringing them "back to their start."[30] By this he means measures to instill in the people at large that wholesome fear of punishment which was present at the institution of the regime. Republican laws make for virtue when they are enforced, but with corruption lawbreaking always goes unpunished. The renovator, in a position of authority, will insist on the fullest enforcement of the laws and on the severe punishment of the culprits. He will carry out a purge of all those whose behavior undermines the principles of the system. The history of Rome showed frequent renovations of this sort before her final corruption and decline.

> Notable amongst such drastic actions, before the taking of Rome by the Gauls, were the death of Brutus's sons, the death of the ten citizens, and that of Maelius, the corn-dealer. After the taking of Rome, there was the death of Manlius Capitolinus, the death of Manlius Torquatus's son, the action taken by Papirius Cursor against Fabius, his master of horse, and the charge

[30]*Ibid.,* III.1.1.

brought against the Scipios. Such events, because of their unwonted severity and their notoriety, brought men back to the mark every time one of them happened; and when they began to occur less frequently, they also began to provide occasion for men to practise corruption, and were attended with more danger and more commotion.[31]

The renovator will usually be a single crusading individual—an Archibald Cox prosecuting high-placed Watergate conspirators—who fights uphill to enforce the laws "despite the power of those who contravene them."[32]

A renovator should not suppose that patience, mercy, and rewards for those who wish to subvert the regime will succeed in controlling them or transforming their intentions. Sticks, not carrots, are required in such instances. Piero Soderini, Gonfalonier of the Florentine Republic in Machiavelli's time, a public-spirited man, made just this error, and as a consequence he lost his own position and the republic was overthrown. One reason that he failed to act vigorously against the ambitious men around him was his recognition that he would have had to enlarge his authority greatly in order to deal with them, and that this might have threatened the future integrity of the office which he considered an important institution of the republican order. "Such a course and such authority, even though he did not henceforth use it tyranically, would so alarm the general public that, after his death, they would never again agree to appoint a gonfalonier for life, an office which he thought it would be well to strengthen and to keep up."[33] What he did not recognize was that a failure to act decisively against his opponents would bring a far greater and more immediate evil to the system, which would overwhelm the good he sought to do. The choice here was not between good and evil but between two evils, and he should have chosen the lesser, which might have saved the republic. Machiavelli probably would have applauded Lincoln's decision to use extraconstitutional powers in order to deal promptly with the Southern secessionists: laying down a blockade, enlisting troops, and suspending the writ of habeas corpus—all prerogatives of the Congress; for though the "act accused, the result excused."[34] The temporary eclipse of the presidency after Lincoln was a necessary price to pay for the territorial integrity of the republic.

Transformation of Republic. When corruption has run its course, nothing can be done, according to Machiavelli, to renovate the "matter." Under such circumstances, the maintenance of order requires the concentration of power in one man, "so that those men whose arrogance is such that they cannot be corrected by legal processes, may yet be restrained to some

[31]*Ibid.,* III.1.5.
[32]*Idem.*
[33]*Ibid.,* III.3.2.
[34]*Ibid.,* I.9.2.

extent by a quasi-regal power."[35] It is likely, though, that the establishment of such a royal system will more often than not lead to tyranny rather than a reform dictatorship, for "very rarely will there be found a good man ready to use bad methods in order to make himself prince; though with a good end in view."[36] Even if such a good man is found, as soon as he is dead the corrupt people "will relapse into their former habits. . . . No individual can possibly live long enough for a state which has long had bad customs to acquire good ones."[37]

This being the case, Machiavelli freely prescribes for the man who wishes to acquire power and glory in a corrupt republic by becoming a tyrant rather than a public-spirited reformer, for Machiavelli's criterion of value is desire, and desires are equal, the desires of republicans and of tyrants alike. Desire contains in itself no principle of legitimacy. Furthermore, he assumes that under conditions of public corruption, only an enlightened tyranny can produce the things that are universally desired, though the total quantity of satisfactions will not be as great as that which can be achieved in a republic. But, in the midst of corruption, republics cannot be constructed, and attempts to build them will necessarily be futile and lead to anarchy, which no one finds desirable. The reverse side of the coin, of course, is that attempts to set up tyrannies when the "matter" is virtuous will also fail, the result being losses rather than profits all around, due to the futile commotion.[38]

Principalities

The brief companion piece to the *Discourses, The Prince,* is addressed to Lorenzo di Piero dei Medici, a ruler who occupied a new throne in a society in which the "matter" was corrupt. It has the form of a book of general precepts for the guidance of all persons who seek to obtain and maintain a position of absolute authority. The emphasis throughout the book is on new principalities, constructed amid general institutional ruin. Hereditary and ecclesiastical monarchies, in which established institutions provide support for the rulers, receive scant treatment, as the problems they present are few in Machiavelli's eyes. "It is in the new monarchies that difficulties are found."[39]

If virtue is absent from the body politic of a princely system, it must be present in the head of the system for the regime to be stable. A "virtuous"

---

[35]*Ibid.,* I.18.7.
[36]*Ibid.,* I.18.6.
[37]*Ibid.,* I.17.4-5.
[38]*Ibid.,* III.7.8.
[39]*The Prince,* Chapter 3, p. 2.

prince must have all the mental, moral, and physical qualities which are also characteristic of a virtuous people—the will to exercise power over others, physical power, courage, intelligence, foresight, a capacity to plan and execute difficult schemes, self-control, a desire for glory and honor above all other things, and an ability to identify one's own good with the common good. A prince's virtue is the central ingredient of his power, and without it all the blessings of fortune and all the most learned recipes for power are of no avail. Virtue is the capacity whereby the prince is able to seize opportunities presented by circumstance (to which Machiavelli gives the name "fortune") and to master the recalcitrant elements in circumstance. It allows him to foresee future links in the causal chain of fortune and to build "levies and dikes so that when the river rises it may follow a channel prepared for it, or at least have its first onrush rendered less impetuous and harmful."[40] The theme of the entire essay in fact is the relationship, the interplay, of virtue and fortune. As institutions drop from view, the personality of the prince necessarily holds the center of the stage as the pivot of the orderly society.

Fortune, Virtue, and the Problem of Acquisition. In discussing the acquisition of royal power, Machiavelli tells us that those who rely chiefly on their own virtue will be more successful than those who are the creatures of fortune, that is, those who rely on the influence of others to win power for them. The most excellent princes of the past have risen to greatness through their own abilities, owing nothing to fortune but the occasion which gave them an opportunity to act, men such as Moses, Cyrus, Romulus, and Theseus. These were all founders of great states, and their work lasted not only for their own lifetimes but for hundreds of years. By contrast, Machiavelli describes the meteoric career of Cesare Borgia, who owed his throne in the first instance to the power and favor of others—to his father, Pope Alexander VI, and to the King of France. Despite the fact that he himself had great capacities, he put them to work too late in the game. He worked feverishly to create for himself an independent position, but time ran out on him. The death of his father, coming at a time when he himself was ill and unable to exert his great virtue, quickly brought ruin to his state-building enterprise.

> Had he succeeded [in taking Pisa, Lucca, Sienna, and Florence] (and the matter was in hand the very year that Alexander died) he would have acquired such strength and prestige that he would have been able to stand on his own feet, dependent only on his own power and skill and not on the forces or fortunes of another. But Alexander died only five years after the Duke had first drawn his sword, and Valentino was left with the state of Romagna well consolidated but all the rest still in the making, placed between two very powerful hostile armies and himself sick unto death.[41]

[40]*Ibid.,* Chapter 25, p. 73.
[41]*Ibid.* p. 21.

It is significant that Machiavelli refuses to call virtuous a man like Agathocles, who rose to become ruler of Syracuse through the use of "excessive cruelty and inhumanity, and . . . infinite crimes."[42] Here was a man who relied only on his own talents and owed nothing to fortune. He succeeded in building a strong power position, but he was hated, and so was unable to win the greatest prize that men covet—the praise and adulation of others. Hence, Machiavelli will not call him a man of virtue, for virtue brings to its possessor the highest goods.

Virtuous Strategies for the Maintenance of Power. Machiavelli devotes several chapters of *The Prince* to a detailed description of the moral qualities a prince must have and their role in the maintenance of his power. In the first place, the prince must shake himself free of the scruples which plague adherents of traditional morality. Machiavelli does not believe there are many thorough Christians in the world, but he knows that most people trained in the Christian tradition will at least occasionally feel pangs of conscience and try to conform to the moral code. This produces a haphazard behavior which can be called rational and good in no sense of the word, and which brings with it great hazards to the man engaged in politics and to his followers.

> Most men prefer to steer a middle course, which is very harmful; for they know not how to be wholly good nor yet wholly bad.[43]

The man of Machiavellian virtue, by contrast, puts aside traditional morality as a code that has any absolute claim on him. He rids himself of conscience. He will frequently have to perform acts which traditional morality enjoins, but he must not be emotionally bound to the code. "It is necessary for a prince, if he wishes to remain in power, to learn how not to be good and to use his knowledge or refrain from using it as he may need."[44] He must train himself to make systematic use both of what men call virtue and of what men call vice, as the occasion demands. He must be good and bad by turns, not as conscience alternating with passion dictates, but coolly, rationally, dispassionately, as expediency dictates.

Thus Machiavelli advises the prince that it is well to be *considered* generous, merciful, trustworthy, and religious, and yet be able to perform acts which are entirely contrary to these qualities. Miserliness is better than generosity, because it keeps taxes down and develops support for the regime. Cruelty, when properly used, is better than mercy, for it controls men through fear, which is a stronger bond than love. "Cesare Borgia was regarded as cruel, yet his cruelty reorganized Romagna and united it in

[42]*Ibid.*, Chapter 8, p. 24.

[43]*Discourses*, I.26.3

[44]*The Prince*, Chapter 15, p. 44.

peace and loyalty."[45] A prince should always be ready to break his word, if it will serve his advantage, for since men are "wicked and will not keep faith with you, you are not bound to keep faith with them."[46]

The release of the prince from the obligations of the moral law and the consequent reduction of the political art to the technique of effective control give rise to a new theme in political theory—"appearances" or "seeming." Emphasis shifts from the moral character of the ruler to his "image." What people think of the ruler and his policies is important, for it affects his ability to remain in power, but what he is in his heart of hearts is politically irrelevant.

> The mass of mankind is always swayed by appearances and by the outcome of an enterprise. And in the world there is only the mass, for the few find their place only when the majority has no base of support.[47]

The way is open for a theory of propaganda and of public relations techniques, powerful instruments because "men are so simple and so ready to follow the needs of the moment that the deceiver will always find some one to deceive."[48] We all know how important a role the concept of "image" plays today in the age of mass media.

Machiavelli recognizes that his advice constitutes a sharp breach with the traditional ideal of human behavior, so he summarizes it by telling the prince that he must descend to the level of the subhuman and "know how to play the beast as well as the man. . . . A prince must know how to use either of these two natures and that one without the other has no enduring strength."[49] He must in particular seek to embody the characteristics of the lion and the fox.

Machiavelli paints his ideal ruler, who is driven by a master passion for power and glory, as a man of perfect self-control. He restrains his lust, his passion for wealth, and whatever sadistic tendencies he may have, for to give free rein to them is to incur hatred and the loss of the greatest good. Though all good things are merely objects of desire, we are required to establish a hierarchy amongst them and sacrifice those which we deem less important to those which we cherish more. The man of virtue is a disciplined man even though he is a beast-man.

Support Groups. The question of support for a regime, within Machiavelli's frame of reference, can always be reduced to a question of the greatest force. Should the prince build on the force represented by the many, or by the few?

[45]*Ibid.*, Chapter 17, p. 47.
[46]*Ibid.*, Chapter 18, p. 51.
[47]*Ibid.*, Chapter 18, p. 52.
[48]*Ibid.*, Chapter 18, p. 51.
[49]*Ibid.*, Chapter 18, p. 50.

The few, in a state of corruption, are blindly and ferociously ambitious. Their object, like that of the prince, is power, and they seek it through intrigue and conspiracy. They are one another's enemies and the enemies of the prince. Hence, they cannot be effectively organized as a support group. By contrast, the many in a state of corruption seek simply "not to be oppressed." Their primary objects are security of person and property, and these the virtuous prince can guarantee them. Their values and those of the prince are mutual. The support of the many assures power and glory for the prince, and his leadership in turn safeguards their security by keeping in check the few who otherwise would be continually stirring up disorder and conflicts. The many will applaud the prince's cruelty, for it will be directed not against them but against the arrogance of the few.[50]

> A prince should care nothing for the accusation of cruelty so long as he keeps his subjects united and loyal; by making a very few examples he can be more truly merciful than those who through too much tender-heartedness allow disorders to arise whence come killings and rapine. For these offend an entire community, while the few executions ordered by the prince affect only a few individuals.[51]

The many may not necessarily be the best foundation for every royal regime, however. The rule is not to offend the dominant groups, *whoever* they may be. A new prince, for example, may find himself in the situation of the Roman emperors, who had not only an aristocracy and a populace to deal with, but a powerful professional soldiery as well. Machiavelli says that they "bent their efforts to satisfying the soldiers and thought little of injuring the people" and that this was a "necessary choice."[52] Thus we see that the values of the majority have no special sacredness for Machiavelli. We have already noted that his motive in writing both *The Prince* and the *Discourses* was selfish, to receive praise for demonstrating the principles of policy whereby individuals and groups may maximize their satisfactions. Since *The Prince* is addressed to the few who desire to be absolute rulers, it is their praise that he seeks for his advice. Thus their interest, not that of the many, provides the framework within which Machiavelli must work. It is only coincidental that for the *most part* the interests of king and common people are complementary.

Foreign Affairs. The prince who is engaged in the expansion of his territories is advised by Machiavelli to employ a principle which closely resembles that recommended generally for domestic affairs. The imperialist should appear as the defender and leader of the weaker states in the area he enters, and break the power of the established rulers, just as the prince at

[50]*Ibid.,* Chapter 17, p. 48.
[51]*Idem.*
[52]*Ibid.,* Chapter 19, p. 56.

home draws together the many, who are individually weak, against the individually powerful nobility. The Romans, he notes, met with eminent success in applying this principle to the conquest of Greece.

In all foreign policy situations, both offensive and defensive, the prince is advised to adopt a strategy of coalitions rather than try to "go it alone." Neutrality, which is impossible in domestic politics, is equally impossible abroad. It is always best "to take sides and wage an honest war." Otherwise you will fall a prey to the victor or at least find that you are isolated from support in a later crisis. "The best policy is to join the weaker side, and to avoid joining a prince more powerful than yourself," since victory may place you at your ally's mercy if he is greater than you. However, one may be "absolutely drawn by necessity" to take such a risk, for if there is no other choice, such a risk is better than that involved in neutrality.

Machiavellian realism produces at this point in the text a striking passage in which Machiavelli tells his reader that there are no final solutions in international politics and that a ruler can make no decision that does not have drawbacks. We are reminded of Augustinian realism.

> Let no state think that it can always adopt a safe course; rather it should be understood that all choices involve risks, for the order of things is such that one never escapes one danger without incurring another: prudence lies in weighing the disadvantages of each choice and taking the least bad as good.[53]

Fortune. Machiavelli devotes an entire chapter, the last but one of the book, to the subject of fortune, the great cause of the prince's inability to work out final solutions to his problems. He tells us that we are masters of only half our actions, that only 50 percent of the time can we hope to predict and control the results of our actions. Fortune, incalculable and uncontrollable circumstance, is master of the rest. But Machiavelli does not counsel despair, and advises that measures can be taken to minimize, if not to eliminate, her role in our affairs.

An important principle is to keep one's behavior in tune with the temper of the times and to shift with shifting circumstances—to understand when boldness or caution is called for. However, this is a hard principle to apply, for it involves a flexibility in basic character traits, which few people have. Men are by nature bold or cautious, either lions or foxes, and cannot easily change as occasion requires. "For if nature could be changed with the variation of times and circumstances fortune would not change."[54] Since this is the case, Machiavelli notes that as between the two courses, boldness is usually the better, "for fortune is a woman and whoever wishes to own her must importune and beat her, and we may observe that she is more fre-

[53]*Ibid.,* Chapter 21, pp. 66, 67.
[54]*Ibid.,* Chapter 25, p. 74.

quently won by this sort than by those who proceed more deliberately."[55]
The rigidities of human nature, though, rule out a foolproof control of the
shifting sands of fortune. Machiavelli's prescriptions, both in *The Prince*
and in the *Discourses,* carry with them no "money-back guarantee."

The Separation of Ethics from Politics

We have followed Machiavelli on his voyage of political discovery,
and we have seen that his prescriptions for the happiness of the citizens of
the Earthly City have carried him far beyond the land's end of traditional
morality. What are the full ethical implications of his work?

Some writers have said that Machiavelli's separation of politics from
ethics represents no more than the dispassionate stance of any scientific
enterprise. James Burnham, for example, writes:

> Machiavelli divorced politics from ethics only in the same sense that every
> science must divorce itself from ethics. Scientific descriptions and theories
> must be based upon the facts, the evidence, not upon the supposed demands of
> some ethical system.[56]

Max Lerner tells us that it is unfair to malign Machiavelli as the "father of
power politics," that it is like speaking of Harvey as the "father of the cir-
culation of the blood."

> Power politics existed before Machiavelli was ever heard of; it will exist long
> after his name is only a faint memory. What he did, like Harvey, was to
> recognize its existence and subject to it scientific study.[57]

Both these statements imply that Machiavelli limits himself to the
description of phenomena and to scientific generalizations. But we have seen
that this is not so. Neither *The Prince* nor the *Discourses* is a descriptive
work like Thucydides' *Peloponnesian War,* nor does Machiavelli pretend
that they are. Each is a collection of maxims, prescriptions for action. Both
openly advocate villainy as a necessary ingredient of political success. According to Machiavelli, we must simply recognize that the price of temporal
happiness is the abandonment of the rules of Christian morality, which do
not fit human nature. Augustine had hoped for the occasional accession to
power of a just man, whose rule would be happy because it applied the
moral law which most rulers neglect. But as Machiavelli sees it, such a
person, surrounded by depraved subjects, would be beaten at the outset. His

[55]*Ibid.,*Chapter 25, p. 75.

[56]James Burnham, *The Machiavellians* (New York: The John Day Company,
Inc., 1943), p. 38.

[57]Lerner, *op. cit.,* p. xlii.

code would not allow him to take the strong measures necessary to establish and defend his regime, be it a principality or a republican order.

> A man striving in every way to be good will meet his ruin among the great number who are not good. Hence it is necessary for a prince, if he wishes to remain in power, to learn how not to be good and to use this knowledge or refrain from using it as he may need.[58]

Needless to say, Augustine and even more St. Thomas would have been surprised at Machiavelli's belief in the incompatibility of Christianity with vigorous and successful government. We have seen that Thomism adjusts the application of moral principles to circumstance, and sanctions for crisis situations measures which would be unacceptable in the normal course of events. Maritain has given us an interesting Thomist comment on Machiavelli's idea of the Christian moral law:

> Machiavelli . . . had a somewhat rough and elementary idea of moral science, plainly disregarding its realist, experimental and existential character, and lifting up to heaven, or rather up to the clouds, an altogether naive morality which obviously cannot be practiced by the sad yet really living and labouring inhabitants of this earth. . . . Accordingly, what he calls vice and evil . . . may sometimes be only the authentically moral behavior of a just man engaged in the complexities of human life and of true ethics: for instance, justice may call for relentless energy—which is neither vengeance nor cruelty—against wicked and false-hearted enemies. Or the toleration of some existing evil . . . may be required for avoiding a greater evil. . . . Or even dissimulation is not always bad faith and knavery. It would not be moral, but foolish, to open up one's heart and inner thoughts to any dull or mischievous fellow. Stupidity is never moral, it is a vice.[59]

Where did Machiavelli get his conception of Christian morality? Apparently from a variety of Neo-Augustinian doctrines that dominated the formal philosophies of the intellectuals and the popular religious revival and reform movements of the Italian Renaissance. Both sets of ideas represented a reaction against the official, but decreasingly authoritative, scholastic moral theology. "The production of popular religious and ascetical literature was increasing during this period," writes P.O. Kristeller, "and many of its ideas and motives may be attributed to the influence and inspiration of Augustine. . . . No less significant is the influence of Augustine . . . [on Renaissance] Platonism." The new ideas were quietistic and perfectionist, providing no canons for the active life. It was probably decisive in the formation of Machiavelli's concept of Christian morality that the pious monk Savonarola, preacher of political and moral reform, failed

---

[58]*The Prince,* Chapter 15, p. 44.

[59]Jacques Maritain, *The Range of Reason* (New York: Charles Scribner's Sons, 1953), p. 138.

to organize force to achieve his political objectives and hence failed miserably.[60]

As a consequence of all this, Machiavelli simply gave up the problem of reconciling morality with effective politics. In doing so he paved the way for a whole literature which treats the study of politics as a purely technical affair.

Machiavelli and the Natural Science of Politics in the United States

Early Political Science in the United States

The Age of The Founders.   A Machiavellian influence on American political science can be found at the outset of the republic, in the thought of the Federalist founders—men like James Madison, Alexander Hamilton, and John Adams. It is clear that pessimistic assumptions about the nature of man, like those of Machiavelli, account for the complex system of separated, checked, and balanced powers of the Federal government. The expression, "civic virtue," with a Machiavellian connotation, was also on everyone's lips, and the problem of its maintenance and cultivation was a question to which statesmen of the time thought it most important to give their systematic attention. The concept of the "public interest" had also entirely supplanted the traditional notion of the "common good."[61]

Nothing like a systematic school of political science succeeded to the theoretical and empirical research involved in making the Constitutional order, though some leaders of the time thought systematic leadership training was desirable. George Washington left funds for the creation of a "National University," provided Congress would match his legacy, "to which youth of fortune and talent from all parts" might repair to complete their education in the arts and sciences, especially to the end of "acquiring knowledge in the principles of politics and government."[62] But the university did not materialize. A widespread assumption of the time was that political science could not be set down in systematic academic treatises, but existed rather in the practice of intelligent statesmen. (As we have seen, it was from the careful study of the practice of "virtuous" leaders that

[60]P.O. Kristeller, *Studies in Renaissance Thought and Letters* (Rome: Edizioni di storia e letteratura, 1956), esp. pp. 294, 299, 323, 359-60, 367, 369.

[61]See Stanley Rothman, "The Revival of Classical Political Philosophy," *American Political Science Review,* LVI (1962), 352; H.F. Russell Smith, *Harrington and His Oceana,* Cambridge: Cambridge University Press, 1914, pp. 7, 19, 20, 33, 125, 186, 278.

[62]George Washington's will, cited in Bernard Crick, *The American Science of Politics* (Berkeley: University of California Press, 1959), p. 4.

Machiavelli derived the precepts of his science.) It was supposed by eighteenth-century Americans that their leaders would always be men of broad learning and experience, and would on their own cull from their reading the maxims needed for the execution of their political tasks.[63]

The Tradition of Moral Philosophy and Jurisprudence. During the years between 1787 and the Civil War, the only formal academic training in politics received by students in American institutions of higher education took the form of moral philosophy and jurisprudence. Francis Wayland's *Elements of Moral Science* and William Whewell's *Elements of Morality, Including Polity* (1856) were typical texts. After the trauma of the Civil War, leaders in American education, such as Andrew D. White, first President of Cornell University, renewed Washington's call for systematic education in political science for the leaders of our expanding democracy. But in fact what developed was a combination of political history and comparative legal-institutional studies, informed by a vague ethos of Hegelian idealism, and in some cases, Darwinian racialism. The books of John W. Burgess, Professor of "History, Political Science and International Law" at Columbia University, are leading examples of the didactic materials that were in vogue down to the turn of the century.[64] Citizenship training was the chief function of this curriculum. We are reminded of the objectives of Protagoras in democratic Athens.

A Naturalistic Political Science. Though it never received widespread academic embodiment in the nineteenth-century college curriculum, the idea of a naturalistic science of politics is clearly expressed in the writings of William Graham Sumner and Lester Frank Ward, whose very different versions of Social Darwinism became popular in intellectual circles during the last quarter of the nineteenth century. Though the immediate source of inspiration for both was the social evolutionism of Herbert Spencer, rather than any earlier naturalistic doctrine, the aggressive individualism of the first, and the communitarianism of the second, when understood as alternative ideologies for a dynamic secular democracy, are reminiscent of the naturalistic political sciences of Periclean democracy in Athens.

Progressivism and the "Chicago School"

Progressive Reform and Political Science. The individualist, competitive evolutionism of Sumner, and the cooperative "sociocratic" evolutionism of Ward (in which the public interest was presided over by scientific experts) gave currency to the idea of a natural science of politics at

[63]*Ibid.,* pp. 5-8.
[64]*Ibid.,* pp. 12-13, 21-31, 69.

the turn of the century, though both were entirely *a priori* in method. As Crick remarks, "It could . . . be protested . . . that such systems of thought, so vastly synthetic, were themselves unscientific; they neither experimented, measured nor accurately predicted."[65] It remained for the "Chicago School" to call for the application of these inductive procedures of the natural sciences to the problem of socio-political order.

The political science of the Chicago School was a direct outgrowth of the reformist politics of the Progressive Era (1900-1916.) Unlike the earlier Populist movement, this new assertion of the rights of the common man eschewed appeal to traditional moral principles in favor of what its proponents took to be a scientific approach to reform. They would unmask the opposition by simply digging through to the facts, to the real processes of power that were operative behind the facade of democratic institutional procedures. The attitude of the Progressives was perfectly epitomized in the statement of Charles Beard that it was "not the function of the student of politics to praise or condemn institutions or theories, but to understand and expound them; and thus for scientific purposes it [the study of politics] is separated from theology, ethics, and patriotism."[66] The "scientific method" of reform was pragmatism—the philosophical pragmatism of James, Peirce, and Dewey, adapted to the critique of political practice as "the method of intelligence," technically applied.[67] In the background, of course, was the great American consensus on constitutional process and the rights of man, and the assumption that America was one great community, unriven by class conflict or fundamental antagonisms of any kind. "Science" would be adequate to bring "the interests" to book before the bar of democratic equity.

In a volume of 1911 entitled *Social Reform and the Constitution*, Frank Goodnow, first President of the American Political Science Association (founded 1904) virtually paraphrased Chapter 15 of *The Prince* in expressing the new realism of the Progressives. "Political theorists and philosophical dreamers" of the past, he remarked, had framed "various utopias" in writing about politics. They had had lovely visions of how the world *ought* to be. What was needed was an investigation of the "facts," of the world as it actually is.[68]

Charles Merriam. The founder of the "Chicago School" of political science, in which Progressive reform was married to scientific empirical inquiry in a systematic faction, was Charles E. Merriam, Professor of Political Science at the University of Chicago from 1903 to 1940. In the decade before

---

[65]*Ibid.,* p. 68.
[66]Charles Beard, *Politics* (New York: 1908), p. 14, cited in *Ibid.,* p. 75.
[67]*Ibid.,* p. 81.
[68]Cited in *Ibid.,* p. 101.

World War I, Merriam was an Alderman in Chicago's old Seventh Ward, an active reformer in city politics, and an enthusiastic Bull-Mooser in 1912. During the Presidential election of that year he met Harold J. Ickes, who was a member of Theodore Roosevelt's following, and during the 1930s was brought by Ickes to Washington to serve in the New Deal Brain Trust of F.D.R.[69]

With the rout of Progressive reform through the Democratic defeat of 1919, and the election that year of Warren G. Harding, Merriam withdrew from active politics for more than a decade to devote himself wholly to scientific politics. The events of the election, Crick remarks, "together with the 'Red Scare' of 1919 and the fierce anti-intellectualism of the popular press in the early 'twenties, must have convinced men like Merriam that they were only burning their fingers in practical politics: they would do better to construct a genuine science of politics that would make such 'jungle' politics impossible."[70] We are reminded once more of Machiavelli, who in 1512, after fourteen years' service in the foreign office of the Florentine republic, quit his post when the republic fell that year and Lorenzo de Medici came to power. He was to remain secluded at his farm the rest of his life, devoted to the development of a science of politics which would be an inspiration for all ages to come.

In constructing a framework around which to organize his own political erudition, and as an agenda for the empirical research he thought ought to occupy the new generation of political scientists, Merriam chose the idea of "power" as his central or focal concept. Here we find him working squarely within the Machiavellian tradition. In a leading work of 1934, *Political Power: Its Composition and Incidence,* he tells us that his purpose was "to set forth what role political power plays in the process of social control," and to do this "with perhaps more realism than is usual." Others had "woven webs of intricate interpretations, apologies, and justifications." But he had no intention of pursuing such an evaluative approach, or to declare whether power . . . must have a moral basis; or whether it is essentially immoral." Instead, he set forth in his book a systematic account of the typical ways in which power is won (Chapter I), of typical techniques by which elites hold on to power (Chapter VII), and of the conditions under which power is lost (Chapter IX)—the same agenda as that employed by Machiavelli in his two great works of political theory.[71]

What new things had Merriam to say on these themes? Had not Machiavelli himself given us detailed and universally applicable information on all facets of the acquisition and loss of power? One chapter of *Political*

[69]*Ibid.,* p. 108.

[70]*Ibid.,* p. 134.

[71]Charles Merriam *Political Power: Its Composition and Incidence* (New York: McGraw Hill, 1934), pp. 3,4.

Power deals with aspects of the subject on which Machiavelli had remained silent: political symbolism and political ideology (Chapter IV). If Merriam had thought through the implications of his reflections on ideology, he would have realized how important it was to distinguish "power" from "authority," which, like Machiavelli, he failed to do.[72] The existence of ideological phenomena proves that conceptions of right have a significance for the stability of governments independent of, though related to, power and material interest. In the ordinary language, "authority" carries connotations of "rightfulness" and "legitimacy" that power does not. Since Merriam wrote his book in 1934, a large literature has developed on both the subjects of political symbolism and political ideology, which reports the empirical findings of political scientists who accepted Merriam's exhortations to uncover the facts of political behavior.[73]

Special aspects of the modern industrial state also required a restatement of classical doctrines on the acquisition and loss of power. As Merriam noted, important institutional changes were taking place in his time "under the influence of science, technology, invention, both social and mechanical."

> The family, the church, the school, industry, agriculture, labor, are undergoing profound modification, fundamentally affecting the basis of political power, and its external forms and manifestations, and compelling a reconsideration of earlier conclusions reached in the light of less adequate data.[74]

In a chapter entitled "The Family of Power" Merriam presented what he had learned on both the private and public aspects of power in these leading social institutions. We can see these pages also as a kind of preface to the vast empirical literature that political scientists have produced during the forty-five years since Merriam wrote his chapter, on the politics of industry, agriculture, and labor. Family, church, and school remain to be as fully researched.

The books that Merriam wrote after 1934 present in more detail what he had learned in traditional ways about political behavior over the long

[72]See Crick, *op. cit.,* p. 150.

[73]See especially Jacob Murray Edelman, *Politics as Symbolic Action* (Chicago: Markham, 1971); Murray Edelman, *The Symbolic Uses of Politics* (Urbana: Univ. of Illinois Press, 1964); Douglas E. Ashford, *Ideology and Participation* (Beverly Hills, Cal.: Sage, 1972); William T. Bluhm, *Ideologies and Attitudes* (Englewood Cliffs, N.J.: Prentice Hall, Inc., 1974); Gerald K. Hikel, *Beyond the Polls: Political Ideology and its Correlates* (Lexington, Mass: Lexington Books, 1973); Robert E. Lane, *Political Ideology: Why the American Common Man Believes What He Does,* (N.Y.: Free Press of Glencoe, 1962); Robert A. Putnam, *The Beliefs of Politicians: Ideology, Conflict and Democracy in Britain and Italy* (New Haven: Yale University Press, 1973); David Apter, ed., *Ideology and Discontent,* (London: The Free Press of Glencoe, 1964).

[74]Merriam, *Political Power,* p. 5.

years of his life. They do not contain the results of systematic empirical research, however.[75] Merriam's role was not to be that of an inductive researcher himself, but rather the prophet and facilitator of empirical investigation. Within the context of the American Political Science Association he organized a "Committee on Political Research" and a "National Conference on the Science of Politics." He was also instrumental in the creation of the Social Science Research Council in 1923, and served as its first Chairman. The Council was organized to promote unity among the social sciences and to raise funds to subsidize social science research.[76]

Though Merriam's conceptual framework was, for the most part, Machiavellian in character, he also modified that framework significantly through his investigations in modern psychology. We must credit Merriam, in fact, with linking Machiavelli to Freud in his groundbreaking endeavors to construct a natural science of politics. In *Political Power*, Merriam pointed out that unconscious motives were as vital, and sometimes more vital, than conscious motives in the determination of political behavior. Notice how the new psychology led him in the following passage to modify Machiavelli's teaching on religious motives in politics:

> It was Machiavelli who said that it is better to appear to be religious than actually to be so, on the ground that too highly developed a conscience might cause a fatal hesitation at the critical moment when action should occur. This is not wholly true, for the most promising type is one who actually is highly religious and interprets all situations which are to his own advantage in terms of religion, and that without any trace of hypocrisy but as the result of the conceit of his nature and his confidence in the infallibility of his own religio-political judgment. He may be able to find moral justification for material advantages.[77]

Most significant for political science were the findings of psychologists about the many kinds of personality that are produced by the variety of unconscious and subconscious individual experience. Here was a dimension of politics that had been overlooked by scholars who stressed the economic and sociological foundations of political behavior. "Types of personalities," wrote Merriam, "must be adapted and adjusted under all systems by whatever means are available—by force, custom, persuasion, social pressure, individual reorientation; otherwise the concern will not go forward,

---

[75]See Charles Merriam *The Role of Politics in Social Change* (N.Y.: New York Univ. Press, 1936); *Prologue to Politics* (Chicago; University of Chicago Press, 1929); *Public and Private Government* (New Haven: Yale University Press, 1944); *Systematic Politics* (Chicago: University of Chicago Press, 1945).

[76]Crick, *op. cit.,* p. 137.

[77]Merriam, *Political Power*, p. 262.

will not function."[78] The new science had enormously proliferated the personality types that had to be taken into account:

> In the older terminology there were good men and bad men; there were just and unjust; there were docile and insubordinate; patriots and traitors; dreamers and doers; there were power hungry and power indifferent persons; masters and slaves.
>
> In later terms there are . . . those with father and mother complexes; there are those with superiority and inferiority complexes; there are sadists and masochists; there are narcissists and exhibitionists; there are obsessives and hystericals; paranoiacs, manic-depressives, acid and alkali types; psychotics and neurotics.[79]

Merriam himself was to play a "John the Baptist" role in the study of politics and personality. His eminent colleague of the Chicago School, Harold Lasswell, was to be the messianic figure in spreading the new gospel amongst empirical students of politics.

Harold D. Lasswell. A student of Merriam's, Harold Lasswell became his colleague at the University of Chicago in 1922, where he taught until 1938, when he removed to the Library of Congress, and thence, in 1946, to Yale. As the second leading representative of the "Chicago School," Lasswell complemented Merriam with his emphasis on the theoretical rather than the empirical requisites of a natural science of politics. Merriam's role was to stress the need for fact-gathering; Lasswell's was to show the importance of careful framework construction. In all his writings on systematic politics, Merriam worked within an unselfconscious Machiavellian framework, modified by Freudian concepts, as we have seen. Lasswell was, by contrast, a perennial and very selfconscious framework builder, though most of the systems he conceived can be ranged within the broad world-view of a Freudian Machiavellism like Merriam's, with some excursions into Marxism.[80]

One of Lasswell's first studies, *Psychopathology and Politics* (1930) embraces both framework-building and the investigation of empirical data that Merriam called for but did not engage in.[81] The book is the result of a detailed examination of psychic case histories collected in part by Lasswell himself through prolonged interviews, using a "free fantasy" technique, and in part by other researchers. Some of the subjects were

[78]*Ibid.,* p. 25.
[79]*Ibid.*
[80]See Crick, *op. cit.,* pp. 176-81.
[81]In *The Political Writings of Harold D. Lasswell* (Glencoe, Illinois: The Free Press, 1951).

normal, others suffered from various kinds of psychic illness. All were persons in public life. Lasswell's intention in this inductive inquiry was to "discover what developmental experiences are significant for the political traits and interests of the mature."[82] Specifically, he wanted to find out what kinds of psychic experience produce the kinds of personality that are correlated with crucial political roles: agitators, administrators, and theorists.

The roles Lasswell chose to investigate for their psychological correlates formed part of the conceptual framework he developed for the inquiry. He selected "agitator," "administrator," and "theorist" rather than categories such as "statesman" or "legislator" because they were not confined to narrowly governmental institutions like the others, and therefore permitted a more comprehensive view of politics.[83] Politics is a process broader than the activities of public government, embracing private institutions such as "banking houses, manufacturing enterprises, distributing services, ecclesiastical organizations, fraternal associations, and professional societies."[84] Types of political leaders therefore had to be formulated in terms that embrace functional processes which take place throughout a broad spectrum of social agencies. The concepts chosen for his research also had to reflect the relevant range of psychic types, which Lasswell defined in terms of three kinds of relation: "a nuclear relation, a co-relation, and a developmental relation."[85] Nuclear types focus on a single kind of activity to display their political prowess, while co-relational types operate in a variety of related roles. Developmental types display in adult political activity traits and goals that are discernible in childhood, and which can be traced developmentally through an individual's case history. This category overlaps the first two, because "every nuclear and co-relational type carries developmental implications."[86] Lasswell's conceptual framework also included an adaptation of Freud's theory of personality.

In writing *Psychopathology and Politics, Power and Personality* (1948), and *Democratic Character* (1951), Lasswell was pursuing a normative as well as a descriptive-theoretical purpose. His research was intended to show how conflict might be mitigated through the reduction of social tension levels, the requisite means to be worked out by social scientists and social administrators. The implication was that politics today, even in democratic societies, is sick, even neurotic. But it can be made well by the social sciences, using the insights of psychology. Lasswell's ultimate intention, therefore, was to improve the workings of democracy, and the quality of

[82]*Ibid.,* p. 8.
[83]*Ibid.,* p. 42.
[84]*Ibid.,* p. 45.
[85]*Ibid.,* p. 49.
[86]*Ibid.,* p. 60.

democratic life—to enhance human freedom.[87] It is interesting to observe that Lasswell has here moved away from the partisan concept of reform originally associated with the Progressive beginnings of the Chicago School, evidenced in the early writings of Merriam, toward a more general, abstract, and, one might say, "non-political" objective. That Machiavelli's works, whose concepts were seminal for the Chicago School, had a similar intention to reform is not as clear, despite the fact that he seemed to admire free republics more than one-man despotisms. He was ready to prescribe for the construction and stabilization both of free societies (in *Discourses*) and of tyrannies (*The Prince*).[88]

More in the normatively-neutral style of Machiavelli is another of Lasswell's books, entitled *Politics: Who Gets What, When, How?* (1936). Here he returned to the framework employed by his teacher, Charles Merriam, and attempted to extend the analysis of the power of political elites—how it is won, lost, and sustained. Lasswell states the intention of his book in these terms in its first paragraph:

> The study of politics is the study of influence and the influential. The science of politics states conditions; the philosophy of politics justifies preferences. This book, restricted to political analysis, declares no preferences. It states conditions.[89]

Like Machiavelli, Lasswell divided the world into two kinds of people: elite (Machiavelli's "The Few") and mass (Machiavelli's "The Many"). And he assigned to them typically Machiavellian values:

> The influential are those who get the most of what there is to get. Available values may be classified as *deference, income, safety.* Those who get the most are *elite*; the rest are *mass*.[90]

Like Machiavelli, Lasswell noted that deference (glory) is peculiarly an elite value, while safety is more equally distributed between the few and the many. Unlike Machiavelli, he presented statistical evidence to document his observations.[91] Lasswell also set forth a more complex classification of elites than Machiavelli, who was content to distinguish leaders with princely virtue from leaders with republican virtue. The new categorization referred elite status to skills (e.g., in fighting, in political organization, in

---

[87]See Crick's analysis of Lasswell's therapeutic intention, *op. cit.,* pp. 198-201.

[88]See *per contra,* James Burnham, *The Machiavellians* (New York: The John Day Company, Inc., 1943).

[89]In *The Political Writings of Harold D. Lasswell,* p. 295.

[90]*Ibid.*

[91]*Ibid.,* pp. 295, 296.

manipulating symbols), to social class, to personality (using Freudian categories), and to attitudes signifying influence based on shared symbols of loyalty to nation, class, occupational role, and authoritative persons).[92] The bulk of the book was taken up with detailed discussion of these bases of elite status. Special attention was given to the ability to manipulate the symbols of universal ideologies, such as communism, a new political reality of our time. The closest parallel in Machiavelli's work is his description of the manner in which Roman generals manipulated religious rituals in order to instill courage into their superstitous troops. Lasswell also took note of the emergence of a new kind of elite in recent times, which might be described as a function of modern ideological dynamics. "Perhaps the distinguishing and unifying political movement of our times," he wrote, "is the emergence of the lesser-income skill groups to hegemony in a world where the partial diffusion, partial restriction of the world-revolutionary pattern of 1917 is taking place atop the world created by the revolution of 1789."[93]

The general scope of Lasswell's study was also broader than Machiavelli's: "influence and the influential," rather than power in specifically governmental form, embodied in kings, princes, generals, Roman Tribunes and Senators, Renaissance Gonfalonieri and Condottiere. As a consequence of this broader focus, Lasswell chose not political office but "shares in values" that are socially prized, as the measure of the influence of a particular person or group.[94]

The Influence of the Chicago School.   Like that of Charles Merriam, the work of Harold Lasswell is as important for the empirical studies it inspired as for the new theoretical insights and empirical revelations it contains. The science of politics conceived by the Chicago School has flourished since 1945 in the form of behavioralism, post-behavioralism, rational choice analysis, and some varieties of functionalism, which make up today's science of politics in the United States. Heinz Eulau, one of the leading behavioral scholars of this decade, pays the following tribute to the Chicago School:

[In the late forties and early fifties] the seeds planted at Chicago had spread across the prairies of academe and grown into plants. Chicagoans turned out to be the most innovative of American political scientists. Herbert Simon published his attack on conventional public administration in 1947; V.O. Key breathed new life into American studies in 1949; Gabriel Almond tackled the ticklish relationship between public opinion and foreign policy in 1950; David Truman established contact with the group notions of the neglected pioneer

[92]*Ibid.*, pp. 297-305.
[93]*Ibid.*, p. 454.
[94]*Ibid.*, p. 309.

Arthur Bentley in 1951; and Lasswell himself, with the help of Abraham Kaplan codified much of his thinking in 1950.[95]

Numerous young empiricists were given encouragement and support by Charles Merriam. Among them were Harold F. Gosnell, who introduced quantification techniques to the study of voting behavior, and Quincy Wright, a pioneer in the empirical analysis of international politics, whom Merriam brought to Chicago from the University of Minnesota. Four of Merriam's students, besides Lasswell, who also became well known for their behavioral research, have served in the office of President of the American Political Science Association: Gabriel A. Almond, V.O. Key, C. Herman Pritchett, and David B. Truman.[96]

Lasswell's influence has been equally extensive among the several generations of American political scientists who have matured since World War II. His largest impact has no doubt been in the area of political psychology, and is found in the work of T.W. Adorno, Arnold Rogow, Herbert McClosky, Robert D. Lane, and James D. Barber. But Heinz Eulau maintains that Lasswell's thought has been equally seminal in many other areas. He has even argued that "there are few ideas in contemporary political science that cannot be found in Lasswell's early work," and that Lasswell "anticipated current interest in system theory, in functional analysis, in the study of roles, in the diagnosis of symbolic behavior, in the science of public policy, and in many methodological topics such as content analysis, participant observation, objectifying interviews, and experimental design."[97] Elite studies, such as those carried out by Ithiel de Sola Pool, propaganda analysis, and trend research also owe much to Lasswell's inspiration.[98]

Machiavelli and the "Group Process" School

Machiavelli and Harrington. A body of American political science clearly related to the approaches pioneered by the Chicago School, and developed by the younger members of that school, though originating in another source, is the literature of "Group Process." The leading concepts of this important literature, which constitutes the most authoritative work done in the field of parties and pressure groups since 1945, derives from the

[95]Heinz Eulau, "The Maddening Methods of Harold D. Lasswell," in Arnold A. Rogow, ed., *Politics, Personality, and Social Science in the Twentieth Century: Essays in Honor of Harold D. Lasswell* (Chicago: University of Chicago Press, 1969), p. 16.

[96]Bruce Lannes Smith, "The Mystifying Intellectual History of Harold D. Lasswell," in Rogow, ed., *op. cit.,* pp. 54, 55.

[97]Rogow, ed., *op. cit.,* p. 16.

[98]See Smith, *op cit.* in *Ibid.,* pp. 68, 75, 88-89.

theoretical work of Arthur F. Bentley, a pragmatist philosopher who was a contemporary of Charles Beard and a friend and collaborator of John Dewey. His study of 1908, *The Process of Government*, was the seminal book for this entire large body of work.

Bentley's thought carried forward the "interest" focus first developed theoretically by a Machiavellian thinker of seventeenth century England, the classical republican, James Harrington, and developed in the American context by James Madison, and John C. Calhoun. In his *Oceana*, a model for a perfectly stable republican system, dedicated to Oliver Cromwell and published in 1656, Harrington expressed his great admiration for Machiavelli. He was for Harrington "the greatest artist in the modern world," "the Prince of Politicians," "the only Politician of later ages," "the sole retriever of this ancient prudence."[99]

Harrington adopted in its entirety Machiavelli's theory of political motivation, together with his observational-historical method. But he went further than did Machiavelli in eliminating from the science of politics such traditional concepts as "virtue."

Machiavelli, the reader will recall, had found the chief cause of political change in social "corruption," the loss of civic "virtue." But "in showing what a *corrupt people* is," Harrington wrote, "[Machiavelli] hath either involved himself or me." He felt that he could "come out of the *Labyrinth*" only by substituting a sociological explanation, by relating changes in the distribution of property to structural changes in the government.[100] Let us say, wrote Harrington, that when the balance alters, a people "as to the foregoing *Government*, must of necessity be *corrupt*."[101] But in this formula he had placed a new meaning on "corruption." It no longer signified psychological and moral decay, to Harrington unmanageable concepts. We have instead a shorthand expression for the empirically observed fact of sociological and political change. It could mean "no more than that the *corruption of one Government (as in natural bodies) is the generation of another*." A government which is out of line with the property balance, dissolves.[102]

---

[99]Cited in H.R. Russell-Smith, *Harrington and his Oceana* (Cambridge: Cambridge University Press, 1914), p. 19.

[100]It is interesting that Arthur Bentley, the father of modern group theory, rejects psychology as a basis for political science with precisely the same metaphor as that used by Harrington. In *The Process of Government*, Bentley says: "Motives? They may be as complex as you will and with them you go into the labyrinth, not into the light." Arthur F. Bentley, *The Process of Government* (Evanston, Ill.: Principia Press, 1935), p. 180.

[101]*Oceana*, p. 55.

[102]See Judith N. Schklar, "Ideology Hunting: The Case of James Harrington," *American Political Science Review*, LIII (1959), p. 675.

The importance of "approach" for the final result of theoretical analysis is clearly seen in a comparison of Machiavelli's and Harrington's estimates of republican stability. Machiavelli could conceive of no institutional arrangement which would guarantee permanent moral stability, to him the foundation of the system. All political orders, he thought, have a natural life cycle which ultimately brings decay. Such stability as there can be depends less on institutional devices than on the periodic appearance of a strong-willed leader who by a "return to the beginnings," that is, by terror, revives public virtue in a population. By contrast, Harrington could see no reason why a republic might not be made to last forever. If "virtue" cannot be engineered, the distribution of property can be. Therefore, if one creates institutions which fix an established balance of property and keep public officials responsible to the dominant social group, there is no reason why a commonwealth cannot be perpetual.

The shift from Machiavelli's pyscho-moral focus to a socio-economic interpretation of political stability and change produced the key concept of Harrington's political theory, the notion of "interest." Governments are founded upon interest and express the demands of interest.

> All Government is Interest, and the predominant Interest gives the Matter or Foundation of the Government.[103]

"Interest" designated for him, except in one unique case, a social group, as in the theories of the modern "group process" writers. As the constellation of groups is, so will the government be.

It is not all groups which counted for Harrington, but chiefly property groups, and especially those which control property in land. These were the decisive interests. In a few places he did broaden the concept to include commercial groups and others whose power rests on money rather than land.[104] But nowhere did he arrive at the broad conception of interest as a shared attitude, a much more general and useful term, which is the special contribution of David Truman, a modern group theorist.

Some have seen Harrington as a forerunner of Marx in his belief in the economic foundations of political order. But the connection is more ap-

[103]*A System of Politics* in John Toland, ed., *The Oceana of James Harrington and His Other Works,* hereafter cited as *Collected Works,* (London, 1700), p. 498.

[104]Thus, in defining "Dominion" he says that it consists in "Propriety . . . in Lands, or in money and goods," and that "in a City that hath little or no Land, and whose revenue is in Trade" the balance of property must be computed in money rather than in land. In the *Prerogative of Popular Government* he spells out in even more detail the political importance of property in money or capital vis-à-vis land. See James Harrington, *Oceana,* ed. S.B. Liljegren (Heidelberg: Winter, 1924), pp. 14-15; and citation in Charles Blitzer, *An Immortal Commonwealth: The Political Thought of James Harrington* (New Haven: Yale University Press, 1960), p. 125.

parent than real, for Harrington saw in the institutions of governmental authority a weapon which groups not in control of economic power could use to gain that power. In the event of a discrepancy between the two, it was not a foregone conclusion that the economic power groups would ultimately "frame the superstructure unto the foundation." Those in control of the government might rather "frame the foundation unto the Government," which implies that officiality, organization, intelligence, vigor, and other elements of power can in a short-run period outweigh economic power, though in the long run the two must be brought together.

In his recognition that the holders of official power are sometimes, *because* of their official status, able to exert power against economic interests and in fact reorganize those interests, Harrington was a step ahead of some of the modern group process theorists who, while they are able to see that organization and other things as well as property are able to yield political power, have a blind spot when it comes to the importance of official institutions of government. They often relegate official processes and structures to the position of mere registers of power generated elsewhere, without independent value. Parties and interest groups are seen as prime movers, and officials become merely their instruments.

Action which is in accordance with interest Harrington called "rational" or "reasonable." But this does not yield an adequate ethical principle, for "there be divers *interests* and so divers *reasons*."[105] How may we choose among these interests and reasons? Harrington spoke of "that *Reason* which is the interest of mankind, or of the whole." This he called a "Law of Nature . . . which is more excellent, and so acknowledged to be by the agents themselves then the right or interest of the parts onely." He made a comparison between men and things "that want sense, that . . . in themselves . . . have a Law which directeth them, in the means whereby they tend to their own perfection." Just so, men have a Law "which toucheth them as they are sociable parts united into one body, a Law which bindeth them each to serve unto others' good, and all to prefer the good of the whole, before whatsoever their own particular."[106] All of this seems rather different from the assumptions of radical self-interestedness which underlie the rest of the book, a strange return to medieval theories of moral perfection. Yet Harrington's boast in *Oceana* was that he could create a perfect commonwealth of sinful and selfish men who are interested in nothing but their own utility and profit.

Perhaps the clause which follows the passage just quoted tells us how we ought to receive it. Harrington proposed a physical simile to his natural law of sociability and disinterestedness. This law operates in us, he said, "as when stones or heavy things forsake their ordinary wont or center, and fly

[105]*Oceana*, p. 22.
[106]*Idem*.

upwards, as if they heard themselves commanded to let go the good they privately wish, and to relieve the present distresse of Nature in common."[107] Perhaps we have here an example of secret writing. Harrington was trying to say that no one naturally has a conception of or desire for the common good, but that the institutions of the political order can channel our self-interests into courses which produce a common good, conceived in the manner of Machiavelli's common good, just as stones can be *made* to fly upward by the human hand, though without that intervention they plunge downward. This makes more sense than the idea that Harrington accepted a traditional natural law conception of the common good.

If, then, we suppose that Harrington did not really hold for a conception of the common good, why did he prefer the republican order? Perhaps hedonist individualism has a majoritarian principle hidden in it; if there is any good better than that of any individual, it is the addition of individual goods, the greatest quantity of them. This seems implied in a passage of *Oceana* in which Harrington said, "whereas the people taken apart, are but so many private interests, but if you take them together, they are the publick interest."[108] He went on to say that "the publick interest of a commonwealth (as hath been shown) is nearest that of mankind, and that of mankind is right reason."[109] But this last is mere window dressing. He simply seems to mean that the only public interest you have results from the adding up of all the particular interests, and that a quantity of such private goods somehow has more value than any one. This assumption also appears to be a chief moral premise of modern theorists of group process.

A republic should accept as natural and healthy the opposition of interests. As long as there is a republican balance of property and a sound system in the superstructure, it can do no harm. In the balance that underlies the republican system there is a large area of common interest.

> Men that have equall possessions, and the same security of their estates and liberties that you have, have the same cause with you to defend.[110]

The area of antagonism and opposition can safely be managed by the well-wrought institutions of a republican superstructure.

> The nature of orders in a *Common-wealth* rightly instituted being void of all Jealousie, because let the parties which she embraceth be what they will, her orders are such, as they neither would resist if they could, nor could if they would.[111]

[107]*Idem.*
[108]*Oceana*, p. 141.
[109]*Ibid.*, pp. 141-42.
[110]*Idem.*
[111]*Idem.*

Again, Harrington pointed forward to modern group theory, which in recent years has given legitimacy to the notion of pressure group activity in America. For many years, under the influence of certain Rousseauistic notions in our political culture which condemn partial interests as inimical to the General Will voiced by "the people," pressure groups were considered odious and detrimental to democracy. Many group theorists, by contrast, see in the free play of interests the very principle of justice. The only thing which can be defined as the "just" is the results of the interaction of groups—of conflict and compromise—within the framework of our republican "orders." Like Harrington, group theory stresses the principle of equality. It is *equal* interests whose interplay has this benign result, and if reform is called for at all it is in this direction. Get more interests organized and on a more equal footing. Group theorists would no doubt agree with Harrington that "if a Commonwealth be perfectly equal, it is void of Sedition, and has attained to perfection, as being void of all internal causes of dissolution."[112]

The interests which Harrington envisaged operating in his model commonwealth were chiefly the property groups whose relationships determine the fundamental balance of the system. There are indications that he had a broader conception of interest; however, unlike the private interest organizations of our own system, his were given a formal status in the constitution. Apparently he tried to conceive a priori what all of the major lines of cleavage would naturally be in a society, and then built the system around them, giving each an official status and function with regard to elections. Thus he listed the "Divisions of the People; first into Citizens and Servants; Secondly, into Youth and Elders; Thirdly, Into such as have an hundred pound a year in Lands, Goods, or Monies, who are of the Horse, and such as have under, who are the Foot. Fourthly, by their usual residence into Parishes, hundreds, and Tribes."[113]

Arthur F. Bentley. The hardheaded categories of interest group theory found a place in the writings of American political scientists both in the eighteenth and early nineteenth centuries, as we have noted. But from the middle of the century down to the appearance of Arthur Bentley's *The Process of Government* in 1908, American political science lost sight of the important place of the interest group in the political system. Under the influence of German philosophy it became preoccupied with the formal analysis of legal institutions within the framework of a mystical theory of the state as the embodiment of "soul" and "idea."

Bentley's book, in fact, is an attack on this kind of political science in

[112]*The Art of Law Giving* in *Collected Works,* p. 394. See also p. 462, and *Oceana,* p. 135.

[113]*Oceana,* p. 198.

the name of a more adequate mode of analysis. A full chapter is devoted to a critique of each of the styles of political inquiry which were fashionable at the turn of the century. Bentley criticizes the comparative study of constitutional forms characteristic of the work of people like Garner and Burgess as "a formal study of the most external characteristics of governing institutions." Such studies proceed with their legalistic classifications and comparisons *in vacuo,* he argues, never mentioning underlying social realities. "They lose all sight of the content of the process [of political activity] in some trick point about the form."[114]

Bentley even hits out against psychological interpretations of politics. Neither the motives nor feelings nor ideas nor ideals of individuals are ascertainable causes of events. They are just as much unreal "soul stuff" as the social mind and will. We have no way of getting at them.

> If we are going to infer a soul quality from the social fact and then use the quality to explain the fact, we put ourselves on a level with animists in the most savage tribes. A branch falls. It was the life in it or behind it that threw it down. Thunder peals. It is a spirit speaking. The grain grows. It is the spirit of the corn pushing it up. This man is a slave. It is because such is his nature. The pigeons are left unharmed. It is because we are growing more humane. We pass child-labor laws. It is because we will not tolerate abuses our fathers tolerated. That man is a boss at the head of a corrupt machine. It is because he is dishonest by nature. This man wrote a great book. It is because he had a giant intellect.[115]

These are crude explanations which Bentley attacks in this paragraph, but he is just as impatient with much more sophisticated motivational theories, such as those of sociologists like Albion W. Small, who developed an elaborate algebra of desires with which to explain the facts of social life. Herbert Spencer also comes in for a drubbing. We are reminded of Harrington's bewilderment at the "labyrinthine" psychological postulates of Machiavelli.

If all these ways of explaining social and political life are sterile, what does Bentley wish to put in their place? The proper object of the political scientist's investigation, according to Bentley, is political activity, political process.

> The raw material can be found only in the actually performed legislating-administering-adjudicating activities of the nation and in the streams and currents of activity that gather among the people and rush into these spheres.[116]

[114]Bentley, *op. cit.,* p. 162.

[115]*Ibid.,* p. 19.

[116]*Ibid.,* p. 180. See Leo Weinstein, "The Group Approach: Arthur F. Bentley," in Herbert J. Storing, ed., *Essays on the Scientific Study of Politics* (New York: Holt, Rinehart & Winston, Inc., 1962), pp. 163-64, 171, 173, 175.

This *must* be his raw material, for this is political reality. It is not found in formal legal norms in a constitutional code, nor in psychic phenomena which cannot be observed. It is especially in the activity of groups of men rather than of individuals that Bentley finds this reality. Individual actions, as he sees it, are always a function of some group to which the individual belongs. The individual does not act in isolation nor can he be understood in isolation.[117]

Bentley uses the word "interest" interchangeably with "group," giving it a "meaning coextensive with all groups whatsoever that participate in the social process."[118] He also has a special category of "underlying groups" which comes close to the Harringtonian conception of interest, though it is not a very clear concept. An underlying group is apparently an inchoate group with boundaries less clearly defined than those of the "highly differentiated" political group. It is less "manifest, . . . palpable, [and] measurable" than the political group, and it is "reflected" in and "represented" by the political group.[119] It determines the political group, and is never determined by it. This is made evident to the observer when changes in the distribution of power occur among the underlying groups. "Both discussion and organization groups yield to the lower-lying groups with surprising rapidity when the actual change in the balance of pressures takes place."[120]

Bentley's classification of groups which have political roles is much broader than Harrington's. This does not mean that he is interested in all groups whatsoever, such as the class of blondes or brunettes, though he is sure that "if ever blondes or brunettes appear in political life as such it will be through an interest which they assert."[121] Like Marx, rather than Harrington, he emphasizes the techniques and organization of manufacture for the character and relationships of the underlying interests.[122] Bentley denies, however, that the economic group is the exclusive basis of political activity,

---

[117]The source of Bentley's particular conception of the group as a constituting social reality, which involves the notion that the real entity to be studied is a set of inter-individual relations rather than individual entities, is not Harrington but German and Austrian sociologists like Georg Simmel and Ludwig Gumplowicz, and American pluralists and pragmatists like Pierce, James, and Dewey. It might be shown, however, that the nominalism and naturalism of the latter can be traced in part to Harringtonian elements in our political culture. Stanley Rothman has noted the underlying stratum of classical liberalism in the work of Bentley's disciple, David Truman. See his article, "Systematic Political Theory: Observations on the Group Approach," *American Political Science Review*, LIV (1960), 28.

[118]Bentley, *op. cit.*, p. 212.

[119]*Ibid.*, p. 209.

[120]*Ibid.*, p. 446. See Weinstein in Storing, *op. cit.*, pp. 166-67.

[121]Bentley, *op. cit.*, p. 212; Weinstein in Storing, *op. cit.*, p. 192.

[122]Bentley, *op. cit.*, p. 463; Weinstein in Storing, *op. cit.*, pp. 206-7.

though he does not say what other bases there are.[123] He maintains that "the most important of these groups assume wealth forms."[124]

Bentley tends to treat public officials as mere registers of the pressures exerted on them from without. "A discussion of the work and defects of a state legislature carries one nowhere as long as the legislature is taken for what it purports to be—a body of men who deliberate upon and adopt laws." Investigation of the whole range of lawmaking activities "from its efficient demand to its actual application" may reveal the legislature as "Moses the registration clerk" rather than "Moses the law giver."[125] The official procedures of government are techniques through which interest groups operate rather than independent forces in the political process. Secretary of War Taft, proclaiming himself provisional governor of Cuba in the Spanish-American crisis, is described as "merely a ganglion" in the body politic.[126]

In one passage Bentley does recognize that he has overstated his argument, and grants that at least sometimes bodies of governing officials can themselves be viewed as interest groups with a substantial weight of their own in the political system, but the bulk of the text does not give this impression.[127] Harrington, before him, clearly recognized that officials might act as an autonomous interest. This was the reason for the limitations which he placed on the functions of the upper legislative house, which contained the aristocracy of brains. Group theorists *since* Bentley have likewise recognized the importance of treating officials as parts of the interest complex. Earl Latham in particular has emphasized this in his study of basing-point legislation. "They exhibit," he writes, "all the internal social and political characteristics of group forms in that infinite universe of plural forms outside the state apparatus."[128]

Even though Bentley's reaction against legalistic analysis leads him to minimize unduly the role of official institutions in the political process, his assumption that the activity within legislative halls and executive and judicial offices is not self-contained is certainly a sound one. He rightly emphasizes the need to observe behavior from the "efficient demand" for policy by social groups "to its actual application" in the society at large, in order to comprehend the policy-making process. Some of the most valuable work which has been done by Bentley's disciples has taken the form of

[123]Bentley, *op. cit.,* p. 209.

[124]*Ibid.,* p. 462.

[125]*Ibid.,* p. 163.

[126]*Ibid.,* p. 291.

[127]*Ibid.,* p. 444.

[128]Earl Latham, *The Group Basis of Politics, A Study in Basing-Point Legislation* (Ithaca, N.Y.: Cornell University Press, 1952), p. 34.

detailed analyses, case studies of particular pieces of policy. Notable in this literature is Stephen K. Bailey's *Congress Makes a Law*,[129] an analysis of the making of the Employment Act of 1946 and the first full-length study of the legislative process at the national level. Important also are Bertram Gross's *The Legislative Struggle* (1953) and Earl Latham's *The Group Basis of Politics* (1952), cited above. Policy-making case studies are being increasingly employed in the teaching of American government to show the student on what kinds of data sound generalizations must be based and to lead him to theorize for himself.[130]

Bentley and some of his disciples are unwilling to grant that there can be an interest of society as a whole. There is no social whole, only parts locked in conflict. "For political phenomena I think I am justified in asserting positively," he writes, "that no such group as the 'social whole' enters into the interpretation in any form whatever. Where we have a group that participates in the political process we have always another group facing it in the same plane . . . On any political question which we could study as a matter concerning the United States, for example, alone, we should never be justified in treating the interests of the whole nation as decisive. There are always some parts of the nation to be found arrayed against other parts."[131] We have already noted that, while Harrington frequently used the concept of the common interest, it is difficult to see how it could be truly "common" in his frame of reference. He really identified it with a dominant partial interest. Bentley is more frank and honest.

Bentley had three reasons, I believe, for excluding the common-sense notion of the public interest from his analysis. One was methodological. Having defined politics as the activity of clashing groups, he restricts his data accordingly to phenomena revealing conflict. The interest of the whole is thus excluded a priori by Bentley's definition of the area of inquiry. One place where he admits that a national interest is visible is in the study of international conflict, "but it is clear that under such circumstances neither nation is the 'social whole'; it takes the two together to make the society whose processes we are at the time studying."[132]

The second ground for Bentley's rejection of the idea of a common interest was emotional. He was tired of hearing the cant of the interests of his

---

[129]Stephen K. Bailey, *Congress Makes a Law* (New York: Columbia University Press, 1950).

[130]See, for example, the Eagleton Foundation Studies published by Holt, Rinehart & Winston, Inc.; Alan F. Westin, *The Uses of Power, Seven Cases in American Politics* (New York: Harcourt, Brace & World, Inc., 1962); and the publications of the Inter-University Case Program.

[131]Bentley, *op. cit.*, p. 220.

[132]*Idem.* On this point, see R. E. Dowling, "Pressure Group Theory: Its Methodological Range," *American Political Science Review*, LIV, No. 4 (Dec. 1960), 945 and Weinstein in Storing, *op. cit.*, pp. 168-69, 197 ff.

time, who liked to dress their obviously selfish ends in the garb of the general good. A third reason was philosophical. He could think of no way of objectively demonstrating the ethical superiority of any particular claim made in the name of the general interest.

This does not mean that Bentley excludes from his political science all of the things which we commonly range under the idea of community, or of the whole. He admits for example the importance of understanding the "habit background" against which group activity is cast. These "habits" are the "rules of the game," the norms according to which politics are carried on. "This habitual activity is commonly discussed in terms of moral factors."[133] Such elements of political consensus we would say in the common sense are clearly considered by all to be the joint or common interest of all. Perhaps Bentley refuses to give them this name for fear that his reader will confuse two levels of analysis. In his scheme the common elements of the "habit background" constitute only the environment of the political world. Its substance is pressure group activity, and it is this activity that Bentley wishes to designate as "interest." Words with a clear and univocal meaning are the most useful in science.

There is one more Bentleyan notion which should be discussed in connection with the idea of common interest. This is the concept of "adjustment," which specifies for Bentley what all governments aim at. "Government is the process of the adjustment of a set of interest groups in a particular distinguishable group or system."[134] The process may operate without any differentiated activity or organ, or there may be an elaborate organizational structure. By adjustment Bentley seems to mean the resolution of matters at issue in a society, or at least an agreement on a given procedure for reaching solutions. A society in "adjustment" is one in which policy is made with the least amount of friction, with peaceful processes operating to produce decisions. If particular interests aim at advantage in terms of power, the system as a whole aims at peace.[135] "Adjustment" is the end, the terminal point of politics in a stable system. We can classify governments according to the quantity and variety of techniques which groups use to produce adjustment.[136] In a sense, in Bentley's politics, "adjustment" substitutes for the "common good" of traditional political theory.

After one has determined that a system is in "adjustment," it is possible to estimate the "balance" of interests within the system, the particular weights to be assigned to the units. "Once given an organization of the in-

[133]Bentley, *op. cit.*, p. 218. Cf. Dowling, *op. cit.*, pp. 953-54.

[134]Bentley, *op. cit.*, p. 260.

[135]*Ibid.*, p. 301. See Myron Q. Hale, "The Cosmology of Arthur F. Bentley," *American Political Science Review*, LIV, No. 4 (Dec. 1960), 960-61; Weinstein in Storing, *op. cit.*, pp. 217-18.

[136]Bentley, *op. cit.*, p. 305.

terests, held in position by effective groups," Bentley writes, "and with no clashes with changing group interests, then that organization may persist indefinitely. There is no reason why it should not be continued—which is just another way of saying that there is no interest group in action powerful enough to alter it."[137] We are reminded of Harrington's vision of a "perpetual commonwealth," though unlike Harrington, Bentley prescribes no device for maintaining a system in permanent adjustment, no "equal agrarian" nor rotational elections. He merely states a theoretical possibility.

The Group Process School Today.   David Truman, in *The Governmental Process,* follows Bentley's lead in rejecting the concept of a social whole with a common interest. "In developing a group interpretation of politics," he writes, "we do not need to account for a totally inclusive interest, because one does not exist."[138] Given the concepts which he employs, however, his rejection of the idea makes less sense than Bentley's. Instead of defining interest as conflict activity, Truman says that "shared attitudes . . . constitute the interest."[139] Thus the "rules of the game" constitute interests. Truman speaks of them as unorganized interests, "competing with those of various organized groups."[140] He even says that they "are dominant with sufficient frequency in the behavior of enough important segments of society so that . . . both the activity and the methods of organized interest groups are kept within broad limits."[141]

The "serious disturbance" of these unorganized interests "will result in organized interaction and the assertion of fairly explicit claims for conformity."[142] It would seem from this that it is a misnomer to call these "shared attitudes" or procedural norms of the society at large "unorganized interests." The last quotation indicates the public agencies which daily enforce "the dominant interests" against those who create "serious disturbances" are properly viewed as the organization of the general interest. The general interest, therefore, instead of being only a "potential group," is at least at times also actual, and not only an organized but the best-organized interest in the society.[143]

The existence of an organized general interest, operating through the machinery of public government, also follows from Truman's definition of the "association," a particular variety of interest group organization which

---

[137]*Ibid.,* p. 266.

[138]David Truman, *The Governmental Process* (New York: Alfred A. Knopf, Inc., 1951), p. 51.

[139]*Ibid.,* p. 34.

[140]*Ibid.,* p. 514.

[141]*Ibid.,* p. 515.

[142]*Ibid.,* p. 512.

[143]See Dowling, *op. cit.,* p. 954.

typically appears in a complex industrial society. "The function of the association . . . is to stabilize the relations among their members and to order their relations as a group with other groups."[144] The example with which Truman follows this definition is a labor union, but it could as well be the political society as a whole, which is the broadest associational form, whose interest is the common interest. In the work of Earl Latham we have a clear recognition that the common interest is, after all, a genuine reality.

> In civil polities, some association does in fact represent the consensus by which the groups exist in mutual relations. This is the state. It establishes the norms of permissible behavior in group relations and enforces those norms. The fact that men have other group loyalties than the one they bear to the state does not in itself prescribe any limits to the activity of the state. The state is not necessarily confined to a few police functions at the margins where the intersecting and overlapping groups touch each other, nor is it limited to the role of referee in the group conflict. It is established to promote normative goals, as a custodian of the consensus, and to help formulate these goals, as well as to police the agreed rules. In the exercise of its normative functions, it may require the abolishment of groups or a radical revision of their internal structure.[145]

How shall we evaluate the "group process" approach to the study of politics? What are its virtues, what its shortcomings? While Arthur Bentley claimed that his purpose in writing the *Process of Government* was to "fashion a tool" of investigation rather than to present a theory, some writers have argued that his book hardly amounts to this. So far as methodology is concerned, the *Process of Government* has chiefly a negative value. It is a thorough and persuasive critique of the older fashions of political inquiry. But it does not succeed in replacing the old categories of understanding with new ones, nor does it develop a set of analytical techniques. We are told that we must analyze group activity, but we are not told how to proceed. We are told to measure, but not what nor how.[146]

Bentley urges that we dismiss "spooks" and "grasp social facts just for what they are, study them for what they are, analyze and synthesize them for what they are."[147] Surely, though, it is not evident just what those "social

[144]Truman, *op. cit.,* p. 56.

[145]Latham, *op. cit.,* p. 14.

[146]See Dowling, *op. cit.,* pp. 994, 951, 952, and Bernard Crick, *The American Science of Politics* (Berkeley: University of California Press, 1959), Chapter 8. Crick claims Bentley does not show us how we can recognize a significant political fact (p. 122). Roy Macridis says that Bentleyites place exaggerated demands on empirical research and data gathering, and criticizes the conceptual adequacy of group theory. Differences in group organization cannot be explained with the tools at hand. See Roy C. Macridis, "Interest Groups in Comparative Analysis," *The Journal of Politics,* XXIII (1961), 32-35.

[147]Bentley, *op. cit.,* p. 56.

facts" are. What are the concepts with which we are to reduce the observed phenomena to intelligibility? Bentley says that we must get all of the phenomena "stated . . . as differentiated activity" before we have ready the raw material from which we can construct "theories about the relations of the activities."[148] However, he gives us only the vaguest notion of the concepts we must employ to differentiate this activity into its proper classes. Words like "group," "interests," "pressure," and "habit background" are not enough. We must have an entire conceptual order, but Bentley supplies hardly the rudiments of one. In emphasizing the need to give close regard to "efficient causes," he has virtually neglected "formal cause."

In disregarding the psychological, legal, and moral anaysis of the past, Bentley insists that he does not mean to throw out the political realities for which the symbols used in that analysis stand. He wants rather to state those realities more clearly and validly than did the older political science. "The ideals must count," he says. "There is no doubt about it. They are involved in the social fact. But they must be properly stated at their real value, not at their own allegation as to that value." "I think it will be apparent that in casting out the concrete feelings and ideas we are not necessarily casting out the values and meanings they represent. . . . If we can read the values and meanings into another manner of statement which will aid us to interpretation where the concrete feelings and ideas prove themselves incoherent, then we suffer no loss while making a very great gain." This makes it evident that he also wanted to keep "final causes." But again, we are not shown exactly how it can be done.

Contemporary "group process" theorists are attempting to fill in the skeleton conceptual framework which Bentley supplied in his early work. Truman's concept of "equilibrium," though it contains difficulties, is more adequate than Bentley's "adjustment." The notion of "potential groups" is also a refinement of a Bentleyan concept. Latham has reintroduced the individual motives of "self-expression" and "security" as the "impulses which animate the group motion."[149] Nevertheless, the methodology and conceptual framework of group analysis still remain quite crude and simplistic. The importance of group analysis does not lie in methodology but rather in its concrete findings about the American political system.[150] The value of these findings stems from these theorists' faithfulness to two important assumptions: (1) the only true raw material of political analysis is political events, things that are happening, not the words of constitutional documents, and the interpretation of these events must not do violence to them; and (2) organized groups, both within and outside the official network of authority,

[148]*Ibid.,* p. 211.
[149]Latham, *op. cit.,* p. 27.
[150]See Dowling, *op. cit.,* p. 952, and Rothman, *op. cit.,* p. 29.

play a key role in the making of public policy and have a particularly promi-nent place in American politics. As we saw above, Harrington's work is significant for a similar reason, not for its methodological sophistication.

One important difference between the work of Harrington and that of the American group theorists is the absence of prescriptions in the latter. We find nothing like a formula for an "equal agrarian" to establish a republican balance or maintain it, for example. Group theory is wholly descriptive and analytical, and if there is any normative content to it at all, it is a vague flavor of conservatism. In the writings of Truman and Latham there is a note of marvel and admiration at the symmetry and balance of the American political order. Latham, for example, concludes *The Group Basis of Politics* with the following paragraph:

> An awareness of the nature of the group struggle, ubiquitous and constant, is basic to an understanding of what went on in the Eightieth and Eighty-first Congresses. But, at the same time, it is impossible to witness the process in Congress without admiration for the strength of this vital institution of a free people in a democracy. Congressmen looked and sounded inept, and even silly and confused, in various stages of the passage of S. 1008 from committee con-sideration to final enactment. And many would have disagreed with the way in which Congress finally acted on this particular issue. But when so much is said, the fact remains that a fantastically complicated question of public policy was refined and sifted as it went through the mechanism of legislative procedure, at each stage reducing the number of alternatives to be decided, un-til the final stage was reached, and it was then possible for Congressmen to say "aye" or "nay" to a specific and simplified, even over-simplified, choice about which they could make up their minds.[151]

Conclusion

The thought of Machiavelli, historically extended, appropriately culminated in the natural science of politics. Though Machiavelli's own language was that of the moral tradition, the language of inherent good and evil, right and wrong, virtue and vice, his redefinition of its terms pointed away from that tradition toward a new world of naturalistic freedom.

Like Machiavelli, the natural science of politics takes its point of departure from behavior, from what is done, rather than from moral ideals, from what ought to be done. And it theorizes on the basis of systematically collected empirical evidence. Its emphasis throughout is on accurate description, and it eschews moral evaluation. Yet, as we have seen, in the work of the Chicago School, its ultimate purpose was prescription—for a therapeutic method to be used in the scientific enhancement of freedom. Lasswell in particular was fond of the conception of a policy science of

[151]Latham, *op. cit.,* pp. 226-27.

freedom. We are led back in thought to the beginning of Western political philosophy, to the natural science of freedom planned, but abortively executed by Democritus, Protagoras, and the later Sophists.

In its post-Chicago phase, the natural science of politics in the United States has sought to eschew prescription altogether, and to confine itself to a purely descriptive stance.[152] This stance is evident in what we have written above about the group process school, though it is less clear in other branches of scientific politics, such as the rational-choice school which we discuss in the next chapter. While explicit prescription can be renounced, it appears not to be the case that all moral content can be drained from a political theory. For the group process effort at pure description sometimes gives the impression of being a moral celebration of the *status quo,* an admiration of the marvellous way in which the interplay of particular interests automatically gives rise to the interest of the public at large, defined as "adjustment."

Bibliographical Note

Perhaps the most insightful study of Machiavelli's political theory is by Leo Strauss. See his *Thoughts on Machiavelli,* New York: Free Press of Glencoe, Inc., 1958. While Strauss is an anti-Machiavellian, his book is not a polemic but a carefully reasoned interpretation. The author's hostility to Machiavelli remains in the background. Other leading commentaries are Herbert Butterfield, *The Statecraft of Machiavelli,* London: G. Bell & Sons, Ltd., 1955, and John H. Whitfield, *Machiavelli,* Oxford: B. Blackwell, 1947. An interesting monograph on Machiavelli's scholarly method is Leonardo Olschki, *Machiavelli the Scientist,* Berkeley, Calif.: The Gillick Press, 1945. Lord Acton's introduction to the Burd edition of *The Prince* is a classic commentary (L.A. Burd, ed., *Il. Principe,* by Niccolo Machiavelli, Oxford: Clarendon Press, 1891). Leslie Walker's introduction and very extensive notes to his two-volume edition of *The Discourses* are extremely useful. The notes compare Machiavelli's treatment of the historical events which he interprets with that of his sources. See Leslie J. Walker, ed. and trans., *The Discourses of Niccolo Mahiavelli,* 2 vols., New Haven, Conn.: Yale University Press, 1950. For an admirer's commentary on Machiavelli, see Max Lerner's introduction to the Modern Library edition of *The Prince and the Discourses,* New York: Random House, 1940. See also another pro-Machiavellian book, James Burnham, *The Machiavellians,* New York: The John Day Company, Inc., 1943, which contains a discussion of the political theory of several modern Machiavellian political theorists, Mosca, Pareto,

[152]See David Easton, *The Political System* (New York: Alfred A. Knopf, 1953).

and Michels. Two useful collections of interpretive essays are Anthony Parel, ed., *The Political Calculus: Essays on Machiavelli's Philosophy,* Toronto: University of Toronto Press, 1972, and Martin Fleischer, ed., *Machiavelli and the Nature of Political Thought,* New York: Atheneum, 1972. An important new study of Machiavelli's ideas in relation to modern political culture is John G. Pocock, *The Machiavellian Moment: Florentine Political Thought and the Atlantic Republican Tradition,* Princeton, N.J.: Princeton University Press, 1975.

A bibliography of the Chicago School and of theories of group process is found in the footnotes of this chapter.

PART TWO

Theories of Political Freedom

With Thomas Hobbes, the axial concept of political philosophy shifted from "Virtue" to "Freedom," and has remained there to the present time. Machiavelli prepared the way for this change, as we have seen, by his startling redefinition of "virtue," and by celebrating the democratic republic as the best political order. But he did all this within the language of the aristocratic and organicist moral tradition. In the philosophy of Hobbes, the old language was largely stripped away, and a new world of equal and autonomous individuals came into view.

Hobbes's world was a naturalistic and atomistic one, like that of Democritus, in which human freedom resembled the freedom of particles of matter in space, moving toward and away from one another, according to "gravitational" princi- ples of attraction and repulsion. That the attractiveness of this mechanical metaphor should reassert itself so markedly in seventeenth-century political philosophy is a testimony to the enormous impression of power made on the minds of Renaissance men by the new science of Copernicus, Galileo, Kepler, Newton, and others. It is also a tesimony to Hobbes's disenchantment with the language of religion and ethics. The bloody and cruel wars of religion of the sixteenth and seventeenth cen- turies had been fought about the nature of divine truth; disagreement about "the Good," about virtue, seemed to Hobbes the root of the barbarous behavior of his time. Scientific rationality and individual freedom, mechanically ordered, might well show the way to peace out of the disorder of the English Civil War.

Hobbes's system of freedom was a paradoxical one, however. For his effort to unite man with physical nature made "freedom," defined as the absence of exter- nal impediments to motion, compatible with the unfreedom of purely mechanical behavior. It ruled out freedom of the will, free choice. In a state of nature, "rational" behavior was conflictual; in a state of civil society it was peaceful. But in each case, the rationality displayed was that of the machine.

In Chapter 7 we describe Hobbes's solution to the problem of freedom and order, via the institution of a leviathan state, and we explore the problematical consistency of his theory of mechanical rationality. The utilities and difficulties of the Hobbesian approach we then investigate in contemporary "rational choice" theories of public policy, which rest on premises about the nature of man that we can trace back to Hobbes.

In the writings of John Locke, naturalism relaxed its theoretical rigor. Empirical and experimental in his approach, Locke eschewed any effort to construct a mathematically proportioned political machine, governed by necessary principles of causation. He was content instead to present a utilitarian scheme for marrying freedom to order, by showing how a social majority devoted to defending the individual's freedom to acquire an unequal share of property, could be formed. Specifically in view was an explanation of how the Glorious Revolution of 1688 came about, why it was legitimate, and why the settlement that was its outcome would last. In Chapter 8 we explore Locke's propertarian theory of freedom, and its dependence on his naturalistic theory of ideas, the foundation of modern associationist psychology. We also attempt to display its significance for the political culture of middle-class America, and the academic political theories that express the norms of that culture.

In the work of Rousseau we meet a naturalism born of an atomized French society like that of Hobbes's State of Nature, a society on the verge of revolutionary change. Unlike Hobbes, however, Rousseau supposed that the "atoms" could be transmuted into functions of a moral organism, participants in a shared community life, in which "freedom" would be defined as a "General Will." Thus sentiment and will, not reason, became the keys to freedom and order. And we are not surprised that this approach yielded a Cassandra-warning that scientific rationality and the technological society that was its product might point the way to doom rather than freedom. Rousseau's naturalism thus led in aspiration, out of the modern state, back to the simpler lifestyle of yeoman democracy—to an early Geneva, rather than to modern Paris. In chapter 9 we spell out Rousseau's theory of the "General Will," and then see how modern political scientists, of a Rousseauistic persuasion, have attacked the problem of finding that will in large, urban, technological states like our own—a problem Rousseau himself believed insoluble.

By requiring that natural man, the radical individualist, be educated to sociality, to a sharing in the "General Will," Rousseau had subtly reintroduced the concept of virtue within the rubrics of freedom. Hobbes and Locke had taken natural man as they found him. Their educational schemes enlightened calculating reason. But they did not aim at the reformation of character. Rousseau had precisely such an end in view, a reshaping of the soul—according to an implicit idea of sociality as a virtue. That his social man was conventionally, not naturally sociable—for Rousseau's naturalistic world contained no natural tele or perfections—made problematical the sort of virtue that this was. We therefore call Rousseau and his successors "teleo-naturalists." Rousseau himself insisted on retaining the language of freedom. Social man remained "as free as he was before," subject only to the "General Will," which was " his will."

In the writings of Kant, the return of virtue was less ambiguous. For the Kantian man of good will who obeyed the rule of the "Categorical Imperative" obeyed a rule of Absolute Right. The noumenal world of tele indeed remained closed to mankind. That Right exists was now a presupposition, not a moral fact which our minds can know. But it was for Kant a necessary presupposition, if words like "ought" and "should" were to have any meaning, if our sense that we are obliged to do what is Right was not to be a mockery. Kant's dutiful man was therefore a virtuous man of faith. He was also a free man, who gave laws to himself, constrained only by the principle of law itself—universal and equal applicability—and by the recognition that others must be treated with dignity, for they also are free men, capable of listening to the voice of right. Moral freedom made a man a member of the noumenal world of ends, though he remained also an actor in the phenomenal world, in which every end is only a means to another end, in an infinite chain of causality.

In Chapter 10 we present Kant's free man of good will (or good man of free will), and his representative republic, the political structure within which all men were required to act as though they were men of good will, required to treat each other as ends, never as means only. This was Kant's halfway house from the naturalism of phenomenality to noumenal virtue and freedom. The world was moving toward it, he believed, through the confusion of the French Revolution, and the shock waves it set up throughout traditional Europe. We also examine in this chapter the important place of Kantian ethics in the work of two eminent moral philosophers of our time.

Kant had described how the free man ought to act. But he had only hope, not certainty, that virtue and freedom would in fact be brought together–that a "Kingdom of Ends" would someday exist without the coercive law of republican order. It remained for Hegel, more closely tied to the fervid faith and optimism of the French Revolution than Kant, to show that this noumenal world of freedom is actually coming into being, through the conflictual dialectics of history. For Hegel, the naturalistic processes of the world were given noumenal meaning as the alienated self of a "World Spirit," or Universal Idea of Right and Freedom, striving in the particularities of historical existence to fulfill itself. Through dialectical alienation, and the overcoming of that alienation, the world of moral freedom was being completed in the life of mankind. In every age Hegel discerned progressively higher levels of freedom—for one, for some, ultimately for all. Napoleon, a "world historical figure," was carrying freedom forward in his time, laying the groundwork of liberal order.

In Chapter 11 we describe the salient features of the dialectical politics of Hegelian freedom, and the culminating structures of the modern liberal state, as Hegel understood them to be emerging from the work of early 19th century German reformers, who had caught the spirit of the Revolution. We also examine the literature of phenomenology, a humanist extension, in our post-liberal time, of Hegelian developmental theory, which seeks to point the way to human freedom and authenticity through "praxis." Praxis pits the creative human idea and will against the obstacles of the technological world of impersonal givens, and shows us the way to overcome our own alienation, born of technical rationality and inequality.

For Karl Marx, the economic dimension of alienation loomed large, and the wrenching, dehumanizing experience of capitalist industrialization during the nineteenth century seemed manifest evidence of the validity of his analyis of it. The centralization of production in the factory system, together with its enormously complex division of labor, had pushed the alienation of man from himself, from others, and from nature to its furthest point, while at the same time creating the superabundant productivity which Marx believed to be the chief precondition of overcoming that alienation once and for all. In collaboration with Frederick Engels, Marx spent a lifetime redefining the dialectical process in economic terms, in order to develop a scientific instrument for understanding (and ultimately predicting and controlling) the historical emergence of the non-alienated communist society of free, creative persons. Paradoxically, a perfectly impersonal, scientific comprehension of the naturalistic forces which produce selfishness, greed, competition, and the desire to dominate, would yield insight into the personal, humane, unselfish, cooperative and equal world of autonomous persons of the communist future.

In Chapter 12, we review the outlines of the original Marxist theory, both in its humanist and scientific aspects, and then its twin contemporary culminations in totalitarian scientism and liberal humanism, emphasizing the latter's growing role in American political studies.

John Stuart Mill, who lived through most of the experience of nineteenth-century industrialization, gave us a rather different account of it from Marx, although we discern a similar Hegelian influence in the background of his thought. For Mill, the great impediment to freedom was not capitalist exploitation but the tyranny of mass taste and opinion that had accompanied the development of mass production in large urban centers. Capitalism's bad features could be mitigated by public regulation and by competition from cooperative enterprises in selected areas, and its enormous efficiency in the productive process would continue to benefit mankind. More problematical was the establishment of political and social institutions which would insure the freedom of creative individuals to conceive and express new ideas and lifestyles, the necessary leaven of mass culture if human progress were to continue.

In Chapter 13, we describe Mill's theories of liberal progress, in which cultural elitism, defined as the guaranteed freedom of the creative few from mass control, is combined with the institutions of representative political democracy. We also look into the writings of a modern philosopher who agrees with Mill that the expansion of individual freedom of expression and style of living is the crucial problem of our time. We also note this writer's frank naturalism, which eventuated in an extreme individualism, unbounded by the teleo-naturalist organicism of Mill's own thought. Despite his emphasis on individual liberty, Mill insisted on the essential sociality of mankind, and implied, although ambiguously, a noumenal ideal of virtue as the ultimate justification of the human quest for personal freedom.

Nietzschean nihilism and Nietzche's prophecy of the over-man close our study of theories of virtue and freedom. Nietzsche's thought dissolved all systems, both noumenal and naturalistic, which sought to express in comprehensive, rational form the ideal order of human existence. Neither virtue nor freedom, nor any teleo-naturalist combination of the two, as a public order of ultimate right, was for him the primary reality and end of the human enterprise. It was rather the subjective will to power that counted. From this primal irrational urge, not mechanistic drive but free will to self-assertion, in the past had come all dreams of virtue and freedom, all cultures and polities, all social and economic systems. No noumenal or natural world that might be known either by the teleological or scientific reason, preexisted this urge and will. Nor was there any "World Spirit" or communal human person for whom there was a preexisting historical plan of self-realization. There was only creative self-will, which over the years might be dragged down to passivity and banality of expression by its own creations, eventuating in the whimpering and stupid "mass man" of today's liberal democratic and socialist societies. But this too would pass, with the appearance of the over-man, who would set aside all systems of order, of right and wrong, of virtue and freedom, and create again, out of his will to power, a new world.

In Chapter 14, we explore the Nietzschean denouement of our story of virtue and freedom, in which both ideas are simply reflexes of the will to power in its eternal cycles of creativity and nihilism. We also look at two recent products of Nietzsche's thought—the domineering will to power of Nazi totalitarianism and the humanist self-assertion of the existentialist in the face of the bewildering situation into which he has been cast by unknown fates.

In Chapter 15, we reflect on the nihilistic character of our time, in which nothing is true and everything is permitted. We also note that the language of ordinary men still retains signs of a human hunger for goodness and a love of freedom, but that it expresses as well an existential puzzlement about what these might mean today, if we try to combine them, as we must.

Chapter 7

Individual Preferences
and the Free Society:
Hobbes and "Rational Choice" Theory

Thomas Hobbes has been something of a bogy man of political thought because of the authoritarian doctrines of his famous *Leviathan*. Both in his own time and in ours, his theory of sovereignty has shocked people, especially those who have not studied it carefully. He has even earned the name, though undeservedly, of first theorist of totalitarianism.[1] Less shocking than the Leviathan notion, more difficult to understand, and of far greater significance is Hobbes's distinctive method of political analysis, on which we shall focus in this chapter.

With the exception of Plato, the writers whom we have studied to this point all assumed that the method of purely abstract disciplines such as mathematics had no relevance for the study of politics. Politics, as an activity of the changing empirical world, they believed, must be understood with what Aristotle called the "practical reason," and political prescriptions had to take the form of prudential rules rather than of universal and necessary truths. In the work of Hobbes we have an attempt to bring mathematics back into the study of politics, but in a way quite different from the mystical dialectic of Plato. Like Machiavelli and Thucydides, Hobbes rejects transcendentalist explanations and casts his theory in a mechanistic and naturalistic framework. His world-view is much like that of modern science, and his use of mathematics approaches that of the physical scientist.

Between Hobbes's time and the present we find very little evidence of such investigative techniques in the literature of political theory. Only the "felicific calculus" of Bentham approaches it. Since about 1950, however, great strides have been made in the mathematization of politics, and the second part of this chapter will be devoted to the work of two strategy

[1]Joseph Vialatoux, *La Cité Totalitaire de Hobbes* (Lyons: Chronique Sociale de France, 1952).

theorists, Anthony Downs and William H. Riker, whose methods of analysis bear striking resemblance to that of Hobbes.

Hobbes used to say that fear and he were born twins and were ever thereafter inseparable. His mother was frightened by the approach of the Spanish Armada in 1588, when she was carrying him, and he was born prematurely. Nor were the events of Hobbes's boyhood to compensate for his prenatal insecurity; precisely the opposite, for his father, though a vicar, was a brawling ne'er-do-well who deserted his wife and three children. Remembering the anxieties attendant upon unstable domestic authority, Hobbes must have suffered more than normal alarm at the unsettled politics of the 1620s and '30s, which culminated in the collapse of the public power in 1642, when the tensions between King and Parliament erupted into open war. He fled immediately to France, the first of the *émigrés*. It is not surprising, in view of these personal experiences, that the causes of stable authority should be the central concern of Hobbes's political theory.

Hobbes early demonstrated unusual intellectual powers, and his uncle undertook to educate him. At the age of fourteen he matriculated at Oxford, and after finishing there he entered the service of the Cavendish family as a kind of resident scholar and tutor. It was as traveling companion to the scion of this noble family and, another time, to the son of Sir Gervase Clifton that he had the opportunity to tour the Continent, where he came under the influence of the classical scholarship and the new science of the High Renaissance which were to shape his method of political analysis. From his visit to Italy he came home in love with classical literature and set about translating Thucydides, an experience to which we may attribute many of the concepts of Hobbes's psychology. On another trip abroad he discovered Euclidean geometry, an event that was for him virtually a religious revelation. And from men like Galileo and Mersenne, whom he met on his travels, he learned the mechanistic world-view of the new physics which was then turning the intellectual world upside down.

The *Elements of Law,* Hobbes's first political work, was finished in 1640, two years before the civil war broke out, and it reveals both the writer's concern with the problem of stability and his reliance on mathematical method. It was fear that the doctrines of the book might lead to persecution by the men of the Long Parliament that made Hobbes an *émigré* to Paris, where he remained until 1651. The publication that year of *Leviathan,* which some have read as an apology for Cromwell, sent him back to England, this time fearful of the animosities of Royalist sympathizers in France. At the Restoration, however, the King treated him with good grace and welcomed him at Court. Except for a brief stir in 1666, caused by some of the Anglican Bishops over the atheistic doctrines of *Leviathan,* Hobbes's life was quiet enough from then until his death in 1679.[2]

²For a delightful account of Hobbes's life see Oliver Lawson Dick, ed., *Aubrey's Brief Lives* (London: Secker & Warburg, 1950), pp. 147 *ff.* See also Richard S. Peters, *Hobbes* (Baltimore: Penguin Books, Inc., 1956).

Physics, Geometry, and Politics:
Hobbes's Method

Values and Motives

In his theory of value Hobbes is a Machiavellian, for he holds that it is appetite or passion which designates the good for man. His naturalism is in fact more throughgoing than Machiavelli's, who, in making the distinction between how men actually live and how they ought to live, acknowledged the authority of the traditional ethic, albeit in a rather extraordinary manner. The impossible ideal of Christianity remained a shadowy presence in the background of his work, but real enough to taint his prescriptions for power with the smell of evil. Hobbes entirely exorcises the wraith of transcendent goodness. His break with tradition is complete. "Whatsoever is the object of any mans Appetite or Desire; that is it, which he for his part calleth *Good;* And the object of his Hate, and Aversion, *Evill;* And of his contempt, *Vile* and *Inconsiderable.* For these words of Good, Evil, And Contemptible are ever used with relation to the person that useth them: there being nothing simply and absolutely so; nor any common Rule of Good and Evil to be taken from the objects themselves."[3]

Appetite, to Hobbes, is utterly selfish. "Of the voluntary acts of every man, the object is some *Good to himselfe.*"[4] And if the pursuit of his own values leads a man to deprive another of a good, he is guilty of no moral wrong. "The Desires, and other Passions of man, are in themselves no Sin. No more are the Actions that proceed from those Passions, till they know a Law that forbids them: which till Lawes be made they cannot know."[5]

Hobbes's theory of values and motives is not, as was Machiavelli's, simply the product of empirical observation of behavior, but a deduction from a general theory of reality, his materialistic metaphysics, which contains the axioms from which all the parts of his political theory, method of inquiry as well as substantive doctrines, proceed. A brief review of its essential elements will show us how the various aspects of Hobbes's thought can be integrated.

Matter in Motion. The theories of space, mass, and motion with which seventeenth-century mechanics undertook to describe and explain the movements of physical bodies Hobbes embraces as a complete philosophy of life, adequate for the understanding of the whole of reality. The clarity, precision, and simplicity of mechanical explanations appeal to his neat, well-ordered mind. And they exclude all distressing mystery. Thus man can best be understood as a machine.

[3]Thomas Hobbes, *Leviathan* (New York: E.P. Dutton & Co., Inc. [Everyman's Library], 1950), Chapter 6, 41; J.M. Dent & Sons, Ltd., London.
[4]*Ibid.,* Chapter 14, p. 109.
[5]*Ibid.,* Chapter 13, p. 104.

For seeing life is but a motion of Limbs, the beginning whereof is in some prin-
cipall part within; why may we not say, that all *Automata* (Engines that move
themselves by springs and wheeles as doth a watch) have an artificiall life? For
what is the *Heart* but a *Spring*; and the *Nerves,* but so many *Strings;* and the
Joynts, but so many *Wheels* giving motion to the Body, such as was intended
by the *Artificer?*[6]

Even those things in us which appear to be nonmaterial—all our
thoughts, hopes, fears, desires, loves, hates—can be reduced to mere internal motions, brought into play by the stimulus of an external body and
eventuating in action on the outside world. The pressure on our sense
organs of some external thing gives rise to those motions which we call sensation. This is in turn transmuted into an "apparence to us," a "Fancy,"
and thence into "Imagination" or "Memory," all of these things being
simply "decaying Sense." These motions stimulate still others, the appetites,
which take the form either of attraction to or repulsion from the thing "fan-
cied." All the states of our consciousness can be explained as other internal
motions resulting from these feelings of attraction and revulsion. Thus,
delight or pleasure is the "apparence" of appetite or of good (the name we
give to a "fancy" which attracts us); fear is the "opinion of Hurt" from an
"apparence" that repels us; courage is "the same, with hope of avoyding
that Hurt by resistance"; kindness is the "Love of Persons for society."[7]
And all of our voluntary animal motions—such as walking, running, and
speaking—are an extension and result of this internal passionate activity.
"Will" is simply the name we give to the last passion which precedes action.[8]
    Man is thus nothing but sensations, activity, constant motion, a
restless bearing of the world machine. Whether there are things beyond the
confines of sensation and action, Hobbes does not know. Our feelings are
the only things of which we are aware, and we delude ourselves if we think
we can intuit ends and essences behind them. There are no "intelligible
species" such as the scholars in the universities prate of. "A man can have
no thought, representing anything, not subject to sense."[9] We can name
only the affections of our consciousness with clarity, not that which causes
an appearance or fancy in us. And it seems clear to Hobbes that the same
object will produce different appearances in different men, due to the diversity of passions.[10]
    How can we describe the happiness of a creature such as this? Ob-

    [6]*Ibid.,* Introduction, p. 3.

    [7]*Ibid.,* Chapter 6, pp. 42, 43, 44.

    [8]See Leo Strauss, *The Political Philosophy of Hobbes* (Oxford: Clarendon
Press, 1936), p. 9. The author argues that Hobbes is not consistently a mechanist in
his psychology. See also the argument on pp. 166-70 to the effect that mechanistic
materialism does not provide the foundation of Hobbes's political philosophy.

    [9]*Leviathan,* Chapter 3, p. 21.

    [10]*Ibid.,* Chapter 4, p. 30; Chapter 8, p. 58.

viously, the traditional concepts of fulfillment and perfection, or the contemplation of intelligible reality, either as form or as mystical vision of the Godhead, are quite meaningless. "The Felicity of this life, consisteth not in the repose of a mind satisfied. For there is no such *Finis ultimus,* (utmost ayme,) nor *Summum Bonum,* (greatest Good), as is spoken of in the Books of the old Morall Philosophers. . . . Felicity is a continuall progresse of the desire, from one object to another; the attaining of the former, being still but the way to the later."[11]

Power. In our search for happiness, thus understood, we wish not only to provide for present enjoyment, but, being creatures of foresight, also to assure a contented life in the future. Hence we aim above all at storing up the means "to obtain some future apparent Good." Hobbes uses the word "power" to signify these means, and he assumes as "a generall inclination of all mankind, a perpetuall and restlesse desire of Power after Power, that ceaseth only in Death."[12]

This does not mean that Hobbes considers the desire to dominate others the chief human passion, however. For "power," as he uses the word, does not mean only domination but, more broadly, the ability to secure a good. Wealth is power, friends are power, good luck is power. Sometimes, indeed, domination is the means sought. Interests collide in the race to acquire "Riches, Honour, Command, or other power." And "the way of one competitor, to the attaining of his desire, is to kill, subdue, supplant, or repell the other." But it is also true that men like to live at ease, and to enjoy themselves. Stronger than all passions is the "Fear of Death, and Wounds." These dispose men to live peacefully with one another, under "a common Power."[13]

From this we may infer that men will count as power the knowledge of constituting stable commonwealths that can assure for the long future the "apparence" of the goods of ease, sensual enjoyment, and freedom from fear. It is the restless mind of Hobbes, with its fear of death and lust for power over the future, that has won this knowledge for himself and mankind.

Knowledge as Power. How does the idea of knowledge fit into the framework of material motions which we have been describing? Of what sort is political knowledge? Like all other aspects of life, thought and reasoning are motions, according to Hobbes. Arthur Child sums up Hobbes's thought on this point with particular succinctness.

[11]*Ibid.,* Chapter 9, p. 79.

[12]*Idem.* (I do not agree with MacPherson that "power" in this passage means specifically or only power over other men. See C.B. MacPherson, *The Political Theory of Possessive Individualism* [Oxford: Clarendon Press, 1962]) p. 35.

[13]*Ibid.,* p. 80.

Ratiocination is a causal progress, not by analogy in that without the premises the conclusions could not exist, but in the very same way in which causation holds of external bodies. For reasoning is conducted through names and their connection, which constitute speech; speech is a voluntary motion begun in imagination; imagination is decaying sense; and sense, again, is a motion within a living body: whence reasoning itself is certain motions of a body; and the premises, therefore, are literally the first efficient—and indeed corporeal—causes of the conclusion.[14]

Our reasonings are generated by the desire for power. "Anxiety for the future time, disposeth men to enquire into the causes of things: because the knowledge of them maketh men the better able to order the present to their advantage."[15] "The Thoughts, are to the Desires, as Scouts, and Spies, to range abroad, and find the way to the things Desired."[16] It is only reasoning about causes and effects that can be truly called reasoning, for as we have seen, Hobbes has reduced reality to process. Its fruit is "science," which is "the knowledge of consequences, and dependence of one fact upon another."[17]

Science and Political Science

How is science, and especially political science, acquired? Contrary to what is commonly held, I find a considerable empirical element in Hobbes's method.[18] In the *Elements of Law,* Hobbes says plainly that science has its origin in "some beginning or principle of sense."[19] And several passages in *Leviathan* emphasize the importance of observation for the knowledge of causes and effects. Beasts cannot provide for the future "for want of observation, and memory of the order, consequence, and dependence of the things they see." But "Man observeth how one Event hath been produced by another; and remembereth in them Antecedence and Consequence." This is caused in us by desire, from which "ariseth the Thought of some means we have seen produce the like of that which we ayme at; and from the thought of that, the thought of means to that means." He defines science as "the knowledge of Consequences, and dependence of one fact upon another; by which, out of that we can presently do, we know how to do

[14]Arthur Child, "Making and Knowing in Hobbes, Vico, and Dewey," *University of California Publications in Philosophy,* XVI, (1954), 275-76.

[15]*Leviathan,* Chapter 11, p. 85.

[16]*Ibid.,* Chapter 8, p. 59.

[17]*Ibid.,* Chapter 5, p. 36.

[18]For a traditional statement, see George H. Sabine, *A History of Political Theory,* rev. ed. (New York: Holt, Rinehart & Winston, Inc., 1950), p. 458, or Sheldon Wolin, *Politics and Vision* (Boston: Little, Brown & Co., 1960), p. 251.

[19]Thomas Hobbes, *The Elements of Law* (Cambridge: Cambridge University Press, 1928), Vol. I, Chapter 4, p. 19.

something else when we will, or the like, another time," and to this he immediately adds a statement which describes the process of observation— "Because when we see how anything comes about, upon what causes, and by what manner; when the like causes come into our power, we see how to make it produce the like effects." He also insists that "whatsoever . . . we conceive, has been perceived first by sense, either all at once, or by parts."[20]

Science is not, of course, identical with such observations and prudential calculations as these. It consists rather, says Hobbes, in reducing the consequences thus calculated to "generall Rules, called *Theoremes,* or *Aphorismes.*" For one can "reason, or reckon, not onely in number, but in all other things, whereof one may be added unto, or subtracted from another."[21] The first step in the reduction of prudence to science is the careful fashioning of "generall names" out of the data acquired by observation, the precise definition of universal concepts. Care must be taken in designating them so that they correspond to actual sensations, "fancies" that we have experienced, and not to supersensible things. "Naturall sense and imagination are not subject to absurdity."[22] But Hobbes argues that the terminology of the Schools, which embodied such notions as "incorporeall substance" and "In-powred vertue," contained nothing but "insignificant sounds."[23]

With our definitions settled, we may proceed to reckon the logical relationships which obtain among them, "the consequences of one Affirmation to another." The product of our reckoning is science, and its model is geometry, which Hobbes calls "the onely Science that it hath pleased God hitherto to bestow on mankind."[24] With these operations we have moved out of the empirical world of our "fancies" into the world of "names" or

[20]*Leviathan,* Chapter 13, p. 87; Chapter 3, p. 17; Chapter 5, p. 37; Chapter 3, p. 21.

[21]*Ibid.,* Chapter 5, p. 34.

[22]*Ibid.,* Chapter 4, p. 27.

[23]*Ibid.,* pp. 28, 29. Percy Bridgman's notion of an "operational concept" is an extension of Hobbes's idea. Both insist that only ideas which represent measurable experience permit the development of science. "If experience is always described in terms of experience, then there must always be correspondence between experience and our description of it, and we need never be embarrassed, as we were in attempting to find the prototype of Newton's absolute time." P.W. Bridgman, *The Logic of Modern Physics* (New York: The Macmillan Company, 1928), in Herbert Feigl and May Brodbeck, eds., *Readings in the Philosophy of Science* (New York: Appleton-Century-Crofts, Inc., 1953), p. 37. See also Vernon Van Dyke, *Political Science: A Philosophical Analysis* (Stanford, Calif.: Stanford University Press, 1960), pp. 63-70. The author argues for the importance of clear operational concepts in the study of politics and against the use of words such as "state," which represent reified abstractions. Cf. Hobbes's caution against the use of metaphysical and rhetorical figures (*Leviathan,* Chapter 5, p. 36).

[24]*Leviathan,* Chapter 4, p. 26.

what in the terminology of Hobbes's methodological successors of today is commonly called the "model world." We can describe the relationships which obtain between these "names" of the model world with perfect exactitude, since we are merely drawing out by deduction the logical implications of definitions and rules of behavior we have ourselves made. But the knowledge we have always remains knowledge of an abstract world, and Hobbes calls it "Conditional" knowledge, by contrast with "Absolute" knowledge, which is knowledge of "fancies"—sense experience or memory. "No man can know by Discourse, that this, or that, is, has been, or will be; which is to know absolutely: but onely, that if This be, That is; if This has been, That has been; if This shall be, That shall be."[25]

However, if we are good at fitting the right "generall names" to the particular "fancies" that inhabit our psyches, and if the rules we establish correspond to empirical laws, our scientific knowledge provides us with a powerful instrument of prediction and control over the world of sensible particulars. We can interpret the real world in the light of the model, and thus establish power over it, power undreamed of by those who hold that politics is properly only the realm of experience and prudence.

> As, much Experience, is *Prudence;* so, is much Science, *Sapience.* For though wee usually have one name of Wisedome for them both; yet the Latines did always distinguish between *Prudentia* and *Sapientia;* ascribing the former to Experience, the later to Science. But to make their difference appeare more clearly, let us suppose one man endowed with an excellent naturall use, and dexterity in handling his armes; and another to have added to that dexterity, an acquired Science, of when he can offend, or be offended by his adversarie, in every possible posture, or guard: The ability of the former, would be to the ability of the later, as Prudence to Sapience; both usefull; *but the later infallible.*[26]

Here we have a statement of Hobbes's great break with the philosophical tradition, in his assertion that the theoretical reason is not a device for understanding and contemplating eternal objects, but an instrument for manipulating the world of sense, because the world of sense has a logical structure to it, susceptible of being known under the categories of a model world of "generall names."

We cannot call Hobbes's method "scientific method" in the modern sense, since it entirely omits the empirical check which forms the last and essential ingredient of that method. Hobbes assumes that if one is careful in the first instance to make one's concepts precise and to ground them on empirical observation, the development of scientific propositions and their proof can proceed entirely by deduction, without reference to the empirical

[25]*Ibid.,* Chapter 7, p. 51.
[26]*Ibid.,* Chapter 5, p. 38. (Emphasis supplied.)

world, in the manner of geometry. Indeed, if we could be sure that our working concepts and rules always did fit reality, we should not need empirical checks, whose prime function is to signify the validity of these starting points of our reasoning. But of course we cannot.

Politics as a Demonstrable Science.   Hobbes is fond of comparing the method of political philosophy with that of geometry, and always insists that it is a science whose conclusions are capable of logical demonstration. His clearest argument on this point is found in a minor work on mathematics. It is worthwhile reproducing the full statement, which runs as follows:

> Of arts, some are demonstrable, others indemonstrable; and demonstrable are those the construction of the subject whereof is in the power of the artist himself, who, in his demonstration, does no more than deduce the consequences of his own operation. The reason whereof is this, that the science of every subject is derived from a precognition of the causes, generation, and construction of the same; and consequently where the causes are known, there is place for demonstration, but not where the causes are to seek for. Geometry therefore is demonstrable, for the lines and figures from which we reason are drawn and described by ourselves; and civil philosophy is demonstrable, because we make the commonwealth ourselves. But because of natural bodies we know not the construction, but seek it from the effects, there lies no demonstration of what causes be we seek for, but only of what they may be.[27]

When Hobbes says that civil philosophy is demonstrable "because we make the commonwealth ourselves," he must mean that the civil philosopher creates the political system in a manner which resembles the drawings and descriptions of the geometer. Now behind the drawings of figures by the geometer lie certain definitions and axioms that serve as the efficient causes of his construction, along with the initial physical motions of the pen. Corresponding to the construction itself, and as a means of knowing it are the true propositions about the construction which the geometer obtains by the addition and subtraction of the geometric definitions.

Hobbes's analogy of civil philosophy to geometry is somewhat misleading, for the civil philosopher cannot make up the first causes of the commonwealth as the geometer lays down, arbitrarily, his rules and definitions. He can only make propositions which state what the causes are. It is not he who constructs the commonwealth from its causes, but rather every man, by the keeping of his covenants. However, the civil philosopher *can directly*

---

[27]Thomas Hobbes, *Six Lessons to the Professors of Mathematics,* . . . Epistle Dedicatory: *The English Works of Thomas Hobbes of Malmesbury,* Sir William Molesworth, ed. (10 vols.; London: John Bohn; Longmans, Green and Company, Ltd., 1839 *et seq.*), VII, p. 183 f., quoted in Child, *op. cit.,* pp. 271-72. The following analysis of the paragraph quoted is a summary of Child's exegesis of it, especially pp. 277, 280, 281 of his article.

know the prime causes, which he defines, by introspection, as indeed can every man. Hobbes points out the significance of introspection for his political philosophy at the beginning of the *Leviathan,* and asserts that its principles permit of no other demonstration.

> Whosoever looketh into himself, and considereth what he doth, when he does think, opine, reason, hope, feare, etc., and upon what grounds; he shall thereby read and know, what are the thoughts, and Passions of all other men, upon the like occasions. . . . When I shall have set down my own reading orderly, and perspicuously, the pains left another, will be onely to consider, if he also find not the same in himself. For this kind of Doctrine, admitteth no other Demonstration.[28]

Thus the proof of the theorems and of the validity of the definitions "like the proof of the principles of geometry, comes by the exposition to sense of the beginnings of the thing itself," even though those beginnings are given, and not man-made, and this sets political philosophy and geometry together and apart from physics.[29] Such demonstrations of the motions of natural bodies are not possible, because the generative causes are not known to us. The first principles of physics cannot be observed, but only supposed from the effects we observe. Hobbes would probably argue that modern procedures of empirical verification do not alter the situation a whit, and that physics by its nature must always remain only probable knowledge. But since the first causes of politics *are* laid bare to us, empirical verifications, other than the introspective act, are irrelevant. We must rather look to the clarity and precision of our definitions and to the exactness of our reasoning to assure the validity of our science.

The Commonwealth
as a Geometrical Construction

Let us review, with Hobbes, the procedures for fashioning the Commonwealth. We proceed as in the construction of a geometrical figure. "The skill of making, and maintaining Common-wealths, consisteth in certain Rules, as doth Arithmetique and Geometry; not (as Tennis-play) on Practise onely."[30] Our starting point is a blank page, the "state of nature," or society as it would be without the institution of government. First we observe the most politically significant characteristics of men which would also be present in a state of nature. What strikes Hobbes most forcefully is the equality of men in the faculties of both mind and body. For despite certain obvious

[28]*Leviathan,* Introduction, p. 5.
[29]Child, *op. cit.,* p. 281.
[30]*Leviathan,* Chapter 20, p. 176.

differences in bodily strength and intellectual agility, it seems to him evident that "the weakest has strength enough to kill the strongest, either by secret machinations or by confederacy with others, that are in the same danger with himselfe."[31] This forms one of our basic axioms.

Why does Hobbes emphasize so macabre an aspect of human equality? Because it means that the state of nature constitutes a state of war, of each person against everyone else, if we also specify the egoistic character of human motives. "From this equality of ability, ariseth equality of hope in the attaining of our Ends, and therefore if any two men desire the same thing, which nevertheless they cannot both enjoy, they become enemies; and in the way to their End, endeavor to destroy or subdue one another."[32]

On the basis of these observations we are prepared to define the central axiom, or rule, which describes human behavior in a state of nature. As a "generall name" it is the "Right of Nature," or *Jus Naturale*. Its definition is "the Liberty each man hath, to use his own power, as he will himselfe, for the preservation of his own Life; and consequently, of doing any thing, which in his own Judgment, and Reasons, hee shall conceive to be the aptest means thereunto."[33] In this remarkable redefinition of the traditional terminology of moral obligation to fit his own mechanistic assumptions, Hobbes effects his "Copernican revolution" in the field of political ethics. The normative language of the *Jus Naturale* in which, from Cicero to Aquinas, the teleological reason had legislated the obligation of perfection to the free will of man, Hobbes now uses descriptively to characterize the determined behavior of interacting motions (human passions). The *Jus Naturale* becomes a scientific generalization, like the law of gravity, and thereby man ceases to be a moral animal. Not obligation but right, translated as unimpeded power, becomes the prime fact of human nature. And unbridled license in the search for security and contentment is found to be the basic characteristic of human behavior. "Every man has a right to every thing; even to one anothers body."[34]

Another postulate which we formulate after considering, on the one hand, the "apparent goods" towards which men are by their passions impelled, and on the other, the effect of the operation of the Right of Nature is that the state of nature is an ill, unhappy, and intolerable situation.

> [In the State of Nature] men live without other security, than what their own strength, and their own invention shall furnish them withall. In such condition, there is no place for Industry; because the fruit thereof is uncertain; and consequently no Culture of the Earth, no Navigation, nor use of the com-

[31]*Ibid.,* Chapter 13, p. 101.
[32]*Ibid.,* p. 102.
[33]*Ibid.,* Chapter 14, p. 106.
[34]*Ibid.,* p. 107.

modities that may be imported by Sea; no commodious Building; no Instruments of moving, and removing such things as require much force; no Knowledge of the face of the Earth; no account of Time; no Arts; no Letters; no Society; and which is worst of all, Continuall feare, and danger of violent death; and the life of man, solitary, poor, nasty, brutish, and short.[35]

Our description of Hobbesian man in a state of nature is still incomplete, for the *Jus Naturale* designates only the passionate aspects of his behavior. Natural man is also rational. Hence we have another axiom, that there are certain precepts of reason which guide his behavior. Hobbes calls them *Leges Naturales,* Natural Laws, and describes them as "generall Rules found out by Reason." The line of reasoning which produces them is set in motion by the feeling of pain experienced from wounds received in the mortal struggle of the war of all against all.[36] The experience of pain brings a man face to face with violent death, from which he recoils in horror, and sends his thoughts abroad to scout out the causes of his peril. His analysis of the chain of causes and effects makes clear to him that his own actions as well as those of others in the unreasoned quest for "power after power" imperil his life, whose security is the precondition of all other enjoyment. This is expressed in a set of precepts forbidding natural man "to do, that, which is destructive of his life, or taketh away the means of preserving the same; and to omit, that, by which he thinketh it may be best preserved."[37]

Our fundamental axiology is now complete. We have described the motives and capabilities of our political actors and specified the basic rules of their interaction in an anarchic environment. Our natural men (1) are engaged in a passionate struggle over apparent goods, such as wealth, status, and power, which (2) because of men's equality of strength and ability (3) threaten to destroy them. (4) They are free of external hindrances in the use of their power, and (5) their only obligation is to self-preservation. How far we have departed from the classical and Christian conceptions of man and society is clear from this summary. Man is no longer a creature with a natural inclination to self-fulfillment through a social life, nor has he any natural obligation to his fellows. There is no such thing as community or common good, but only an aggregation of individuals who are merely interacting masses of matter in motion. The ends of life are not presented to reason by a purposeful God, but are "fancies" generated by blind pressures on the organs of sense, which eventuate in meaningless motions. Reason has become an instrument of the passions, and reason and passion are both simply motions. Hobbes rests the argument for his conception on the ground that it avoids the ambiguities of the tradition, is precise and clear,

[35]*Ibid.,* Chapter 13, p. 104.
[36]See Strauss, *op. cit.,* pp. 18-21.
[37]*Leviathan,* Chapter 14, p. 107.

and corresponds to the experience our senses register, which is the best evidence of reality we have.

We now proceed, by logical inference from our postulates, to develop a set of theorems about other aspects of human behavior, with which, as the geometer makes his figures, we may construct, as a model world, the commonwealth. Our theorems will be specifications of the Laws of Nature, for all of politics has to do with preservation. The first inference which Hobbes calls "the first, and Fundamentall Law of Nature" is *"To seek Peace, and follow it."* For it is the continuance of the state of war that is the chief peril. The precept is not unqualified, however, but has for its corollary, *"By all means we can, to defend ourselves."* If aggressors set upon the peace seekers it would be folly for them not to resist destruction, since the only object of their quest for peace is self-defense.[38]

The second law or theorem follows immediately, by inference from the first theorem and the basic axioms—"That a man be willing, when others are too, as farre-forth, as for Peace, and defence of himselfe he shall think it necessary, to lay down this right to all things; and be contented with so much liberty against all other men, as he would allow other men against himselfe."[39] This theorem prescribes the abandonment of the state of nature and the establishment of civil society, on the condition of mutual willingness of all to do so.

The essential element of this operation is the conclusion of a covenant, or agreement, to transfer all Right or Liberty of the state of nature to a third party, who thereby becomes the sovereign power, unhindered by all limitation. It is interesting that this creates no new rights for the sovereign, nor any obligation either. For the contractants merely agree to diminish the "impediments to the use of [the sovereign's] own Right originall," not to hinder him in the use of his own natural liberty. The contractants themselves, however, are by the contract "Obliged, or Bound, not to hinder" the sovereign. The expectation is that the power of the sovereign will stand as a threat of punishment to all who might be tempted to return to the practices of the state of nature, and it is, therefore, a guarantee of peace.[40]

What other Laws of Nature, or theorems, does Hobbes infer from the

[38]*Idem.*

[39]*Ibid.,* pp. 107-8.

[40]J. Roland Pennock has pointed out some of the ambiguities and inconsistencies in Hobbes's apparently clear and precise use of the word "liberty." Among other things, he shows that if Hobbes intended "liberty" (in his definition of the Right of Nature) to signify a power to act, unimpeded by external hindrances, such "liberty" is not transferred in accepting the obligations of the social contract, but rather the right to use it. See J. Roland Pennock, "Hobbes's Confusing 'Clarity': The Case of 'Liberty,' " *American Political Science Review,* LIV, No. 2, (June 1960), 428 ff.

fundamental axioms, and from the initial theorems? The ancient maxim of *Pacta sunt servanda,* "That men perform their Covenants made," is the next in the order of his exposition. Since the whole structure of social obligation depends on convenant, to deny this principle is to return to the state of nature, which is against reason. A fourth law enjoins gratitude, for men act benevolently with the hope of being praised for their generosity. Ingratitude frustrates this desire, and with it, charity and mutual help. Others enjoin sociable behavior, a willingness to pardon past offenses, the avoidance of vengeful punishments, hatred, and contemptuous attitudes, the guarantee of safe conduct to mediators, and acceptance of the obligation to arbitrate disputes.

Five precepts (the ninth through thirteenth laws) reveal the democratic character of Hobbes's thought. Every man is bidden to "acknowledge other for his Equall by Nature" and forbidden "to reserve to himselfe any Right, which he is not content should be reserved to every one of the rest. . . . The observers of the law, are them we call *Modest,* and the breakers *Arrogant* men."[41] These are central principles of the system, for in Hobbes's reckoning of causes and effects, he names arrogance and vainglory as the great cause of conflict in the state of nature. Vain men, caught up in the delusive fancies of their own self-conceit, try to force others to recognize their superiority. But since their fellows are of equal power, as we have seen, they will not willingly bow down, but choose instead to fight. The shock of wounds received in battle confronts the arrogant with the vision of violent death, and brings them to their senses, and to a willingness to accept the equalitarian principles of the Laws of Nature.[42]

The string of inferences from our basic rules is now finished. We have the full set of rules of peaceful behavior. Our model world is complete. Out of the single obligation of the individual to preserve himself we have constructed a whole set of social obligations, linking the individual to his fellows and to his sovereign in an orderly pattern of rules.

The Nature of Hobbesian "Obligation"

Let us pause for a moment to ask what the word "obligation" must mean for the radically selfish men of Hobbes's nominalistic world. It can never signify something accepted as abstractly and inherently good and proper, which one ought to do simply because it is right. The acceptance of obligation is always prompted by the desire of good to himself by the person obliged, and its only sanction is fear. Obligation can never be imposed, but is always the product of free consent and contract. Thus, by the social contract, one accepts an obligation to live in peace and respect the lives of

---

[41] *Leviathan,* Chapter 15, p. 128.

[42] *Ibid.,* Chapter 17, pp. 141-42, and Strauss, *op. cit.,* pp. 18-21.

others from a desire for the contentment of a peaceful life and from fear of the consequences of continued existence in a state of nature.

No precept of the Laws of Nature becomes an obligation binding one to the prescribed behavior before the conclusion of the social contract and the erection of a sovereign power. Hobbes says that in the state of nature the Laws of Nature oblige only *"in foro interno,"* that is to say, they bind to a desire they should take place."[43] In a state of nature one feels only compelled to try to get out of it, to undertake negotiations, so to speak, but not to give up the procedures of self-help. When the sovereign has been created, however, obligation is complete. But it now rests on fear of the consequences of disobedience, punishment at the hand of authority, and *not* on the sense of security which civil society creates. "There must be some coercive Power, to compel men equally to the performance of their Covenants, by the terrour of some punishment."[44] For men always remain at heart beasts of prey, desirous not only of security but of glory and power, which lead them into depredations.

Even in civil society one cannot be obliged not to resist the sovereign if he assaults a subject and threatens his life. "For though a man may Covenant thus, *Unlesse I do so, or so, kill me;* he cannot Covenant thus, *Unlesse I do so, or so, I will not resist you, when you come to kill me."* [45] Such an obligation would be contrary to the purpose for which the social contract was made, protection. Hobbes goes so far as to say that no one can be obliged to serve as a conscript in the armed forces, because of the risks involved! In short, he keeps the concept of obligation throughout confined to things which a perfectly selfish but rational person will feel compelled to accept in the way of self-limitations, through hope of gain to himself and fear of the consequences of disobedience.[46]

The Hobbesian Sovereign. It should be noted that for Hobbes the contract which creates the commonwealth is not an agreement to abide by the principles of the Laws of Nature, but an agreement, by mutual alienation of Natural Right, to create a sovereign power. Holding that "covenants, without the sword, are but words," it is useless, Hobbes believes, to make agreements until a sword is in being.[47] Thereafter, in place of covenants to keep the peace, we have legislation by the sovereign, "of whose Acts a great Multitude, by mutuall Covenants one with another, have made themselves every one the Author, to the end he may use the strength and

---

[43]*Leviathan,* Chapter 15, p. 131.

[44]*Ibid.,* p. 119.

[45]*Ibid.,* Chapter 14, p. 116.

[46]For a thorough discussion of Hobbes's theory of obligation, see Howard Warrender, *The Political Philosophy of Hobbes* (Oxford: Clarendon Press, 1957).

[47]*Leviathan,* Chapter 17, p. 139.

means of them all, as he shall think expedient, for their Peace and Common Defence."[48]

Hobbes insists that the alienation of power to the sovereign must be absolute and irrevocable, without conditions. And he argues that sovereignty must be concentrated in one man or a single group of men; otherwise there is no assurance that peace, the end of the civil order, will be achieved. For these things he has been called an authoritarian, even a totalitarian, and his name has become anathema to the liberal world. Actually, these doctrines are fully compatible with a liberal theory of government, and Hobbes is properly understood as the intellectual forerunner of utilitarianism rather than fascism. The British political system is known today as the epitome of the liberal order, and yet the central principle of its constitutional law is the legal omnipotence of Parliament. Hobbes's doctrine of sovereignty merely recognizes that somewhere in a commonwealth there must be a legal agent who has the right to say with final authority what the law is. Such an agent is necessarily himself outside the law, the author and judge of it.

Ambiguity as to the location of the sovereign authority, or denial of the principle, is an invitation to everyone to interpret the law in his own interest, and to appeal all acts of public authority with which he is dissatisfied to another tribunal, in an endless series. If a belief that the sovereign power in seventeenth-century England was divided was not the major cause of the civil war as Hobbes believed, it nevertheless contributed to the conflict. The debates leading to open warfare, from 1628 to 1642, all turn on the question of jurisdiction. In our own case, the ambiguity of sovereignty within a federal system, written into the Constitution of 1787, contributed to the division between North and South which culminated in the Civil War of 1861 to 1865. Even today, the conflict over integration often takes the form of a clash between claimants to sovereign authority. This is not to say that the Civil War would not have been fought if a sovereign authority had been identified in 1787. But it does mean that when, for other reasons, tensions developed between North and South, the principle of unity which mutual recognition of a sovereign power creates was lacking, a principle which might have mitigated if not prevented the conflict.

We might ask, however, whether we would be inclined to give a Hobbesian interpretation to the *causes* of the ambiguity of sovereignty in the Constitution of 1787. Would we chalk it up to ignorance of the Laws of Nature or to excessive passion, as he would? Or would it make more sense to inquire into the degree of community and lack of community between North and South at the time of the Convention, a concept which has no place at all in Hobbes's terminology? Political unity for him consists only in the unity of the sovereign, not the society, which is always absolutely many,

[48]*Ibid.*, pp. 143-44.

but which, paradoxically, can agree to be represented by one, and can authorize him to act for all, from considerations of private utility and expediency alone.

Law and Morality.   Hobbes is much maligned for his assertion that until a sovereign is created to define and enforce obligations, there is no distinguishing the just from the unjust. Justice is simply that which the sovereign commands, and injustice what he forbids. Many have understood this to mean that in Hobbes's view there are no principles of morality until the sovereign has spoken. "Right" and "wrong" are purely conventional, meaning simply what the sovereign says they mean.

This is really an overstatement of Hobbes's position. What he is trying to say is that without a sovereign to define obligations, no common standard of right will be enforced. As Howard Warrender puts it, "Without such an authority morality is frustrated, either through men's passions or their insecurity."[49] Abstract words like "justice" and "right" lose common meaning and tend to be used simply as disguises for the selfish claims of rival interests. But this is not to say that for Hobbes there is no rational standard of right apart from the definitions of a sovereign. Hobbes acknowledges just such a standard in the natural law of self-preservation, which, while not the noblest of moral standards, is nevertheless a standard. He does not think that the precepts deducible from it can be *enforced,* however, outside civil society. And the definition of obligations is necessarily involved in their enforcement.

Hobbes's position is readily understandable from a glance at the ideological condition of England in his time. The seventeenth century represented the culmination of the Reformation, which, having discredited the precepts of the Catholic Church as the standard of right behavior, had substituted no commonly accepted moral authority. Catholics, Anglicans, Presbyterians, Independents, and the many inner-light groups of the far left of the spectrum all had their own ideas of moral obligation which they wished to see dominate the political order, and the clash of principles was one of the chief causes of the war. Hobbes was particularly alarmed at the extreme individualists of the ecclesiastical left wing who claimed that they owed allegiance to no authority at all other than their own private revelations. Under such circumstances, how could a person interested in peace and order place the validity of positive law elsewhere than in its formal source? It was in view of this that Hobbes went to the extreme of declaring the sovereign power the author of moral truth. It seemed to him the only alternative to constant strife.

When there is ideological agreement, the problem of relating political commands to an abstract standard of right does not appear. And when

[49]Warrender, *op. cit.,* p. 143.

ideological community is lacking, public authority may readily, though falsely, be seen as a cause rather than a reflection of community standards. A Hobbesian would argue that the problem of international order cannot be solved until a supranational sovereign is created, who can define and enforce principles of universal right. Until then, he would say, periodic violent conflict is inevitable, and actions proclaimed by one side to embody the highest morality will be denounced by the other as the rankest knavery. Perhaps the Hobbesian argument inverts the causal order, however. The development of a world value consensus may be the precondition rather than the product of a world sovereign whose acts are accepted as morally right, rather than as the arbitrary fiats of a monopolist of force.

Prerogatives of the Sovereign. What powers of government is the Hobbesian sovereign expected to wield? In theory, they are limited to accomplishing the limited aim for which the sovereign is instituted—the maintenance of social peace and the defense of the society against foreign aggressors. This is a narrower purpose than that of our own constitutional order, which, in addition to ensuring domestic tranquillity and providing for the common defense includes the broad obligation of promoting the general welfare. But Hobbes's sovereign is empowered to be his own judge of the means necessary to execute his mandate and is even given the right to "be Judge of what Opinions and Doctrines are averse, and what conducing to Peace."[50] This is probably more scandalous to the liberal reader than any other part of Hobbes's doctrine, but it is interesting to note how far our own Supreme Court has gone in recent years toward accepting the principle. Its decision in *Dennis v. United States* (1951) is a case in point. It must also be remembered that Hobbes was writing for an England torn wide open with ideological strife, while our experience has until recently been one of overwhelming agreement.[51] Under circumstances like our own, heretical opinions pose no threat to social peace, while in a deeply divided society, differing opinions on the good and the just are the very heart of the problem of peace and order.

Another prerogative of the sovereign is the definition and enforcement of property rights, which in the older liberal theory was the chief end of government. Another is the maintenance of courts, in which the laws of *meum* and *tuum* are enforced. Another is the making of war and peace. Others include rewarding those who serve the commonwealth and punishing those that break the law, appointing civil and military officials, and distributing titles and other public honors.

[50]*Leviathan,* Chapter 18, p. 148.

[51]See Louis Hartz, *The Liberal Tradition in America,* (New York: Harcourt, Brace & World, Inc., 1955). The author is impressed by the breadth and strength of what he calls the Lockean consensus of Americans.

These are the very limited functions of the Hobbesian sovereign, who passes over large areas of action, leaving their regulation wholly to the private judgment of individuals. Civil freedom consists in "the Liberty to buy, and sell, and otherwise contract with one another; to choose their own aboad, their own diet, their own trade of life, and institute their children as they themselves think fit; and the like."[52] This passage more than any other gives the lie to claims that Hobbes was a totalitarian. It makes him rather the theorist of the nineteenth-century liberal "nightwatchman state."

The Problem of Effective Limitation.   The chief flaw that one finds in Hobbes's theorems is that they provide no institutions to keep the sovereign within the narrow confines just described, and to prevent the tyrannous use of his concentrated legal authority. In one place Hobbes actually admits that the sovereign may work "iniquite," though never injustice (since Hobbes has defined the just as that which is legally prescribed).[53] He makes the somewhat weak argument that in monarchy, which is the form of sovereignty which he prefers, "the private interest is the same with the publique. The riches, power, and honour of a Monarch arise only from the riches, strength and reputation of his Subjects. For no King can be rich, nor glorious, nor secure; whose Subjects are either poore, or contemptible, or too weak through want or dissention, to maintain a war against their enemies."[54] He quite ignores all the empirical evidence of thousands of years to the contrary.

It seems to Hobbes that the troubles of his own time in England were due not to royal oppressions but rather to the ambitions and quarrels of overmighty subjects. From this he generalizes: "The condition of man in this life shall never be without Inconveniences; but there happeneth in no Common-wealth any great Inconvenience, but what proceeds from the Subjects disobedience, and breach of those Covenants from which the Common-wealth hath its being."[55] Anarchy always seems to him a greater evil and a likelier threat than tyranny. We must read Locke to find a concern for hedging the agents of the sovereign power without destroying the principle of sovereignty itself.

The Model World and the Real World

We have completed the construction of Hobbes's commonwealth of the model world. We are prepared to demonstrate the theorems which compose it by showing how they can be deduced from our axioms, the

---

[52]*Leviathan,* Chapter 21, p. 180.
[53]*Ibid.,* Chapter 18, p. 148.
[54]*Ibid.,* Chapter 19, p. 157.
[55]*Ibid.,* Chapter 20, p. 176.

generative causes of the system. What, now, can we say of the relation of our model polity to the real world? If men are rational, in an instrumental sense, and Hobbes gives this as a characteristic property of human nature, do they act upon the Laws of Nature known by reason? Have we described, in our model, the structure of the empirical world? George Sabine, writing of Hobbes's intent, says, in effect, that we have.

> Since [Hobbes] assumes that in the large men really do act this way [i.e., rationally], the laws of nature state hypothetical conditions upon which the fundamental traits of human beings allow a stable government to be founded. They do not state values but they determine causally and rationally what can be given value in legal and moral systems.[56]

But there is a problem here. For Hobbes himself says that political systems are in fact *not* built according to his canons. He lists half a dozen flaws in actual systems which typically cause their overturn. One has the feeling that if the world actually did operate according to the laws of reason which Hobbes lays down, his political works might never have been written. They plainly have a reformist intention. In one place, for example, he notes "how different [his] Doctrine is from the Practice of the greatest part of the world."[57] And in another, he laments that "if men had the use of reason they pretend to, their Common-wealths might be secured, at least, from perishing by internall diseases."[58]

These passages seem to say that men are, after all, *not* rational, and that real and model worlds do *not* correspond. Yet plainly Hobbes believes that his model is derived from the world as it is, and not from a conception of how it ought to be. It is not an ideal commonwealth of philosophical aspiration, like that of Plato. We will recall Hobbes's insistence that our concepts correspond to phenomenal reality, and his avoidance of vague and mystical notions. How, then, can we resolve this, a paradox, incidentally, which also crops up in the work of Hobbes's methodological descendants, the theorists of games and of economic behavior, whom we shall discuss later on in this chapter?

Perhaps what Hobbes is trying to say is that men in the empirical world are indeed rational in the instrumental sense, but that their reason is often uninformed and is subject to error. We all, indeed, take our values from the promptings of passion, and we seek to maximize them through the quest of "power after power." We also send our thoughts abroad as scouts and spies to find the means of getting what we want. We all engage in

[56]Sabine, *op. cit.*, p. 461.
[57]*Leviathan*, Chapter 31, p. 318.
[58]*Ibid.*, Chapter 29, p. 275.

reasoning about causes and effects in our effort to achieve the objects which satisfy us. But most of us reason faultily. Hobbes says that "from defect in Reasoning, (that is to say, from Errour,) men are prone to Violate the Lawes, three wayes. First, by Presumption of false Principles . . . Secondly by false Teachers, that . . . mis-interpret the Laws of Nature . . . Thirdly, by Erroneous Inferences from True Principles."[59] It is not, then, that we are irrational, but that we are badly schooled, unlettered, or corrupted by bad teachers. And "without the help of a very able Architect" we cannot help but construct "any other than a crasie building, such as hardly lasting out [our] own Time, must assuredly fall upon the heads of [our] posterity."[60]

However, Hobbes believes that he has at last reduced politics to science and presents himself for our hire as a "very able Architect." By diligent study he has acquired the "art of making fit Lawes." He will instruct us, if we let him. Like Plato, he requires the help of a sovereign who would, "in the protecting the Publique teaching of it, convert this Truth of Speculation, into the Utility of Practice."[61] Like Plato of the Socratic dialogues, he also asks that every man reason out the laws of nature for himself and cease to rely on the authority of blind tradition. But unlike Plato of the *Republic*, he does not require a "turning about of the soul," moral conversion, a new orientation to life. He takes man as he finds him and only asks that he think more, and more clearly. Also unlike the Plato of the *Republic*, he relies on the common man rather than on the elite to effect reform. By contrast with the intelligentsia of the schools, everyman's reason is incorrupt. "The common sort of men," he writes, "seldom speak Insignificantly," while the philosophers are ever bandying about obscure expressions.[62]

Vested interest as well as erroneous reasoning can blind us to the laws of nature. "Potent men, digest hardly anything that setteth up a Power to bridle their affections; and Learned men, any thing that discovereth their errours, and thereby lesseneth their Authority." But "the Common-peoples minds . . . are like clean paper, fit to receive whatsoever by Publique Authority shall be imprinted in them."[63] Thus, if a sovereign, instructed in the Laws of Nature, would take it upon himself to teach them to the people, a commonwealth might be built that would last forever. The model world of our discourse would then be "positive" in the fullest sense, a perfect description of empirical reality, rather than (though rooted in reality) a standard of improvement, as it now is.

[59]*Ibid.*, Chapter 27, p. 253.
[60]*Ibid.*, Chapter 29, p. 276.
[61]*Ibid.*, Chapter 30, p. 319.
[62]*Ibid.*, Chapter 8, p. 65. See Strauss, *op. cit.*, p. 139 ff., for an interesting comparison of Plato and Hobbes.
[63]*Ibid.*, Chapter 30, p. 291.

"Rational Man" Analysis Today:
An Economic Theory of Democracy

"Rational man" analysis, employing mathematical forms of statement, has been little used in the study of politics since Hobbes. (The work of Jeremy Bentham is the great exception.) By contrast, the study of economics as a scholarly discipline was founded on "rational man" assumptions by Adam Smith, and remains so grounded today. It is not surprising, therefore, that it was a scholar trained as an economist who recently restored this method of inquiry to politics.[64] He is Anthony Downs, a student of Kenneth Arrow, whose work on a theory of social choice inspired Downs's effort.

The purpose of Downs's book is "to provide a behavior rule for democratic government and to trace its implications."[65] By this Downs means the construction of a model of rational political behavior, in terms of economic costs of alternative choices and within the framework of a democratic system of government. Or to put it still another way, his object is to specify the principles or rules of behavior which are implied by the notion of rationality in the pursuit and use of power in a democratic order. Downs was prompted to write such a book, he tells us, by a recognition of the fact that, though government has come to play a dominant role in the making of economic decisions for the modern community, economic theory has not provided a model of rational governmental behavior analogous to that traditionally employed for the understanding of consumer and producer behavior, a necessary ingredient of any general equilibrium theory. His focus is therefore on the classic economic problem, the efficient employment of scarce resources. But broadly conceived, of course, efficiency has also been a classic focus of political theory as well, at least since the time of Machiavelli.

The similarity of Downs's mode of analysis to that of Hobbes is evident at the outset. Downs tells us that his system is deductive, "since it posits a basic rule and draws conclusions therefrom." His basic rule is the rational pursuit of power, which is formally analogous to Hobbes's first Law of Nature, the rational pursuit of self-preservation. Both writers specify the environment in which the rule operates—for Hobbes, the state of nature, which gives way to civil society under an absolute sovereign; for Downs, a democratic polity. In each theory, the elaboration of the model system takes the form of a series of conclusions from the primary rule and from the axioms which describe the environment. Empirical observation plays a role only in the formulation of the "general names" or concepts employed in each system, and of the basic axioms. The heart of each work is logical in-

[64]Anthony Downs, *An Economic Theory of Democracy* (New York: Harper & Row, Publishers, 1957).
[65]*Ibid.*, p. 3.

ference. The conclusions of each writer form an abstract world and are, therefore, "conditional knowledge," or Hobbesian "science," rather than "absolute knowledge" of the world as it actually is. Yet, in each case, the model is "positive" rather than "normative," for it describes "what will happen under certain conditions, not what should happen."[66]

Rationality

The common key concept of both systems is the notion of "rationality." We have seen what this word means for Hobbes. How does Downs use it? To him, as to Hobbes, it is an instrumental rather than a teleological concept and refers to the efficiency of means rather than the goodness of ends. A rational politician or voter is one who seeks the most efficient means of getting what he wants. Ends are simply posited.

Downs specifies one end in particular as the criterion of value, or goal value—power, defined as control over public policy—just as Hobbes gave primacy to self-preservation. But unlike Hobbes, Downs does not assert that the posited value is of overriding importance in the real world as well as in the world of the model. He grants that men will often sacrifice political rationality to other ends. In the model world "we do not take into consideration the whole personality of each individual when we discuss what behavior is rational for him," he writes. "We do not allow for the rich diversity of ends served by each of his acts, the complexity of his motives, the way in which every part of his life is intimately related to his emotional needs." The single-minded "political man" of the model world, therefore, does not correspond to the citizen of the empirical world; he is an abstraction. But analysis is impossible, Downs believes, unless we work with this abstract construct. "If multiple goals are allowed, means appropriate to one may block attainment of another; hence no unique course can be charted for a rational decision-maker to follow."[67]

A critic would object at this point that the "rational" decision of our model-world citizen will be a useless fiction if we make the decision situation artificial in this way, useless both as a description of how men act and as a prescription for behavior. It would be urged, in fact, that the model evades the central decision-making problem of the real world, which sets criteria of choice in the midst of the human situation of multiple, competing, and often contradictory ends. Hobbes, it should be noted, is not open to similar criticism, for he really believed that preservation was the overriding human concern.

Downs is also open to criticism for the definitional sleight of hand by which he identifies political rationality with rationality *as such*. This identification is particularly vulnerable in view of his own admission that the political represents only one dimension of the human moral life. Though he starts out saying (p. 4) that he will use the word "rational" only to specify efficient *means to a given end,* a few pages along (p. 9) we find him invidiously labeling behavior which is irrational from the point of view of political ends as "neurotic." This is to make political *ends* the criterion of the rational. "Neurotic behavior," he writes, "is often a necessary means of releasing tensions which spring from conflicts buried deep within the unconscious. But we are studying rational political behavior, not psychology or the psychology of political behavior."[68] Downs does not realize that behavior which, viewed from the political standpoint, might be deemed irrational, from the standpoint of the total moral and psychic economy of the individual *might* be the highest form of rationality rather than a symptom of neurosis. The expression "political irrationality" which Downs uses in other places seems to me a more appropriate expression, though Downs's tendency throughout is to identify political rationality with rationality as such, and political irrationality with irrationality as such. In other words, he moves covertly rather than directly, like Hobbes, to the judgment that political values are overriding.

This tendency is rather strikingly revealed in another passage in which Downs says "a party which perennially makes false promises can gain votes if it convinces voters to believe its lies. It is rational for this party to encourage voters to behave irrationally."[69] A classical or Christian moralist would add: "though in the larger human scheme of things it would be immoral, and therefore not to be dignified with the name 'rational,' which always conveys the notion of fitting and proper." Downs does not add this, because he believes that the only scheme of things larger than the political is not a rational moral order but an irrational emotional chaos.

Other Axioms of the Model: Democracy

We have said that Downs formulates his rule of rational politics within the framework of a democratic polity. Following "Occam's razor" principle, he constructs his model democracy with great parsimony. It consists of only a very few elements. What does he give as its characteristic features?

Given the assumption of the basic rule, that the motive behind political activity is power, Downs must exclude social welfare functions in assigning a purpose to democratic politics. The members of a government can have only selfish private ends; hence the assumption "that every govern-

[68]*Ibid.,* pp. 9-10.
[69]*Ibid.,* p. 10.

ment seeks to maximize political support."[70] The "purpose" of the government (i.e., of those in control of the government) is simply to stay in power. The author states, however, that a welfare principle does enter the model indirectly in the assignment of one vote to every adult citizen. "We admit openly that we are adopting an ethical principle—equality of franchise." The government assigns equal weight to all welfare preferences. But, in effect, he immediately takes the statement back, noting that the government has really no interest in welfare, but only in votes, and that the "ethical principle" is incorporated in the model "simply as a factual parameter, not a normative one."[71] The model must be "positive" throughout, *à la* Hobbes.

Another notion of purpose in the model which can, however, be stated in terms of process, is the conception that "every government is the locus of ultimate power in its society; it can coerce all the other groups into obeying its decisions, whereas they cannot coerce it. Therefore its social function must at least include acting as the final guarantor behind every use of coercion in the settlement of disputes."[72] The assumption that only one organization in a given area can fit this definition makes it much like Hobbes's notion of sovereignty.

The processes of government assumed are (1) periodic elections, (2) involving contests between two or more parties (electoral coalitions), (3) in which the party receiving a plurality of the votes wins. (4) The winning party then operates the government without the mediation of a parliament until the subsequent election. (5) The only restrictions on the incumbent government are a prohibition on interference with the freedom of the opposition to express itself and to campaign, and a prohibition on alteration of the periodicity of elections. The author recognizes the problem of indirect interference with opposition freedom through government economic policies.

An additional axiom (6) specifies that citizens as well as government act rationally, which means that "each citizen casts his vote for the party he believes will provide him with more benefits than any other."[73] Somewhat inconsistently with his description of the politician's motive as the selfish desire for power, Downs here says that utility which the citizen seeks need not be selfish in the narrow sense of the word, "because self-denying charity is often a great source of benefit to oneself. Thus our model leaves room for altruism in spite of its basic reliance upon the self-interest axiom."[74] It is interesting that Hobbes explained his own frequent charitable acts in similar terms.

[70]*Ibid.*, p. 11.
[71]Ibid, pp. 18, 19.
[72]*Ibid.*, p. 23.
[73]*Ibid.*, p. 36.
[74]*Ibid.*, p. 37.

From Downs's primary axiom, that "democratic governments act rationally to maximize political support," and from his definition of democratic procedures, he proceeds to deduce an entire theory of rational political behavior, an elaborate set of "positive" norms which describe how rational men behave under specified conditions. Each chapter contains an exposition and deductive "proof" of a set of behavioral propositions. In the last chapter Downs formulates the salient propositions as three sets of hypotheses to be tested by empirical observation. One set is derived from the proposition that government, or more generally, "political parties in a democracy plan their policies so as to maximize votes," the second from the proposition that "every citizen rationally attempts to maximize his utility income," and the third from the two axioms taken together. In offering his hypotheses for empirical verification, Downs of course departs radically from the procedure adopted by Hobbes, who would have considered the deductive proofs in the various chapters to be sufficient demonstration.

Typical of Downs's hypotheses is the thesis that "both parties in a two-party system agree on any issues that a majority of citizens strongly favor." A related proposition is that "in a two-party system, party policies are (a) more vague, (b) more similar to those of other parties, and (c) less directly linked to an ideology than in a multiparty system."[75] One wonders whether this particular hypothesis was drawn by Downs by inference from his axioms or from observation of the actual workings of the American party system. For he is compelled to note that, as parties becloud the issues and move together ideologically (when voter preferences peak towards the center of a distribution graph), it becomes extremely difficult for voters to make a rational choice, and they are forced to judge on some basis other than the issues. Yet one of the axioms of the model holds that voters act rationally. The theorem about beclouding also conflicts with another theorem which Downs derives from the basic axioms, according to which the parties in competition are reliable and honest.[76] Thus we have contradictions in the model, though the author attempts to find a way out of them.

One interesting proposition, which Downs adapts from the work of Kenneth Arrow, involves circumstances in which voter preferences in a three-alternative situation are structured so that no alternative has a majority support for first choice. In this case, neither government nor voters can adopt a rational strategy, Downs argues, because of the disparity of preferences. Under these circumstances, the incumbents will always be defeated by the opposition. This finding of the dependence of instrumental

[75]*Ibid.,* p. 297.

[76]See the discussion of these problems in William H. Riker, *The Theory of Political Coalitions* (New Haven, Conn.: Yale University Press, 1962) pp. 98–101. For Riker's interpretation of the beclouding phenomenon in the light of his own model, see pp. 95–98 and pp. 58–59.

rationality on community or consensus seems to testify to the truth of another of the classic theories which we shall examine somewhat later, that of Jean Jacques Rousseau, though it goes quite beyond any argument of Hobbes, who simply did not see "community."

Leadership. Notably lacking in Downs's model democracy is a leadership function. There seems to be a hidden assumption in the model that voter preferences, both on individual issues and as total structures, are fully formed apart from politics, and that the only function of the parties competing for power is to register an already crystallized opinion. The decision-makers are completely passive. Thus, "when a newly elected (or reelected) government sets up its plan of action, it asks about each expenditure, 'Is it worth its cost in votes in terms of votes gained?' ", as though a public judgment about each expenditure, and a schedule of expenditure preferences, existed.[77] We have statements to the effect that "the government subjects each decision to a hypothetical poll and always chooses the alternative which the majority prefers," as though there were always "given" in some way a winning opinion waiting to be discovered, either as majority consensus or coalition of minorities.[78] The simplest opposition strategy, Downs writes, involves adoption of the majority-pleasing principle by formulating a "program which is identical with that of the incumbents' in every particular."[79] He believes, however, that under special conditions, the government can be defeated by supporting the minority. But the assumption behind both strategies is that a majority and minority position exist to begin with. Thus, formulation of alternatives does not appear as a party function in this theory. The author does not seem to be aware that public opinion is often inchoate, waiting to receive form from imaginative leadership.

In one place, indeed, Downs seems to recognize the need for leadership, but the presuppositions of his model lead him, in the end, to deny it. As an economist, he notes that scarcity of time will not allow a citizen to become an expert on all questions involving his interest, and that he must often delegate his decision to another. This is a rational procedure if the delegation is to a person with the same general goals as the citizen but with better judgment. "In short, *S*'s most rational course is to make no decisions himself except deciding who should make decisions."[80] Yet in the next paragraph to this statement he denies that it is rational to make this delegation to the competing parties in an election. "If they eschew thinking about policies and select a party because its personnel are well-informed and have good judgment, they are acting irrationally."[81] He then goes on to deny the

[77]Downs, *op. cit.,* p. 69.
[78]*Ibid.,* p. 54.
[79]*Ibid.,* p. 55.
[80]*Ibid.,* p. 233.
[81]*Ibid.,* p. 234.

rationality of the common real-world phenomenon of party-furnished leadership.

The reason for the denial, is of course, obvious—the prior assumption of the model that those who put themselves forward as political leaders are merely self-centered power lovers, who will say and do anything for votes, and with whom a citizen can have no real community of interest or purpose. If these people become opinion- and interest-fashioners, the citizens are merely clay in their hands. At this point the validity and utility of Downs's assumptions about motives come radically in question for, as we have seen, they lead him to call irrational one of the most widespread democratic practices, party leadership. But Downs chooses to cleave to his axiom and to deny the real world. We are not told to whom the citizen *can* rationally turn for leadership, with the parties ruled out. Though the leadership hypothesis is therefore not repudiated in so many words, we are in fact thrown back into a leaderless world.

It is perhaps only this assumption of politically preformed majority opinions that allows Downs to hold that purely selfish rulers will always, in a democratic system, produce government policy in the interest of the majority of the ruled. There is a perfect complementarity of interest between rational rulers and rational subjects (though the minority is left out in the cold). It is in the interest of the rulers to govern in the majority interest, for if they did not, they would not stay in power. Thus enlightened selfishness produces the results of unselfish government, and without the aid of a social welfare function or any moral standard other than the rulers' greed.[82] But if party politicians were recognized as leaders and opinion formers, this could not be maintained. With such an axiom added, we would have the worst of tyrannies!

Downs might reply to our objection by arguing that he is under no obligation to give a complete picture of an empirical democratic system in his model. He might even employ axioms which, as in the case cited, appear to contradict reality. Such a practice is not uncommon in the construction of natural science models. The proper test for a model is its predictive ac-

---

[82]We have an interesting echo here of a central Benthamite principle, good evidence that Hobbes is the forerunner of Utilitarianism. Bentham's thought on this point is summarized in a recent article by Warren Roberts: "It will be in the interest of the governors to will to do whatever is conceived to be in the general interest, and since we live in a dynamic society, quite clearly change will be the general interest . . . the will to make changes in the common interest will be in the self interest of the power holders if they are to stay in power." Warren Roberts, Jr., "Behavioural Factors in Bentham's Conception of Political Change," *Political Studies,* X, No. 2 (June 1962), 169. In Bentham's view, of course, this complementarity of interest holds only for a representative and democratic form of government.

curacy, not an intuition about its conformity to the phenomenal world. If it predicts successfully events in which the theorist is interested, the model is adequate.

This is surely a valid contention when the writer has clearly specified his objectives, when we know precisely what prediction he wishes to make. But Downs states his purpose far too broadly and vaguely to meet this criterion. We are told at the outset of the book that he intends to provide "a behavior rule for democratic government, and to trace its implications." This seems tantamount to a complete description of the democratic system, which surely includes a leadership function, though the specific hypotheses with which Downs closes the book seem to narrow his purpose somewhat. All that we can say is that the author has been very ambiguous on this crucial question, while the very beauty of the kind of analysis which he undertakes and its claim to superiority over traditional scholarship lie in precision and detail.

Real World and Model World

By calling it a positive, as contrasted with a normative, model, and by saying that his object is to fashion a rule of behavior similar to those used "to predict the actions of consumers and firms," Downs implies that his model world is meant to mirror the real world, to depict in abstract fashion what actually goes on in a democracy. Yet time and again he insists that his statements are "true of the model world, not the real world, unless they obviously refer to the latter," and that his unqualified remarks "about how men think, or what the government does, or what strategies are open to opposition parties," are not references to "real men, governments, or parties, but to their model counterparts in the rational world of our study."[83] He adds that this must be kept in mind throughout, for otherwise "the reader may condemn many of our statements as factually erroneous, when they are really not factual assertions at all." If we suppose an assertion to be empirically false, we are told to assume provisionally that it "refers solely to the model," and thus set our minds at ease, implying that there need be no correspondence whatsoever between real world and model world.[84]

The ambiguity, I believe, arises from the fact that Downs's model world is not a case study, an empirical description of some particular democratic state, but an abstract representation of a democratic system. It is nevertheless intended as a representation of actual systems, and not as a polity of aspiration, like Plato's *Republic*. Therefore there must be a *certain* correspondence to actual democracies, and it is puzzling that in some places,

[83]Downs, *op. cit.*, p. 34.
[84]*Idem.*

as we have seen, the author flatly denies the correspondence. But perhaps these are simply careless phrases which do not convey his meaning well. What *kind* of correspondence does the author seem to intend? Perhaps it is analogous to the physicist's model of an atomic particle, which in a way represents actual particles, yet cannot be identified with any particular one. Perhaps the model is intended as a kind of average, or "normal" system in the scientific sense, towards which actual democracies tend to conform, a kind of Aristotelian entelechy with the conception of perfection expunged from it.[85]

Downs also seems to intend his model, however, not only as a positive representation to which actuality tends to conform, but as a standard of performance in a normative sense as well. He says, for example, that the model can be "used to discover (1) in what phases of politics in the real world men are rational, (2) in what phases they are irrational, and (3) how they deviate from rationality in the latter."[86] It is interesting that he does not say that the discovery of phases of irrationality in actual behavior would invalidate his model as a positive model, though it seems clear that it would. A new, corrected model, including a representation of both rational and irrational components of the real system, would be called for. The discovery of such discrepancies would of course not discredit the model as a normative one. It could still serve the purpose of judging the rationality of actual systems, with a view to correcting deviations in the real world, as I believe Downs actually intends it. It is puzzling, however, that in the passage cited Downs does not say that he is thinking of the model as a normative one, though in other places he does say that it may be *reduced* to a normative model.

Ambiguities of this kind are not found in physical theories, perhaps because we attribute nothing called "rationality" to the purely physical world. Irrationalist political theory is in the same happy position. But such ambiguities are inevitable in any political theory which admits the rationality concept, yet insists on the use of a scientific mode of analysis adapted from the nonrational world. The ambiguity is not as marked in Hobbes as in modern theories like that of Downs, because of Hobbes's frank admission that he wanted to set a standard of political improvement. Nonetheless, there is to be found throughout Hobbes's work a penchant for reducing what appear to be prescriptive and normative notions, like the Right of Nature, to purely descriptive formulas, and there is constant tension between the conception of freedom implicit in the rationality notion and the determinism of Hobbes's mechanical world.

[85]For another discussion of this problem, see W. Hayward Rogers, "Some Methodological Difficulties in Anthony Downs's *An Economic Theory of Democracy*," *American Political Science Review*, LIII, No. 2 (June 1959), 483-85.

[86]Downs, *op. cit.*, p. 33.

Game Theory

Another deductive, rational-man theory à la Hobbes is William H. Riker's.[87] Though the game-theoretical concepts which form the core of the work have entered the study of politics by way of economics,[88] Riker himself is a political scientist, well grounded in the traditional modes of political analysis, and his work is consequently more sophisticated than that of Downs, avoiding many of the pitfalls into which that economist stumbled.

Riker's object is broader than that of Downs. It is no less than an attempt to formulate the central proposition of a general theory of politics. His book appears to be a response to the challenge thrown down to political scientists by David Easton in his book *The Political System* (1952). Easton criticizes modern students of politics as grubbers of isolated behavioral and legal facts which, when put together, constitute only an unorganized miscellany rather than a systematic body of knowledge. Both Easton and Riker are impressed by the symmetry and power of natural science, which long ago overcame such narrow empiricism as politics is now a prey to.

Riker believes that the way to create a true political science is through the imaginative development of a broad general theory of politics from which, by deductive procedures, lower-level hypotheses can be generated, and which can also serve to unify such low-level generalizations as have already been formulated. Procedures of empirical measurement, in his view, enter into the picture after rather than before the business of theory-making, as a test of theory rather than as a means of generating it.

From the definitions that have become legion in the last ten years, Riker selects that proposed by Easton as the most precise, comprehensive, and meaningful for the "generall name," "politics." In this view, politics is an activity revolving around the authoritative allocation of values in society, a definition which combines the traditional emphasis of political studies on public authority and on ethics (in the words "authoritative" and "values") with the newer behavioral focus (in the word "allocation"). And it fits "political science into the tradition that selects motion and action as the proper concern of science."[89]

From Easton, Riker turns to the game theorists for material. It seems evident to him that the chief ingredient in the political decision-making process today is the construction of coalitions among the decision-makers.

[87]William H. Riker, *The Theory of Political Coalitions* (New Haven, Conn.: Yale University Press, 1962).

[88]The leading work in game theory is John von Neumann and Oskar Morgenstern, *The Theory of Games and of Economic Behavior* (Princeton, N.J.: Princeton University Press, 1944).

[89]Riker, *op. cit.,* p. 10.

Accepting the validity of the "iron law of oligarchy," he asserts that few significant decisions are made by individuals. Even in a dictatorship it is a group, not one man, that rules in fact. And group decision-making necessarily involves "a process of forming a subgroup which, by the rules accepted by all members, can decide for the whole. This subgroup is a coalition."[90] A further premise is that most important political decisions are conscious acts rather than the result of a quasi-mechanical process. Thus, the self-conscious process of coalition building for the purpose of authoritatively allocating social values becomes the focus of Professor Riker's analysis. "And for this study, a model is at hand. It is the von Neumann-Morgenstern theory of *n*-person games, which is essentially a theory of coalitions."[91] Riker notes that it is not strange that game theory should have relevance to politics, since many games like chess, or poker, for the analysis of which game-theoretic principles were developed, are make-believe politics.[92]

The Axioms

What are the axioms of the model? As in the work of Hobbes and Downs, an assumption of "rationality" lies at the basis of Riker's study. Reason legislates the end as well as the means for Riker's political animal, as it does for Hobbes's rational man, though not (at least explicitly) for Downs. "Political rational man is the man who would rather win than lose, regardless of the particular stakes. This definition accords with the traditional sense of the rational political man having the character of a trim-

[90]*Ibid.*, p. 12.

[91]*Idem.*

[92]For a pioneering discussion of the relevance of game theory to political studies, see Martin Shubik, ed., *Readings in Game Theory and Political Behavior* (Garden City, N.Y.: Doubleday & Company, Inc., 1954). It is interesting that Hobbes in the *Leviathan* draws a parallel between politics and games. "It is in the Laws of a Common-wealth, as in the Lawes of Gaming: whatsoever the Gamesters all afree on, [sic] is Injustice to none of them." (p. 299). Though he makes no reference at all to modern game theory, Sheldon Wolin calls the Hobbes chapter in his recent reinterpretation of Western political culture "Hobbes: Political Society as a System of Rules," and makes frequent comparisons between Hobbes's theories and the phenomena of games. Thus "to want to play tennis, for example, means that we want to engage in a form of activity defined by the rules of tennis. This is comparable to being a member of Hobbesian society, for in both cases one agrees to abide by a system or rules." And again, "The rules of a card game are operative only on those who choose to play the game; and when they are not playing they cease to be bound by them. Similarly, the laws and agreements of Hobbesian society were meant to cover only a certain selected range of activity and to leave substantial areas open to individual discretion." Or again, "This was similar to the rules of a game: one player may perform a different role from another within the game, but each has the same rights in relation to the rules." *Politics and Vision* (Boston: Little, Brown & Co., 1960), pp. 267–68, 269.

mer and it is consonant with all the previously mentioned definitions of power."[93] And in the next paragraph he speaks of "rational or winning behavior."[94]

Riker does not attempt to demonstrate, as Hobbes did, however, why winning should be a peculiarly rational value. For Hobbes, self-preservation was rational in the sense that reflection on the constellation of human desires and the consequences of their pursuit demonstrated that this value was the precondition of enjoying all others. But Riker does not spell out what he means by the peculiar rationality of "wanting to win," though he does say that he chooses this goal rather than the notion of power because of its greater clarity. It would seem that what he has in fact done is to specify the end of the political act, that he has defined "political" rather than "rational." The ambiguity probably arises from the fact that Riker has borrowed elements of his notion of rationality from economists such as von Neumann and Morgenstern, who typically speak of "maximizing" behavior as rational. The ambiguity tends to disappear in Riker's most extensive definition of rationality:

> Given social situations within certain kinds of decision-making institutions (of which parlor games, the market, elections, and warfare are notable examples) and in which exist two alternative courses of action with differing outcomes in money or power or success, some participants will choose the alternative leading to the larger payoff. Such choice is rational behavior.[95]

Here, rationality refers clearly to means rather than ends—whichever participant acts most efficiently, by choosing the alternative that produces the largest payoff, is rational. We assume that all participants are "political,"— i.e., that they all desire to win, but that only some are "rational," i.e., clever enough to select a winning strategy.

"Winning" as the political value par excellence is not for Riker an entirely selfish object, as the political object is for Downs. This is so because in the democratic political system at least, the office holder acts in a fiduciary capacity. He is always a representative of another's interest as well as his own, in the eyes of society, Riker points out. This does not mean that he is unselfishly motivated, but rather that the system requires that he behave in the same way as an unselfish person, with nothing but his constituents' well-being in mind. The requirement is not a dictate of enlightened self-interest in this case, but a moral and legal norm. It gives to the representative's victory-oriented acts, in the eyes of society, an ethical character they would not otherwise have. It gives them legitimacy.

The second axiom of the model is the "zero-sum" condition. This

---

[93]Riker, *op. cit.*, p. 22.

[94]*Idem.*

[95]*Ibid.*, p. 23.

specifies that the winners gain an amount which exactly equals the losses of the vanquished, an assumption which usefully simplifies the model and makes possible the use of certain mathematical procedures. Riker grants that not all politics involves zero-sum issues, and that the model therefore does not cover the whole spectrum of political decisions. Certain bargaining situations, for example, are excluded. Nevertheless, many issues do fit the condition, he argues. A total war, which is a fight to the death, is probably the best example.

He also claims that elections fit the zero-sum condition, since only one side gains, and losers forfeit exactly what the victors acquire—office. However, it would seem that this is true only in a limited, artificial sense. It could be argued, in terms of voters' utilities, that the supporters of the losing candidates for office, in a democratic consensual society at least, gain something as well as the victors, simply by the fact that the functions of government continue after the election. Their very acceptance of the outcome and refusal to resort to bullets after the failure of ballots indicates that the "enemy" government has some value for them and does not strike at their vital interest. Value is received even from the hands of the opposition in office—fire protection continues, roads are paved, schools are kept open, the aged and infirm are cared for, the mails move, the national defense is secured. The winners do not literally take all.

Riker then moves on, *à la* Hobbes and Downs, to generate theorems by logical inferences from his axioms. A consideration of one theorem in particular occupies the bulk of the book. This is the proposition that:

> In *n*-person, zero-sum games, where side-payments are permitted, where players are rational, and where they have perfect information, only minimum winning coalitions occur.[96]

Riker notes that this conflicts with Downs's thesis that political parties, if they are rational, seek to *maximize* their support. Riker contends that maximization is irrational, because it requires a broader than necessary distribution of the winnings and hence diminishes the value of the coalition for its members. Therefore, not maximal but minimal winning size is the rational object of the political man or group.

After announcing his size principle, Riker proceeds to show in a brief chapter the logical processes whereby he inferred the principle from his axioms, and then presents empirical evidence for its validity, after translating the principle into the form of a sociological law. He examines two kinds of evidence, experimental and historical. The first consists of the findings of small-group research, carried out by the author himself, which involved college boys and groups of the writer's friends playing parlor games.

The experimental evidence was conflicting, and showed that the size

[96]*Ibid.*, p. 32.

principle does not operate constantly in all environments but only in certain situations. The college boys refused to perceive the game as a zero-sum affair and consistently built larger-than-winning coalitions. This would seem to indicate that in a consensual but nevertheless loosely knit society, in which competition for individual distinction is a chief value, the short-run advantages of financial gain from a parlor game will be sacrificed to longer-range and more important success values which can be served through the purchase of good will and esteem by magnanimous behavior in the game, i.e., by spreading the winnings more widely than required to assure the coalition's victory.

The size principle did operate in the case of the close friends, however, who played a cutthroat game. Here it would seem the bond of friendship among the players ruled the game out as an instrument in the larger competition for status. It was perceived as mere entertainment, and, as such, seemed to call for a mock all-out war. Thus, the influence of social parameters on perceptions of the game by the players was decisive, and the applicability of the size principle varied with these perceptions. The parameters involved were (1) the degree of community among the players, which determined (2) the extent to which external and overriding values were imported into the game.

Historical evidence is drawn by the author from a variety of data—American presidential elections in three periods in which the opposition party disappeared, international coalition-building at the time of the Napoleonic and two World Wars, and the experience of the Indian Congress Party in the last two decades. In each case the evidence shows that a winning coalition that began as a grand coalition, or coalition of the whole, soon diminished in conformity with the size principle. The author points out, however, that the uncertainty of the real world by contrast with the systematically complete and perfect information of the model world may produce coalitions which are only subjectively, and not objectively, minimal. The appearance of absolute weapons in international politics "makes for complete information in the sense that we can say that a government so armed can destroy any opponent."[97] Thus, international coalitions should tend to be objectively, as well as subjectively, minimal. In domestic elections, however, information is very imperfect, despite the disclosures of opinion polls, and in this sphere winning coalitions tend to be larger than necessary for victory. Riker formulates from this another theorem which he calls the "information effect," a corollary to and qualification of the size principle, and in part derived from it.

> The greater the degree of imperfection or incompleteness of information, the larger will be the coalitions that coalition-makers seek to form and the more

[97]*Ibid.*, p. 79.

frequently will winning coalitions actually formed be greater than minimum size. Conversely, the nearer information approaches perfection and completeness, the smaller will be the coalitions that coalition-makers aim at and the more frequently will winning coalitions actually formed be close to minimum size.[98]

Riker suggests that the theorem can be empirically tested more directly than the size principle, and attempts to do it with the findings of V.O. Key and others on periods of critical elections. During such periods, in which coalitions of electors, stable for a long time, are fundamentally altered and reorganized, information in the system declines radically. Evidence shows that the reorganized coalitions are larger-than-winning groups, as the information theorem holds.

The Function of a General Theory

Riker next attempts to show that his two theorems have the explanatory and systematizing value which a general theory must have. They can be used to explain "hitherto observed but unexplained facts and relationships" and "to reconcile conflicts between more particularistic or casuistic theories developed to explain observed phenomena."[99] The size principle gives a more plausible explanation of a relationship discovered by V.O. Key between the presence of a Republican minority and the persistence of organized factions in Southern Democratic parties than that offered by Key himself. And the size principle, taken together with the information effect, allows us to reconcile the apparently conflicting interpretations of American political parties as ideologically "empty bottles" on the one hand, and as coherent and distinct ideological groupings on the other. "Since, according to the size principle and the information effect, coalition builders are actually engaged simultaneously in clarifying and rendering ambiguous (for, however, different sets of voters), it should surprise no one that both theories are advanced."[100] Parties have no interest in being absolutely ambiguous, since they seek only to win, not to maximize votes, in Riker's model.[101] Also, beclouding is necessary only of issues concerning voters about whom the parties have perfect information.

Riker's study also includes an abstract description of the dynamics of coalition building (the logical steps involved in the process of coalition formation) and a chapter on strategies. It is at this point that the author makes the most liberal use of the mathematical formulas borrowed from the theory

[98]*Ibid.*, pp. 88-89.
[99]*Ibid.*, p. 95.
[100]*Ibid.*, p. 101.
[101]Note the disagreement with Downs, *op. cit.*

of games.[102] This section also significantly adds to the body of game theory, for, as the author notes, it has "been generally assumed by game theorists that the theory did not offer much basis for the discussion of strategy in *n*-person, zero-sum games."[103] The technical character of Riker's explanation does not permit a ready summary here. Suffice it to say that he develops a set of calculations with which the managers of proto-coalitions (coalitions in process of formation) can determine whether or not they will be in an advantageous or disadvantageous position in the end-play, and a set of prescriptions for extricating them from disadvantaged positions and for building more advantageous ones.

One major theoretical observation which emerges from the discussion of strategy is that, as proto-coalitions move toward the end-play, the smaller rather than the larger will have the uniquely advantageous position which leads to victory. A striking example is the outcome of the election of 1824, which was decided in the House of Representatives. Though Jackson entered the end-play with the largest proto-coalition (eleven electors to Adams's seven, Crawford's three, and Clay's three), he lost to Adams as a result of the so-called "corrupt bargain" struck between Adams and Clay. Riker sees the bargain, which resulted in a stable *minimal* winning coalition, as produced by calculations of advantage that correspond to the abstract strategies of his own game-theoretical model.

A Strategy for America

Riker devotes the last chapter of his book to an application of his theorems to the problems of American foreign policy today. He assumes that, under present conditions, a winning coalition would comprise about two-thirds the total "weight of the world" engaged in the international game. (The significance of the figure is not clear, since we are not told how it is derived, nor how power is to be measured.) If two-thirds is a reasonable figure, he concludes that the United States, by attempting to sustain a coalition which is more than half but less than two-thirds, is pursuing an uneconomic policy which depletes our resources without yielding returns.

[102]Here the theory ceases to be descriptive and becomes normative. The use of game-theoretical constructs as positive and descriptive concepts is unusual. Thus, Rapoport and Orwant say that "game theory is normative rather than descriptive; that is to say, its conclusions state how 'rational' people ought to behave rather than how real people do behave." Anatol Rapoport and Carol Orwant, "Experimental Games: A Review" in *Behavioral Science,* 7, No. 1 (Jan. 1962), 1. It would seem that game theory cannot properly be *both* positive and normative, as Riker holds, for if the actual behavior of men can be described as rational, there is no *need* for teaching them strategies. The strategies are already in operation.

[103]Riker, *op. cit.,* p. 133.

One would expect the analysis at this point to apply the formulas derived in the chapter on strategies in order to show how the American proto-coalition might be placed in a uniquely advantaged position for the end-play with the Soviet Union. But Riker does not do this. Instead, he advises that we reduce our uneconomic commitments, what seems to be an application of the size principle. However, the reduction which he recommends would not produce a minimal *winning* coalition, but what one would probably call a minimal *blocking* coalition. Our strategy should be to prolong for as long as possible "The Age of Maneuver," a stalemate period of relatively balanced blocking coalitions. We can do this by avoiding uneconomically large side-payments in buying allies which would exhaust our resources. This would also be a rational strategy for the Soviet Union, the author holds. It would forestall the (inevitable?) day when both the chief antagonists are so weakened that their places must be filled by other powers. Apparently, he does not think it rational for either the United States or the USSR to bid for victory by coalition expansion through competitive bidding for allies. This would only precipitate a mutually destructive nuclear war. Victory is impossible in a zero-sum nuclear game. This is a rather strange, though understandable, conclusion for a book based on a conception of politics as a struggle to win. It seems to lead to the Hobbesian admonition that politics, so defined, is irrational and should be given up.

A State-of-Nature Theory

Riker devotes one section of his book to a discussion of the implications of his model for social equilibrium. The model, taken alone, he points out, has radically disequilibrating implications, as our last paragraph indicated. It moves by its nature immediately to a decision, and there is nothing in it which puts a ceiling on the stakes set. This means that "pure" politics today spells annihilation. Perhaps we can call the model a description of politics as it operates in Hobbes's state of nature, prior to the discovery of the laws of reason which enjoin peace. For the model is one of pure conflict—rational conflict, indeed, in that the participants use efficient procedures in their pursuit of victory. But it is victory, not peace and order, that is the posited value. This means that another model altogether is required to establish the rules for mitigating conflict in such a way as to make it compatible with peace, order, community, good feeling, and all of the good things which go with these social conditions, if, indeed, *any* logical model can accomplish this.

This recognition leads the author to the discovery of conflicting rules in balance of power theories such as that of Morton Kaplan, which restate in a precise fashion traditional conceptions of the balance of power system.[104] These theories commonly hold "that there is some kind of inner, hidden stability in the rational conduct of politics" as conflict.[105] In particular, it is argued that the *logic* of the decision-making process *itself* secures the continued existence of the members of the system. But Riker points out that there is no logical connection between such rules as "Act to increase capabilities" and "Fight rather than pass up an opportunity to increase capabilities," on the one hand, and "Stop fighting rather than eliminate an essential national actor," on the other. The rules are in conflict, with one another, and the rule about actor-maintenance is not properly a rule of rational politics as decision-making process. Nor is the rule against joining the strongest proto-coalition universally rational. There are circumstances under which it is rational to join the strongest side.[106]

Riker concludes that the conflicts which he has uncovered in balance of power theories produce radical and inherent disequilibrium in those systems and make for a high degree of probability of practical disequilibrium in the real system. As he sees it, "no rules of balance can be formulated for n-person, zero-sum games."[107] The players are required to choose between conflicting rules at some point in the game. And "there is no constraint in the system that forces them to follow the equilibrating rule as against the nonequilibrating one."[108] Stability can be guaranteed only by some factor outside the system—by a moral principle of restraint or an institutional arrangement. The logic of victory is incompatible with the logic of peace and order.

It should be noted here that Riker's chapter on American foreign policy implies a rule of behavior which is incompatible with the victory-oriented norms of his own model. In effect he advises an equilibrating strategy for both the United States and the USSR. But, as we have just seen, a purely logical model, based on the single value of victory, does not permit this. His advice must therefore derive from another model than the one he has described.

The discovery of logical incompatibilities in balance of power theories is an excellent demonstration of the results of confining the notion of rationality to the "scientific" (logical) realization of a single value. Such a restriction does not allow us to integrate the various concerns of social life into an orderly whole. Perhaps this signifies that the work of integration is

[104]See Morton A. Kaplan, *System and Process in International Politics,* (New York: John Wiley & Sons, Inc., 1957).

[105]Riker, *op. cit.,* p. 160.

[106]Cf. Machiavelli, *The Prince* (New York: Appleton-Century Crofts, Inc., 1947), p. 66.

[107]Riker, *op. cit.,* p. 169.

[108]*Ibid.,* p. 173.

not the proper province of man's calculating or "scientific" faculties, by which he demonstrates causes and effects. Perhaps the integration of conflict and order is, as the classical and Christian philosophers supposed, and Machiavelli as well, the province of prudential judgment, not of science, and therefore not subject to demonstration and not infallible. It is this integrating work of the practical reason that the traditional writers *meant* by "politics," as an area of knowledge that does not afford scientific or mathematical certainty. Hobbes demonstrated that the logic of peace was incompatible with conflict, and so advised the end of conflict by absolute obedience to the sovereign. Riker has demonstrated the same incompatibility in the realm of logic. Both have left to other theorists the work of showing how prudence can effect a practical synthesis of the two.

Bibliographical Note

Useful biographies of Hobbes are Richard S. Peters, *Hobbes,* Baltimore, Md.: Penguin Books, Inc., 1956, and Sir Leslie Stephen, *Hobbes,* New York: The Macmillan Company, 1970. Monographs on his political theory are Leo Strauss, *The Political Philosophy of Hobbes, Its Basis and Genesis,* E.M. Sinclair, trans., Oxford: Clarendon Press, 1936, a careful study based on extensive research in the collection of Hobbes's papers at Chatsworth, the ancestral home of the Dukes of Devonshire, and J. Howard Warrender, *The Political Philosophy of Hobbes: His Theory of Obligation,* Oxford: Clarendon Press, 1957, a highly disciplined and tightly reasoned book which focuses on the central problem of Hobbes's work—the nature and basis of obligation in a materialist theory. An interesting new interpretation of Hobbes, from a socialist standpoint, is C.B. Macpherson, *The Political Theory of Possessive Individualism,* Oxford: Clarendon Press, 1962. Another important monograph is Raymond Polin, *Politique et Philosophie chez Thomas Hobbes,* Paris: Presses Universitaires, 1953. M.M. Goldsmith, *Hobbes's Science of Politics,* New York: Columbia Univ. Press, 1966 reviews the major interpretations of Hobbes. New studies are F.S. McNeilly, *The Anatomy of Leviathan,* New York: St. Martin's Press, Inc., 1968; David P. Gauthier, *The Logic of Leviathan: The Moral and Political Theory of Thomas Hobbes,* Oxford: Clarendon Press, 1969; Sheldon S. Wolin, *Hobbes and the Epic Tradition of Political Theory,* Los Angeles: Clark Memorial Library, 1970; Thomas A. Spragens, *The Politics of Motion: The World of Thomas Hobbes,* Lexington: University of Kentucky Press, 1973; and Michael J. Oakeshott, *Hobbes on Civil Association,* Berkeley, California: University of California Press, 1975.

"Rational man" theory *à la* Hobbes constitutes a rather large literature. See John von Neumann and Oskar Morgenstern, *The Theory of Games and Economic Behavior,* Princeton, N.J.: Princeton University Press,

1944, a seminal work. Martin Shubik, ed., *Readings in Game Theory and Political Behavior,* Garden City, N.Y.: Doubleday & Company, Inc., 1954, contains articles which discuss the application of game theory to politics and which point out some problems in these applications, e.g., a conservative strategy bias. Morton A. Kaplan, *System and Process in International Politics,* New York: John Wiley & Sons, Inc., 1957 attempts to state in detail the "rules" implicit in the various patterns of international politics and their strategic implications. See also Thomas C. Schelling, *The Strategy of Conflict,* Cambridge, Mass.: Harvard University Press, 1960, and Kenneth J. Arrow, *Social Choice and Individual Values,* New York: John Wiley & Sons, Inc., 1951. A useful textbook review of social choice theory is William H. Riker and Peter Ordeshook, *An Introduction to Positive Political Theory,* Englewood Cliffs, N.J.: Prentice-Hall, Inc., 1973. See also James M. Buchanan and Robert Tollison, eds., *Theory of Public Choice,* Ann Arbor: University of Michigan Press, 1972. A general work on the application of mathematics to political studies is Hayward R. Alker, Jr., *Mathematics and Politics,* New York: Crowell Collier and Macmillan, Inc., 1965.

Chapter 8

Lockean Freedom:
Focus on Property

It has recently been said that Americans, as a group, are Lockeans; that is, we think the way Locke did in deciding what things government ought to do and the way it ought to do them. This discipleship has not been a conscious one. What we call the "American way of life" is "a nationalist articulation of Locke which usually does not know that Locke himself is involved." Ours is "a society which begins with Locke" and which "stays with Locke, by virtue of an absolute and irrational attachment to his principles."[1]

The political philosophy of John Locke, therefore, occupies a very special place in this volume, for it forms the context in which all of the modern American theorists whom we have been comparing with the classic writers have fashioned their ideas on the nature of politics. In the thought of each of these contemporaries can be found the stamp of one of the classic philosophers who has had a special significance for him in interpreting the politics of our time. But Locke is in the experience of all of them in the commonplaces about liberty and equality they learned in school. All of them react to him, some affirming the values of the general political culture, others emphatically denying them.

Perhaps it is because of this unique place which Locke holds in our political culture that we cannot single out a particular group of writers in the ranks of modern American political science who are distinctly Lockean. Lockeanism is the genus to which, in one way or another, they all belong. If one bears this in mind in reading other chapters of this book, he will see that the polemic of Neo-Platonists such as Walter Berns is directed not against the Sophists, but against the naturalism of Locke, and that the individual rights which Maritain has embedded in his Thomist world-view are Lockean in origin. We shall not, therefore, discuss particular modern students of

[1] Louis Hartz, *The Liberal Tradition in America* (New York: Harcourt, Brace & World, Inc., 1955), pp. 6, 11.

politics in detail in the second part of this chapter, but shall attempt rather to point up some of the aspects of American political culture which are Lockean in character, and their significance for the study of politics today.

The political writings of John Locke should be read as companion pieces to those of Thomas Hobbes, for they were inspired by the same civil conflicts which produced *Leviathan* and *Behemoth,* and they share the rationalist and mechanistic world-view of Hobbes's work. We can say, indeed, that Locke and Hobbes were two chief fashioners of the rationalist naturalism which was to be the common intellectual currency of the European elite for the next hundred years.

Locke was born in 1632, four years after the Petition of Right, and he was a youth of seventeen when Charles I went to the block. He was a member of one of the rising Puritan families of Somerset, the son of a captain in the parliamentary armies, and grandson to a clothier who built the family fortune and raised the Lockes into the growing class of capitalist entrepreneurs.

As a student at Oxford, Locke's chief interest was medicine, though he did not complete the doctorate in that field. It was, indeed, through his medical skills that he entered politics. In 1666 he performed an operation which saved the life of Anthony Ashley Cooper, then Chancellor of the Exchequer and one of the foremost statesmen of the Restoration, best known to history as the Earl of Shaftesbury, the founder of the Whig party. Lord Ashley was as much impressed by Locke's intellect in general as by his medical skill, and so drew him into his entourage as a kind of executive secretary, adviser, and friend. A recent student of Locke's work thinks the *Two Treatises of Civil Government* were inspired by the battle over the Exclusion Bill, an attempt by Shaftesbury and his Whigs during the period 1679 to 1681 to prevent the accession of the Duke of York, later James II, a Catholic, to the throne.[2]

Shaftesbury died in exile in Holland in 1683, and Locke found it expedient to take refuge there also later that summer, following the famous Rye House plot in which the Whig leaders were implicated. Returning to England with the Glorious Revolution of 1688, Locke became a close friend and adviser of Lord Somers, the man who had taken Ashley's place as leader of the Whigs, and the principal member of William III's government. Through this relationship, and through a little group of members of Parliament who were his disciples, Locke played the role of philosopher reformer. "It would almost seem that during these years after the Revolution," Peter Laslett writes, "there was a sense in which Liberal or Whig philosophy did in fact inform government and affect politicians in the person of Locke the Whig philosopher."[3]

[2]John Locke, *Two Treatises of Government* ed. Peter Laslett (Cambridge: Cambridge University Press, 1960), Editor's Introduction, pp. 45-66.
[3]*Ibid.,* p. 40.

In 1689, the first year of the new regime, *A Letter on Toleration,* the *Two Treatises of Government,* and Locke's most important philosophical work, the *Essay Concerning Human Understanding,* all long in process of composition, were completed and given to the world. Locke became famous, and in the remaining fifteen years of his life "he twisted his fingers around the haft of English intellectual life and got so firm a grasp that it pointed at last in the direction which he had chosen."[4]

The revolution which Locke helped to accomplish was profound, reaching from the practices of the constitution down to the philosophical and theological roots of English life. Behind the liberal transformation in political practice and theory lay an even more profound intellectual revolution. Yet the surface of things remained remarkably undisturbed. The old institutions of King, Lords, and Commons enjoyed their accustomed places in the constitution. And the traditional pieties continued to be expressed from the pulpits of an established High Church. Locke is representative in this also, for we find the new doctrine subtly wrapped in the traditional vocabulary in his writings, and the cloak cleverly stitched together with familiar quotations from Scripture and from Hooker, the orthodox Anglican theorist of ecclesiastical polity.

Science and Myth

The inconsistencies, even contradiction, between the *Essay Concerning Human Understanding* and the *Two Treatises of Civil Government,* and within the *Two Treatises* have been a great puzzle to scholars until very recently. What could explain the apparent muddleheadedness of so brilliant a thinker as Locke? Some said that the magnitude of the problems defied solution within a closed logical system. Still others argued that the doctrines of the two works were presented on very different levels of understanding for different purposes, and were not inconsistent but simply not connected with each other. Recent scholars, unhappy with these explanations, made the assumption that the great mind must be consistent, and that contradictions had to be purely superficial. A careful reading of the text would reveal their fundamental harmony.[5]

[4]*Ibid.,* p. 37.

[5]George Sabine's textbook, *A History of Political Theory,* 3rd ed. (New York: Holt, Rinehart & Winston, Inc., 1961), pp. 537-38, states the most generally accepted doctrine, that Locke's inconsistencies arise from the difficulty of the questions and because Locke never fully made up his mind what he believed on political matters. Laslett, *op. cit.,* pp. 83-91, inclines to the belief that the *Essay* and the *Treatises* are on different levels. Leo Strauss suggested in *Natural Right and History* (Chicago: University of Chicago Press, 1953), Chapter 5, an ingenious way of reconciling the apparent inconsistencies, and in 1960 a student of Strauss's did a

The work of this last group of scholars has shown that Locke intentionally obscured the meaning of his political works. It appears that his purpose was not primarily that of a man who wishes to escape the censor's condemnation, though this was one consideration. More apt is a comparison with the doctor who coats a bitter pill with sugar. Perhaps Locke's medical pursuits even suggested an analogous practice for his political teaching. The patient who takes the pill remains unaware of its hidden unpleasantness, and it can quietly work to cure his ill. Without the sugar coating he might spit it out and remain as sick as before.[6]

In our analogy, Hobbes is the unwise doctor who tried to force the bitter medicine on his unwilling patient and failed. Locke, the wise physician, profited by his example and used the saccharine ruse to get the sick man unknowingly to down the same vile cathartic. The trick was a success. As we have seen, Locke was lionized in his lifetime and his work acclaimed to the skies. The fame of the *Essay* and *Two Treatises* guaranteed the success of all his later work. In other words, the pill went down whole and stayed down.[7]

To return from the language of the sickroom to political discourse, how shall we describe what Locke did? He himself would probably agree, in the language of Plato, that he communicated in the metaphor and allegory of a political myth to the ignorant and prejudiced, i.e., to most men, the difficult truths which his science had discovered. Let us see now what his science contained, and then observe the deft process by which Locke converted it into a wholesome myth.

---

monograph based on extensive research in Locke's unpublished papers and on careful textual analysis of the published works which establishes, I believe definitively, the Strauss interpretation. See Richard H. Cox, *Locke on War and Peace* (Oxford: Clarendon Press, 1960). The Strauss-Cox thesis holds that Locke's ambiguities are deliberate, and are intended to cloak his real meaning. Walter M. Simon argues that there is a fundamental consistency between Locke's theory of knowledge as presented in the *Essay* and the political theory of the *Treatises,* but that there is a basic inconsistency within each work, flowing from an attempt to combine "the radical empiricism of Bacon and the new rationalism of Descartes," "John Locke: Philosophy and Political Theory," *American Political Science Review,* XLV (1951) 386 ff.

[6]It is interesting that Locke uses a similar metaphor to explain the secret writing technique of his opponent, Filmer: "Like a wary physician, when he would have his patient swallow some harsh or corrosive liquor, he mingles it with a large quantity of that which may dilute it that the scattered parts may go down with less feeling and cause less aversion." *Two Treatises of Government,* I, Sec. 7, cited in Cox, *op. cit.,* pp. 34-35.

[7]Laslett believes that an undiscovered manuscript to which he found frequent references in Locke's correspondence, which bore the name of a disease, was the *Two Treatises* disguised by a cover name. Locke's choice of a medical cover for his political treatise fits our analogy well. See Laslett, *op. cit.,* pp. 62-65.

The philosophical foundations of Locke's political thought are found in his *Essay Concerning Human Understanding,* in which he discusses the nature of reality as it is known to us, and the ways whereby we know it.[8] Two ideas in particular stand out as we survey this monumental work. First is Locke's emphasis on practical knowledge. As a scion of a rising bourgeois family, he was unwilling to give the highest place to contemplation. Life is work, activity, business; and we know in order to act. Thus he says in the introductory chapter:

> Our business here is not to know all things, but those which concern our conduct. If we can find out those measures whereby a rational creature, put in that state which man is in in this world, may and ought to govern his opinions, and actions depending thereon, we need not be troubled that some other things escape our knowledge.[9]

The other outstanding characteristic of the work as a whole is its humility about what men are capable of knowing. The world of essential meaning in which medieval philosophy delighted is closed to us. We are not equipped to know the interior being of things, not even of ourselves. Our knowledge extends no further than our ideas, which in their primary form may indeed be *caused* by the real world but do not give us a representation of that world as it is *in itself.* Ideas produced by sensation are "in the mind no more the likeness of something existing without us than the names that stand for them be the likeness of our ideas, which yet upon hearing they are apt to excite in us."[10] This does not mean that they are "Fictions of our fancies." They are indeed the "natural and regular production of things without us, really operating upon us." But they carry with them only that conformity to the thing itself "which is intended, or which our state requires."[11]

We may note here a certain resemblance to the espistemology of Hobbes, who also denied the cognitive character of essence and purpose. The parallel is incomplete, however, for Locke does not reduce reality to matter in motion. He does not say that ideas are only material particles stirred into motion by other particles impinging on the senses, but rather signs in us of an external reality. We have also ideas of an internal reality, ideas of

---

[8]See Sterling P. Lamprecht, *The Moral and Political Philosophy of John Locke* (New York: Columbia University Press, 1918), for a thorough analysis of Locke's epistemology.

[9]John Locke, *An Essay Concerning Human Understanding,* ed. A.S. Pringle-Pattison (Oxford: Clarendon Press, 1924), Book I, Chapter 1, Sec. 6, p. 13.

[10]*Ibid.,* Book II, Chapter 8, Sec. 7, p. 66.

[11]*Ibid.,* Book IV, Chapter 4, Sec. 4, p. 288.

the activity of our own minds, which are the product of reflection rather than sensation, ideas of "perception, thinking, doubting, believing,reasoning, knowing, willing."[12] This reality is different from that which gives us ideas of sensible qualities such as hardness, whiteness, smoothness; it is spiritual rather than material. Locke is a dualist. Nevertheless, we cannot know what spirit is in itself, but only through our ideas the effects which it produces in us, known to us by reflection. Locke is indeed much humbler about our cognitive faculties and more careful about the claims he makes for them than Hobbes. Hobbes goes beyond ideas to make a judgment on the nature of the universe, while Locke confines himself to the world of our minds and is simply agnostic concerning the whole.

The Hierarchy of Ideas. What, then, can we know, and how do we know it? Locke's point of departure, in his theory of knowledge, is the theory of innate ideas. He denies the validity of this doctrine and returns in effect to the theories of medieval scholasticism for his basic principle of cognition, though he does not stay with the scholastics on other points. St. Thomas had written that nothing can be in the intellect which is not first in the senses; we know only through our experience of the world. Locke affirms that the faculties with which we acquire this experience are indeed innate, but our ideas are not. Sensation and reflection, one the product of our experience of the external world, the other of our experience of the world of our minds, produce in us what Locke calls "simple ideas." In the case of sensation these are sensible qualities, or what in the scholastic tradition had been called "accidents"—perceptions of color, texture, extension, shape, odor, for example, but not the "things" in which these qualities appear to inhere. Reflection gives us ideas of the processes of our mind—such as thinking, doubting, and believing, which we have already enumerated above.

These simple ideas Locke calls both "real" and "adequate." Their reality consists in "a conformity with the real being and existence of things," "that steady correspondence they have with the distinct constitution of real beings. But whether they answer to those constitutions as to causes or patterns, it matters not; it suffices that they are constantly produced by them." "Adequacy" lies in their perfect representation of "those archetypes which the mind supposes them taken from."[13]

Simple ideas form the raw material of all our knowledge. We combine them in various ways in our efforts to know. One of these Locke calls "mixed modes," a term which stands for abstract notions that have no counterpart in external reality but only a purely intellectual existence. Examples are the ideas of obligation, of justice, of drunkenness, of a lie.

[12]*Ibid.,* Book II, Chapter 1, Sec. 4, pp. 43-44.
[13]*Ibid.,* Book II, Chapter 30, Sec. 1, pp. 208, 209.

Mathematical entities are also ideas of "mixed modes." These are real and adequate because they are identical with their archetypes, which are within our own minds and created by our minds out of simple ideas.

Mixed modes are to be distinguished from "ideas of substance," which are also compounded by us from simple ideas, but which are meant to represent real beings rather than abstractions—ideas such as "man," "horse," "gold," "water." These words name the beings which we conceive as the underlying realities that support the qualities known to us through sensation. Our ideas of substance are real, since "they are such combinations of simple ideas as are really united, and coexist in things without us,"[14] though they are inadequate to represent the being for which they stand. They are not adequate even in the sense that simple ideas are, since they are not produced in us by the action of external objects but are compounded by our mental faculties from simple ideas. Nor can they be adequate in the sense that mixed modes are, since their archetypes exist outside us, not in our minds, like the archetypes of mathematics and ethics. Thus our knowledge of substantial things is dim. *That* there are such entities we know, but *what* they are is hidden from us—we cannot know the essential nature either of God, or of a pebble, or of ourselves. When we describe these things, we must confine ourselves to the external qualities they exhibit, which is all we know of them. For example, we must define the sun as "bright, hot, roundish, having a constant regular motion, at a certain distance from us," a definition which reminds us of a Hobbesian "generall name," and of the "operational concept" of modern science, since it employs only observable, measurable elements.

Locke completes his classification of ideas with "relation." This type of idea is like the mixed mode, since it is abstract, not meant to stand for a substance, and is identical with its archetype which our mind creates. By definition, an idea of relation "cannot but be adequate."[15] Ideas of relation "are often clearer and more distinct than those of substances to which they belong," since they can often be produced by one simple idea, while substances are always complex collections of ideas. Thus, what we mean by "father" is clearer than what we mean by "man."[16]

All of our knowledge is built of ideas of these five kinds, and consists in nothing but them. It is knowledge adequate for our human purposes, but a hopelessly puny thing by comparison with the perfect knowledge of the whole, which must remain obscure to us.

Calvinist God and Hedonist Ethics. We must consider Locke's treatment of two ideas in particular—God and the moral relation—in order to

[14]*Ibid.*, Book II, Chapter 31, Sec. 5, p. 209.
[15]*Ibid.*, Book II, Chapter 31, Sec. 14, p. 214.
[16]*Ibid.*, Book II, Chapter 25, Sec. 8, p. 178.

grasp the full meaning of his political theory. The idea of God is an idea of a substance, compounded from such simple ideas as existence, duration, knowledge, power, pleasure, and of happiness "enlarged" by an idea of infinity.[17] That this idea is real and not chimerical, says Locke, we can know with mathematical certainty. Its reality can be deduced from our intuitive knowledge that we ourselves exist and that nothing cannot produce a being. From these two propositions we can pass, by inference, to the idea of an eternal, most powerful, and most knowing being. This limited knowledge of the Supreme Being is all we need for "the great concernment of our happiness," though it is inadequate to represent perfectly the Being for which it stands. We cannot know God in His own essence, but only in His "accidental characteristics."[18]

Our notion of the moral relation arises from our complex idea of God, compounded with the simple ideas of pleasure and pain. Locke gives a long list of synonyms for pleasure and pain—"satisfaction, delight, . . . happiness . . . on the one side, or uneasiness, trouble, . . . torment, anguish, misery . . . on the other." As ideas, pleasure and pain are mental beings which are, however, both physical and spiritual in origin. They arise from sensation and from reflection, and "join themselves to" nearly all our other simple ideas, even underpinning concepts of morality.

> What has an aptness to produce pleasure in us is that we call good, and what is apt to produce pain in us we call evil; for no other reason but for its aptness to produce pleasure and pain in us, wherein consists our happiness and misery.[19]

From the constant association of pleasure and pain with our actions we become aware of rules of behavior which specify what is good (pleasurable) and evil (painful). These are operative in us as passions or drives before we are aware of them and as laws of our nature even though we may never consciously know them. Since we have an idea of God as creator, the first efficient cause of all that is, we know that He must be their legislator. Hence, we recognize that the laws of nature constitute moral obligations for us. We come in this roundabout way to the idea of the moral relation and of our moral duty.

> *Morally good and evil* [behavior] then, is only the conformity or disagreement of our voluntary actions to some law, whereby good or evil is drawn on us from the will and power of the lawmaker; which good and evil, pleasure or pain, attending on our observance or breach of the law, are the decrees of the lawmaker, is that we call *reward* and *punishment* . . .

[17]*Ibid.,* Book II, Chapter 23, Sec. 33, p. 172.
[18]*Ibid.,* Book IV, Chapter 10, Secs. 1 to 5, pp. 310-12.
[19]*Ibid.,* Book II, Chapter 21, Sec. 41, pp. 145-46. Scholars remain at a loss to explain how Locke's hedonist ethics can be logically joined to his rationalist theology. I think the following discussion shows how the connection is made.

That God has given a rule whereby men should govern themselves, I think there is nobody so brutish as to deny. He has a right to do it; we are his creatures. He has goodness and wisdom to direct our actions to that which is best; and he has power to enforce it by rewards and punishment, of infinite weight and duration in another life: for nobody can take us out of his hands. This is the only true touchstone of moral rectitude.[20]

Locke, the epistemologist, produces in this way Locke, the hedonist moral philosopher, whose definition of good and evil is the same as Hobbes's before him and Hume's and Bentham's afterward. Unlike the Hobbesian notion of the moral good, we find Locke's conception tied, in the cognitive order, inextricably to the idea of God. Yet in the realm of action, of behavior, the moral rules are realized by passion alone, independent of the rational recognition of their source, through the promptings of pleasure and pain. Calvinism and hedonism are ingeniously joined together in (unholy?) matrimony.

It is a fair guess that Locke's theory of knowledge and his hedonist ethical theory are *both* the product of his Calvinism. The Calvinist God is above all an all-powerful will, which commands the order of the heavens, the earth, and of our lives, a will which is manifest to us as the laws of nature. These are everywhere the same, rigorous and inexorable, whether they drive the planets in their motion around the sun, or the thought and actions of men. The mind and reasons of God, which direct His mighty will, are, however, inscrutable to puny and unworthy man. God is a mysterious, cold, withdrawn figure. Our reason, naturally weak, has been shattered by the Fall.

His Calvinism leads Locke to conclude that we cannot know the ultimate why and wherefore of things, the divine purpose, but only the "how" of things as it is disclosed to us in the processes of the world, God's laws. These laws must be inexorable, inescapable uniformities, the same in the moral and in the physical world. The laws of human nature are imprinted in the passions which move our minds and limbs. We can become conscious of them indeed, but their operation does not depend on our understanding of them. The procedure of analysis is more like that of modern psychology than traditional moral theory.

Locke's inquiry is not so much into how we *should act* as into *how we do act* and into the efficient causes of our actions. A law of nature, he writes in another work, "should not be called the dictate of reason for (a) it is the decree of the Divine will issuing commands and prohibitions, and (b) it is implanted in men's hearts by God so that reason can only *discover and interpret it.*"[21] Thus, as the Divine Reason withdraws from our view, God's

---

[20]*Ibid.,* Book II, Chapter 28, Secs. 4, 8, pp. 201, 202.

[21]John Locke, *Essays on the Law of Nature,* ed. W. von Leyden (Oxford: Clarendon Press, 1954), Analytical Summary, Sec. 1, p. 95.

power and will are doubly manifest to us. God becomes above all a source of energy, the prime mover and first efficient cause of a world which, like that of Hobbes, is a machine. Our passions are in us the drive shafts. From this conception we move readily to the naturalistic world-view of modern science, which has dispensed with the first cause, God, as an unnecessary hypothesis, but which retains faith in the idea of a universal and immanent order.

While this view of reality, I believe, is derived from Calvinism, it is not identical with but rather a distant extension of Calvinist theology by Locke. As I have formulated it, if applied to an analysis of man's social and political behavior, it would indeed be distasteful, even shocking, to the average Calvinist believer and quite unacceptable to other Christians. Its emphasis on pleasure and pain as the motors of moral behavior reminds us of Hobbes, and we wonder whether this does not necessarily imply Hobbesian political theory.

Science Into Myth

Locke realized that the technical and abstract formulas of the *Essay Concerning Human Understanding* would never be the intellectual fare of the common man, and that the small elite that understood them was sophisticated enough to absorb their lesson without dismay. But to apply the theory in a political essay was another matter. Politics, especially in an age of revolution, is everyone's concern, though espistemology is not. Hobbes had shocked the common consciousness from top to bottom, and he had been repudiated by every faction on both sides of the political struggle. How could Locke teach a Hobbesian lesson about human nature and politics without incurring the disapproval which fell like an avalanche on "the Monster of Malmesbury"?

Secret Writing

Locke found an answer to his problem in the art of secret writing. It prescribes the use of an outer and an inner line of argument, the former innocently presenting a facade of traditional doctrine in traditional terms, the second carrying the author's shocking revolutionary doctrines.[22] The intellectual elite, as careful and erudite readers, would readily find the blazes of the hidden trail, while the many would digest the new doctrine quite unaware, supposing it to be only a novel application of familiar ideas. As Richard Cox puts it, "Locke, by very careful writing, achieves his true end of insinuating the central tenets of heterodox doctrines while at the same

[22]See Leo Strauss, *Persecution and the Art of Writing* (New York: Free Press of Glencoe, Inc.), 1952.

time he protects himself from persecution and also, perhaps even more important, gains a hearing for his works by seeming to reject those very doctrines."[23]

The *Two Treatises of Civil Government* have the form of a dual essay against the political theories of Sir Robert Filmer's *Patriarcha Non Monarcha,* an absolutist tract of 1680 which argues the case for the indefeasible hereditary right of the legitimate monarch. This was the period when the Exclusion Bill was being hotly debated, and the Filmer piece was used to good advantage by the partisans of the Duke of York. Absolutism was by no means yet a dead horse, and the tract caused quite a stir. Locke's *Two Treatises* constituted the Whig rebuttal, though they did not appear in their present form, nor publicly, under the author's signature, during the exclusion controversy. Locke waited until the year after the Glorious Revolution to put them in their final form and to publish them. Even then he withheld his name and did not acknowledge authorship until 1702.[24] Like Hobbes, he was a cautious man.

The first of the *Two Treatises* is a rather dull affair, and to a modern reader it seems to have only antiquarian interest. It is a refutation of Filmer's thesis that royal power is analogous to parental authority, and that it is grounded in and descends from the power of Adam, the first king. We need hardly say that no one would seriously entertain the idea today. Yet the book is still of some importance, for, as Cox has pointed out, it contains the rules for reading the secret message of the *Second Treatise* with understanding.

In the *First Treatise,* Locke claims that Filmer has disguised his meaning in order to make it more acceptable to his readers. Then Locke demonstrates Filmer's technique, which consists mainly of two methods. One is to "scatter" his meaning "up and down" in the text and to write ambiguously, shifting the sense of a word between the beginning and the end of a chapter, varying the meaning of words from context to context, yet retaining the appearance of consistency in usage. The other is to use "authority" in such a way as to support his thesis in the surface argument while demolishing it on the second level.[25] In this way, Cox contends, Locke presents the code for deciphering the meaning of his own *Second Treatise,* his theory of government in which we find stated the principal assumptions of modern liberal politics.

The State of Nature and Its Laws. Like the *Leviathan,* Locke's *Second Treatise* opens with a description of society from which government has been abstracted, the state of nature. It seems quite a different condition

---

[23]Cox, *op. cit.,* p. 27.

[24]On the dating of the *Treatises,* see Laslett, *op. cit.,* pp. 45-66.

[25]See Cox, *op. cit.,* pp. 34-37.

from that described by Hobbes, however. While Locke calls it a "state of perfect freedom [where men are able] to order their actions, and dispose of their possessions and persons as they think fit," and while he makes it "a state also of equality, wherein all the power and jurisdiction is reciprocal," he does not extend liberty of action to the seizure and use of one's neighbor and his property in the manner of Hobbes's "right of nature." Even the freedom to use oneself is confined "within the bounds of the law of nature"[26] "Reason, which is that law, teaches all mankind who will but consult it, that being all equal and independent, no one ought to harm another in his life, health, liberty, or possessions." Men "living together according to reason without a common superior on earth, with authority to judge between them, are properly in the state of nature," which is a "state of peace, good will, mutual assistance and preservation."[27]

The picture is an idyllic one that seems far removed from the rapacity of Hobbes's natural man. It is the traditional picture of man in his perfection, a sociable and rational animal, living in harmony with his fellows. Yet, scattered through the chapter on the state of nature are traces of quite a different picture, much like that drawn by Hobbes. And in the subsequent discourse "of the state of war" its details are filled in. The statements are subtle. The first and chief qualification of individual liberty in the state of nature is that one "has not liberty to destroy himself." A few lines further on the idea is rephrased in more positive language. "*Everyone, as he is bound to* preserve himself." (Emphasis supplied.) The formula looks remarkably like Hobbes's first law of nature, the law of self-preservation. Immediately, however, Locke broadens the mandate and makes his natural man a sociable animal—one ought also "as much as he can to preserve the rest of mankind." Yet this is interestingly qualified by the phrase, "when his *own* preservation comes not in competition." (Emphasis supplied.) Duty to self always comes first. We are plainly in the self-oriented world of the *Essay*.[28]

We are also brought to wonder whether the state of nature is, as Locke says, one of "peace and good will." There are aggressors in it, for we are told the law of nature needs an executor "that all men may be restrained from invading other's rights, and from doing hurt to one another." In the state of nature this executive power is given to every man, who has the right and obligation to "preserve the innocent and restrain offenders." Some offenders will be no better than wild beasts, and men will find it necessary to

[26]John Locke, *Second Treatise on Civil Government*, Chapter 2, Secs. 4, 5, in Ernest Barker, ed., *Social Contract* (London: Oxford University Press, 1947), p. 5.

[27]*Ibid.*, Sec. 19, pp. 17, 18.

[28]*Ibid.*, Chapter 2, Sec. 6, pp. 6, 7. For a new interpretation of the "state of nature" which contradicts the Strauss-Cox view presented in these paragraphs see Richard Ashcraft, "Locke's State of Nature: Historical Fact or Moral Fiction?", *American Political Science Review* (Sept. 1968), pp. 898-915.

"destroy things obnoxious to them."[29] Fully three-quarters of the chapter is devoted to the restraint and punishment of the transgressors of the law of nature by its equal executors. Then Locke states an objection that may be made to the mode of law enforcement:

> I doubt not but it will be objected, that it is unreasonable for men to be judges in their own cases, that self-love will make men partial to themselves and their friends: and on the other side, ill nature, passion and revenge will carry them too far in punishing others; and hence nothing but confusion will follow.[30]

This is a description of Hobbes's jungle. The peace of the state of nature will be broken not only by an occasional offender but by all its members, who are all ill-natured, passionate, and vengeful. Therefore, the objection continues, the state of nature should be abandoned for a governmental order, which God himself has appointed "to restrain the partiality and violence of men." *Locke capitulates at once to the objection and grants the truth of its argument!*

> I easily grant that civil government is the proper remedy for the inconveniences of the state of nature, which must certainly be great where men may be judges in their own cases.[31]

The rest of his reply warns against the establishment of absolute monarchies as the particular remedy, for the freedom of such a ruler to judge in his own case makes the whole society a prey to his passion, and no one is safer than before. Thus Locke enters an objection to the Hobbesian solution to the state of nature problem at the same time that he adopts Hobbes's premises about the nature of man and of politics.

The last paragraph of the chapter on the state of nature returns to the surface argument, to the theme stated at the beginning—the social nature of man. Man comes into society for perfection, to fill the wants of isolated existence. The thought is fittingly expressed in a quotation from a traditional clerical writer of Elizabethan times, Richard Hooker.

> For as much as we are not by ourselves sufficient to furnish ourselves with competent store of things, needful for such a life as our nature doth desire, a life fit for the dignity of man; therefore to supply those defects and imperfections which are in us, as living singly and solely by ourselves, we are naturally induced to seek communion and fellowship with others.[32]

[29]*Ibid.,* Secs. 7, 8, pp. 8, 9.
[30]*Ibid.,* Sec. 13, pp. 12, 13.
[31]*Ibid.,* p. 13.
[32]*Ibid.,* Sec. 15, p. 15.

This is a Platonic or Aristotelian description of the origin of society. But Locke has in the paragraph before this adopted the Sophistic theory set forth by Glaucon, and by Hobbes.

The succeeding chapter contrasts the "state of nature" with the "state of war" in the surface argument, while showing clearly below the surface that the two are identical. Its theme is the right of defense against unjust aggressors. A "declared design of force" and aggression creates a state of war, which gives the defender the right to use all means to protect himself, even to kill the aggressor if that is needed.[33] But this is an intolerable condition.

> To avoid this state of war (wherein there is no appeal but to heaven, and wherein every the least difference is apt to end, when there is no authority to decide between the contenders) is one great reason of men's putting themselves into society, and quitting the state of nature.[34]

The state of nature *involves* the state of war because of the passionate nature of man. There can be no "living together according to reason" in the state of nature. If this is meant as a key element of the definition of the state of nature, then that state simply does not exist. There is only the state of war, and it is excluded only by the creation of governmental authority. This is the way in which Locke "scatters" his meaning up and down the text and hides his Hobbesian natural right theory under the respectable garb of the traditional natural law.

Locke also disguises the irrationalist and utilitarian ethic of the *Essay* in the rationalist language of natural law in the pages of the *Second Treatise*. While the surface argument says that the law of nature is plainly "writ in the hearts of all mankind"—which looks strangely like the Cartesian notion of innate ideas that Locke rejects in the *Essay*—the subterranean argument shows that by "hearts" Locke means here the passions. The law of nature governs our behavior as irrational drive, not as rational principle, though it may be made conscious as rational principle. Locke nowhere gives an account of the whole content of the laws of nature as a rational system. He speaks in the *Second Treatise* only of the "first and fundamental law of nature," which is everyone's passion for self-preservation. We must indeed grant that in the *Essay* Locke says he thinks that ethics can be made a deductive and demonstrable science, like mathematics. But neither there nor anywhere else in his writings does he attempt to deduce a systematic code. Nor does he anywhere clarify the concept of "natural law" or show how it fits into the epistemology of the *Essay*.

What of the use that Locke makes of "authority"? Cox has described

[33]*Ibid.,* Chapter 3, Sec. 19, p. 18.
[34]*Ibid.,* Sec. 21, p. 19.

a typical example of Locke's deft sleight of hand with passages of Scripture. Locke's object is to cite authority for the proposition that man in his natural state has a right to punish infractions of the law of nature and to destroy offenders. He cites *Genesis* to prove that God gave man this right in his original state:

> Cain was so fully convinced, that everyone had a right to destroy such a criminal, that after the murder of his brother, he cries out, *everyone that findeth me shall slay me;* so plain was it writ in the hearts of all mankind.[35]

But he neglects to quote God's reply to Cain:

> And the Lord said to him: no, it shall not be so; but whosoever shall kill Cain, shall be punished sevenfold. And the Lord set a mark upon Cain, that whosoever found him should not kill him.[36]

It is not until the covenant with Noah that God gives man the right to sentence others to death. Therefore, Locke, in making it an original right of nature and "tacitly ignoring God's reservation of that power to himself, already at this point reveals the extent to which his underlying argument tends toward a completely secular conception of man's original condition— a conception, one hardly need add, which Locke is not likely to have openly acknowledged, given the pressure of religious orthodoxy."[37] Revolutionary doctrine is thus subtly insinuated in the guise of traditional teaching.

Locke's Leviathan

Property

Lockean man quits the state of nature to protect more than life and limb. His property is also threatened by marauders, and the natural state sets a limit to what he can acquire. Locke actually assimilates property to the person of his natural man, who enjoys property in his person, which is the foundation of all other property.

In the discussion of property, Locke presents another aspect of his ambivalent view of the state of nature. In some places he speaks of "the plenty God has given" man in the state of nature, or of nature having furnished "the materials of plenty." Yet in others he speaks of the "penury of [man's] condition" in this state. In the condition in which God has given goods to man they are of little value. "Tis labor indeed that puts the

---

[35]*Ibid.*, Chapter 2, Sec. 11, pp. 11, 12.
[36]*Genesis*, 4: 15.
[37]Cox, *op. cit.*, pp. 55-56.

difference of value on everything." "Of the products of the earth useful to the life of man, nine-tenths are the effect of labor: nay . . . ninety-nine hundredths are wholly to be put on the account of labor."[38] The value that labor creates can be realized by the individual in large amounts only through the facilities which political society makes available. Abundant value cannot be had in a state of nature, for spoilage limits the right of acquisition. In good Calvinist fashion Locke sees the law of nature prohibiting waste, which is hurtful to the community and to the individual who makes the waste. No one profits from it; it causes only universal pain, and is therefore forbidden. The system of exchange which society makes possible is necessary for our hedonist to acquire to his satisfaction, for money can be stored in unbounded quantities.

The Political Compact

Like Hobbes, Locke grounds all political authority in covenant. Authority is conventional and can have no other origin than popular consent, for by nature every man is his own sovereign lord. By agreement, then, men give up their natural authority, but the cession is to the society as a whole rather than to an individual or a small group. The compact, in effect, creates a democratic sovereign. It is specifically the executive power of the law of nature that is ceded, and each contractant pledges to support the decisions of the general authority with his own force. This seems a narrower grant of authority than the one involved in the Hobbesian contract, by which the men of the state of nature divest themselves of their "natural right." Hobbes's contract creates a sovereign who not only executes but also defines the principles of right. Rather than create a different system, however, I think Locke has merely clarified Hobbes's intention here. Only Hobbes's sovereign can define what principles of right will be universal legal obligations. But Hobbes clearly expected that the sovereign would define a particular set of principles, those of his law of nature, which in the state of nature are merely "theorems," obliging only to a desire that they be enforced. The sovereign's true freedom of decision lies in the realm of application and enforcement rather than in the definition of general principles. Locke's formula is clearer.

Majority Rule. Except for the original compact which creates the political society, the decisions of the group are taken by a majority vote rather than by unanimous agreement. Why so? Locke attributes no special wisdom to the majority, but bases the argument on expediency. Unanimous decisions would be preferable, but human nature does not make them possible. Free men, who are also individualists, cannot be expected to manifest

[38]*Second Treatise,* Secs. 40, 43, in Barker, *op. cit.,* pp. 35, 37.

such absolute concord in the normal course of things. But why a majority rather than a minority? As Calvinist turned mechanist, Locke asks himself what will in fact occur when each principle is applied. Which principle will produce an effective decision? He concludes:

> For that which acts any community, being only the consent of the individuals of it, and it being one body, must move one way, it is necessary the body should move that way whither the greater force carries it, which is the consent of the majority, or else it is impossible it should act or continue one body, one community.[39]

Interpreting the problem as analogous to a question of physics, Locke decides for majority rule. He may be mistaken in his belief that numbers are the chief ingredient of *force majeure*. Often they are not. The interesting point here is that Locke sees politics, like Hobbes, as an aspect of mechanics. Might must determine at least what is legally right. One cannot legislate against the natural motions of social bodies.

The mechanical analogy puts Locke in a predicament from which he is unable to extricate himself. The basic law of nature is the preservation of the individual. Obligation is first to self, and only thereafter to the preservation of all mankind. The law of nature says nothing of the majority. Yet Locke's voting formula guarantees only the majority, and not the individual against whom the majority may range itself or in which the majority finds no interest. Locke is himself aware of the problem. Thus he writes in a chapter on tyranny:

> For if it reach no further than some private men's cases, though they have a right to defend themselves, and to recover by force what by unlawful force is taken from them, yet the right to do so will not easily engage them in a contest wherein they are sure to perish; it being as impossible for one or a few oppressed men to disturb the government where the body of the people do not think themselves concerned in it, as for a raving mad man or heady malcontent to overturn a well-settled state, the people being as little apt to follow the one as the other.[40]

In the next chapter, on the "dissolution of government," Locke repeats the thought. "The examples of particular injustice or oppression of here and there an unfortunate man moves them not."[41] In both cases he is, of course, describing what he thinks does usually happen; he is not prescribing. He seems to think there is no prescription for the absolute security of the individual, that if God makes man an individualist, He is himself a majoritarian. The odd thing is that Locke really does not seem concerned with

[39]*Ibid.,* Chapter 8, Sec. 96, p. 81.
[40]*Ibid.,* Chapter 18, Sec. 208, p. 174.
[41]*Ibid.,* Chapter 19, Sec. 230, p. 192.

the individual's plight. It does not shock him. In fact, the tone of the passages is almost one of relief. It is well that injustice to an isolated individual will not upset a government. Peace and stability are for Locke, as they were for Hobbes, a greater value than individual justice. Perhaps we can explain Locke's attitude by noting that the problem of individual liberty and security in the face of majoritarian tyranny was not the problem of his time. Rather, it was a question of securing the right of the many, or virtually a whole society, against the arbitrary actions of the royal individual.[42]

The social majority is not competent to do more than settle basic questions of governmental form. What kind of superstructure should it raise? The object is to create an effective power which can keep peace and order and defend property, but which will not be an arbitrary power and become itself a threat to these values. Hobbes secured only the first object and quite ignored the second. Locke's solution aims at both. Let us consider the institutions through which he hopes to achieve them, taking them up in reverse order.

Limited but Energetic Government: Combining Opposites. How does Locke attempt to prevent the abuse of governmental power? He lays down at the outset the principle of the primacy of the law of nature, as a kind of bill of rights to his constitution and as a permanent limitation on governmental authority. The law of nature stands "as an eternal rule to all men, legislators as well as others . . . and the fundamental law of nature being preservation of mankind, no human sanction can be good or valid against it."[43] Another limitation is the principle that the government may not take property without consent; the object of government is to secure property as well as persons. As we have seen, Locke actually assimilates these values to one another in the grand concept of "property." Consent is registered either directly in referendum, or in the representative assembly by majority decision. In addition, there is a constitutional prohibition against the delegation of legislative power. Responsibility can be maintained only as long as authority rests in the hands of those on whom the social majority has conferred it. Lastly, there is a requirement that legal rules have the form of "promulgated standing laws" which deal equally with all citizens.

How are these limiting principles to be enforced? Locke provides two institutional safeguards. The first is the provision that the legislature be a representative body subject to periodic reelection, and that it sit for only part of the year. The necessity of defending their policies in the electoral struggle, and the requirement that they go home and live as simple citizens

[42]See Willmoore Kendall, *John Locke and the Doctrine of Majority Rule* (Urbana, Ill.: University of Illinois Press, 1959), and J.W. Gough, *John Locke's Political Philosophy* (London: Oxford University Press, 1950).

[43]*Second Treatise,* Chapter 11, Sec. 135, in Barker, *op. cit.,* p. 114.

under the laws they have made may help to keep the legislators honest. A second device is the separation of powers. Those who make the laws should not also enforce them. To permit this "may be too great temptation to human frailty, apt to grasp at power."[44]

It is the executive who provides the energetic action needed to secure the first set of values—peace, order, and the security of property—for laws are active only as they are enforced. To this end the executive must be unified and constantly in operation. With it, Locke believes, should be joined the "federative power," that power which derives not from the cession of individual authority to society, but from the existence of the society itself as a member of the international community. This comprises the power to make peace and war, and to carry on all transactions with foreign states. Though distinct from executive power in its function, the federative should not be placed in different hands, "for both of them requiring the force of the society for their exercise, it is almost impracticable to place the force of the commonwealth in distinct and not subordinate hands."[45] Energetic government also requires that the executive wield a prerogative power, a discretionary authority to act in the absence of a legal directive, and at times even against the prescriptions of the standing law. Law cannot provide for every contingency of political hazard, nor can the legislature be assembled to deal swiftly enough with every emergency.

Is this not a backdoor restoration of the arbitrary sovereign of Hobbes's Leviathan state? Locke would argue that is is not, for he has made the elective legislature the supreme authority in his system. The *Second Treatise* does not revive the "balanced" medieval constitution in which no agency had the final legal word; it enshrines the principle of 1688, legislative supremacy. The royal prerogative is subject to parliamentary definition and limitation to prevent its abuse, and the executive is responsible to the parliament for its acts. The legislature may withdraw authority from the executive agency and may also punish acts of maladministration. At every point, the executive-federative agents are responsible and subordinate to the legislature.

The "Appeal to Heaven." In this way Locke has attempted to provide energetic government which is at the same time responsible and law-abiding, at all times guided by the principles of natural law. He recognizes, however, that no paper prescription can provide an absolute guarantee against arbitrary government. No matter how cleverly contrived to restrain power, legal rules can be broken. The legislators may flout their trust and unlawfully delegate away their powers. They may legislate elections out of existence and confiscate the property of their enemies, contrary to the

---

[44]*Ibid.,* Chapter 12, Sec. 143, p. 122.
[45]*Ibid.,* Chapter 12, Sec. 148, p. 125.

natural law. The executive may refuse to convene the legislature or otherwise avoid legal sanctions which the legislature might use against it. What recourse does Locke provide his social majority in contingencies such as these? In all such cases the only recourse is an "appeal to heaven," that is, to arms. The people reserve the right of revolution, and the government is "dissolved" by any of the foregoing acts.

Formation of the Social Majority

We have reviewed the institutional arrangements whereby Locke's social majority protects itself against tyrannical government. But we have not yet learned on what principle the social majority is put together. What guarantee is there within the Lockean system that there will *be* a consensual social majority?

Locke never mentions social classes in the *Second Treatise;* he presents us a society that appears to be made up of individuals, who are all pretty much alike in their motives and interests—especially in their common interest in property. He seems to assume that a majority of these individuals will always be able to agree on the need to protect individual rights to life, liberty and property, and on appropriate means to accomplish this. We know, however, that the model of a uniform, classless society does not correspond to Locke's England, and that Locke intended his *Second Treatise* to have applicability to that society. There appears to be a gap in the argument.

Several Locke scholars have demonstrated that the gap is only apparent, and that in various tacit and indirect ways, which include statements in his other writings, Locke has filled it in. C.B. Macpherson has pointed out that Locke believed only a minority of men will be politically active. These are the acquisitive, property-minded individuals of his *Second Treatise.* Most men he expected to be politically passive, and to accept the political leadership of the propertied few. The poor he did not regard as fully rational, whereas the men of his model world are rational, and have the Law of Nature stamped on their minds. The poor can be taught by the elite to accept the Law of Nature as a matter of faith, however, both Macpherson and Hans Aarsleff have pointed out. And they can be made to accept the obligations it lays down to respect the rights of private property, out of fear of everlasting punishment by a wrathful God.[46] The social majority will therefore be held together by an enlightened elite which, by teaching the Law of Nature as Divine Writ, creates a value consensus, at least among a majority of the society. This dominant majority will leave the conduct of

---

[46]See C.B. Macpherson, *The Political Theory of Possessive Individualism,* (London: Oxford University Press, 1962), pp. 222-29; Hans Aarsleff, "The State of Nature and the Nature of Man in Locke," in John W. Yolton, ed., *John Locke: Problems and Perspectives,* (Cambridge: Cambridge University Press, 1969), pp. 132-33.

daily politics up to the elite, but it can be mobilized by them for direct action to protect the rights of property when a threat arises, due to the breakdown of normal political and legal processes.

The Rights of Conscience

Proceeding from the same individualist and hedonist assumptions as Hobbes, Locke has constructed a political order which he thinks can better secure the values of life, liberty, and property than the Hobbesian Leviathan. What both writers have in common with Machiavelli is now clear. In all three theories the political order has a purely utilitarian purpose and has nothing to do with the moral perfection of man. The theme is preservation and enjoyment rather than perfection. In the Hobbesian system, indeed, the sovereign has ecclesiastical functions, but for the purpose of executing his civil purposes rather than for the moral improvement of his subjects. The sovereign defines religious doctrines and prescribes ecclesiastical practices to which outward conformity is required for the sake of peace and order. Diversity of religious beliefs in England in the seventeenth century had bred civil war, from which Hobbes concluded that uniformity would make for peace. He did not care what people believed in private as long as their public actions followed the prescribed rule.

Locke deals with the spiritual order differently. He does not think that religious diversity itself is the cause of conflict, but rather that the persecution of diversity breeds turmoil. In his view, if religion is treated as a purely private and individual affair, and if churches are declared voluntary and private organizations, with equal legitimacy before the law, peace and order will be secured.

> Believe me, the stirs that are made proceed not from any peculiar temper of this or that church or religious society, but from the common disposition of all mankind, who when they groan under any heavy burthen endeavor naturally to shake off the yoke that galls their necks.[47]

Locke's theory is a new variation of the traditional value of ecclesiastical independence of civil power. The "things of God" used to be set apart from those of Caesar in the keeping of a public church with coercive jurisdiction. In the Lockean system, they have become "rights of individual conscience," an area of privacy withdrawn from public control. Caesar must confine himself to the protection of life and property, and leave all other things to the individual to work out in perfect freedom according to the dictates of his own conscience.

[47]John Locke, *A Letter Concerning Toleration* (New York: Liberal Arts Press, 1950), p. 54.

The commonwealth seems to me to be a society of men constituted only for the procuring, preserving, and advancing their own civil interests. Civil interests I call life, liberty, health, and indolency of body; and the possession of outward things, such as money, lands, houses, furniture, and the like.[48]

Traditionally, it had been enormously difficult to draw a clear line between civil and spiritual affairs, and the politics of the entire Middle Ages was filled with disputes between ecclesiastical and temporal rulers about the relationship between the two powers. Locke finds it equally difficult to establish watertight compartments. What if religious practices involve human sacrifice? Must they be tolerated as a right of conscience? Locke says no, for such things threaten the values which government is instituted to secure. The protection of life is a legitimate concern of Caesar's, and he may therefore forbid murder even when it is done in the name of conscience. This resembles the medieval doctrine which declared that the church might interfere in the affairs of the civil ruler to accomplish a spiritual end. Locke turns this around and claims that conscience may be infringed for a civil end. When life, liberty, limb, or property are threatened by religion, Caesar may step in.

Why must religion be a private affair? As Locke sees it, simply because its object—eternal salvation—cannot be furthered by coercive measures, and for him the essential mark of the commonwealth is organized force. Public force can protect life and property, but it cannot persuade a recalcitrant conscience. Only the individual himself, by an act of faith, can gain salvation for himself. True belief is always free. He argues further that persecutors who claim their object is the glory of God and the welfare of the church are only using religion as a cloak for their own selfish lust for power. The use of force in the name of religion is always "upon pretense of religion"; it is never sincere. Locke repeats this thought eight times in the *Letter Concerning Toleration.*

It is often said that the basis of Locke's belief in religious toleration is his poor opinion of the cognitive powers of the mind, as stated in the *Essay.*[49] If the mind is a fallible instrument and if we cannot know the true nature of things, then we ought to tolerate one another's opinions, for none of them can be established with certainty. This argument assumes, however, that Locke regards revealed religion as belonging in the same category as the rational truths discussed in the *Essay,* which he quite clearly does not. Revealed religion is a matter of faith and has nothing to do with the knowledge obtainable by the ordinary powers of the mind. Surely, if Locke had intended this as a principal argument for toleration, he would

[48]*Ibid.,* p. 17.

[49]See Patrick Romanell's introduction in *ibid.,* pp. 7, 8.

somewhere in the *Letter* have stated it. But he did not. He merely says in several places that "everyone is orthodox to himself," but does not say why.

In one place he writes that matters debated among Christians are "for the most part about nice and intricate matters that exceed the capacity of ordinary understandings."[50] But this is not a comment on the weakness of the mind but upon the frivolousness of theological hairsplitting. It is interesting that in one place he writes that Christians are in fundamental agreement on basic things.[51] His main point, it seems to me, is that faith is a matter of inner conviction, the "inward and full persuasion of the mind." It cannot be coerced but only persuaded. It is a personal act of submission to the divine will. This, not the fallibility of the mind, is the reason for toleration. The emphasis is on freedom and spontaneity as the central characteristics of the act of faith, characteristics that exclude it by nature from the realm of politics, which is the province of power and domination.

Religion and Social Duty.   Locke's theory of the purposes of religion and of church organization also influences his toleration theory. Religion consists solely in helping individuals achieve salvation in the hereafter, and the business of salvation is everyone's private affair, and only his affair. Locke assigns the church no role in educating men for the good social life in the here and now. Religion is entirely otherworldly. Hence, social justice is not a concern of the church, but of the civil order only. And its content is clear—to guarantee to every individual the fruits of his labor, as much as he is honestly able to pile up. Though Locke does say that property is subject to regulation, since storing it up is made possible only by social institutions, he sets down no secular principle of justice which might guide such regulation. He mentions no limit on the right of individual acquisition for any obligations in the use of property. In Locke's law of nature, the preservation of property is its chief and, apparently, only object. The great purpose of the political order designed to fulfill the natural law is, therefore, to protect life and property, not to secure its just distribution and use.

This is all in the order of justice. Even in the order of charity Locke says nothing of the obligations of property. His frequent mentions of charity mean love for one's fellow man in a general sense, not helping the poor as a special instance of such love. At any rate, whatever men feel they ought to do for their fellow men, as a dictate of religion, is wholly voluntary and unrelated to political obligation.

The Intolerable. The Civil Uses of Religion.   Locke makes two exceptions to his general doctrine of toleration. Atheists are not to be tolerated,

---

[50]*Ibid.,* p. 15.
[51]*Ibid.,* p. 31.

nor are those whose religion dictates political allegiance to a foreign power (by which he probably means Roman Catholics). The atheist cannot be trusted to keep his word; his assent to the political contract which underlies the whole civil order has no effective sanction.

> Promises, covenants, and oaths, which are the bonds of human society, can have no hold upon an atheist. The taking away of God, though but even in thought, dissolves all.[52]

The pleasures and pains of this life are insufficient leading strings for God's human puppets. Fear of eternal punishment and the prospect of heavenly pleasure alone are sufficient to guarantee the operation of the natural law.

In this exception to the toleration principle, if it is to be taken seriously, we have further evidence that Locke does not found that principle on the fallibility of the human mind. Here he says, in effect, that if men are adherents of none of the many revealed faiths, they must fall back on the powers of their natural faculties. When natural reason comes in to play in religious questions, it is not, for Locke, a helpless instrument. On the contrary, the mind is capable of knowing with certainty that God exists and that He demands obedience to the natural law. God has allowed us to know what is necessary for our conduct. There is a natural religion whose tenets are sure, and towards them the commonwealth can tolerate no doubts, based on the claim of cognitive fallibility or anything else.

Lockean America

"The true role of government is to protect life and property and to stop killing incentives." This might be an excerpt from the *Second Treatise.* Actually it comes from a twentieth-century periodical.[53] The sentiment has been a popular one in the United States since the country's birth. At the Constitutional Convention, for example, one delegate spoke of property as "the principal object of government," and another went further and said that "property was the sole end of government."[54] Or note the still more striking words of James Madison, written in defense of the Constitution, words which out-Locke Locke. "The protection of [the unequal faculties of acquiring property] is the first object of government."[55]

[52]*Ibid.*, p. 52.

[53]Henry Hazlitt, "The Growth Mania," *Newsweek,* Mar. 18, 1963, p. 88.

[54]James M. Burns and Jack W. Peltason, *Government by the People,* 4th ed. (Englewood Cliffs, N.J.: Prentice-Hall, Inc., 1960), p. 50.

[55]*The Federalist,* No. 10.

Jefferson's Declaration of Independence has played in the life of the American polity much the same role as Moses' Ten Commandments did in that of the ancient Jewish nation. It has been both a civil "credo," which every child learns in elementary school, and a moral and legal rule of action. Its doctrine is almost pure Lockeanism. The underlying assumption, understood as self-evident truth, is the equality of men with respect to certain rights, legislated by God in the laws of nature—life, liberty, and the pursuit of happiness (which Jefferson substituted for "property"). The security of these rights is given as the reason for instituting government and as the purpose for which government exists. Governments draw their just authority only from the consent of the governed. When a form of government becomes destructive of these rights, the people may alter it by their reserved right of revolution. Yet the people are conservative. They will not upset the civil order for "light and transient causes" but only when "a long train of abuses and usurpations . . . evince a design to reduce them under absolute despotism."[56]

Gunnar Myrdal has called these ideals the "cement" of American society, and he has said that the "American creed" has "the *most explicitly expressed* system of general ideals in reference to human interrelations. This body of ideals is more widely understood and appreciated than similar ideals are anywhere else."[57] Why have they so long remained the American creed? Why are they so widely understood and appreciated? Alexis de Tocqueville's famous nineteenth-century answer and Louis Hartz's twentieth-century elaboration of it emphasize the congruence of the doctrine with the conditions of American life.[58] Its eqalitarianism fits well with the fact of equality among Americans, particularly in respect to legal and political status. The institutions of feudalism were never imported into the colonies nor was the aristocratic ideal which goes with the fact of legal stratification. American's cultural tone was set by the English middle classes from which most of the early settlers came, and we have seen that Lockeanism is preeminently a bourgeois philosophy. Life on the frontier,

[56]Cf. Locke, "Such revolutions happen not upon every little mismanagement in public affairs . . . but if a long train of abuses, prevarications, and artifices, all tending the same way, make the design visible to the people . . . 'tis not to be wondered that they should then rouse themselves, and endeavor to put the rule into such hands which may secure to them the ends for which government was at first erected." *Second Treatise,* Chapter 19, Sec. 225, in Barker, *op. cit.,* p. 188.

[57]Gunner Myrdal, *An American Dilemma* (New York: Harper & Row, Publishers, 1944), p. 3, quoted in Marian D. Irish and James W. Prothro, *The Politics of American Democracy,* 2nd ed. (Englewood Cliffs, N.J.: Prentice-Hall, Inc., 1962), p. 54.

[58]Hartz, *op. cit.*

which dominated American life until 1900, promoted a rugged individualism that found the individualist sentiments of Lockean theory most appealing.

Indeed, Locke's discussion of the state of nature has many references in it to America, which perfectly exemplified his idea. The resources of a virtually empty continent lay open for the individual to mix his labor with, and it was an environment where he could acquire property without hindrance. To sustain life in the wilderness would have been impossible, however, if every man had had only his own resources to fall back on, so cooperation became as much an aspect of American manners as individualism. But it is cooperation among self-reliant and, in many ways, self-sufficient men, and its spirit is equalitarian, voluntarist, and contractual in the Lockean manner. Americans have always been known for their pragmatic cast of mind, their avoidance of philosophizing in the grand manner, which in political philosophy means a refusal to blueprint utopias to serve as standards for reform.

We have believed that such theory as we need was given us, preformed by the Founding Fathers, and that it is in our experience of life in America that we find guidance for the future.[59] This is typically Lockean. The *Second Treatise* has no detailed description of ideal institutions. It gives only the barest outline of the structure of a good government. Locke had little use for "ideas of government in the fancy."[60] And so the Lockean consensus which developed in the seventeenth and eighteenth centuries has remained strong down through the present. Hartz speaks of it as complete and overwhelming, a unanimous agreement.

God and Enlightened Hedonism

Is there any other explanation available, not only of the fact of our Lockeanism but of our conscious knowledge and application of its principles? A most interesting and cogent one has been given by Harry Jaffa, a modern American Platonist of the Straussian persuasion. Jaffa suggests that the popularity of Lockean values lies in their correspondence with the strongest human passions. He sums up the intention of the framers of the Declaration of Independence in these terms.

> Let us assume that by the right to life and liberty, the framers meant the right of self-preservation, and all the means necessary thereto. Let us assume that they regarded self-preservation as a right, because they regarded it as the strongest human passion, and all other human passions, including the passion

[59]See Daniel J. Boorstin, *The Genius of American Politics* (Chicago: University of Chicago Press, 1953), Introduction and Chapter 1.

[60]See Cox, *op. cit.,* p. 68.

for truth, as weak and ineffective when opposed to it. Suppose that, for this reason, they regarded the true morality an enlightened self-preservation, and that they regarded all other moralities as false, because they were, inadvertently or otherwise, at war with human nature itself, which universally sought preservation above all else. . . .

When the framers thought of some men as maimed in their intellects, they thought of the grounds alleged by divine right monarchy, and feudalism, as the basis for political obligation. These grounds they thought gross superstition, which no one with the knowledge of natural causes provided by modern science could believe in. The strength of the passion of self-preservation throughout all nature was in fact attested to by science. Hence governments constructed to satisfy this passion they thought in accordance with nature, and in this sense in accordance with natural right.[61]

Jaffa in effect says here that the Framers made the same hedonist assumptions about human nature that Locke did, and were ready to accept Locke's view of the values and institutions which corresponded to those assumptions. Popular enthusiasm for the system indicates that the society in general makes the same assumptions. In short, Lockean naturalism in America has become tradition.

The combination of hedonism, utilitarianism, and religion, which we found in Locke, also appears as a characteristic of American political culture. De Tocqueville speaks of their role in American life:

> In the United States hardly anybody talks of the beauty of virtue, but they maintain that virtue is useful and prove it every day. The American moralists do not profess that men ought to sacrifice themselves for their fellow creatures *because* it is noble to make such sacrifices, but they boldly aver that such sacrifices are necessary to him who imposes them upon himself as to him for whose sake they are made.[62]

Americans are like the Lockean men of the state of nature, who contract to form a political society which imposes obligations on them and takes away some of their natural freedom, out of the recognition that these natural obligations are useful. Also, like Lockean men, Americans are religious, a quality not ordinarily thought of as a concomitant of hedonism. Their religion is typically Lockean—rationalist rather than emotional ("It would seem as if the head far more than the heart brought them to the foot of the altar"), and useful for the commonwealth. Thus, de Tocqueville says, American preachers "to touch their congregations, . . . always show them how favorable religious opinions are to freedom and public tranquility; and

---

[61] Harry V. Jaffa, "Comment on Oppenheim," *American Political Science Review,* LI (1957), 55, fn. 2.

[62] Alexis de Tocqueville, *Democracy in America* (New York: Alfred A. Knopf, Inc., 1951), Vol. II, pp. 121-22.

it is often difficult to ascertain from their discourses whether the principal object of religion is to procure eternal felicity in the other world or prosperity in this."[63] Fear of divine retribution is necessary for the safety and stability of the commonwealth. If he were writing today, de Tocqueville would probably find a modern example of utilitarian religion in the slogan that "the family that prays together stays together."

What has been the influence of this Lockean context on the academic study of politics in America? To the traditionally oriented student of politics, the historian, student of law and governmental institutions, and *litterateur,* it has furnished ideals to celebrate, refine, evaluate with, and exhort with. To the behavioralist and proponent of a natural science of politics it has given "goal values" to realize through the application of scientific understanding to the manipulation of political events. It has also reinforced, if not prompted, the belief in a scientific politics. To the noumenalist—the neoclassical and neo-orthodox philosopher—it has supplied an ideological whipping boy.

Locke and the Natural Science of Politics

The Lockeanism of the "scientists" is perhaps the most interesting of the three. It is a primary dogma of this persuasion that "goal values," the ultimate purposes and objectives of political society, cannot be scientifically or rationally demonstrated. One might suppose that the result of such a judgment for an intellectual who holds it would be *anomie,* a condition of skepticism about all value systems and detachment from political commitment. Many of the "scientists," however, affirm with zeal the established values of Lockean democracy and see their role as implementing these values through the creation of a "policy science" of democracy.

On what grounds can an intellectual make such an affirmation, after declaring the whole area closed to rational inquiry? Harold Lasswell shrugs off the question with a statement that the "dignity of the individual" does not require justification in terms of "higher abstractions." Is this value then a self-evident truth, like the natural rights of Locke's surface argument or of the Declaration of Independence? Surely, Lasswell cannot think so.

Perhaps Lasswell is saying indirectly that freedom values do not need justification because they are passionately desired. They are a fact of action, of the political process as it actually operates (just as Locke describes the right of self-preservation in his subterranean argument). This would be consonant with Machiavellian premises, which we saw in Chapter 6 are Lasswell's point of departure. It is also compatible with his definition of "value" in *World Politics and Personal Insecurity* as "the word we use to in-

[63]*Ibid.,* pp. 126, 127.

dicate that there are some impulses with which we associate our ego symbol at a given time."[64]

Locke's naturalism—his rejection of the idea that the human mind can penetrate to the essence of things—has led, as we have seen, to a sharper focus on the externals with which we are in contact. If we cannot know purpose, we can know process and we can describe the way things actually happen. This is, of course, what science aims at doing, and it is therefore not strange that a Lockean political culture should give rise to the idea of a scientific politics, though in Locke himself we have hardly more than a scientific attitude. The individualism and egalitarianism of Lockean doctrine also create a favorable environment for the development of a scientific politics. Scientific generalization is possible only where there is regularity and uniformity, and a society of equal, and therefore comparable, political "atoms" lends itself well to such generalization. As Bernard Crick writes, "the assumption of an atomic unity between individuals as a basis for a science of politics was noticed explicitly in W.B. Munro and implicitly in all the other figures of the movement. . . . That pleasant uniformity of decent competence, as De Crevecoeur had hailed the character of this new man, this American, slipped gradually into an assumption that individuals were or should be so much alike that all their behavior in political and thus group activities could be reduced to measurable and recurrent uniformities."[65]

A crude but interesting measure of the importance of their Lockean context for theorists such as Lasswell is found in the number and importance of citations of Locke's work in their writings. To give just one example: Lasswell and Kaplan's *Power and Society* (1950) bears a quotation from Locke as an epigraph on the title page, and the definition of the book's primary concept, "power," is a modification of Locke's definition in Chapter I of the *Second Treatise*. The authors also refer to Locke in defining "authority," "naked power," "state," and "elite." Of the great classics of political thought, only Aristotle and Machiavelli are cited more frequently than Locke.[66]

Platonist Dissent. The neoclassicists who challenge the possibility and desirability of a natural science of politics are naturally enough also anti-Locke. This is especially noticeable in Leo Strauss's *Natural Right and History* (1953). In this book Locke is described as the great architect of "modern" natural right theory and liberalism, building upon foundations laid down by Machiavelli and Hobbes, who also destroyed "traditional"

[64]Harold Lasswell, *World Politics and Personal Insecurity,* p. 271, in *A Study of Power* (New York: The Free Press of Glencoe, Inc., 1950).

[65]Crick, *op. cit.,* p. 235.

[66]See Harold D. Lasswell and Abraham Kaplan, *Power and Society* (New Haven, Conn.: Yale University Press, 1950).

natural right doctrine. For Strauss, "traditional" natural right, as a teleological politics, a theory of moral order, is all that is good and holy, while "modern" natural right, in its naturalism and hedonism, is a devilish doctrine. It produces a society in which "life is the joyless quest for joy."[67] It also gives rise to modern technology. In Stanley Rothman's paraphrase, "the classics, if not hostile to technological change, at least regarded it as inimical to an ordered society. However, if the only goal is a satisfaction of individual and collective passions, then the development of technology becomes a supreme good."[68]

As Rothman, a critic of Strauss, sees it, the Straussian attack on positivist social science and on Locke as its progenitor amounts to an attack on the American political tradition and puts Strauss outside the American liberal consensus. He notes that Strauss "makes much of the fact that, as he puts it, America is the only country which was founded on the basis of an anti-Machiavellian tradition, and he is fond . . . of citing Jefferson or even Tom Paine to bolster particular philosophical points." But Rothman believes this is all window dressing. "The whole thrust of Strauss's analysis is that the American tradition stems from Hobbes and Locke. In other words, the American tradition is Machiavellian."[69] This amounts to saying that Strauss's praise of Paine and Jefferson is prudent camouflage of the sort that Locke so dearly loved, and also that Strauss, like Locke, is a revolutionary in the realm of political doctrine.

Rousseauist dissent. Dissent from Lockean political science comes also from another quarter, from exponents of the communitarian tradition in American political culture, whose roots are in the thought of Jackson, Jefferson, and ultimately Rousseau. Today many of these persons are found in the Caucus for a New Political Science, which for almost fifteen years has opposed, with slates of its own candidates, the official nominees of the American Political Science Association, and at annual meetings of the Association has sponsored an alternative series of panels to the official program. Leading members of this group include Peter Bachrach, H. Mark Roelofs, and Henry Kariel.

The targets of the communitarian critique are members of the "Group Process" school we described in Chapter six, who are sometimes referred to as "pluralists" and at other times as "democratic elitists." They include V.O. Key, David Truman, and Rober Dahl. Peter Bachrach has pointed out that these three scholars have all argued that the workability of American democracy rests on elites, not on the masses of the people. He quotes Key,

[67]Leo Strauss, *Natural Right and History* (Chicago: University of Chicago Press, 1953), p. 251.

[68]Stanley Rothman, "The Revival of Classical Political Philosophy," *American Political Science Review,* LVI (1962), 347-48.

[69]*Ibid.,* p. 352.

who wrote that there must be consensus "among the upper-activist stratum" on the "rules of the game by which the system operates" and Truman who holds that the existence of democratic process depends on the "consensus of elites."[70] We are reminded of the agreement of Locke's propertied elite to the principles of the "Law of Nature."

Associated with the notion of the importance of elite responsibility is the idea that the mass are neither interested nor well enough informed to be politically responsible. Lindsay Rogers writes,

> Most men and women do not study public questions and endeavor to form rational opinions. They have neither time nor interest. What they learn from newspapers or the radio gives them incomplete . . . distorted information.[71]

It follows, therefore, that political apathy on the part of the many, is a good thing for democracy—a logical deduction from the Lockean view. Jack L. Walker tells us that several elitists suggest "that democracies have good reason to fear increased political participation. They argue that a successful (that is stable) democratic system depends on widespread apathy and general political incompetence."[72]

Kariel and other communitarians have lamented that as the elitists prepare their readers to pay the price for limited politics, "they unwittingly clarify precisely how high the price happens to be." The elitist's approach, Kariel concludes, "keeps him from seeing to what extent individuals are deprived of such possibilities for personal growth as inhere in the act of participating in public life."[73] In chapter nine we shall explore the participatory view of democracy that Rousseauist political science would substitute for the Lockean model.

Bibliographical Note

A good biography of Locke is Maurice Cranston, *John Locke,* New York: The Macmillan Company, 1957. John Y. Yolton, *John Locke and the Way of Ideas,* London: Oxford University Press, 1956 is an excellent historical study of the generation of Locke's theory of knowledge. Important analyses of Locke's political theory include Wilmoore Kendall, *John*

---

[70]Peter Bachrach, *The Theory of Democratic Elitism,* (Boston: Little, Brown and Co., 1967), pp. 48-49.

[71]Lindsay Rogers, *The Pollsters,* (New York: Alfred A. Knopf, 1949), in H.M. Bishop and S. Hendel, *Basic Issues of American Democracy,* (New York: Appleton-Century-Crofts, 1951), p. 255.

[72]"A Critique of the Elitist Theory of Democracy," *American Political Science Review,* LX (June 1966) 287.

[73]Henry Kariel, *The Promise of Politics,* (Englewood Cliffs, New Jersey: Prentice-Hall, Inc., 1966), p. 109.

Locke and the Doctrine of Majority Rule, Urbana, Ill.: University of Illinois Press, 1941, which points out some of the unarticulated implications, assumptions, and problems of Locke's majoritarianism, and Sterling Lamprecht, *The Moral and Political Philosophy of John Locke,* New York: Columbia University Press, 1918, which contains an excellent study of the psychological theory of the *Essay Concerning Human Understanding* and of its relevance for Locke's political theory. Another excellent analysis of the *Essay* is Richard I. Aaron, *John Locke,* Oxford: The Clarendon Press, 1965. Richard Cox, *Locke on War and Peace,* New York: Oxford University Press, Inc., 1960, and Peter Laslett's introduction to his edition of John Locke, *Two Treatises of Civil Government,* London: Cambridge University Press, 1960, are of very great help in working out some of the ambiguities and apparent contradictions in Locke's political thought. Also valuable, for Locke's theory of natural law, is John W. Gough, *John Locke's Political Philosophy: Eight Studies,* Oxford: Clarendon Press, 1950. M. Seliger, *The Liberal Politics of John Locke,* New York: Frederick A. Praeger, Inc., 1968, reviews and criticizes the leading interpretations of Locke. In particular he takes issue with the Strauss-Cox thesis that Locke engaged in secret writing and that his work is a disguised Hobbism. He also argues that Locke's "state of nature" contains several kinds of situations and cannot be reduced either to an idyllic or to a warlike condition. John Dunn, *The Political Thought of John Locke,* Cambridge: Cambridge University Press, 1969, criticizes C.B. MacPherson's interpretation of Locke as an exemplar of "possessive individualism" (see Bibliographical Note for Hobbes) and of the thoroughly hedonic and materialist standpoint represented by that concept. He stresses the importance of the afterlife to Locke and argues that his conception of rationality is theologically based. John W. Yolton, ed., *John Locke: Problems and Perspectives,* Cambridge: Cambridge University Press, 1969, is an important collection of recent interpretive essays on Locke's political theory.

For Lockean theory as ideology in America, see Louis Hartz, *The Liberal Tradition in America,* New York: Harcourt, Brace & World, Inc., 1955, which defends the thesis that American political culture is and always has been dominantly Lockean in tone, and spells out some of the implications of this. The student may also find it interesting to search out Lockean concepts in two reflections on the American creed and on the need for its reinvigoration. One is *Goals for Americans.* Englewood Cliffs, N.J.: Prentice-Hall, Inc., 1960, published by the American Assembly at Columbia University, which contains the report of the President's Commission on National Goals. The other is Oscar Handlin, ed., *American Principles and Issues,* New York: Holt, Rinehart & Winston, Inc., 1961, which contains a collection of ideological statements by outstanding Americans of yesterday and of today.

Chapter 9

Freedom and Community:
Rousseau, Dewey, and Bachrach

With the work of J.J. Rousseau we leave the Machiavellian world of calculating mind and egostic reason which we have traversed in the last four chapters to investigate still another moral continent, the land of the sympathetic heart and the general will. The politics of interest balancing gives way to the politics of interest fusion, and liberal conflict to democratic cooperation.

As with Locke we can find strong traces of Rousseau in the popular political culture of the United States ever since the time of Jefferson and Paine. His thought also defines the parameters of the social theory of America's greatest philosopher, John Dewey. Rousseau's good-hearted common man is an integral part of our national mythology. But while Americans are Lockeans first, last, and always, they are Rousseauists only periodically and by parts. Rousseauist concepts can be used to discriminate one American from another as Locke's cannot. They set Paine and Jefferson over against Madison and Hamilton, and Jackson against Calhoun.

One culmination of the Rousseauist strand in American political culture is the recent work of Peter Bachrach, an American political theorist who has trenchantly criticized the Lockean aspects of the natural science of politics, and has suggested an alternative communitarian approach. In the latter part of this chapter we shall see how he grapples, in the American context, with the problem to which Rousseau addressed himself on the eve of the French Revolution: how, in a post-traditional and naturalistic culture to find a more acceptable ground of value than individual selfishness. Like Rousseau, he has a nostalgia for the virtues and values which go along with community, the common good. Neither believes that viable political society can be constructed on the basis of a pure individualist naturalism. Both also see man as a creature capable of moral development, not as the eternal and irreformable hedonist. Yet neither can accept the noumenalist metaphysics which in the past have always been associated with values which transcend the individual self and with the idea of moral perfection. We shall therefore call them "teleonaturalists," to signify their wish to find *telos,* or purpose, in a world which must be ontologically apprehended from a naturalist standpoint. Mill, Marx, and Nietzsche, philosophers with whom we deal in the succeeding chapters, were also engaged in such an attempt. The reader will have to ask himself how well they have succeeded and whether the problem they have posed themselves is not at the heart of our modern crisis of culture.

While Jean Jacques Rousseau lived his entire life in the eighteenth century (1712-1778) and while his literary product is contemporaneous with the great writings of the Age of Reason, his thought stands apart from the main schools of his day. This is true despite the fact that many of his chief concepts, such as the state of nature, natural man, and the social contract constituted the fashionable jargon of eighteenth-century philosophic salons. Rousseau is the theorist of will and sentiment, and as such is the father of romanticism, which had its fullest flowering in the nineteenth century.

Rousseau's antirationalism was at least in part the result of personal unhappiness flowing from the clash of his neurotic personality with the society of his time. We would say of him today that he was not a "well-adjusted" person. He was born in 1712 to an impoverished Genevese dancing master. His mother died in childbirth, and Jean Jacques grew up almost a wild thing under the unsteady tutelage of his father, who abandoned him at the age of ten. His intellectual biographer, Charles Hendell, writes that, unlike men who grow up in settled families and acquire their moral principles slowly as habits, Rousseau discovered himself as a moral being only late in manhood, a discovery which was "a sudden and transforming disclosure."[1] He lived for many years the life of a tramp, absolutely without discipline or responsibility, though attractive to others for his amiability. Recovering from a serious illness in his twenty-sixth year, Rousseau appears to have recognized the worthlessness of his early life, and resolved to make better use of the time ahead. This led to an intensive self-education in philosophy, mathematics, and science, made possible by the leisure and comfort supplied by the bounty of a wealthy patroness, Mme. de Warens. His self-education was followed by a short stint of work as secretary to the French ambassador to Venice, who failed to compensate Rousseau for his services, causing him to go into debt. An appeal to the Ministry of Foreign Affairs brought Rousseau no help at all, and "the injustice of the situation, and the utter helplessness, were to rankle long within his breast, and stir up defiant sentiments."[2]

[1]Charles W. Hendell, *Jean Jacques Rousseau, Moralist,* Vol. I (New York: Oxford University Press, Inc., 1934), p. 1.
[2]*Ibid.,* p. 20.

Rousseau knocked about after this as a jack of all trades and dabbled in a variety of artistic pursuits, including the composition of opera. His career as a literary figure dates from the success of his *Discourse on the Arts and Sciences,* which was awarded a prize by the Academy of Dijon in 1749. It is a vigorous condemnation of the sophisticated world which had received him so badly. The success of his essay gave Rousseau entry to the smart intellectual salons of Paris, but his neurotically sensitive personality did not allow him to be happy there. Charles Frankel writes that Rousseau felt out of his element in Paris. "The conversation of the *salon,* the politely shocking epigrams, the frivolous dialectical twists, the books written in public" he found repulsive. "The continual talk about civic virtue seemed cold and hypocritical, and the freedom of Parisian life seemed licentious to a man brought up in austerely Calvinist Geneva."[3] Deeply hurt by the coolness of members of the intellectual elite whom he sought to make close friends, Jean Jacques withdrew from the fashionable world of French society to a hermitlike existence. He sought comfort there in the arms of a mistress. Thérèse Levasseur, a simple, uneducated peasant woman with whom he lived for most of the rest of his life. We must understand his violent attack on civilization and the eulogy of the primitive and commonplace, his attack on philosophic reason and praise of sentiment and emotion, in this context.

That Rousseau's assault on the high French culture of his time also constituted an attack on the established social and political system is, however, as much a result of the real illness and decrepitude of those institutions as of Rousseau's unhappy personal experience. The morbid condition of the *Ancien Régime* in the middle of the eighteenth century has been described too often to require treatment here. Symptomatic of trouble was the widespread character of the critique of political and social institutions then in progress among the French intelligentsia. Rousseau was but one of a host of critics, which included such luminaries as Montesquieu, Voltaire, Diderot, Holbach, and Helvetius. These were the *philosophes* who laid the intellectual groundwork of the French Revolution in the very salons of the French "establishment." The ideologies of the revolution were distilled from the writings of all of them, though the name of Rousseau was invoked the most frequently.

The writings which were to establish Rousseau's reputation as a political theorist were produced in a twelve-year period, from 1750 to 1762. The prize essay on the arts and sciences was followed by a second effort of a similar genre, also entered in competition for a Dijon prize. This was a *Discourse on the Origin and Foundation of Inequality among Men.,* which Rousseau published in 1755. It is in effect a continuation of the argument of the first essay—that all our social ills can be attributed to our civilized state,

---

[3]Charles Frankel, Introduction to Jean Jacques Rousseau, *The Social Contract* (New York: Hafner Publishing Co., Inc., 1955), p. xiii.

especially the inequalities which have grown up with complex culture. The essay includes a lengthy eulogy of the idyllic life of the primitive natural man. A *Discourse on Political Economy* also appeared in 1755 as a contribution to the *Encyclopedia,* the great effort of the *philosophes* to compile all the knowledge of the time. Here Rousseau drops the wholly negative attitude of the other essays and begins to sketch out a constructive political and social theory, which is brought to completion in *The Social Contract* and the *Émile* of 1762, a theory in which Rousseau attempts to import the values which he found in nature into the structure of a reorganized conventional order.

The defenders of the *Ancien Régime* saw the clear threat to the established system represented by Rousseau's theories and proceeded against him with censorship and threats of arrest. Fleeing from Paris, he wandered from place to place around Europe, living now in Germany, now in France, now in England. He was not permitted to return to his native Geneva, where his works were condemned. In 1770 Rousseau was allowed to return to Paris, where he lived in sickness, both mental and physical, for eight years. In May of 1778 he died at Ermenonville, a nearby town.

A Brief Note on Method

Rousseau appears to be the least systematic writer we have discussed to this point, and if it is at all proper to speak of Rousseau's method of presentation we should call it "intuitional." This does not mean that he writes "from the top of his head," or without information, or in a chaotic fashion. Rousseau was widely read, though self-educated, and he displays considerable erudition in his writings. His effort in the *Discourse on Inequality* to reconstruct the character and way of life of primitive man from observations of the life of modern primitives, for example, shows a knowledge of the travel literature and anthropological writings of his own time. *The Social Contract* evidences a fair knowledge of classical and modern history, and it is plain that Rousseau was conversant with the work of other political philosophers—Plato, Machiavelli, Grotius, Locke, Hobbes, Montesquieu. And the *Émile* shows that he was a careful student of psychology and of the epistemological theories of his time.

By "intuitional" we shall rather mean that Rousseau *seems* to apply no conscious principle of data-gathering before writing his political theories, nor any self-conscious conceptual framework in organizing his analysis. He wants to give the impression of writing by inspiration, of allowing his genius, his *daemon,* to guide the pen. There are passages which indicate that he thought of his work as constituting a logical whole. But it is a whole that he apprehends as in a vision. "All my ideas are consistent," he writes, "but I cannot express them all at once." "I must beg the attentive reader not hurriedly to accuse me of contradiction. The terms of which I have made use might give some colour to such a charge, but that is owing to the poverty of human language. But wait." "I warn the reader that he must apply his mind to this chapter slowly and deliberately. I have not the skill to make my meaning clear save to those who concentrate their attention upon it."[4] Rousseau writes as a man whose brain is on fire. Analysis sometimes passes over into sudden prophecy: "The Russian empire will wish to subjugate Europe, and will itself be subjugated. The Tartars . . . will become its masters, and ours as well. Some such revolution seems to me to be inevitable. All the kings of Europe are working together to accelerate it." "There is still one country of Europe capable of legislation—the Island of Corsica . . . I have a premonition that this tiny island may one day astonish Europe."[5]

A Theory of Democractic Fulfillment

L'Enfant de la Nature

In Chapter Five we noted that St. Thomas' attempt to synthesize the mundane ideas of the classical world with the otherworldly values of Christianity produced a political theory essential different from its Aristotelian and Patristic components, yet one in which the constituent strands of thought are clearly discernible. We noted also that the synthesis is somewhat problematical, that there remains a certain unresolved tension between the diverse elements in its structure. We may describe the political ideals of Rousseau in a similar way, as a blend of the post-Christian naturalistic individualism (laced with traces of Augustinianism) which was dominant in the intellectual world of his time and some elements of the teleological collectivism of the classical tradition. The "teleonaturalist" synthesis is not complete, and the theory appears kaleidoscopic, presenting in turn radically different patterns, ranging from anarchy to totalitarianism.

Though the differences between the political theories of Rousseau and those of Hobbes and Locke are of the greatest significance, it is also important to note that they share much common ground. In seeking to define the political good, the proper goal and object of the political order, each turns to the hypothetical behavior of man in a prepolitical, presocial "state of nature" for a standard. The hypothesis is worked out in each case by an a priori separation of original from acquired human characteristics, rather than by the teleological analysis of man as a perfect form or idea, as in the classical and Christian tradition. In each case the description is naturalistic

---

[4]Jean Jacques Rousseau, *The Social Contract,* in Ernest Barker, ed., *The Social Contract* (London: Oxford University Press, 1947), pp. 284, 277 (fn), 315.
[5]*Ibid.,* pp. 299–300, 308.

rather than noumenalist. Each writer thinks of the subject under analysis as an "ingenious machine."[6] Rousseau builds his bridge from the naturalistic side of the chasm.

What does Rousseau's natural man strive for? While "self-preservation . . . [is] his chief and almost sole concern," he is not the rapacious egoist of Hobbes and Locke.[7] His wants are so simple and he is so isolated from his fellows that he does not aggress against his neighbors or try to dominate them. Contrary to Hobbes, in the state of nature "the care for our preservation is the least prejudicial to that of others, [and] was consequently the best calculated to promote peace, and the most suitable for mankind."[8] Also, Jean Jacques' primitive has a compassionate, sympathetic side to his character which is entirely absent from the other two versions of natural man. He finds no obstacle to identifying himself with the other, in being glad and sad with his fellows. He feels a compulsion to aid them in distress. Is this a trace of the classical theory that man is a social animal? In one place Rousseau says that "from this quality alone flow all [of man's] social virtues."[9] But he does not say that natural sympathy is coupled with a felt need for society, and a recognition that one can be fulfilled as a man only in society, propositions which are at the heart of the classical noumenalist doctrine. Sympathy is unconnected with any sentiment of moral community or community of interest. Natural men have "no moral relations or determinate obligations with one another."[10] They are independent and self-sufficient.

Another characteristic of natural man is his radical freedom. He is his own master and his own provider, beholden to no one. His only authority is his own will. Rousseau sees this as a fitting condition of life for an animal whose distinctive faculty is free will, the ability to determine his own acts. This, rather than the understanding, is what distinguishes the motion of "the human machine" from "the operations of the brute." "The one chooses and refuses by instinct, the other from an act of free will."[11] Rousseau calls it "the noblest faculty of man."[12]

In the *Discourse on the Origin of Inequality* one frequently senses in Rousseau a great nostalgia for this naturalistic Eden. It appears as a condition in which man's fundamental needs are fulfilled, rather than frustrated,

[6]See Jean Jacques Rousseau, *A Discourse on the Origin of Inequality,* in G.D.H. Cole, translator and editor, *The Social Contract and Discourses* (New York: E.P. Dutton & Dutton Co., Inc., 1946), p. 169.

[7]*Idem.*

[8]*Ibid.,* p. 181.

[9]*Ibid.,* p. 183.

[10]*Ibid.,* p. 180.

[11]*Ibid.,* p. 169.

[12]*Ibid.,* p. 210.

as they are in the Hobbesian and Lockean states of nature. Every comparison of life in politicallly organized society with the supposed primeval condition favors the savage state and condemns social life as depraved. We expect the conclusion that the natural life is the best and happiest life, and that its values can be achieved only by a return to primordial anarchy. Yet Rousseau does not draw this conclusion as a general precept for all men,[13] and even in the passages which seem to argue for the superiority of nature over society, there is a sense of incompleteness, of something lacking in the life of natural man. It is neither a virtuous nor a vicious state. It is a state of potential rather than actual happiness. If man had remained in it, "he would have spent his days insensibly in peace and innocence."[14] But is insensibility happiness? As a person and a moral agent, man is incomplete in the state of nature. This is the implicit judgment of the *Discourse,* though it never appears as an express proposition. How different is this condition from that of Hobbesian and Lockean man, who is quite complete as a person, though terribly discommoded and uncomfortable, in the state of nature.

Society as Bane.   In the classical and scholastic tradition, the notion that original man is only potentially rather than actually fulfilled and happy is connected with the proposition that he enters society in order to accomplish this completeness, in order to live the full life, and that society is therefore a part of the natural order, since nature wills fulfillment. Both in the *Discourse* and in *The Social Contract* Rousseau treats society as purely conventional and utilitarian in origin, in the manner of Locke and Hobbes. Society is not part of a universal teleological order but a human invention. In the *Discourse* he describes the condition which probably gave rise to it—a gradual growth in the human population through which "men's cares increased," presumably from the increased pressure on the meager resources of nature. In response to this challenge to human existence, man became inventive, and his intellectual powers increased. This soon gave him superiority over the beasts, and from the recognition of this superiority

---

[13]In an appendix to the *Discourse on Inequality,* Rousseau indeed advises those who are able to break away from society to do so. They should not be apprehensive of degrading their species by renouncing society's advances in order to renounce its vices. But this is not for all men, particularly men like himself. For such persons, "whose passions have destroyed their original simplicity, who can no longer subsist on plants or acorns, or live without laws and magistrates" the injunction is to "respect the sacred bonds of their respective communities," even though they ought to hold the system in contempt. See *ibid.,* p. 229. He speaks vaguely in this passage of the "eternal prize" which those who resign themselves to social living can hope for "from the practice of those [social?] virtues, which they make themselves follow in learning to know them." This seems to be a dim echo of the Augustinian injunction to the citizens of the Heavenly City who abide in patience this painful pilgrimage here below. He reserves the return to nature for those "who have never heard the voice of heaven." *Ibid.,* p. 228.

[14]*Ibid.,* p. 171.

sprang the sentiment of pride. Rousseau connects the latter with man's first reflective act, with his first self-awareness, saying, "Thus, the first time he looked into himself, he felt the first emotion of pride; and, at a time when he scarce knew how to distinguish the different orders of being, by looking upon his species as of the highest order he prepared the way for assuming pre-eminence as an individual."[15]

Man's new intellectual power also taught him the utility of association, Rousseau writes.

> Taught by experience that the love of well-being is the sole motive of human actions, he found himself in a position to distinguish the few cases, in which mutual interest might justify him in relying upon the assistance of his fellows; and also the still fewer cases in which a conflict of interests might give cause to suspect them. In the former case, he joined in the same herd with them, or at most in some kind of loose association, that laid no restraint on its members, and lasted no longer than the transitory occasion that formed it.[16]

From these utility-inspired acts of association, according to Rousseau, arose the habit of living together in family groups, and from this in turn a new development in man's moral life. Family life "soon gave rise to the finest feelings known to humanity, conjugal love and paternal affection."[17] Thus a social relationship prompted only by considerations of utility gave rise incidentally to moral awakening, a theme which we find restated and developed in *The Social Contract*. In this way Rousseau brings together the teleology of traditional noumenalist theory with the naturalist utilitarianism of Renaissance and Enlightenment thought.

Other moral changes accompanying the growth of intelligence in Rousseau's pseudo-history of man were not so noble, however. As his power of invention increased, man acquired new wants and desires, and from them flow all the ills which dominate the social state. With the division of labor, which was introduced in order to satisfy these growing needs, Rousseau associates the development of property and the loss of natural equality. The abler and stronger outstripped the less well-equipped members of society. Disorder resulted. "Usurpations by the rich, robbery by the poor, and the unbridled passions of both, suppressed the cries of natural compassion and the still feeble voice of justice, and filled men with avarice, ambition, and vice."[18] Fearful for life and property, the rich man sought to dupe the poor into erecting institutions of law and government.

> Let us join, said he, to guard the weak from oppression, to restrain the ambitious, and secure to every man the possession of what belongs to him: let us

[15]*Ibid.*, pp. 193-94.
[16]*Ibid.*, p. 194.
[17]*Ibid.*, p. 195.
[18]*Ibid.*, p. 203.

institute rules of justice and peace, to which all without exception may be obliged to conform; rules that may in some measure make amends for the caprices of fortune, by subjecting equally the powerful and the weak to the observance of reciprocal obligations.[19]

The weak agreed, and "all ran headlong to their chains."[20] At first, before inequality had reached its extreme form, governments were relatively equitable in form and in behavior, but as the gulf increased between rich and poor, despotism developed with it. With the emergence of despotism, man lost his freedom altogether and thus suffered the degradation of his nature to the level of the brute, for his noblest faculty of free choice was thereby sacrificed.

At the conclusion of the *Discourse* we are left with the impression that society has not only failed in the long run to produce the utilities for which it was created, but that it is also responsible for the destruction of man's potential for happiness by the perversion of his moral character. Man seems fatally condemned to an unhappy lot.

Society as Blessing.   In *The Social Contract* Rousseau removes the curse. It is not society as such but simply society as we have known it that is corrupt. There is one form of social order which is a blessing, not a bane, in which the moral potential of the state of nature is fulfilled rather than frustrated. Membership in this society "substitutes justice for instinct in [man's] behavior, and gives to his actions a moral basis" which was lacking in the state of nature. "The voice of duty replaces physical impulse" and "right replaces the cravings of appetite." All of man's faculties are enlarged, "his ideas take on a wider scope, his sentiments become ennobled, and his whole soul [is] elevated." He is turned "from a limited and stupid animal into an intelligent being and a Man."[21]

What is this society like? It must be so organized that many of the aspects of life in a state of nature, features which make it a happier place than most of the forms of organized society, are preserved. The simplicity of the state of nature, its equality, and especially its freedom must be brought intact into society, for on them depend man's moral development and happiness. Society must be organized in such a way "that each when united to his fellows, renders obedience to his own will, and remains as free as he was before."[22]

How can this be accomplished? In the *Discourse on Inequality*, Rousseau had implied that the very fact of interdependence, which is of the essence of society, subjects the members of society to one another and

[19]*Ibid.*, p. 205.
[20]*Idem.*
[21]Rousseau, *The Social Contract*, in Barker, *op. cit.*, pp. 262, 263.
[22]*Ibid.*, p. 255.

destroys freedom. "Each became in some degree a slave even in becoming the master of other men: if rich, they stood in need of the services of others; if poor, of their assistance; and even a middle condition did not enable them to do without one another."[23] Even at the beginning of *The Social Contract* Rousseau speaks of *all* political society as "chains" in a much quoted passage:

> Man is born free, and everywhere he is in chains. Many a man believes himself to be the master of others who is, no less than they, a slave. How did this change take place? I do not know. What can make it legitimate? To this question I hope to be able to furnish an answer.[24]

Here he does not offer to build a society which will not constitute "chains"; he merely hopes to discover legitimate chains.

Freedom and Fulfillment Through the General Will

How is it possible for man in society to render obedience only to his own will and be as free as he was in a state of nature? The problem of individual freedom, as Rousseau explains it, is to avoid organizing society in such a way as to establish relationships of personal dependence. That society implies dependence he does not deny, but freedom is secure if the individual is made dependent on the collectivity rather than on an individual or a partial group. "Freedom," he writes, "is that condition which, by giving each citizen to his country, guarantees him from all personal dependence."[25] "In short, who so gives himself to all gives himself to none."[26]

How can Rousseau call this a definition of personal freedom, the social counterpart to the freedom of the state of nature? Two assumptions are fundamental to the argument. One, which derives from the naturalistic part of Rousseau's thought, is that a society can only arise on the basis of some common interest. If it is absent, there is no true society, only an aggregate. In the matter of common interest in which the society is grounded, the citizens are as one being in their sharing of it, and Rousseau makes it clear that the society must be governed only on the basis of this common interest.[27] The second assumption, which represents the noumenalist in Rousseau, is that a true society constitutes a moral unity as well, a life shared in common, a community of values. He goes so far as to say that the act of association *"substitutes* for the person of each of the contracting parties a

[23]Rousseau, *Discourse on the Origin of Inequality,* in Cole, *op. cit.,* p. 202.

[24]Rousseau, *The Social Contract,* in Barker, *op. cit.,* p. 240.

[25]*Ibid.,* p. 262.

[26]*Ibid.,* p. 256.

[27]*Ibid.,* p. 269.

moral and collective body made up of as many members as the constituting assembly has votes."[28]

As a moral being, society makes choices, just as the individual does; it therefore has a will, which is the motor force in its act of choice. Since through shared interests and shared moral values the individual is identical with the society, in being subject to society's will (which Rousseau calls the "general will") he remains subject, in Rousseau's logic, only to himself. "The Sovereign People, having no existence outside of the individuals who compose it, has, and can have, no interest at variance with theirs . . . it is impossible that the body should wish to injure all its members, nor . . . can it injure any single individual. The Sovereign, by merely existing, is always what it should be."[29]

This does not mean that everything *called* a political society possesses a general will, or, though possessing it, is able to express it. Several conditions must obtain for the general will to be operative. In the first place there must be truly present a common interest and a common agreement on principles of right. "The bond of society is that identity of interests which all feel who compose it. In the absence of such an identity no society would be possible."[30] "What makes the will general is not the number of citizens concerned but the common interest by which they are united." It is "the admirable identity of interest and justice which gives to the common deliberations of the People a complexion of equity."[31] Community of interests presupposes certain social conditions. The society must be quite small, its members must share a roughly equal social and economic status, and it must be simple in its way of life and simple in its economic organizations. In *The Social Contract,* Rousseau stresses the first three conditions, while in the constitution which he drafted for the island of Corsica he emphasizes the latter. Specialization is to be avoided at all costs, to prevent the development of dependence by one partial group on another. Even single farms should produce a variety of crops, so that agricultural trade will be minimized. Various devices are proposed to restrict the development of industry.[32]

There are a number of procedural conditions which must be met in formulating the general will. All of the citizens must take part in the process of legislation through which the general will is expressed. The act of legislation is a sovereign act; no legal process overrides it, and all citizens are subject in an absolute manner to the laws. "The sovereign who is a collective be-

---

[28]*Ibid.,* p. 257. (Emphasis supplied.)

[29]*Ibid.,* p. 260.

[30]*Ibid.,* p. 269.

[31]*Ibid.,* pp. 279-80.

[32]See the excellent discussion of this matter by I. Fetscher, "Rousseau's Concepts of Freedom in the Light of His Philosophy of History," in Carl J. Friedrich, ed., *Nomos,* Vol. IV, *Liberty* (New York: Atherton Press, 1962), pp. 44-51.

ing only, can be represented by no one but himself. Power can be transmitted, but not will." "Since laws are nothing but the authentic acts of the general will, the sovereign cannot act save when the People are assembled."[33] Representative assemblies therefore play no role in Rousseau's ideal order. The legislature is the whole people assembled, as in the popular Roman assemblies, a New England town meeting, or the popular assembly of the Swiss canton. The latter in particular is the model which Rousseau has in mind. He speaks of the "happiest country in all the world" in which one beholds "groups of peasants deciding the affairs of State beneath an oak-tree, and behaving with a constancy of wisdom."[34]

The general will is announced through voting, and every citizen enjoys a vote equal to every other citizen's. "Far from destroying natural equality," the legal equality thus acquired "compensates for all those physical inequalities for which men suffer."[35] In voting, the citizen is required to abstain from all communication, which would encourage the formation of partial groups, or factions, based not on the general shared interest, but on a special or particular interest. He must consult only his own conscience and ask himself what the general will, which is his own will, requires. Rousseau assumes that the lack of communication will not prevent the citizens' being adequately informed to make a sound judgment. Decisions are to be taken by a majority, whose required size should depend on the importance and solemnity of the matter under consideration.

In what position does this place the minority? Rousseau says that its members must simply suppose that they were mistaken, and what they "took to be the general will was no such thing."[36] How does he meet the objection that the losers might be the victims of majority tyranny? In effect he points to the underlying social and moral conditions which we have just described. He says that he "assumes that all the characteristics of the general will are still in the majority."[37] In other words, community is so strong that the opposition between majority and minority can be understood as a merely technical disagreement as to how best to serve a common end which all desire, not as a clash of interests. Why the majority should have this technical wisdom rather than the minority Rousseau does not attempt to demonstrate, however. Perhaps he reasoned that the majority is closer to being the whole than is any minority.

Equality before the law as well as in its making is a central principle of Rousseau's system. The decisions which emerge from the deliberative process which we have just described must always take the form of general

[33]Rousseau, *The Social Contract,* in Barker, *op. cit.,* pp. 269, 365.

[34]*Ibid.,* p. 384.

[35]*Ibid.,* p. 268.

[36]*Ibid.,* p. 390.

[37]*Idem.*

laws, rather than administrative acts aimed at particular persons. "Law is concerned with the subjects of a State taken as a whole, and with actions considered as purely abstract. It never treats a man as an individual nor an act as special or exceptional."[38] This does not mean that law may not establish classes and categories, but in doing so it must not assign particular individuals to a class.

When it comes to administering the law, Rousseau recognizes that the absolute democracy which he requires for the making of fundamental policies cannot obtain. The sovereign people must delegate executive power to a few if the public business is to be accomplished, but the act of delegation creates a special interest by virtue of the privileged status which it erects. The necessary limited departure from the principle of equality threatens thereby to destroy the entire egalitarian structure. The executive, which Rousseau refers to as "the government" must, therefore, be hedged around with all sorts of restrictions in order to ensure the primacy of the general will. Such restrictions are particularly needful if economic inequality is combined with political, as in an aristocratic government. This form "involves inequalities of fortune, . . . in order that the administration of public affairs may be in the hands of those best able to give all their time to it."[39] There must, therefore, be fixed meetings of the popular assembly, which convenes without being specially called by the executive. At the opening of each such meeting the sovereign people are asked whether they desire to retain the established form of government and to leave the administration in the hands of the incumbent magistrates.

Such is the system by which Rousseau supposes it possible to import into man's social condition the freedom and equality of his state of nature, and, by preserving these values, to make possible individual moral development, thus transmuting innocence into perfection.

Liberal or Totalitarian?

How sound in logical structure is the synthesis of individualism and collectivism represented by the theory of the general will? Is it a true synthesis, or does one element give way to the other? Rousseau's insistence that society should be governed solely on the basis of the common interest implies that there is a legitimate realm of particular interests outside the scope of public authority, and that it may even stand in need of protection against encroachments by that authority. In Book I of *The Social Contract* he formulates the purposes of the political association in restrictive terms like those of Hobbes and Locke, "the protection of the person and property of each constituent member." If the social compact is modified or violated in

[38]*Ibid.*, p. 287.
[39]*Ibid.*, p. 336.

the slightest degree, he says, "each associated individual would at once resume all the rights which once were his, and regain his natural liberty."[40] On the other hand, the passages immediately following speak of the "complete alienation by each associate member to the community of *all his rights*" and of the substitution of the collectivity for the persons of the contractants. Each individual becomes a part, and only a part, of the social whole.[41]

In all subsequent discussions of particular interests and the particular will, Rousseau treats them as enemies of the general interest and the general will, to be conquered and destroyed, never as legitimate private affairs. Nor does he think of the general interest as the result of a negotiated compromise among conflicting interests.[42] He says explicitly that the general will does not arise from an "addition" of particular wills. It flows from the common interest which is present to begin with, not negotiated into being. And whatever groups do not recognize its paramountcy, "whoever shall refuse to obey the general will must be constrained by the whole body of his fellow citizens to do so."[43] This "is no more than to say," writes Rousseau, than "that it may be necessary to compel a man to be free," which he proceeds to define as the condition of being given to one's country. From this integration, he shortly adds, arises "Moral Freedom which alone makes a man his own master. For to be subject to appetite is to be a slave, while to obey the laws laid down by society is to be free."[44]

The autonomous individual thus disappears altogether and is absorbed wholly in the category of citizen. Rousseau embraces a totalitarian conception of the political order, reminiscent of classical theory. Society is conceived as a single monolithic unity, and the men who form it are required to think of themselves only as parts of the monolith and to divest themselves of all allegiance to their private concerns as individuals and as members of lesser societies within the great society. The only legitimate order is the public order, and its value is absolute, because it is the instrument of human perfection and happiness. To give any freedom to the private self is to invite it to become radically antisocial and vicious, destructive of one's own happiness and that of all with whom one comes in contact. Virtue is identified in all its parts with good citizenship, with devotion to the collectivity.

[40]*Ibid.,* pp. 255-56.

[41]*Ibid.,* pp. 256, 257.

[42]In one passage there is a hint of such a conception of the general interest, but not a very clear one, and its force is offset by many other passages in which the general interest appears as a monolith. The passage runs as follows: "Take from the expression of the separate wills the pluses and minuses—which cancel out, the sum of the differences is left, and that is the general will." *Ibid.,* p. 274.

[43]*Ibid., p. 261.*

[44]*Ibid.,* p. 262, 263.

Some scholars have suggested that Rousseau conceived of the political order as a church in which the individual finds a kind of secular salvation through the subjection of his particular will to the general will, which stands as a surrogate for the will of God.[45] The Christian church, however, as an organization was never a totalitarian society but always shared authority with an autonomous civil order. More apt a parallel is the classical *polis* which, like Rousseau's society of the general will, was both state and church.

Rousseau says of Hobbes that "he only has dared to propose that the two heads of the eagle should be united, and that all should be brought into a single political whole."[46] His own union of the eagle heads is much more complete than that proposed by Hobbes, which was external only and left the spirit free.

Some writers have argued that if Rousseau's concept of the general will is totalitarian, it is nonetheless mitigated by a principle of rationality, as was the totalitarianism of antiquity. Frederick Watkins says that the rationalistic element in the general will concept is most evident in Rousseau's insistence that the general will can only be expressed in law. "The idea that the process of legislation, which forces men to think in general rather than in specific terms," he writes, "is intrinsically more rational than the process of administration, was well-known even in the time of Aristotle. . . . True rationality is possible only when men transcend their particular interests and purposes and devote themselves to a consideration of general problems."[47] By "rationality" Watkins here means, presumably, "fairness," "equity," "justice," or even "inherent rightness," in a teleological sense. It should be stressed, however, that this single procedural principle, that laws be general, is the only standard of rationality, or rightness, in *The Social Contract*. No substantive principles of right are given us whatsoever. Carl Friedrich properly points out that the dictates of the general will "are not 'rational' in the sense in which that word was used by the traditional natural law schools" of classical and medieval times, a sense which always signified substantive right.[48]

So far as foreign affairs is concerned, Rousseau never establishes any standards of right at all. Rousseau's theory of right order, therefore, in its substantive emptiness, in its obscurity, in its social relativity, and in its

---

[45]F.J.C. Hearnshaw, ed., *The Social and Political Ideas of Some Great French Thinkers of the Age of Reason* (London: George G. Harrap & Co., Ltd., 1930), p. 189.

[46]Rousseau, *The Social Contract,* in Barker, *op. cit.,* p. 429.

[47]Frederick Watkins, *The Political Tradition of the West* (Cambridge, Mass.: Harvard University Press, 1948), pp. 103, 104.

[48]Carl J. Friedrich, *Inevitable Peace* (Cambridge, Mass.: Harvard University Press, 1948), p. 173.

emphasis on will is radically different from the teleological classical and Christian standards of right and from the naturalistic standards of Hobbes, Locke, and Harrington, all of which were detailed, clear, universalist, and rationalist. Rousseau comes close to saying that whatever norms a particular society sets for its behavior and that of its members are right simply because they are willed. The way lies open from this position to the perfect nihilism of a Nietszche.

The Legislator.   The extent of Rousseau's irrationalism is most clearly shown in Chapters Six and Seven of Book II of *The Social Contract.* Here he admits a doubt that the general will can always find expression through the democratic legislative processes we have described above. "Left to themselves, the People always desire the good, but left to themselves, they do not always know where that good lies. The general will is always right, but the judgment guiding it is not always well informed. . . . That is why a legislator is a necessity."[49] Rousseau describes the "legislator" as a "superior intelligence which can survey all the passions of mankind, though itself exposed to none: an intelligence having no contact with our nature, yet knowing it to the full; an intelligence, the well-being of which is independent of our own, yet willing to be concerned with it."[50] He does not say where this extraordinary being is to discover his values, however. Unlike Plato's philosopher-king, his intelligence is subject to no form of the Good. Rousseau says rather that "only Gods can give laws to men."[51]

Does this mean that the charismatic legislator, like a god, makes up the values of the society which he founds from the dictates of his creative mind, without any external standards? This seems to be the implication. For in another place Rousseau says that "by genuine genius I mean the power to create everything from nothing."[52] The legislator is called on by Rousseau to "change, as it were, the very stuff of human nature; to transform each individual who, in isolation, is a complete but solitary whole, into a part of something greater than himself, from which, in a sense, he derives his life and his being; to substitute a communal and moral existence for the purely physical and independent life with which we are all of us endowed by nature."[53] Using the individualist raw materials supplied by nature he creates new social beings, according to a pattern of his own invention, and gives them their standards, their way of life, their institutions. Since his work is so radically creative,the legislator is enjoined by Rousseau to use the tricks of Machiavelli's prince and claim divine sanction and inspiration for

[49]Rousseau, *The Social Contract,* in Barker, *op. cit.,* pp. 289-90.
[50]*Ibid.,* p. 290.
[51]*Ibid.,* p. 291.
[52]*Ibid.,* p. 299.
[53]*Ibid.,* pp. 291-92.

his work, for it is only to divine agency that men are willing to grant such an awesome license to shape their lives. He must attribute "to the Gods a Wisdom that [is] really [his] own."[54] Thus, in place of an objective order of right, discoverable by the teleological reason, Rousseau's hunger for righteousness in a naturalistic world substitutes a human artifact. Master of nature, man creates at will, even his own values. The moral world has become the world of pure imagination and art. Everything is permitted to the political artist. The restraints on him are only natural, not ethical—that which he is simply unable to force his subject to perform.

A Descriptive Footnote

Whatever the horrendous implications of the general will idea for ethical theory, it is clear that with it Rousseau expressed an important fact about the way political societies actually operate which is quite missing from the individualist theories we have been examining in the last several chapters. This is the recognition that men in political society do *not* live in a merely utilitarian relationship with one another, each morally complete apart from his social involvements. The individual receives from the society in which he is educated a way of life and a way of looking at the world. He becomes, as Rousseau supposed, in large part what society makes of him. The moral dependence of the individual on society is a fundamental principle of the modern science of sociology, and its validity has been demonstrated time and time again in the literature of that discipline.

The dependence is not necessarily on a single, all-inclusive "reference group," a fact which Rousseau also recognized, though he did not approve it. An individual becomes "socialized" through a variety of primary and secondary groups which wrap him in an intricate web of social influence. The political society remains, however, a most significant reference group in a pluralist society, and operates through a variety of specific structures and processes to influence important aspects of individual behavior. Understanding how these processes operate, how men become "politicized," has recently become an important subject of empirical research in American political science.

A Problem of Democratic Policy

Despite the utopian aspects of his thought, therefore, Rousseau was a realist, much more so than Hobbes or Locke, in his clear recognition of the moral impact of society on its members. He also saw a moral problem in that impact—the problem of reconciling the value of freedom with the value

---

[54]*Ibid.*, p. 295. Rousseau actually cites Machiavelli in a footnote at this point— *Discourses* I, xi.

of political cohesion based on a common way of life—though he seems to have solved it by giving up freedom. The problem of cohesion bedevils any society which is democratic and also wishes to be pluralistic, and it has been raised many times and in many forms in the history of the American political system.

Graphic and typical statements of the problem are found in the record of two Supreme Court cases which were argued in the 1940s, when the problem was particularly acute in the face of the pressures of a world war. The "Flag Salute Cases," as they are called, arose out of the refusal of children of some members of the Jehovah's Witnesses sect to comply with state statutes requiring the observance of a flag salute ceremony in public schools. The children were expelled from school for failure to participate in the ceremony. The first case came before the Supreme Court in 1940 from Pennsylvania, and the court was asked to decide whether the Pennsylvania statute infringed without due process of law the liberty of conscience guaranteed by the Fourteenth Amendment. The Witnesses claimed that the salute was a violation of the First Commandment, which forbids obeisance to "graven images."

Justice Frankfurter delivered the opinion of the court. He noted at the outset the grave responsibility of the justices in any case in which they are required to reconcile the conflicting claims of public authority and individual liberty, and that "judicial conscience is put to the severest test" when liberty of conscience is involved, "and the authority is authority to safeguard the nation's fellowship." "The ultimate foundation of a free society," he said, "is the binding tie of cohesive sentiment," the theme of *The Social Contract*. "Such a sentiment is fostered by all those agencies of the mind and spirit which may serve to gather up the traditions of a people, transmit them from generation to generation, and thereby create that continuity of a treasured common life which constitutes a civilization." Without such a unifying sentiment, he continued, "there can ultimately be no liberties." He could see no reason why a society might not "in self-protection utilize the educational process for inculcating those almost unconscious feelings which bind men together in a comprehending loyalty." The only issue in the case for him was whether things such as flag salutes were efficient means for attaining this plainly legitimate end. Freedom of conscience was not a valid claim against an effective measure to create that unity which is the foundation of all freedoms. But courts, he concluded, had no special competence in judging the efficiency of means to the end. This was simply a question of public policy, properly to be settled in a legislative, not a judicial, forum. The Pennsylvania statute was therefore upheld, on typically Rousseauistic grounds.[55]

[55]See *Minersville School District v. Gobitis.* 310 U.S. 586, 60 S.Ct. 1010, 84 L. ed. 1375 (1940).

A few years later, however, the Supreme Court changed its mind. In *West Virginia Board of Education v. Barnett,* the court, speaking this time through Justice Jackson, took a Lockean as against a Rousseauist position and said that the First Amendment freedoms, brought to bear through the Fourteenth Amendment against the states, have a special position within our constitutional system and "are susceptible of restriction only to prevent grave and immediate danger to interests which the state may lawfully protect."[56] Justice Jackson also chose to consider the question of utility, which Justice Frankfurter had concluded was beyond the competence of the court. Historical experience has shown, he argued, that a spirit of unity is something which cannot be compelled. "Ultimate futility of such attempts to compel coherence is the lesson every such effort from the Roman drive to stamp out Christianity as a disturber of its pagan unity, the Inquisition, as a means to religious and dynastic unity, the Siberian exiles as a means to Russian unity, down to the fast failing efforts of our present totalitarian enemies. . . . Compulsory unification of opinion achieves only the unanimity of the graveyard."

In two passages Justice Jackson even seemed to say that public authority in a free society does not have the responsibility for creating and maintaining a sentiment of unity, which Frankfurter had claimed for it. "Authority has to be controlled by public opinion, not public opinion by authority," he said. "If there is any fixed star in our constitutional constellation," he added, "it is that no official, high or petty, can prescribe what shall be orthodox in politics, nationalism, religion, or other matters of opinion. . . . If there are any circumstances which present an exception, they do not now occur to us." Not sentiment or feeling but enlightened reason is the true basis of our unity, in Justice Jackson's view. To think that patriotism will languish if patriotic ceremonies are spontaneous instead of a compelled routine "is to make an unflattering estimate of the appeal of our institutions to free *minds.*" (Emphasis supplied.) This Lockean view is presently the controlling one for the court. Whether this or the Rousseauist position is the sounder one, only the future can show.

Freedom, Virtue, and Participatory Politics: The Critique of Democratic Elitism

The Rousseauan Tradition in America

The Rousseauan tradition has found frequent expression in American life—in the thought and practice of Jefferson, in that of Andrew Jackson and of the Jacksonian intelligentsia, and, so far as philosophical elegance is

[56]See *West Virginia State Board of Education v. Barnette,* 319 U.S. 624, 63 S.Ct. 1178, 87 L. ed. 1628 (1943).

concerned, pre-eminently in the thought of John Dewey. In each restatement, the problem of freedom is posed precisely as Rousseau posed it: How can individual liberty be combined with the natural equality of men, with fellow-feeling, and with community?

John Dewey.   The most difficult formulation of the problem in its American form came from the pen of Dewey. For he posed the democratic question in the context of the vast, complex, urban and industrial society of our own century, a society far more complex, more "rationalized" than France under the *Ancien Regime,* or Jacksonian America. We still have to learn whether a definitive answer can be given to the question. Dewey came at the "General Will" problem as one of working out a system of communications which could convey to the public the truth about all the consequences of individual (both private and official) and group behavior at large. Existing agencies of publicity, said Dewey, misuse the communications media for private ends. We live in the age of the public relations man and the advertising agency who are skilled in the manipulation of taste and opinion. We are confronted with superficially pleasing and reassuring "images" rather than with the whole truth about the consequences of socially related behavior. A way must be found to make the system produce the truth.

> Opinions and beliefs concerning the public presuppose effective and organized inquiry. Unless there are methods for detecting the energies which are at work and tracing them through an intricate network of interactions to their consequences, what passes as public opinion will be "opinion" in its derogatory sense rather than truly public, no matter how widespread the opinion is.[57]

When this kind of communication develops, "democracy will come into its own, for democracy is a name for a life of free and enriching communion."[58] A key role in the organization of the public as an effective communications system can be played by the social sciences by developing a public experimental mode of social inquiry.

Rousseau, it will be recalled, solved the problem of communication by establishing equality in voting and requiring that the sovereign people meet as a single body to voice their opinions on what the "general will" demanded. Assuming a sensed community of interest among the people (itself, in part, a function of small size) Rousseau believed that the conditions of equality and face-to-face communication would produce policies conformable to the "general will." He did not envisage the problem as one of obtaining accurate measures of the consequences of alternative policies, but rather of compelling individuals to communicate honestly their subjec-

---

[57]John Dewey, *The Public and its Problems* (New York: Holt, Rinehart & Winston, Inc., 1927), p. 177.

[58]*Ibid.,* p. 184.

tive opinions on social policy. Given the comparatively simple character of life in the eighteenth century, the relatively small populations of the time, and the still undeveloped division of labor, not to speak of the relatively small range of alternative uses of social resources, Rousseau's recipe is persuasive.

A Policy Science for Democracy. The complex nature of modern mass society, however, evidently demands that the science which created complexity also serve society by developing an understanding of the consequences of its many-faceted use. Dewey's concern was to find a way to develop a social science which would be at the disposal of the democratic "public," and which, in fact, would make it possible for this public to have genuine existence. He envisaged this not as a laboratory science but an experimental method of policy-making. Social science needs to show that policies and proposals for social action must be treated as working hypotheses, not as rigid programs. The experience of consequences will indicate the need to alter or retain the original hypothesis. "The social sciences will be an apparatus for conducting investigations and for recording and interpreting its results."[59] This was not a call for government by experts Dewey claimed. Experts would be asked simply to supply the facts on which the rational framing and executing of policies (hypotheses) depends. The latter—the framing and executing—would be done by the public itself within improved processes for discussing and evaluating policies (processes which Dewey only very hazily lined out.) He simply told us that face-to-face communities of the public must be reconstructed (but how?) and local communication be articulated in a larger whole (again, how?).

Communitarian Political Theory Today

Among contemporary political theorists, numerous writers have been addressing themselves to the solution of the American problem of the "General Will," the conversion (to use Dewey's language) of the "Great Society" into a "Great Community." One of the most articulate and insightful of them is Peter Bachrach, who has focussed some of his most important work on a critique of the prevalent Lockean view of society, especially as it is represented in the natural science of politics.

Peter Bachrach. In a study entitled *The Theory of Democratic Elitism,* Peter Bachrach challenges the assumption of the natural science of politics that the chief role of the political theorist today is to develop explanatory models of politics. Such models are drawn from the empirical observation of actual political behavior. They help us to understand in precise terms exactly what is happening in the contemporary political world,

[59]*Ibid.,* p. 203.

and to account for events in terms of psychic motivation, social and economic structure, and "rational choice," understood as the efficient pursuit of given sets of preferences. But for Professor Bachrach such models are inadequate because they do not give us guidance for the future. They assume that the behavior observed today must reoccur tomorrow, that the future will be like the past, and that one can predict the future by extrapolating present trends and value patterns. But in doing this they assume away human moral freedom and intentionality.

> Democratic theory must provide an ideal upon which the political system can be judged and toward which a free people can strive. To be content with an explanatory model of democracy, or, indeed, of polyarchy - albeit useful - is to be left aimless, without direction and perspective, and without the inspiration and fire to reach that which is presently unattainable.[60]

Bachrach is especially distressed that despite divergent technical approaches to political decision-making, most political scientists have concluded that small minorities do and must dominate our organizational life, both public and private. He cites with alarm Robert Dahl's remark that "It is difficult—nay, impossible—to see how it could be otherwise in large political systems."[61] Giving up on the possibility of meaningful participation in politics by mass publics, theorists like Dahl are content to settle for a conception of democracy which emphasizes constitutionalism, the liberal character of the system of elite pluralism, institutions of elite accountability, elite competition, and the breadth of political access afforded by our system. Analysis of the theory of elite pluralism, however, indicates to Bachrach that the pluralists themselves do not rely on traditional institutional processes but have rather turned "to some form of 'elite consensus' as a means to curb or direct elite power effectively."[62] But Bachrach finds this reliance quite unrealistic, and expresses fear that strategically placed elites today have maneuvered themselves substantially free of meaningful democratic control.[63]

To cope with the problem of maintaining effective control over elites, and also to realize the values that participatory politics have for the self-development of democratic man, values that the elitist theorists ignore, Bachrach proposes that we work for extension of the participatory base of the many private bureaucracies which are omnipresent in modern life, and which are closely interlocked today with public authority.

[60]Peter Bachrach, *The Theory of Democratic Elitism* (Boston: Little, Brown & Co., 1967), p. 6.
    [61]*Ibid.*, p. 7.
    [62]*Ibid.*, p. 62.
    [63]*Ibid.*

Is there any sound reason . . . why participation in political decisions by the constituencies of 'private' bureaucratic institutions of power could not be widely extended on those issues which primarily affect their lives within these institutions? . . . If private organizations . . . were considered political — on the ground that they are organs which regularly share in authoritatively allocating values for society — then there would be a compelling case, in terms of the democratic principle of equality of power, to expand participation in decision-making within these organizations.[64]

The result of such an endeavor would be a learning experience, the learning by mass publics of how social decision-making takes place, and of the importance of popular control. It would also help fill the growing gap in contemporary structures of democratic control over elite behavior. And it would be an opportunity for the average man for personal growth by participating in the formation of the democratic "General Will."

Bachrach himself is especially concerned for the last-named value of democratic participation, self-development, which for him is a euphemism for the attainment of "virtue" or goodness. Following Rousseau, he believes that what makes a man a moral person is participation in the life of society, by which he is formed, and on which he also leaves his own imprint. He furthermore believes that this hypothesis is borne out by experiments such as those conducted by Kurt Lewin and his associates in the 1930s "contrasting the impact of authoritarian and democratic leadership on group behavior."[65] The responsible behavior developed in the democratic experimental groups substantiated the testimony of the philosophic tradition since Rousseau "that man's development as a human being is closely dependent upon his opportunity to contribute to the solution of problems relating to his own actions."[66]

Bibliographical Note

Useful intellectual biographies of Rousseau are Frederick C. Green, *Jean-Jacques Rousseau,* London: Cambridge University Press, 1955; Charles W. Hendell, *Jean Jacques Rousseau, Moralist,* 2 vols., New York: Oxford University Press, Inc., 1934; and Daniel Mornet, *Rousseau,* 4th ed., Paris: Hatier, 1950. Frederick M. Watkins, in a lengthy chapter on Rousseau in *The Political Tradition of the West,* Cambridge, Mass.: Harvard University Press, 1948, while recognizing the presence of totalitarian implications, emphasizes the liberal elements in Rousseau's political thought. J. L.

[64]*Ibid.,* pp. 95-96.

[65]*Ibid.,* p. 98. Bachrach cites Kurt Lewin *et al.,* "Patterns of Aggressive Behavior in Experimentally Created Social Climates," *Journal of Social Psychology,* X, (1939), 271-99.

[66]*Ibid.,* p. 9.

Talmon, in *The Rise of Totalitarian Democracy,* London: Secker & Warburg, 1952, makes Rousseau an intellectual progenitor of modern totalitarian movements. John W. Chapman canvasses both sides of the argument in *Rousseau—Totalitarian or Liberal?,* New York: Columbia University Press, 1956. Annie M. Osborn has done an interesting comparative study of the thought of the Great Democrat and the Great Conservative, and has found an amazingly large amount of common ground between the two in *Rousseau and Burke: A Study of the Idea of Liberty in Eighteenth-Century Political Thought,* New York: Oxford University Press, Inc., 1940. Irving Babbitt, *Rousseau and Romanticism,* Boston: Houghton Mifflin Company, 1919, is a violently anti-Rousseau book by a noted conservative. Roger D. Masters, *The Political Philosophy of Rousseau,* Princeton, N.J.: Princeton University Press, 1968, is an impressive new study of Rousseau's political thought. His analysis of Rousseau's theory of knowledge as set forth in *Émile* and its connection with his politics is especially important.

A useful selection of Dewey's political and social essays is John Dewey, *Philosophy, Psychology and Social Practice, Essays,* ed. Joseph Ratner, New York: G.P. Putnam's Sons, 1963. Another is John Dewey, *Problems of Men,* New York: Philosophical Library, 1946. In addition to *The Public and Its Problems,* Dewey's major treatises on politics are *Individualism, Old and New,* London: G. Allen and Unwin, Ltd., 1931, and *Liberalism and Social Action,* New York: G.P. Putnam's Sons, 1935. For early and late statements of the philosophical framework of Dewey's thought, see John Dewey, *Human Nature and Conduct,* New York: Holt, Rinehart & Winston, Inc., 1922, and John Dewey, *Reconstruction in Philosophy,* enl. ed., Boston: Beacon Press, 1949. Other writings of Peter Bachrach include *Power and Choice: The Formulation of American Population Policy* (with Elihu Bergman), Lexington, Mass.: Lexington Books, 1973, and *Power and Poverty: Theory and Practice* (with Morton S. Baratz), New York: Oxford University Press, 1970, which focus on two areas of public policy. See also *Problems in Freedom,* Harrisburg, Pa.: Stackpole Co., 1954.

Chapter 10

The Reunion of Freedom
with Virtue:
Kant, Hare, and Rawls

The definition of freedom had become a highly problematical affair in the work of Rousseau. Instead of adding to the concept a moral (i.e., social) dimension, one that was lacking in the theories of Hobbes and Locke, Rousseau complicated the problem of individual autonomy. As we have seen, some commentators believe that his concept of freedom amounts to a theory of totalitarian social control.

In the philosophizing of Immanuel Kant we find another significant effort to join freedom to moral value, not by processes of social indoctrination, but by the redefinition of what it means to be a human being. Kant's solution was, at base, metaphysical rather than psychological and political. The life of social and individual freedom had to be grounded, as he saw it, in a concept of moral agency that embodies the person's freedom to act according to the sheer idea of duty, independently of all influences from the world of empirical causation. It was this unique human capacity that, for Kant, warranted institutional guarantees of personal freedom.

The Philosopher of Koenigsberg

Frederick the Great's Prussia, the society in which Immanuel Kant thought and wrote his philosophy of freedom, contained none of these institutional guarantees. Its principles embodied no notion of right other than dynastic right—expressed as *Raison d'etat,* a frank political realism—and contained no principle of human freedom. Kant was born in the city of Koenigsberg in the eastern reaches of this dour northern kingdom, on April 22, 1724, the son of the descendant of a Scottish immigrant. He lived there almost continuously until his death in 1804. From 1732 to 1740 he prepared for university studies at the Collegium Fredericianum. And from 1740 to 1746 he studied physics, mathematics, philosophy, and theology at the University of Koenigsberg, where he made a brilliant record. Kant took his doctorate in 1755 and became immediately thereafter a lecturer in the University. (His studies were interrupted for lack of money from 1746 to 1755, when he served as tutor to several Prussian families.) As lecturer, Kant concentrated first in mathematics and physics, and published several scientific works. Thereafter his interests turned toward metaphysics. In 1770 he was promoted to the chair of Professor of Logic and Metaphysics, which he held until his death, serving the University also as Dean and Rector.

There is little to report about Kant's life, which was totally lacking in external romance, quite unlike the adventurous and strenuous sojourn of Rousseau in this world. In its visible character, Kant's existence was one of scholarly asceticism and routine. The farthest he ever travelled from home was some sixty-five miles, during his service as tutor. He never ventured abroad, but lived entirely, and most intensely, the life of the philosopher in Koenigsberg.

Kant was not only a great scholar, but a careful and very prudent one as well. He waited until the age of fifty-seven (1781) to publish his first major philosophical work—the *Critique of Pure Reason,* an epistemological masterpiece that lays a groundwork for the modern philosophy of science. This was followed seven years later by a *Critique of Practical Reason* (1788), which sets out parallel canons of moral reasoning, and in 1791 by the *Critique of Judgment.* Kant's substantive moral philosophy and his political philosophy are expressed chiefly in *The Groundwork of the Metaphysics of Morals* (1785), *The Metaphysics of Morals* (1797), and the brief essays, *Idea for a Universal History* (1784) and *Perpetual Peace* (1795).

Influence of Rousseau

Despite the differences between his own philosophical position and that of Rousseau, we shall see that Rousseau's politics is Kant's point of departure, and that the thought of Kant contains many Rousseauistic elements. Important contributions of Kant were to be the clarification of "freedom" as the autonomous legislation of law for oneself, a development of the "general will" as the governing principle of an ideal "Kingdom of Ends," and the liberation of the "general will" concept thereby from totalitarian overtones and its establishment on a basis of transcendence. Kant's admiration of Rousseau is revealed in the fact that the sole adornment of Kant's study was a portrait of the great Genevese. It is also noteworthy that the only time he is said to have missed the daily constitutional, by which the citizens of Koenigsberg regulated their watches, was when Kant found himself enthralled by Rousseau's *Émile.*

Altogether, Kant's express statement of political ideas occupies less than 5 percent of the total volume of his work, and appears peripheral to his main intellectual contribution. *Perpetual Peace,* the most important of the political books, was presented as a collection of "reveries," "views hazarded at random." Also, Kant was never active in politics. When the authorities began to look askance at some of his political utterances after the death of Frederick the Great, and to curtail his freedom, Kant remarked that "When the world's strong men are in a state of intoxication, a pygmy who values his skin is well advised to stay clear of their quarrels".[1] Kant never developed a political program, and stood at arm's length from the ideologists of the French Revolution who wanted to put his critical philosophy to political work.[2] Nevertheless, Kant's metaphysics and ethics were to have profound implications for political philosophy, and a large impact on the world of practical politics as well. Hans Saner tells us that "Kant's political thinking is suggested throughout his work, that it is an organic outgrowth of that work." And he sees Kant's political thinking as "original and central."[3] Variations of Kant's political ideas continue to play a role in contemporary political debate between philosophers of the "right" and the "left," as we shall see in a glance at the work of John Rawls later in this chapter.

Kantian Dualism: Metaphysics and Method

Hume's Challenge

If the point of departure for Kant's politics was Rousseau, his metaphysical starting point was Hume. The Scottish philosopher, in the tradition of British empiricism, had taken apart the Cartesian world, which was bound together by necessary mathematical realtionships, and had argued that the regularities that we posit about the movements of natural bodies rest only on our observation of them. We can only say that the "laws of nature" have obtained in the past as a matter of empirical fact, but not that they exist by logical necessity. It is only probable that the sun will rise tomorrow. Hume's assertion seemed to Kant to destroy the possibility of philosophical order. In Hume's world, anything at all might happen. Certain knowledge is impossible, and we must content ourselves with pragmatically useful information.

[1]Hans Saner, *Kant's Political Thought* (Chicago, London: University of Chicago Press, 1967), pp. 1, 2.
[2]*Ibid.*
[3]*Ibid.,* p. 4.

On the moral side, Hume had developed out of the individualist "Law of Nature" proclaimed by Locke a frank utilitarianism. He made explicit the hedonistic view of man that Locke had hidden between the lines, veiled in secret writing. Hume's moral doctrine was, in fact, more a psychological description than an ethics. And it rested, as did all of his ideas, on an empirical rather than a theoretical base. Morality became a code of enlightened interest: "The distinguishing impressions by which moral good or evil is known are nothing but particular pains or pleasures."[4] We are reminded of Locke's sanctions of the "Law of Nature." The motive forces of human nature are the desires, or passions, some of which are self-centered, others altruistic and centered on society. His view of the substantive character of motives is, then, Rousseauistic. Hume's statement of the relationship of the passions to "mind" and "reason," however, is very reminiscent of Hobbes. "Reason" said Hume, "is, and ought only to be, the slave of the passions, and can never pretend to any other office than to serve and obey them."[5]

From these assumptions, Hume moved to a theory of justice founded on the pragmatic conception of public utility. Each of us comes to identify with society, and to accept the norms of the society in which we live as principles of moral obligation. But the minimally ethical character of his doctrine on this subject is also converted into empirical description. For Hume is unable to tell us who is a suitable judge of what is socially useful, or to adumbrate general principles of utility. His thought therefore eventuates in the judgment that whatever group in society has the power to control public decisions will establish criteria of utility. His politics in this way becomes a descriptive doctrine of a nontheoretical sort, a statement of empirical laws at the most.

The Restoration of Reason

Kant set himself the task of restoring a theoretical dimension to our knowledge, both in its descriptive and in its moral, or prescriptive aspects. "Reason," reduced by Hume to a confined tool of our desires, had to be restored to its former sovereign position in human life, if we are to do justice to our human possibilities. As Edward Ballard has expressed it, "Kant aspired to show the way across the boundary . . . between Humean skepticism and scientism to a renewed rational and humanistic tradition . . . to reason understood as 'the whole higher faculty of knowledge.' [Reason] takes as its task not only the understanding of the physical universe but also

[4]David Hume, *Moral and Political Philosophy,* H.D. Aiken, ed (New York: Hafner, 1948), p. 44.
[5]David Hume, *A Treatise of Human Nature,* C.A. Selby-Bigge, ed (Oxford: Clarendon Press, 1888), Bk. II, Part III, Section 3, p. 415.

the acquiring of insight into human-being and the world of its possible experience, its limits, its ideals, and its goals."[6]

Reflecting on Hume's denial of necessary causation, Kant discovered a gap in the Humean argument. Our experience of causation cannot be purely empirical, he decided, because without certain *a priori* ordering principles we could make no sense of our experience nor discern the relationships of events to one another. And yet, Kant was unable to say that these ordering principles, e.g., that there are no uncaused events, were the product of Reason solely. For if they were, "any coherent flight of fancy would rate as metaphysical truth."[7] They must therefore occupy a mixed status, partly the work of Reason, partly of experience, but necessary in their character, like the realities of Reason, for without them we would find that organized experience was impossible. Hence knowledge would be impossible. While Reason does not furnish the content of our ideas, combined with our experience it does supply a necessary element for their interpretation and intelligibility. "The formal conditions which render the organization of the given possible for knowledge are said to be constituted by Reason."[8]

Understanding the Phenomenal World.   Abstracting the formal principles from specific experience yields, according to Kant, transcendental knowledge of phenomena which is necessary. The resulting propositions are true in all possible worlds and about all possible experience. They are, therefore, not to be classed as logical or analytical realities only, pure definitions, autonomously legislated by the mind, but as synthetic *a priori* knowledge, compounded of Reason and experience.[9] As such, they establish predictable order in the world and the limits of intelligible discoveries about that world.

An example of the importance of transcendental concepts of this sort is the imagination of a ship sailing backwards up a river, in which we reverse the experienced sequence of events. It is clear the imagination here produces another event, different from the observation of a ship sailing down a river in the usual way. Thus it is not from the regular concomitance of particular events (the constant observation of boat together with river) that we derive the notion of the causal order of events. "The manifestation of irreversible time order is just the manifestation of causality in nature," and this derives

---

[6]Edward G. Ballard, *Philosophy at the Crossroads* (Baton Rouge: Louisiana State University Press, 1971), p. 116.

[7]Jeffrie Murphy, *Kant, The Philosophy of Right* (London: Macmillan, 1970), p. 28.

[8]*Ibid.*, p. 29. See Immanuel Kant, *The Critique of Pure Reason*, N.K. Smith, tr., (New York: St. Martin's Press, 1929), p. 126 (A94).

[9]Murphy, *op. cit.*, pp. 30-31.

from the concept of causality itself.[10] Other regulative principles that lie partly beyond experience and yet state the necessary conditions of all experience include our ideas of quality, quantity, space and time. All these are valid because they are shared by all; they are universal principles of mind or Reason as such.

Knowledge of this sort, though it has a transcendental aspect to it, was for Kant only knowledge of the phenomenal world, the world as it appears to be. This is the world of body, or extension. With this knowledge one can predict the motions of the phenomenal world, though never with certainty, and also to a degree establish control over it. It does not give us direct access to the inner reality of the objects we perceive, however, but only represents them in sensible appearances. The knowledge one so obtains is also always hypothetical, and our science of the phenomenal world is made up of hypothetical statements. Thus we have such propositions as the following: "If XYZ under circumstances abc, then def."

This kind of knowledge is important in action as well as in contemplation, and yields norms, or "ought" statements, albeit these are also of a hypothetical sort. Thus we say that *if* our goals and ends are such and such, under circumstances abc we should act so-and-so to obtain them, but under circumstances def, in a different fashion. The connection of ends and means here, then, rests on the same notion of causality as our purely descriptive statements. But we learn nothing of the goodness or badness (correctness) of our ends; we merely posit them. Nor do we ascertain anything about the inherent goodness or propriety of our means. We have rather established a technical relationship, in the order of efficiency, between ends and means.

Noumenal Reality. When we contemplate the motions of the phenomenal world, we see that the behavior of persons, ourselves included, can be calculated and predicted in the same manner as the behavior of physical objects. We can assign causes to that behavior in the surrounding environment of physical, economic, and social reality. And we can also discover the mechanics of psychological automatism. We can study people as things. But we know that in doing so we have not exhausted human reality. We are observing only the outer man, his appearance in the world of phenomena. We believe that behind the world of apparent objects there lies another world of noumenal reality, of things as they exist in themselves—a world like Plato's Forms, Aristotle's entelechies, Augustine's Divine Ideas. But this is foreclosed to observation by the senses. In ourselves, however, we have some direct experience of this noumenal world, which is the world of value and meaning. Our experience consists in our conviction that there is an order of Right, and that we must do our duty. In our consciences we experience an obligation to do that which is inherently meaningful and right.

[10]*Ibid.,* p. 33.

And this is an experience that takes us out of the world of mechanically-moved objects into the world of free persons. For the motive to do right comes from no stimulus to action anywhere in the measurable world of empirical causality, but from the pure concept of Right. In responding to Right, we stand beyond the phenomenal world of cause and effect; we are entirely free and self-determining in our behavior. We determine our actions by our good will. This noumenal world of moral freedom constitutes the foundation of Kantian politics. Lewis Beck has paraphrased Kant's conception of the free moral will in the following succinct paragraph:

> *Willkuer,* the faculty of spontaneity, is wholly spontaneous only when its action is governed by a law of pure practical reason, not when it accepts a rule given by nature for the accomplishment of some desire. Pure reason is effective . . . only upon the ascription of its law as a motive by *Willkuer.* Its law is never a law of action, but a law for the choice of maxims for an action: it leaves specific actions undetermined, and *Willkuer*—desire, plus the logical use of reason, plus consciousness of the maxim which expresses the condition of the rule—determines the action itself.[11]

Noumenal Ethics

A Kingdom of Ends

The ability of a human person to act according to his sense of moral obligation puts him into a class of beings quite different from those of the object world. He deserves to be treated as a person, not a thing, and therefore he deserves not to be used as a means to any end in the causal nexus of phenomenal reality. He is, in fact, an end in himself. No other person has the right to treat him as an object that can be moved hither and yon at will, but is obliged to deal with him as a free and autonomous moral agent. Collectively, the community of persons as a whole constitutes what Kant calls a "Kingdom of Ends," a society of free individuals. The problem of politics is so to structure the institutions of society as to insure the reality of this right of every person to autonomy, and to encourage the full development of human moral responsibility. There is no method of Reason by which we can *demonstrate* our moral freedom, and the noumenal existence of a "Kingdom of Ends." But we are compelled to act *as if* they are realities, if our experience of obligation is to be meaningful. An act of faith underlies our analysis of the principles decreed by the Practical Reason.[12]

[11]Lewis W. Beck, *Studies in the Philosophy of Kant* (Indianapolis: Bobbs-Merrill, 1965), p. 220.

[12]Kant tells us that the existence of God and the immortality of the soul must also be posited, though they cannot be demonstrated, if obligation is to be complete.

In this fashion Kant sought to restore to politics a moral value that encompasses the autonomy of every individual and at the same time the common good of society. This was the problem Rousseau had set himself—the problem of the "General Will." Since Kant assumed that everyone already possesses the capability of moral action, no charismatic figure with unlimited powers needs to be brought in to mold him into a moral and social person. It is rather through the guarantee of autonomy that moral behavior is encouraged on the part of every individual. Here Kant departs from Rousseau.

The Categorical Imperative

But what is the code of right conduct, substantively, that free moral persons are supposed to observe? What does our sense of obligation tell us must be done in particular cases, and how is such knowledge inculcated without infringing our autonomy? Unlike the ancient codes of right and models of virtue such as those outlined by Plato and Aristotle or embodied in the Jewish Decalogue or taught authoritatively by Christian churches, Kant's conception of Right is purely formal. It enjoins no substantive "shalts" or "shalt nots." The substantive character of the noumenal world remains closed to us, and rightly so, if we are to remain truly free persons. It is up to each of us to fill in his own model of the virtuous life and to decide on his own maxims of action. In doing so, we need to observe only one formal prescription if we are to be sure we are on the side of Right, which means behaving in such a way as to safeguard every other person's freedom. Kant states this prescription as a Categorical Imperative. In deciding on any particular course of action we must be sure that our intended behavior conforms to this rule, which is statable in various ways. One is: "Act only on that maxim through which you can at the same time will that it should become a universal law," or, "Act as if the maxim of your action were to become through your will a universal law of nature." The rule can also be stated: "Act in such a way that you always treat humanity, whether in your own person or in the person of any other, never simply as a means, but always at the same time as an end." "Act as though you were a member of an ideal Kingdom of Ends." "Every rational being must so act as if he were through his maxims always a law-making member in the universal Kingdom of ends."[13]

A person who measures his conduct by rules such as these is truly a free and rational being, i.e., a being who is subject to self-given laws, which are confined only by the principle of what it is to be a law—a rule capable of

---

[13]Immanuel Kant, *Groundwork of the Metaphysic of Morals,* H.J. Paton, tr. and ed. (New York: Barnes and Noble, 1964), pp. 52, 53, 67, 83.

being universalized without contradiction, the principle of moral necessity. "Every one must admit," Kant tells us, "that if a law is to have moral force, i.e., to be the basis of an obligation, it must carry with it absolute necessity."[14] In this fashion, Kant develops moral laws of freedom for the noumenal world that, as law, are analogous to the physical laws of the phenomenal world. They differ only in that moral necessity is compatible with empirical freedom, while physical laws produce empirical invariability in the behavior of the objects they describe. "Everything in nature," writes Kant, "works in accordance with laws. Only a rational being has the power to act *in accordance with his idea [Vorstellung] of laws,*—that is, in accordance with principles."[15]

Using the Imperative.   Let us now test our maxims for action according to the rule that Kant has articulated for us. Suppose that we wish to determine whether it is right to lie when we find it convenient to do so (a favorite example of Kant's). We must first state the maxim, or rule, that underlies the intention to lie as a universal principle or rule: "All men should lie to one another whenever they find it convenient to do so." According to W.T. Jones, a Kant scholar, an effort to envisage such a rule in universal operation produces a logical impossibility, and thus makes it impossible to act upon the rule.

> What is meant by saying that it is impossible is simply that if I try to think through what is meant by my willing *A* to lie to me, I see that it involves a contradiction. For I must have the thought of him as lying, since I could not otherwise will that he lie; on the other hand, I must not think that he is lying, since, if I think that he is saying what is not the case, I am not taken in by it. But my willing to be lied to by *A* involves my willing to be taken in by what *A* says, since when I lie to *A* I will to take him in. For it would be absurd to lie to *A* unless I hoped to take him in, and I may not claim any special advantages for my lies to *A* which I deny to *A*'s lies to me . . . .
> I can, in a word, believe, suspect, or know that *A* intends to deceive me; but I cannot know that I am deceived, for if I know *that,* I am not deceived.[16]

Another example has to do with promise-keeping, and can be illustrated by borrowing money in bad faith. The maxim of my will would be: "Keep your promises only when it is convenient to do so." More specifically, I might frame the rule: "If I am short of money, I will borrow and promise return—knowing I never will." Universalized, such promises and their purposes would become impossible, for I should have to imagine

---

[14]Cited in W.T. Jones, *Morality and Freedom in the Philosophy of Immanuel Kant* (London: Oxford University Press, 1940), p. 72.

[15]*Groundwork,* p. 36.

[16]Jones, *op. cit.,* pp. 83-84.

everyone employing the maxim, and hence everyone knowing that when someone wished to borrow, the debt would not be repaid. Under such circumstances, no money would be lent, and so the object of the maxim would be frustrated.[17]

The test of universalization does not work in all cases, however. There are numerous actions that Kant deemed immoral whose rules can be universalized without contradictions of this sort. Suicide is one of them. "Supposing there were some one who thought that in certain circumstances suicide was a moral end," writes Jones, "the test of universalization would not show him to be mistaken: he could perfectly well will that everybody commit suicide under these circumstances. We can certainly conceive of a 'system of nature' in which every one took his own life."[18]

The Alternative Formula.   Kant scholars tell us that the alternative formulation of the Categorical Imperative, by which we are enjoined to treat others always as ends, never as means, provides a much more comprehensive test of moral actions than the universalization of the first form of the Imperative. In all our actions we should consider the effect that they will have on other persons and on the community. If the action would be such as to involve our "using" the other person, treating him as a means rather than as an end, we know that it would be wrong. We express our moral duty by treating others with the respect that is due to free and rational creatures who are also capable of recognizing the obligation of obeying the moral law. "Duty," writes Kant, "is the necessity of acting from respect for the law."[19] And as Jones puts it, "Respect . . . is the unique and distinctive attitude which characterizes our recognition of the worth of reason, that 'higher nature' which distinguishes us in our own eyes from brute animals."[20] In sum, then, it is "simply the function of the moral law to disclose to us the worth and dignity we have as persons."[21] Jeffrie Murphy has synthesized the principle of universalizability and the criterion of respect for persons as ends in the following succinct sentence:

> For any code of conduct C, C is a system of rational morality (or is a real moral system) if and only if the maxims of the actions prescribed in C are such that their universal performance would leave secured the value of each rational being as an end in itself having absolute worth, i.e., would leave each rational being free to pursue his own ends in action.[22]

[17]See S. Koerner, *Kant* (Hamondsworth: Penguin Books, 1955), p. 137.
[18]Jones, *op. cit.,* p. 85.
[19]*Ibid.,* p. 90.
[20]*Ibid.,* p. 91.
[21]*Ibid.,* p. 92.
[22]Murphy, *op. cit.,* pp. 75-76.

The Best Regime

Kant's conception of the best political regime is grounded in his idea of a transcendent Kingdom of Ends. This is a kingdom to which we all belong in idea, because of our capacity to make moral choices, i.e., to live according to the dictates of universal laws that we give ourselves. And in this Kingdom all persons are treated as ends, never as means.

What institutions are required to make the "Kingdom of Ends" an empirical reality? We will find that they embody a conception of political goals resembling those of Rousseau, but a conception of means more like those of Locke. The ends are stated in *Perpetual Peace* as "freedom of the members of society (as men); . . . dependence of all upon a single common legislation (as subjects); and . . . by the law of their equality (as citizens)."[23] How can these ends, which define basic procedures for giving expression to the "General Will," such that everyone in a society will be subject to laws which are the product of his own will (to which he "could have given consent"), be achieved?[24] The reader will recall that Rousseau, in order to obtain this result, called for a large-scale educational process for developing the strength of the *moi commun,* the sharing self, in each of us and for inhibiting the action of the *moi propre,* or selfish, individualistic self. This involved the activity of a charismatic leader as the founder of the society's political culture, whose work was to form a sharing mentality in the citizenry by giving them common beliefs and values and by patriotic indoctrination. Coupled with this was a requirement of strict economic equality in a context of austerity or simplicity. Only when souls had been thus formed into such a sharing or communal form could it be expected that equality of mass participation in the legislative process would produce a truly general will rather than factions and parties acting as exploitive and domineering majorities.

Kant's solution is very different, and consists in the creation of legal institutions designed to confine the behavior of all individuals in such fashion that each person is compelled to respect the rights of all others, i.e.,

[23]From Immanuel Kant, *Perpetual Peace,* edited by Lewis White Beck, copyright © 1957 by The Liberal Arts Press, Inc., reprinted by permission of the Bobbs-Merrill Company, Inc., p. 12.

[24]In *Perpetual Peace,* Kant describes external (juridical) freedom as "the privilege to lend obedience to no external laws except those to which I could have given consent. Similarly, external (juridical) equality in a state is that relationship among the citizens in which no one can lawfully bind another without at the same time subjecting himself to the law by which he also can be bound" (p. 11, fn. 2). Note the difference from Rousseau's concept of freedom as self-determination within the General Will.

to respect the right of everyone to be treated only as an end, not as a means. Instead of educating a majority so that it will embody a truly general will, Kant establishes institutions to prevent the rule of any homogeneous majority. The devices that he counts upon to do this are the institutions of republican and representative government.

Republican Government

Canvassing "forms of sovereignty," understood in terms of the location of ultimate authority, Kant finds three types: a democratic, an aristocratic, and an autocratic.[25] But the principle of sovereignty provides no solution to the problem of the "General Will," for each form tends to despotism. More important, writes Kant, is the form of administration or form of government, which is either republican or despotic. Republicanism he defines as the separation of executive from legislative power, which is a guarantee of protection against the unlimited sway of any individual or group.[26] The most vicious of the despotic forms of administration Kant tells us is the democratic, because "it establishes an executive power in which 'all' decide for or even against one who does not agree; that is, 'all,' who are not quite all, decide, and this is a contradiction of the general will with itself and with freedom."[27] In effect, Kant is asserting that the problem of good government is not to establish sovereignty in a virtuous social group, but to break up and diffuse the weight of sovereign authority as much as possible, to limit the exercise of governmental power by such devices as the separation of powers.

Representative Government.   Representation, his second grand principle, operates in the same direction, by filtering the passions of constituents through the more dispassionate minds of elected representatives who are psychologically one step removed from the interests of those who elect them. In spelling out the character of his ideal representative system, Kant tells us that "the smaller the personnel of the government (the smaller the number of rulers), the greater is their representation and the more nearly the constitution approaches to the possibility of republicanism."[28] The underlying thought seems to be that in a small assembly each delegate will represent a larger number of persons than in a large assembly, and will thus have to effect more compromises and reconciliations of interests in public policy decisions. In this fashion all the particular wills are cancelled out, and the General Will emerges as a lowest common denominator.

[25] *Perpetual Peace*, p. 13.
[26] *Ibid.*, pp. 13-15.
[27] *Ibid.*, p. 14.
[28] *Ibid.*, p. 15.

The spirit of Kant's prescription seems well expressed in James Madison's discussion of the virtues of representative government in one of his contributions to *The Federalist,* in which he, Alexander Hamilton, and John Jay attempted to persuade the citizens of New York State to adopt the Constitution of 1787 which they had helped create at the Philadelphia Convention:

> Each representative of the United States will be elected by five or six thousand citizens; whilst in the individual States, the election of a representative is left to about as many hundreds. Will it be pretended that this difference is sufficient to justify an attachment to the State governments, and an abhorrence to the federal government? . . .
> Is it supported by *reason*? This cannot be said, without maintaining that five or six thousand citizens are less capable of choosing a fit representative, or more liable to be corrupted by an unfit one, than five or six hundred. Reason, on the contrary, assures us, that as in so great a number a fit representative would be most likely to be found, so the choice would be less likely to be diverted from him by the intrigues of the ambitious or the bribes of the rich.[29]

Kant's prescription for getting government according to the "General Will" thus relied primarily on the opposition and compromise of particular interests, through institutions of limited government, rather than on the social and psychological formation of a single shared interest. The "generality" of the emergent will, that is, its character as a *shared* will, derives from the fact that everyone *could* will the policy result when listening to the voice of the Categorical Imperative. Policies emerging from Kant's representative process would guarantee that everyone be treated as an end, never as a means, to be exploited or used by any closed group, whether majority or minority.

A League of Nations

Kant also deduces an international as well as a national political order from his concept of moral autonomy. Just as individuals severally have the right to self-government, so also do collectivities. Kant writes:

> A state is not, like the ground which it occupies, a piece of property (*patrimonium*). It is a society of men whom no one else has a right to command or to dispose except the state itself. It is a trunk with its own roots. But to incorporate it into another state, like a graft, is to destroy its existence as a moral person, reducing it to a thing; such incorporation thus contradicts the idea of the original contract without which no right over a people can be conceived.[30]

[29]James Madison *et al., The Federalist* (New York: Modern Library, 1937), p. 374 (#57).
[30]*Perpetual Peace,* p. 4.

This is perhaps the first theoretical statement of the right to national self-determination, which has become a leading ideological principle throughout the world and in all political cultures today.

To keep the peace and insure the security of a world of autonomous nations Kant envisioned the formation of a league of states. It would be a league that

> does not tend to any dominion over the power of the state but only to the maintenance and security of the freedom of the state itself and of other states in league with it, without there being any need for them to submit to civil laws and their compulsion, as men in a state of nature must submit.[31]

Its creation might come about, he believed, under the leadership of a "powerful and enlightened" republic, which would give a "fulcrum to the federation with other states so that they may adhere to it and thus secure freedom under the idea of the law of nations."[32] Such a league would provide a "negative surrogate of an alliance which averts war, endures, spreads, and holds back the stream of those hostile passions which fear the law."[33] The League of Nations of the 1920s and the present United Nations Organization, in their ideal if not in their actual working, embody Kant's vision of a liberal world order.

Creating the Kingdom of Ends

To prescribe legal institutions is one thing. But to bring them into being and to make them effective in the processing of social issues is another. How did Kant hope to accomplish these results? To answer this question Kant had recourse to a philosophy of history, which he set forth in *Perpetual Peace* and in his *Idea for a Universal History*. Looking back over the ages of mankind, Kant observed that the pressures of war and invasion had driven people to the farthest reaches of the earth. The same pressures could be credited with the construction of states; for reasons of self-defense the peoples had formed themselves into structured political systems. And in recent years Kant observed the increasing tendency of these states to adopt republican forms of organization. Also, between states there was a growing body of international law to regularize the relations of peoples with one another and to mitigate conflict.

The Mechanism of Nature. In all of these events the ruling motive was self-interest, self-protection. Yet paradoxically, the results so obtained were precisely those that the principle of Right—the Categorical

[31]*Ibid.*, p. 18.
[32]*Ibid.*, p. 19.
[33]*Ibid.*, p. 20.

Imperative—called for in the name of Duty! There appeared to be in nature a mechanism, working through the selfish passions of mankind, which could be seen as a guarantee that Right would triumph. "Nature inexorably wills that the right should finally triumph. What we neglect to do comes about by itself, though with great inconveniences to us."[34]

In describing the "mechanism of nature" Kant had shifted from the categories of freedom (the noumenal world of right) to the categories of necessity (cause and effect patterns in the world of phenomena). One might suppose that the discovery that the mechanical action of the passions was bringing about the end of political freedom and world peace, which every rational creature desired as its good, would eliminate the very concepts of "Right" and "Duty." For of what use are they if human values are being realized without the operation of moral obligation? In one place Kant even writes:

> The problem of organizing a state, however hard it may seem, can be solved even for a race of devils, if only they are intelligent. The problem is: 'Given a multitude of rational beings requiring universal laws for their preservation, but each of whom is secretly inclined to exempt himself from them, to establish a constitution in such a way that, although their private intentions conflict, they check each other with the result that their public conduct is the same as if they had no such intentions.'[35]

Yet elsewhere we find him saying that the mechanism of nature favors "man's moral purpose," and that "nature guarantees perpetual peace by the mechanism of the human passions . . . making it our duty to work toward this end."[36] How can we solve this riddle?

To begin with, we must recall what we said earlier in this chapter about the character of our knowledge of the phenomenal world. It rests upon synthetic *a priori* propositions of Reason, which allow us to make sense of our experience. The concepts of Reason, however, our minds supply to our experience, they do not indwell it. And though they are certain, they do not guarantee us certain knowledge of the natural world. The predictability that they establish in nature is only probable. Thus, when writing about the mechanism of nature guaranteeing perpetual peace, Kant tells us that "she does not do so with sufficient certainty for us to predict the future in any theoretical sense." For she operates "as a necessity working according to laws we do not know."[37] Thus, while we think that we discern a pattern in political history, we cannot be certain of it. An opposite pattern might emerge without any contradiction. But if this is the case, we are also

[34]*Ibid.,* p. 31.
[35]*Ibid.,* p. 30.
[36]*Ibid.,* pp. 29, 32.
[37]*Ibid.,* pp. 32, 24.

assured of our freedom of moral choice. For our actions are not determined by the mechanism of nature after all. However, the fact that we have discovered an uncertain pattern has other moral implications. For it has shown that the end that Duty legislates—that we work for universal freedom and perpetual peace—"is not just a chimerical one."[38] We need to know this, for if "we cannot do our duty, . . . this concept would itself drop out of morality *(ultra posse nemo obligatur)*."[39]

The Politics of Prudence and the Politics of Right. Kant also canvasses another approach to the problem of peace and freedom, and sets it aside in favor of the way of duty. If we insist on looking at the problem naturalistically (i.e., in terms of the motives of the phenomenal world), we need not be fatalists, and suppose that the reign of freedom will come about passively, through the purely mechanical operation of the passions. A naturalist as well as a believer in Absolute Right can perceive the problem of certainty in the working out of the mechanism of nature. But his conclusion will be that instead of letting nature work blindly, we should harness and control the blind operation of the passions; we should develop a policy science of peace and freedom based on the laws that nature has imperfectly revealed to us. It is not, however, sufficient to teach the rationality of republican order and international federation. "The will of each individual to live under a juridical constitution according to principles of freedom . . . is not sufficient to this end . . . A uniting cause must supervene upon the variety of particular volitions in order to produce a common will from them."[40] The solution is that men must be manipulated and forced into the relationships by conscious political acts. And the "pretended practical man" has a list of principles at hand to employ in this venture. They are not the principles of morality, but a Machiavellian technique which Kant sums up as "an immoral doctrine of prudence."[41]

This approach Kant finds just as inadequate as a blind reliance on the mechanism of nature. "For the solution of . . . the problem of political prudence" he writes "much knowledge of nature is required so that its mechanism may be employed toward the desired end; yet all this is uncertain in its results for perpetual peace."[42] For "reason is not yet sufficiently enlightened to survey the entire series of predetermining causes, and such vision would be necessary for one to be able to foresee with certainty the happy or unhappy effects which follow human actions by the mechanism of

[38]*Ibid.,* p. 32.

[39]The Latin means, "We cannot be obliged to do things which are beyond possibility." *Ibid.,* p. 35.

[40]*Ibid.,* p. 36.

[41]*Ibid.,* p. 41.

[42]*Ibid.,* p. 43.

nature."[43] It turns out that sophisticated calculation is just as helpless in the end as passive fatalism; both come to grief on the uncertainty of the mechanism of nature.

The way of Duty, however, does promise certainty. For having established that the goals which it posits are realizable, the unconditional character of the laws of Right are our final and perfect guarantee of the human hope for peace and freedom.

> The solution of the . . . problem . . . of political wisdom presses itself upon us, as it were; it is clear to everyone and puts to shame all affectation. It leads directly to the end . . .
> Then it may be said, 'Seek ye first the kingdom of pure practical reason and its righteousness, and your end (the blessing of perpetual peace) will necessarily follow.' For it is the peculiarity of morals, especially with respect to its principles of public law and hence in relation to a politics known *a priori,* that the less it makes conduct depend on the proposed end, i.e., the intended material or moral advantage, the more it agrees with it in general.[44]

Thus, Kant's ultimate solution to the problem of establishing the institutions of freedom that we described in an earlier part of this chapter is to enjoin us to adopt the rule of the Categorical Imperative in all our actions. If we do this, which requires a careful attention to the morality of the means we employ in our political dealings, we have a certain guarantee that our moral end will be achieved.

Problems of Kantian Dualism

Applying the Categorical Imperative

How adequate is Kant's attempt to restore a moral dimension to political theory? Is the Categorical Imperative in its various formulations a sufficient principle of moral choice? And are the republican institutions of Kantian freedom a warrant that the Imperative will be politically operative?

The universal human right always to be treated as an end, not only as a means, certainly seems to follow from Kant's conception of moral autonomy, albeit that the existence of the noumenal self is for Kant a matter of faith, not Reason. Also persuasive is the assertion of a correlative obligation of every man to treat all other men as ends, to avoid "using" them as though they were things. But these are extremely abstract notions, and we may wonder whether Kant's philosophy provides an adequate guidance in the endless complexities of particular choice situations.

Take the case of lying, for example. It seems clear that Kant thought

[43]*Ibid.,* p. 36.
[44]*Ibid.,* p. 44.

that a lie was always wrong, even when altruistically intended. We might wish to save a terminal cancer patient, who is a beloved relative, great anxiety by giving him a false account of his illness. But according to the Kantian principle, this would be helping his body at the expense of his rational personality. "It is not so much making use of another man's body that makes lying wrong" writes W.T. Jones, "as it is that a lie makes use of his person, that is, of the rational part of him which understands and believes what one says."[45] But it is not self-evident that the rational nature of our moral being implies that each of us must be capable of stoic fortitude in the face of a horrible death—that the requisites of rational personality be set so sharply over against natural inclination, in this case, the desire to avoid excessive pain. Yet Kant insisted on so opposing them. In one place he writes that "Man feels in himself a powerful counterweight to all the commands of duty presented to him by reason as so worthy of esteem—the counterweight of his needs and inclinations, whose total satisfaction he grasps under the name of happiness. But reason, without promising anything to inclination, enjoins its commands relentlessly."[46] One wonders how Kant expected the voice of duty *ever* to prevail in so thoroughgoing a conflict with all our natural inclinations.

What about a lie to an evil-hearted enemy who might hope to overthrow our republican institutions were he in possession of true information about the disposition of American military forces? Here the circumstances seem overwhelmingly to predominate over the principle of truth-telling, since it is difficult to see how a lie could do injustice to the enemy's rational principle, when he himself is bent against acting according to such a principle. But assessing the circumstances comes under the heading of calculating the mechanism of nature—pragmatic planning—and Kant rejects such a procedure in moral choice, which he reduces wholly to the logic of principles. Is this not pressing the dualism of observed phenomenality and abstract noumenality too far?

Right as a Cause of Political Events

The problem of radical dualism also enters in when we ask whether it is possible to know that Right and Good Will, as Kant conceived them, can ever be causes in the world of phenomenal events. Can we *know* whether, when we act, it is at the prompting of the sometimes subtle demands of inclination, or according to the decrees of Right? Kant himself gives up on the question when he writes, "How pure reason can be practical—All human reason is totally incapable of explaining this, and all the effort and labor to

---

[45]Jones, *Op. cit.,* p. 94.
[46]*Groundwork,* p. 73.

seek such an explanation is wasted."[47] Edward Ballard points up in the following terms the magnitude of the problem Kant has engendered:

> Man as phenomenal can be known to be causally determined; nevertheless as rational (noumenal) man may be believed to act freely and to initiate sequences of events for which he is responsible (*Pure Reason,* A66, B679). But it also follows that we cannot *know* ourselves to be both moral and empirical. We cannot in principle know that our will is completely undetermined by empirical inclinations and desires. Moreover, we cannot discover a schematic structure of the will which shows that moral law (the law of rational being) necessarily applies to any sort of value objects, for example, to our experienced motives. Strictly speaking, therefore, we cannot know that our motives are moral even if they are.[48]

What all this adds up to is a picture of an atemporal noumenal will. But if the moral will is atemporal, "there seems to be no alternative but to admit that the real self cannot be said to make moral progress."[49] The *real* (or rather ideal) self as noumenal reality, *always* acts well. But can it influence the empirical self—the self of our phenomenal experience? This does not seem to be demonstrable within the Kantian framework. Yet in places Kant seems to say that such progress does take place. Thus in *Perpetual Peace* he writes:

> Providence is justified in the history of the world, for the moral principle in man is never extinguished, while with advancing civilization reason grows pragmatically in its capacity to realize ideas of law.[50]

To believe this, however, is an act of faith, though one that is necessary. For "if we assume that humanity never will or can be improved, the only thing which a theodicy seems unable to justify is creation itself, the fact that a race of such corrupt beings ever was on earth."[51]

Kantianism Today

Kant's Influence

The influence of Kant on all later philosophy, and on the methodology of the particular sciences, has been enormous. We find a significant Kantian mark on the work of men who are known for their own

[47]*Ibid.,* p. 129.
[48]Ballard, *op. cit.,* p. 158.
[49]*Ibid.,* p. 159.
[50]Perpetual Peace, p. 46.
[51]*Ibid.*

originality and for their *departure* from Kant—Fichte, Schelling, Hegel, and Schopenhauer, for example. And between 1865 and 1920 there emerged in Germany five distinct, self-consciously Neo-Kantian schools of thought. Through the work of Georg Simmel (1858-1918) and Karl Mannheim (1893-1947) the Kantian influence is brought from the realm of pure epistemology into the philosophy and methodology of the modern social sciences.[52] And in the legal theories of Hans Kelsen, a Kantian outlook has found its way into the precincts of American political science. Kelsen taught law and legal philosophy in Austria and Germany for many years, and climaxed his career as a Professor of Political Science at the University of California (Berkeley). His *Pure Theory of Law* (1939, 1960) is an effort to establish a frame of reference for the scientific analysis of legal normative systems.[53] It presents "a way of interpreting certain acts of will as the issuing of norms and a way of explaining what it means to say that a norm exists, is valid, or ought to be obeyed."[54] Like Kant, Kelsen developed his theory in purely formal and procedural terms, both in its descriptive and normative function, and eschewed all discussion of substantive principles. In a voluminous and monumental study of the Charter of the United Nations, Kelsen applied his Kantian theories to the analysis of a most important legal institution.

In the balance of this chapter we shall focus on Kantian themes in the work of two contemporary political philosophers, who are eclectic in their general world views, rather than strict Kantians or members of a Neo-Kantian school. Their work has received special attention from students of political philosophy during the past few years, and one of them has become known popularly because of the special significance of his work for the crisis of American welfare politics. The writers are R.M. Hare, a Fellow of Balliol College, Oxford (who has also taught and researched in the United States) and Harvard Professor John Rawls.

The work of these men, as well as that of Simmel, Mannheim, and Kelsen, reveals very clearly the capacity of Kantian concepts to develop new forms and applications, to grow into new ideas as other minds work with them. This aspect of Kantian philosophy has been well described by James Collins in a chapter entitled, "Kant Our Contemporary," in which the author writes of the "essentially open texture and implicatory power of the Kantian text, its successful resistance to any effort to finish off its significance with an altogether definitive historical presentation. There is no topic

[52]See Lewis White Beck, "Neo-Kantianism," in P. Edwards, Gen. Ed., *Encyclopedia of Philosophy*, Vol. 5 (New York: Macmillan and Free Press, 1967), pp. 468-73.

[53]See Hans Kelsen, *The Pure Theory of Law*, M. Knight, tr. (Berkeley: Univ. of California Press, 1967). For an analysis of Kelsen's work see William Ebenstein, *The Pure Theory of Law* (Madison: Univ. of Wisconsin Press, 1945).

[54]M.P. Golding, "Hans Kelsen," in *Encyclopedia of Philosophy*, vol. 4, p. 328.

in Kant . . . which does not hold a surprise for the next reading and present a new visage in some other philosophical context."[55]

Freedom and Reason

Like Kelsen, R.M. Hare understands his work as descriptive, rather than prescriptive, even though his subject matter has a normative character. The intention of his major published work is to display in clear relief the logical structure of language about moral questions, the structure of ethical discourse. Again, like Kelsen and Kant, his concern is with a clear exposition of form and process, leaving content to the hidden world of noumenal reality and to the variety of its cultural interpretation. His logical intention also makes him a member of the modern school of analytical philosophy, a largely English offshoot of Logical Positivism, whose origins we can trace back to one brand of Neo-Kantian thought.

Professor Hare does not share the view of analytical philosophers like A. J. Ayer or scientific value relativists like Max Weber that values belong to the world of irrational preference, the province of the emotions. (Weber actually held this view as a way of safeguarding moral freedom by insisting on the absolute privacy and uniqueness of every individual's values.) Hare's purpose in studying the structure of moral reasoning is to reestablish the cognitive character of moral judgment and thereby to overcome the strict "dichotomy of facts and values" that has been a major assumption of modern social science. In this he shares common ground with Kant, who, despite his confinement of scientific cognition to the phenomenal world, insisted that there was a mode of ethical cognition as well. Though the "Practical Reason" was different from the "Pure Reason" it was still a faculty of Reason, and therefore a producer of knowledge.

Like Kant, Hare is a believer in moral freedom, and his central problem is to show that establishing a rational and cognitive ethics does not interfere with that freedom. "For one of the most important constituents of our freedom, as moral agents, is the freedom to form our own opinions about moral questions."[56] Like the positivist proponents of the heterogeneity of facts and values, he does not assert that there can be a "logical deduction of moral judgments from statements of fact."[57] He puts forward, rather, as a criterion of their rationality, that moral judgments are "distinguished from other judgments of [the] class [of prescriptive judg-

[55]James Collins, *Interpreting Modern Philosophy* (Princeton, N.J.: Princeton University Press, 1972), pp. 268-69.

[56]R.M. Hare, *Freedom and Reason* (London: Oxford University Press, 1963), p. 2.

[57]*Ibid.*

ments] by being *universalizable*."[58] He asserts also "that it is possible for there to be logical relations between prescriptive judgments, including even imperatives."[59]

Universalizability. The affinity of Hare's thinking to that of Kant should already be apparent, and Hare himself recognizes this. At an early point in the book, however, Hare makes it clear that he is not prepared to follow Kant in recognizing universalizability as a moral principle in *itself.* Presumably this disclaimer carries with it a rejection of Kant's conception of the individual's moral agency as residing in a sense of obligation to do Right (as an Absolute obligation) and in our capacity to be governed by the pure concept of law in our moral decisions. Perhaps he thinks this concept implies a substantive, rather than purely formal idea of Right, and therefore that it willy-nilly asserts something about the unknowable noumenal world. In any case, Hare wishes to confine *his* concept of a "Categorical Imperative" to pure logic. Thus he tells us that "the principle of universalizability . . . is a purely formal principle, following from the logical character of the moral words; no substantial moral judgments follow from it unless the substance is put in by arguments [of a certain kind], and these require other ingredients besides logic."[60] Nevertheless, "it is capable of very powerful employment in moral argument when combined with other premisses."[61] Thus the principle of universalizability itself is kept morally neutral, while moral substance is treated as subjective preference.

Hare's object in insisting on the ethically neutral character of universalizability puts his work into the category of "meta-ethics" rather than prescriptive ethics; it is confined to a description of the structure of ethical argument, without making any commitment at all to a substantive ethical principle. His intention is to establish a parallel between the canons of moral reasoning and those of scientific reasoning, and in this fashion to put ethics back on a cognitive foundation. He writes:

> We must . . . notice an analogy between [a logical moral argument] and the Popperian theory of scientific method. What has happened is that a provisional or suggested moral principle has been rejected because one of its particular consequences proved unacceptable. But an important difference between the two kinds of reasoning must also be noted; it is what we should expect, given that the data of scientific observation are recorded in descriptive statements, whereas we are here dealing with prescriptions.
> . . . Just as science, seriously pursued, is the search for hypotheses and the testing of them, by the attempt to falsify their particular consequences, so

[58]*Ibid.,* pp. 4, 5.
[59]*Ibid.,* p. 4.
[60]*Ibid.,* p. 118.
[61]*Ibid.,* p. 35.

morals, as a serious endeavour, consists in the search for principles and the testing of them against particular cases. Any rational activity has its discipline, and this is the discipline of moral thought: to test the moral principles that suggest themselves to us by following out their consequences and seeing whether we can accept them.[62]

In effect, Hare is suggesting that we somehow deal with the rational assessment of moral arguments with the categories of scientific reason, which Kant confined to the phenomenal world. He is unwilling to grant that we have even the limited access to the noumenal which Kant described in his *Critique of the Practical Reason* and in the *Groundwork of the Metaphysic of Morals.* How successful has Hare been in this attempt?

Assumptions About Human Nature: Empathic Man. In the latter portion of *Freedom and Reason* Hare attempts to show that the principle of universalizability can resolve not only conflicts of interest, but can even arbitrate between opposed moral ideals. In particular, he attempts to show that a fanatic Nazi, when made aware of the idea of universalizability, will reject extermination of Jews as a moral end. He will, in effect, be led to grant the superiority of liberal ethics. Hare achieves this result by having his fanatic Nazi imagine that he and his family are themselves Jews, and then asks him to give the order that he and his family be sent to the gas chamber. This is not put forward as an argument based on enlightened self-interest— the subject must truly imagine that he *is* the other, hated person—but one designed to show that when the Nazi empathizes himself into the place of the Jew, he will realize that he has the facts wrong—that what he took to be significant differences between Jews and non-Jews, warranting differential treatment, really were not. Hare applies the principle of universalizability also to the believer in racial discrimination against blacks, by requiring that he put himself in the place of the black.

> The operation is to consider the hypothetical case in which he himself has lost the quality which he said was a sufficient ground for discrimination, and his present victims have gained it—and to consider this hypothetical case as if it were actual. There are two stages in the process of universalization. The first is passed when we have found a universal principle, not containing proper names or other singular terms, from which the moral judgement which we want to make follows, given the facts of our particular situation. . . . for example, by adducing the principle that it is all right for black people to be oppressed by white people. But the next stage is more difficult. It is necessary, not merely that this principle should be produced, but that the person who produces it should actually hold it. It is necessary not merely to *quote* a maxim, but (in Kantian language) to *will* it to be a universal law. . . . For willing it to be a universal law involves willing it to apply even when the roles played by the parties are reversed. And this test will be failed by all maxims or principles which look attractive to oppressors and persecutors on the first test.[63]

[62]*Ibid.,* p. 92.
[63]*Ibid.,* p. 219.

What is the chief operative factor in the "ethical conversion" of Hare's two examples—the Nazi and the racist? At the outset, we are led to suppose that it is the desire to be logical, as a morally neutral fact, that is governing; that truly moral cognitions are distinguished by their logical character. But as we get into the argument we discover that this is not so. Hare himself admits that even after they have mentally exchanged places with the hated Jew or black, some people will remain fanatically attached to their original position and accept extermination or discrimination for themselves, without violating any logical criteria. He therefore must grant that his argument rests

> not upon logic itself—though without logic we should never have got to this point—but upon the fortunate contingent fact that people who would take this logically possible view, after they had really imagined themselves in the other man's position, are extremely rare.[64]

Without realizing it, Hare at this point has committed himself to a theory of human nature. Empathizing reflection produces the judgment that all men are equal, in the sense of having equal rights to life, liberty and the pursuit of happiness. The liberal, who is able to empathize readily, able mentally to exchange places with persons in very different life situations, is the normal (good?) man, and most people, when they reflect on the matter, will so empathize.

In making this judgment on the basic structure of normal human nature, Hare has asserted, willy-nilly, a substantive ethical doctrine, which the student of meta-ethics, committed to purely formal analysis of ethical language, is supposed to avoid. Apparently unwilling to accept Kant's substantive doctrine of human moral agency, Hare has shown himself unable to complete his discussion of cognitive ethics without introducing a substantive doctrine of his own. For it is not logic but an undefended substantive assertion about human nature that underlies Hare's meta-ethical analysis. John Gunnell has pointed out that while "current ethical philosophy is concerned with the logical analysis of moral language and with the characteristic forms of reasoning in morals," it has become a very controversial issue as to "whether ethics can address itself to the logic of moral reasoning without implicitly making normative ethical judgments."[65] And in another place he finds it "something more than a coincidence that rationality and liberal democratic ideals appear to always complement one another" in the work of Hare.[66] An adequate political ethics would require that Hare argue *to* the

---

[64]*Ibid.*, p. 172.

[65]John Gunnell, *Philosophy, Science, and Political Inquiry* (Morristown, N.J.: General Learning Press, 1975), p. 269.

[66]John Gunnell, "Reason and Commitment: Political Values and the Problem of Justification," Paper presented at the 1969 meeting of the American Political Science Association, pp. 33, 46.

liberal democratic view of human nature, not *from* it, as an assumption. Making this view an assumption of the analysis simply gives it the character of parochial ideological or cultural prejudice. But philosophy is devoted to the exposition of first principles in such fashion as to go beyond the habits of particular cultures. Kant at least had the good grace to acknowledge that his doctrine of the noumenal self was a matter of faith. It remains the work of philosophy to determine whether noumenalism or a similar concept can be brought fully within the purview of unaided Reason.

A Theory of Justice

John Rawls, Professor of Philosphy at Harvard University, describes his recent book, *A Theory of Justice,* as an effort to "present a conception of justice which generalizes and carries to a higher level of abstraction the familiar theory of social contract found, say, in Locke, Rousseau, and Kant." Specifically, he wishes to establish what the principles are "that free and rational persons concerned to further their own interests would accept in an initial position of equality as defining the fundamental terms of their association."[67] What, he asks, is the logical order of basic goal values and procedural rules that underlie a political system of rational freedom? And following upon that, he wishes to show what public policy programs derive logically from the initial commitment to ground rules. The two together define the just society.

Rawls's intention is to present a viable alternative to utilitarian doctrines "which have long dominated our philosophical tradition," and which define justice in terms of the greatest net balance of satisfactions.[68] His concern is to develop a theory of justice that enshrines the principle of equal freedom, building on a conception of right rather than on individual or group interests or satisfactions. (He attempts, however, also to show that his view will accommodate the demands of rationally self-interested individuals.) Rawls describes his conception as "a deontological theory, one that either does not specify the good independently from the right, or does not interpret the right as maximizing the good. The concept of right is prior to that of the good."[69] He also considers his work a contribution to the theory of rational choice, a utilitarian version of which we have discussed in the chapter on Hobbes. A theory of justice he believes to be "perhaps the most significant part of the theory of rational choice."[70]

[67]John Rawls, *A Theory of Justice* (Cambridge, Mass.: Harvard University Press, 1971; and, Oxford: The Clarendon Press, 1972), pp 3, 11. Copyright © 1971 by Harvard University Press.

[68]*Ibid.,* pp. 3, 22, 26.

[69]*Ibid.,* pp. 30, 31.

[70]*Ibid.,* p. 16.

The Original Position. The "original position" with which Rawls begins his discourse, and on which he focuses in developing his major thesis, plays a role analogous to the "state of nature" in earlier social contract theory. Explicitly following Kant, he treats this as a hypothetical rather than an historical conditon.[71] Rawls contends that in the original position all persons

> would choose two rather different principles: the first requires equality in the assignment of basic rights and duties, while the second holds that social and economic inequalities, for example inequalities of wealth and authority are just only if they result in compensating benefits for everyone, and in particular for the least advantaged members of society. These principles rule out justifying institutions on the grounds that the hardships of some are offset by a greater good in the aggregate. . . . But there is no injustice in the greater benefits earned by a few provided that the situation of persons not so fortunate is thereby improved.[72]

In a second formulation he specifies the two basic principles more precisely as

> First: each person is to have an equal right to the most extensive basic liberty compatible with a similar liberty for others.
> Second: social and economic inequalities are to be arranged so that they are both (a) reasonably expected to be to everyone's advantage, and (b) attached to positions and offices open to all.[73]

Efficiency. Rawls wishes to show that equal freedom is entirely compatible with the principle of economic efficiency. The "everyone's advantage" phrase of the second principle therefore is meant to imply Pareto Optimality, a concept which holds "that a configuration is efficient whenever it is impossible to change it so as to make some persons (at least one) better off without at the same time making other persons (at least one) worse off."[74] The "equally open" phrase guarantees that careers will be open to talents and that equality of fair opportunity will be increased, thus compensating for initial differences in "historical and social fortune."[75] Limited inequalities are to be permitted only on the basis of inequalities in natural endowment, and then only to the extent that the least privileged also benefits by them.

Welfare State Equality. On this foundation of basic social agreement, Rawls proceeds to build a theory of justice focused politically on in-

[71]*Ibid.,* p. 12, fn. 5.
[72]*Ibid.,* p. 15.
[73]*Ibid.,* p. 60.
[74]*Ibid.,* p. 67.
[75]*Ibid.,* pp. 65, 74.

stitutions of constitutional democracy and economically on policies that produce a relative equality of distribution of such basic values as wealth and status. Rawls terms his doctrine "justice as fairness," a theory which, in effect, constitutes a justification of welfare state principles like those which have been in the ascendancy in American political culture since the 1930s. Rawls argues that in adumbrating the principles of his "original position" he did not take an esoteric view of the matter. Rather, he attempted to define, clarify, and extend the deepest convictions of our society. For he writes that one way of

> justifying a particular description of the original position . . . is to see if the principles which would be chosen match our considered convictions of justice or extend them in an acceptable way. We can note whether applying these principles would lead us to make the same judgments about the basic structures of society which we now make intuitively and in which we have the greatest confidence; or whether, in cases where our present judgments are in doubt and given with hesitation, these principles offer a resolution which we can affirm on reflection.[76]

While questions of religious intolerance and racial discrimination are fairly settled in the arena of public debate, "we have much less assurance as to what is the correct distribution of wealth and authority."[77] And it is in this area of distributive justice that Rawls offers philosophical guidance.

Kantian Elements.   The concept of the "original position," on which Rawls raises his welfare state edifice, constitutes the heart of his theory. It is interesting that some of its elements bear a striking resemblance to Kant's theories of human freedom and moral agency, and that Rawls acknowledges his debt to Kant for key ideas. Half way through the book, Rawls tells us that the

> original position may be viewed . . . as a procedural interpretation of Kant's conception of autonomy and the categorical imperative. The principles regulative of the kingdom of ends are those that would be chosen in this position, and the description of this situation enables us to explain the sense in which acting from these principles expresses our nature as free and equal rational persons.[78]

Rawls expects that others will accept the principles of justice of the original position not from any calculation of interest but because of their sense of justice. The purpose of the conditions and rules he lays down is to "represent equality between human beings as moral persons, as creatures having a conception of their good and capable of a sense of justice." And he assumes

[76]*Ibid.,* p. 19.
[77]*Ibid.,* p. 20.
[78]*Ibid.,* p. 256.

"that each person beyond a certain age and possessed of the requisite intellectual capacity develops a sense of justice under normal circumstances."[79] He also argues that the experience of living in the kind of society he describes as a just one will enhance this sense of justice.

Since the basis of agreement is in the category of right rather than interest, Rawls drops a "veil of ignorance" over the persons who imagine themselves contemplating his principles in the original position. The veil erases all knowledge of a person's social position, and of his "natural assets and liabilities, his intelligence and strength, and the like. Nor, again, does anyone know his conception of the good, the particulars of his rational plan of life, or even the special features of his psychology such as his averseness to risk or liability to optimism or pessimism."[80] Knowledge of all these things belongs to the phenomenal self, but the noumenal self is concerned only with principles of right that derive from its freedom and rationality as a moral person. "The description of the original position interprets the point of view of noumenal selves, of what it means to be a free and equal rational being."[81]

The utilitarian doctrines which Rawls criticizes at length for their individualist and aristocratic bias are grounded, by contrast, on a conception of the phenomenal self like that developed by Hobbes, which gives full rein to natural liberty. But for Rawls such an approach is "arbitrary from a moral perspective. There is no more reason to permit the distribution of income and wealth to be settled by the distribution of natural assets than by historical and social fortune." "Inequalities of birth and natural endowment are undeserved."[82]

Thus it is upon the Kantian conception of the equality of moral persons that Rawls builds his prescription for relative political, social, and economic equality that is the substance of the Liberal welfare state. He is here extending the implications of Kant's view of human nature beyond the conclusions that Kant himself drew, which were confined largely to the political and constitutional sphere. In dealing with the concept of property, Kant presents only a justification of the right of private ownership and an explanation of the political conditions under which such a right can be made secure. However, in one passage of *The Metaphysical Elements of Justice,* in which Kant describes the public welfare functions of the political sovereign, we do find a statement about the obligations of society to the underprivileged which moves in the egalitarian direction that Rawls has taken. Kant's prescription is to mitigate poverty through limited distributions of wealth via the power to tax.

[79]*Ibid.,* p. 46.
[80]*Ibid.,* p. 137.
[81]*Ibid.,* pp. 255-56.
[82]*Ibid.,* pp. 74, 180. See also pp. 65, 72, 79.

The general Will of the people has united itself into a society in order to maintain itself continually, and for this purpose it has subjected itself to the internal authority of the state in order to support those members of the society who are not able to support themselves. Therefore, it follows from the nature of the state that the government is authorized to require the wealthy to provide the means of sustenance to those who are unable to provide the most necessary needs of nature for themselves. Because their existence depends on the act of subjecting themselves to the commonwealth for the protection and care required in order to stay alive, they have bound themselves to contribute to the support of their fellow citizens, and this is the ground for the state's right to require them to do so. [In order to fulfill this function, the state may] tax the property of the citizens or their commerce or establish funds and use the interest from them; ... The money should not be raised merely through voluntary contributions, but by compulsory exactions as political burdens, for here we are considering only the rights of the state in relation to the people. ... In this connection, we might ask whether the funds for the care of the poor should be raised from current contributions so that each generation will support its own poor or whether it would be better to have recourse to permanent funds that are collected gradually.[83]

The last sentence of the quotation seems to prophesy a modern social security system based on long-term funding.

Opposition to Hare. It is interesting that, in the course of describing his theoretical debt to Kant, Rawls rejects the reading given to Kant's doctrine by R.M. Hare, which we have reviewed above. Rawls's own point of departure is the idea of a Kingdom of Ends, whose members are treated only as ends never as means, rather than the principle of universalizability of maxims. He writes in a footnote that "to be avoided at all costs is the idea that Kant's doctrine simply provides the general, or formal, elements for a utilitarian (or indeed for any other) theory. See, for example, R.M. Hare, *Freedom and Reason,*"[84] We recall that Hare attempted to abstract the principle of universalizability from the philosophy of Kant as a purely logical (and therefore morally neutral) principle which might be of use in giving moral argument a cognitive (i.e., a rational because logical) status, without commitment to a substantive moral position that might be difficult to defend as cognitive matter. We saw, however, that Hare was nevertheless led to develop a view of the empathic personality as the normal being, which involved embracing, after all, a substantive ethical view, and one of a somewhat ambiguous character. It is possible to understand the empathic man as a utilitarian (a pragmatic person of enlightened interest), as Rawls apparently does.

[83]Immanuel Kant, *The Metaphysical Elements of Justice* (Part I of *The Metaphysics of Morals*), John Ladd, tr. (Indianapolis: Bobbs-Merrill Co., Inc., 1965), pp. 93-94.

[84]*A Theory of Justice,* p. 251, fn. 29.

Reception of the Theory.   Rawls's effort at public guidance has been accorded a very mixed reception. The publication of *A Theory of Justice* was heralded by Liberals as magisterial, the most formidable defense ever made of the social contract tradition, "the most penetrating contribution to systematic political philosophy since John Stuart Mill."[85] Contrastingly, Conservatives have damned it as "an ideological tract," "an elaborate catalogue of political prejudices," "vague, abstract, and inconsistent."[86] In 1975, Robert Nozick, a Harvard colleague of Rawls, brought out a work entitled *Anarchy, State, and Utopia,* which may be read as a Libertarian answer to Rawls's egalitarianism. (We shall present a critique of Nozick's book in Chapter 13.)

In December of 1972, the staff of *The New York Times Book Review* selected *A Theory of Justice* as one of the five most significant books of the year. Citing a passage in which Rawls proclaims that the specially gifted "may gain from their good fortune only on terms that improve the situation of those who have lost out," the editors conclude that "Rawls's arguments for this proposition are persuasive; its political implications may change our lives."[87] Political philosopher John Chapman writes in *The American Political Science Review* that *A Theory of Justice* is "an achievement of the first order," saying that its significance "lies in its accommodation of the liberal principles of liberty, equality and fraternity," and calling the book "the high water mark of liberalism." "Once again a 'Legislator' has appeared in our midst," Chapman concludes.[88]

Negative critiques of *A Theory of Justice,* however, also abound. A particularly caustic one by Allan Bloom, a leading proponent of the neo-Platonist Straussian approach to political philosophy that we discussed in Chapter 2, appears in the same issue of *The American Political Science Review* as the John Chapman review.[89] Bloom berates Rawls for failing to present a defense of his first principles, especially of the assumption that the rational determination of values is possible. Rawls fails to take account of the Marxian and Nietzschean critiques of rationalism in political philosophy, and if these theorists are right, he must be put down as "only a deluded myth maker." Bloom wonders whether Rawls's teaching is "meant to be a permanent statement about the nature of political things, or just a collection of opinions that he finds satisfying and hopes will be satisfying to others." He thinks that Rawls "takes it for granted that we are all egalitarians." "We start from what we are now and end there, since there is

[85]Marshall Cohen, in *The New York Times Book Review,* July 16, 1972.

[86]David L. Schaefer, "The 'Sense' and Non-Sense of Justice: An Examination of John Rawls's *A Theory of Justice," Political Science Reviewer,* III, (Fall 1973), pp. 1, 3.

[87]*The New York Times Book Review,* December 3, 1972, p. 1.

[88]*American Political Science Review,* LXIX (June 1975), No. 2, pp. 591, 592, 593.

[89]*Ibid.,* pp. 648-62.

nothing beyond us. At best Rawls will help us to be more consistent, if that is an advantage. The distinctions between opinion and knowledge, and between appearance and reality, which made philosophy possible and needful, disappear."[90]

Bloom's point is well taken, for as we have shown, Rawls's point of departure is what he takes to be the general sense of justice in contemporary American society, which he thinks has a basically Kantian character, an opinion about justice which he does not seek to verify but to clarify by working out its implications for social policy. His work is therefore likely to have an "appeal to the typical liberal in Anglo-Saxon countries," because such a person happens to share Rawls's assumptions. But what meaning will it have for someone from another culture? If philosophy is the search for universal truth, the philosopher must argue to and not from his first principles. We saw that this kind of parochialism was also a problem in Hare's *Freedom and Reason,* in which the desire for self-consistency and the conception of the empathic person as the normal human being are taken as self-evident truths rather than as problematic assertions.

Bloom also argues that Rawls has misused the Kantian doctrines which we have described as central to his basic philosophical position. He writes that Rawls does not know "what Kant means by morality" which "must be chosen for its own sake; it must be a good, or rather the highest good." According to Bloom, "Rawls has done nothing to establish such an interest. Surely it is not interest in morality that motivates men in the original position, whose goal is to enjoy as much happiness as possible." "Rawls's men in the original position act in terms of individual desire."[91]

Utilitarian Admixture. This seems a strange appraisal of Rawls's standpoint, in view of the description we have given of that standpoint above, and the citations with which we have supported that description. Bloom's critique, is indeed overdrawn, and in part incorrect. But there is some ground for the view that he takes in the fact of Rawls's electicism. For Rawls combines with his Kantian justification of the principles of the original position what clearly seems a utilitarian theory of rational choice in another part of his book in which he recommends the "maximin" concept as a criterion of judgment for members of his hypothetical society faced with a choice situation. "The maximin rule," writes Rawls, "tells us to rank alternatives by their worst possible outcomes: We are to adopt the alternative the worst outcome of which is superior to the worst outcomes of the others." Since because of the "veil of ignorance" the chooser does not know what place he occupies in society, what resources he can summon to his aid in achieving his life goals, the maximin rule is the most rational to select. For

[90]*Ibid.,* pp. 648, 649.
[91]*Ibid.,* p. 656.

in the absence of information, a chooser may properly believe that he needs to protect himself against the contingency that the society might be designed so that "his enemy is to assign him his place."[92] Under the maximin rule it would be rational for the individual to accept the principle that inequalities will be tolerated only if they result in compensating benefits for all members of the society. In thus recommending the maximin principle, Rawls has presented a utilitarian criterion of choice, based on the calculation of interest. In other words, Rawls tries to show that rational interest and one's sense of justice and right decree the same behavior.

Bloom quite rightly points out that "for Kant, the moral man acts with full awareness of his particular circumstances and chooses to obey the universal rule in spite of them. Particular desire and universal law are only coincidentally harmonious, so that the man who always acts according to the law shows that he is free."[93] Unlike Rawls, Kant does not attempt to lay down rules of pragmatic choice which are precisely congruent with the rules of right, and in his discussion of the "political moralist" and the "moral politician" in *Perpetual Peace,* Kant tells us that the moral man will reject the pragmatic calculations of the first in favor of the moral principles of the second. Kant is not perfectly consistent in this view, however, for we have also shown that in his description of the "mechanism of nature" he attempted to demonstrate that the dictates of rational interest in the world of phenomenal men are bringing about precisely the kind of republican world order that the voice of Duty requires the man of good will to construct simply because it is right. Also, we must not forget that it was Kant who in the same essay wrote,

> The problem of organizing a state, however hard it may seem, can be solved even for a race of devils, if only they are intelligent. The problem is: 'Given a multitude of rational beings requiring universal laws for their preservation, but each of whom is secretly inclined to exempt himself from them, to establish a constitution in such a way that, although their private intentions conflict, they check each other, with the result that their public conduct is the same as if they had no such intentions.[94]

It seems more appropriate to charge Kant with inconsistency than to say that Rawls has misused the noumenalist categories of Kant's theory of political right. We may read Rawls's work as an effort to rectify this inconsistency in Kant, by showing that at least some utilitarian theories of rational choice, as logical systems, may well be wholly congruent with the logic of noumenal right.

[92]*A Theory of Justice,* pp. 152-53.
[93]*Op. cit.,* p. 656.
[94]*Perpetual Peace,* p. 30.

Problems of the maximin rule.   This does not mean that Rawls's use of the maximin rule is entirely unproblematical. Several theorists of rational choice who have reviewed *A Theory of Justice* have attempted to show that in the circumstances in which Rawls employs it, it is not the most rational behavior for individuals to adopt. Nor, viewed from the standpoint of social groups in its formulation of the "difference principle" (whereby elite privileges are to be permitted only when compensations for the disadvantaged are also forthcoming), is it a rational criterion of justice to adopt, they claim. Thus John Harsanyi asserts that after an initial period of popularity among students of social choice during the 1940s and 50s, there "came a growing realization that the maximin principle and all its relatives lead to serious paradoxes because they often suggest wholly unacceptable practical decisions" when employed as a decision rule under uncertainty. He goes on to describe several hypothetical cases in which applying the maximin rule would produce "a highly irrational conclusion." Social choice theorists have found the Bayesian principle of expected-utility maximization a more adequate rule for conditions of uncertainty.[95]

Douglas Rae, of Yale University, tells us that Rawls has raised exactly the question that a Liberal society needs to face. We should give up the pretense of being just because we have established equality of opportunity and equality before the law, and because we have proscribed vulgar racism. "For these practices . . . pass over the fundamental problem of social allocation: which strata of society are entitled to which claims on the control and use of our common resources?" But despite this initial praise, Professor Rae goes on to say that he thinks "Rawls's theory fails."[96] As Rae sees it, "(1) . . . maximin justice is insensitive to the wellbeing of many social positions, and for this reason, (2) . . . it is possible under Rawls's principles to make choices which at once increase social inequality and decrease total social welfare, thus ignoring both equalitarian and utilitarian urgings at a single stroke."[97] The rest of his review is an attempt to demonstrate the cogency of this criticism.

Despite all these difficulties, we must applaud Rawls's effort to spell out for a modern industrial society the implications of the Kantian view of human morality, and also to bring interest and right together in a single theoretical system, to bridge the gap between Kantian noumenality and phenomenality. For this gap is the single largest problem of the political philosophy framed by Immanuel Kant himself.

---

[95]John Harsanyi, "Can the Maximin Principle Serve as a Basis for Morality? A Critique of John Rawls's Theory," *American Political Science Review* LXIX, (June 1975), No. 2, pp. 594, 595.

[96]Douglas Rae, "Maximin Justice and an Alternative Principle of General Advantage," in *Ibid.,* p. 630.

[97]*Ibid.,* pp. 630-31.

Bibliographical Note

A good collection of Kant's political writings is Hans Reiss, ed., *Kant's Political Writings*, H.B. Nisbet, tr., Cambridge: Cambridge University Press, 1970. Kant's moral theory and noumenal epistemology, which underlie his political philosophy, are succinctly set forth in his *Groundwork of the Metaphysics of Morals*, H.J. Paton, tr., New York: Harper and Row, 1956. An excellent analytical commentary on Kant's moral and political theory is Jeffrie G. Murphy, *Kant: The Philosophy of Right*, New York: St. Martin's Press, 1970. For the development of Kant's political thought, see Hans Saner, *Kant's Political Thought*, E.B. Ashton, tr., Chicago: The University of Chicago Press, 1967. Mary J. Gregor, *Laws of Freedom*, New York: Barnes and Noble, 1963, is a study of Kant's application of the Categorical Imperative in his *Metaphysics of Morals*. Carl J. Friedrich places Kant's thought in the context of Western theories of peace and law from the Renaissance to the formation of the United Nations, in *Inevitable Peace*, Cambridge, Massachusetts: Harvard University Press, 1948.

In addition to *Freedom and Reason*, R.M. Hare is the author of *The Language of Morals*, Oxford: Clarendon Press, 1952, an earlier statement of his view of the logical character of moral judgments. For a capsule statement of John Rawls's theory of justice, in which the Kantian element is not as evident as in *A Theory of Justice*, see his article, "Justice as Fairness," *Philosophical Review* LXVII (1958), 164-94. For its application to the problem of constitutional liberty, see John Rawls, "Constitutional Liberty and the Concept of Justice," *Nomos* VI (1963), 98-125. An acute and detailed analysis of Rawls's theory of justice is Brian Barry, *The Liberal Theory of Justice*, Oxford: The Clarendon Press, 1973.

Chapter 11

Freedom
and the Dialectics of Mind:
Hegel and Some Phenomenologists

Can right be a cause in the world? Though Kant had reestablished the credentials of absolute right by connecting it intimately with the idea of freedom, he had been unable to demonstrate that the noumenal and empirical worlds could effectively be brought together. In other words, the Kingdom of Ends, the best regime, remained a free republic of moral aspiration only. Within Kant's dualistic framework its potential reality as an historical order of justice seemed problematical. For Kant was unable to show how the voice of rational duty could command desire in such fashion as to produce, empirically, the order of political freedom.

Georg Friedrich Hegel began his philosophizing with the Kantian dilemma. To be meaningful, he believed, the order of Right had to be shown to be more than a hypothetical possibility; its power as a cause of events had to be revealed. The right and the rational had to be actual, according to the root meaning of the German word for "actual" — *wirklich,* that which "works" *(wirkt),* in the sense of that which causes motion and growth, like yeast in the process of baking bread.[1] Yet it was also clear to Hegel that, in a very real and obvious sense, right does not control and shape the world. What is and what ought to be are different; our behavior often clashes with our moral ideals.

Hegel's solution to the puzzle we have just sketched lies in his concept of reality and of right as dialectical—i.e., as a process of developmental change in which opposite principles are fused in a context of tension, sometimes of conflict. Conceived dialectically, right is the order of universal freedom, which is coming into being through the historical combination of that which ideally *is* (the abstract idea of freedom in the mind of a "World

[1]Cf. Shlomo Avineri, *Hegel's Theory of the Modern State* (Cambridge: Cambridge University Press, 1972), p. 126.

Spirit"), with that which it concretely *is not* (the necessities of human existence in a world of pure particularity). History is thus for Hegel a process of freedom, as an idea, becoming actualized in empirical existence. In this way, the sharp traditional distinction between thought and action falls away. And Hegel's fusion of the two ultimately culminates in Marx's famous remark that until our time "Philosophers have only contemplated the world; the point is to change it."

Commentators disagree on the extent to which Karl Marx, intellectually formed by the Hegelian system, differs from Hegel on the nature of freedom and ultimate reality. Some believe that the mature Marx, in his collaboration with Engels, radically inverted the Hegelian dialectic by propounding a thoroughgoing materialist metaphysic in which economic forces rather than ideas blindly and mechanically determine human events. Others believe that the Marxian emphasis on the material forces of production in shaping human life was merely intended to draw our attention to the importance of economic factors in society. These interpreters assert that Marx remained throughout his life an Hegelian, and that he affirmed the primacy of spirit over matter. These same interpreters, however, show that Marx also eliminated the reified Hegelian abstraction called "Spirit" *(Geist)* from his philosophy and substituted as ultimate reality the rational action of free human persons. For those who read Marx in this way, he becomes the outstanding humanist philosopher of our age, and much more truly a humanist than Hegel.

Reason, Romanticism, and Revolution

Georg Friedrich Hegel was born in Stuttgart in 1770, the son of an official of the government of Wuerttemberg, a middle-sized German duchy surrounded by a congeries of minute principalities, bishoprics, and free cities that typified the fragmented character of Germany at the end of the eighteenth century. Legally independent both in domestic and foreign affairs, the duchy and surrounding mini-states belonged to the Holy Roman Empire, the wraith of traditional political culture that was to disappear altogether from the European scene just thirty-six years after Hegel's birth. Closer to the border of France than Kant's Prussia, and lacking the power potential and political discipline of Frederick the Great's barracks state, Wuerttemberg presented a very open window to French philosophy and a very open door to the power of French arms. After the winds of Enlightenment rationalism and cosmopolitanism and the countercurrent of Rousseauistic romantic nationalism had swirled dizzily through the window, the armies of Napoleon were to sweep through the door and occupy the house. The influences from the old and new culture that played on the young Hegel, and from the interaction of the two cultures, were many and varied, a wealth of ideas as kaleidoscopic in pattern as the crazy political mosaic of fragmented Germany. Hegel would attempt their synthesis, both in his own varied life experience and in the complexities of his dialectical reasoning.[2]

Hegel's Philosophical Career

Hegel's academic career began in the context of tradition, as a theology student at the University of Tuebingen, where he took a certificate in theology in 1793. But the Tuebingen years were also a time of enthusiasm for the classical-humanist ideals of the Enlightenment and the classical republicanism of the French Revolution. Together with F.W.J. Schelling, Hegal planted a "freedom tree" in the town square of Tuebingen in a transport of delight at the new way of ideas.[3] After tutoring briefly in Berne and Frankfurt, Hegel went in 1801 to Jena to teach metaphysics and logic as a lecturer at the University there, where critical Rationalism and Romanticism both held sway in the work of such notable academics as Schiller, Novalis, the Schlegels, Fichte and Schelling. It was in Jena that Hegel wrote *The Phenomenology of Mind,* which evidences a turning away from the French Revolution because of the excesses of its Jacobin phase. His loyalty to the ideals of the Revolution remained, but his conception of their realization became evolutionary and gradualist, with stress on the values of social continuity. When Napoleon rode into Jena as a conqueror in 1805, Hegel's house was burned and the university was shut down. He thereupon removed east to Bamberg and later Nuremberg, but despite his personal suffering remained enthralled by the changes that were taking place around him and with the idea of political and social modernization on a liberal pattern.[4] In Nuremberg, where he was a high school principal, Hegel published his *Logic* (1812-1816), which was so well received that he was invited to the philosophy faculty of the University of Heidelberg. In 1818 he moved to Berlin, to take the chair of Fichte, a moving spirit of Romantic conservative nationalism. In Berlin were penned his other major works. *The Philosophy of Right,* his chief statement on politics, appeared in 1821, followed by *The Philosophy of History* and *The Philosophy of Religion.* In 1830 Hegel became rector of the University and died the following year.

Beginning in the Berlin days, Hegel's influence spread out over all Europe. Persons of all ideological persuasions were to find something in his work that spoke to them—nationalists, liberals, conservative traditionalists, and ultimately Marx and the Marxists—a counterpoint of intellectual influences to match the counterpoint in which Hegel had grown up and lived his mature life.

[2]*Ibid.,* pp. 1 ff.
[3]*Ibid.*
[4]*Ibid.,* p. 63.

Hegel's World View and Method

The scientific revolution of the sixteenth century in its repudiation of teleology wrought a major alteration in the philosophical conception of truth, overturning a tradition dating back to Plato. Barely three hundred years later, Hegel was to propose an even more radical change. Whether teleologically or scientifically descriptive, formal thought had always been an instrument of truth-saying, understood as a mirroring or reflection of a permanent and unchanging natural reality, according to rules of Aristotelian logic. For Hegel, however, truth as thought *embraced* natural reality, and was enshrined in it. Truth is not found in contemplation, but made in action.

> Philosophy . . . does not deal with a determination that is non-essential, but with a determination so far as it is an essential factor. The abstract or unreal is not its element and content, but the real, what is self-establishing, has life within itself, existence in its very notion. It is the process that creates its own moments in its course, and goes through them all; and the whole movement constitutes its positive content and its truth.[5]

Dialectical Truth

Truth, for Hegel, cannot be expressed in a logic of static words, but only in a dialetic of experience. Its dynamic and organic character requires that its elements not be represented as wholly discrete, mutually exclusive ("A" and "Not-A") but as opposites which fuse. ("A" becomes "Not-A"). Over time, opposites cease to be opposites and become identified with one another.

Hegel illustrates his meaning in *The Phenomenology of Mind* with a discussion of "the now" in relation to changes in time.

> To the question, What is the Now? we reply for example, the Now is night-time. To test the truth of this certainty of sense . . . write that truth down . . . If we look again at the truth we have written down, look at it *now, at this noon-time,* we shall have to say it has turned stale and become out of date.
>
> The Now that is night is kept fixed, i.e., it is treated as what it is given out to be, as something which *is*; but it proves to be rather a something which is *not*. The Now itself no doubt maintains *itself,* but as what is *not* night.[6]

The meaning of "Now," Hegel tells us, is revealed in its dialectical mediations. The "Now" is displayed "by and through negation, which is neither

---

[5]G.W.F. Hegel, *The Phenomenology of Mind,* tr. J.B. Baillie (New York & Evanston: Harper & Row, 1967), p. 105.

[6]*Ibid.,* pp. 151-52.

this nor that, which is a *not-this,* and with equal indifference this as well as that—a thing of this kind we call a Universal."[7] Here we have the traditional idea of "universal" absolutely inverted; instead of an abstract and static concept of logically self-consistent elements it has become an idea of concrete reality consisting of a combination of successive and opposite "moments." In this fashion, Hegel rejects the traditional concept of "Being" as the basic category for conceiving reality, and places in its stead "Becoming." Nothing in the world statically "is"; all is in process of change, development into something else, different from and often opposite to the "being" that it displays at any particular moment. Knowledge, or truth, can therefore only be expressed dialetically, as a process of combining opposites.

Geist As Actor

If Truth is made in action, then there must be an actor to do the making. And this, for Hegel, is Mind or Spirit *(Geist).* For it was clear to him that without Mind, experience would have no form. Whenever we act in the world, it is the processes of Mind which give form and meaning to events— both in shaping and understanding them. Here is a striking expression of the idea in Hegel's own words:

> Through consciousness spirit intervenes in the way the world is ruled. This is its infinite tool—then there are bayonets, cannon, bodies. But the banner [of philosophy] and the soul of its commander is spirit. Neither bayonets, nor money, neither this trick nor that, are the ruler. They are necessary like the cogs and wheels in a clock, but their soul is time and spirit that subordinates matter to its laws. An *Iliad* is not thrown together at random, neither is a great deed composed of bayonets and cannon: it is spirit that is the composer.[8]

While we commonly say that each of us observes and acts through the resources of his own particular mind, Hegel believed that this was an inadequate statement of the full reality involved. For the individual thinks and acts only through the intellectual resources of the community of which he is a member. There is no such thing as individual thinking in general. The symbols and meanings of individuals are derived from the language and other symbols of the culture of which they are a part. The individual's way of conceptualizing and evaluating things is derived from society, and he in turn contributes to the further development of social symbolism.

[7]*Ibid.,* p. 152.

[8]From a fragment printed by Nicolin in *Hegel-Studien* IV, 14, in Avineri, *op. cit.,* p. 64.

Looking at the total social process of thought as an historical reality, Hegel discerned a pattern of meaningful change in it: gradual movement toward greater and greater human self-consciousness, and consciousness of the character and interrelationships of natural processes, and therefore toward greater freedom of mind to control the world through increased understanding of its laws—a conception of freedom realized in the context of necessity. Thus there emerged for Hegel the idea of *Geist,* the Absolute Idea, Mind as such, as the primary reality of the world, which is becoming self-conscious and, thus, free. In this fashion Hegel eliminated "the Kantian distinction between the noumenal and the phenomenal. Hence the title *Phenomenology of [Mind],* which implies that ultimate reality, *Geist,* is manifest in its phenomenological appearances and intelligible through them."[9]

The process whereby the self-awareness of *Geist* occurs—through which its ultimate truth is made and then understood—is dialectical. Beginning as a perfectly *abstract universal,* the Idea is converted into that which it initially is not: *particular ideas,* concretized as the thoughts and institutions of human beings. These persons, as individuals and groups, exist in a dialectical relationship to one another also. Each is for itself a subject (personal mind), ranged over against a world of objects (impersonal body). The relationship can also be expressed in the opposition of "self" to "other." Through the medium of historical social interaction, which is frequently one of conflict, the *particularity* (i.e., fragmentation) of the Idea is gradually overcome, and its *universality* restored—but now as a new reality, a *concrete universal,* in which essence and existence are perfectly fused. The synthesized new reality will be a community of "selves," who have overcome their alienation from "others," and become one with them as a unity of plurally embodied, self-conscious, freely creative Mind. The process of "becoming" will have moved toward its completion or fulfillment. George A. Kelly has succinctly restated Hegel's conception in the following elegant passage:

> The *Phenomenology* is the dramatically ordered account of a mind coming to represent humanity by learning continually through painful rebuffs and deceptions and then circling back again and again on the materials of its education in order to fortify its self-awareness up to a complete appropriation of its experience in trans-subjectively meaningful form. At the point in this Daedalian ascent where 'reason' (of the scientific observer) passes over into 'spirit' (of the collective enterprise), the thinker and his total culture become at ease with one another and are no longer indicative of an alien mind posited against all other manner of traditional resistance and locked in a deadly strug-

[9]*Ibid.,* p. 65.

gle with them. 'It is the nature of humanity,' Hegel writes, 'to struggle for agreement with others, and humanity exists only in the accomplished community of consciousness.'[10]

The Dialectical Politics Of Freedom

It is evident from our review of his theory of knowledge and reality that for Hegel the dialectical process of "becoming" is preeminently political. For the self-expression of the Idea at every point in its development occurs through the shared institutions of human beings, institutions which are created and transformed through acts of power.

Hegel's mature political philosophy is set forth in two major works. In *The Philosophy of History* he represents the historical dialectic of political forms and meanings from ancient times to the present. And in *The Philosophy of Right* he attempts to depict the essential pattern of the Idea of freedom as it was maturing in his own time, within the forms of European constitutional monarchy, especially in Germany, the area of his own personal experience of political change.

From Oriental Despotism to the Modern State

The most primitive form of the "Idea" as political institution was for Hegel the oriental despotism of China and India, old before Greek democracy was conceived, persistent into the nineteenth century, and finally in radical decline. In this system only one person, the despot, is conscious of his freedom. In the Chinese embodiment the subjective consciousness of the ruler is not differentiated from the objective institution of the realm: his will is law. The regime is also perfectly static and unchanging. Sacred and profane remain identical, and the despot appears as an incarnate god. Individual and social morality remain undifferentiated.[11] In Hegel's special use of the term, this is the most "abstract," i.e., undifferentiated and inadequately particularized embodiment of the Idea or Spirit.

> The Orientals do not know yet that mind or man as such are in themselves free; because they do not know it, they are not. They know only that one single man is free. That is why such a freedom is only caprice and barbarism.[12]

Ancient Greek society represented an advance of spirit. Here a large democratic citizenry was conscious of freedom. It was not, however, a sub-

[10]George Armstrong Kelly, "Politics and Philosophy in Hegel," *Polity,* IX, 1976, 7.

[11]Avineri, *op. cit.,* pp. 223-24.

[12]Georg F. Hegel, *The Philosophy of History,* tr. J. Sibree (New York: Dover, 1956), p. 18.

jective, individual freedom, but that of the undifferentiated *Polis*.[13] Also, they confined the concept of freedom to those of Greek blood, and saw the rest of mankind as barbarians fit only to be their slaves. The concept did not reach full generality. The Greeks "as well as the Romans, knew only that some are free, not man as such."[14]

Christianity, in recognizing the dignity and autonomy of the human person as a child of God signified an advance of the dialectic, the transformation of the limited objective freedom of the Greek and Roman political systems into subjective freedom. It also set up a series of dialectical tensions "between the conscience and the world, the other world and this one, piety (which commands chastity, poverty, and obedience) and terrestrial morality (which recommends marriage, work, and reasonable freedom), the clergy and the laity, the church and the state."[15] In Lutheran Christianity, however, Hegel believed the tensions had been resolved, with the full generalization of transcendent and subjective freedom. This was manifest in the assignment of moral value to marriage, work, and crafts, the transformation of the hierarchical priesthood into the priesthood of all believers, and in the recognition of the autonomy of individual conscience.[16]

The culminating phase of dialectical development of the Idea Hegel saw in his own time, with the conversion of subjective into an increasingly universal and objective freedom, embodied in the institutions of the emerging liberal state. Hegel was particularly optimistic about what was happening in the German area under the inflluence of ideas disseminated by the revolutionary armies of France. The French Revolution itself, however, while seminal for development elsewhere, had retained the Idea in France in a still largely "abstract" form—carried in the minds of individuals as a dynamic idea, indeed capable of causing vast institutional change, but not developed into effective and viable socio-political institutions, not adequately particularized as an *objective* universality.[17] But in the Prussia of 1818, incipiently modernized on liberal lines as a result of the Vom Stein and Hardenberg reforms, Hegel thought he saw this dynamic subjectivity passing over into a workable institutional form.[18] In the modern liberal state,

[13]Avineri, *op. cit.*, pp. 225-26.

[14]*The Philosophy of History*, p. 18.

[15]Pierre Hassner, "Georg W.F. Hegel," in L. Strauss and J. Cropsey, eds., *History of Political Philosophy*, 2nd. ed. (Chicago: Rand-McNally, 1972), p. 694.

[16]*Ibid.* Cf. Avineri, *op. cit.*, pp. 227-28.

[17]Hassner, *op. cit.*, pp. 691-92.

[18]Avineri, *op. cit.*, pp. 116-17. Avineri insists that the common view that Hegel apotheosized Prussia is incorrect. His positive references to the Prussian constitution were prompted by the fact that after the Napoleonic Wars liberalizing influences were at work in it, even though they later became abortive. In *The Philosophy of Right*, Hegel also indirectly criticized Prussian practices by inserting into his ideal political system institutions such as the election of representative bodies which were manifestly lacking in Prussian practice.

though still not fully developed, all the "moments" of freedom were independently visible: subjective liberty was paired with objective liberty, freedom was revealed as the essence of human nature, and men had become capable of realizing freedom *in* the state rather than against it.[19]

Geist in the Liberal State

The Philosophy of History brings us up to Hegel's present. In *The Philosophy of Right* the author presents a dialectical cross section of that reality; the book abstracts descriptively the characteristic elements of liberal politics as Hegel had experienced them. But Hegel's descriptions are not like the allegedly "value-free" descriptions of our modern science of politics. They are intended to display the manner in which ethical substance manifests itself in institutional life.

The Three "Moments" of the Spirit. It is in the shared life of the family that individuals find their initial ethical realization and selfhood, the first "moment" of the Spirit. It is not as individuals but as husband (subject) and wife (object) in the institution of marriage (synthesis) that a man and a woman receive concrete ethical rights and obligations. One of the obligations is the moral formation of the offspring of their union.

When the grown citizen emerges from the shelter of family life, the work of spirit is complete at this level, and the "subject" resulting from the synthesis of the family goes out into civil society to experience the next phase of dialectical development. In the new context the other-regarding, and group-regarding morality learned at home (subject) passes over into particularist egoism (object). "Civil society," the second "moment" of the Spirit, was for Hegel an expression for the individualist and atomistic atmosphere of middle-class commercial society, in which relationships are external, governed by the "unseen hand" of the economic laws (by market relations), rather than by the self-conscious will of persons. In this context, however, the individual stands out and receives ethical recognition as such. He acquires property rights and other civil rights simply as a person.

> It is part of education, of thinking as the consciousness of the single individual in the form of universality, that the ego comes to be apprehended as a universal person in which all are identical. A man counts as a man in virtue of his manhood alone, not because he is a Jew, Catholic, Protestant, German, Italian, etc. This is an assertion which thinking ratifies and to be conscious of it is of infinite importance. It is defective only when it is crystallized, e.g., as a cosmopolitanism in opposition to the concrete life of the state.[20]

[19]Hassner, *op. cit.,* pp. 693, 696.

[20]G.F. Hegel, *The Philosophy of Right,* tr. T.M. Knox (London and New York: Oxford University Press, 1952), para. 209-A, p. 134.

Individual right cannot be complete and secure in civil society, however. This requires the state, whose role is to protect the universality implicit in the particularity of civil society through its institutional order and coercive powers. This is the third "moment" of the Spirit, in which universal and particular are brought into final synthesis.

The Three "Moments" of the State. Hegel opens his discussion of the constitution of the emerging liberal state, which in his model has the form of a constitutional monarchy, with an analysis of the division of powers, organically considered. He rejects out of hand the mechanical conception of an equilibrated constitution of opposed forces, enshrined in the free constitution of Kant and his English-empiricist predecessors.

> This view implies that the attitude adopted by each power to the other is hostile and apprehensive, as if the others were evils, and that their function is to oppose one another and as a result of this counterpoise to effect an equilibrium of the whole, but never a living unity.[21]

This false view he calls a product of the "abstract Understanding." But the state is not a self-consciously constructed mechanism. It is an historically emergent organism. When the concrete Understanding grapples with the question it sees in the division of power the "inner self-determination of the Concept" *(der Begriff)*. This is the Universal Idea of *Geist,* seeking organic institutional embodiment. It is the nature of the Idea to determine itself inwardly in dialectical thought, passing from universality through particularity to individuality (the synthesis of these two). Thus in the division of powers, the organic thought process is institutionally embodied, as follows:

> The state as a political entity is . . . cleft into three substantive divisions:
>   (a) the power to determine and establish the universal—the Legislature;
>   (b) the power to subsume single cases and the spheres of the particularity under the universal—the Executive;
>   (c) the power of subjectivity, as the will with the power of ultimate decision—the Crown. In the crown, the different powers are bound into an individual unity which is thus at once the apex and the basis of the whole, i.e., of constitutional monarchy.[22]

As Hegel's description of the state further unfolds, we are presented with a picture of a highly differentiated socio-legal organism, a complex symbiotic union of functionally different parts, each of which subsumes a portion of the citizen body; a corporative state.

The corporative character of Hegel's political system is especially evident in the composition of the legislature. This is not based on the territorial

---

[21]*Ibid.,* para. 272, p. 175.
[22]*Ibid.,* para. 273, p. 176.

distribution of individuals, but on occupational clusterings, which Hegel calls "Estates" *(Staende),* using the traditional aristocratic concept of corporative order. These he envisages as constituted by two classes of persons, one unofficial, the other official. The unofficial class is composed of two parts. One is the agricultural estate, embracing all families engaged in agriculture, which "is summoned and entitled to its political vocation by birth without the hazards of election."[23] This estate he considers a stable hereditary interest. The other "comprises the fluctuating element in civil society," the kaleidoscope of ever-changing groups in which urban society organizes itself: businessmen's associations, professional organizations, labor unions. Through these corporations the individual receives indirect representation in the legislature. The official class of the legislative body is made up of civil servants, who are recruited from the entire society by competitive examination—an estate of experts. Working together, though voting in separate assemblies, the three estates draft legislation for presentation to the Crown, which has the right of final determination.

The estates have a double function in the exercise of their power "to determine and establish the universal."[24] One takes place within the occupational organizations of which the estates are composed, which serve as units of self-government as well as electoral constituencies. It consists in establishing rules of conduct for the members of the various groups—an ethos, principles of behavior, the ethical life of civil society *(Sittlichkeit).* These are the *mores* proper to the various occupational groups, rather than principles of inter-individual morality *(Moralitaet).* But like morals so defined, they lead away from egoism and particularity toward the universal. The culmination of the work of the estates in determining the universal is found in their participation in legislation, the establishment of enforceable standards of right for the state (organized society) as a whole.

The second "moment" of the state is the executive function, "the power to subsume single cases and the spheres of particularity under the universal."[25] This is the province of the civil service, the official estate, acting as the administrative branch of the political system. This was for Hegel the lynch-pin of the entire system, the "universal class" in its vital work of translating abstract directives of the legislature into practical decisions affecting the entire life of society in all its members. The work of the civil service is to provide rational government, defined as nonpartisan expert judgment in the application of general principles to particular cases. As mediator between universal and particular, it was thought this "universal class" in its administrative functions best exemplified the work of *Geist* in the modern liberal state. Hegel's vision is the same as that of the American

[23]*Ibid.,* para. 307, p. 199.
[24]*Ibid.,* para. 273, p. 176.
[25]*Ibid.*

reformers who in 1883 accomplished the enactment of the Pendleton Act, which replaced the earlier spoils system of Jacksonian democracy with the merit principle, and established procedures of competitive examination to recruit technical experts for public service. Like Hegel, they were seeking a method for introducing technical rationality into government in order to cope with the problems of an increasingly technical and complex society.

The third "moment" of the Hegelian state is the Crown, which in culminating the work of legislation and in acting as general overseer of the administrative process provides a synthesis of the other two "moments."

> The power of the crown contains in itself the three moments of the whole . . . viz . . . the *universality* of the constitution and the laws; . . . counsel, which refers the particular to the universal; and . . . the moment of ultimate decision, as the self-determination to which everything else reverts and from which everything else derives the beginnings of its actuality.[26]

Hegel makes it clear that he thinks of the crown in institutional, not in personal terms. It is not his intention to write an *apologia* for absolute, but for constitutional monarchy.

> The individual functionaries and agents are attached to their office not on the strength of their universal and objective qualities. Hence it is in an external and contingent way that these offices are linked with particular persons, and therefore the functions and powers of the state cannot be private property.[27]

The Problematic Character of Hegelian Freedom

Hegel and Welfare Liberalism

How successful was Hegel's effort to show that right can be a causal force in the world, and that it is working through historical processes to build the kingdom of freedom? It is certainly undeniable that Hegel's philosophy furnished a coherent theoretical explanation for many aspects of the modern liberal democratic experience, in which conceptions of freedom (defined in terms of rights of individuals) are brought together with moral obligation, conceived as the reciprocal duties of citizens and governments. The Welfare Liberal conception of the positive state, which requires that governments take legislative and administrative action to make real the rights of individuals is a distinctly Hegelian idea. The state is obliged, ac-

[26]*Ibid.*, para. 275, p. 179.

[27]*Ibid.*, para. 277, p. 179. While this statement is written in very general terms, and seems applicable to every public official, it is significant that it does not appear in the section of *The Philosophy of Right* which deals with the Executive— the civil service—but in the section on the Crown.

cording to Hegel, not only to establish the Lockean values of security of person and property, but to secure "every single person's livelihood and welfare."[28] One can trace a line of intellectual influence, reaching from Hegel through such English theorists as Thomas Hill Green and Americans such as John Dewey to the social reformers who developed the principles of welfare liberalism (the positive state) into programmatic form (e.g., Roosevelt's "New Deal"). Thus, individuals are understood to enjoy rights to freedom from want and from fear, freedom to develop as persons. The long list of human rights in the United Nations' Universal Declaration of Human Rights and in the American Bill of Rights, together with its judicial interpretation and legislative extension, fit well with Hegelian theory.

Anti-Liberal Ideas: Hegel and Fascism

Despite the similarity of Hegel's conception of the rights of humankind with that of welfare liberalism, it is also the case that Hegel was rather skeptical about the importance of two traditional liberal values—freedom of speech and of the press. Thus, while he writes in *The Philosophy of Right* that "Public opinion . . . is a respository not only of the genuine needs and correct tendencies of common life, but also . . . of the eternal, substantive principles of justice, the true content and result of legislation, the whole constitution, and the general position of the state," he argues in the very same paragraph that it frequently "becomes infected by all the accidents of opinion, by its ignorance and perversity, by its mistakes and falsity of judgment." He goes on to say that it should therefore be "despised for its concrete expression" and that "to be independent of public opinion is the first formal condition of achieving anything great or rational whether in life or in science." In the sequel he adds that "to define freedom of the press as freedom to say and write whatever we please is parallel to the assertion that freedom as such means freedom to do as we please." And he concludes by saying that "the contemptuous caricature of government, its ministers, officials . . . defiance of the laws are all crimes or misdemeanours."[29] No liberal would accept such a view. Nor can Hegel's glorification of war fit into a liberal's outlook.[30]

In view of these qualifications of the liberal reading of Hegel, we are not surprised to learn that Hegel's influence moved in an anti-liberal as well as a liberal direction. The philosophy of Giovanni Gentile, chief theoretician of Fascist Italy, is Hegelian through and through.[31] Gentile makes

[28]*Ibid.*, para. 230, p. 146.

[29]*Ibid.*, paras. 317, 318, pp. 204-207.

[30]See *Ibid.*, paras. 324-29, pp. 209-12.

[31]See Giovanni Gentile, *Genesis and Structure of Society*, tr. H.S. Harris (Urbana, Ill.: Univ. of Illinois Press, 1960).

extensive use of Hegel's conception of *Geist* as the creator of the state, and identifies as its bearer, Benito Mussolini, the founder of the Italian Fascist state, which was organized along corporative lines, vaguely reminiscent of the Hegelian corporative order. Ready to hand to legitimate this identification of the charismatic *Duce* was Hegel's concept of the "World Historical Individual," celebrated in *The Philosophy of History* as a hero figure who appears at crucial intervals in the evolution of the *Weltgeist* in order to initiate a new phase of the development of the Idea. Alexander, Caesar, and Napoleon are examples with whom Hegel illustrates his concept. He wrote of them:

> They may be called Heroes, inasmuch as they have derived their purposes and their vocation, not from the calm, regular course of things, sanctioned by the existing order; but from a concealed fount — one which has not attained to phenomenal, present existence, — from that inner Spirit, still hidden beneath the surface, which, impinging on the outer world as on a shell, bursts it in pieces, because it is another kernel than that which belonged to the shell in question. They are men, therefore, who appear to draw the impulse of their life from themselves; and whose deeds have produced a condition of things and a complex of historical relations which appear to be only *their* interest, and *their* work.
>
> Such individuals had no consciousness of the general Idea they were unfolding, while prosecuting those aims of theirs; on the contrary, they were practical political men. But at the same time they were thinking men, who had an insight into the requirements of the time — what was ripe for development.[32]

In Gentile's view, and in that of Mussolini himself, it was fitting that the *Duce* be added to Hegel's list of World Historical Figures.[33]

An Ambiguous Connection

What all this points up is a fundamental ambiguity in Hegel's dialectical connection of the normative notion of Creative Spirit, seeking its self-realization in freedom, with the empirical institutions of particular states. Though Hegel's concept centrally involved the particularization of the Idea in phenomenal reality, Hegel did not wish to identify the bearer of the World Spirit with *every or any* empirical polity that happens to exist. T.M. Knox points out, for example, that "whatever Hegel meant by his identification of the real with the rational, he did not mean to justify the *status quo,* because the rational State described in ... *[The Philosophy of*

[32] *The Philosophy of History,* p. 30.

[33] See for Mussolini's conception of Fascism, his article that appeared originally in the *Encyclopedia Italiana,* "The Doctrine of Fascism," in Michael Oakeshott, *The Social and Political Doctrines of Contemporary Europe* (Cambridge: Cambridge University Press, 1939), p. 169ff.

Right] was not a description of any state actually existing at that time."[34]
And Avineri argues that a famous passage from *The Philosophy of History,*
in which Hegel appeared to hold that every period of history has a particular
World Historical Nation, which has a right to political hegemony for that
period, is a misinterpretation. "The *absolute right* is not in the realm of international politics, but in the sphere of cultural leadership." And so far as
the last phase of historical development is concerned, Hegel termed it *"die
germanische Welt* (the Germanic World) and not *die deutsche Welt* (the
German World." The expression, "the Germanic World," Avineri maintains, is not a designation of a particular state, but a reference to Western
Civilization in general.[35] Thus Hegel does not give us a perfectly clear rubric
for relating the true form of his ever-evolving Idea to the welter of historical
political reality.

Hegel and Marx

As the liberal state, whose beginnings Hegel celebrated, began to
develop into its industrial phase, problems for the realization of human
freedom and dignity which Hegel had recognized in some of his minor
writings (but strangely excluded from *The Philosophy of Right)* began to
develop in an acute form. For Hegelians such as Karl Marx, they raised the
question of the ultimate compatibility of capitalist institutions with the universality of freedom.

The new industrial order, growing up under the guidance of a con-
scienceless economic individualism, had created massive dislocations which
would take decades to repair. Wholly new cities, like Manchester, England,
had sprung up overnight, and into them had been herded as factory workers
masses of people from the impoverished countryside.

> The working people [lived] like rats in the wretched little dens of their dwell-
> ings, whole families, sometimes more than one family, swarming in a single
> room, well and diseased, adults and children, close relations sleeping together,
> sometimes even without beds to sleep on when all the furniture had been sold
> for firewood, sometimes in damp, underground cellars which had to be bailed
> out when the weather was wet, sometimes living in the same room with the
> pigs; ill nourished on flour mixed with gypsum and cocoa mixed with dirt,
> poisoned by ptomaine from tainted meat, doping themselves and their wailing
> children with laudanum; spending their lives, without a sewage system, among
> the piles of their excrement and garbage; spreading epidemics of typhus and
> cholera which even made inroads into the well-to-do sections. . . .

[34]T.M. Knox, "Hegel and Prussianism," in W. Kaufmann, ed., *Hegel's
Political Philosophy* (New York: Atherton Press, 1970), p. 18.

[35]Shlomo Avineri, "Hegel and Nationalism" in Kaufman, *Hegel's Political
Philosophy,* p. 130.

Children, fed into the factories at the age of five or six, receiving little care from mothers who were themselves at the factory all day and no education at all from the community which wanted them only to perform mechanical operations, would drop exhausted when they were let out of their prisons, too tired to wash or eat, let alone study or play, sometimes too tired to get home at all. In the iron and coal mines, also, women and children as well as men spent the better part of their lives crawling underground in narrow tunnels, and emerging, found themselves caught in the meshes of the company cottage and the company store and of the two-week postponement of wages. They were being killed off at the rate of 1,400 a year through the breaking of rotten ropes, the caving-in of workings due to overexcavated seams and the explosions due to bad ventilation and to the negligence of tired children; if they escaped catastrophic accidents, the lung diseases eventually got them.[36]

Such was the condition of the proletariat of whose deliverance and glorious transfiguration Marx was to become the prophet.

Hegel himself had accepted capitalism, in the belief that the social distortions it produced could be rectified by the political controls of his corporative state over the egoistic formlessness of "civil society." Marx was to come to the conclusion that Hegel's idealist legalism fundamentally misstated the basic realities of the historical process of freedom. But he was to take as his point of departure the critique that Hegel himself had made of capitalism.

Hegel's Critique of Capitalism

In three early writings of his Jena period, the *System der Sittlichkeit* and two versions of the *Realphilosophie* (1802-1806), Hegel attacked the problem of understanding the workings of "Objective Spirit" (the embodied Idea) by reflecting on the institution of property. His reflection began with the observation that human consciousness, in its earliest moments, seeks to overcome the painful separation of "subject" from "object" by absorbing the outer world into itself. But the gratification is only momentary, and results in the destruction of the object. (Hegel is here thinking of the compulsive, "grasping" behavior of infants.) The institution of property Hegel saw as another, more developed effort to appropriate nature to the self. And in his own time, in the emergence of the bourgeois class, he found the passion for property generalized into an entire life style.

The power of this estate is thus so determined that it consists in possession generally and in a system of law relating to possession. It constitutes an interrelated system, and . . . the relationships of possession are integrated into a

[36]From *To The Finland Station* by Edmund Wilson, pp. 134-35. Copyright 1940 by Edmund Wilson. Reprinted by permission of Doubleday & Company, Inc., and W. H. Allen & Company, London.

formal unity. Everyone, who is thus capable of holding possession, relates to all as a universal—as a burgher, in the sense of *bourgeois*.[37]

In seeking to understand the phenomenon of capitalist acquisition, Hegel, in *Realphilosophie* II, uses language reminiscent of Locke's *Second Treatise:* "Man has a right to take into possession as much as he can as an individual. He has this right, it is implied in the concept of being himself: through this he asserts himself over all things."[38] But both Locke and Hegel observed that possession becomes property right only when it is recognized by society. For Locke, however, this recognition is merely a pragmatic device for guaranteeing individual right, and for establishing a rule of comity among individuals. Property remains assimilated to the individual, an extension of the self. Locke underlines this notion by telling us that the beginning of property right is the fact that we have a property in our persons. Hegel, however, comes to a very different philosophical conclusion; since recognition is central to the establishment of the individual's right, property must be an attribute of society, not of the individual as such.[39] Since, moreover, society is the vehicle of the ethical life, the context in which an individual becomes a moral person, and since society is the determiner of property right, property must have another significance than the individual's sensuous enjoyment of it. It must have a moral significance. This Hegel sets forth in a theory of labor.

A Theory of Labor.   In laboring on an object, the individual does not consume what he has appropriated, but transforms it into something else—a new reality in which the self (subject) is combined with the raw materials of nature (object). Thus "the accidentality of coming into possession [is] transcended *(aufgehoben)*."[40] It is because his labor has, as a creative act, imprinted the self on objects, that a man receives recognition from others. In labor "man becomes a universal for the other, but so does the other."[41]

> Consciousness, by desiring an object, moves man to create it, to transform need from a subjective craving and appetite into an external, objective force. Labour is therefore always intentional, not instinctual for it represents man's power to create his own world. Production is a vehicle of reason's actualization of itself in the world.[42]

[37]*Gesammelte Werke,* IV, 458 in Avineri, *Hegel's Theory of the Modern State,* p. 86. In this section I follow closely Avineri's report and analysis of Hegel's critique of capitalism, *Ibid.,* pp. 81-98.

[38]Cited in Avineri, p. 88.

[39]*Ibid.,* p. 89.

[40]*Realphilosophie* II, 217 in Avineri, *op. cit.* p. 89.

[41]*Schriften zur Politik,* p. 428 in Avineri *op. cit.,* p. 89.

[42]Avineri, *op. cit.,* pp. 89-90.

The process of material production thus becomes central for human fulfill-ment, and therefore also central for the ultimate self-realization of *Geist*. But the fulfillment seems far away. Under capitalism the "externalization" (or "alienation," *Entaeusserung*) of the self in labor had created widespread misery, not fulfillment.

The Division of Labor.   Hegel focusses on the effect on the working-man of the increasingly complex division of labor that he observed develop-ing around him.

> Because work is being done for the need as an abstract being-for-itself, one also works in an abstract way . . . . General labour is thus division of labour, saving . . . . Every individual, as an individual, works for *a* need. The content of his labour [however] transcends *his* need; he works for the satisfaction of many, and so [does] everyone. Everyone satisfies thus the needs of many, and the satisfaction of his many particular needs is the labour of many others. Since his labour is thus this abstraction, he behaves as an abstract self, or ac-cording to the way of thingness, not as a comprehensive, rich, all-encompassing spirit, who rules over a wide range and masters it.[43]

This is a graphic picture of the dehumanizing effects of factory production. In the new economic regime, a man was less and less able to "see himself" in the objects of his toil. His alienation (externalization) was complete. Yet at the same time, capitalism produced an advance. For it had increased a thousand-fold the dependence of each individual on the other; it had made the individual into a universal being. And through mechanization it had also increased the number of goods that could be produced. But under capitalism man had lost control over the direction of production. The im-personal forces of the market had taken over, and were producing an ever-increasing supply of commodities to satisfy an increasing number of new tastes and fashions. Instead of finding his human self in his objects, man was becoming a slave to meaningless commodity production. At the same time, the market had sharply divided society into two classes—a small one of rich capitalists dominating a large one of poor workers.

> Aspects of class-domination appear in a very prominent way in Hegel's description when he expresses his awareness of the fact that the wealth of na-tions can be built only at the expense of the poverty of whole classes. 'Fac-tories and manufacturers base their existence on the misery *[Elend]* of a class,' he remarks. And, in another context, his description is no less brutal in its can-dour: '[This power] condemns a multitude to a raw life and to dullness in labour and poverty, so that others could amass fortunes.'[44]

Such is Hegel's critique of early capitalism in Europe. Strangely enough, only vestiges of it can be found in Hegel's major social treatise, *The*

[43]*Realphilosophie* II, 214-15 in Avineri, *op. cit.,* pp. 91-92.
[44]Avineri, *op. cit.,* p. 96.

Philosophy of Right. Avineri suggests that this is the case because Hegel had in that book developed a solution to the problem of class domination and the morally destructive egoism of "civil society"—the institution of the "universal class." Thus the critique was placed in a secondary position.[45] Marx, as a young Hegelian, unsatisfied with Hegel's "solution" was to return to the radical critique of the Jena writings for his own point of departure. His own analysis would lead him to conclusions about social reform far removed from the optimistic rationalism of *The Philosophy of Right.*

Hegel and Phenomenology

Karl Marx and the myriad subsequent Marxists are, of course, the best known Hegelians of our time. We shall have occasion to deal with them extensively in the next chapter. But Hegel's influence has moved in a variety of directions, as we have seen, and can be found in the background of several important intellectual schools of our time. In the field of political philosophy, one school of growing importance is existential phenomenology.

Purpose and Consciousness

American phenomenologists working in the area of political studies have concentrated their efforts in a critique of the positivist basis of behavioral political science, the natural science of politics. Like Hegel, phenomenologists insist that an adequate grasp of politics cannot be derived from behavioral observation, that such observations can be made intelligible only when they are seen as a correlate of human thought. With Hegel, they also hold that mind is not a passive recorder of reality, but an active shaper of it. As one writer puts it:

> The essence of the contemporary critique . . . emphasizes the inadequacy of natural science methods to the study of society. Men are not mere objects, the critique maintains, but are purposive beings, capable of thought and conscious of themselves and their setting.[46]

This critique resembles that made by the Straussians, which we described in Chapter 2, and that of the Thomists like Maritain, mentioned in Chapter 5. It differs from them, however, in failing to assert the existence of a transcen-

[45]*Ibid.,* p. 98.

[46]Peter J. Steinberger, "Hegel as a Social Scientist," *American Political Science Review,* LXXXI, 1977: 99. In this article Steinberger writes of Hegel as the father of the entire interpretive critique of positivist political science in the present decade. Among the interpretive approaches that Steinberger discusses is the phenomenological school. See especially pp. 102-3.

dent world of right and moral purpose, from which the concept of human purpose is derived. Rather, it affirms that human purposes are a function of human freedom. Transcendent meaning is foreclosed to us. According to Edmund Husserl, the father of phenomenology, "objects *have reality for us* only through the meanings we attach to them."[47] Transcendence is "bracketed" out by the phenomenologists, and the world of meaning confined to the realm of interaction between knowing subject and its object, the latter as an element of consciousness.

Edmund Husserl.   Edmund Husserl (1859-1938) grew up in Moravia, in his time a province of the Austrian Empire, and today part of Czechoslovakia. After pursuing his education in Leipzig, Berlin, and (both formally and informally) in Vienna, he taught philosophy at the universities of Goettingen and Freiburg in Germany, until retirement in 1929. The immediate inspiration of Husserl's philosophical approach was the work of the Viennese priest-philosopher, Franz Brentano, whose "psychognosy" emphasized the importance of intentionality in the causation of human behavior and of psychic data as the material of metaphysical and ethical analysis. For Husserl, intelligible reality was confined (as for Hegel) to consciousness, which contained "intention" as the subjective pole, and the psychic object as its objective pole.[48] "Thus in one fundamental move he eliminated the question of whether the object of the act of consciousness is 'real' and revealed consciousness itself as a source of objectively valid data on which universal philosophical principles can be based."[49] This amounted to an adaptation of the Hegelian insistence that thought and mind, including ideas of absolute right and meaning, are intelligible only as aspects of consciousness, but with the Hegelian assumption omitted that a mysterious *Geist* seeks self-realization in human consciousness. Interpretive psychic analysis is thus converted by Husserl from reified Idealism into an empirical humanism. The difference is of great importance, even though Husserl came to refer to his own philosophical position as idealism. The thrust of the difference is away from idealism toward existentialism, as shown by the thought of Husserl's great pupil, Martin Heidegger.

Phenomenology and Behavioral Political Science

Though a vital focus of intellectual attention in Europe since the turn of the century, phenomenology began to stimulate the interest of Americans only in the present decade. As one account notes, "With its accent on 'objec-

---

[47]*Ibid.,* p. 102.

[48]For a brief intellectual biography of Husserl, see the article by Joseph Lyon in *The International Encyclopedia of the Social Sciences,* Vol. 7 (New York: Macmillan and the Free Press, 1968), pp. 27-31.

[49]*Ibid.,* p. 28.

tive' processes, large-scale technology and technical rationality, America was a poor breeding ground for a philosophy grounded on such notions as consciousness intentionality, and the *Lebenswelt*." Instead, phenomenology came to be caricatured as a kind of mentalistic subjectivism. Though admitted to some academic departments of philosophy, it remained insulated from contact with "the social sciences in general and political science specifically."[50]

The disillusioning experiences of the 1960s changed the situation. The sense of injustice about the Vietnam War, and outrage at the apparent loss of a sense of human values by a military concerned with "body counts" and with the technical effectiveness of monstrous methods of modern warfare, led numerous intellectuals to question the moral adequacy of utilitarian culture. The liberal society "seemed to be on the verge of paradigm breakdown," as did the political science which had celebrated and been enveloped by the Lockean ethos and which had existed in "long-standing symbiosis with the governmental bureaucracy and public policy."[51] In particular, the "value-free" descriptions of contemporary society given by this science seemed of questionable usefulness in a time that required moral direction. Behavioralists themselves proclaimed the coming of the "post-behavioral" era, and other political scientists began to look to phenomenology to infuse the systematic study of politics with moral categories.

Importance of the Lebenswelt. In the phenomenological perspective, the basic reason that the natural science of politics is of no use in moral judgment is that the vocabulary of that science has abandoned the "life world" of daily political experience. Maurice Natanson, in the introduction to a two-volume anthology of phenomenological essays on the social sciences, points out that "there has come to be a replacement of man's self-understanding in mundane life by a fundamental abstraction out of recognizable experience into a mathematical-physical formalism whose roots go back directly to Galileo."[52] In the process, the moral content of the life-world had been lost. Beyond that, the scientific understanding of "subjectivity" has made values equivalent to individual preferences, understood as arbitrary wish, something which may profitably be described, but not evaluated. "Not only has 'subjectivity' been made synonymous with the purely psychological sense of individual attitude, it has been made an object

[50]Herbert G. Reid and Ernest J. Yanarella, "Toward a Post-Modern Theory of American Political Science and Culture: Perspectives from Critical Marxism and Phenomenology," *Cultural Hermeneutics,* II, 1974, p. 95.

[51]*Ibid.,* p. 97.

[52]Maurice Natanson, ed. *Phenomenology and the Social Sciences,* I (Evanston: Northwestern University Press, 1973), p. 38.

for behavioral investigation, the assumption being that the main consideration in the analysis of the subjective is what the observer can make of it."[53]

Hwa Yol Jung.   One of the most incisive and detailed phenomenological critiques of political science is by Hwa Yol Jung, who contributed
to the Natanson symposium and who has edited a selection of writings on
Existential Phenomenology and Political Theory.[54] In the introduction to his
reader, Professor Jung presents an analysis of the work of Anthony Downs
(which we have already described in Chapter 7) as an example of political
science which lacks moral meaning because of its abandonment of the
vocabulary of the "life world." Jung notes that Downs constructed his
"positive" model of the democratic polity for the purpose of prediction,
rather than to understand the meaning of the phenomena of politics. This
was accomplished "by selecting a few crucial variables as relevant while ignoring others which may have a vital influence on the real world of
politics."[55] In accomplishing this, "the preconceptual reality of how *real*
men behave in the *real* world of politics" was treated as "materially imperti-
nent to his conceptual framework."[56] This might be acceptable when prediction rather than description or explanation is the writer's intention. But
Jung suggests that Downs's model actually appears as more than a predictive
device in *An Economic Theory of Democracy.* For Downs presents the reader
with a motivational theory, and contends that people in party politics seek
to fulfill "their personal desires for the income, prestige, and power which
come from holding office."[57] In the eyes of Jung, he has introduced into his
political science "a one-sided, hence false image of man"—the image of a
"consumer who maximizes his own utilities," and whose behavior is
described as "rational to the degree that it is directed primarily towards
selfish ends."[58] The image of economic man has been put forward by Downs
"for allegedly analytical reasons," but it actually serves to teach a moral (or
immoral) lesson. For it contains a substantive judgment on human moral
character.

Jung also comments on Heinz Eulau's study, *The Behavioral Persuasion in Politics.*[59] He notes that Eulau, a leading member of the "behavioral
persuasion," has written that "the function of political science is to understand and interpret the political world rather than to change it."[60] He thus

[53]*Ibid.*
[54](Chicago: Henry Regnery, 1972).
[55]*Ibid.,* p. xxxi.
[56]*Ibid.*
[57]*Ibid.,* p. xxxviii.
[58]*Ibid.*
[59](New York: Random House, 1963).
[60]*Ibid.,* p. xxxiv.

appears to be substantively in agreement with the phenomenological conception of what the discipline is all about — the study of meaningful human behavior. But as behavioralist he nevertheless parts company with the phenomenologist in his judgment of what are appropriate methods to employ. For Eulau believes that "there are no 'natural limits' to the use of scientific methods and techniques in political science," by which he means standard devices of behavioral observation and measurement. Jung thus concludes that "in the final analysis Eulau chooses to opt for what is external, rather than what is internal, as the only legitimate means of scientific discourse and observation."[61] In another essay Jung notes that Eulau insists that intentions, beliefs, values and such "must be either translated into the 'observable contexts' or inferred from overt behavior."[62] But in doing this Eulau is really reducing human behavior to its overt or external components. Phenomenology opts instead for a wholly different method of intentional analysis, which takes account of "the radical difference between what is human and what is merely natural."[63]

Jung lays stress on the phenomenological insight that man as an active being is preeminently social. He goes so far as to say that "he is nothing but a nexus of relationships."[64] As such, man must be understood, not as an autonomous reality existing in an environment, but as a being who is in constant dialectical interaction with his environment—an intersubjective reality. "Man is capable of both internalizing the external and externalizing the internal; the dialectical process of this capability constitutes the self-making of an individual on the one hand and the history of a society or a civilization on the other."[65] Even when behavioral scientists try to take account of consciousness, they ignore the importance of this interaction. Thus Robert Lane and Karl Deutsch interpret consciousness only as a reflex, as "sensitivity or the internal feedback of secondary messages." They lose sight of its intentional structure, in which internal and external worlds meet and interact.[66] This makes all the difference in the world, for it affects the scientist's understanding of causation in the social world and substitutes a mechanical theory of causality for a properly intentional and voluntarist one.[67]

Other contributors to the phenomenological critique of the natural science of politics are Ira Strauber, Randal Ihara, Marvin Surkin, and

---

[61]*Ibid.*, p. xxv.

[62]Hwa Yol Jung, "A critique of the Behavioral Persuasion in Politics: A Phenomenological View," in Natanson, ed., *op cit.*, Vol. II, p. 142.

[63]*Existential Phenomenology and Political Theory*, p. xxxv.

[64]*Ibid.*, p. xl.

[65]*Ibid.*, p. xli.

[66]"A Critique" in Natanson, ed., *op. cit.*, Vol. II, p. 143.

[67]*Ibid.*, p. 145.

Charles Taylor. Taylor is also the author of a well-received study of Hegel's philosophy.[68]

Conclusion. Just as Hegel himself, in *The Phenomenology of Mind,* criticized the incompleteness of the analytical method of the natural sciences of his time, so today the phenomenologists have carried forward his message that in the study of human affairs in particular, we must not allow the attractiveness of analytical precision to prevent us from attempting a synthetic account of the whole. The "social researcher must go beyond those unambiguous data that present themselves, and seek a level of facticity that demands a degree of sympathetic interpretation." He must "confront his world in a total way." From Hegel and from today's phenomenologists we learn that spiritual context is what gives significance to political and social structures. They are unintelligible apart from the work of the minds (if not of "mind") which inhabit them. We can understand behavior only "by grappling first with the nature of human thought."[69]

Bibliographical Note

The metaphysical and epistemological foundations of Hegel's political thought are set forth in detail in his *Logic,* William Wallace, tr., Oxford: Clarendon Press, 1975, and in *The Phenomenology of Mind,* J.B. Baillie, tr., New York: Harper & Row, 1967. *The Philosophy of Right* is Hegel's chief statement of political theory. A good English edition is by T.M. Knox, London: Oxford University Press, 1967. Additions, derived from notes taken at lectures given by Hegel, are included as an appendix. There are also extensive notes by the translator. See also *The Philosophy of History,* J. Sibree, tr., New York: Dover Publications, Inc., 1956.

A good general commentary is Walter Kaufmann, *Hegel: a Reinterpretation,* Garden City, New York: Doubleday, 1965. A wide range of interpretations of Hegel's political theory is found in Walter Kaufmann, ed., *Hegel's Political Philosophy,* New York: Atherton Press, 1970, which is organized as two multi-sided debates. See also Z.A. Pelczynski, ed., *Hegel's Political Philosophy,* Cambridge: Cambridge University Press, 1971, and Shlomo Avineri, *Hegel's Theory of the Modern State,* Cambridge:

[68]Charles Taylor, *Hegel* (Cambridge: Cambridge University Press, 1975). See also Taylor's frequently cited essay on behavioral political science, "Neutrality in Political Science," in P. Laslett & W.G. Runciman, eds., *Philosophy, Politics, and Society,* 3rd series (Oxford: Basil Blackwell & Mott, Ltd., 1967). Taylor does an excellent job of showing that every "scientific" analysis of politics rests upon a special view of human nature and of reality in general, i.e., upon a special metaphysics, which includes a special ethical position. For a discussion of the phenomenological work of Jung, Taylor, and Ihara see Reid and Yanarella, *op. cit.,* pp. 99-107.

[69]Steinberger, *op. cit.,* pp. 99, 109.

Cambridge University Press, 1972. The latter is particularly lucid and contains an excellent comparison of Hegel's little known early political and economic thought with his later writings on politics and society.

An interesting essay on recent Hegelian thought, which constitutes a critique of the natural science of politics, is Peter J. Steinberger, "Hegel as a Social Scientist," *American Political Science Review,* LXXXI, 1977: 95-110. An extensive review of the applicability of phenomenological analysis to the study of politics is Maurice Natanson, ed., *Phenomenology and the Social Sciences,* Vol. II, Evanston: Northwestern University Press, 1973.

Chapter 12

The Freedom of a "Species Being": Humanist Marxism and Dialectical Materialism

The apocalyptic quality of Marxism has frequently been remarked by scholars. The Marxian philosophy of history, which is the framework of Marxian political and economic theory, seems in fact to be a secularized version of the Judaeo-Christian philosophy of history and eschatology. It portrays a stricken mankind, laboring through centuries of wickedness, suffering, and injustice, but emerging finally and suddenly into a paradise of well-being and righteousness, in which the Chosen People of the race, who have endured lengthy oppression, are given seats of honor. Naturalist necessity is apocalyptically replaced by noumenalist freedom and justice.

It is not surprising that a Rhenish Jew should understand the questions of life, death, and transcendence in these terms. Karl Marx was born in Trier (Trèves), a German Rhineland city, in 1818, into the family of a Jewish lawyer. The Prussian discriminatory legislation which relegated Jews to an inferior legal position was particularly burdensome to the Jews of the Rhineland, because they had enjoyed a brief moment of equality during the Napoleonic period. Like Moses, they had seen the Promised Land but were not allowed to enter it, and they felt their deprivation the more sorely.

It was quite natural that a sensitive intellectual like Marx, as a member of one oppressed group, and indignantly aware of its oppression, should identify himself with another disinherited segment of society, the urban working class, whose growing numbers held a power potential for sundering the bonds of injustice to which unhappy Jewry could never aspire.

Following a stormy student life of drunken brawling at the University of Bonn and ferocious asceticism and overwork at Berlin, where he buried himself in Hegelian philosophy, Marx began his public career of angry protest in 1842 as editor of the *Rheinische Zeitung,* a newspaper devoted to the cause of liberal reform—parliamentary representation and civil rights.

After a few months of Marx's editorship the paper was suppressed by the Prussian government, and Marx went to Paris to study and write. There he met the man who was to be his lifelong friend and collaborator, Friedrich Engels, the son of a wealthy German manufacturer who was disenchanted with his father's world. Engels had seen close at hand the misery of industrial life in the factory town of Barmen-Elberfeld, where he was brought up, and in Manchester, where his father had textile interests, and it was he who focused Marx's genius and outraged soul on the condition of the working classes. The two of them hammered out together the central doctrines of dialectical materialism, which found a public audience for the first time in the *Communist Manifesto,* a polemical tract they wrote together in Brussels in 1848 for the revolutionary Communist League.

That was a year of revolutionary explosions throughout Europe, and Marx is alleged to have played at least a minor role in one of them. He was expelled from Belgium on the basis of a police report that he had contributed to the purchase of arms for Belgian workers. Returning briefly to Paris, he set up a Communist League headquarters there, and then went back to Germany to play once more the part of a publicist, this time as editor of the *Neue Rheinische Zeitung,* in whose columns he lashed at the fumbling inactivity of the timid Frankfurt Assembly.

In 1849, Marx was expelled by the Prussian government and went to England, where he remained until his death in 1883. He lived in London in poverty, supporting his family chiefly on loans from his wealthy friend Engels, who had gone to work in Manchester for his father's firm. Marx spent most of his time in the British Museum, working away on the manuscript of his *magnum opus, Capital,* in which he applied the principles of historical materialism to an analysis of the development of capitalist economy. The massive work, not published in its entirety until after Marx's death, fills three stout volumes.

Marx as Humanist

Karl Marx did not begin his career as philosopher and revolutionary as a dialectical materialist, even though that label today has great currency in descriptions of his thought. The "scientific" Marx (a correlative expression), for whom man is assimilated to nature and whose social relations are controlled by laws as rigid as the laws of physical motion, was to develop only gradually, in his collaborative work with Friedrich Engels. Some writers, indeed, are prepared to maintain that the necessitarian and materialist categories of Marxist dialectics are wholly the work of Engels. According to this view, Marx, in his early works, transmuted Hegel's Idealism into humanism, by dropping the mysterious concept of *Geist* from his philosophical vocabulary, and remained a humanist—a believer in the irreducible autonomy of human thought and action—all his life.[1] We shall see later in this chapter that the controversy about the "real Marx" is not a merely academic dispute, but has political ramifications of the greatest importance.

Materialism

The transformation of Hegel's idealist formulation of dialectical process into a materialist theory was not accomplished by Marx himself, but was borrowed by him from the writings of Ludwig Feuerbach, a German Hegelian who was Marx's contemporary. In a volume of 1841, entitled *The Essence of Christianity,* this writer argued that Hegel was wrong in understanding history as the progress of *Geist,* or spirit, through alienation to self-realization in the life of mankind. Such a view of things required the positing of causal reality quite beyond our consciousness—initially autonomous *Geist.* More true to our experience was a view of things that began and stayed within human consciousness. Seeing things this way, it made sense to say that Spirit (or God) should be understood as self-alienated man.

> When man, the human species, projects an idealized image of itself into heaven as 'God' and worships this imaginary heavenly being, it becomes estranged from itself; its own ungodly earthly reality becomes alien and hateful. To overcome this alienation man must repossess his alienated being, take 'God' back into himself, recognize in man—and specifically in other human individuals—the proper object of care, love, and worship.[2]

This is the starting point of Marx's reinterpretation of the Hegelian worldview. Its implications were worked out by Marx in several writings of 1843-45, before the beginning of his collaboration with Engels, and these writings today form the basis of the humanist interpretation of Marxism.[3]

Though Marx, in these early writings, calls the position that he espouses "materialist," it was a standpoint worlds away from the mechanistic materialism which can be discerned in his later writings in collaboration

---

[1]See Shlomo Avineri, *The Social and Political Thought of Karl Marx* (Cambridge: Cambridge University Press, 1968), See also the discussion of this question by Robert C. Tucker, in the Introduction to his excellent anthology of Marxist writings, *The Marx-Engels Reader* (New York: W.W. Norton Co., Inc., 1972), pp. xvi-xvii, xxii-xxiii.

[2]Robert Tucker, summarizing Feuerbach's argument. Reprinted from *The Marx-Engels Reader,* edited by Robert C. Tucker, with the permission of W.W. Norton & Company, Inc., copyright © 1972 by W.W. Norton & Company, Inc., pp. xviii-xix.

[3]These include an unfinished commentary on Hegel's *Philosophy of Right* (1843), an essay on "The Jewish Question," published in the *Deutsch-Franzoesische Jahrbuecher* (1843), *The Economic and Philosophic Manuscripts* of 1844 (unpublished until 1932), and Part I of *The German Ideology* (1845).

with Engels, and still further from the "Dialectical Materialism" which his philosophy became in the hands of its Russian interpreters from Plekhanov to Lenin and Stalin.[4] Marx's commitment to materialism at this time consisted in his conviction that the truth about the human situation can only be understood by viewing man in his material involvement, as a producer of material goods, a fully sensuous activity. But this does not make man a mere reflex of the productive process. On the contrary, it is in the context of economic activity that man defines and expresses himself as an historical actor.

> Men . . . begin to distinguish themselves from animals as soon as they begin to *produce* their means of subsistence, a step which is conditioned by their physical organization . . .
> . . . This mode of production must not be considered simply as being the reproduction of the physical existence of the individuals. Rather it is a definite form of activity of these individuals, a definite form of expressing their life, a definite *mode of life* on their part.[5]

In his *Theses on Feuerbach* Marx makes it quite plain that this position is a marked qualification of Feuerbach's own more thoroughgoing materialism.

> The materialist doctrine that men are products of circumstances and upbringing, and that, therefore, changed men are products of other circumstances and changed upbringing, forgets that it is men who change circumstance and that it is essential to educate the educator himself.[6]

This way of looking at things is intimately tied in with Marx's espousal of revolution as a way out of the unhappy situation in which humankind finds itself. Feuerbach's materialism had been contemplative. But for Marx, as for Hegel, thought and action were not to be separated. In his XIth thesis on Feuerbach Marx tells us that "philosophers have *only interpreted* the world in various ways; the point, however, is to *change* it."[7]

To be effective, of course, revolutionary activity has to be grounded in a theoretical understanding of the situation to be revolutionized. If man had created God in the image of his own dream of a possible self and established this "in the clouds as an independent realm," this unnatural situation could

---

[4]Tucker has pointed out that the expression "Dialectical Materialism" was given currency by Georgi Plekhanov, a 19th-century Russian Marxist revolutionary, and that the authoritative exposition of the doctrine in Communist circles was for a long time an essay by Joseph Stalin which appeared as a section of his *History of the Communist Party of the Soviet Union (Bolshevik)*, a textbook. See Tucker's Introduction to *The Marx-Engels Reader, op. cit.*, p. xvi, fn. 2.

[5]*The German Ideology*, Part I, in Tucker, *op. cit.*, p. 114.

[6]*Theses on Feuerbach* in Tucker, *op. cit.*, p. 108.

[7]*Ibid.*, p. 109.

only "be explained by the cleavage and self-contradictions within [the] secular basis. The latter must itself, therefore, be understood in its contradiction and then, by the removal of the contradiction, revolutionized in practice."[8] It was in the *Economic and Philosophic Manuscripts of 1844* that Marx presented his first extensive analysis of the alienated or "contradictory" condition of the life of mankind, and of what might be done about it.

Man as Species Being

The leading theme of the 1844 manuscripts is that man's true self or essential nature is to be a "species being" *(Gattungswesen)*. When the term is translated "community being" or "universal being" we immediately see that Marx's thought on this fundamental question has evolved from the earlier speculation of Kant and Hegel, and indeed, that it has roots much further back—in the thought of Plato and Aristotle at the beginning of the Western tradition. For in Western philosophy the idea of the "universal" has always been a concept of intelligibility, goodness, and fulfillment. By contrast, the "particular" or purely individual has meant that which is unintelligible, and bad, in the sense of the partial or incomplete. And as for Kant and Hegel, to be conformed to the world of the universal meant "freedom," so too for Marx, the human being as a *Gattungswesen* is a free person. Marx expresses his thought in these terms:

> Man is a species being, not only because in practice and in theory he adopts the species as his object (his own as well as those of other beings), but—and this is only another way of expressing it—but also because he treats himself as the actual, living species; because he treats himself as a *universal* and therefore a free being."[9]

As a free and universal being, man is also a producer, a creative actor, harmoniously united in the work of free creation with nature and with other men, and thus with himself. "The productive life is the life of the species. It is life-engendering life. The whole character of a species—its species character—is contained in the character of its life-activity; and free, conscious activity is man's species character. Life itself appears only as a *means to life*."[10]

Alienated Man. But all this expresses the end of the historical process, when man finds his fulfillment—a teleonaturalist wish. The present reality is one of estrangement, alienation. Man sees himself now as a pure particular, an individual, set against and hostile to other persons as objects.

---

[8]*Ibid.*, p. 108.
[9]*Economic and Philosophic Manuscripts of 1844*, in Tucker, *op. cit.*, p. 61.
[10]*Ibid.*, p. 62.

He is avaricious and competitive; and he seeks to dominate and exploit both his fellow men and the natural environment. In this situation of egoistic isolation, man finds work a merely external affair, useful only to satisfy animal desires. It is also carried out under compulsion—from the necessity to live. And it has no human meaning for him, is not a creative enterprise in which the human personality is revealed.

In this unhappy situation man has only a dream of his true self, and it takes the form of religion, in which he imagines his universal life as the life of a transcendent god. Man comforts himself in this false consciousness with the idea that he will participate in that transcendent world after death. But this is merely the expression of his "*alienated* self-consciousness."[11]

Capitalist Alienation

Such has been the unhappy situation all through history, since from early times the mode of production, the basic institution of human life, has been organized on a particular rather than a universal basis. It has been built upon private property. Under capitalism, however, the most developed form of property, alienation has achieved a most extreme and degrading form. Every one of the natural unities of the equal life of man as a *Gattungswesen* are missing. Labor has been radically separated from capital and reduced to pure "thingness," bought and sold as a commodity on the market. And the division of labor has proceeded so far that each man plays only a meaningless small role in the production process.

The capitalists who preside over this system are as much one-sided "non-persons" as the workers. They can think only of piling up profits and have no conception of creative work. They compete with one another in a struggle of mutual destruction. Workers obtain only a subsistence wage and live like animals. They are subordinated as subjects to their objects—their product—in a production system of inequality and domination. They are therefore unfree to be creative persons. The production process remains physically life-engendering (at a low level), but is throughout spiritually stultifying.

Communist Fulfillment

This analysis is not far removed in tone, even in detail, from Hegel's reflection on the effects of capitalism on human consciousness. Marx's program for the future, however, is radically different from that proposed by Hegel. The future for Marx does not belong to a liberal corporative state governed by a class of moral-technical experts. It belongs instead to a thoroughgoing communist organization of human life, in which all the

[11]*Ibid.,* p. 96.

natural unities are completed in a situation of equality and mutual cooperation. The division of labor is abolished in favor of perfect versatility,
founded upon an achieved superabundance. Alienation is done away with as
free persons participate creatively in communal enterprise. Man is restored
to unity with nature, with his fellow man, and with himself. As a fulfilled
species being man can at last recognize himself in his product. The production process has become life-engendering at all levels.

> In place of the *wealth* and *poverty* of political economy come the *rich human
> being* and rich *human* need. The *rich* human being is simultaneously the human
> being *in need of* a totality of human life-activities—the man in whom his own
> realization exists as an inner necessity, as *need.*[12]

Transition to Communism

How is this transformation of the historical order to occur? Marx
found the movement toward communism already under way. In the circumstances of developing capitalism, the outline of universal man was already
evident. The productive forces necessary to the superabundance of the day
of perfect universality were being enormously increased by capitalist
enterprise. And the spread of capitalist industry over the globe that was
working these miracles of production had revealed man's essence as a
creator. Along with this went the development of natural science as the basis
of industrial production, the emergence of a science of man, and the dimly
foreseen unity of all the sciences.

> History itself is a *real* part of *natural history*—of nature's coming to be man.
> Natural science will in time subsume under itself the science of man, just as the
> science of man will subsume under itself natural science: there will be *one*
> science.[13]

Negative Universality. The emergence of communism Marx also
found visible in the development of a number of negative equalities or un-
iversalities in capitalist life. He wrote ironically of the universalizing effects
of money in the market economy. The man who has money can buy his way
out of the confining particularities of his original situation.

> Thus, what I *am* and *am capable* of is by no means determined by my in-
> dividuality. I am ugly, but I can buy for myself the most *beautiful* of women.
> Therefore I am not *ugly,* for the effect of *ugliness*—its deterrent power—is nul-
> lified by money. I, in my character as an individual, am *lame,* but money fur-
> nishes me with twenty-four feet. Therefore I am not lame. I am bad, dishonest,
> unscrupulous, stupid; but money is honoured, and therefore so is its possessor.

[12]*Ibid.,* p. 77.
[13]*Ibid.,* p. 76-77.

. . . . Does not my money therefore transform all my incapacities into their contrary?

The overturning and confounding of all human and natural qualities, the fraternization of impossibilities—the divine power of money—lies in its *character* as men's estranged alienating and self-disposing *species-nature.* Money is the alienated ability of mankind.[14]

Crude Communism.   More ironies are involved in Marx's picture of the "crude communism" that would eventually emerge from the historical process. This would reveal in universal form the vile and negative things of the reign of private property. It would be exemplified in "the bestial form of counterposing to *marriage* . . . the *community of women,* in which a woman becomes a piece of the *communal* and *common* property."[15] In its early stages the communist order would also be "only a community of *labour,* and an equality of *wages* paid out by the communal capitalist—the *community* as the universal capitalist."[16] In the political order, "the annulment of the state" would be "yet still incomplete" and would take a form that might be either "democratic or despotic."[17] We have here a vague foreshadowing of the idea of the "dictatorship of the proletariat."

The Fulfillment of Communism.   Once the negative aspects of universalization had been lived through, the pendulum would swing the other way and the human community would enter into its own as a true *Gattungswesen.*

> *Communism* as the *positive* transcendence of *private property,* or *human self-estrangement,* and therefore as the real *appropriation of the human essence* by and for man; communism therefore as the complete return of man to himself as a social (i.e., human) being—a return become conscious, and accomplished within the entire wealth of previous development. This communism, as fully-developed naturalism equals humanism, and as fully-developed humanism equals naturalism; it is the *genuine* resolution of the conflict between man and nature and between man and man—the true resolution of the strife between existence and essence, between objectification and self-confirmation, between freedom and necessity, between the individual and the species. Communism is the riddle of history solved, and it knows itself to be this solution.[18]

From Humanism to Historical Materialism

It is important to notice that in his early writings Marx focuses his effort on painting a picture of human nature and the human situation, both in its actual and potential forms. His intention is to depict the free human

[14]*Ibid.,* p. 81.
[15]*Ibid.,* p. 68.
[16]*Ibid.,* p. 69.
[17]*Ibid.,* p. 70.
[18]*Ibid.,* p. 70.

person, in his alienation and in his fulfillment. Little is said of historical process, or, in detail, of the place of revolution in that process. These were the subjects that were to occupy Marx in his collaboration with Engels in the years to come. And in the course of this work, the categories of humanist freedom would gradually give way to the categories of necessary dialectical process. Whether this was the result of the subject matter—the search for a science of history based on a discovery of historical laws—or due to the influence of Engels is not clear. It is certainly the case that Engels was much more interested in natural science than Marx, and that he attempted to extrapolate dialectical theory from the history of culture to physical nature.[19] In the section which follows, the Marx-Engels theory of "historical materialism" is set forth as an explication of the dynamic of history, especially of its capitalist phase, embracing a theory of class struggle and revolution, together with a projection of the post-revolutionary political and social order. The reader will notice that many of the references to the impersonal, necessitarian elements of the theory are to the solo writings of Engels, especially the *Anti-Duehring*.

Marxism as Science: Historical Materialism

The first fruit of Marx's collaboration with Engels was *The German Ideology* (1845), in which an effort was made to discover the structure of the historical process that would lead from alienation to free consciousness. As Tucker notes, the concept of alienation itself now falls away, and "we are in the more impersonal world of Marxian social theory as made familiar in the later writings."[20]

> The social structure and the State are continually evolving out of the life-process of definite individuals, but of individuals, not as they may appear in their own or other people's imagination, but as they really are; i.e., as they are effective, produce materially, and are active under definite material limits, presuppositions and conditions independent of their will. ... Morality, religion, metaphysics, all the rest of ideology and their corresponding forms of consciousness, thus no longer retain the semblance of independence. ... Life is not determined by consciousness, but consciousness by life.[21]

What precisely is involved in the activity of man as producer? The activity has three main aspects: "what is produced and how it is produced, and

[19]Tucker, Introduction to *The Marx-Engels Reader, op. cit.*, pp. xxii and xxxiii.

[20]*Ibid.*, p. xxii.

[21]Karl Marx and Friedrich Engels, *The German Ideology* (New York: International Publishers, 1947), pp. 13-15.

how the product is exchanged."[22] An economy may be predominantly pastoral, agricultural, or industrial. This is the "what" of production. The "how" constitutes the technology and social organization of production. There may be, for example, handicrafts manufacture in the home, which is individual, not social in character. Or there may be highly mechanized mass production techniques, requiring the cooperation of many men in an intricate organization. Next there is the "how" of exchange—primitive barter or a highly developed money and credit system, for example. Added to these three fundamental elements are a set of property relations—individual or social ownership of capital, the separation or conjunction of labor and capital. These are the sum total of the conditions and relations of production.

Over and over again, Marx and Engels underline the unique causal importance of the economic order. From it "*alone* can be explained, the political and intellectual history of [an] epoch." It is "the *basis* of every social order." When the mode of production changes, men "change *all* their social relations." The mode of production "*conditions* the whole process of social, political, and intellectual life."[23] Nevertheless, here and there they introduce a qualification, to avert an overly simple interpretation of their meaning. Engels, for example, in a letter of 1890, says that in the materialist conception of reality "the determining element . . . is *ultimately* the production and reproduction in real life," but that if "somebody twists this into the statement that the economic element is the *only* determining one, he transforms it into a meaningless, abstract and absurd phrase." Other things, including philosophical and religious ideas, also exercise an influence, and "there is an interaction of all these elements," an infinite series of "parallelograms of forces" in the causal complex, plus an "endless *host* of accidents." Any particular event therefore may not be explicable in economic terms. For example, it could not be argued, Engels says, "that among the many small states of North Germany Brandenburg was specifically determined by economic necessity to become the great power embodying the economic, linguistic, and after the Reformation, also the religious differences between north and south." Nevertheless, other causes remain subordinate in the large picture and "the economic movement finally asserts itself as necessary."[24]

[22]Friedrich Engels, *Herr Eugen Duehring's Revolution in Science* (hereafter cited as *Anti-Duehring*) in Emile Burns, A Handbook of Marxism (New York: Random House, 1935), p. 279.

[23]Karl Marx and Friedrich Engels, *The Communist Manifesto* (New York: Appleton-Century-Crofts, Inc., 1955), p. 5; Engels, *Anti-Duehring,* in Burns, *op. cit.,* p. 279; Karl Marx, *The Poverty of Philosophy* in *ibid.,* p. 355; Karl Marx, *A Contribution to "The Critique of Political Economy,"* in *ibid.,* p. 372. [Emphasis supplied.]

[24]Engels to J. Bloch, London, Sept. 21, 1890, in Karl Marx and Friedrich Engels, *Correspondence, 1846-1895* (New York: International Publishers, 1934), pp. 475, 476.

The necessary laws of the materialist social world produce neither a static nor cyclical order, but one which is constantly changing and which is unilinear in its change. The world in fact is *fundamentally* flux in this conception, for *"motion is the manner of existence of matter."*[25] This is one of the things that Marx and Engels had learned from their early discipleship to Hegel, that the world cannot be understood "as a complex of ready-made things, but as a complex of *processes,* in which the things apparently stable no less than their mind-images in our heads, the concepts, go through an uninterrupted change of coming into being and passing away."[26] Darwin had confirmed the truth of the proposition for physical nature; Marx and Engels would apply it to society.

Unlike the Darwinian laws of physical evolution, however, the economic laws of Marx are teleological, though in a rather special sense, for they tend toward a definite end, the expansion of the "forces of production" to a capacity which ensures a superabundance of material goods. History is a process of development from universal poverty to universal abundance. It proceeds dialectically.

In its materialist formulation by Marx and Engels, the dialectic involves the opposition and synthesis not of ideas but of physical states. One microcosmic example of its operation given by Engels is the process of raising orchids. When a seed of an orchid is planted, it disappears, is "negated," and in its place grows an orchid plant which is the "negation of the negation." But this process gives us "not only more seeds, but also qualitatively better seeds, which produce more beautiful flowers, and each fresh repetition of the process, each repeated negation of the negation increases this improvement."[27] To cast the same example into other dialectical terms, the initial seed is the "thesis," the orchid flower the "antithesis," and the new and better seed the "synthesis."

In the macrocosm, the dialectic operates through the negation and synthesis of modes of production, until the superabundant system emerges, bringing the process of negation to an end. At the most general level and in the broadest perspective, the development has three stages. In the initial stage we have primitive communism, or communalism. This dissolves away into its opposite, private property and individual production. As the forces of production grow under the new dispensation, the new order itself is gradually negated. From individual production for individual needs we pass to social production for social needs. For a while the old individualist *relations* of production—private property—are maintained, but they become a

[25]Engels, *Anti-Duehring,* in Burns, *op. cit.,* p. 237.
[26]Engels, *Ludwig Feuerbach,* in *ibid.,* p. 225.
[27]Engels, *Anti-Duehring,* in *ibid.,* p. 262.

fetter on the expanding forces. "At a certain stage of their development the material productive forces of society come into contradiction with the existing productive relationships . . . the property relationships within which they had moved before." These are finally burst asunder. "An epoch of social revolution opens. With the change in the economic foundation the whole vast superstructure is more or less rapidly transformed."[28] We then enter into communist relationships once more—the negation of the negation. We have moved from communal poverty through an opposite form of social organization to communal abundance.

Engels tells us that dialectical analysis permits us to see only general trends with accuracy. "Dialectics is nothing more than the sum of the general laws of motion and development of Nature, human society and thought." It does not give us the ability to see exactly where things stand at a particular time. Mistakes will be made in detailed analysis. "I do not say anything concerning the *particular* process of development," he writes. "I leave out of account the peculiarities of each separate individual process."[29] One must always be "conscious of the necessary limitations of all acquired knowledge, of the fact that it is conditioned by the circumstances in which it was acquired."[30] Often we may feel that the events we examine are pure accidents. Even the appearance of Marx as the first thinker to have a genuine insight into the law of the dialectic, Engels regards as "not an inevitable event, following of necessity in the chain of historical development, but a mere happy accident."[31] He might have appeared five hundred years earlier or later than he did. Nevertheless, we know that "the so-called accidental is the form behind which necessity hides itself."[32] We are able to see the general line of development and predict the final outcome, but exact analysis of links in the causal chain is not possible.

From Necessity to Freedom.   When the dialectic has worked itself out and the superabundant economy has come into being, a rather remarkable change will take place in the fundamental relationship of man to nature, according to the Marxian prediction. Through the course of the ages, the expansion of productive power, and the myriad changes in social organization, art, philosophy, and religion which have accompanied it, have occurred independently of human volition and reason. But when superabundant production is achieved, the roles of man and nature will be reversed. After a long assimilation to nature, man will finally emerge as the conqueror

---

[28]Marx, *Critique of "Political Economy,"* in *ibid.,* p. 372.

[29]Engels, *Anti-Duehring,* in *ibid.,* p. 266.

[30]Engels, *Ludwig Feuerbach,* in *ibid.,* p. 225.

[31]Friedrich Engels, *Socialism: Utopian and Scientific,* in Arthur P. Mendel, ed., *Essential Works of Marxism* (New York: Bantam Books, 1961), p. 47.

[32]Engels, *Ludwig Feuerbach,* in Burns, *op. cit.,* p. 225.

and lord of nature. We return at last to the humanist language of the manuscripts of 1844.

> The laws of his own social activity, which have hitherto confronted him as external, dominating laws of Nature, will then be applied by man with complete understanding, and hence will be dominated by man. Men's own social organization which has hitherto stood in opposition to them as if arbitrarily decreed by Nature and history, will then become the voluntary act of men themselves. . . . It is only from this point that men, with full consciousness, will fashion their own history; it is only from this point that the social causes set in motion by men will have, predominantly and in constantly increasing measure, the effects willed by men. It is humanity's leap from the realm of necessity into the realm of freedom.[33]

Engels explains that the Marxian conception of freedom does not abolish the natural laws which have operated inexorably throughout history. Freedom consists rather in "the control over ourselves and over external nature which is founded on knowledge of natural necessity."[34] In this context it is another word for power. Marx and Engels would probably accept an analogy to the "freedom" which mankind has acquired through the discovery of the secrets of atomic energy. Atomic energy gives us the power to exert a control over nature never before dreamed of, and therefore freedom from control by nature. But our newly acquired power rests on *knowledge* of physical laws, not on their supersession.

Bridge Building: A Teleonaturalist Theory

To what ends should (or will) mankind use this new-found freedom and power? About this Marx and Engels say nothing except that there will be a "settled plan" of action. They do not say what the "settled plan" will be, with which liberated mankind will create its paradise. It will not be according to the scheme of any traditional philosophy or religion, which Marx labels the "mystical veil" of the "life-process of society, . . . based on the process of material production."[35] Religion is merely a fiction which helps realize the goal of superabundance but has no other function. The naturalistic metaphysics of Marx seems, in fact, to rule out of court all values but technical mastery, power. Yet one has always the feeling that Marx and Engels are trying to say that the freedom of their utopia is only the necessary condition for the realization of man's age-old dream of righteousness, justice, and the flowering of the spirit. In one place Engels

[33]Friedrich Engels, *Anti-Duehring* (New York: International Publishers, 1939), pp. 309-10.
[34]*Ibid.,* p. 125.
[35]Karl Marx, *Capital,* Vol. I, tr. Samuel Moore and Edward Aveling (Chicago: Charles H. Kerr and Company, 1915), p. 92.

speaks of "a really human morality" as possible only in the society which will postdate the dialectic.[36] What we call history is really only a kind of prehistory of mankind.

In this prehistory, man is simply one animal among others, struggling for existence. But in the new society he "cuts himself off from the animal world, leaves the conditions of animal existence behind him, and enters conditions which are really human."[37] Man as man, i.e., man as the rational and social animal of the tradition, will come into his own only after he has mastered the laws of physical necessity.

The Exploitative State and Beyond

What is the character of the political order within the framework of dialectical materialism? In what way is it produced by ultimate economic causes, and what functions does it perform? How does it change? What differences will be found between politics in the period of necessity and politics under freedom? Let us first sketch out a generalized answer to these questions and then present, in Marxian fashion, an analysis of the evolution of a particular political system, the "bourgeois-capitalist" state.

An Instrument of the Ruling Class

The reader will recall that Marxian theory posits an original communal order as the thesis in the great triad of the historical dialectic. This is identified by Engels with the primitive Greek and Roman tribal society which predated the emergence of the *polis* of Mediterranean antiquity and with the German tribal order of the Dark Ages which antedated feudalism. Engels describes the government of these societies as "primitive natural democracy." Its apparatus (chief and council) is extremely simple, and it is responsible to the entire society. There is "no place for domination and subjection." It receives the "free, voluntary respect" of all.[38] What is its economic base? Primitive society is a poor society. There is virtually no division of labor, and little exchange. Those tools which a man makes himself he alone owns, and with them he produces just enough for his own consumption. But land is held in common as are all the instruments of production which are *socially* made and used, such as the long-boat. The social order is egalitarian; there are no class distinctions.

As more efficient tools and methods of production are developed (Engels does not say *why* there is technical progress in primitive society),

[36]Engels, *Anti-Duehring,* in Burns, *op. cit.,* p. 249.
[37]*Ibid.,* p. 298.
[38]Engels, *The Origin of the Family,* in *ibid.,* pp. 314, 326, 330.

production increases "in all branches—cattle raising, agriculture, home handicrafts."[39] It becomes possible now to produce a surplus, which enters into exchange, and wealth increases. But the new efficiency of tools puts pressure on the labor supply, for it is now clear that there are no fixed limits on what can be produced, and each member of the tribe must work longer and harder in order to swell the quantity of the surplus. Still more labor is needed and so the tribe goes to war to procure slaves. This constitutes the "original sin" in the Marxian scheme. Society is now divided into two great classes of exploiters and exploited. Wealth grows rapidly, but it is individual, not communal, wealth. Still new classes develop, the rich and the poor. The division of labor proceeds further, which gives rise to yet further class distinctions based on occupation. The land is divided up and becomes private property.

From the thesis of communal, classless society in this way arises the antithesis of individualist, class-organized society, the "negation" of the thesis. With the change a new political order arises—the "state." It is organized territorially rather than on the blood group; it is a complex affair, and it is expensive to maintain. Taxes become necessary. The heart of the system is an elaborate public force, which is required to keep in check the class antagonisms of the new society. Sometimes it has a kind of independence of all elements of society and operates as an arbiter of the class conflicts, but usually it appears simply as an instrument of the ruling, economically dominant class for the repression of the exploited segments of society. In antiquity the state was used by the free citizenry to control the slave population; in medieval Europe it was a tool of the feudal aristocracy; today it is a weapon of the bourgeoisie against the proletariat. Its authority rests not on free consent and spontaneous respect but on fear of coercion.

This remains the character of the political order from the breakup of original communism through all the stages of the dialectic down to the appearance of the final communist society. As the forces of production expand, new forms of society and of the state are brought into being, and in turn give way to others. But every form of state represents only a particular class, never the social whole. Each passing system dies hard, and the new emerges amid fierce class struggles. "The history of all hitherto existing society," write Marx and Engels in the *Communist Manifesto*, "is the history of class struggles. Free man and slave, patrician and plebeian, lord and serf, guild master and journeyman, in a word, oppressor and oppressed, stood in constant opposition to one another, carried on an uninterrupted, now hidden, now open fight, a fight that each time ended, either in a revolutionary reconstruction of society at large, or in the common ruin of the contending classes."[40]

[39]*Ibid.,* p. 317.
[40]Marx and Engels, *Communist Manifesto,* p. 9.

The class struggle frequently involves the exercise of force and violence, both by the ruling class, through the public authority, and by the revolutionary elements. Force acts as a salutary instrument in the Marxian scheme. It "is the midwife of every old society which is pregnant with the new, . . . it is the instrument by the aid of which social movement forces its way through and shatters the dead, fossilized, political forms."[41] When employed by the public authority, it may occasionally work against economic development rather than for it; there will be rear-guard actions. But in these cases, force succumbs ultimately to the power of economic development. Exceptions are a few instances in which a barbarian people destroy a more civilized, with the result that productive capacity is destroyed.—At least occasionally, the dialectic moves backwards! Engels writes, however, that when an internal public force stands against economic development, it always loses.[42]

Marx and Engels did envisage the possibility of peaceful change, of evolution as opposed to revolution in the political order, at least in exceptional instances. Thus Engels writes in his preface to the first English translation of *Capital* in 1886 that in England "the inevitable social revolution might be effected entirely by peaceful and legal means."[43]

The Role of Religion and Morality in History

Marxian theory associates with each form of politico-economic order a particular religious and ethical belief system. While only primitive democracy rests on a spontaneous and general consensus as to its goodness and legitimacy, religious and ethical dogmas which support the regime will be widespread in any particular system, furnishing it with an aura of legitimacy. The state does not rest *purely* on force and violence. But every morality is only a class morality. It derives always in the last resort "from the practical relations on which [the] class position is based—from the economic relations in which [men] carry on production and exchange."[44] For example, "Thou shalt not steal!" to Marx and Engels is a norm peculiarly fitted to a society based on private property. A given moral code, therefore, will have broad acceptance only in the heyday of a system. As a society moves toward its end, the veils are lifted, and the revolutionary class sees injustice lurking behind the moral system and understands it only as a rationalization of the interest of the ruling class. This realization gives a further impetus to the demand for change.

[41]Engels, *Anti-Duehring*, in Burns, *op. cit.*, p. 278.
[42]*Ibid.*, pp. 277, 278.
[43]Marx, *Capital*, I, p. 32.
[44]Engels, *Anti-Duehring*, in Burns, *op. cit.*, p. 248.

Marx and Engels adopt a strangely ambivalent position in their own moral judgments of political and social events, but one which is easily explicable by what we have just said. At times their writings virtually scream with moral indignation against what they deem the wicked behavior of various ruling classes, especially the capitalist bourgeoisie. At other times we find them praising harsh and oppressive institutions. In one place Engels, for example, feels "compelled to say . . . that the introduction of slavery under the conditions of that time was a great step forward."[45] And there are also passages of praise for the accomplishments of the hated bourgeoisie. By subjecting the countryside to the city, they write, the bourgeoisie "has rescued a considerable part of the population from the idiocy of rural life." During its brief rule, the bourgeoisie "has created more massive and colossal productive forces than have all preceding generations together."[46]

The contradictions are, of course, explained by the recognition that Marx and Engels judge with two different moralities. When ranting against the bourgeoisie, presumably they are engaging in a revolutionary act as the vanguard of the proletariat, and are seeing questions of good and evil through proletarian eyes. When saying that force is salutary and that slavery was beneficial, and when lauding the achievements of capitalism, they are looking at things from outside the dialectic, so to speak, and with reference to the final result of the dialectical process, economic superabundance, which assumes the status of sole value in the system.

The Withering Away of the State

With the achievement of the superabundant economy, the state will have finished its historical work, in the Marxian scheme of things. "The first act in which the State really comes forward as the representative of society as a whole—the taking possession of the means of production in the name of society—is at the same time its last independent act as a State." "The society that organizes production anew on the basis of a free and equal association of the producers will put the whole State machine where it will then belong; in the museum of antiquities, side by side with the spinning wheel and the bronze ax."[47] Since the final phase of the dialectic re-establishes common ownership of the instruments of production, contending classes, which are the result of private property, will disappear, and with them class conflict. And since the function of the state is conceived as the moderation of class conflict and the repression of the ruled classes, its utility will then be at an

[45]*Ibid.,* p. 275.
[46]Marx and Engels, *Communist Manifesto,* p. 14.
[47]Engels, *Anti-Duehring, The Origin of the Family,* in Burns, *op. cit.,* pp. 295-96, 332.

end. "The government of persons is replaced by the administration of things and the direction of the process of production. The State is not 'abolished,' *it withers away*."[48]

Accompanying the economic, social, and political changes of the last great act of the dialectic, Marxian theory foresees a radical change in human behavior as we have known it. Aggressiveness disappears along with the "furies of private interest."[49] Men become perfectly socialized creatures, with only benevolent and cooperative impulses. Unlike the prescriptions of the classical and scholastic traditions for the good society, however, the Marxian recipe does not call for a soul-struggle by individuals, for the interior conquest and mastery of the self. Indeed, the men of the Marxian utopia remain interested in the things of the self; they remain individualists, who are now guaranteed "the completely unrestricted development and exercise of their physical and mental faculties."[50]

The point is that in the new environment the development of one individual does not interfere with the development of another. There is nothing to fight about, for *all* are guaranteed the material conditions for their self-realization. The creation of moral and social behavior is not seen as a problem of interior education and the mastery of antisocial motives by discipline of mind and will, but as an exterior affair only. In effect, the moral problem is reduced to a technical one, the proper organization of the environment. In this we are reminded of Rousseau. If the original sin was not an act of bad will but an alteration of the social environment quite independent of human willing, redemption occurs in a similarly impersonal, one might even say inhuman, way. This is a function of the underlying naturalistic framework.

Theory of Capitalist Development

Let us now bring our Marxian camera in for a close-up of a particular segment of the dialectical process, the period of capitalist emergence, fulfillment, and crisis. The analysis begins with medieval society, for every stage of the dialectical process is rooted in and grows out of the preceding stage. Every thesis begets its own antithesis.

Medieval economy was predominantly agricultural. Land and, to some extent, labor as well (serf labor) were owned or otherwise controlled by the feudal nobility, who were the ruling class. Manufacture was carried on by the burghers of the towns, who, though free men, constituted "an oppressed estate liable to pay dues to the ruling feudal nobility, recruited from serfs and villeins of every type." Production was small-scale, and technology

[48]Engels, *Anti-Duehring*, in *ibid.*, p. 296.
[49]Marx, *Capital*, I, p. 15.
[50]Engels, *Anti-Duehring*, in Burns, *op. cit.*, p. 298.

was primitive. Implements "were the instruments of labour of individuals, intended only for individual use, and therefore necessarily puny, dwarfish, restricted." Production was also highly decentralized—each manor produced only for itself—and there was little exchange. In addition, the handicrafts industry of the town was "hemmed in by all the thousandfold guild privileges and local provincial customs barriers."[51]

The dynamic factor within this system was the bourgeoisie. Despite all the limitations of feudal society, this class developed handicrafts manufacture and exchange "to a relatively high level." And with the voyages of discovery at the end of the fifteenth century, its horizons broadened measurably. Trade, formerly carried on only with the Middle East, was extended to America and India. An enormous expansion of wealth ensued. Gold poured into Europe, and the demand for goods increased sharply.[52]

The rising demand could not be met within the confines of feudal society, because the structure of that society severely limited the scale of production. It became a "fetter" on production, to use a favorite term of Marx and Engels. As a consequence, the growing bourgeoisie came into conflict with the feudality, and a class struggle ensued which was to culminate in the triumph of the bourgeoisie as the new ruling class. The French Revolution represented, in the political order, the climax of the movement from feudalism to capitalism.

"Freedom and equality of rights" were the objects of the bourgeois revolution. These were required if production was to expand. "Trade on a large scale . . . world trade, requires free owners of commodities who are unrestricted in their movements and have equal rights as traders to exchange their commodities on the basis of laws that are equal for them all."[53] And the transition from handicraft to manufacture demanded a working class free of guild restrictions, free to contract away their labor to the capitalist entrepreneur. The political superstructure created by the bourgeoisie was republican, theoretically a vehicle for representing *all* the interests of society. Actually, it became simply a committee of the new ruling class, through limitations of the franchise and other devices.

No sooner was the bourgeoisie triumphant than contradictions began to appear in the new, but still imperfect, society, according to Marx and Engels. While the property relations of the new order were built on individualist principles, production came to be organized more and more on a social basis. No longer did the workman produce with instruments of his own, alone in his own cottage, for a limited market. Now the capitalist owned the instruments of production and brought together large groups of

[51]*Ibid.,* pp. 269, 270, 281.
[52]*Ibid.,* p. 251.
[53]*Ibid.,* pp. 251-52.

men to operate them socially in the factory and to produce *en masse* for an ever expanding market.

Still other antitheses emerge as the system develops. Beginning as widespread competition among a host of individual entrepreneurs, capitalism develops into a monopoly of a few very powerful owners, according to Marxian analysis. "One capitalist always kills many."[54] The centralization and the socialization of production proceed together. As the number of the capitalist bourgeoisie declines, the proletariat, which is created as a class by the capitalist system, expands and becomes ever more revolutionary. It takes up the demand for freedom and equality first voiced by the bourgeoisie and adds to it a new and broader meaning quite incompatible with the capitalist system. Along with these events the forces of production expand colossally under capitalism. But a point is reached where effective demand fails and the vast product cannot be consumed. It becomes a glut on the market.

Value and Surplus Value.   To understand these elements in Marxian theory, we must inquire into the Marxian conception of capitalist motivation, and this leads us first to the Marxian theory of value. Marx sees human labor as the only source of value. Natural resources acquire social value only when they have been removed from nature and mixed with human labor. So far as the act of production goes, "productive activity . . . is nothing but the expenditure of human labour-power."[55] Capital goods are merely stored-up past labor.

Under capitalism, according to Marx, the whole product properly belongs to all the workers who create it, but instead it is appropriated by the capitalist, who himself contributes nothing to the production process. The capitalist must, of course, pay the worker something of his product in order to keep him alive. But it is only a subsistence wage that he pays. If the worker produces twelve hours of value in his working day, he may receive back four hours' worth of wages. The rest of his product, which Marx calls "surplus value," is appropriated by the entrepreneur.

Now, the Marxian capitalist is a single-minded person whose only desire in life is to increase the amount of surplus value (or "profit") which he can wring from the workers. He can do this either by lengthening the working day or by increasing the efficiency of the worker, so that he can produce a subsistence wage in a shorter period of working time. The capitalist accomplishes this by revolutionizing technology and by replacing less efficient by more efficient machinery. If it takes four hours under technology *"a"* for the worker to earn his keep, under technology *"b"* he can produce a subsistence wage in only two hours. This allows the capitalist to appropriate ten instead of only eight hours of value.

[54]*Ibid.,* p. 259.
[55]Marx, *Capital,* I, p. 51.

The capitalist's revolutionizing of production in search of increased surplus value produces three results: (1) It moves the economy toward monopoly, as the poor and inefficient entrepreneurs, who cannot afford new capital equipment, go under and are cast into the proletariat. (2) Machines replace men, and workers are thrown out of jobs. A "reserve army" of labor builds up, which is virtually destitute and lives in abject misery. (3) The capitalists who remain cannot realize their surplus value, because there is not enough purchasing power to take the goods from the market. Overproduction occurs, and vast quantities of commodities lie on the shelves unsold.

The Crisis of Capitalism. At this point, capitalism becomes as feudalism before it, a fetter on production, according to Marx and Engels. While earlier capitalists had effected an enormous expansion of productive forces, they now begin to limit production and to solve business crises by destroying productive forces. This is the death knell of the system.

The revolutionary proletariat steps in to expropriate the capitalists and institute the communal ownership of property. This is virtually all that remains to be done in laying the foundations of the new society. Capitalism has already centralized and socialized production, created a worldwide market, "given a cosmopolitan character to production and consumption in every country," destroyed the distinction between city and country, and brought the forces of production to the verge of superabundance. It has destroyed the illusions of religion and "drowned the most heavenly ecstasies of religious fervor, of chivalrous enthusiasm, of Philistine sentimentalism, in the icy waters of egotistical calculation." Capitalism has also created the beginnings of a world culture and made "national one-sidedness and narrow-mindedness more and more impossible" (one of the least perceptive of Marx's observations on the trend of things!).[56]

While earlier class struggles were complex affairs, the conflict has been simplified for the final "Armageddon" of the dialectic. Only two classes, the bourgeoisie and the proletariat, now stand locked in opposition. The world is on the verge of the proletarian revolution. Through the irony of the dialectic, the capitalists by their own acts in quest of surplus value are preparing their own destruction by creating the proletariat and swelling its numbers.

The proletariat is led on to battle by the Communist Party. Communists are the "philosopher-kings" of the Marxian world, for they alone fully understand the dialectical movement of history and hence know what action is called for. They are "that section which pushes forward all others."[57] Thus theory and practice are joined at the barricades. The dialectic has not produced a uniformly developed capitalism; different parts of the

[56]Marx and Engels, *The Communist Manifesto,* pp. 12, 13.
[57]*Ibid.,* p. 23.

world are at different stages of evolution. It is the mission of communists to support every revolutionary movement wherever it may be found, even bourgeois revolutions where the feudal order has not been completely erased. Their work is one of universal agitation and protest, hastening the movement of the dialectical process.

Marx and Engels say virtually nothing of the structure of society after the proletarian revolution. All we are told is that it will be an apolitical world, without conflict because of its material abundance and because it will be without classes. Government will no longer involve the coercion of men but merely the administration of social benefits. Presumably, the men who are to inherit this promised land will be enlightened by their new condition as masters of physical necessity and will see clearly what has to be done. Marx and Engels, writing this side of Armageddon, could but see as "through a glass darkly."

From Historical to Dialectical Materialism

Since the time of Marx and Engels, "historical materialism" has been transformed into the theoretical edifice of "dialectical materialism." The bulk of this work has, of course, been done in the Soviet Union, by the theoreticians of the established authoritarian regime. Lenin added a theory of revolutionary tactics to the sacred writ, and some doctrine on the postrevolutionary development of communist society. Stalin, Khrushchev, Mao Tse-Tung and others have added still more, and the end of the literature is not in sight. But we have no room here to describe and analyze these later Marxian writings.

Much has been said about what is orthodox and what is unorthodox Marxism in these writings, and about whether Marx was right or wrong. Such debate is futile. The original scriptures are so general in their formulas that they are susceptible of a variety of readings and a variety of applications in the interpretation of particular historical events.

There is no theoretical way by which any individual Marxist can establish his application as the correct one or prove the validity of the theory. Marx and Engels themselves denied that particular events were perfectly intelligible, which implies that particular events cannot be predicted. Only the general laws of historical motion could be understood, they claimed. But how are they to be verified? When Marxists succeed in coming to power, they take this as a demonstration both of the validity of the original theory and of their own development and application of it. There is little doubt that Messrs. Brezhnev and Kosygin, who have seen the USSR rise to the first rank of power in a little over fifty years under communist auspices, are true believers in Marx, in Lenin, and in their own additions to the gospel. Russian success is sufficient demonstration of the validity of Marxism, just as to the common man the explosion of an atom bomb is a demonstration of the truth of nuclear physics as a theoretical system.

There is, of course, one substantial difference between nuclear physics and Marxist political science. Atomic particles do not think about their behavior, and are controlled by laws which operate quite independently of their "will." While Marxists claim that men are similarly controlled, they grant that behavior is at least *proximately* conditioned by ideas in people's heads. If a proletarian revolution is to be achieved, men must think that they are proletarians and they must will the revolution. They must be taught about the dialectic. Atomic particles do not need to know nuclear physics in order to explode. But no Marxist has *demonstrated* that certain men are *bound* to think themselves revolutionary proletarians, or that men in general have as little intellectual and spiritual autonomy as Marxism claims. Therefore, Marxian political science cannot be a science as physics is a science. It is rather a vision, a faith, a prophecy, a wish. As Alexander Gray put it so well, "To consider whether Marx was 'right' or 'wrong' . . . is, in the last resort, sheer waste of time; for when we consort with Marx we are no longer in the world of reason or logic. He saw visions—clear visions of the passing of all things, much more nebulous visions of how all things may be made new. And his vision . . . awoke a responsive chord in the hearts of many men."[58]

Whether science or myth, however, it is clear that "dialectical materialism" has become a powerful instrument of authoritarian social control in the hands of the Soviet "scientists" who occupy the positions of authoritative interpreters and appliers of the doctrine. Since these men predict a long period of struggle (albeit a peaceful one) with the forces of capitalism, they have also postponed the "leap from necessity to freedom" to the distant future. Their excuse is that the continued existence of capitalism shows that the dialectic has not yet run its impersonal course. And until it has, "scientific" elite management of affairs, helping the dialectic along, is the order of the day, not freedom. For freedom to be established now, they claim, would permit access to the Socialist homeland for ill-willed capitalists bent on setting the dialectical process back.

Humanist Protest

Within the Soviet Union and the satellite states of the Iron Curtain perimeter, the plausibility of dialectical materialism as a doctrine of total authoritarian control has worn thin, especially in an age of detente with capitalism, and one in which the chief competitor of Soviet power is

[58]Alexander Gray, *The Socialist Tradition* (New York: Longmans, Green & Co., Inc., 1946), p. 331.

manifestly not international capitalism but another Communist state—the People's Republic of China. Demands for "freedom now" have therefore been heard on all sides, and especially from poets and natural scientists who have experienced the brunt of the official control system commanded by party bureaucrats. To give theoretical support to this protest, dissident intelligentsia have searched the corpus of Marxist thought for a counterweight to the official line, and have found it in the early work of Marx himself that we have sketched above. The *Economic and Philosophic Manuscripts of 1844,* unpublished down to the 1930s, have become a humanist "counter gospel" to the official party doctrines of dialectical materialism throughout the Iron Curtain lands.

Humanist Marxism in the Liberal Democratic World

Humanist Marxism has had currency not only behind the Iron Curtain as an ideological weapon against Communist totalitarianism, but also in the liberal democratic western world. It serves there as the basis of a running critique of what its exponents consider to be the unreconstructed and unreconstructible aspects of capitalist culture, which are seen as a continuing bar to human authenticity and freedom in the widest sense. In continental Western Europe, Humanist Marxism has had an especial vogue, frequently in combination with insights from Freudian psychology, as in the critical philosophy of the Frankfurt School (T.A. Adorno, Juergen Habermas and others) and in the writings of existential phenomenologists such as Jean Paul Sartre and Maurice Merleau-Ponty.

Marxism and American Political Science

As we have seen in earlier chapters, modern American political studies exhibit a diverse structure of competing paradigms of inquiry, in which can be seen the influence of numerous of the classic writings from Plato to J.S. Mill. The largest number of these paradigms are employed in the empirical study of political behavior, and these draw most heavily on the Aristotelian, Machiavellian, and British empiricist traditions. Platonists, like the Straussians, Rousseauists, such as Wolin, Bachrach and Kariel, and Hegelians like the phenomenologists discussed in Chapter 11 argue for speculative-philosophical and interpretive approaches instead. And they subject to searching philosophical critique the work of the behavioralists and other empiricist schools, as we have noted in earlier chapters.

Until recently, there was in American academia no representative of Marxist political science, with the possible exception of C. Wright Mills, the political sociologist, whose *Power Elite* we critiqued in two earlier editions of this book. As we noted there, Mills' work evidences a good deal of eclecticism, and he himself denied that he was a Marxist.[59] In the heartland of liberal democratic capitalism, Marxist concepts were not respectable or acceptable categories of political inquiry.

With the New Left upheaval of the 1960s, however, the ghost of Karl Marx finally found its way into the halls of American academe. But his new presence has tended to be polemical rather than philosophical or scientific. As Herbert Reid and Ernest Yanarella have pointed out:

> Despite the fact that the revival of political controversy in the United States in the sixties radicalized an impressive minority of scholars in various academic disciplines, no significant school of Marxist-minded political scientists was generated . . . instead, the response of radical political scientists in the discipline to the failure of liberalism, like that of the New Left in the larger social arena, has tended to be political and ideological.[60]

Within the "Caucus for a New Political Science," a clustering of ideologically diverse dissidents opposed to the behavioralist-empiricist political science "establishment" of the American Political Science Association, Marxists played a significant political role during the 1960s and continue to do so today. (The "Caucus" now annually runs a series of panels at the annual meeting of the APSA, as an alternative to the "establishment" panels.) But they have not produced a political science of their own, nor even a significant critique of the philosophical bases of modern political science.[61]

Herbert Marcuse

The possible beginnings of a Marxian political science is found in the work of Herbert Marcuse, a philosopher of German origin who now lives and teaches in the United States. Marcuse's name got to be widely known in New Left circles during the 1960s, though the lack of rigor of thought among student protesters prevented the scholarly assimilation and development of his subtle and complex work by the alienated intelligentsia of that time. Marcuse contributes to the literature of "Critical Philosophy."

One-Dimensional Man. Marcuse's *One-Dimensional Man: Studies in the Ideology of Advanced Industrial Society,* is an interesting example of Marxist humanism. It holds an important critical message for modern technological society, whether that society is organized under communist or capitalist auspices. Marx himself, no doubt, would find it a great irony

[59]See *Theories of the Political System,* 2d ed., 1970, pp. 472-77.

[60]Herbert G. Reid and Ernest J. Yanarella,"Toward a Post-Modern Theory of American Political Science and Culture: Perspectives from Critical Marxism and Phenomenology, *Cultural Hermeneutics,* II, 1974, p. 107.

[61]*Ibid.*

that his philosophy should be used today to condemn communist regimes, in which he placed so many hopes, together with the technically developed economic order which for him was the foundation of the good life.

Marcuse's leading assertion is that advanced industrial society has brought "contained" qualitative social change to an end. He finds that society is wholly irrational, for instead of serving as the material foundation of human development and creative freedom, he believes that its affluence destroys free development.[62] In capitalist society, bourgeois and proletarian share a common interest in preserving the status quo, and Communist society has also become stultifyingly conservative.[63]

Were we to analyze the situation with the categories of the older Marx, we should have to come to the conclusion that the dialectic had come to an abortive halt. Instead of working out mechanically to its own dissolution in an era of free creativity, it had produced a static system of impersonal, mechanistic domination. Technology, meaningless mechanical activity, had triumphed over human freedom and meaning. But such a result would hardly have been consonant with Marx's conception of the dialectic as the instrument of history for realizing, not destroying human freedom and meaning. It would, however, be consonant with the more open-ended categories of Humanist Marxism, as expressed in the *Manuscripts of 1844*. For those manuscripts left the future undetermined, to be formed or malformed by human intention.

The False Consciousness of Consumerism. According to Marcuse, modern technological society retains its hold over humankind by fostering a false consciousness composed of fear and consumerism. Within capitalist society, capitalists and workers have closed ranks in fear of communist aggression.[64] Together with this, the technological revolution has created an enormously affluent society. "Its supreme promise is an ever-more-comfortable life for an ever-growing number of people who cannot imagine a qualitatively different universe of discourse and action."[65]

As a consequence of these two things—the welfare state and the warfare state—alienation has substantially disappeared, at certain crucial levels. Mechanization has reduced the worker's expenditure of energy. He no longer experiences the conscious alienation that flows from the physical pain of exhausting manual labor, and from the meager life allowed by subsistence wages. At the same time, the routine of mechanized work has dulled his mind and senses to the importance of free creativity. The worker no longer consciously realizes that he cannot see himself in his product. And he is

[62]Herbert Marcuse, *One-Dimensional Man* (Boston: Beacon Press, 1964), p. ix.
[63]*Ibid.,* p. xiii.
[64]*Ibid.,* p. 21.
[65]*Ibid.,* p. 23.

diverted from this thought by the growing assortment of available creature comforts, which increase his passivity by producing a kind of euphoria. He has thus become *unaware* of his fundamental alienation. He labors under a false consciousness, no longer of religion, promising transcendent happiness, but of hedonic present enjoyment. And this false consciousness hides the alienation, the "thingness" of the worker from him.[66]

The organizational counterpart of euphoric consumerism is an intricately bureaucratized society, on either side of the Iron Curtain. In the capitalist world, the old-style employer, visible to all and identifiable by all as the exploiter, has been transformed into the manager, who disappears in the rationalized order of the corporation.[67] In the world of socialism, a similar thing has occurred. The liberating party elite have been transformed from charismatic messiahs into bureaucrats whose work of liberation has become the administration of a system of total control.[68] Marcuse spends a good deal of space showing how the high culture of society—works of graphic and plastic art, literature, music—once the intellectual register of alienation from an unfree world, pointing toward a better age, have been brought into the service of the technological society and transmuted into material culture. The ideal has been assimilated to reality.[69]

Social Science and Social Control. The reduction of alienated thought to an instrument of the status quo Marcuse finds also in the language of science, especially as that language has been adapted for use in the social sciences. The concept of "operationalism" is especially revealing. According to this idea, scientifically meaningful words must always be defined in terms of observable operations or in terms of observable behavior for which the words stand. Thus scientific language lacks all critical content. It is wholly drawn from the motions that it measures. Even when normative judgment is called for, it takes place within parameters laid down by the reality that is being evaluated. To illustrate his point, Marcuse describes a paper by Morris Janowitz and Dwaine Marvick, two behavioral political scientists, whose intention was to measure the effectiveness of elections in expressing the concept of democracy, through an analysis of the American elections of 1952.

> The criteria for judging a given state of affairs are those offered by the given state of affairs. The analysis is 'locked'; the range of judgment is confined within a context of facts which excludes judging the context in which the facts are made, man-made, and in which their meaning, function, and development are determined.

[66]*Ibid.,* p. 33.
[67]*Ibid.,* p. 32.
[68]*Ibid.,* p. 43.
[69]*Ibid.,* p. 65.

Committed to this framework, the investigation becomes circular and self-validating. If 'democratic' is defined in the limiting but realistic terms of the actual process of election, then this process is democratic prior to the results of the investigation.[70]

Can Freedom be Restored?   Is there a way out of this state of affairs? How can qualitative social change be set in motion again? How can human alienation once more be restored to consciousness so that intentionality can move the world toward freedom? Marcuse has little to offer by way of a solution. As a humanist, Marcuse's great resource for change must be human will and intention. And if he is to make use of the dialectic he must do so in a humanistically modified form. "As historical process, the dialectical process involves consciousness: recognition and seizure of the liberating potentialities. Thus it involves freedom. To the degree to which consciousness is determined by the exigencies and interests of the established society, it is 'unfree.' "[71] But how can free will be developed in the midst of euphoric consumerism? Marcuse can call upon only those who live at the margins of society to act as the catalyst of change. Only those who have not participated in the false consciousness of the affluent society can be motivated to act—"the substratum of the outcasts and outsiders, the exploited and persecuted of other races and other color, the unemployed and the unemployable."[72] But he has no guidelines for them. "The critical theory of society possesses no concepts which could bridge the gap between the present and the future."[73] It can only enjoin the Great Refusal, the will to negate, the will not to go along.

Bibliographical Note

An excellent anthology of the writings of Marx and Engels, in which both humanist and "scientific" writings are represented, is Robert C. Tucker, ed., *The Marx-Engels Reader,* New York: W.W. Norton and Company, Inc., 1972.

Useful studies of the thought of Marx and Engels are Isaiah Berlin, *Karl Marx: His Life and Environment,* New York: Oxford University Press, Inc., 1948; Mandell M. Bober, *Karl Marx's Interpretation of History,* 2nd rev. ed., Cambridge, Mass.: Harvard University Press, 1948; Sidney Hook, *From Hegel to Marx,* London: Victor Gollancz, Ltd., 1950; Franz Mehring, *Karl Marx,* trans., Edward Fitzgerald, New York: Covici, Friede, 1935; and Edmund Wilson, *To the Finland Station,* Garden City, N.Y.: Doubleday &

[70]*Ibid.,* pp. 115-16.
[71]*Ibid.,* p. 222.
[72]*Ibid.,* p. 256.
[73]*Ibid.,* p. 257.

Company, Inc., 1953. For a sympathetic but nevertheless critical treatment by a writer who was a Marxist during part of his intellectual pilgrimage, see Harold Laski, *Karl Marx: An Essay,* London: G. Allen & Unwin, 1925. An anti-Marx essay is Edward H. Carr, *Karl Marx, A Study in Fanaticism,* London: J.M. Dent & Sons, Ltd., 1938. An interesting collection of essays is Bertrand Russell et al., *The Meaning of Marx, a Symposium,* New York: Farrar, Straus & Company, 1934. On Marx as a scientist, see a Marxist comment by J.D. Bernal, *Marx and Science,* London: Lawrence and Wishart, Ltd., 1952, and a non-Marxist essay which demolishes the thesis that Marxism represents a scientific system, Max Eastman, *Marxism, Is It Science?,* New York: W.W. Norton & Company, Inc., 1940. An important humanist interpretation of Marx is Shlomo Avineri, *The Social and Political Thought of Karl Marx,* London: Cambridge University Press, 1968. A representative sample of the leading views of Marx's work is found in V. Stanley Vardys, *Karl Marx: Scientist? Revolutionary? Humanist?,* Lexington, Mass.: D.C. Heath and Company, 1971.

Herbert Marcuse's most important book, in which he attempts a synthesis of concepts from Freud with Marxism is *Eros and Civilization,* Boston: Beacon Press, 1955. See also his earlier study of Hegel as a political liberal, *Reason and Revolution,* London: Oxford University Press, 1941. Recent works of philosophical, social, and cultural criticism include *Negations; Essays in Critical Theory,* Boston: Beacon Press, 1968, *An Essay on Liberation,* Boston: Beacon Press, 1969, and *Studies in Critical Philosophy,* London: NLB, 1972.

Chapter 13

Freedom, Progress, and Experiments in Living: J.S. Mill and Robert Nozick

John Stuart Mill, the ardent crusader for individual liberty, is only a half-hearted democrat. He differs from the other liberals we have studied, especially Locke and Rousseau, in his awareness that the democratization of society does not of itself solve the problem of freedom and may even aggravate it. The autonomy of the individual, he believes, must be defended against the power of democratic majorities, both political and social, as well as against kings and aristocrats.

The defense of individual liberty requires, first, its justification as a primary value and, second, a complex of safeguarding institutions. Mill devoted his life to these two problems at the theoretical and at the practical level. His attempt to solve the first of them led him to raise the vexed question of "Freedom for what?" which is so much discussed in our own day. In answering it, Mill felt compelled to reject the narrow hedonism which was implied in the earlier liberal theories of Hobbes and Locke, and which was quite explicit in the work of his immediate predecessor and friend, Jeremy Bentham. Liberty was meaningful to Mill only as it might contribute to human happiness, but happiness could not signify merely pleasure, as it had for Bentham. It could mean only the highest and most refined pleasures which accompany the noble life. The idea of a noble life, however, implies an objective standard of moral perfection such as we find in classical and Christian teleology. This conception fitted with difficulty into the naturalistic world-view which Mill inherited from his liberal predecessors and which he wished to retain. We have seen the difficulties into which Rousseau and Marx fell in similar attempts to reunite virtue with freedom. The pitfalls involved in such an enterprise are even more evident in the writings of Mill, which are marked throughout by contradiction, ambivalence, and ambiguity.

John Stuart Mill was born in London in 1806, into the family of a scholarly author and social reformer of Scottish descent. His father, James Mill, was a friend and disciple of Jeremy Bentham, and a leading exponent of the philosophical and social doctrines which have been variously labeled "utilitarianism," "Benthamism," and "philosophical radicalism." The elder Mill earned his living until 1819 by his contributions to periodical magazines and, according to his son, ardently spread the new faith in his writings. He "invariably threw into everything he wrote, as much of his convictions as he thought the circumstances would in any way permit."[1]

James Mill also tried to see to it that his oldest son would share these convictions and carry on the cause of utilitarianism when he and Bentham had passed away. From infancy on, Mill was trained by his father according to utilitarian rules and in the principles of the utilitarian creed. And a most rigorous training it was. Tuition in Greek began at age three, to which were soon added Latin, arithmetic, and history. At twelve, young John was introduced to logic, both classical and modern, the modern writings including those of Hobbes, which his father "estimated very highly." Mill says in his *Autobiography* that he prized this part of his education particularly, and felt indebted to it "for whatever capacity of thinking" he had attained.[2] The "Socratic method" of reasoning of the dialogues of Plato, which Mill read about this time, he also counted a valuable part of his training in precise thinking, though the "dogmatical conclusions" of some of the dialogues impressed him but little. Mill wondered in fact whether Plato himself regarded them "as anything more than poetic fancies or philosophic conjectures."[3] A course in political economy, delivered by Mill's father as a series of lectures during their daily morning walks together, completed his early education up to age fourteen. All of it was administered personally by the elder Mill in a most severe and demanding manner.

Religion was entirely excluded from Mill's training. His father had found both revealed and natural religion wanting in persuasive argument, had rejected both, and had adopted an agnostic position. To fill the place of religion, the elder Mill imbued the boy with a spirit of logical analysis and a penchant to disputatiousness, a habit of dissecting and challenging any idea presented to him. The philosophy of life and moral principles which James Mill "delivered" to his son along with this analytical method consisted of a mixture of Stoic, Epicurean, and Cynic elements. The "moralities" instilled in young John by "brief sentences . . . of grave exhortation, or stern

[1]John Stuart Mill, *Autobiography* (London: Longmans, Green & Company, Ltd., 1873), p. 4.

[2]*Ibid.*, pp. 18, 19.

[3]*Ibid.*, p. 22.

reprobation and contempt" were "justice, temperance (to which he gave a very extended application), veracity, perseverance, readiness to encounter pain and especially labour; regard for the public good; estimation of persons according to their merits, and of things according to their intrinsic usefulness; a life of exertion in contradiction to one of self-indulgent ease and sloth." The abstract moral standard his father taught him was "Epicurean, inasmuch as it was utilitarian, taking as the exclusive test of right and wrong, the tendency of actions to produce pleasure or pain." But Mill tells us that his father, nevertheless, had "scarely any belief in pleasure" and "deemed very few of them worth the price which . . . must be paid for them." Thus temperance became for him "almost the central point of educational precept . . . 'the intense' was with him a by-word of scornful disapprobation," and all passionate emotions he condemned. Intellectual satisfactions he rated above all others, and "the pleasures of the benevolent affections he placed high in the scale."[4]

At fourteen, young Mill spent a year in France as the guest of General Sir Samuel Bentham, the philosopher's brother, and there he studied chemistry, zoology, philosophy of science, and mathematics at Montpellier. Returning to England the next year, he resumed his studies with his father, and was now introduced to the works of Bentham. While his whole earlier tuition had in itself been a training in Benthamism, the reading of the doctrine made it "burst upon [him] with all the force of novelty." "The feeling rushed upon [him] that all previous moralists were suspended, and that here indeed was the commencement of a new era of thought." He was particularly taken with "the scientific form" of Bentham's moral analysis. When he found "scientific classification applied to the great and complex subject of Punishable Acts, under the guidance of the ethical principle of Pleasurable and Painful Consequences, followed out in the method of detail introduced into these subjects by Bentham, [he] felt taken up to an eminence from which [he] could survey a vast mental domain, and see stretching out into the distance intellectual results beyond all computation." To this were added "the most inspiring prospects of practical improvement in human affairs."

He felt like a new person as he laid down the last volume. Bentham had provided the "keystone" which held together and gave unity to the formerly separate fragments of his knowledge. He now "had opinions; a creed, a doctrine, a philosophy; in one among the best senses of the word, a religion; the inculcation and diffusion of which could be made the principal outward purpose of a life. And [he] had a grand conception laid before him of changes to be effected in the condition of mankind through that doctrine."[5] Bentham was above all things a democrat, and it was the

4*Ibid.*, pp. 46-49.
5*Ibid.*, pp. 64-67.

democratization of aristocratic Britain that formed the core of the grand Benthamite conception.

Mill's formal education was completed with reading in Locke, Condillac, and Helvetius under his father's direction, and the reading of Roman law with his father's friend, the jurisprudent John Austin. He emerged from his training a fighting utilitarian, and in 1822 he was ready to enter the lists to do battle for the intellectual and social reform of England. It was in that year that he founded the Utilitarian Society, a study and discussion group of young Benthamites, and published his first essays in an evening newspaper. The following year he helped Bentham establish *The Westminister Review* as a propaganda organ of philosophical radicalism. His professional occupation began the same year with an appointment in the East India Company under his father, who had accepted employment there a few years earlier as an assistant to the examiner of India correspondence. The younger Mill was to stay with the India Company for thirty-five years.

The excessive intellectualism and emotional aridity of Mill's education produced its effect in the form of a severe mental crisis and depression when Mill reached twenty. He suddenly found that he could take no pleasure in contemplating the thought of realizing all his grand dreams of reform. He had been taught that feelings of love and hatred were the results of associating, through training or experience, the ideas of pleasure and pain with the objects toward which our feelings are directed. His father had inculcated in him from an early age, through the "old familiar instruments, praise and blame, reward and punishment," a love of mankind and a desire for social reform. But he had also instilled the analytical spirit, and to an extraordinary degree. Mill now concluded that "the habit of analysis has a tendency to wear away the feelings," especially those which he thought to be, in his own case, artificially produced. His analytical habit had become "a perpetual worm at the root both of the passions and of the virtues." He remained convinced that the pleasure of sympathizing with humanity was the greatest source of happiness. But to *know* that such a feeling would gladden him did not *produce* the feeling in him. His education, he decided, "had failed to create [those] feelings in sufficient strength to resist the dissolving influence of analysis, while the whole course of [his] intellectual cultivation had made precocious and premature analysis the inveterate habit of [his] mind." There he was, "stranded at the commencement of [his] voyage, with a well-equipped ship and a rudder, but no sail." All desire had dried up, and he had become Pure Utilitarian Reason.[6]

Mill emerged from his "dry heavy dejection" about six months after its onset. The change for the better began one day in the spring of 1827,when he was reading Marmontel's *Memoires.* He reached the passage in which the author describes his father's death and was inspired, though only a boy, to

[6]*Ibid.*, pp. 136-39.

take upon himself the direction of the family. Suddenly Mill found himself in tears. He realized that he could "feel" again, that he could get excited about things and take pleasure in life. This must have represented to him the symbolic death of his father's total influence over him. And it was also the death in him of his commitment to a pure Benthamism. After this he came to believe that happiness can be achieved only by *not* making it a direct end. Whether the object one sets for oneself is the happiness of others, mankind's improvement, or the pursuit of an art, it must be followed "not as a means, but as itself an ideal end." The only chance to happiness is to treat "not happiness, but some end external to it, as the purpose of life."[7]

Mill also came to recognize the importance of nurturing the feelings, and therewith the significance of music and poetry for a balanced and happy life. In reading Wordsworth he found special comfort. In Wordsworth's poems he "seemed to draw from a source of inward joy, of sympathetic and imaginative pleasure, which could be shared in by all human beings; which had no connection with struggle or imperfection, but would be made richer by every improvement in the physical or social condition of mankind. From them [he] seemed to learn what would be the perennial sources of happiness, when all the greater evils of life shall have been removed."[8]

What Mill had experienced, without fully realizing it, was the transcendent, the divine, for which Benthamite utilitarianism had no place at all. Throughout the rest of his life Mill tried to unite Wordsworth with Bentham, so to speak, "purpose" with "process," "virtue" with "freedom" in a single unified philosophy. He never succeeded because he never quite understood the problem with which he contended—building a bridge from naturalism to noumenalism—and because he insisted on trying to derive the one from the other—noumenalist conclusions from naturalistic premises—which simply cannot be done.[9]

We have no room to detail the story of Mill's relationship with Harriet Taylor, his intellectual companion, collaborator, critic—his *Seelenfreundin*—for nearly thirty years and his wife for eight. In a sense she filled the place in Mill's manhood which his father had occupied in his early life, and he submitted to her judgment and advice in his work as to a superior and guiding intellect. Harriet was a dominant influence during the composition of Mill's most important writings. The *System of Logic,* his great treatise on scientific method, appeared in 1843. In 1848 he published the first edition of the *Political Economy.* He revised it, in accordance with Harriet's recommendations, with a result not entirely beneficial to the book,

---

[7]*Ibid.,* p. 139-42.

[8]*Ibid.,* p. 148.

[9]For an interesting account of Wordsworth's influence on Mill, see Thomas Woods, *Poetry and Philosophy, A Study in the Thought of John Stuart Mill* (London: Hutchinson and Co., Ltd., 1961).

according to one commentator. The deletion of crucial passages and the alteration of others had the effect of "completely confusing his position on communism." "He admitted that he still preferred the old version and could not see the logic of the new," but he made the changes anyway. He wrote to Harriet that he was bound to make the changes "even if there were no other reason than the certainty [he felt] that [he] never should long continue of an opinion different from [hers] on a subject which [she had] fully considered."[10] She also had a hand in drafting the *Essay on Liberty, Considerations on Representative Government,* and *Utilitarianism,* though they were not published until after her death, in 1859, 1861, and 1863, respectively.

After their marriage in 1851, the Mills spent most of the time in seclusion, and after Harriet's death, Mill became a virtual recluse, living in a villa near Avignon which had been a favorite spot of his wife's. In 1865 he emerged from his retreat, however, to stand for a seat in Parliament for Westminister, and he won it. (He had earlier been invited to stand for an Irish constituency but had declined because of his administrative position in India House, from which he retired, however, in 1858). He was a member of the Commons during the three sessions of Parliament which passed the great Reform Bill, a fitting climax in the practical order to a life devoted to the causes of radicalism, though one which fell far short of the objects which Mill himself had in view.

Mill died at Avignon in 1873. *Three Essays on Religion,* composed in the last years of his life, were published posthumously. In them Mill had begun haltingly to outline a theistic philosophy, which was implicit in his admiration of Wordsworth's poetry, but to which he could not give clear form until these declining years, after all his life's important work was over.

A Theory of Ultimate Values

The Benthamite Premise

Building on epistemological and psychological foundations laid by Hobbes and Locke, Jeremy Bentham proposed as the grand object of political endeavor the "greatest happiness of the greatest number." By happiness he meant simply pleasurable sensations. According to his psychology, pleasure is the only thing that men actually pursue, and pain that which they always seek to avoid. Since he could find no teleological reason operative in the world, nor any transcendental system of values which demanded fulfillment, it seemed to him reasonable to take as the standard of good that

---

[10]John Stuart Mill, *Essays on Politics and Culture,* ed., Gertrude Himmelfarb (Garden City, N.Y.: Doubleday & Company, Inc., 1962), p. xxv.

which men in fact, in his view, pursue as good. He could find no principle to distinguish the merit of one man's demand for pleasure from any other man's, and so he reached the democratic conclusion that, from the point of view of a disinterested public authority, the pleasures of all men must be treated as equally valuable. On this premise, the maximization of as many of these individual pleasures as possible seemed to him the only rational standard of right political action.

Motives counted for nothing in Bentham's view, nor did abstract principles such as natural right and contract—this part of the Hobbesian and Lockean apparatus he chose to discard. The probable consequences of a measure were everything. If they were likely to increase the general stock of pleasure, the measure was good; if the results would diminish this stock and increase the general pain, it was bad. The utility of an act to produce pleasure was the sole yardstick of its worth. This is the conception of political good which John Stuart Mill learned from his father.

Criticism of Bentham.   As we have noted, the mental crisis of 1826 and Mill's subsequent immersion in Wordsworth, and then in the works of Coleridge and Carlyle, led him to question the adequacy of Benthamism as a philosophy of life and of politics.

In an essay on Bentham which he published in 1838, Mill praises Bentham for introducing clarity of concept and precision of reasoning into moral and political philosophy, but he then proceeds to criticize the conception which Bentham held of human nature, a conception which "furnished him with an unusually slender stock of premises." To Mill in 1838, Bentham's method is "a security for accuracy, but not for comprehensiveness." His knowledge of man is "wholly empirical; and the empiricism of one who has had little experience." Mill is shocked at the readiness with which Bentham dismissed all of past philosophy as so many "vague generalities," not heeding "that these generalities contained the whole unanalyzed experience of the human race."[11]

The incompleteness of his own mind as a representative of universal human nature simply disqualified Bentham as a philosopher, Mill writes. "In many of the most natural and strongest feelings of human nature he had no sympathy; from many of its graver experiences he was altogether cut off." Bentham's greatest fault lay in his failure to recognize that men pursue goods which lie beyond and apart from utility. "Man is never recognized by him as a being capable of pursuing spiritual perfection as an end; of desiring, for its own sake, the conformity of his own character to his standard of excellence, without hope of good or fear of evil from other

[11]John Stuart Mill, *Essay on Bentham* in *Utilitarianism, On Liberty, Essay on Bentham,* ed., Mary Warnock, (New York: Meridian Books, 1962) pp.92, 96, 94, 97. Hereafter cited as *Utilitarianism.*

source than his own inward consciousness. Even in the more limited form of conscience, this great fact in human nature escapes him."[12]

Here Mill seems to have abandoned the utilitarian standard altogether. He speaks of the "moral part of man's nature" as "the desire of perfection," and of the good as something inherently valuable. These are noumenal ideas. The political good takes the form, in Mill's essay, of a conception of "the spiritual interests of society" and of "national character." Bentham's theory provides nothing for these things, Mill asserts. It can only "teach the means of organizing and regulating the merely *business* part of the social arrangements," and Mill thinks it a mistake to assume that this "part of human affairs was the whole of them . . . that the legislator . . . had to do with." The implication is that the public government should be charged with the task of building national character and promoting the spiritual well-being of a society. But the theme is not developed. Mill drops it suddenly and turns at this point of the essay to another subject.[13]

The Greatest Happiness Principle Restated

In *Utilitarianism,* which he published in 1863, twenty-five years after the essay on Bentham, we find a radical reversal of Mill's position. Mill returns to the utilitarian fold in his theory of political value. The romantic influence has faded, and Mill once more holds in high esteem the creed of his youth. The definition of utilitarianism which he presents in this essay has an orthodox Benthamite ring to it.

> The creed which accepts as the foundation of morals, Utility, or the Greatest Happiness Principle, holds that actions are right in proportion as they tend to promote happiness, wrong as they tend to produce the reverse of happiness. By happiness is intended pleasure, and the absence of pain, by unhappiness, pain, and the privation of pleasure. . . . All desirable things . . . are desirable either for the pleasure inherent in themselves or as means to the promotion of pleasure and the prevention of pain.[14]

[12]*Ibid.,* pp. 96, 100.

[13]*Ibid.,* pp. 100, 105, 106. In *Representative Government* (1861), Mill gives as the measure of the merit of governments "the degree in which they promote the general mental advancement of the community, including under that phrase advancement in intellect, in virtue, and in practical activity and efficiency, and partly of the degree of perfection with which they organize the moral, intellectual and active worth already existing, so as to operate with the greatest effect on public affairs." *Utilitarianism, Liberty, and Representative Government* (New York: E. P. Dutton & Co., Inc., 1951), p. 262.

[14]Mill, *Utilitarianism,* in *Utilitarianism,* p. 257.

Hedonism does not necessarily mean egotism, however. With Bentham, Mill rejects an egotistic conception of happiness. That is good which tends to produce "the greatest amount of happiness altogether," which tends to increase "the sum total of happiness."[15] It may even be good for some particular individual to sacrifice his own happiness to that of others, if this augments the general stock of happiness.

How can Mill demonstrate that the general happiness is the greatest good? Like Bentham, he wishes to confine the entire argument within the realm of phenomenal reality, the world of "facts." To leave this realm is to destroy all possibility of objective statement and of objective measurement. So he attempts to derive his "social happiness" value from the "facts" of human motivation. "The sole evidence it is possible to produce that anything is desirable," he writes, "is that people do actually desire it. If the end which the utilitarian doctrine proposes to itself were not, in theory and in practice, acknowledged to be an end, nothing could ever convince any person that it was so."[16] He then goes on to assert it as a fact that each person wishes his own happiness. Evidently, he thinks this is readily established by common-sense observation. He concludes that if "each person's happiness is a good to that person . . . the general happiness [is], therefore, a good to the aggregate of all persons."[17]

A problem enters the argument at this point. In utilitarian metaphysics, only the individual is real, and society consists merely of a collection of individuals. The "aggregate of all persons" therefore has no existence as such; only the individuals in the addition are real. Hence the aggregate has no desire and no will; only individuals desire and will. If good is what is desired, and only individuals have desires, the notion of "the general happiness [as] a good to the aggregate of all persons" is a meaningless expression. What Mill must show is that the individual desires the general happiness as well as, or *even rather than*, his own happiness. He attempts such a demonstration.

Mill finds a "natural basis of sentiment for utilitarian morality," i.e., for the general happiness principle, in "the social feelings of mankind." Apparently a foundation is laid in reason as well as in sentiment, for a few passages later Mill speaks of the "deeply rooted conception" which man has "of himself as a social being," which "tends to make him feel it one of his natural wants that there should be harmony between his feelings and aims and those of his fellow-creatures," and "that his real aim and theirs do not conflict; that he is not opposing himself to what they really wish for, namely their own good, but is, on the contrary, promoting it."[18] The *idea* of man as

[15]*Ibid.*, pp. 262, 268.
[16]*Ibid.*, p. 288.
[17]*Ibid.*, pp. 288-89.
[18]*Ibid.*, pp. 284, 287.

a social animal leads a man to *feel* an identity of his happiness with that of the whole, and to *desire* the general happiness.

Not all persons have in equal degree the conception of man as a social being nor the social feelings which go with it. In fact in *most* individuals Mill finds the desire for the general good "much inferior in strength to their selfish feelings." And in some "it is wanting altogether." "The moral feelings are not indeed a part of our nature, in the sense of being in any perceptible degree present in all of us." Nevertheless, these feelings can be developed by education, and with the spread of civilization Mill believes that they are in fact becoming more widely accepted and more refined. Man is gradually becoming "conscious of himself as a being who *of course* pays regard to others"; sociability becomes built into us as an *acquired nature* and as a habit.[19]

What is the content of the general happiness which all of us *potentially* can desire, and which, gradually, more and more of us do *actually* desire, though it is still a "comparatively early state of human advancement in which we now live" ? Bentham had been content with a simple equation of happiness with pleasure, counting all pleasures qualitatively equal. (Witness his well-known *mot* that "push-pin is as good as poetry.") This led to a claim by antiutilitarians that Benthamism made no distinction between the happy human life and that of the beast and was, therefore, "a doctrine worthy only of swine." Mill's happiness principle is a very different one. There are specifically human pleasures, he argues, which are of higher quality, "more elevated" than animal delights. These are "the pleasures of the intellect, of the feelings and imagination, and of the moral sentiments." The greatest social happiness, therefore, cannot be conceived merely in quantitative terms. The good society will not be one merely of contented pigs. It will be "as rich as possible in enjoyments, both in point of quantity and quality.[20]

But who decides what the qualitatively best pleasures are which society *ought* to want? And by what criterion will he judge? Mill tells us that we should receive the judgment of the majority of those who have experienced the broadest range of pleasures. In our time these men of sophisticated feelings, as in the past, are only a few, an Epicurean aristocracy. They correspond to the wise men of traditional philosophy.

> Of two pleasures, if there be one to which all or almost all who have experience of both give a decided preference, irrespective of any feeling of moral obligation to prefer it, that is the more desirable pleasure. If one of the two is, by those who are competently acquainted with both, placed so far above the other that they prefer it, even though knowing it to be attended with a greater amount of discontent, and would not resign it for any quantity of the other

[19]*Ibid.*, pp. 287, 283, 285.
[20]*Ibid.*, pp. 287, 258, 262.

pleasure which their nature is capable of, we are justified in ascribing to the preferred enjoyment a superiority in quality, so far out-weighing quantity as to render it, in comparison, of small account.[21]

The man of developed social feelings who wishes to serve the general happiness will strive to create a society in which the higher pleasures, discerned by the moral epicure, have their proper place.

After weighing all the foregoing considerations, Mill asks whether and how his doctrine can be validated. The test, he asserts, is a psychological one. "If the opinion which I have now stated is psychologically true . . . we can have no other proof, and we require no other." The psychological test is an empirical and a scientific test. The question to be answered "is a question of fact and experience, dependent, like all similar questions, upon evidence. It can only be determined by practical self-consciousness and self-observation, assisted by observation of others."[22]

Method of Proof

At this point we expect Mill to say that the full demonstration of his value theory waits upon the development of the social science whose need he proclaimed and whose structure and method he outlined in the *System of Logic* (1843). Would not the discovery and the validation of the laws of mind and the laws of formation of character of which he speaks there give us a scientific test of Mill's ethical doctrine? In the pages of the *Logic*, Mill, however, *denies* that the problem of ends is one for science.

> A scientific observer or reasoner, merely as such, is not an adviser for practice. His part is only to show that certain consequences follow from certain causes, and that to obtain certain ends, certain means are the most effectual. Whether the ends themselves are such as ought to be pursued . . . it is no part of his business as a cultivator of science to decide, and science alone will never qualify him for the decision.[23]

There are "first principles of Conduct" as well as "first principles of Knowledge." But they are different, and the former are not derived from the latter, which are the province of science.[24] At the very end of the *Logic*, Mill states his belief in the general happiness principle as a universal standard of ethical conduct, but adds that it would be out of place to discuss the foundations of morality in a scientific work or even to define the kind of justifica-

---

[21]*Ibid.*, p. 259.

[22]*Ibid.*, p. 292.

[23]John Stuart Mill, *A System of Logic, Ratiocinative and Inductive*, 7th ed., Vol. II (London: Longmans, Green & Company, Ltd., 1868), pp. 551-52.

[24]*Ibid.*, p. 552.

tion proper to his moral theory. He merely declares his "conviction" of the rightness of the general happiness idea. The editor of the 1868 edition of the *Logic* at this point refers the reader to *Utilitarianism* for an "express discussion and vindication of this principle."[25] Yet, as we have seen, the passages on the proof of the doctrine in this essay *seem* to refer back to the system of proof outlined in the *Logic*. We are caught in a vicious circle.

We must conclude that when Mill in *Utilitarianism* speaks of "fact," "experience," and "observation" as the tests of his ethical doctrine, he is not thinking about scientific facts, scientific experience, or scientific observation. What other kinds of facts, experience, and observation could he have had in mind? Unfortunately, he does not take the trouble to tell us, and his doctrine is muddled as a result.

If Mill really intended to be consistent in his conclusions from the axiom that our conception of the desirable must be derived from the facts concerning the things which are desired, and from his postulate that the test of ethical doctrine is a psychological one, he would have confined himself to a scientific description of human behavior with the method outlined in the *Logic* and then pronounced the described behavior "good." Instead, he wrote *Utilitarianism*. And the kinds of facts that he talks about there are not scientific facts. They are teleological facts. In asserting that some pleasures are higher than others, Mill implies that there exists a criterion by which these distinctions can be made, a criterion which cannot itself be pleasure. To say that we should follow the judgment of those who have the broadest range of experience in pleasures begs the question, for it does not tell us what the criterion is which these judges use. But plainly there must be some such criterion, for without it the judges could only pronounce that there are differences in intensity and duration of sensation among pleasures and in such "circumstantial advantages" as "permanency, safety and uncostliness." But Mill rejects all such quantitative criteria and insists on one, which, he says, must refer to the "intrinsic nature" of the pleasures.[26]

In using expressions such as the "nobler feelings," Mill implies that the criterion, if it is a feeling or sentiment, is a sentiment not of pleasure but of nobility, a word which expresses inherent goodness. If the criterion is an idea, it is a conception of what goes into the structure of a noble life, a conception of human perfection. In saying that a "highly endowed being" will account every happiness that he can hope for as "imperfect" because of the way "the world is constituted," he implies that the human mind can have intuitions of perfection which are not derived from empirical facts but from some transcendental order beyond those facts. How can Mill know that the world is imperfect unless he can pass beyond the world to an idea of perfection? In saying that man has a "conception . . . of himself as a social be-

---

[25]*Ibid.*, p. 553, fn.

[26]Mill, *Utilitarianism,* in *Utilitarianism*, p. 258.

ing," he is not saying that man looks around him and judges merely that he in fact lives with other men, but rather that those facts suggest a standard of *ideal* being, not yet realized which gives rise to a value and to an obligation—to the idea "that there *should* be harmony between his feelings and aims and those of his fellow-creatures."[27]

Mill is indirectly saying in all this that observation will show us that it is a fact that some men have feelings and conceptions of a transcendent and perfect order of being, from which spring conceptions of moral obligation, and that he is convinced that these feelings and conceptions represent true insights into the true and the good and the beautiful. He leads us into a transcendent order, and we hear echoes of Plato, Aristotle, and St. Thomas. (Mill had, after all, not shaken off the influence of the "intuitionists.") But it is an order that logically has no place in the explicit utilitarian premises on which Mill wishes to build. He would like to acknowledge it, but finds himself unable to do so expressly. Hence the muddle—the ambiguities and contradictions of his doctrine. Mill's utilitarianism remains suspended halfway between Bentham and Wordsworth.[28]

Progress and Freedom:
A Theory of Instrumental Values

The Idea of Progress

We have seen that the notion of higher and lower pleasures, and the notion that there are noble and ignoble feelings and actions, imply a doctrine that there is an objectively good and noble way of life to which men are morally obliged to conform. We have also seen that Mill is reluctant to state the doctrine explicitly. He is doubly reluctant to spell out in detail the characteristics of the noble way of life. We are told that it will give full play both to the rational and to the emotional faculties of man, and that conscience and reason will be in control of impulse and desire. In this case, however, Mill's reluctance does not seem to flow from a sense of incompatibility of such a doctrine with utilitarian premises but rather as a logical conclusion from another of his doctrinal principles. This is the doctrine of progress, which Mill shared with most other nineteenth-century liberals, and which stemmed originally from certain elements of the thought of the French Enlightenment.[29]

[27]*Ibid.*, pp. 260, 287. (Emphasis supplied.)

[28]Cf. Woods, *op. cit.*, pp. 73-76, and Arthur Pap, *Elements of Analytic Philosophy* (New York: The Macmillan Company, 1949), p. 44.

[29]See Marie Jean de Caritat, Marquis de Condorcet, *Outlines of an Historical View of the Progress of the Human Mind* (Philadelphia: Carrie, Rice, Orwood, Bache and Fellows, 1796). See also J.B. Bury, *The Idea of Progress: An Inquiry into Its Origin and Growth* (New York: The Macmillan Company, 1932).

In the essay *On Liberty*, Mill tells us that the utility which he regards as "the ultimate appeal on all ethical questions" is a utility "grounded on the permanent interests of man as a *progressive* being."[30] The formula seems to imply that change, or dynamism, is a fixed characteristic of man's nature. That Mill uses the word "progressive" rather than "dynamic" implies that man is not merely a creature who changes, but one who changes for the better. His life involves movement toward a goal, toward the fulfillment of some standard of the good.

However, the notion of progress, at least as we find it in Mill, also implies that at all the stopping points on the way to the goal, in all the stages of human development short of its perfection, man's vision is severely limited. He cannot see the goal clearly nor envisage all that is involved in the perfection toward which he moves. Only when he has reached the goal and is himself perfected will he see clearly and fully where it was that he was heading all along.

We cannot be sure that Mill supposed that there would be a static utopia some day. Perhaps he conceived of progress as an indefinite affair. He does use some expressions which may imply that there is a static goal to be reached, but they are ambiguous. To say that such and such a principle should hold "while mankind are imperfect," and "until mankind are much more capable than at present of recognizing all sides of the truth," "in an imperfect state of the human mind," seems to imply that there will be a time of perfection when other principles will hold.[31] At any rate, Mill does not expect it to arrive tomorrow. He speaks of the "comparatively early state of human advancement in which we now live."[32] And the words "improvement" and "development" appear much more frequently in the pages of his books than "perfection." The noble life, then, is something of which we get a better and better idea as time goes on, and which we realize ever more fully over the ages. But what its completion is we do not know. That is something that will take care of itself if we devote our energies to progressive change.

But if we do not know what perfection is like, how can we know whether change is progressive or regressive? If we do not know where we are going, how do we know whether we are on the way? Mill does not, like Marx, think that progress is inevitable. It can flow only from man's free agency, from his rational desire to achieve it. And he never fully solves the problem of the obscure ultimate standard. He assumes that some particular things will be part of the ideal order—the end of violence and the establishment of peaceful human intercourse, the harmonization of interests, the

[30]John Stuart Mill, *On Liberty* (New York: The Liberal Arts Press, 1956), p. 14. (Emphasis supplied.)

[31]*Ibid.*, pp. 68, 62.

[32]Mill, *Utilitarianism,* in *Utilitarianism,* p. 287.

growth of benevolent and cooperative behavior, the diminution if not the end of compulsion, a high general level of material well-being, technical improvement, the high development and wide diffusion of knowledge. Progress toward these goals will be a sufficient index of progress as such.

Liberty

The concept of the utilitarian good as something progressively achieved leads us to the means of ensuring that progress will occur. It is at this point that we arrive at Mill's conception of individual liberty, which he cherishes as the great instrument of progress. At a certain stage of human development, Mill believes, freedom becomes conducive to, one might even say it becomes the necessary and sufficient condition of, further development or progress. This is the period which follows the inculcation in a people of habits of obedience to regular authority and the development of an industrious spirit. The first may require quite illiberal, even despotic, government. Creating the second stage even justifies slavery.[33]

Mill likes to make a parallel between childhood and the primitive condition of a social body. Neither the child nor the savage can claim freedom. He must first learn social habits under another's control. But when the child comes of age, or when the barbarian has attained civilization, freedom becomes for each a moral necessity. It is vital both for his own happiness and that of the society as a whole. So far as the individual is concerned, he needs it to exercise and develop his specifically human attributes. "The human faculties of perception, judgment, discriminative feeling, mental activity, and even moral preference are exercised only in making a choice."[34] Freedom *means* the making of choices. So far as society is concerned, free choice for its members is the necessary condition for the appearance and development of new and original ideas and modes of living, without which society cannot change but labors in the doldrums of a static imperfection.

What Kinds of Freedom?   Mill is not an anarchist and does not demand a perfect liberty of choice in all things. The notion that we now live in an imperfect society implies the need to maintain some social controls. Where and how does Mill draw the line between individual freedom and social authority? He gives us both an abstract formula for drawing the line and some specific examples of utilitarian liberties.

The formula sets up a dichotomy of self-regarding and other-regarding acts. Those things belong to freedom which "directly and in the first instance" affect only the individual, in which society "has, if any, only

---

[33]Mill, *On Liberty*, p. 14, *Representative Government,* in *Utilitarianism, Liberty, and Representative Government,* pp. 265-66.

[34]Mill, *On Liberty*, p. 71.

an indirect interest." The area of freedom also involves acts which affect others if they freely and undeceivedly consent to them. Those things are properly under social control which directly and in the first instance affect others against their will and without their undeceived consent. In another place Mill describes the distinction as one between "the part of life in which it is chiefly the individual that is interested" and the part "which chiefly interests society." In still another place he says that "mankind . . . individually or collectively" may interfere with an individual's liberty of action for "self-protection" and to "prevent harm to others," but never for "his own good."[35]

Taken alone, the abstract formula is of little use, for by what criterion do we establish whether in any particular case society's interest is direct or only indirect? And what regulation of the individual cannot be justified as an effort to protect society and prevent harm to others? Then too, we have already seen that in Mill's ethical theory the chief value is the social good, the greatest happiness of society as a whole, not that of the individual. His standard of utility is grounded on "the permanent interests of *man* as a progressive being," not the permanent interests of *men*. Individual liberty is important because it makes for social progress. Society has a most weighty and direct interest in the individual's very freedom. Perhaps a better dichotomy would be: acts which, if left free, presumptively contribute to social progress and acts which, if left free, presumptively do not contribute to social progress. In fact, this seems to be the dichotomy which is illustrated by the examples Mill supplies.

The area of freedom should include, according to Mill, "the inward domain of consciousness," which means that liberty of opinion and feelings on all matters whatsoever should be absolute. Freedom of expressing these opinions should also be absolute. (Here Mill ought to have recognized the unworkability of his abstract formula, for he notes that the expression of ideas affects others. He justifies this freedom as an exception to the rule because he considers it "practically inseparable" from freedom of opinion. It would have made his argument more precise if he had abandoned the formula.) The utility of these "First Amendment" freedoms stems, in Mill's belief, from the notion that no single mind or single group of minds is likely to grasp fully a perfect truth. Prevailing or dominant opinions in particular he thinks never likely to represent the whole truth on a matter. There must, therefore, be freedom for dissent to be expressed, in the hope that in the "collision of adverse opinions . . . the remainder of truth . . . [may be] supplied."[36] Even if we grant the theoretical possibility of a single opinion representing an absolute truth, the only test of its validity, according to Mill,

[35]*Ibid.*, pp. 15, 16, 91, 13.
[36]*Ibid.*, p. 64.

is the constant possibility of disproof in the free competition of ideas. (This amounts to a variation on the Burkean theme that wisdom resides in social processes rather than in a particular mind or group of minds, though Burke found that wisdom in particular institutional procedures rather than in an abstract freedom.) Since truth is useful to social progress, the freedom which produces it, or rather which makes possible its emergence, is also useful.

A second great area of liberty is what Mill calls "liberty of tastes and pursuits," which he defines as "doing as we like . . . without impediment from our fellow creatures . . . even though they should think our conduct foolish, perverse, or wrong."[37] Again, social progress is the purpose. Only through such spontaneity, through "experiments in living," can mankind work toward that perfect way of life for which we are destined. Mill casts the argument into a metaphor which opposes an image of organic growth to one of mechanical contrivance. Human nature, he argues, is not a machine which we can build according to a model or a blueprint prescribing precisely how it should run. It is rather a tree which develops and grows "on all sides according to the tendency of the inward forces which make it a living thing."[38] We have no definite model or blueprint of the perfect society; its nature is obscure to us. Yet we can see a kind of model working from within society, as a principle of growth. It is like an Aristotelian entelechy or a Hegelian Idea, developing over the great stretches of historical time and thriving on freedom. Through a process of free competition of all possible modes of life, a kind of dialectical opposition of ways of living, we move toward utopia. This dialectical conflict is for Mill a peaceful one, not a bloody warfare of classes ranged under opposing ideological banners. And it has no special relationship to economic change.

From freedom of expression and of tastes and pursuits derives a third freedom, freedom to combine "for any purpose not involving harm to others."[39] Mill takes an entire chapter to describe each of the two primary areas of freedom, but he enunciates this corollary in only a brief statement.

Institutions of Freedom

Mill is not so foolish as to suppose that freedom will grow simply from sermons, such as his own essay *On Liberty,* which preach the need for it. Freedom requires institutional safeguards. What form do they take in the Millian prescription?

It is in his *Considerations on Representative Government,* published in 1861, two years after the essay *On Liberty,* that Mill gives us his most

[37]*Ibid.,* p. 16.
[38]*Ibid.,* p. 72.
[39]*Ibid.,* p. 16.

thorough treatment of this subject. The first requisite of a government for free men is that it be democratically based. Only when every man can look forward to full citizenship on an equal basis with all others is the "maximum of the invigorating effect of freedom upon the character" obtained.[40] Widespread participation in public affairs educates the participants and raises markedly the intellectual standard of a society. As evidence, Mill cites the high intelligence of the ancient Athenian citizenry, which he attributes to the democratic *ecclesia*, and the cleverness of modern lower-middle-class Englishmen, which he believes they owe to jury service and to service in parish offices.[41]

A democratic order does not require that all take part in the entire business of government, however. This would be impractical except in the smallest communities, and Mill sees no need to restrict the boundaries of the political community as Rousseau did. For large societies the democratic principle is preserved in representative institutions. In a representative system "the whole people, or some numerous portion of them, exercise through deputies periodically elected by themselves the ultimate controlling power."[42] Mill is not a legalist and so he sees no need for the principle of popular control to receive express form in a constitutional law. It may depend only on custom, on the "positive political morality" of the country, as it does in Great Britain.[43] The important thing is that it be an operative principle, whether express or tacit.

The representative no more than the citizen will actually execute the work of government. The chief function of popular elections is to control the representative parliament, and the chief business of parliament is to control the policy-makers. These will be the leaders of the representative assembly, organized in a body such as the British Cabinet, using and directing the expert knowledge of professional bureaucrats.

Tyranny of the Political Majority

Democratic control over public policy, through popular election of parliamentary watchdogs, is a central ingredient of good government. But it has its vices as well as virtues, Mill believes, and instead of promoting the greatest degree of individual freedom, it may be used to destroy freedom and prevent that social progress from which the greatest social happiness derives. How might this occur?

Mill is by no means a thoroughgoing democrat. His view of human

[40]Mill, *Representative Government*, in *Utilitarianism, Liberty, and Representative Government*, p. 289.

[41]*Ibid.*, p. 290.

[42]*Ibid.*, p. 305.

[43]*Ibid.*, p. 306.

nature is, as we have seen, aristocratic. Only a few persons, at least in the imperfect condition of mankind as it now is, are capable of higher pleasures. Only a few can be expected to have great and original ideas. And only a few will adventurously engage in experiments in living. "But these few are the salt of the earth; without them, human life would become a stagnant pool."[44] It is on them, and therefore on their freedom especially, that social progress depends, according to Mill. But a pure majoritarian democracy would swamp and perhaps, therefore, destroy the intellectual elite. All deviations from the standards set by the mediocre many would be persecuted.Thus, while promoting freedom in one way, democracy threatens it in another. Somehow, within the framework of democracy, a position must be created for the talented and virtuous natural aristocracy from which its influence can flow out into and mold the whole society, steering it on the road to progress and improvement.

In *Representative Government,* Mill recommends two institutions through which the influence of the virtuous few can be secured against the deadening hand of the selfishness and mediocrity of the majority. These are proportional representation and plural voting. He approves in particular of the Hare system, invented by a countryman of Mill's, which was designed to give expression in a parliamentary assembly to the broadest possible spectrum of opinion. The majority system entirely excludes from influence about half the electorate, as Mill sees it, while with the Hare system, minorities receive representation in proportion to their numbers.[45]

> It secures a representation, in proportion to numbers, of every division of the electoral body; not two great parties alone, with perhaps a few large sectional minorities in particular places, but every minority in the whole nation. . . . No elector would . . . be nominally represented by someone whom he had not chosen.[46]

Though the men of superior intellect and lofty character are bound to be outnumbered, this system guarantees that they will at least be heard. This makes a great difference, for the ignorant many may be influenced by their words or at least be forced to give reasonable arguments for the measures they propose.

Mill is not clear as to whether his "instructed minority" should act in concert as an organized pressure group or as so many individuals. The democrat in him speaks in one place where he writes that "a separate organization of the instructed classes, even if practicable, would be invidious." But as members of Parliament, representing simply a numerical

---

[44]Mill, *On Liberty,* p. 78.

[45]For the details of the system see *Representative Government,* in *Utilitarianism, Liberty, and Representative Government,* pp. 351-54.

[46]*Ibid.,* p. 354.

fraction of the population on the same basis as all other members, the elite of the educated groups would be offensive to no one, he thinks.[47] Presumably, these will be elected to Parliament under one or other of the usual party banners, or perhaps as isolated independents who win simply by force of character and intellectual merit. A few pages further on, however, Mill ponders the importance of organization for political success. He writes that it is assumed to be legitimate for "every petty interest" to add to its power by organization, and then asks why we should suppose "that the great interest of national intellect and character would alone remain unorganized."[48]

The influence of intellect on public policy may also be extended, Mill contends, by giving plural votes to the intelligentsia. But what sort of standard should be used to measure intelligence? The democratic side of his nature leads Mill to reject property as a criterion out of hand, though he thinks it may be considered a kind of test. The ideal measure would be some system of general education, but this poses the problem of working out a reliable examination procedure. As a practical substitute he suggests occupational status as a criterion, and he gives us a hierarchy of intelligence which runs from the unskilled laborer at the bottom of the list through foreman and employer up to the members of the liberal professions at the top. An alternative or supplement to this might be certificates of educational achievement, with university degrees at the head of the hierarchy.

Tyranny of the Social Majority

By institutions such as these, Mill hopes that in an egalitarian age the freedom and influence of the intelligent and morally superior few may be secured against the tyranny of ignorant and selfish majorities in the political order. But political oppression he sees as only part of the problem. Far more of a threat to freedom of expression and to individuality is the pressure of public opinion which "leaves fewer means of escape, penetrating much more deeply into the details of life, and enslaving the soul itself."[49] Society tends in a thousand subtle ways to prevent the formation of characters not in harmony with prevailing custom, and to mold all life to a single model. We speak of this today as "conformity," and a spate of books have recently been written which describe and deplore the problem.

Mill found the tendency to conformity especially marked in his own Victorian England. "Society has now fairly got the better of individuality," he writes. If the defect of feudal culture was the too unbridled individuality and excessive passion of the nobility, which constantly threatened to destroy

[47]*Ibid.*, p. 361.
[48]*Ibid.*, p. 367.
[49]Mill, *On Liberty*, p. 7.

law and order, the democratization of English life had produced precisely the opposite defect. There was neither passion nor self-assertion of any kind to be found in any level of society. "From the highest class . . . down to the lowest, everyone lives as under the eye of a hostile and dreaded censorship." No one asks "what do I prefer? or, what would suit my character and disposition? . . . They ask themselves, what is suitable to my position? What is usually done by persons of my station and pecuniary circumstances? . . . It does not occur to them to have any inclination except for what is customary."[50] Mill found himself surrounded by a host of what we today have learned from David Riesman to call "other-directed" men, and from William Whyte "organization men." Persons of genius and of potential originality are stifled by the conformist spirit, and progress ceases. The existence of the very concept of diversity is threatened.

All the circumstances of democratic life, as Mill sees it, contribute to the spirit of conformity. The various ranks of traditional society lived as in different worlds, and diversity of condition made for diversity of temperaments, ideas, ways of life. But in a democratic age, people "read the same things, listen to the same things, go to the same places, have their hopes and fears directed to the same objects, have the same rights and liberties, and the same means of asserting them. Great as are the differences of position which remain, they are nothing to those which have ceased."[51] All the political and technical changes of his time Mill sees pointing toward an ever more pronounced leveling—the extension of education, improvements in the means of communication, the increase of commerce and manufacture.

What will stem the tide? For the problem of conformity and of the tyranny of public opinion Mill has no institutional solution. He can only rely on the influence of voices like his own, crying in the egalitarian wilderness.

Freedom and Property

We have seen that in the liberalism of Locke as in that of Hobbes, the rights of private property are closely tied in with the idea of individual liberty. This is also true of Bentham's liberalism. What does Mill have to say of the relationship of property to freedom?

It is chiefly in his *Principles of Political Economy* that Mill expounds his views on the subject. The first edition of the book was published in 1848, a year of widespread revolutionary explosions throughout Europe, and the same year that the *Communist Manifesto* first appeared. At least part of the volume was written, like the *Manifesto*, as a response to the social and political questions raised by the great technological revolution which for some fifty years had been radically altering European life. The answers

[50]*Ibid.*, p. 74.
[51]*Ibid.*, p. 89.

which Mill makes to these questions are rather different from those of Marx, however.

Mill's theory of property builds on the assumption that the social benefits of the modern industrial order of large-scale enterprise are so great and the system so well established that it must be taken as a "given." He also assumes that no man's freedom is complete if he is radically dependent on another for support, in the form of wages, and that a good society is a democratic one of equally free and independent souls. The first assumption rules out a pattern of widespread small holdings as the economic foundation for the good society. The alternative, if we assume a necessary connection between property and freedom, is some sort of system of collective ownership.

Mill has been called a socialist, but the kind of collectivism he envisages is a far cry from the system of government ownership which most people identify with the word "socialism" today. His scheme is more accurately described as profit-sharing, or as cooperative enterprise. Mill cites several examples of experimentation with the profit-sharing idea, and hopes that wise capitalists will see the virtues of distributing surplus profits to their workers proportionately to the value of their contribution to the enterprise. It is in the interest of the capitalists to do this, Mill thinks, in order to increase the efficiency of their labor. "Capitalists are almost as much interested as labourers in placing the operation of industry on such a footing, that those who labour for them may feel the same interest in the work, which is felt by those who labour on their own account."[52] More significant, he thinks, would be the proliferation of firms wholly owned by the workers themselves. He grants the difficulty with which such enterprises are made into profitable affairs, due to the difficulty they have of obtaining working capital, but he finds several French examples of their success based on the temporary privation of the worker-stockholders and the careful saving and investment of their slender joint means. (The fifth edition of 1862 is particularly optimistic about the future of such cooperative firms.)

As cooperatives gain acceptance, the owners of capital will find it advantageous to lend to them, Mill believes. And gradually the system will be transformed into a fully cooperative order. Mill does not think it desirable, however, that cooperative societies should wholly supplant the profit-sharing capitalists at once. The unity of authority of the capitalist firm has many advantages. The private owner will "run judicious risks, and originate costly improvements" which the association might be tempted to avoid, and these things make for progress.[53]

The "civilizing and improving influences" of business associations based on lines such as these, not involving relationships of dependence, but

[52]John Stuart Mill, *Principles of Political Economy,* ed., W. J. Ashley (New York: Longmans, Green & Co., Inc., 1909), p. 762.

[53]*Ibid.,* p. 791.

of free and equal cooperation for a common interest, Mill considers inestimable. Public-spiritedness and "generous sentiments" would be developed in all who took part in the creation of a fully cooperative society. The spirit of selfish acquisition would decline, and the narrowness of family life, dominated by a father who sees the family group "as an expansion of self," would be overcome. A society would emerge which combines "the freedom and independence of the individual, with the moral, intellectual, and economical advantages of aggregate production." The triumph of the cooperative "would be the nearest approach to social justice, and the most beneficial ordering of industrial affairs for the universal good, which it is possible at present to foresee."[54]

Though cooperation is the principle of internal organization for Mill's firms, competition must exist among them. Mill is an inveterate foe of monopoly, both private and public. Economic competition is as important for progress as is the competition of ideas and ways of life. Monopoly encourages "the natural indolence of mankind" and leads to stagnation.[55] Men are naturally slaves of habit and must be prodded into originality and innovation. Every restriction of competition he therefore regards as evil. Competition is the midwife of progress.

What is the role of government vis-à-vis economic activity? Since trade is a social act, it is subject to public regulation in Mill's scheme. Wage and hours laws and similar restrictions on the economic activities of individuals and groups are legitimate and necessary. Public ownership, however, means monopoly, and Mill draws the line sharply against it, except for the municipal ownership of utilities which are only efficient as monopolies. Government can be of great help to private firms by serving as a depository and distributor of information which is turned up by the competitive process. Public funds may be used to stimulate economic activity, but they should always be expended to stimulate private cooperative enterprise, never to supersede it.

As far as public welfare functions are concerned, Mill does not think they should be so extensive as to diminish the energy and self-exertion of the population, but he prefers public to private charity as a guarantee against absolute destitution. The government ought to secure a certainty of subsistence to all, though no more than that.

A Natural Science of Politics

In his general methodological treatise of 1843, the *System of Logic*, Mill tells us that "the most effectual mode of showing how the sciences of Ethics and Politics may be constructed, would be to construct them." But he

[54]*Ibid.*, pp. 763, 791, 792.
[55]*Ibid.*, p. 793.

goes on to add that this is a task which he is "not about to undertake."[56] Nevertheless, he thinks he may be able to point the way to the construction of such a science by laying down the canons of scientific procedure in the study of society. He does this in Book VI of the *Logic*, a section which he entitles "The Logic of the Moral Sciences."

None of the propositions about the utility of liberty to progress and about the institutionalization of liberty which we have just surveyed, that Mill gives us in *Liberty, Representative Government,* and *Political Economy*, appear to be the product of applying these canons to the study of social phenomena. They are rather the shrewd intuitions of an erudite man of wide experience. If Mill had been a quite consistent person, he would have written these books not as definitive statements, which they appear to be, but as hypotheses to be tested and revised by future generations of social scientists. By what procedures does Mill think that such hypotheses could be turned into scientific facts?

The General Science of Society

Mill thinks that it is impossible to create a separate and independent science of government. Government more than all other social phenomena, he tells us, is inextricably "mixed up, both as cause and effect, with the qualities of the particular people or of the particular age." Thus, he concludes, "all questions respecting the tendencies of forms of government must stand part of the general science of society."[57] By this he seems to mean that the functions and effects of government are broad and their boundaries indefinite, and that they change from place to place and from age to age as a result of cultural differences. There can be independent social sciences, however, which deal with more specialized and fixed institutions of society than government. Political economy, for example (what we today call "economics"), Mill describes as an autonomous discipline, despite the interdependence of all the parts and aspects of society, for it is clear in this case that "the immediately determining causes are principally those which act through the desire for wealth." The phenomena which political economists study are those which "take place in consequence of the pursuit of wealth."[58] We can, therefore, build a science around the single concept of wealth-getting. But with the phenomena of government we can associate no such single-minded activity. Government, as he says in another work, affects the aggregate interests of society.[59] Its study is, therefore, coextensive with the study of society as a whole.

[56]Mill, *A System of Logic*, Vol. II, p. 415.

[57]*Ibid.*, p. 500.

[58]*Ibid.*, p. 493.

[59]Mill, *Representative Government*, in *Utilitarianism, Liberty, and Representative Government*, p. 249.

What are the central problems of social science so considered? Mill observes that societies and cultures are quasi-organic wholes; all the parts of a society fit together. One problem which the social scientist tackles is the determination of the conditions under which these clusters of social phenomena are stable. This problem, in fact, defines an entire branch of social analysis, which Mill labels "social statics," borrowing from the terminology of Auguste Comte. When social change takes place, not one part of society alone but the entire organism is ultimately affected. We notice in comparing past states of society with those of today, and the various cultures of our own time one with another, that there are "Uniformities of Coexistence," and that these patterns alter as wholes.[60] What Mill wishes to discover are the causal laws determining how one "state of society" is transformed into another. The answer to the question of how governments change, and what kind of government goes with what kind of society, will be a by-product of this inquiry, for there is a "necessary correlation between the form of government existing in any society and the contemporaneous state of civilization." "To fix the laws according to which any state of society produces the state which succeeds it and takes its place" therefore defines the second great branch of social science, "social dynamics." This problem also constitutes "the fundamental . . . problem of the social science."[61]

Millian social science in its second and principal branch is, then like Marxian social science, pre-eminently a science of history. Unlike Marx, however, Mill does not claim to have worked out the historical pattern. He writes in the *Logic* from the position of a person at the beginning of an inquiry rather than at the end. He does not claim to know, for example, what the final product of historical change will be, or whether the direction of change is for the better or for the worse. He *believes* that he sees a general tendency of improvement. But this has at present only the status of a "theorem," a proposition which awaits proof. And he finds it "conceivable that the laws of human nature might determine, and even necessitate, a certain series of changes . . . which might not on the whole be improvements."[62]

Is there an underlying causal agent which figures as the prime mover in Mill's theory of historical development, analogous to the Marxian technological dialectic? In one place, Mill speaks of the "great assistance" it would be to social scientists "if it should happen to be the fact, that some one element in the complex existence of social man is pre-eminent over all others as the prime agent of the social movement." Borrowing again from Comte, he thinks that there is such an element, and that it consists in intel-

---

[60]Mill, *A System of Logic*, Vol. II, p. 507.
[61]*Ibid.,* pp. 508, 516.
[62]*Ibid.,* p. 509.

lectual development. Material advances and great social changes have always been preceded by changes in opinion and in modes of thought, he believes. "The state of the speculative faculties, the character of the propositions assented to by the intellect, essentially determines the moral and political state of the community . . . [as well as] the physical." But again he is more modest than Marx, for while he is sure of the dependence of all else on intellectual change, he does not claim to understand the dynamics of mind. "The question remains," he writes, "whether this law ['the law of the successive transformations of human opinions'] can be determined."[63]

The Inverse Deductive
and the Concrete Deductive Method

How may we proceed to determine the law of intellectual development? The first step is inductive, and consists in a thorough examination of the entire historical record of human life, especially the history of ideas. From this examination we attempt to formulate an empirical law, a statement of the uniformities or order discovered in our reading of the record. (Mill cites Comte's law of the three stages as an example of what he has in mind.) This is only a beginning, however, for descriptions of empirical uniformities do not constitute science. An explanation must be given for the uniformities which we discover. The law must be "converted into a scientific theorem by deducing it a priori from the principles of human nature."[64] Mill calls this procedure the inverse deductive method of analysis.

For this method to be employed, two other disciplines must be constructed as foundations for the general science of society. These are psychology and what Mill calls "ethology." Psychology treats of the "laws of mind" and composes "the universal or abstract portion of the philosophy of human nature."[65] Its laws specify the way in which one mental state succeeds another. As examples, Mill gives the "Law of Association" developed by Hume, Hartley, and by his father—e.g., that "similar ideas tend to excite one another," or "that when two impressions have been frequently experienced . . . either simultaneously or in immediate succession, then whenever one of these impressions, or the idea of it, recurs, it tends to excite the idea of the other."[66] These and all of the laws which describe the workings of the human mind are built up, Mill believes, by experimental inquiry. Psychology is, therefore, constructed through the use of an inductive method, by which we move from observations of empirical events to generalizations concerning uniformities of behavior.

[63]*Ibid.*, pp. 523, 524, 525.
[64]*Ibid.*, p. 525.
[65]*Ibid.*, p. 445.
[66]*Ibid.*, p. 436.

When we compare the universality of our laws of mind with the diversity of human behavior throughout the world, we realize that circumstances vitally modify the operation of the general laws. Psychology alone cannot explain the different patterns of behavior which we discover. Englishmen do not act in the same way as Frenchmen, nor Germans like the Chinese. Another science is needed, therefore, before we are able to explain the various empirical laws which we form on the basis of observation of different patterns of behavior. We need a science of the laws of the formation of character, which Mill dubs "ethology," to allow us to connect our general psychological laws with these empirical laws. By contrast with psychology, and with the process of forming empirical laws, ethology would be deductive rather than inductive. "The laws of the formation of character are," Mill writes, "derivative laws, resulting from the general laws of mind; and are obtained by deducing them from those general laws; by supposing any given set of circumstances, and then considering what, according to the laws of mind, will be the influence of those circumstances on the formation of character."[67] Observation and experiment enter into ethological analysis as the last rather than the first step. Having "deduced theoretically the ethological consequences of particular circumstances of position," we compare our deductions "with the recognized results of common experience."[68] If they correspond, we can consider our ethological hypotheses validated. An analogue to ethology in the physical sciences is astronomy. Its laws can be deduced from mechanics, the general science of motion, and verified by observation of the motion of the heavenly bodies. Mill calls the method by which his ethological laws are derived the "physical" or "concrete deductive method."

If we were able to complete the sciences of psychology and ethology, should we not be able to deduce a priori the law of succession of states of society? Should we not be able with this to reconstruct a priori all of past history and to predict a priori the whole pattern of the future, using direct observation only as an empirical check? Why, in solving the riddle of social and political dynamics, must we instead use the much more laborious procedure of the inverse deductive method, which Mill insists be our tool? Why must we build inductively, from observation, the laws of social dynamics and only then show that they could have been deduced from the laws of human nature?

Mill answers this question in detail. The reason that social dynamics cannot be an a priori science lies in the complexity of the social data, the extraordinarily large number of variables which are involved. With the resources of psychology and ethology we should indeed be able to determine

---

[67]*Ibid.*, p. 454.
[68]*Ibid.*, p. 459.

the effect of any one cause on society. "But when the question is that of computing the aggregate result of many coexistent causes; and especially when, by attempting to predict what will actually occur in a given case, we incur the obligation of estimating and compounding the influence of all the causes which happen to exist in that case; we attempt a task, to proceed far in which, surpasses the compass of the human faculties."[69] This does not mean that there are no laws operative, or that they are not certain. It is simply a problem of the complexity of the data to which the laws must be applied.

This is true only of the general science of society, however, according to Mill. In the particular sciences, such as political economy, where the data are more confined and the operative causes fewer, one can employ the concrete deductive method with success. But even here one must realize that "all the general propositions which can be framed by the deductive science, are . . . in the strictest sense of the word, hypothetical. They are grounded on some supposititious set of circumstances, and declare how some given cause would operate in those circumstances, supposing that no others were combined with them."[70] If the supposed circumstances have been taken from the actual circumstances of a particular society, the conclusions will hold for that society, provided that all modifying factors not taken into account can be excluded.

Very limited political questions might also be answered in this way, Mill says, by the deductive method. We might endeavor "to ascertain what would be the effect of the introduction of any new cause, in a state of society supposed to be fixed." Thus we might produce knowledge "sufficient for the more common exigencies of daily political practice." But it would be "liable to fail in all cases in which the progressive movement of society is one of the influencing elements; and therefore more precarious in proportion as the case is more important."[71] Therefore, in general, we are constrained in the study of politics to adopt not the concrete but the inverse deductive method which requires us to generalize first from historical observations and then to relate these generalizations to the laws of human nature.

What exactly do we prove when we perform this kind of analysis? We cannot demonstrate that the empirical law which we have discovered is the only one which our psychological and ethological laws could have produced. We cannot demonstrate anything of necessity but can only show "that there were strong a priori reasons for expecting it, and that no other order of succession or coexistence would have been so likely to result from the nature of man and the general circumstances of his position." Often we

[69]*Ibid.*, p. 487.
[70]*Ibid.*, p. 491.
[71]*Ibid.*, p. 511.

cannot even do this. We might not be able to show "that what did take place was probable a priori, but only that it was possible."[72] Nevertheless, Mill considers the inverse method to be a "real process of verification"[73] and a genuine means of explaining empirical laws.

The laws which we might work out in this manner would not be adequate for prediction, Mill grants. But they would be useful for guidance, if they made it possible "in any given condition of social affairs . . . to understand by what causes it had . . . been made what it was; whether it was tending to any, and to what, changes; what effects each feature of its existing state was likely to produce in the future; and by what means any of those effects might be prevented, modified, or accelerated, or a different class of effects superinduced."[74] It was not a chimerical hope that "general laws" might be ascertained which could answer these questions. Presumably, their development and demonstration would constitute the acid test of the entire body of Mill's own theories of liberty and representative government.

From Science to Art

If Mill has no hope that social science can be put on a footing that would permit precise prediction, what does he think of its utility for purposes of greater social control, of manipulation? What effect would the development of political science have on the art of politics? The rules of the art, Mill tells us, are adapted from the laws and theorems of the science. In one place he, in fact, seems almost to identify the two. "Art in general," he writes, "consists of the truths of Science, arranged in the most convenient order for practice, instead of the order which is the most convenient for thought."[75] We receive the impression that all that art does is to transform the propositions of science from the indicative into the imperative mood. "Science . . . lends to Art the proposition (obtained by a series of inductions or deductions) that the performance of certain actions will attain" some specified end. "From these premises Art concludes that the performance of these actions is desirable, and finding it also practicable, converts the theorem into a rule or precept."[76]

From these passages we conclude that a sophisticated social science would be a powerful instrument, indeed, in the hands of the political practitioner. But here Mill is speaking very generally of science and art, and not

[72]*Ibid.*, p. 512.

[73]For some of the difficulties involved in the idea that this is a genuine process of verification, see Fred Kort, "The Issue of a Science of Politics in Utilitarian Thought," *American Political Science Review*, XLVI (1952), 1150-52.

[74]Mill, *A System of Logic*, Vol. II, p. 464.

[75]*Ibid.*, p. 549.

[76]*Ibid.*, p. 546.

specifically of the general science of society, of which politics is an aspect. In another place we are given quite a different picture. Indeed, Mill writes, we might be able some day to lay bare all the causes on which social phenomena depend, and we might also discover that the manner in which those causes act could be reduced to rather simple laws. "Yet," he writes, the political artist might find that "no two cases . . . admit of being treated in precisely the same manner." The variety of circumstances on which the outcome depends in different cases might be so great, "that the art might not have a single general precept to give, except that of watching the circumstances of the particular case, and adapting our measures to the effects which according to the principles of the science, result from those circumstances." Despite the fact that social phenomena conform to universal laws, it may be impossible to lay down "practical maxims of universal application."[77] It is not to be supposed, therefore, within the confines of a Millian political universe, that the computer will some day substitute for the prudential faculties of the statesman.

Freedom and the "Invisible Hand" of Libertarian Process: Robert Nozick

Mill Plus Locke

Robert Nozick, a young Professor of Philosophy at Harvard, has recently taken up the Millian cause of defending the external liberty of individuals against political and social encroachments peculiar to a democratic age. Like Mill, he is concerned with safeguarding freedom of expression, especially freedom of life style. On the first page of his preface, in order to underline the importance of individual autonomy, he announces that governments may not coerce citizens "for their *own* good or protection," an expression reminiscent of Mill's injunction that a person's "own good, either physical or moral, is not a sufficient warrant" for state interference. However, Nozick is also worried about the Lockean value of inviolable property right, which Mill considerably modified. He therefore couples with this statement the assertion that the state may not compel people to help others, a position with which it is doubtful Mill would agree.[78] It is also significant that Nozick is not concerned, as Mill was, with the utility of generic man "as a progressive being" (i.e., as a developing social animal) but only with the rights of individuals as such. Like Locke, he is a pure individualist.

---

[77] *Ibid.*, p. 463.

[78] Robert Nozick, *Anarchy, State and Utopia* (New York: Basic Books, Inc., 1974), p. ix; J.S. Mill, *On Liberty*, p. 13.

Nozick and Rawls.   A chief target of Nozick's book is John Rawls, his Harvard colleague whose philosophical defense of neo-welfarism we analyzed in Chapter Ten. Nozick spends about fifty pages of text in an effort to refute Rawls's argument.[79] The attack on Rawls is of special significance in a time in which established centralized modes of welfare administration have been discredited as corrupt and inefficient. The book appears at least at one level, as a political tract, though the author denies that it was his intention to polemicize.[80] Nozick denies the justice of any redistributive scheme whatsoever, beyond what is required to provide peace, order, and the security of property, and he particularly denies the justice of Rawls's scheme. The reader will recall that Rawls's argument begins not with individual right but with social obligation, and permits inequality of wealth and authority "only if they result in compensating benefits for everyone, and in particular for the least advantaged members of society."[81]

Justification of a Minimal State.   The starting point of Nozick's libertarian argument is a Lockean state of nature. (Nozick cites Locke's description of the state of nature copiously in his own description of it.) But while it takes Locke forty-six octavo pages to get the reader into a state of political society, Nozick requires one hundred thirty-seven quarto pages. He moves first to private protection associations, thence to an ultraminimal state, and finally to the minimal state. (An ultraminimal state, like the minimal state, monopolizes the use of force, but provides protection only to those who purchase its services in the market.)[82] The justification probably takes so long because Nozick's starting point is simply an aggregate of separate persons.

> The moral side constraints upon what we may do, I claim, reflect the fact of our separate existences. They reflect the fact that . . . there is no moral outweighing of one of our lives by others so as to lead to a greater overall *social* good. There is no justified sacrifice of some of us for others. This root idea . . . also . . . leads to a libertarian side constraint that prohibits aggression against another.[83]

Though he cites it in describing the state of nature, Locke's Law of Nature plays no part in Nozick's moral theory, nor does a legislating God, who requires of us mutual protection (either as a reality or as a convenient myth). Nozick must therefore establish the state entirely on the basis of a

[79]Nozick, *op.cit.*, pp. 183-231.

[80]*Ibid.*, p. xii.

[81]John Rawls, *A Theory of Justice* (Cambridge, Mass.: Harvard University Press, 1971), p. 190.

[82]See *ibid.*, pp. 26ff.

[83]*Ibid.*, p. 33. The word "sacrifice" in this context embraces any coerced sharing of goods or resources with other individuals.

demonstration of what the enlightened interest of property-loving individuals requires, and which the free market is simply unable to provide, e.g., adequate compensation for certain kinds of aggression against persons.[84] Another reason for the lengthy argument is that Nozick realizes that even a minimal state is to a *degree* redistributive, in that it requires tax money, i.e., the taking of property, a problem that Locke apparently overlooked.

Nothing Beyond the Minimal State. Having justified a minimal state, Nozick goes on to argue that nothing beyond the maintenance of peace and the security of persons and property by the state can be justified.[85] His state turns out to be more minimal than that of Locke, who required that the state be the guardian of public morals. For Nozick there exists no public criterion of morality, nor any shared principle of right that might require the slightest redistribution of social resources in the name of redistributive justice. Rawls, the reader will remember, based his conception of rational behavior in the "original position," from which he derives his welfare state, on the Kantian conception of universal Right. It was a "procedural interpretation—of Kant's conception of autonomy and the categorical imperative. . ."[86] But Nozick has no concept of universal right which serves as a principle of community, of sharing among individuals. His world is populated by *absolutely* autonomous individuals, who share nothing by nature or by right but their individuality.

The logical culmination of Nozick's theory of the human condition is what he calls an "entitlement theory" of justice, which he states in the following terms:

> From each according to what he chooses to do, to each according to what he makes for himself (perhaps with the contracted aid of others) and what others choose to do for him and choose to give him of what they've been given previously . . . and haven't yet expended or transferred.[87]

In a society so ordered, any redistribution will be the result either of the "invisible hand" of impersonal market forces or of free gifts by individuals. Coerced redistribution is illegitimate.

From Locke to Mill

To this point the reader may think that Nozick's book fits better in a chapter on Locke than in one on Mill, since our concern has been to show the grounds of Nozick's theory of the minimal night-watchman state. If the

[84]See *ibid.*, pp. 65-66.
[85]*Ibid.*, p. 149.
[86]Rawls, *A Theory of Justice,* p. 256.
[87]*Op.cit.*, p. 160

book went no further than this, the reader would be right. But having arrived here in his argument, Nozick pronounces the result to be quite dull! He asks: "Doesn't the idea, or ideal, of the minimal state lack luster? Can it thrill the heart or inspire people to struggle or sacrifice?"[88] Here we sharply diverge from the Lockean frame of reference, for Locke was quite unconcerned with utopian luster, as were the men who rallied to the banners of the cause which the *Second Treatise* justifies. They were interested in the security of persons and properties, and nothing more. Mill, by contrast, was chiefly concerned with the promotion of the "higher pleasures," and hence with life styles, and with cultural change and development. In the last brief chapter of his book, entitled "A Framework for Utopia," Nozick reveals his clear affinity with Mill in his shared concern for these values.

Freedom and Utopia.   Nozick's agreement with Mill that man is a developing creature, that his values are not statically given as Locke believed, is revealed in his interest in utopia-building. A utopia is a world that we creatively imagine, in which our ideal life can be led to the fullest. And Nozick assumes that human utopias will be multiform and infinite in number. For we all have different conceptions of the good society and the good life.[89] Since the efficient protection of property is surely a matter of potential universal agreement, the institutional diversity celebrated by Nozick reveals a concern for freedom in the working out of diverse life styles, each one the special product of a free man's creative imagination. Nozick fantasizes a condition of society in which all individuals enter a market in life style groups. Acting upon their private conceptions of goodness, each seeks like-minded persons in the open market of association. The market then functions like an "invisible hand," as in Adam Smith's model of competitive enterprise, to produce, over time, an optimal clustering of dynamically stable groups. The advantages of this device, which can only operate within the parameters of a minimal state, are, according to Nozick, that nearly every utopian will find it acceptable, and that it allows nearly all utopian conceptions to be realized, without guaranteeing the triumph of any individual utopia.[90]

Life style, is, of course, a lived representation, an expression of meaning and significance, as well as a pattern of enjoyment. So the quest for utopia implies that it is a basically human characteristic to seek or to imagine meaning and significance in the world, something that Locke did not write about, but which was central to Mill's idea of man as a "progressive being." Nozick speaks quite openly about the problem of meaning for the free man. Early in his book, he presents a tentative effort at defining the es-

[88]*Ibid.*, p. 297.
[89]*Ibid.*, pp. 297-98.
[90]*Ibid.*, pp. 318-19.

sential characteristics of human nature, his normative view of the human person. A (good?) person is a being that is "not merely the plaything of immediate stimuli, [but rather] a being that limits its own behavior in accordance with some principles of or picture it has of what an appropriate life is for itself and others."[91] He then goes on to say that it is through this ability that a person gives meaning to his life.[92]

Having raised the question of meaning, however, Nozick finds himself unable to give an answer to it—to how meaning can be defined. Instead, he raises a series of difficult correlative issues, such as, are there certain modes of treating individuals (including ourselves?) that are incompatible with meaningful life, whether utilitarian "happiness" might be substituted for "meaningfulness," and whether one is morally obligated to have a meaningful life. He concludes this pregnant passage with the statement that he hopes "to grapple with these and related issues on another occasion."[93]

Having thus sidestepped the issue of "meaning," Nozick has (at least for the time being) foreclosed the possibility of establishing a public criterion, comparable to Mill's concept of man as a "progressive being," that would give coherence and moral significance to his chapter on utopia, which as we have seen, calls for creative experiments in group living. He contents himself, instead, with attempting to show that this (as yet) unjustified enterprise would best be carried out within the parameters of the minimal state, guided by the "invisible hand" of market forces (the economist's surrogate for "Divine Providence"). In addition to safeguarding Lockean property, this is what the minimal state is good for. But we are given no careful argument that what this state is good for, is itself good. Nozick has taken one butterfly-step from the confines of propertarian hedonism toward the definition of a moral ideal for freedom, toward "virtue." Mill took at least three. This seems to be something of a commentary on the present state of liberal political culture, at least in its academic representation. A chapter on Nietzschean nihilism is an appropriate sequel.

Bibliographical Note

The *Collected Works* of John Stuart Mill have been published by the University of Toronto Press, 7 volumes, 1963-69. J.S. Mill's *Autobiography*, New York: Columbia University Press, 1944, is an extremely interesting work and an important key to the structure of his entire thought. See also the excellent biography by Michael St. John-Packe, *The Life of John Stuart Mill*, London: Secker & Warburg, 1954. Analyses of his political theory in-

[91]*Ibid.*, p. 49.
[92]*Ibid.*, p. 50.
[93]*Ibid.*, pp. 50, 51.

clude R. P. Anschutz, *The Philosophy of J. S. Mill,* Oxford: Clarendon Press, 1953; John M. Robson, *The Improvement of Mankind: The Social and Political Thought of J. S. Mill,* Toronto: University of Toronto Press, 1968; the sections on Mill in John MacCunn, *Six Radical Thinkers,* London: Edward Arnold Publishers, Ltd., 1907; Sir Leslie Stephen, *The English Utilitarians,* New York: G. P. Putnam's Sons, 1900; and W. L. Davidson, *Political Thought in England, The Utilitarians from Bentham to J. S. Mill,* New York: Holt, Rinehart & Winston, Inc., 1916. Thomas Woods, *Philosophy and Poetry,* London: Hutchinson & Co., Ltd., 1961, emphasizes Mill's debt to Wordsworth and other romantic writers, and reveals the fundamental cleavage in the structure of his thought. Joseph Hamburger, *Intellectuals in Politics; John Stuart Mill and the Philosophic Radicals,* New Haven, Conn.: Yale University Press, 1965, discusses the effort to effect a comprehensive social and political reform based on Millian principles by parliamentary action in England. In a new study, Gertrude Himmelfarb distinguishes two Mills, the one of *On Liberty,* and another whom she identifies with the organicist, conservative, and elitist liberalism of Montesquieu and de Tocqueville. See *On Liberty and Liberalism. The Case of John Stuart Mill,* New York: Alfred A Knopf, 1974.

Many modern theorists develop Millian themes. See, for example, J. Roland Pennock, *Liberal Democracy, Its Merits and Prospects,* New York: Holt, Rinehart & Winston, Inc., 1950, which makes an argument for the individual and social utility of civil rights. Ernest Barker, *Reflections on Government,* New York: Oxford University Press, Inc., 1958, which eulogizes the virtues of government by discussion, is written squarely within the Millian tradition. See also Thomas L. Thorson, *The Logic of Democracy,* New York: Holt, Rinehart & Winston, Inc., 1963, which builds methodologically on the work of British analytical philosophy, of which the utilitarians are forebears, and comes up with a Millian justification for liberal democracy.

Chapter 14

The Freedom of the Over-Man: Nietzsche, Nazism, and Humanist Existentialism

The logical culmination of naturalism is the philosophy of Friedrich Nietzsche. In his scorn of the moral tradition Nietzsche is more thorough-going than any of his predecessors. At the same time, the moral vacuum of naturalism is felt keenly by him, and his hunger for noble values is more demanding than that of the other teleonaturalists we have discussed— Rousseau, Marx, Mill. At times he foresees with prophetic vision the cataclysm which the naturalistic revolution was bringing on the world: "If the doctrines of sovereign Becoming, of the fluidity of all . . . species, of the lack of any cardinal distinction between man and animal . . . are hurled into the people for another generation . . . then nobody should be surprised when . . . brotherhoods with the aim of robbery and exploitation of the non-brothers . . . will appear on the arena of the future." (This is not an inexact description of the Nazi stormtrooper.) Elsewhere he writes that if it becomes widely known that we have killed God, the night will close in, "an age of barbarism begins," and "there will be wars such as have never happened on earth."[1] (The last line was published just six years before the outbreak of World War I.)

Nietzsche's hope for the future was to create, with his own philosophy, a way to value beyond "good and evil," which were dying, and beyond the chaos which their destruction implied. In seeking the new way he insisted on remaining firmly within the naturalism which had brought it about. Perhaps naturalism, expressed in an extreme conception of in-dividual freedom, could somehow be brought to yield noble value. Was there a way beyond nihilism, not to the old "transcendence" but to an

[1] *Untimely Meditations,* II, 9; XI, 20; *Ecce Homo,* IV, 1, quoted in Walter Kaufmann, *Nietzsche,* 3rd rev. and enl. ed. (N.Y.: Vintage Books [Random House], 1968), p. 98. Copyright © 1968 by Princeton University Press.

"over-man," nature heightened and ennobled by being embraced to the full, by giving free reign to the ego, giving it the place of the old God? This is not only the problem which Nietzsche set for himself. It is the problem which modern man as such sets for himself. Will the final thinking-through end in nobility and the dignity of man, or in mad laughter, as in the case of Nietzsche?

Friedrich Nietzsche was born on October 15, 1844, into the world which had been created by the naturalism of Hobbes, Locke, and Rousseau. Advancing liberalism had enshrined the values of equality and sociability and the idea of the dignity of man as the right to property, security, and the pursuit of happiness. Commerce and industry were conquering chivalry, and the middle class was coming into its own. Socialism stood in the background, demanding a universalization of the values of the middle class. A façade of the moral tradition remained in social practice. As Locke had softened the strong language of his naturalism with traditional-sounding references to God and divinely bestowed values, so the nineteenth-century European world draped its materialism in the gentle pieties of Christian religion.

Nietzsche was born the son of a Lutheran minister in the small German city of Roecken, in Saxony. His grandfathers on both sides had also been members of the Lutheran clergy, and one of them had written a pious book on the deathlessness of Christianity. The family of the good pastor, happily bowing to Paul's dictum about every soul being subject to the higher powers, were enthusiastic patriots. As a sign of it they had named the new baby Friedrich Wilhelm after the Prussian King.[2]

When the boy was only four, his father died after a period of mental disorder brought on by a brain injury suffered in an accident, and the family moved away to Naumburg. There young Nietzsche grew up in the gentle company of five women relatives. Friedrich Wilhelm was the only male in the household. Even Walter Kaufmann, an admiring intellectual biographer of Nietzsche who is reluctant to explain Nietzsche's philosophy as a protest against this environment, admits that it must at least have influenced the beginnings of his mature thought. Surely "the will to power" manifest in the caustic directness and overstatement of Nietzsche's writings was the opposite of the gentility and meekness in the midst of which he grew up.[3]

After six years at a boarding school, where he excelled in religion and the classics, Nietzsche was sent to the University of Bonn. The fraternity life into which he threw himself there, however, proved uncongenial. When his favorite classics teacher, Friedrich Ritschl, moved to Leipzig, Nietzsche followed him there. It was while he was a student at Leipzig that he came upon

[2]Walter Kaufmann, *op. cit.,* p. 22. The following biographical sketch relies heavily on this study.
[3]*Ibid.*

Schopenhauer's *World as Will and Representation,* a book whose doctrine was to be the starting point of Nietzsche's own philosophizing, a doctrine in which, despite its pessimism, we find the kernel of the concept of the "will to power," Nietzsche's theory of value.

Though he had not yet finished his doctorate, Nietzsche was called in 1869 to a chair of classical philology at the University of Basel. The unusual and signal honor was accorded him on the recommendation of Ritschl, who had recognized his precocious genius in the classroom and in professional articles which the young scholar had published. He taught there for ten years, until he was compelled by ill health to retire in 1879. The rest of his life was to be a recurrent struggle with pain and illness, a tragic background for the exercise of Nietzsche's own "will to power," both in personal discipline and in philosophical exposition. The origin of his illness, which may also have been the origin of his final madness, is not clear. Biographers speculate that it may have been a fall from a horse which occurred during a period of military training in 1867 or during a brief service as a medical orderly in the Franco-Prussian War of 1870, when he fell ill with dysentery and diphtheria.

During his years as a professor of philology at Basel, Nietzsche began to develop and publish his philosophy in the form of studies in the classics. His first book, *The Birth of Tragedy* (1872) contained a new and important thesis on the character of Greek culture, though its breezy style and lack of apparatus (no footnotes) brought scathing reviews from some scholarly quarters. Alongside the Apollonian themes of form, restraint, and balance, which earlier scholars had seen as central and dominant, Nietzsche had discovered the Dionysian quality of Greek life—the theme of wild ecstasy represented by the satyr and the bacchanal and by the rites of the god Dionysus. From the pages of the Greek classics Dionysus entered into Nietzsche's own life as his guiding spirit, the symbol of "the will to power" and of the dynamic, ebullient, overflowing Nature which the philosopher celebrated in all his works. From *The Birth of Tragedy* to his last book, Nietzsche worked on the task of integrating in a single, naturalistic whole the two conflicting elements of Greek life, the Apollonian and the Dionysian, as a standard of value for himself and one which might produce the "over-man" of the future.

After his retirement from Basel, Nietzsche passed his time as a semi-invalid alternately in Sils-Maria, in the Upper Engadine valley of Switzerland, in the summer and in Nice or Genoa in the winter. Sometimes he suffered for several days from painful migraine headaches combined with retching fits in which he coughed up phlegm. The period was philosophically a productive one, however. In 1882 he published *The Gay Science* and in 1883 to 1885, his masterpiece, *Thus Spake Zarathustra,* a long allegorical poem in which he set forth the final version of his philosophy of the "will to power." In 1886 appeared *Beyond Good and Evil,* in which Nietzsche repeated the central elements of his doctrine in a clearer, less masked style than he employed in *Zarathustra*. *Toward a Genealogy of Morals*, a most important statement of his political thought, he brought out in 1887.

The Case of Wagner appeared in 1888. Nietzsche had met Richard Wagner when he was in Leipzig late in 1867. From Basel he went to visit the composer at his villa at Triebschen, a town within easy reach. He later wrote of these days as the happiest of his life. In Wagner Nietzsche found something of the father he had missed as a young boy. He also must have found in him a magnificent embodiment of the "will to power," the continued possibility of great creativity in our time. He also had loved Wagner's music from his student days, and *Tristan* called up images of the frenzied Dionysian bacchanal which was so central a symbol in Nietzsche's philosophy of life.

Despite all that it meant to him then and later, Nietzsche broke off his friendship with Wagner after the composer moved to Bayreuth. At the cultural center there Wagner became the high priest of the ideals of the new Wilhelmine Reich. Wagner's sentimental German nationalism, set forth in racist and anti-Semitic political essays which were later to play a significant role in the formation of the ideology of the Third Reich, Nietzsche detested. To Nietzsche, Bayreuth represented cultural philistinism of the worst kind, and in embracing Bayreuth, Wagner, as he saw it, had sold his independence of soul. To maintain his own, the break with his friend was a necessity. "What did I never forgive Wagner?" Nietzsche wrote in *Ecce Homo*, one of his last works, "that he became *reichsdeutsch*."[4] That his love for Wagner's fascinating wife Cosima may have played a role in the decision ought not to be discounted.

The extravagant egoism of *Antichrist* and *Ecce Homo*, which Nietzsche wrote along with the essay on his relationship to Wagner in 1888, may be a sign of his impending mental collapse. The breakdown came the next year, during a visit to Turin. The remaining decade of his life was spent in an asylum in Jena and in Weimar, the city of Goethe, where he died on August 25, 1900. Moments of lucidness were surrounded by wild ravings in which Nietzsche sometimes declaimed his own prophetic poetry at the top of his voice and penned notes to his friends, signed "Dionysus."

Life as Art and Will:
Nietzsche's *Weltanschauung*

Aphorisms and Metaphysics

The aphoristic method which Nietzsche employed to set forth his ideas is a clue to his metaphysics. It appears to be rambling, unsystematic, a stream of consciousness style. This was precisely the way Nietzsche con-

[4]Quoted in *ibid.*, p. 38.

ceived the world to be—a torrent of life and movement. There was no possibility of capturing it in a grand and definitive philosophical system. In rejecting systematic philosophy Nietzsche was reacting not only against the noumenal ontologies of writers like Plato and Aristotle but also against the great naturalistic systems produced by moderns such as Marx, and Mill. In their attempt to save reason and order and intelligibility, these writers had transmuted noumenal transcendence and immanence into a teleological historical mechanism, from whose naturalistic movements they saw emerging at the end of the historical process a new world of value. The metaphysical status of the new world, as we have seen, is difficult to determine.

Nietzsche takes a radically skeptical stance. No ultimate reality can be known, whether conceived as transcendent form or historical law. The flux of empirical events, of which we are directly aware, is all that we can know. "There is no 'being' behind doing, effecting, becoming," he writes in *The Genealogy of Morals.* " 'The doer' is merely a fiction added to the deed—the deed is everything. The popular mind in fact doubles the deed; when it sees the lightning flash, it is the deed of a deed: it posits the same event first as cause and then a second time as its effect."[5] We are reminded of Dewey's insistence on action and process as the prime reality. As in Dewey, it is not a mechanical but a willed reality. We are the causes of human events in the flux of which we participate. Even what appears in the nonhuman world to be the result of mechanical causation Nietzsche would like to reduce to the effect of will. In *Beyond Good and Evil,* for example, he writes:

> The question is in the end whether we really recognize the will as *efficient,* whether we believe in the causality of the will: if we do—and at bottom our faith in this is nothing less than our faith in causality itself— then we have to make the experiment of positing the causality of the will hypothetically as the only one. . . . One has to risk the hypothesis whether will does not affect will whatever "effects" are recognized—and whether all mechanical occurrences are not, insofar as a force is active in them, a will force, effects of will.[6]

One might ask whether, in making will the first and efficient cause of reality, Nietzsche has not imported into his philosophy a metaphysical "spook," a single principle of "ultimate" explanation like the dialectical *Geist* of Hegel which he had just exorcised. His reply would probably be that his own hypothesis was based on direct personal experience and was not a dubious metaphysical inference from external empirical observations. In his own life the daily battle against the weakness of femininity and of physical illness had made him plenteously aware of the causal power of will.

[5]Friedrich Nietzsche, *On the Genealogy of Morals,* in Walter Kaufmann, trans. and ed., *Basic Writings of Nietzsche* (New York: Modern Library, 1968), p. 481.

[6]*Beyond Good and Evil in ibid.,* p. 238.

If the primary reality is creative will, what models does it employ? Once more like Dewey, Nietzsche's reply is: "No models." No standards are given by Nature. The watchword is, therefore, "Experiment! See what works." Here once more Nietzsche breaks sharply with tradition. Of the system-builders of the past he writes:

> The small single questions and experiments were considered contemptible. . . . To solve all with one stroke . . . that was the secret wish. . . . The unlimited ambition . . . to be the 'unriddler of the universe' made up the dream of the thinker.[7]

Nietzsche's experiments are without moral horizon or limit. Christian morality is specifically and unequivocally rejected. "The unconditional will of Christianity to recognize *only* moral values, [is] the most dangerous and uncanny form of all possible forms of a 'will to decline.' . . . Confronted with morality . . . life *must* continually and inevitably be in the wrong, because life *is* something essentially amoral."[8] The dangers hidden in such an approach, especially since experiment for Nietzsche meant an experience to be lived, not a laboratory affair, are hinted at in the following passage from *Beyond Good and Evil:*

> A new species of philosophers is coming up . . . these philosophers of the future might require in justice, perhaps also in injustice, to be called *attempters [Versucher]*. This name is . . . only an attempt and, if one prefers, a temptation [*Versuchung*].[9]

The Nietzschean experimenter is more artist than scientist, for his inquiries are not directed toward the discovery of laws but are rather aspects of a creative enterprise. From the beginning of his philosophical work Nietzsche thought primarily in the categories of aesthetics, and the figure of the man who experiences preeminently "the will to power," and who is capable of becoming the "over-man" is the figure of the artist. (Nietzsche speaks of saints, artists, and philosophers in this connection. In the later works, however, as Kaufmann notes, the saint drops out. In the way that Nietzsche viewed the world, surely the philosopher must be deemed a kind of artist.) In his first book, *The Birth of Tragedy,* he declares that the task of his "audacious book" is "to look at science in the perspective of the artist."

[7]Quoted from *The Dawn* in Kaufmann, *Nietzsche,* p. 86.

[8]*The Birth of Tragedy,* in *Basic Writings,* p. 23.

[9]Quoted in Kaufmann, *Nietzsche,* p. 86. The English translation of *Versucher* offered here by Kaufmann seems hardly adequate. *Versucher* means "tempter, seducer, the Devil, experimenter." That the former rather than the latter meaning is intended here seems indicated by Nietzsche's use of the word "temptation" in the next sentence. This is an excellent example of the way Nietzsche, the philologist, enjoyed playing games with similar-sounding words.

He also says that "the existence of the world is *justified* only as an aesthetic phenomenon." And in another passage he remarks that he is convinced "that art represents the highest task and the truly metaphysical activity of this life."[10]

The supreme artist, like Rousseau's "Legislator," or Hegel's "World Historical Figure" becomes a god-figure in Nietzsche's philosophy. His archenemy is the Christian God. "Christian teaching . . . with its absolute standards, beginning with the truthfulness of God, . . . negates, judges, and damns art."[11] Since he has no models laid down to him by Nature, the creations of the Nietzschean artist must be peculiarly his own, the outpouring of his creative ego on the world. He makes up the world and its values as he works, out of the inspiration of his own genius. The good life is artistic and amoral.

Nietzsche's artist does not work in a void. If Nature presents him no ends, it does furnish beginnings. "Will" may be the primary causal force, but it must have materials to work with, and these are given by Nature. But what things are given by Nature? To find them one must examine the beginning of things. This means going back in time to historical beginnings (which are also presocial beginnings) and down beneath consciousness to beginnings in unconscious motives.

The Origins of Morality

The beginnings of things are symbolized for Nietzsche by the figure of the satyr, an imaginary being with whom the ancient Greeks peopled their tragic choruses.

> I believe, the Greek man of culture felt himself nullified in the presence of the satyric chorus, and this is the most immediate effect of the Dionysian tragedy, that the state and society and, quite generally, the gulfs between man and man give way to an overwhelming feeling of unity leading back to the very heart of nature. The metaphysical comfort . . . that life is at the bottom of things, despite all the changes of appearances, indestructibly powerful and pleasurable—this comfort appears in incarnate clarity in the chorus of satyrs, a chorus of natural beings who live ineradicably, as it were, behind all civilization and remain eternally the same, despite the changes of generations and of the history of nations.[12]

The joyful will to power, as represented by the amoral satyr then, is the beginning of things, both historically and now. Here we have a strong contrast with the naturalism of Hobbes. For Hobbes, the beginning of things is the universal drive for self-preservation. It is the foundation stone of society,

[10]*The Birth of Tragedy*, in *Basic Writings*, pp. 19, 23, 31-32.
[11]*Ibid.*, p. 23.
[12]*The Birth of Tragedy*, in *Basic Writings*, p. 59.

the state, all organized life. Nietzsche explicitly repudiates it. "Physiologists should think before putting down the instinct of self-preservation as the cardinal instinct of an organic being," he writes. "A living thing seeks above all to *discharge* its strength—life itself is *will to power;* self-preservation is only one of the indirect and most frequent *results.*"[13]

Those who possess the greatest capacity to exert power—" 'the powerful,' 'the masters,' 'the commanders' "—call themselves "the truthful." The root of the Greek word for this (Nietzsche used his philological knowledge in all his works as an instrument to demonstrate his philosophy) means "one who *is,* who possesses reality, who is actual."[14] They also fashion the terms of morality as well as those of truth and arrogate to themselves the words which mean "good" and "noble." "The noble, powerful, high-stationed and high-minded . . . felt and established themselves and their actions as good, that is, of the first rank, in contradistinction to all the low, low-minded, common and plebeian."[15] Among the ruling tribes, "whoever has the power to repay good with good, evil with evil, and also actually repays, thus being grateful and vengeful, is called good; whoever is powerless and unable to repay is considered bad."[16]

The idea of "justice" originates among those who are equal in power. To fight to resolve a conflict over possession of some good would mean mutual harm, so an understanding is worked out. An exchange is made, so that each partner to the arrangement receives his most urgent values, which are also guaranteed to him. The prudent concern for self-preservation is thus the origin of justice in the world. Nietzsche stresses that it derives from "the egoism of the consideration."[17] After the initial bargain is written into the positive law, into the tradition, being moral or ethical simply means obeying the law, and "*good* is what one calls those who do what is moral as if they did it by nature."[18] Conversely, being "evil" means being immoral, which in turn means resisting tradition.

Thus in going back to the beginning of things one finds everywhere that ego and power are the origins. Morality simply describes the actions of the strong, and justice arises as a utility of the strong and of those who are equal in power to secure their values. Both morality and justice are wholly subordinate and derivative. We are reminded of the Sophistic naturalism of Glaucon and of Thrasymachus in Plato's discourse on justice in *The Republic.* But Nietzsche also explains the morality of the weak and how it develops. Here we are on new ground.

[13]*Beyond Good and Evil,* in *Basic Writings,* p. 211.
[14]*Genealogy of Morals,* in *Basic Writings,* p. 465.
[15]*Ibid.,* p. 462.
[16]*Human, All-too-Human,* in *Basic Writings,* p. 147.
[17]*Ibid.,* p. 148.
[18]*Ibid.,* p. 149.

Nietzsche calls for a transvaluation of values. In doing so he demands a reversal of standards similar to the one which he attributes to the work of the Jews in ancient times. It was they, he claims, who developed out of their resentment of their masters a "slave morality" in which "the wretched alone are good: the poor, impotent, lowly alone are the good; the suffering, deprived, sick, ugly alone are pious, alone are blessed by God." By contrast the noble and powerful are deemed evil, "the cruel, the lustful, the insatiable, the godless to all eternity."[19] The Jewish scheme as well as the original pagan one originated in ego. In this case it is resentful, revengeful, impotent ego seeking a way out of its lowly position. The motives are no different in kind from those of the pagan value makers. With the rise and spread of Christianity the success of the Jewish "table turners" was guaranteed.

The Decay of Culture

To this point Nietzsche has engaged only in description, although at an epistemological and metaphysical level. He has told us what he takes to be the real and how it comes to be known. He has also described the process whereby values are generated. At this point his own preferences enter the picture, and he begins to prescribe. For he finds intolerable the world in which the slave morality of Jews and Christians prevails, and weakness rather than strength is enshrined as the good and noble. He wishes to restore the order of Nature, which he identifies as the *truly* good, and he hopes that this restoration will result from the decay of Christian values which he sees going on around him.

> What if a symptom of regression were inherent in the "good," likewise a danger, a seduction, a poison, a narcotic, through which the present was possibly living *at the expense of the future?* Perhaps more comfortably, less dangerously, but at the same time in a meaner style, more basely?—so that precisely morality would be to blame if the *highest power and splendor* actually possible to the type man was never in fact attained? So that precisely morality was the danger of dangers?[20]

Traditional Christian morality is not the only thing attacked by Nietzsche's pen. He writes also against the materialist liberalism and socialism of his time, which had made comfort and equality prime values and in doing so had also produced a cult of the mediocre in all things. The new doctrine is radically aristocratic. Nietzsche sees the nineteenth century as a leveling age which has destroyed the quality of civilization. The idea of the outstanding and the exceptional has been lost in the new regard for the

---

[19]*Genealogy of Morals,* in *Basic Writings,* p. 470.
[20]*Ibid.,* p. 456.

majority, the welfare of the many. "O Voltaire! O humaneness! O non-sense!" he writes.[21] He calls the French Revolution "that gruesome farce."[22] And he writes of democratic theorists as

> *levelers*—these falsely so-called "free spirits"— being eloquent and prolifically scribbling slaves of the democratic taste and its "modern ideas." . . . they are unfree and ridiculously superficial, above all in their basic inclination to find in the forms of the old society . . . just about the cause of *all* human misery and failure. . . . What they would strive for with all their powers is the universal green-pasture happiness of the herd, with security, lack of danger, comfort, and an easier life for everyone; the two songs and doctrines which they repeat most often are "equality of rights" and "sympathy for all that suffers"—and suffering itself they take for something that must be abolished![23]

A third devil to castigate is the Western cult of knowledge together with the optimistic spirit which hopes that all things can ultimately be known and all mystery dispelled. Nietzsche is thinking chiefly of the optimistic rationalism of the Enlightenment and its doctrine of progress, but he weaves it, strangely enough, together with the Socratic noumenalism which equated knowledge with virtue, and condemns the entire rationalist tradition of the West, in all its forms. Original man lived by instinct, like the satyr of the Greek chorus. And "in all productive men it is instinct that is the creative-affirmative force," while "consciousness acts critically and dissuasively."[24] When Socrates dethroned instinct and made knowledge the supreme guide, the natural order was inverted. Its final evil product was the "insatiable optimistic knowledge" of the nineteenth century.[25] The basic error of Socrates was to ascribe "to knowledge and insight the power of a panacea, while understanding error as the evil *par excellence*."[26]

All four enemies—Christian morality, liberalism, socialism, and rationalist science—were soon to have their day of reckoning. This would come in part because they had too long suppressed men with a will to power, who were bound to have their revenge, in part because the growing hunger for myth and mystery which spreading rationalism had occasioned would have to be satisfied, but chiefly because rationalist liberalism had simply promised too much and would be unable to make good on its promises, because they were based on false assumptions.

> We must not be alarmed if the fruits of this optimism ripen—if society, leavened to the very lowest strata by this kind of culture, gradually begins to

[21] *Beyond Good and Evil*, in *ibid.*, p. 237.
[22] *Ibid.*, p. 239.
[23] *Ibid.*, p. 244.
[24] *The Birth of Tragedy*, in *ibid.*, p. 88.
[25] *Ibid.*, p. 99.
[26] *Ibid.*, p. 97.

tremble with wanton agitations and desires, if the belief in the earthly happiness of all, if the belief in the possibility of such a general intellectual culture changes into the threatening demand for such an Alexandrian earthly happiness, into the conjuring up of a Euripidean *deus ex machina*.[27]

At this point Neitzsche becomes the prophet of universal calamity, a calamity which would clear the ground for the appearance of a new great artist, the "over-man," who will create culture anew and on a grander scale than ever before.

The Will to Power: The "Over-Man"

The Transvaluation of Values

Nietzsche does not only play the role of prophet. He also, by his writing, contributes to developing nihilism. He is an iconoclast, a smasher of idols, who by telling the truth about Nature helps to prepare the way for the triumph of Nature in the "over-man." He is a destroyer, but the work of destruction is itself creative. (Here we have one of the dialectical formulations of which Nietzsche, as well as Marx, was fond.) "I contradict as has never been contradicted before and am nevertheless the opposite of a No-saying spirit. I am a bringer of glad tidings. . . . For all that, I am necessarily also a man of calamity. For when truth enters into a fight with the lies of millennia, we shall have upheavals, a convulsion of earthquakes, a moving of mountains and valleys, the like of which has never been dreamed of. . . . There will be wars the like of which have never yet been seen on earth. It is only beginning with me that the earth knows great politics."[28]

What is the way beyond nihilism that Nietzsche offers? In expounding it we face problems of interpretation which have stirred profound controversy down through the years about what Nietzsche was trying to say. He tells us himself, and frequently, that he does not write openly but uses "masks." We must not always take him literally. In *Beyond Good and Evil* he advises philosophers to "Flee into concealment. And have your masks and subtlety, that you may be mistaken for what you are not, or feared a little." And later in the same essay he tells us that "Whatever is profound loves masks; what is most profound even hates image and parable. Might not nothing less than the *opposite* be the proper disguise for the shame of a god? . . . I could imagine that a human being who had to guard something precious and vulnerable might roll through life, rude and round as an old green wine cask with heavy hoops: the refinement of his shame would want

[27]*Ibid.*, p. 111.
[28]*Ecce Homo*, in *ibid.*, p. 783.

it that way." And in another place he says: "Every philosophy also *conceals* a philosophy; every opinion is also a hideout, every word also a mask."[29]

The possibility that he is using a mask must make us especially cautious in our interpretation of the frequently bloody and immoralist statements which abound in Nietzsche's work. In one place he even warns us that "Our highest insights must—and should—sound like follies and sometimes like crimes when they are heard without permission by those who are not predisposed and predestined for them."[30] But there is an ambiguity even in passages like this one. We could understand Nietzsche to mean that we are not to take his statements which approve of violence and cruelty literally, that they are merely masks behind which he seeks to convey a spiritual truth of a complicated sort. Or we could understand his sentence to mean that those readers who cannot break with traditional morality, who do not understand that what we have always called "good" is really the opposite, who are not ready to overturn, to transvalue existing social norms, will think his statements are crimes, because they are using the old and rejected frame of reference. They are not "predisposed" or "predestined" to hear them. The result of all this is that Nietzsche's influence has been in many directions. His sister, Elisabeth Foerster-Nietzsche, edited his works so as to make him an apologist of the ideals of Nazism, some of which—racism, anti-Semitism, German nationalism—he himself explicitly repudiated. He was claimed by the Nazi leaders as their own, as a precursor. (We shall have more to say about all this later on.) On the other hand, Nietzsche's writings also had a profound influence on Liberal thought, as represented by the existentialist philosopher, Karl Jaspers, for example. So when we attempt to interpret Nietzsche's subtle thought, and especially to condense it in a few textbook paragraphs, we are engaged in a perilous enterprise.

In my own reading ot Nietzsche, I cannot avoid the conclusion that he meant to be taken seriously when he wrote that the canons of traditional morality must be overturned, that we must accept the challenge of becoming immoralists. If this is not a starting point for the transvaluation of values, it is difficult to know where that effort, which Nietzsche believes is necessary to restore high culture, should begin. His contempt for Christianity, not only the hypocritical practice of it, but the norms themselves, and his disdain for the new "slave morality" of Liberal egalitarianism are too manifest to be misunderstood. The "Nature" which he celebrates, at least in its beginnings, is rough and raw. And his message is that civilization must make a new beginning. What else can he mean by passages like the following?

Man has all too long had an "evil eye" for his natural inclinations, so that they have finally become inseparable from his "bad conscience." An attempt at the

[29]*Beyond Good and Evil* in *Basic Writings,* pp. 226, 240-41, 419.
[30]*Ibid.,* p. 232.

reverse would *in itself* be possible—but who is strong enough for it? that is, to wed the bad conscience to all the *unnatural* inclinations, all those aspirations to the beyond, to that which runs counter to sense, instinct, nature, animal, in short all ideals hitherto, which are one and all hostile to life and ideals that slander the world. To whom should one turn today with *such* hopes and demands?

One would have precisely the *good* men against one; and, of course, the comfortable, the reconciled, the vain, the sentimental, the weary.[31]

He speaks of speculations such as these as a profound "world of insight," an "almost new domain of dangerous insights" revealing itself to daring travelers and adventurers. His experiments have taken him, like Machiavelli, across strange and wonderful seas to new lands. He understands the voyage as one which has carried him down below the veil of consciousness to the world of unconscious urge and desire. "Psychology is now again the path to the fundamental problems," he writes.[32] A link with Freud has been established.

Perhaps what is not clear to those who are unwilling to take Nietzsche's rude sayings at face value is that Nietzsche was thinking very much in terms of the future. He did not intend that we should stop at the beginnings, but rather expected that out of the suffering and cruelty of a return to Nature, a frank facing of and acceptance of the enormous egoism which he saw at the heart of Nature, the opposite values of gentleness and charity would emerge. Nowadays we are afraid to look Nature in the face. We feign an attachment to benignity, the other-regarding virtues that we do not genuinely feel. We try to deny our egos, and this makes us hypocrites. Were we to be frank, and finally assert ourselves, we should find that the dialectic of Nature would in the end add the gentle virtues to us. Perhaps this is what he intended by his phrase "the Roman Caesar, with Christ's soul."[33]

Time and again Nietzsche sounds the theme that things must get worse before they get better, that good will ultimately emerge from evil. "Speaking frankly, it is necessary that we once become rather evil that it may get better."[34] Even more clearly, he says in an early fragment: "Man, in his highest and most noble capacities, is wholly nature and embodies its uncanny dual character. Those of his abilities which are awesome and considered inhuman are perhaps the fertile soil out of which alone all humanity . . . can grow."[35] It would not seem that Nietzsche is here thinking

[31]*Genealogy of Morals*, in *Basic Writings*, p. 531.

[32]*Beyond Good and Evil* in *ibid.*, pp. 221, 222.

[33]Friedrich Nietzsche, *The Will to Power*, trans. and ed., Walter Kaufmann (New York: Random House, 1967), p. 513.

[34]*Untimely Meditations*, 4, quoted in Kaufmann, *Nietzsche*, p. 170.

[35]*Homer's Contest*, II, 369, cited in *ibid.*, p. 193.

of an apocalyptic process, like that described in Christian theology and in the Marxian dialectic, by which, after a period of necessary sin and suffering the "Heavenly Kingdom" comes. Nietzsche rejects the idea of an historical teleology and holds instead the doctrine of "the eternal return of all things." Thus from some passages it appears that he did not think of an eventual "humanity" replacing the harsher traits in man. These would remain, as the precondition, the background, the foil to other-regarding virtues. This is what the following seems to say:

> For all the value that the true, the truthful, the selfless may deserve, it would still be possible that a higher and more fundamental value for life might have to be ascribed to deception, selfishness, and lust. It might even be possible that what constitutes the value of these good and revered things is precisely that they are insidiously related, tied to, and involved with these wicked, seemingly opposite things—maybe even one with them in essence. Maybe!

And shortly afterward he remarks: "To recognize untruth as a condition of life—that certainly means resisting accustomed value feelings in a dangerous way; and a philosophy that risks this would by that token alone place itself beyond good and evil."[36] The dialectical duality of Nature, completed, embraces both what we call "good" and what we call "evil" as our true natural "good."

We should still remember, however, that we may be dealing here with one of Nietzsche's masks. Perhaps he is simply trying to make morality appealing, to give it life and verve. For in *The Gay Science* he writes: "Say that *morality is something forbidden.* Perhaps you will in that way gain the support for these things of the only type of men that matter—those who are *heroic.*"[37] This is in the context of an aphorism entitled "To the Preachers of Morals," whom he accuses of making popular currency out of "the happiness of virtue, peace of soul, of justice and immanent retribution" by preaching about them morning and night and thus wearing all the gold off them—"all the gold that was *in* them will have been changed to lead."[38] One should write of the *unity* of good and evil, the inseparability of the one from the other, make good more attractive by giving it violent and exciting company. But my own belief is that he was genuinely convinced of the duality of Nature. It is a theme that is frequently repeated. Nietzsche writes of the nobility of the ancient Athenians, who saw and accepted the duality. Pericles says in his funeral oration that Athenian boldness had raised monuments everywhere "to its goodness *and wickedness.*" Elsewhere he tells us there is no more decisive mark of a "higher nature" than to be "a genuine battleground" of the opposed values of "good and bad." He symbolizes this

---

[36] *Beyond Good and Evil,* in *Basic Writings,* pp. 200, 202. See also pp. 221, 244.
[37] *The Gay Science,* in *ibid.,* p. 174.
[38] *Ibid.*

battle as the conflict of "Rome against Judaea, Judaea against Rome"—the elite morality versus the slave morality—the union of Caesar with the soul of Christ.[39] What a grand experiment to attempt to put the two together.

The Over-Man

What, precisely, is the "over-man" to whom we should aspire? Does Nietzsche spell out the qualities of spirit which characterize him? Sometimes he does this by telling us what it is that he does *not* admire. In writing of the decline of modern man he deplores the tendency to "go down, down, to become thinner, more good-natured, more prudent, more comfortable." Thus, we conclude that the "over-man" is not good-natured, not prudent, not comfortable. If an historical model is available of the "over-man," it is found among the Romans, of whom Nietzsche writes that "nobody stronger and nobler has yet existed on earth or even been dreamed of." In speaking specifically about a future man Nietzsche calls him "the *redeeming* man of great love and contempt, the creative spirit." Above all, he is the supreme egoist. "He does *not* deny 'existence,' he rather affirms *his* existence and *only* his existence. Let there be . . . me." This affirmation Nietzsche sees as "optimum condition for the highest and boldest spirituality."[40]

One writer has culled from Nietzsche's work a list of six groups of qualities which constitute his standard of revaluation, the qualities of the "over-man." They are (1) uniqueness, individuality; (2) integrity, purity, sincerity, and, correspondingly, dislike for falsity and duplicity; (3) subtlety, delicacy, *nuances,* intellectuality, culture, nobility—things lacking in mass culture, in the mass man; (4) greatness of soul, in contrast with greatness measured merely by success; (5) measure, limitation, form, style—the Apollonian virtues, both in life and in art; (6) ripeness, serenity, perfection, "the golden nature."[41] Nietzsche makes it clear that although these particular traits will be found in all superior men, he does not wish to propose a wholly uniform standard of virtue. The stress is rather on variety, "an abundance of *aesthetic, equally justified* valuations: each the ultimate fact and measure of things for an individual."[42]

"Overcoming" Politics and Self-Control. The process of producing a new nobility of spirit, the "over-man," Nietzsche writes of in terms of "over-coming." Again we are faced with the problem of masks. When he speaks of *political* overcoming, of conquest, are we to take him literally; or

[39]*Genealogy of Morals,* in *Basic Writings,* pp. 477, 488.

[40]*Ibid.,* pp. 480, 489, 532, 544.

[41]George Allen Morgan, Jr., *What Nietzsche Means* (Cambridge, Mass.: Harvard University Press, 1941), pp. 119-120.

[42]Quoted in *ibid.,* p. 120.

does he rather intend such statements as allegories of spiritual overcoming, of the conquest of self? My own reading is that he means both. One writer has pointed out that while Nietzsche disparages *mere* external success, external power, he nevertheless "prizes outer controls very highly as means to the development of intrinsic power."[43] The two go together. Greatness of soul will beget and will build upon external power. So for example he writes, "Wherever the superior is *not* the more powerful *there is something missing in the superior himself:* he is only a fragment and shadow at most."[44] Thus it would seem that we must take seriously what Nietzsche says about political conquest and about the cruelty which is its inevitable counterpart.

In one passage in *Genealogy of Morals* Nietzsche writes of political conquest as a natural need of men of superior nature, which from time to time must be fulfilled.

> One cannot fail to see at the bottom of all these noble races the beast of prey, the splendid *blond beast* prowling about avidly in search of spoil and victory; this hidden core needs to erupt from time to time, the animal has to get out again and go back to the wilderness: the Roman, Arabian, Germanic, Japanese nobility, the Homeric heroes, the Scandinavian Vikings—they all shared this need.[45]

It is startling that Walter Kaufmann, a proponent of the spiritual and allegorical interpretation of Nietzsche, selects this passage to support the contention that Nietzsche did not have a racist conception of the "over-man." "The 'blond beast' is not a racial concept and does not refer to the 'Nordic race' of which the Nazis later made so much," he writes. True, as is obvious on the face of the quotation. Who would deny it? But by what evidence can Kaufmann also claim that "This alleged historical process . . . is viewed suprahistorically as an allegory or symbol of the extirpation of the impulses"?[46] The examples cited by Nietzsche are well known *historical* examples of political conquest. And he tells us equally plainly that "this hidden core needs to erupt from time to time." What the allegorical element might be is by no means clear. It is clear that Nietzsche *is* describing a pattern of historical recurrence. He is also advocating it. For he asks, a little later on in the same essay, "Must the ancient fire not some day flare up much more terribly, after much longer preparation? More: must one not desire it with all one's might? even will it? even promote it?"[47]

External overcoming in the future means for Nietzsche more than Viking raids. It means deep social and political revolution, a radical over-

[43]*Ibid.*, p. 123.

[44]Quoted in *ibid.*, p. 123.

[45]*Genealogy of Morals*, pp. 476, 477.

[46]Kaufmann, *Nietzsche*, p. 225.

[47]*Genealogy of Morals*, in *Basic Writings*, p. 490.

turning of the existing order. In *Ecce Homo,* one of the last essays penned before he went mad, Nietzsche prophesies that "the concept of politics will have merged entirely with a war of spirits; all power structures of the old society will have been exploded—all of them are based on lies."[48] Presumably they are based on lies, as Nietzsche sees it, because they enshrine to one degree or another the liberal democratic ideal. (This essay was written in 1888 when governments everywhere were giving at least lip-service to liberal and democratic ideals, even Wilhelmine Germany.) But the future, to conform to Nietzsche's conception of nobility, would have to be radically antidemocratic. The age of the "over-man" would be an aristocratic age.

In the new age of "truth," of looking Nature in the face and fulfilling her commands, the new order emerges as it has in past ages of truth. "Some pack of blond beasts of prey, a conqueror and master race, . . . organized for war and with the ability to organize, unhesitatingly lays its terrible claws upon a populace perhaps tremendously superior in numbers but still formless and nomad." The act of organization is by force and violence. "I think that sentimentalism which would have it begin with a 'contract' has been disposed of. He who can command, he who is by nature 'master,' he who is violent in act and bearing—what has he to do with contracts!"[49]

The aristocratic organizers are amoral artists. For as we have seen, morality is derivative, and we are here at the beginning of things. The primary social cause is the creative will and imagination of artists. "They do not know what guilt, responsibility, or consideration are, these born organizers; they exemplify that terrible artists' egoism that has the look of bronze and knows itself justified to all eternity in its 'work.' "[50] The canons of creation are *purely* esthetic, quite beyond the "good and evil" which involves human feelings, human suffering. Men are used as the sculptor uses the marble or the potter his clay, as insensible objects. But since man is not insensible, the result is cruelty. In writing of the origin of justice and the inculcation of habits of compliance to its commands—in other words, the beginning of a state, as an artistic creation—Nietzsche says, "It is here, one suspects, that we shall find a great deal of severity, cruelty, and pain." This is nothing to shrink from, for it is universally the way of animal nature. The "optimistic theoretical man" of today shrinks from it, because he is only half a man, half natural. "He no longer wants to have anything whole, with all of nature's cruelty attaching to it."[51]

Perhaps one reason that Nietzsche can so cheerfully celebrate cruelty and violence in the building of societies is that he assumes a vast gulf

[48]*Ecce Homo,* in *ibid.,* p. 783.
[49]*Genealogy of Morals,* in *ibid.,* p. 522.
[50]*Ibid.,* p. 523.
[51]*Genealogy of Morals,* in *ibid.,* p. 500; *The Birth of Tragedy* in *ibid.,* p. 113.

between the high-spirited elite and the average man, a gulf so deep as to demarcate two different species. His attitude is like that of the Southern slave owner who justifies the practices of slavery by seeing the slave as something less than a man. Even Walter Kaufmann, who emphasizes the spiritual aspects of Nietzsche, calls this doctrine "dynamite."

> It is dynamite. He maintains in effect that the gulf which separates Plato from the average man is greater than the cleft between the average man and a chimpanzee. While Nietzsche may agree with Christianity, as Simmel insists, in ascribing infinite worth to the individual soul, Nietzsche does not ascribe this worth to every man as such, but only to some men. . . . Most men are essentially animals.[52]

We are thus placed in a radically aristocratic frame of reference in which rulers are paired not with citizens or subjects but with slaves or, better still, with beasts of burden and domestic animals. Within such a frame of reference the most extreme tyranny is justified.

With all the blood and thunder to be expected with the appearance of the "over-man" there will also be, Nietzsche insists, great spiritual development involving self-discipline, self-overcoming ascetiscism of a high order. The artist will have to be cruel even to himself if he is to attain the highest level of being. Nietzsche writes of

> this secret self-ravishment, this artists' cruelty, this delight in imposing a form upon oneself as a hard, recalcitrant, suffering material and in burning a will, a critique, a contradiction, a contempt, a No into it, this uncanny, dreadfully joyous labor of a soul voluntarily at odds with itself that makes itself suffer out of joy in making suffer . . . as the womb of all ideal and imaginative phenomena, also brought to light an abundance of strange new beauty and affirmation, and perhaps beauty itself.

But to be capable of such self-overcoming the artist must be a person who also can subdue the external world. "The attainment of this goal" of self-conquest "would require a *different* kind of spirit from that likely to appear in this present age: spirits strengthened by war and victory, for whom conquest, adventure, danger and even pain have become needs . . .; it would require even a kind of sublime wickedness, and ultimate, supremely self-confident mischievousness in knowledge that goes with great health; it would require, in grief and alas, precisely this great health!"[53]

The achievement of the "over-man" is not to be understood as an apocalyptic moment like the coming of the Christian Kingdom of Heaven or the Marxist Classless Society, in which the old order is once and for all "transvalued" and done away with *in perpetuo*. No historical teleology is in-

---

[52]Kaufmann, *Nietzsche,* p. 151.

[53]*Genealogy of Morals,* in *Basic Writings,* pp. 523. 532.

volved. The frame of reference is purely naturalistic. There are no final ends in Nature.[54] Nietzsche says explicitly that the "over-man" is not the "last man." He utterly rejects the Liberal and Marxist conception of historical progress. The "over-man" is in reality a return to an earlier time, to pre-Christian Greece and Rome, when Nature was better understood and more fully embraced than today. The paganism he embodies, however, will be "raised up" (*aufgehoben*) in dialectical fashion. The Jewish-Christian experience will be imprinted on it. For the "over-man" will not be just Caesar, but Caesar with the soul of Christ. If he is attained, however, we are not at the end of history. A new decline will come in the cycle of years, which brings no final fulfillment but "the eternal return of all things." Nature is infinite and recurrent process, change, eternal Becoming.

The Charges Against Nietzsche

The Sense in which the Charges are False

We must deal more fully with the charges against Nietzsche. Certainly there is plenty of evidence in his writings that he was not a German nationalist, that he did not accept the idea of a Nordic or Aryan superrace, that he did not glorify "the State," and that he was not an anti-Semite. There is evidence that he actively disliked Germans, condemned the state, and liked and approved of Jews. He found German literature sadly wanting. "Everything ponderous, viscous, and solemnly clumsy, all long-winded and boring types of style are developed in profuse variety among Germans." Even Goethe's style did not escape infection by the German spirit. Nietzsche writes of himself as "so alien in [his] deepest instincts to everything German that the mere proximity of a German retards [his] digestion." Of the pompous jingoism of the Wilhelmine *Reich* he writes devastatingly:

> That *no* kind of swindle fails to succeed in Germany today is connected with the undeniable and palpable stagnation of the German spirit; and the cause of that I seek in a too exclusive diet of newspapers, politics, beer, and Wagnerian music, together with the presuppositions of such a diet: first, national construction and vanity, the strong but narrow principle *"Deutschland, Deutschland, ueber alles,"* and then the *paralysis agitans* of 'modern ideas.'[55]

In a preface to *The Will to Power* (which his sister neglected to use in its posthumous publication) Nietzsche specifically repudiates any connec-

---

[54]See, however, Kaufmann, *Nietzsche*, p. 172 which discusses Nietzsche's doctrine that Nature purposes perfection but leaves its actualization up to man.

[55]*Beyond Good and Evil*, in *Basic Writings*, p. 230; *Ecce Homo*, in *ibid.*, p. 703; *Genealogy of Morals*, in *ibid.*, pp. 594-95.

tion between the strong language of his own philosophy and the nationalist political aims of Germany:

> *The Will to Power*. A book for *thinking*, nothing else: it belongs to those to whom thinking is a *delight*, nothing else. That it is written in German is at least untimely: I wished I had written it in French in order that it might not appear as a confirmation of any *reichsdeutschen* aspirations.[56]

His regard for genius among the Jews was so great that in one place Nietzsche writes of them as the carrier of nobility of spirit *par excellence* in the Europe of his time. Of his English friend Helen Zimmern, he writes: "Of course Jewish:—it is terrific to what extent this race now holds the 'spirit' in Europe in its hands." And in another letter he says: "May heaven have mercy on the European intellect if one wanted to subtract the Jewish intellect from it."[57] Of anti-Semitic agitations he writes in *Genealogy of Morals,* "I do not like these latest speculators in idealism, the anti-Semites, who today roll their eyes in a Christian-Aryan-bourgeois manner and exhaust one's patience by trying to rouse up all the horned-beast elements in the people by a brazen abuse of the cheapest of all agitator's tricks, moral attitudinizing."[58] It is particularly passages like this which make one sympathetic to the interpretation of Nietzsche's approval of cruelty and violence as a mask. But there is, of course, always the possibility that *this* passage is the one which wears the mask!

Nietzsche's repudiation of political romanticism and nationalist chauvinism is just as clearly stated as the other disclaimers. "Now almost everything on earth is determined by the crudest and most evil forces, by the egotism of the purchasers and the military despots. The State, in the hands of the latter . . . wishes that people should lavish on it the same idolatrous cult which they have lavished on the Church."[59] With the Existentialist, of whom he is a precursor, Nietzsche refuses to glorify any institution. He is an individualist, and the doctrine of the "will to power" has to do with the power of the outstanding individual, not that of the collectivity or of its institution, the state.

The Sense in which
the Charges are True

Despite all this we are left with the manifest fact that the Nazis *thought* they were living up to Nietzsche's spirit and living out his doctrine. Misunderstood or not, his greatest political influence has been in this direction. And it can be shown that in *fact* the parallel between the doctrines of

[56]Quoted in Kaufmann, *Nietzsche*, pp. 247-48.
[57]Quoted in translator's preface, *Basic Writings*, p. 185 and footnote 11.
[58]*Genealogy of Morals*, in *ibid.*, p. 594.
[59]Quoted in Kaufmann, *Nietzsche*, p. 166.

Nietzsche and those of Nazism was, at a certain level, a very close one. Nazism was not one but two doctrines—one for the few, the initiated, the elite, another for the many, the average man, the crowd. German nationalism and Aryan racism (as a biological or pseudo-biological doctrine) were elements of the exoteric, not the esoteric philosophy. They were intended as a useful myth for the consumption of the "Many." They were not believed by the "Few." And the statism which Nietzsche condemned was never a part of either doctrine. Hitler made it clear that nation and *Volk* always took priority over "state," that "state" was only an instrument of the *Volk* and of the *Volksgeist*.

The evidence is abundant that the esoteric doctrines of Nazism, the creed of the elite group who made the Nazi revolution, was much more abstract and subtle than the crudities of Hitler's speeches about the German nation and the Aryan superrace. The more elaborate spinning out of such themes in books like Alfred Rosenberg's *Myth of the Twentieth Century* was also for popular consumption. (Hitler said disdainfully that he had never read Rosenberg.) The evidence is found in Hermann Rauschning's *Voice of Destruction,* which reports the private conversations of Hitler of the early 1930s, in *Hitler's Secret Book,* written in 1928 but not published until 1961, and in two volumes of Hitler's table talk, taken down by Martin Bormann during the war years and published in 1953 and 1961.[60]

Rauschning reports, for example, that at the very time that Hitler was inspiring the German people to a super-heated nationalism he was already thinking in quite different terms. "The conception of the nation has become meaningless," Hitler is alleged to have said to his cronies. "The conditions of the time compelled me to begin on the basis of that conception. But I realized from the first that it could have only transient validity. . . . The new order cannot be conceived in terms of the national boundaries of the peoples with an historic past, but in terms of race that transcend those boundaries."[61] Rauschning also shows that Hitler's conception of "race" was quite different from the biological claptrap concocted by people like Rosenberg and Houston Stewart Chamberlain out of the theories of the Comte de Gobineau and Richard Wagner. It was a conception remarkably akin to Nietzsche's idea of the "over-man," the man of power.

I know perfectly well . . . that in the scientific sense there is no such thing as race. . . . I as a politician need a conception which enables the order which has hitherto existed on historic bases to be abolished and an entirely new and antihistoric order infused and given an intellectual basis. France carried her great

[60]Hermann Rauschning, *The Voice of Destruction* (New York: G. P. Putnam's Sons, 1940); Telford Taylor, ed., *Hitler's Secret Book* (New York: Grove Press, 1961); Adolf Hitler, *Table Talk,* 1941-44 (London: Weidenfeld & Nicolson, 1953); H. R. Trevor Roper, ed., *The Testament of Adolf Hitler* (London, Cassell & Co., Ltd. 1961).

[61]Rauschning, *op. cit.,* pp. 231-32.

Revolution beyond her borders with the conception of nation. With the conception of race, National Socialism will carry its revolution abroad and recast the world. . . . I shall bring into operation throughout the world the process of selection which we have carried out through National Socialism in Germany. . . . The active section in the nation, the militant, Nordic section will rise again and become the ruling element over these shopkeepers and pacifists, these puritans and speculators and busybodies. . . . There will be an understanding between the various language elements of the one good ruling race.[62]

This amounts to saying that the superrace are simply men of talent, of capacity and power who can appear anywhere, quite independently of biological origins. It is a matter of pure will and intellect. What could be more Nietzschean? In Hitler's last conversations, just before the collapse, he speaks of the Oriental peoples as the superrace of the future.

"A month after issuing [his] last testament," writes Telford Taylor, "Hitler summarized the result to his old disciple, Albert Speer. Germany . . . had failed him: therefore let it be destroyed: the future belongs solely to the stronger Eastern nation!"[63] We are reminded of the passage in *Genealogy of Morals* in which Nietzsche enumerates the historical "blond beasts of prey," and includes Japanese and Arabians along with Scandinavian Vikings.

Again, in the *Secret Book*, Hitler makes it clear that his conception of "race" was not biological but psychological. "The importance of the blood value of a people," he writes, "becomes totally effective only when this value is recognized by a people, properly valued and appreciated." Not genes but consciousness is the important thing.[64] And in his last testament, written in February 1945, Hitler makes it clear that his antagonism to the Jews has nothing to do with blood or race, but rather with an almost metaphysical notion of counter-elite: competitors for the status of "over-man."

I have never regarded the Chinese or the Japanese as being inferior to ourselves. They belong to ancient civilizations, and I admit feeling that their past history is superior to ours. . . . Our racial pride is not aggressive except in so far as the Jewish race is concerned. We use the term Jewish race as a matter of convenience, for in reality and from the genetic point of view there is no such thing as the Jewish race. . . . The Jewish race is first and foremost an abstract race of the mind. . . . It is the characteristic mental makeup of his race which renders him impervious to the process of assimiliation. And there in a nutshell is the proof of the superiority of the mind over the flesh![65]

One of the last entries in the Bormann diaries (April 2, 1945) presents us with a Nietzschean figure of the purest naturalist sort unconnected with biologism. Hitler speaks of the yellow races invading America, armed with "the sole right that history recognizes—the right of starving people to as-

[62]*Ibid.,* p. 232.
[63]Trevor Roper, *op. cit.,* p. 24.
[64]Taylor, *op. cit.,* p. 28.
[65]Trevor Roper, *op. cit.,* pp. 53, 55, 56.

suage their hunger . . . backed by force!"[66]Rauschning gives us a fragment of conversation in which Hitler actually invokes the authority of Nietzsche. It contains on the one hand a glaring error and misunderstanding but on the other a perfect insight into Nietzsche's thought (itself a very Nietzschean duality).

> Man has to be passed and surpassed. Nietzsche did, it is true, realize something of this, in his way. He went so far as to recognize the superman as a new biological variety. But he was not too sure of it. Man is becoming God— that is the simple fact. Man is God in the making. Man has eternally to strain at his limitations. The moment he relaxes and contents himself with them, he decays and falls below the human level. He becomes a quasi-beast. Gods and beasts, that is what our world is made of.[67]

Nietzsche and Existentialism

Existence Versus Essence

Nietzsche's influence also goes in quite another direction. He is a father of the existentialist philosophies and theologies of our time, which combine the Apollonian and Dionysian aspects of the human psyche in ways quite different from those conceived by the prophets of Nazi totalitarianism. Nietzsche's exclamation, "God is dead!" did not become a fascist slogan but rather the watchword of a new and vital Christian theology. And Karl Jaspers, whose *Future of Mankind* is an exciting secular restatement of Liberal ideals for the world that emerged from the catastrophe of World War II, is an avowed disciple of Nietzsche.

Existentialists learned from Nietzsche the inadequacy, indeed the deceptiveness, of the great nineteenth-century philosophical systems, especially those of Hegel and Marx, which pretended to explain all reality and to tell us just where history is going, as a final truth. "The basic human situation is to be in the world, and not to know whence or whither," writes Jaspers.[68] And this is well, for acceptance of a total system takes away our humanity, by taking away our autonomy, our responsibility to be active and creative. The rationalist philosophies of history that emerged from the Enlightenment have made of us events in a vast mechanical causal process, effects of irresistible laws rather than independent persons.

> The fact that history cannot be foretold and that every attempt to foretell it changes *ipso facto* the course of that which has been foretold, is, for Jaspers, a sign of that freedom which does not exist objectively. The attempt to deter-

[66]*Ibid.,* p. 109.

[67]Rauschning, *op. cit.,* p. 246.

[68]Karl Jaspers, *The Future of Mankind* (Chicago: University of Chicago Press, 1961), p. 4.

mine history in advance is scientifically false and philosophically destructive. It is scientifically false because it moves toward that totality which we ourselves are and which science cannot apprehend. It is philosophically destructive because it denies our freedom and responsibility. If we could determine our future in advance by scientific means we would no longer be men. We would be God. Or dead.[69]

Nietzsche had shown that these philosophies of history were nothing but the psychological autobiographies of particular men, fantasies arising from their personalities, not eternal truth. And thereby we have become free to act again as autonomous, responsible persons who must work out for themselves the meaning of life and of history. We must affirm our *existence* against these false *essences*. "The totality of man lies way beyond any conceivable objectifiability," wrote Jaspers. "He is incompletable both as a being-for-himself and as an object of cognition."[70]

The existentialists, as did Nietzsche, also seek to free the individual from the toils of an increasingly "rationalized" society, from the impersonal, bureaucratically-ordered life of our time, and from its accompanying mediocrity—another sort of abstractness. William Barrett has stated the problem in terms to which Nietzsche would warmly respond.

> It is not so much rationalism as abstractness that is the existentialists' target; and the abstractness of life in this technological and bureaucratic age is now indeed something to reckon with. The last gigantic step forward in the spread of technologism has been the development of mass art and mass media of communication: the machine no longer fabricates only material products; it also makes minds. Millions of people live by the stereotypes of mass art, the most virulent form of abstractness, and their capacity for any kind of human reality is fast disappearing.[71]

Existential Dread

Unlike Nietzsche, the existentialist typically experiences a certain dread at the recognition of his aloneness in a nihilistic time, in which the old value symbols have become lifeless, and the individual must work out the meaning of life in terms that correspond to new realities. Barrett has captured this aspect of the existential situation in these terms:

> Alienation and estrangement; a sense of the basic fragility and contingency of human life; the impotence of reason confronted with the depths of existence;

[69]Golo Mann, in Paul A. Schilpp, ed., *The Philosophy of Karl Jaspers* (New York: Tudor Publishing Co., 1957), pp. 553-54.

[70]"Philosophical Autobiography," in Schilpp, ed., *The Philosophy of Karl Jaspers*, p. 19.

[71]William Barrett, *Irrational Man* (Garden City, N.Y.: Doubleday, 1958), p. 239.

the threat of Nothingness, and the solitary and unsheltered condition of the individual before this threat. One can scarcely subordinate these problems logically one to another; each participates in all the others, and they all circulate around a common center. A single atmosphere pervades them all like a chilly wind: the radical feeling of human finitude.[72]

Perhaps it was the sense of human finitude that Karl Jaspers experienced in reflecting on the existential situation that led him away from the solipsistic arrogance that is so strong a characteristic of Nietzsche's thought and character toward a new openness to "Being" and "transcendence" as concepts of a reality which man does not create out of his own will, but for which he perpetually reaches out. Jaspers also lived through the catastrophe of two world wars, and therefore experienced the terror of Nothingness which Nietzsche apparently escaped. Barrett notes that Jaspers' *Man in the Modern Age* was written in 1930, "three years before Hitler came to power and precisely at the end of a postwar decade in Germany of great intellectual brilliance and greater economic bankruptcy under the Weimar Republic. The book is thus saturated from beginning to end with the dual feeling of the great threat and the great promise of modern life."[73]

Self, Other, and Transcendence

It was the catastrophe of the two wars that led, for Jaspers, to self-discovery—to the recognition of himself as an *Existenz,* which earlier contemplation of the essence of universal man and of God, through universal propositions, through theology, could not awaken. And the discovery of himself, in the midst of moral anguish, was to lead Jaspers to "the other" and to God. But like the experience of himself, these were now authentic realities, not abstractions. "The existential way of philosophizing is intensely personal, active, and autonomous . . . . There is no room in Jaspers' dispensation for a receptive attitude, wherein the thinker receives truth as a gift from another. He must not only appropriate truth to himself; he must regard as true only that which is an outflow from his own act of faith and original dynamism. In this unexpected way, Jaspers comes to agree with Sartre that any initiative taken by a personal, transcendent God would be an attack upon one's freedom, an intrusion from the outside."[74] Significantly, it was in this same context that Jaspers rediscovered "Reason." The "Will to Power" for him would entail the submission of Dionysus to Apollo, of "Freedom" to "Virtue."

[72]*Ibid.,* p. 31.
[73]*Ibid.,* p. 28.
[74]James Collins, *The Existentialists* (Chicago: H. Regnery Co., 1963), p. 113.

Bibliographical Note

Oscar Levy, ed., *The Complete Works of Friedrich Nietzsche,* New York: The Macmillan Company, 1924, 18 vols., contains all of Nietzsche's finished works. Walter Kaufmann, a leading contemporary Nietzsche scholar, is critical of many of the translations, however. His own selection of *Basic Writings of Nietzsche,* New York: Modern Library, Inc., 1966, contains careful and authoritative translations of most of the principal works. References in this chapter to original sources are to this volume. In Kaufmann's *Portable Nietzsche,* New York: The Viking Press, Inc., 1945, there is a complete translation of Nietzsche's masterpiece, *Thus Spake Zarathustra* and of *Antichrist,* which do not appear in the other anthology.

A leading study of Nietzsche's psychology is Ludwig Klages, *Die psychologischen Errungenschaften Nietzsches,* Leipzig: Barth, 1926. Klages, along with Freud, Jung, and others, in their own work in psychology built on many Nietzschean insights. Karl Jaspers, *Nietzsche: Einfuehrung in das Verstaendnis seines Philosophierens,* Berlin: De Gruyter, 1936, treats Nietzsche as a precursor of Existentialist philosophy.

Works critical of Nietzsche include Arthur H. J. Knight, *Some Aspects of the Life and Work of Nietzsche,* New York: Russell and Russell, 1933, which analyzes inconsistencies in Nietzsche's thought and calls in question the philosopher's sincerity. Knight interprets the "Superman" or "Over-man" as Darwinian. Crane Brinton, *Nietzsche,* Cambridge, Mass.: Harvard University Press, 1941, sees Nietzsche as partially a Nazi. Thorough and sympathetic accounts of Nietzsche's thought are George A. Morgan, Jr., *What Nietzsche Means,* Cambridge, Mass.: Harvard University Press, 1941, and Walter Kaufmann, *Nietzsche,* Cleveland and New York: Meridian Books, 1950. See also Karl Loewith, *From Hegel to Nietzsche,* New York: Holt, Rinehart & Winston, Inc., 1964.

Karl Jaspers' leading ontological work is *Reason and Existenz,* New York: Noonday Press, 1955. His most important expressions of political theory are *Man in the Modern Age,* New York: Henry Holt and Company, 1933; *Existentialism and Humanism,* New York: R.F. Moore Company, 1952; *The Origin and Goal of History,* New Haven: Yale University Press, 1953; and *The Future of Mankind,* Chicago: University of Chicago Press, 1961.

Chapter 15

Bridge Building:
The Problematic Relation
of "Virtue" and "Freedom"
in Our Time

What have we learned from our survey of political theories and modes of political theorizing? That the great theoretical systems which come to us from the Greek, the Roman, the medieval, the Renaissance, the Victorian past are not time and culture-bound, I think, has been amply demonstrated by our comparisons of classic and modern writings. To an extraordinary extent, modern political analysis restates and develops the great theories. It does not supplant them. We may borrow a metaphor from the language of music and speak of modern political science as variations on an array of themes. Hopefully, our study of the themes has enriched our understanding and appreciation of the variations.

Let us press our metaphor a bit further and ask whether our collection of themes and variations (if we play them all together) represents cacophony or a fugue? Must we only appreciate the beauty of each alone, or can we put them together? If we were indeed talking about music, perhaps this would not be an important question, for a concert of lovely pieces played in succession is just as satisfying as a fugue constructed of the whole. But we are talking about politics. Political theories are not (or at least not only) objects of aesthetic contemplation, but representations of practical truth. By "practical truth" I mean images of reality which lead to practice. Every political science not only explains reality but also, either expressly or tacitly, prescribes conduct. Is a man who understands the political system as a cluster of Bentleyan pressure groups likely to behave politically the same as one who subscribes to the politics of Rousseau, even though Bentleyan theory may contain no explicit prescriptions? We seek to understand the world of politics in order to act politically. There are few Crusoes today. We may indeed decide not to act, to withdraw from politics and to contemplate the political hurly-burly in utter passivity. Augustinian theory, as we have seen, points in this direction. But this, too, is an action of a sort.

Theory also affects practice in another sense, the practice of political inquiry. None of the theories we have considered is a finished system, a complete explanation of the political. Each rather furnishes guideposts for further investigations and for further speculation. The search to reveal the political world goes on and will never be finished, just as the work of discovering the physical world continues from generation to generation of scholars. Plato furnishes a point of departure for the inquiries of Leo Strauss; Aristotle is reflected in the work of Maritain, Anscombe, and Lipset; Machiavelli in the inquiries of the "Chicago School"; and so for other classical thinkers. Some of you who read this book will become professional students of politics. And you will need a theory to guide you.

If our purpose in studying political theory is to know how to act in the forum and in the study, plainly the canons which we adopt must be in harmony with one another. Does this mean that we must select one or another of the great explanations? Or can we draw from all of them? Can we create our "fugue"? Plainly, if they are guides for action, it would not be wise to "play" a different theme each day of the week. We must either write our fugue, or pick and choose.

The scholarly polemics of recent years in the field of political studies are evidence that no one has yet written the fugue, and they also underscore the problematical character of its composition. There seems to be an unbridgeable intellectual gulf today as in the past between the noumenalist political philosophers and the exponents of naturalist behavioral political science. Associated with it is the same sort of acid debate as characterized the disputes between Plato and the Sophists.[1] And, as we have also seen, this opposition implies as well the problem of viable definitions of "virtue" and "freedom."

The division can be seen, in fact, throughout the history of political ideas. On the one hand, we have those who think that an adequate political science can only be founded on insight into "true" virtue, understood as transcendent value. On the other, there are those who deny the existence of such an order and celebrate man's freedom to pursue values that are empirically (i.e., psychologically) given, or to create his own values. We have grouped the theorists whom we have studied in terms of this dichotomy, placing Plato, Aristotle, St. Augustine, St. Thomas, Kant, and (probably) Hegel together as noumenalists. Machiavelli, Hobbes, Locke, Rousseau, Marx, Mill, and Nietzsche form the second group, whom we have called naturalists.

[1]See Herbert J. Storing, ed., *Essays on the Scientific Study of Politics* (New York: Holt, Rinehart & Winston, Inc., 1962), a violent attack on behavioral science by a group of Professor Strauss's former students, and the vituperative rebuttal of Sheldon Wolin and John Schaar in a review article in *American Political Science Review,* LVII (1963), 125-62.

We have noticed, however, that not each of our theorists has been content to affirm in a narrow, parochial way his own metaphysical persuasion and to expend his intellectual capital in preparing self-righteous anathemas against an opposing group. Several of them have been bridge builders. Aristotle was the first of our noumenalists who attempted to cross over the metaphysical gulf to the naturalist side in constructing his theory of actual states. Unfortunately, none of his intellectual progeny have been as catholic in their theoretical insights. Thomist Aristotelians have confined their studies to the noumenalist world of the good polity. Modern political sociologists, who owe a debt to Books IV to VI of the *Politics,* have, by contrast, quite ignored the Aristotelian doctrines of entelechy and final causation, so that their work is difficult to distinguish from that of the "Chicago School" who build upon Machiavellian naturalism. St. Augustine, in order to exculpate Christianity from any responsibility for the demise of the Roman Empire, developed a theory of political change founded on naturalistic principles of causation. Reinhold Niebuhr has drawn freely on the findings of modern psychological science in the development of his neo-Augustinian theory, and has ingeniously wedded Freudian analysis to the Christian doctrine of Original Sin. In the work of Kant we have a valiant effort at bridge-building through cognitive separation, with naturalistic science specialized to the phenomenal world of necessity and noumenal science to the ethical world of freedom. In the thought of Kant we also find the concept of freedom, formerly the chief value-word of hedonistic naturalism, transformed into a conception that embraces absolute and transcendent right and virtue. But, unfortunately, Kant was unable to connect the phenomenal and noumenal worlds in the realm of action, because he had drawn too severely the lines of cognitive division. In his dialectical effort to erase this line, Hegel drew the phenomenal world of naturalistic law into the moral universal of "Geist" to produce a problematic combination of virtue and freedom within the confines of necessity. His modern counterparts among the phenomenologists, by contrast, see necessity as something to overcome or to mold by intentionality, but they have as yet found no way of coming to terms, in the cognitive order, with necessitarian science. To the present they have chosen to oppose it, but have not shown what they would put in its place.

While some modern noumenalists, such as the phenomenologists, have entirely absorbed the concepts of right, good, and virtue into free human intentionality, freedom of the creative will, others, such as the Straussian Platonists, seek to restore traditional concepts of virtue to their old pre-eminence. But as we have seen, they share common ground with the phenomenologists in their unwillingness to find any good in naturalistic social science and have rather felt compelled to do battle against it.

Both schools have condemned as a kind of heresy the entire corpus of modern behavioral research and have not stopped to wonder whether the knowledge of empirical uniformities contained in that research and the scientific explanations of them by the behavioralists might contain matter of importance for their speculations about the political good. They seem to think that rationalist value theory is the only legitimate scholarly enterprise in the field of politics and that an adequate experiential basis for it is supplied by everyday life—the experience of association with others in the family, in the classroom, in the market place, in the forum, at church, at the club, in the tennis match. In one place Professor Strauss speaks of the utility of the "judicious collections" of facts made by behavioral scholars.[2] But he does not show how they may be used, nor does he use them.

The Aristotelians are less at fault on this count. St. Thomas and Maritain both nodded approvingly in the direction of naturalistic description and explanation as a proper counterpart to their metaphysical endeavors. But neither of them wrote a "politics of Books IV to VI." Maritain has not condemned but rather blessed the behavioral science of our time, but he has used none of its findings in constructing his own theory of the good order. This is typical of the modern Thomist. Yves Simon, another Thomist of note, in a lengthy volume on the theory of democracy, which assumes all sorts of facts about the psychological and sociological conditions and results of democractic government, cites exactly one survey which could in any way be called empirical and scientific as authority for facts which he alleges. All the other facts which he assumes in his theorizing are either from the experience of everyday life, or from literary sources, or are entirely speculative.[3]

Among the more recent classics, and in modern thought as well, we find our bridge builders chiefly among the naturalists. Rousseau, reacting to the extreme individualism and egoism of Enlightenment thought, is the first of them. Unfortunately, he restored to the conception of human nature only one of the traditional aspects of noumenal "virtue," the idea of man as a social animal who is fulfilled in the company of his fellows. But here he stopped, and as a consequence his theory swallows man up in the category of citizen more completely than classical theory ever did, for no objective norms are laid down to delimit the character of the good social life. Human goodness is equated with *mere* sociality, and the way is open to the totalitarianism of "1984."

Marx and Engels, we have seen, embrace Rousseau's doctrine of sociality as a historical goal for man to achieve, and combine with it a conception of individual freedom from social restraints and a conception of in-

[2]Leo Strauss, *What Is Political Philosophy?* (New York: Free Press of Glencoe, Inc.), 1959.

[3]Yves R. Simon, *Philosophy of Democratic Government* (Chicago: University of Chicago Press), 1951.

dividual fulfillment which, at least in the utopian postproletarian order, mitigates the collectivist concept. But beyond a radical freedom and sociality, they have nothing to say of the qualities of the good life.

Among modern naturalists, John Stuart Mill has done more than others to unite naturalistic freedom and scientific law to noumenal freedom and virtue, in his conceptions of the "higher pleasures" and of "man as a progressive being." But his metaphysical framework is incomplete and frequently obscure, sometimes appearing as a crazy quilt combination of Benthamite and Hegelian notions. The project for experiments in group living of his young counterpart, Robert Nozick, seems even more wide of the mark of naturalist-noumenalist synthesis, since it is entirely lacking in a worked-out metaphysical and epistemological base. In the work of Nietzsche we find most striking evidence that a purely naturalistic freedom is not capable of supporting a bridge toward noumenal values. Pressed to its logical extreme, voluntarist naturalism eventuates in a radical irrationalism (patternlessness in Nature) and a deification of undirected, unfettered "Will." On the other hand, we have seen that existentialist "will," sobered by dread recognition of its finitude, has opened itself to transcendence. In the hybrid school of existential phenomenology the combined resources of Hegelian dialectical law and Nietzschean intentionality perhaps give promise of future bridge-building. But at present the phenomenologists seem to have lost track of "law."

Today we need a dialogue and a sharing of insights. Plato must sit down with the Sophists. Surely, both those among the naturalists who prescribe instrumental values (means to specified ends) and those who confine themselves to descriptions and scientific explanations of observed regularities could profit from a reexamination of the model of man from which they derive their basic axioms. The prescription of means to a given end ought to be carried on with an awareness of the problem of how the many ends of man are related to one another. And, presumably, political descriptions are made with some practical aim, if only a very distant one. (It is a hopeful sign that "post-behavioralists" have abandoned the behavioralist fear of a "premature policy science.") The very act of description requires that the describer know what a man is, as distinct from other animals and from machines, if the descriptions are to be of *human* behavior.[4]

In a political science created by the union of noumenalism and naturalism, political ethics would not swallow up descriptive science, nor would ethical questions be reduced to behavioral ones. Each part of the discipline would proceed autonomously, but in cooperation with the other. As

[4]Heinz Eulau, a leading behavioralist, entitled the first chapter of his book, *The Behavioral Persuasion in Politics* (New York: Random House, 1962), "The Root Is Man," and the last chapter "The Goal Is Man." But he glosses over many large philosophical problems which are implicit in the use of these expressions.

in any happy marriage, neither partner would be destroyed, but would be rather enriched by the other. Ethical speculation about virtue and freedom would be grounded in an awareness of the facts of process, which specify the limits of the freedom the notion of ethics presupposes, limits, however, which are also the laws by which purposes are achieved. But the logic of ethical inquiry, as a logic of man's freedom and virtue, would continue to be a discipline in some sense different from scientific inquiry.

In such a unified science the Socratic dialectic of the Platonists would not be outmoded. It would work with more elaborate and sophisticated data. The desirability and the possibility of the universal polity of the common man would be tested in the light of a broader ethical and scientific inquiry than the one in which the theory of the common man was conceived; so would the hypotheses of Marx about a proletarian paradise. There would surely be room in such a science for theories of group process like those of the Bentleyites, for theories of the conditions of democratic stability like those of Lipset, and for Nozick's experiments in living. In each case, the categories for collecting data and for analyzing it would be more distinctly and more accurately drawn, to emerge more significant than they are now. Lasswell's recipes for power would not be outlawed but would be combined with, and perhaps modified by, a theory of the uses of power. And game theory, from which the students of political ethics can learn canons of clear and precise reasoning about ends and means, could no longer be criticized as a science of sharp practice but would become one aspect of a science of the human political good. Ultimately, the mathematical vocabulary which has been developed by the game theorists and some of the other decision-making theorists might become a vehicle for expressing the principles of the entire unified discipline, in both its ethical and behavioral dimensions. Plato's numbers in such a science would lose their mysticism without losing their moral value.

It is evident that the procedures of what we ordinarily call science must be in use from the outset, in collecting, sorting, collating the anthropological-ideological-psychological data which must constitute the raw material of the philosophic enterprise. But science as explanation and prediction must also play a large, indeed a major role. For how can we choose among values or arrange them in a hierarchy of priorities unless something is known about the consequences of their pursuit? Here is an area where Dewey has pointed to a profound truth. It is precisely the occurrence of unforeseen and undesired consequences in living out our ideologies that has been the reason for ideological revision from age to age and for political instability. And it is therefore especially in the area of its capacity to explain and predict consequences that value-free social science can make a contribution to a philosophy of values.

One answer to the question of how the social science of causality, that is, of outcomes, can be placed at the service of value theory is found in the work of C. West Churchman, philosopher-cum-decision-making analyst. In a volume entitled *Prediction and Optimal Decision* he writes: "The empirical investigation of what men really want is possible only if men are educated as well as possible concerning the outcome of policies, and only if men are free to choose. Evidence of man's true values is to be found in his spoken words, or his consumer practices, or his voting behavior only if he is free of ignorance and other constraints."[5] He suggests that science, at least ideally, can verify prudential recommendations. And he defines such a recommendation as "a prediction of behavior when the decision-maker acts in a state of complete knowledge, either knowledge that predicts with certainty, or knowledge of the true probabilities of outcomes."[6] Thus " 'X ought to do A' means 'X would do A' if he were aware of all alternative actions and knew the probabilities of the possible outcomes."[7]

Surely to suggest that science is capable of predicting even with the most elaborate computers all possible outcomes of all possible combinations of actions based on all possible combinations of values is utopian. Prudence has since ancient times been a central concept of ethics and must remain the virtue which supplies gaps in our scientific patterning of the world. As another part of the enterprise of constructing an ethics for today I think we need to inquire more than is now fashionable into the concept of prudence and into its contemporary role in moral judgment.

The information we need to construct a rational political ethic cannot be obtained in an armchair via the inspiration of categorical imperatives but only by a careful study of what men do in fact try to live as social morality, and by working out as far as we are able the causal implications of these facts. The object remains ethics, but much of the method must be that of empirical science. This does not mean that it can be wholly science. The traditional concepts of metaphysics and ethics must finally be brought to bear in the work of selection and synthesis. It is also clear that creative imagination must also be at work in the business of metaphysical discovery. Here we must thank Nietzsche for an important emphasis. If slide rules have never by themselves produced science, it is not to be supposed that they can produce ethics.

Similarly, science must today involve ethics if it is not to become ideology masquerading as description. Pure scientific description, at least in the case of man and society, is not possible at any very general level, for it presupposes an identity in the thing to be described—human and social nature—a subject which in comparison to the identity of the atom and the molecule is problematical and controversial. For social scientists to assume

[5]C. West Churchman, *Prediction and Optimal Decision* (Englewood Cliffs, N. J.: Prentice-Hall, Inc., 1961), p. viii.

[6]*Ibid.,* p. 19.

[7]*Ibid.*

that identity without even recognizing that an assumption has been made is both arrogant and parochial. It can also produce irrelevance. In alliance with students of values, however, as helpmates in the quest for human nature and the prediction of its consequences (its fulfillment) the building of scientific models and their application to empirical situations can be of deep significance for the human enterprise. Instead of ideology this science could become, in the broadest and best sense, philosophy. And "virtue" would be reconciled to "freedom."

Index

Anscombe, G.E.M., 107-10
Antichrist, of Nietzsche, 476
Anti-Duehring, of Engels, 417
Antiphon, 20, 21
Aquinas, Thomas, St., 162-98 (*see also* Thomas Aquinas, St.)
Aristocracy (*see also* Elite, Leadership): Aristotle, 88, 91, 94, 97; Kant, 316; Machiavelli, 203-4; Mill, J.S., 447, 456-57; Nietzsche, 480, 482, 489-90; Plato, 42-43, 58n.; Thomas Aquinas, 178, 179
Aristotle, 72-124: aristocracy, 88, 91, 94, 97; character and personality types, 84, 86-87, 104-5; classes, 88-90, 92, 94-97, 104; classification of governments, 91, 92; community, 74-76; consensus, 96-97; criticism of Plato, 73-76; *De Anima,* 12, 79-80; democracy, 88-90, 94-95, 98, 99, 104; education, 105-6; elite (*see* ruling class); empirical order, 90-95, 97-102; entelechy, 76-78; equality, 86, 90, 97, 104; ethics and politics, 82-85, 87, 95-96, 106; family, 85-86; four causes, 76-81; freedom, 88, 94, 95, 98; genetic analysis of *polis,* 81-82; good life, 82-85, 103; good order, 95-97, 102-5; immanentism, 76-82, 107, 127; intention, 73; leadership, 100; life, 72-73; metaphysical bridge-building, 74, 91-93, 97, 106, 120, 123; metaphysical theory, 76-81, 103; *Metaphysics,* 74; method, 73-81, 90-95; monarchy, 88, 93-94, 99; motivation theory, 98; naturalism, 91-93, 106, 123; *Nicomachean Ethics,* analyzed, 82-85; noumenalism, 74, 93, 106, 123; oligarchy, 88, 89, 91, 94-95, 98, 99; and ordinary language philosophy, 106-10; and political

Aristotle *(cont.)*
sociology, 112-19; *Politics,* analyzed, 85-106; polity, 94-97; property, 85-86, 94-95, 100, 104-5; reason, practical, 84, 87, 105, 111; revolution, 98-100; ruling class, 90, 95, 96, 98, 100, 102; and situation ethics, 110-12; slavery, 86; stability, 100, 120; theory of knowledge, 73-81; tradition, 84, 122; tyranny, 89, 91, 99, 101-2, 107; virtue, 21, 22, 82-90, 102
Augustine, St., Bishop of Hippo, 125-61: character types, 138-39, 143-45; church and state, 132, 134, 138; *City of God,* analyzed, 126-49; classes, 144; community, 130-31, 132, 134, 137; contract, 137; elect, 132; elite, 143-45; empire, dynamics of, 140-46; empirical order, 133-40; ethics and politics, 138-40; freedom, 129-30, 131-32, 143, 149; good order, 131-33, 136-37, 139-40; intention, 125-26; justice, 134, 138-39; leadership, 144-45; life, 125-26; metaphysical bridge-building, 137, 143-48; method, 126-31; and modern realism, 149-60; motivation theory, 138, 143-47; naturalism, 148; noumenalism, 146-47; philosophy of history, 127-28; power, 138, 144-45, 147; quietism, 137-38; reason, 126, 128-29; religion and politics (*see* Church and state); revelation, 126-27; sin, 130, 132; slavery, 139; temporal good, 136-37; theology and eschatology, 128-33; theory of knowledge, 127-28; tradition, 148; transcendent good (*see* good order); two cities, 130-40; tyranny, 138, 148; virtue, 21-22, 129, 130, 131-33, 143, 147; will, 128-30, 142

Ethics and Politics *(cont.)*
Rousseau, 332, 333-36; Thomas Aquinas, 176-77
Euthyphro, of Plato, analyzed, 38
Existentialism: 495-97

Facts and Values: 8
Fletcher, Joseph, 110-12
Forms, Plato's theory of: 31, 33-39, 40, 41, 43, 63
Fortune: Machiavelli, 218-19
Freedom, *(see also* Liberty, Rights): Aristotle, 88, 94, 95, 98; Augustine, 129-30, 131-32, 143, 149; Hegel, 14, 15, 250-51, 384, 389, 390-96; Hobbes, ix, 14, 20, 248-49, 264, 266, 271; Kant, 14, 249-50, 350, 351, 356-59, 360, 364; Locke, 14, 20, 249, 305, 311, 315-17; Machiavelli, 204, 206-7, 208-9; Marx and Engels, 14, 15, 251, 413, 416-17, 420-21; Mill, 15, 251, 438, 453-55, 458-60; Nietzsche, 15, 252, 482, 491, 496, 497; Plato, 58; Rousseau, x, 14, 20, 249, 331, 334-46, 339, 342-43; Thomas Aquinas, 167, 172, 173, 179-80; theories of, 14-15, 19-23, 248-52; and virtue, ix-x, 13-15, 19-23, 248, 252, 471, 497, 500, 503, 506

Game Theory *(see also* Rational choice, Theories of): 283-92
Gay Science of Nietzsche, 475, 486
General Will: Kant, 351, 357, 360, 361, 362; Rousseau, 249, 335-38, 339, 340, 341, 342, 345, 346
German Ideology of Marx, 417
Good, Idea of: Plato, 31, 32, 35-37, 41, 49, 62, 66
Good or rational order: Aristotle, 95-97, 102-5; Augustine, 131-33, 136-37, 139-40; Hegel, 393-95; Hobbes, 267-69, 270-71; Kant, 360-63; Locke, 309-17; Machiavelli, 206-10; 211-12; Marx, 420-21, 425-26, 430-31; Mill, 452, 454-60; Nietzsche, 489-91; Plato, 30, 40-48, 53-62; Rousseau, 334-38; Thomas Aquinas, 169-74, 179-80
Groundwork of the Metaphysics of Morals of Kant, analyzed, 357-59
Group process school: *(see* Interest group theory)

Hare, R.M., 370-74
Harrington, James, 231-36

Hegel, George F. 384-408: alienation, 401; civil society, 392; constitutional monarchy, 393-94; corporative state, 393-94; critique of capitalism, 399-402; dialectics, 384-85, 387-90, 390-95; division of powers, 393; ethics and politics, 392-95; and fascism, 396-97; freedom, 14, 50, 250-51, 384, 389, 390-96; good order, 393-95; and Husserl, 403; and Hwa Yol Jung, 405-6; Idea, Absolute, *(see* World Spirit); intention, 384-85; life, 385-86; and Marx, 398-99; metaphysics, 387-90; method, 387-88; moments of the spirit, 392-93; moments of the state, 393-95; motivation theory, 389-90; and phenomenology, 402-7; *Phenomenology of Mind,* 386, 387-90; *Philosophy of History,* 386, 390-92, 397, 398; philosophy of history, 389-92, 397, 398; *Philosophy of Right,* 386, 390, 392-95, 397-98, 402; reason *(see* World Spirit); theory of knowledge, 387-90; Universal Spirit *(see* World Spirit); virtue, 250-51, 392-94; and welfare liberalism, 395-96; World Historical Individual, 397, 479; World Spirit, 250, 384-85, 388-90, 392-93
Hobbes, Thomas, 253-93: community, 264, 268, 279; consent, 266-67; contract, 265-66, 266-67; *Elements of Law,* 254, 258; elite, 273; empirical order, 271-73; equality, 262-63, 266; ethics and politics, 266-67, 269-70; freedom, ix, 14, 20, 248-49, 264, 266, 271; and game theory, 283-92; good order, 267-69, 270-71; justice, 269; laws of nature, 264-67; *Leviathan,* analyzed, 255-73; liberty, 263-65, 271, life, 254; mathematics and politics, 253, 260-62; metaphysics, 255-57; method, 8, 253, 255-62; model world, 266, 271-73; motivation theory, 255-58; naturalism, 248-49, 253, 255-56; natural law *(see* laws of nature); nature, state of, 263-64; obligation, 266-67; power, 257-58; property, 270, 271; and rational choice analysis, 248, 274-92; rational order, 270-71; reason, 258, 260, 263, 264, 272, 273, 275; right of nature, 263-64; science, 258-62; sin, 255; sovereignty, 267-69; theory of knowledge, 255-62; tradition, 255, 260-61; virtue, 248-49, 269, 270
Hume, David, 9, 352-54
Husserl, Edmund, 403

Idea for a Universal History of Kant, 351, 363
Ideas, Plato's theory of *(see* Forms, Plato's theory of)
Ideology, Structure of: 1-4